Texts for Preaching

YEAR A

Also published by Westminster John Knox Press

Texts for Preaching:
A Lectionary Commentary Based on the NRSV—
Year B

by Walter Brueggemann, Charles B. Cousar,
Beverly R. Gaventa, and James D. Newsome

Texts for Preaching:
A Lectionary Commentary Based on the NRSV—
Year C

by Charles B. Cousar, Beverly R. Gaventa,
J. Clinton McCann, Jr., and James D. Newsome

Texts for Preaching

A Lectionary Commentary
Based on the NRSV

YEAR A

Walter Brueggemann, Charles B. Cousar,
Beverly R. Gaventa, James D. Newsome

Westminster John Knox Press
LOUISVILLE
LONDON • LEIDEN

Acknowledgments will be found on page ix.

Book design by Drew Stevens

First edition

Published by Westminster John Knox Press
Louisville, Kentucky

This book is printed on acid-free paper that meets the American National Standards Institute Z39.48 standard. ♾

PRINTED IN THE UNITED STATES OF AMERICA
02 03 04 — 10 9 8 7 6

Library of Congress Cataloging-in-Publication Data
(Revised for vol. 1)

Texts for preaching : a lectionary commentary, based on the NRSV.

Includes index.
Contents: [1] Year A — [2] Year B.
1. Lectionary preaching. 2. Bible—Commentaries. I. Brueggemann, Walter.
BV4235.L43T488 1993 251 93-8023
ISBN 0-664-21927-6 (v. 1)
ISBN 0-664-21970-5 (v. 2)
ISBN 0-664-22000-2 (v. 3)

Contents

Preface			vii
Acknowledgments			ix
First Sunday of Advent			1
Second Sunday of Advent			10
Third Sunday of Advent			19
Fourth Sunday of Advent			28
Christmas, First Proper			37
Christmas, Second Proper			46
Christmas, Third Proper			55
First Sunday After Christmas			64
Second Sunday After Christmas			73
Epiphany			82
First Sunday After Epiphany *(Baptism of the Lord)*		Ordinary Time 1	91
Second Sunday After Epiphany		Ordinary Time 2	100
Third Sunday After Epiphany		Ordinary Time 3	109
Fourth Sunday After Epiphany		Ordinary Time 4	118
Fifth Sunday After Epiphany		Ordinary Time 5	127
Sixth Sunday After Epiphany	Proper 1	Ordinary Time 6	137
Seventh Sunday After Epiphany	Proper 2	Ordinary Time 7	146
Eighth Sunday After Epiphany	Proper 3	Ordinary Time 8	155
Last Sunday After Epiphany *(Transfiguration Sunday)*			164
Ash Wednesday			173
First Sunday in Lent			182
Second Sunday in Lent			192
Third Sunday in Lent			200
Fourth Sunday in Lent			209
Fifth Sunday in Lent			218
Sixth Sunday in Lent *(Palm Sunday or Passion Sunday)*			228

Holy Thursday			237
Good Friday			246
Easter			255
Second Sunday of Easter			264
Third Sunday of Easter			273
Fourth Sunday of Easter			282
Fifth Sunday of Easter			291
Sixth Sunday of Easter			300
Ascension			309
Seventh Sunday of Easter			318
Pentecost			328
Trinity Sunday			337
Proper 4	Ordinary Time 9	May 29–June 4 *(if after Trinity)*	346
Proper 5	Ordinary Time 10	June 5–11 *(if after Trinity)*	355
Proper 6	Ordinary Time 11	June 12–18 *(if after Trinity)*	364
Proper 7	Ordinary Time 12	June 19–25 *(if after Trinity)*	371
Proper 8	Ordinary Time 13	June 26–July 2	380
Proper 9	Ordinary Time 14	July 3–9	388
Proper 10	Ordinary Time 15	July 10–16	397
Proper 11	Ordinary Time 16	July 17–23	406
Proper 12	Ordinary Time 17	July 24–30	416
Proper 13	Ordinary Time 18	July 31–August 6	425
Proper 14	Ordinary Time 19	August 7–13	434
Proper 15	Ordinary Time 20	August 14–20	443
Proper 16	Ordinary Time 21	August 21–27	452
Proper 17	Ordinary Time 22	August 28–September 3	461
Proper 18	Ordinary Time 23	September 4–10	470
Proper 19	Ordinary Time 24	September 11–17	478
Proper 20	Ordinary Time 25	September 18–24	487
Proper 21	Ordinary Time 26	September 25–October 1	496
Proper 22	Ordinary Time 27	October 2–8	505
Proper 23	Ordinary Time 28	October 9–15	515
Proper 24	Ordinary Time 29	October 16–22	525
Proper 25	Ordinary Time 30	October 23–29	534
Proper 26	Ordinary Time 31	October 30–November 5	544
Proper 27	Ordinary Time 32	November 6–12	553
Proper 28	Ordinary Time 33	November 13–19	562
Proper 29 *(Christ the King or Reign of Christ)*	Ordinary Time 34	November 20–26	571
All Saints		November 1 *(or first Sunday in November)*	578
Index of Lectionary Readings			587

PREFACE

The preaching and hearing of the Word lies at the heart of the life of faith. From as early as the time of the rediscovery of the "book of the law" by the people of King Josiah's day (2 Kings 22–23), it has been understood that the written Word contains the power to transform the life of the faith community and of individuals within that community. But, as the king discovered, in order for that transformation to take place, it was necessary not only to read the Word (23:2), but to "perform" it (23:3).

It is the preacher's task—sometimes joyful, sometimes somber, but always profoundly consequential—to facilitate that performance by interpreting the text. Fortunately, she or he does not mount this task in isolation, but does so in the company of many others who, over the centuries, have listened for the Spirit's voice within the Word. It is this "great . . . cloud of witnesses" (Heb. 12:1) that stands in the pulpit with the preacher and that not only offers encouragement and support, but on occasion may point toward fresh understandings of what the Spirit would have the Word say to all who listen.

The authors of this commentary offer it not as some final testimony to what the text may or should mean, but as one witness among many to the vitality of the Word in the life of the church. If our comments also offer insights to the preacher as she or he attempts to lead a congregation from "reading" the text to "performing" it, our purposes will have been achieved.

Although there are occasional variations to it, the general pattern of authorship in this volume is as follows: Walter Brueggemann is responsible for the Old Testament lections from the First Sunday in Advent through Good Friday, and for the Psalms texts thereafter. James Newsome wrote the commentary for the Psalms through Good Friday, and for the Old Testament lections the balance of the year. Beverly Gaventa is the author of the commentary on the Epistles texts, and Charles Cousar on the Gospels. Each of us contributed introductory essays. J. Clinton McCann of Eden Theological Seminary, who collaborated with us on the volume for Year C of this series, wrote the Psalms commentary for the First Sunday in Lent.

We owe a debt of gratitude to the editorial staff of the Westminster John Knox Press for their patience in helping us see this volume to fruition, especially Harold L. Twiss, who provided editorial assistance during the initial stages of manuscript preparation, Timothy G. Staveteig, who was at our side as we moved toward completion, and Esther M. Kolb, copyeditor.

The Faculty Development Committee of Columbia Theological Seminary generously helped us with a grant which lifted much of the clerical burden from our shoulders. And Eugene Lovering, of the office of the Society of Biblical Literature, rendered crucial assistance in the area of electronic data management.

We are also deeply indebted to our colleagues at the institutions where we teach and—by no means of least importance—to our spouses. Without the encouragement of the latter we would not have persevered.

JAMES D. NEWSOME
Editor, Year A

ACKNOWLEDGMENTS

Unless otherwise noted, scripture quotations are from the New Revised Standard Version of the Bible, copyright © 1989 by the Division of Christian Education of the National Council of the Churches of Christ in the U.S.A., and are used by permission.

Scripture quotations from the Revised Standard Version of the Bible are copyright 1946, 1952, © 1971, 1973 by the Division of Christian Education of the National Council of the Churches of Christ in the U.S.A. and are used by permission.

Scripture quotations from *The Jerusalem Bible* are copyright © 1966, 1967, 1968 by Darton Longman & Todd, Ltd., and Doubleday & Co., Inc. Used by permission of the publishers.

Scripture quotations from *The New English Bible* are copyright © 1961, 1970 by The Delegates of the Oxford University Press and The Syndics of the Cambridge University Press and are used by permission.

Scripture quotations from *The Revised English Bible* are copyright © 1989 by Oxford University Press and Cambridge University Press and are used by permission.

Scripture references for the lectionary readings are from the *Revised Common Lectionary,* copyright © 1992, the Consultation on Common Texts. Used with permission.

Grateful acknowledgment is made for permission to reprint "God's Grandeur," from *Poems and Prose of Gerard Manley Hopkins,* ed. W. H. Gardner (London: Penguin Books, 1953).

First Sunday of Advent

Advent is an abrupt disruption in our "ordinary time." It is not only a new season in the church year; it is an utterly new year, new time, new life. Everything begins again. What one marks as new in the *liturgical* sequence we dare to confess is a genuine newness wrought by God *in the world.* That is, liturgy anticipates historical newness, and matches the newness that God is doing in the world. In this season we are at the brink of something utterly new, long yearned for but beyond our capacity to enact. Advent invites us to awaken from our numbed endurance and our domesticated expectations, to consider our life afresh in light of new gifts that God is about to give.

The community of faith has been hoping for a very long time. The substance of that hope, deeply rooted in the Old Testament, is persistent and resilient. As both the prophetic oracle and the psalm attest, Israel hopes for *justice, peace,* and *well-being*. The biblical community knows God's intention for these matters and trusts God's faithful promise. Thus Advent begins in a vision of a healed alternative for the world.

The New Testament church stands in close continuity with the Old Testament. Christians hope with Jews, and hope for the same thing, well-being in a world that has been healed, blessed, and cared for. The New Testament readings, however, intensify the long-standing hopes and make the promises of God immediate prospects. The intensity and present tense of New Testament faith revolves around the presence of Jesus, whose very person initiates a new beginning in the world. Believers are to perceive the world differently and position themselves for the new gifts of God.

These Advent texts of promise and expectation make a claim on us that violates our rationality and jeopardizes our current patterns of security. The church at Advent watches in order to notice where God is doing justice and peace and well-being. Wherever and whenever that happens, God's promises are on the move toward newness. It is for us to notice and receive with eagerness and joy.

Isaiah 2:1–5

In the book of Isaiah, the city of Jerusalem is a vexing and unending problem. The city of Jerusalem is the locus of national pride, self-sufficiency, and self-serving religion. That arrogant enterprise is massively critiqued and condemned by the prophet (see Isa. 1:21–26; 5:1–7). It is not, however, dismissed from purview. Jerusalem would not go away just because the prophet critiqued it. Neither the prophet nor the community can finally finish with Jerusalem, because that vexatious city in fact has a crucial role to play in God's future. The city so much condemned is also the city for which the poet has enormous hope.

This poem is a "word," which Isaiah "saw" (2:1). That is, it is a vision, an act of imagination that looks beyond present dismay through the eyes of God, to see what will be that is not yet. That is the function of promise (and therefore of Advent) in the life of faith. Under promise, in Advent, faith sees what will be that is not yet. The ground for such a daring act of hope is, in the words of the RSV, "It shall come to pass in the latter days" (v. 2). The formula makes two assertions. On the one hand, the promise is very sure, as sure as the intent of God. On the other hand, the poet does not know when. It is in the nature of faithful promise to trust the one who promises, and therefore not to need a timetable.

The promise proceeds by making a sharp contrast between what is and what will be. The city of Jerusalem, in the time of Isaiah, was a marginal and vulnerable operation. Jerusalem lived and flourished, or suffered, at the behest of the great powers.

Against that present shabbiness, the poet imagines a majestic future for the city. For an instant, the poet works in a rhetorical trick (2:2b). He entertains a scenario in which all the other nations, even the superpowers of Assyria and Egypt, will "stream" to Jerusalem. In the moment of utterance, the repressed hopes of ideological Israel flashed to consciousness. This is the long-promised coming greatness of the city.

As quickly as that fantasy is suggested, however, just as quickly is it refuted and withdrawn. Focus on promise not only encourages self-serving anticipation, it also corrects and precludes such a false promise. The poem is not an anticipation of triumph for the Jerusalem political-religious establishment. Quite the contrary! It is the place of God's presence in the "house," that is, the Temple, that is important. God's presence lives in profound tension with the would-be success of human power; it is to God's presence that all the nations shall stream. Thus the poet's vision is a profoundly theological vision, that is, fixed on God.

The journey to God's presence, however, is a journey to the Torah. In Israel, dealing with Yahweh requires acknowledgement of Torah (v. 3). The nations will not only delight in God's person, they will be engaged in God's purpose. In a daring anticipation, the poet foresees that all nations will accept Israel's Torah as their charter for well-being.

As the nations accept the Torah of Yahweh, God is established as the adjudicator of international disputes (v. 4a). The coming rule of God is cast by the poet theologically, but the import of the scenario is profoundly political. The poem envisions a "court of appeal," whereby there will be adjudication of large and deep problems. What a difference if in troubled areas of the world, there were an equitable authority recognized in such disputes! In the ancient world, as in the contemporary world, the warrant for war is that there is no such authority for adjudication, and so nations take matters into their own hands. Now, in the envisioned world of the poem, where God's rule pertains, war as a mode of national policy is not needed. The end of brutality, however, requires submission to this power of adjudication and relinquishment of the privilege of justice by one's own hand.

The poem then offers a lyrical vision of an alternative economy and the dismantling of the weapons of war (v. 4b). The move to a "peacetime economy" requires not only good intentions, but procedures whereby the resources and capacities of the economy are otherwise deployed. It is not enough to end spears and swords as an act of romance or of goodwill. There must at the same time be production of instruments of life, such as plowshares and pruning hooks. Thus human energies and public resources are reassigned to vine-dressing and agriculture. The economy is transformed; the earth is also transformed, from battleground to fertile garden.

Psalm 122

Whereas various Advent motifs may be found in the lections for this day, the readings from Isaiah and Psalms share an interest in the themes of pilgrimage, justice, and peace. Indeed, Ps. 122 might be prayed or sung by anyone who wishes to implement the injunction of Isa. 2:3, for this psalm is, as its ascription attests, a song of pilgrims ascending the hills to the Holy City. It is easy for the imagination to reconstruct a scene in which countless men and women, from all the tribes of Israel, chant the stanzas of Ps. 122 as they converge on Jerusalem for a sacred festival. Aching muscles and gritty feet would be forgotten in the joy and expectancy of the moment.

Joy, in fact, is the emotion that captures the reader of this text (v. 1), a joy that is quite beyond the emotion felt by the modern Sunday churchgoer, however positive that feeling might be. To "go to the house of the LORD" in ancient Israel was to return to that spot which represented the most intimate encounter between the divine and the human. It meant going home again to all those realities which contain purpose and truth. "The place that the LORD your God will choose . . . as his habitation . . . there" is the wording with which Deuteronomy (12:5) describes Israel's central place of worship. And the gladness expressed by our psalmist in returning to that sacred house may be appreciated all the more when compared with the bereavement of another poet over the destruction of the Holy City and its Temple (Lam. 2:7–11). Perhaps it is by experiencing the loss of that which is holy that men and women often come to the deepest appreciation of that reality when they stand in its presence.

The second section of the psalm (122:2–5) elaborates the theme of the centrality of Jerusalem in the life of Israel. Not only is Jerusalem physically strong (v. 3, if NRSV and REB have it right; but see NEB), but it is the place to which all the tribes gravitate, as willed by God (v. 4). Yet, interestingly enough, Jerusalem is important to the life of the people of God not only because of the worship of God that takes place there, but because it is the seat of God's justice. NRSV's "thrones for judgment" (v. 5) may with equal justification be translated "thrones of justice," the thrones in question being, of course, those of the Davidic kings.

Those parts of the Old Testament which celebrate God's gift to Israel of the office of the Davidic monarch frequently describe the human king as the one who is charged with the responsibility to see that the just ways of the divine King are carried out. Psalm 72, which contains the psalm lection for next Sunday and whose opening lines read

> Give the king your justice, O God,
> and your righteousness to a king's son

is a litany of obligations laid on the king to see that justice is carried out in the land. There we are reminded that the king "delivers the needy," "the poor and those who have no helper" (72:12). In a similar, but less expansive manner, Ps. 122 celebrates God's presence in the life of Jerusalem as the One who, through the office of the king, brings justice into human life.

As justice is portrayed as the companion of peace in Isa. 2:1–5 (especially vs. 3–4), the two qualities are also linked in Ps. 122. The celebration of Jerusalem as the city of God's justice in the second section gives way to a prayer for peace in the third section (vs. 6–9). "Pray for the peace of Jerusalem" (v. 6) has an alliterative power in Hebrew that is quite lost in English translation: *ša'ălû šĕlôm yĕrûšālāim*. This imperative is followed by a petition for wholeness and health among God's people ("May they who love you be tranquil" is another way of translating the second line of v. 6). And the section achieves a climax in the renewal of the psalmist's dedication to work for the good of the city of God (v. 9).

We do not need to be reminded that Advent is a season that celebrates the reality that peace is one of God's great hopes for humankind. During the next several weeks the churches will peal with the sounds of biblical passages, Luke 2:14 among them, that renew our understanding of that fact. However, what is often forgotten is that peace is not an abstraction: the absence of hostility, the presence of material wealth, or whatever. In the biblical view, peace is inevitably linked with justice. Only in the presence of justice—that is, a commitment to the well-being-within-community of one's fellow men and women—can peace be present. Thus, God's hope for peace is, in reality, God's hope that men and women take seriously our mutual responsibility to care about one another. God's hope for peace is God's hope that the members of the human family institute those initiatives by which the hungry are fed and the naked clothed, as well as those initiatives which help to enable persons to be all that God intended for them at creation. And so, as the people of God long for peace at Advent (or any other season of the year), we are reminded by our text that the achievement of that peace rests, in large measure, on the human commitment to justice.

Romans 13:11–14

With its combination of early Christian eschatological expectation and ethical dualism, Rom. 13:11–14 may initially appear to present the preacher with more hazards than opportunities, especially on the First Sunday of Advent. A careful examination of this text, however, will more than repay the investment by revealing its connections with traditional themes of Advent.

Beginning with Rom. 13:1, Paul offers a series of ethical exhortations having to do with the need for mutual respect among believers, appropriate attitudes toward outsiders, and respect for the "governing authorities." This section of exhortations continues in 14:1–15:13, but at the beginning of chapter 14 Paul focuses more intently on conflicts within the Christian community. Romans 13:11–14, then, marks an important transition within the ethical instructions as a whole.

The first words in the text have to do with time: It is time *now* to wake from sleep because "salvation is nearer to us now than when we became believers." Here we catch a glimpse of the dynamic character of Paul's understanding of salvation. Far from being a possession that human beings *acquire*—either by their own achievements or by God's grace—salvation is here personified; it is something that can come closer. In this text salvation is a metonymy, in which the single term stands for the whole of God's actions on behalf of humankind.

Salvation has come closer to us than "when we became believers." We might expect Paul to say simply, "when we converted," but he reserves the traditional language of conversion for reference to Gentiles who "convert" to belief in the one God (see, e.g., 1 Thess. 1:9; cf. Gal. 4:9). Here, as elsewhere (cf. 1 Cor. 15:2, 11), he speaks of the beginning of faith simply as "to believe."

Out of context, we might take the references to time in v. 11 as simple markers of time. That is, time has passed since he began to believe. But the beginning of v. 12 announces that the passage of time is not a simple matter of "marking time." It is urgent: "the night is far gone, the day is near." The salvation that draws near does so, not with the measured pace of sand in a glass or even the beeps of a digital watch, but with the suddenness of an intruder whose schedule is known to no one.

Here the dualistic motif already present in v. 11's imagery of awakening from sleep becomes dominant. Paul contrasts night with day, darkness with light, evil behavior (reveling, drunkenness, and so on) with that of those who have "put on the Lord Jesus Christ." Such dualistic imagery appears, of course, in a wide variety of religious traditions, including the writings of Paul's contemporaries at Qumran and in the community that produced the Fourth Gospel. Paul's contrast between "darkness" and "light" refers, here as elsewhere, to the contrast between the darkness of night and the welcome coming of day's light.

What makes this text difficult for interpreters is that Paul places these two concerns, eschatology and ethics, alongside each other without explicitly articulating what the relationship is between the two. Our initial impulse may be to assume that the eschatological reminder constitutes a warning about ethics. That is, behavior that is not ruled by the light will eventuate in judgment and the wrath of God. For Paul, however, the eschaton is not a threat to employ in order to manipulate human behavior. Nor does he present the eschaton as a reward for living "in the light." Instead, the nearness of the eschaton recalls for him not only an urgency regarding time but also the urgency of the Christian life. Conviction that salvation draws near is, for Paul, inextricably linked with altered behavior, since the way we live always reflects our loyalties. Consistent with this expectation, he opens this section of ethical admonitions in 12:1–2 with a plea that the reasonable service of God consists in the offering of the "body," that is, the entire person.

The ancient Christian connection between the first advent of Christ at his birth and the second at his return emerges forcefully in this reading from Romans, as it does in the reading from Matt. 24. Paul's initial words provide us with an important clue to the meaning of both advents: "Besides this, you know what time it is. . . ." In the RSV the word "hour" translates the Greek noun *kairos,* but it is better translated "time" (NRSV) or "season," since everything that Paul says in these short verses depends on knowing what time it is. In the same way, what is at stake in Advent is knowing what time it is, and this text challenges us to reflect on that "time," perhaps in contrast to the ways in which we use our time or fret over our time during the season of Advent.

Matthew 24:36–44

Preaching on the second advent presents a challenge. Texts such as this one from Matthew's Gospel come from apocalyptic sections where highly symbolic language is used. On the one hand, to interpret the images literalistically or to refashion the biblical worldview as if there were no gap between the first century and the twentieth leads to absurd claims. Most sensitive readers of the text devoutly wish to avoid the excesses of those interpreters who discover in the biblical images specific timetables for the events of the end-time. On the other hand, if we demythologize the texts and ask only about their existential significance for the moment, we rob the early Christian witness of its hope in the fulfilling, consummating activity of God. The task is to listen carefully to the texts and allow the symbols to evoke the sense of urgency and expectancy at God's future.

Matthew 24:36–44 begins and ends with declarations that the hour of the Son of man's coming is unknown. The fact that even Jesus and the angels are not privy to the time of the second advent provides a sharp warning against speculation and an overeagerness to read the signs of the times. In fact, any claim to special insight about the future merely exposes human arrogance and pretense.

But there is also a positive word in the statement of the unknowableness of the hour. Readers are reminded that they live not as speculators guessing about the future nor as prospectors hunting for gold nuggets, but as those to whom a promise has been given. They count on the reliability of the promiser; they wager on the advent of the Son of man. It is not that the future is somehow mysteriously shrouded so that armchair apocalyptists must seek to break the secret code and discover when the end will be. A promise is less scientific; it allows considerable latitude. Since a promise does not depend on the natural possibilities inherent in the present, it may appear unrealistic by current standards. It may (and in fact the text says that it will) come as a surprise, something one cannot calculate. Nevertheless, those receiving the promise are bound to the future. They are oriented toward the outstanding fulfillment, and thus they watch.

Two vivid figures are set forth in this passage. One is Noah, who is strikingly contrasted with his surrounding society. His contemporaries were eating and drinking, marrying and giving their children in marriage, while he engaged in the incredible task of building a boat. They are not faulted for their gross sinfulness (as in Gen. 6:11–13). They simply assumed that business-as-usual would continue forever. Their lives were composed of a seemingly endless series of repeated activities, leaving them neither time nor reason to face the future. Noah could hardly perceive what the future would be any more than they, but he acted on a word of God and built a boat. When the flood came, he entered the ark and they were swept away. The days of Noah brought separation.

The other figure is that of the householder who lacks vigilance in protecting the house. Because he fails to keep watch, the thief succeeds in breaking in and plundering the house. What Noah's contemporaries and the householder share in common is that "they knew nothing" (24:39, 43). Unaware of any impending crisis, they were lulled into a false security by savoring the present, to the detriment of a future-oriented existence. They failed to watch.

The readers, however, are commanded to be ready and to watch for the Son of man's coming. Three parables that follow in Matt. 24 and 25 (24:45–51; 25:1–13, 14–30) reinforce the exhortations, but also lead to a climactic, apocalyptic scene. There, in a vision depicting the actual coming of the Son of man, a judgment is rendered regarding those who have or have not tended to the hungry, the thirsty, the stranger, the naked, the sick, and the imprisoned (25:31–46). The judgment leaves no doubt as to what readiness and watchfulness entail.

As the church observes the season of Advent and is pointed by the lectionary to texts that highlight waiting and watching, it is salutary to recall that what the church currently awaits is not Christmas but the second advent. In one sense, the baby born in Bethlehem fulfills the promise of the Hebrew scriptures; but in another sense, the baby becomes a promise of something more, the coming of the Son of man at an unknown hour. We no longer await the baby's birth. We await his return, his revelation as the Lord of heaven and earth, as the King-Judge, who renders judgment and sets right all that is twisted and distorted. Celebrating Christmas means renewing the promise and standing ready to welcome God's consummation.

Second Sunday of Advent

These Advent readings characterize hope as a visible, public, shared yearning. What God has promised and what God will give is a deep and foundational change in social relations, which are finally submitted to God's purpose and will.

It is for that reason that the Old Testament roots of Advent hope are cast in royal imagery. The psalm marks the king (the present king or the expected king) as one whose work is to bring justice to the weak. The office of the king is to equalize by a powerful intervention a social situation of enormous inequity. The new king makes a new world possible.

That new world, however, is not just a pious expression of hope that will come to fruition automatically or by osmosis. The newness is an intrusive reality that disrupts all that is old and destructive. The reception of the new public possibility requires a decision that is both daring and costly. It is daring because we will not know how to act in a genuinely just community. It is costly because we benefit from and are comfortable with old, deathly patterns of life. The Gospel reading is both invitation and warning that we must make concrete decisions to reorder our life in ways appropriate to God's new intention.

Characteristically Paul, as a pastor, makes the grand, sweeping claim immediate and concrete. The new behavior appropriate to God's new governance is not just a sweeping generalization, but it is the immediate practice in the church of the way the strong and the weak, the haves and have-nots, relate to each other in new faithfulness. Advent is pondering specific decisions about bringing our daily life into sync with God's rule. It is the energy and power of God (that is, the wind of God) that may authorize and enable us to receive the new king and rejoice in a new obedience which attends to the neighbor. When we are so energized, we are dazzled by the fact that the whole of creation can begin again, healed, restored, forgiven. The news of God's newness is indeed very good news. We can embrace it, receive it, and act upon it!

Isaiah 11:1–10

The political situation of Jerusalem is dominated by a "stump." The religious yearning of Israel is powered by "the spirit." The crisis of Israel's present and Israel's future is the deep conflict and contest between the *stump* and the *spirit*. The "stump" is the "stump of Jesse" (Isa.11:1). Allusion to Jesse, father of David, refers us to the dynastic line of David's family, believed to be the carrier of God's goodness and God's faithfulness in the world. That dynasty, however, had come on very hard times. Either the dynasty was ended by the Babylonians (in the exile of the sixth century) or it was humiliated by the Assyrians (in the eighth century), depending on when one dates the text. This "stump" bespeaks a situation of despair and resignation.

Then, however, enters God's "spirit" (v. 2). The poet refers to God's life-giving, future-creating, world-forming, despair-ending power and wind, which can create an utter newness. This "wind of God" is inscrutable, irresistible, beyond human control, management, or predictability. The poem announces that the wind has come to blow over the stump. The wind indicates new possibility; the stump forecloses all futures. The contest is urgent. Some believe the hopeless stump can defeat the wind and leave Jerusalem bereft.

The poet, however, knows otherwise! The spirit will prevail! The wind will win, for the stump is not mentioned again in the poem. The little "shoot" of the David line is so insignificant as to be unnoticed. That little "shoot," however, will be invaded and occupied by the spirit, and therefore massively transformed.

The authorizing of the new king by God's powerful spirit will make the king an advocate of good, fair, and equitable judgment. The wind that will blow over the new governance is marked by wisdom, understanding, and power, contrasted with foolishness, obdurance, and cowardice (v. 2).

The primary responsibilities of the king in the ancient world include dispensation of justice, that is, making decisions about social power and social goods. The poet (and the Bible generally), however, has a quite distinctive notion of righteousness and equity. This equity is a partisan, interventionist, active justice, which is entrusted to the "shoot." The new king, powered by the spirit, will not be open to bribes ("what his eyes see") or convinced by propaganda ("what his ears hear") (v. 3). He will, rather, be the kind of judge who will attend to the needs of the "meek" and the "poor," that is, the socially powerless.

These acts of righteousness and equity are not only occasional acts or arbitrary interventions, but the enduring characteristics of the new governance, so consistent and reliable that they will be the very clothes the king wears. The poet dares to imagine that in place of the usual weapons of military office—sword, spear, and javelin—this king will be dressed in the saving regalia of loyal concern and love.

The poet finally launches into a lyrical celebration of newness that is as broad and large as all of creation (vs. 6–9). In our own time, we are learning, a little at a time, that human acts of injustice wreak havoc with the created order (witness the "greenhouse effect," or the destruction of the Brazilian rain forests). Conversely, acts of human justice permit creation to function in a healthy, fruitful way. Thus the newness envisioned for creation (vs. 6–9) follows properly from the newness of human justice (vs. 4–5).

The upshot of the new governance is a restored, reconciled creation, in which the brutality is tamed and the deathliness is overcome. The oldest of enemies—wolf-lamb, leopard-kid, calf-lion, cow-bear, lion-ox—are made friends. We thought it not possible, but the wind has blown newness. In the midst of the transformed word pairs, three times a child is mentioned: "a little child" (v. 6), "the nursing child," "the weaned child" (v. 8). The little child may be the new shoot of Jesse who will preside over new creation. More broadly, "the little child" bespeaks the birth of a new innocence in which trust, gentleness, and friendship are possible and appropriate. The world will be ordered, so that the fragile and vulnerable can have their say and live their lives.

The new possibilities depend on the wind, which the stump cannot withstand. That wind is blowing. Advent is our decision to trust the new wind against the hopeless stump of what has failed.

Psalm 72:1–7, 18–19

There are two basic foci in this text. The first is on the person of the king, whose rule is here joyously celebrated. It is quite possible that this psalm was originally a coronation anthem sung at the enthronement of a new Davidic monarch, a likelihood heightened by the fact that the "king" (first line of v. 1) is also called "son-of-a-king" (NRSV's "a king's son" in the second line of v. 1; see translation below). That train of thought achieves a climax in vs. 8–11 (outside the lectionary passage), which constitutes a prayer that the empire of David and Solomon remain intact from the River (Euphrates) to the Mediterranean Sea (cf. 1 Kings 4:21).

Yet if this psalm was born as a political statement, it, like many other royalist affirmations in the Old Testament, came over time to be understood as a reference not to any merely mortal ruler, but to the transcendent monarch Jesus Christ. As such, it achieves a place among the lections for Advent, where it celebrates the kingship of the Babe of Bethlehem. And not only does it celebrate. By its presence among the Advent readings, the text also points to the reality that at the first advent God's power was clothed in vulnerability, God's sovereignty in weakness.

The second focus, however, is on the nature of the king's rule, and the psalmist uses the time-honored device of repetition to ensure that no reader or singer of this psalm misses the point. In the literal translation below, which attempts to emphasize the Hebrew word roots, note the manner in which key words are used over and over again:

(1) O God, give to the king your *justice,*
and your *righteousness* to the son-of-a-king.
(2) May he judge your people by means of *righteousness*
and your poor by means of *justice.*
(3) May the mountains bring *peace* to the people,
and the hills bring *righteousness.*
(4) May he render *justice* to the poor of the people,
and deliver the needy
and crush the oppressor.

. . . .

(7) May *righteousness* sprout forth in his days
and *peace* expand
until there be no more moon.

Righteousness, justice, and peace form a litany of the king's responsibilities, those qualities of life whose achievement constitutes the king's role in human affairs. They are chief among those attributes by which the Old Testament understands "kingness" in the dominion of God. Time and again the historians of ancient Israel condemn the nation's rulers because they fail this model of royalty (2 Kings 21:2) or, less frequently, praise them because they attain it (2 Kings 22:2).

Because political expectations once directed at the Davidic kings have become for the church the hope for salvation vested in the one Davidic King, Jesus Christ, the qualities stressed in the lines above stand at the center of that hope. They constitute characteristics not simply of the person of the King, but also of life within the kingdom, in that righteousness, justice, and peace become the qualities by which citizens of the kingdom shape their hearts and conduct their affairs. These qualities are interrelated and do not exist apart from one another.

Thus, righteousness may be described as that orientation of the heart which yearns for the presence of honesty, gentleness, truth, and compassion within the human community. Justice is the actualization within the community of the above qualities, an achievement that is made possible (all too rarely!) by a deep and sincere righteous yearning, while peace is the harmony and concord that result from the presence of justice. Not only the Isaianic tradition among Israel's prophets affirmed this interconnectedness (see Isa. 11:1–10, this Sunday), but others within the prophetic continuum as well (Jer. 5:28; Amos 5:24, etc.).

The seductions of Advent and Christmas are many. They need not take the form of the "crass materialism" so often (and with justification) attacked from the pulpit. They may as easily incarnate themselves as celebrations of little more than what God has done for men and women in the past and will do for us in the future, celebrations in which God is portrayed as the Eternal Giver and humankind shown as the perpetual receiver of God's benevolence. To be sure, that is an important part of the Advent proclamation, for if it is nothing else, the Bethlehem manger is a reminder that God offers to us a Gift that we could not achieve for ourselves. The Christ-event is, after all, an act of God's pure grace.

But texts such as this lection from Ps. 72 are a warning that our vision must not stop at that image, but must include some realization of what the people of the kingdom bring to the experience of expectancy regarding the new King. They/we must, in the spirit of the coming King, live lives of righteousness, justice, and peace—in the Old Testament sense of those words. And they/we must announce, as central to the good news, that Advent is a time of expectancy on the part of God, as well. For while humankind expects the birth of a new King, God expects that men and women will respond to this great gift by building their lives around those very qualities which the new King has come to proclaim. If we fail to do so, we miss the heart of Advent. If we fail to do so, we wait for some other king than Jesus, the Messiah.

Romans 15:4–13

While this reading begins with v. 4, perhaps because of the perceived connection between Paul's use of the Old Testament in vs. 9–12 and his comment in v. 4 about the purpose of scripture, the separation of v. 4 from vs. 1–3 is an awkward one. Verse 4 reflects an attitude toward scripture that pervades all of Paul's letters, but here it is specifically tied to what he has said in vs. 1–3, especially v. 3. Further, vs. 1–6 are formally parallel to vs. 7–13, and that parallel is lost when vs. 1–3 are omitted. Notice that each paragraph begins with an ethical admonition (15:1–2; 15:7), ties that ethical admonition to the action of Christ and to scripture (15:3–4, 15:8–12), and concludes with a prayer-wish (15:6; 15:13).

Romans 15:1–6 brings to a close the comments that began in 14:1 about relationships between the "strong" and the "weak" (labels that may identify various groups in the Roman church according to their attitudes toward the Mosaic law). As is his custom, Paul's sharpest words address the faction that is understood to be the strongest (15:1–2), and he then reminds his audience that Christ did not please himself and applies the words of Ps. 69:9 to Christ. In this context, he claims that scripture ("whatever was written in former days") was written "for our instruction." This claim is not, of course, a historical claim that the psalmist *intended* to refer to Jesus Christ or that the psalmist *intended* to write to a group of Christians living in the first century. It is, instead, a theological claim about the way in which the voice of scripture always speaks a word of hope. Concluding the exhortation and theological rationale is Paul's prayer that God will enable believers to carry out the exhortation.

While the first paragraph addresses the specific conflict between the "strong" and the "weak," the second encompasses all persons. The simple admonition to welcome or to receive or accept one another is attached to an equally simple warrant: Christ welcomed you for the glory of God. What we notice here is that people are not welcomed for their inherent value or their accomplishments or even because of their repentance. They are welcomed because Christ welcomed them—for God's glory.

The complicated explanation that follows seems designed to show how Christ's radical welcome of all people both glorifies God and is reflected in scripture. The NRSV translates Paul's initial comment as "Christ has become a servant of the circumcised," but the Greek phrase is ambiguous. What Paul says is that Christ became a *diakonos peritomēs*, a minister or servant of/to/concerning circumcision. To say that Christ was a servant *of* circumcision or *to* circumcision becomes very problematic in English, because either translation seems to suggest that Christ's role had something to do with circumcision as such. In context, however, the meaning seems to be clear: namely, Christ was a servant who was connected with those who are identified by circumcision—Christ was a Jew. What Paul is affirming here is the very particular identity of Jesus Christ with the people of Israel, an identification that persists even while the "welcome" of Christ is radicalized.

This radicalization comes to expression in vs. 8b–9, as Paul asserts Christ's role both in confirming God's promises to the patriarchs (Christ is for Jews) *and* in bringing Gentiles to glorify God (Christ is for Gentiles). That God's Christ confirms God's faithfulness for both these groups, that is, for all people, lies at the heart of the gospel and simultaneously of its scandal. The scripture citations that follow reinforce the point Paul is making about God's action, especially as that action pertains to the Gentiles. Verse 12, with its reference to the "root of Jesse" and the Gentiles, echoes v. 8's reminder that it is a member of the people of Israel who brings about this radical possibility of including Gentiles within the people of Israel (cf. Rom. 11:17–24). The passage concludes with the second prayer-wish, in which Paul invokes God's own power to enable the life of the community in joy, peace, and hope.

This reading reinforces the theme that has dominated Romans since 1:16–17, namely, the gospel as revealing God's righteousness for all people, "to the Jew first and also to the Greek." That all are alike sinful and that all are alike redeemed by God's grace—these are the themes that Paul asserts over and over again. The subtle references to conflict in Rom. 14 and 15 hint that these are not, for Paul, vague generalizations about reconciliation but powerful assertions about God's righteousness as it alters the lives of real human beings.

The hope that issues forth from this struggle to articulate what God has done in Jesus Christ is the hope that every Advent stirs in the hearts of God's people. It is the hope that not only proclaims the welcome we have received from Christ but also ventures forth to welcome others "by the power of the Holy Spirit."

Matthew 3:1–12

John the Baptist figures in the lectionary readings for both the second and third Sundays of Advent in each of the yearly cycles. His repeated appearances, however, do not make him any easier to understand or his message any more palatable. He is such an unusual character that we modern readers find him hardly believable. He is a rugged, ascetic nonconformist, whose diet consists of grasshoppers and wild honey, and who carries on his crusades outside the cities in the wilderness. It is hard to recast John in Brooks Brothers attire. He seems more like a cartoon figure in the *New Yorker* who walks Park Avenue in a dirty robe, toting a sign that reads, "Prepare to meet thy God!"

But John plays a critical role in the Gospel narrative. He is identified, in the words of Isaiah, as the voice calling for the preparation of the Lord's way. He preaches a message of repentance linked to the confession of sins and practices baptism as a sign of repentance. Crowds from Jerusalem and the surrounding districts flock to hear John and apparently find in his preaching a message worth hearing.

Why do they flock to hear John? Perhaps they are weary of the way their lives are being lived and welcome the call for a change. Perhaps they are glad to know that there really is a God who holds them accountable for their conduct. Perhaps they find reassurance from John that the world in which they live is not amoral after all, that morality is not reduced to a single command—"Thou shalt not get caught." It is terrifying to contemplate the alternative, that we and the terrorists and child molesters and purveyors of racism and sexism might be answerable to no one. John, however, declares a God who cares and demands accountability. To be confronted by such a holy God and to discover who one really is, painful as that may be, brings relief. It is especially good news to those threatened by what seems like a meaningless, haphazard world, who fear that there is no ultimate resolution or justice.

Matthew states that many of the Pharisees and Sadducees came to hear John and to be baptized. What were they doing among the crowd? Could they have been serious seekers? John attacks them with his scorching words: "You brood of vipers! Who warned you to flee from the wrath to come?" The reader is left with the impression that they perhaps were toying with a change of heart, flirting with the message of this strange evangelist. Perhaps they wanted a bit of his message, but not too much—enough to clear the conscience and remove the guilt, enough so that they need no longer to haunted by the past, enough to feel good again.

What John attacks is the presumptuousness of the Pharisees and Sadducees. The prophet had written, "Look to the rock from which you were hewn. . . . Look to Abraham your father" (Isa. 51:1–2). The problem was that the rock had become something behind which to hide, a place of supposed protection, a spot of security. John challenges the privileged position claimed by the Pharisees and Sadducees from being Abraham's descendants, and declares that from ordinary stones in the wilderness God is able to fashion children of Abraham. Repentance has to do not only with remorse over past failures, but also with a new heart and a changed life. "Bear fruit worthy of repentance" (Matt. 3:8) is a warning against cheap grace.

But John does not stop with a call for true repentance; he also points beyond himself to the one stronger than he, who baptizes with the Spirit and who separates the wheat from the chaff. John's role is a preparatory one, both in warning people about the coming wrath and in announcing the ministry of the Messiah. The Holy Spirit, who characterizes Jesus' baptism, signifies the new age, the kingdom of heaven whose nearness John announces. In the ensuing narrative developed by Matthew, the reader is given glimpses of the presence and character of the kingdom of heaven in the words and deeds of Jesus.

John's preaching also needs to be understood in light of the tensions at the time of writing between Matthew's community and the synagogue nearby. The Pharisees and Sadducees mirror the leaders of the synagogue of Matthew's day, who have ignored the wrath that is to come by rejecting the gospel. The children of Abraham whom God has raised from stones turn out to be the Gentiles who have entered the Christian church and who now claim their Abrahamic descendance. The challenge from Matthew's pen is aimed at the Jewish authorities, who are called to repent and to embrace changed lives befitting true repentance. And yet there is a universality about John's preaching, which enables modern as well as ancient readers to hear and sense the urgency of repentance.

Third Sunday of Advent

These readings have a vivid sense that God's coming, or the coming of the Messiah, will be profoundly transformative. The Bible is relentless in its conviction that nothing that is skewed and distorted and deathly need remain as it is. God's power and God's passion converge to make total newness possible. The promises of messianic possibility work against our exhaustion, our despair, and our sense of being subject to fate.

Newness is indeed possible. The community waits for newness; it can do so, however, only because it remembers newnesses given in the past. The psalm provides a comprehensive summary of the miracles wrought by God in the past to make new life possible.

With this legacy of memory and anticipation, we are able to discern Jesus differently. It is in the life and ministry of Jesus that these large expectations of Israel take on concrete body. Jesus is remembered and celebrated as the one who permits human life to begin again.

The prophetic oracle, psalm, and Gospel reading all move toward the practicality of the Epistle reading. The admonition of the Epistle reading is that we permit this claim of new human possibility to permeate all of life, so that the perspective of faithful people is buoyant in the face of seemingly permanent suffering. The community of the faithful believes in cosmic and quite intimate ways that the will of God for the well-being of the world will indeed prevail over all that is distorted and pathological. The church in Advent remembers this newness happening in Jesus and prepares itself for the affirmation that God is at work even now to bring the world to God's powerful well-being.

In embracing this hope, Christians are distinguished both from the despairing, who believe nothing can change, and from the self-sufficient, who believe they themselves will work the newness. Our life, against both temptations, is directed to the reality of God, the very God whom we discern in our present and to whom we entrust our future.

Isaiah 35:1–10

This poem articulates in powerful lyrical abandonment the transformation of creation and history wrought by the coming of God into a people's life. It is divided into two parts: (a) the wondrous transformation wrought by God's coming (vs. 1–7); (b) a response to the newness in glad procession (vs. 8–10).

The described transformation (vs. 1–7) can best be read in a chiastic structure:

(a) the transformation of creation (vs. 1–2)
(b) the transformation of disabled humanity (v. 3)
(c) the assertion of God's coming rescue (v. 4)
(b′) the transformation of disabled humanity (vs. 5–6a)
(a′) the transformation of creation (vs. 6b–7)

1. It may be most helpful to read this text from the center, that is, from the announcement of God's coming rescue (v. 4), because everything hangs on this word from God. Without God's powerful word and powerful presence, both creation and disabled humanity are lost, hopeless, and condemned to deathliness. God's intention is to save; in order to save, God will both "recompense" (that is, make reparations and give good gifts) and "avenge" (that is, defeat the powers of death that prevent full function). God will come in power both to work good and to eliminate threat.

2. The first impact of the news of God's coming concerns disabled humans (vs. 3, 5–6a). The ones addressed are those with "weak hands" and "feeble knees" (v. 3). They are, however, also those with "fearful hearts" (v. 4). It includes all those whose lives are overwhelmed by fear, timidity, vulnerability, lack of courage, lack of the capacity to live a full life—anything that prevents living effectively and joyously.

When the gospel of God's coming is uttered (v. 4), the impact on the disabled ones is immediate and dramatic: the blind see, the deaf hear, the lame walk, the dumb sing (vs. 5–6a; cf. Luke 7:22)! The failure of human creation is inverted. People are given back their lives. Humanity is restored to full function.

3. The impact of God's word on troubled humanity is matched by its impact on troubled creation. Indeed, the situations of humanity

and creation are identical. Both are in pitiful condition, both desperately yearn for rescue, both are incapable of saving themselves. The rhetoric of vs. 1–2, 6b–7 is uttered in an arid climate. The wound of creation (the wilderness) is a massive drought in which all live plants suffer. The wilderness has no surplus resources, and survival for plants is always precarious at best. The rain, however, is promised. God is coming, and the whole of the discouraged wilderness will blossom and flourish, restored to full function (v. 2).

After the oracle of assurance (v. 4), we have an exuberant description of renewed creation (vs. 6b–7). One can easily picture rushing streams of water where there had been cracked earth and dry wadis. In the middle of desolate hot sand, springs well up. Life begins again! New creation emerges because of the power and resolve of God, whose will and purpose are to restore.

The poetry of Isaiah is relentlessly focused on Jerusalem. The Holy City is the place to go. The poet assumes that anyone who is able will use energy to get to Jerusalem to celebrate, to thank, and to enjoy God's new presence. Verses 8–10 thus envision a great procession to Jerusalem on the new road built just for this liturgy of restoration (cf. 40:3–4). Unlike the dangerous road to Jericho, where one can get mugged (see Luke 10:30), this road is utterly safe. There are no attacking lions, no ambush, no threat. The new creation is on its way rejoicing.

All the rescued ones will be on the road. The poet envisions all of creation, all the creatures, in religious pilgrimage—the blind, deaf, dumb, and lame—but also crocuses, grass, and jackals. All are alike. All have in common the new gift of life. All of creation, human and nonhuman, are gathered together in thanksgiving and singing and rejoicing.

Our reading of this text must not tone down or apologize for its lyrical abandonment. The poem is a healing alternative to the church's grim despair and to our modern sense that no real newness is possible. The text invites us out of our managed rationality to affirm that God does what the world thinks is not possible. Advent is getting ready for that impossibility which will permit us to dance and sing and march and thank and drink—and live!

Psalm 146:5–10

Psalm 146 is one of the several hymns of praise which, in the fashion of a crescendo of doxologies, form a climax to the Old Testament Psalter. These all (Pss. 146—150) begin and end with the same affirmation: Hallelujah ("Praise the LORD!") Within this envelope of joyous ascription, these psalms unfurl a litany of mighty acts for which Yahweh is deemed worthy of praise, from the very general ("for he is gracious," 147:1) to the most specific ("he commanded and they [the waters] were created," 148:5).

Yet while the mood of Ps. 146 is consistent with the literary and theological context in which it is set, it is distinctive in important respects. For one thing, it is the most individualistic of these five psalms, almost introspective in its language (vs. 1–2). Although ours may be a time in which the excesses of individualism in religion and in other aspects of life threaten the human need for community, the situation of the psalmist may have been quite different. The ancient world, including Israel-of-old, placed such a premium on community that the individual's life was often submerged to the interests of the larger group. The story of the brutal murder of Saul's seven sons to satisfy the claims of the Gibeonites (2 Sam. 21:1–14) is a tragically prominent instance of community solidarity gone awry. Thus, although other components within this extended doxology which concludes the psalter may stress the importance of corporate praise to Yahweh (e.g., Ps. 149:1–2), Ps. 146 affirms that women and men are to praise God one-on-One.

Another distinctive feature of this psalm concerns the reasons for which Yahweh is to be praised, and it is to this point that this day's lection speaks. Before our passage begins, the psalmist has stated in negative terms the object of valid human trust (vs. 3–4), that is, it should not be vested in puny human strength. And beginning with the first lines of our lection (v. 5), the ancient poet celebrates both the true object of human trust and the mood in which that trust is to be extended: "Happy are those whose help is the God of Jacob!" This is the creator God (v. 6), whose generation of the universe is celebrated elsewhere in the Old Testament (e.g., Gen. 1; Isa. 42:5). This is also the God whose benevolence is unending, who is "faithful forever" (another way of phrasing the second line of Ps. 146:6).

Yet the creativity and perpetuity of Yahweh are not the psalmist's exclusive concern. Rather, the central issue here is Yahweh's role as the liberator and bringer-of-justice. The verbs in vs. 7–9 are crucial. Quite interestingly, the Hebrew releases a string of participial phrases, making of these lines a fountain of splendid epithets concerning the quality of God's person. Yahweh is

a doer of justice
a giver of bread

a liberator of prisoners
an opener of blind eyes
a raiser of fallen ones
a lover of the righteous
a watcher of homeless ones.
The orphan and the widow he will sustain.

It is these phrases which connect directly with other lections for this day (especially Isa. 35:5–6; Matt. 11:5), helping to establish a commonality of purpose among them.

There are, of course, two basic ways in which Yahweh's role as liberator may be understood: literally and metaphorically. And it is interesting that in the list above both modes are described. It was, for example, the deep conviction among many in ancient Israel (notably, the prophets) that Yahweh is a just God, which resulted in their insistence that human society mirror the divine justice. Or, put differently, if Yahweh is a "watcher of homeless ones," Yahweh's people can be no less. On this level, then, the descriptive epithets function in a literal sense (Yahweh is the "giver of bread" in that Yahweh sends the rains that water the earth and make it fruitful).

But there is also a figurative sense in which these statements about Yahweh are made. Yahweh is an "opener of blind eyes," for example, not in casting away all diseases of the eye (blindness was a persistent problem in antiquity), but in sharing with humankind those important realities which give life meaning and purpose, those realities which allow us to "see" where we have come from and where we need to go. (In this connection, it may be worth noting that one way of translating the third line of v. 6 is "keeper of truth forever.") Similarly, while persons who have been released from some form of bondage might justifiably credit their release to God, Yahweh comes to humans as "a liberator of prisoners" and as "a raiser of fallen ones," in that it is Yahweh who reverses the terrible effects of sin and alienation and who creates that freedom of the spirit in which men and women love and serve Yahweh.

Advent is a time of expectancy during which we await the coming of the One who can set us free from the terrible distortions in our relationships with God and with one another. This is the One who liberates us from the power of sin, who salves the hurtful things we do to ourselves and to others, and who gently, yet uncompromisingly (last line of v. 9), sets our feet in ways that are just and true.

Jesus' actual opening of flesh-and-blood blind eyes (the Matthew lection for this day) constitutes a promise, stated in literal form, that the Babe of Bethlehem—who is also our King—is prepared to open our eyes of the spirit. Therefore, we sing with the psalmist of old: "Hallelujah! Praise the Lord!"

James 5:7–10

This passage may initially recall Rom. 13:11–14, with its connection between apocalyptic expectation and ethical admonition, but the two passages actually reflect very different understandings of the "coming of the Lord." For Paul, that day, which he refers to simply as "salvation," seems to be very close at hand and impinges on the present. James shows, apart from this passage, very little expectation of an immediate parousia, and seems to be introducing it to offer some specific ethical teaching, typical of the paraenesis that runs throughout the letter.

James 5: 7–8 introduces and repeats the admonition of patience or endurance. "Be patient, therefore, beloved, until the coming of the Lord." Following the example of the farmer's patience, the admonition is restated: "You also must be patient. Strengthen your hearts, for the coming of the Lord is near." Taken on its own, without further comment, this admonition seems odd. How is it possible to be *patient* if the coming of the Lord is indeed at hand? The urgency that pervades the Son of Man sayings in the Gospels or the eschatological language in Paul's letters is missing here. Why encourage patience in this situation?

The example of the farmer separates the two forms of the admonition and may shed light on this curious interpretation of the parousia: "The farmer waits for the precious crop from the earth, being patient with it until it receives the early and the late rains." Unlike the imagery of the "thief in the night" (1 Thess. 5:2) or the "stars . . . falling from heaven" (Mark 13:25), which conjures up the unexpected, even the violent, this imagery invokes the farmer who must wait for the regular, predictable cycle of Palestinian rains before the arrival of the harvest. For the author of James, the parousia has less to do with God's invasion of the world as it is than it does with the absolute reliability of God's promises. Like the farmer who relies on God to send the needed rain (Deut. 11:14; Jer. 5:24; Zech. 10:1), the faithful may and must rely on God. Patience derives from that certainty about God's protection.

James 5:9 makes concrete and specific the general exhortation to patience: "Beloved, do not grumble against one another." In the Septuagint this same verb (*stenazein*) characterizes the sighing of people who live in situations of oppression, whether as a result of their own sin or that of others (e.g., Ex. 2:23, 6:5; Isa. 59:11). Here it applies to the complaints believers may have against other believers; hence, the repetition of the word "beloved" in the middle of the injunction heightens the scandal of believers engaging in wrongdoing against one another. With his negative view of those outside the church, James is characteristically unconcerned about "grumbling" that may be directed toward the outside. Believers are not to grumble because "the Judge is standing at the doors."

We find in vs. 10–11 other examples of patience and endurance. The prophets are often cited for their suffering (e.g., Acts 7:51–52), but here they serve as examples also of patience. James 5:11 singles out the individual Job, who remained steadfast throughout great suffering. These examples suggest that the call for patience in this text does not arise from some general conviction about the virtue of patience. Instead, the patience referred to is that of suffering people who know that God will vindicate them.

The larger context of this passage reinforces this conclusion. Throughout the letter James rails against those who lack integrity, whose actions do not convey the faith that they assert (1:22–27; 2:14–26). Just prior to our passage comes a warning to the rich about the judgment that will come upon them as a result of their mistreatment of others (5:1–6). The "therefore" at the beginning of v. 7 connects our passage with what precedes it, suggesting that the patience called for is that of believers, even in situations of oppression and injustice.

For the letter of James, then, the advent of Jesus Christ calls for patience, even on the part of the oppressed and suffering. The patience that is called for, however, is not so much passive acquiescence to situations of oppression and injustice as it is active confidence in God, whose promise extends to human beings in every context and every situation. The advent of Jesus Christ, for this letter, also contains a theme of judgment. To say that "the Judge is standing at the doors" is to recall that Jesus' advent brings with it the accountability of human beings before God. The letter of James reminds us that our accountability includes both our convictions and our actions.

Matthew 11:2–11

The Gospel reading for the Third Sunday of Advent returns to the figure of John the Baptist, but now in a far different setting from the reading of last Sunday. No longer in the wilderness preaching his message of judgment and calling for repentance, no longer the baptizer of and witness to Jesus as "the one who is to come," John is now in prison. It is the first mention of John's confinement in Matthew, and only later do the readers learn that the arrest was occasioned by John's denunciation of Herod for his philandering with his sister-in-law. The narrator says that Herod really wanted to kill John, but withheld from doing so because the people took John to be a prophet (14:1–5).

In prison, however, John is troubled. Hearing about "what the Messiah was doing," he sends disciples to Jesus to ask, "Are you the one who is to come, or are we to wait for another?" What precipitates John's uncertainty? How does he move from being the vigorous preacher of repentance to being a questioning doubter? The text provides us with two possible explanations. One reason for his uncertainty could be his situation in prison. This is the explanation often picked up in sermons on the passage and developed psychologically, that is to say, John lies depressed and forgotten in his jail cell, and as his incarceration continues he becomes haunted with doubts. Out of his dejection and discouragement, he sends to question Jesus.

The text, however, offers another, more likely, explanation. In prison John hears about "what the Messiah was doing," presumably those acts of healing and mercy depicted in Matt. 8–9. To a fierce denouncer of the sins of the people, the Messiah's primary task must be to carry out the final judgment, to see that the ax is laid to the root of the trees and to burn every tree that does not bear fruit (3:10–12). What sort of Messiah could Jesus be who teaches in the synagogues, preaches the gospel of the kingdom, and heals every disease and infirmity (9:35)? John seems uncertain, not because of his own plight but because of what Jesus is reputed to be doing. He is not turning out to be the kind of Messiah John expected.

John's question provides an occasion for Jesus to clarify who he is. In the language of two texts from Isaiah (35:5–6; 29:18–19), he invites John's messengers to report what they have seen, what in fact he is doing for the blind, the lame, the lepers, the deaf, the dead, and the poor. His activity fulfills an expectation about the Messiah from the scriptures. To be sure, there is judgment in Jesus' presence; the next few chapters of Matthew relate the various responses to him, many of which are negative and self-condemning. But his primary activity is the restoration of the needy and the giving of life to the lifeless. No wonder that John has doubts about the Messiah!

What John needs is a new understanding of who the Messiah in reality is, what sort of work the Messiah does, and with what sort of people he does it. Jesus acknowledges that such a new understanding may be hard to come by. He pronounces a beatitude on the person who takes no offense at him (11:6). Seeing and hearing that Jesus is preoccupied with people who have been marginalized by their situations, who can do little or nothing for themselves, may represent a threat to some and prevent their accepting Jesus as Messiah. Like John, they expect that the Messiah should be doing more about stopping crime and punishing criminals. They would prefer to wait for another in hopes of finding a leader more to their liking. Jesus alone, however, defines his own messiahship.

From John's uncertainties the focus changes to Jesus' opinions about John. Three times the crowds are confronted with their eagerness to hear John ("What did you go out . . . to look at?" "What then did you go out to see?" "What then did you go out to see?"). He is a prophet, but more than a prophet. He fulfills a special role as the messenger who prepares the way of the Messiah (11:10; Mal. 3:1). There is no one born of woman who is greater than John, Jesus states. Superior accolades for this figure who occupies a distinctive place in the prophetic lineup! And yet, the one who is least in the kingdom of heaven is greater than John. The age of fulfillment toward which John points is so decisive that even Jesus' disciples (named and commissioned in the previous chapter of Matthew's Gospel), who understand and share his fulfilling activity, are greater than John. The comment is not made as a rebuke of John, but as an acknowledgment of the surpassing character of the new age dawning in the person of Jesus. It is an age in which disciples are still vulnerable to arrest and imprisonment (10:17–23), but also are charged and empowered to participate in the very messianic activity of Jesus (10:7–8).

Fourth Sunday of Advent

We are now very close to Christmas. We are close to the birth of the baby. We are close to the reality of Jesus, in whom we have invested so much of our life and faith.

In any season of its life, the church has struggled to recognize, identify, and "explain" Jesus. But it never can do so adequately. Jesus is larger than life. Jesus shatters all the categories of conventional religious recognition. Thus the narratives are pushed to daring testimony, which seeks to honor the concreteness of the coming one, but at the same time honors the inscrutable, sovereign mystery that is present in the person of Jesus. Confronted with the awesome person of Jesus, the testimony of the church takes hold of whatever images it can muster for its memory. As a result, there is an odd tension in the texts. On the one hand, it is asserted that this is the "Son of David," in continuity with the old dynasty and the old promises. On the other hand, this is one "from the Holy Spirit," not at all derived from the dynasty. This twofold way of speaking about Jesus does not reflect vacillation or confusion in the community. Rather, it is an awareness that many things must be said about Jesus, because no single claim says enough, and even the things said about Jesus have a quality of inadequacy about them. The "virgin birth" is understood as a serious, daring effort to utter the unutterable about Jesus, asserting that there is "more" to Jesus than any conventional notion can contain.

As the church reflects on the "more" of Jesus, it is finally driven to utilize references to divine quality in order to witness to Jesus.

Isaiah 7:10–16

The text continues the confrontation between king and prophet from the beginning of chapter 7. The king of Judah is in a foreign policy crisis, fearful of his two close neighbors to the north, Syria and Israel (vs. 4–6). The prophet has just warned that *only faith* will rescue the king from the apparent threat (vs. 7–9).

Our verses continue that high-stakes conversation. Our verses feature (a) a brief exchange of prophet and king (vs. 10–12), and (b) an extended prophetic oracle (vs. 13–17).

The exchange between prophet and king is in fact a confrontation between two contrasting security systems. The prophet has given an assurance that faith in Yahweh will save, even in a political crisis (vs. 7–9). Now, in a defiant challenge to the king, the prophet invites the king to set a test for God, to determine if the prophet does indeed speak God's truth.

The king refuses the defiant offer of the prophet (v. 12). The king's refusal is a gesture of high irony. Ostensibly, Ahaz's response is an act of piety, for Israel has long known the command: "Do not put the LORD your God to the test" (Deut. 6:16; cf. Luke 4:12). The fact, however, is that the king refuses to join a conversation in which the demand of faith is established as valid. If the king demonstrates by "proof" that the prophetic promise is valid, he will be obligated to revise his policy to conform to the assurances of faith. Thus what appears to be an act of profound trust on the part of the king is in fact a clever maneuver of evasion. The king does not want to submit or subject his policies to the claims of faith, because he prefers to act in his foolish autonomy.

The clever but stubborn refusal of the king evokes from the prophet a hard, devastating oracle (vs. 13–17). The prophet puts the royal apparatus on notice. Moreover, the prophet now refers to Yahweh as "my God." By implication, this odd pronoun suggests that Yahweh is no longer "your God." Yahweh has withdrawn from the dynasty. The dynasty wanted autonomy, and now it has it, for the Davidic house no longer is claimed by Yahweh.

"Therefore" (v. 14), because of the king's resistance, the prophet announces a "sign," even though the king has not asked for one. The sign is that a young woman will have a child (v. 14). Her designation "young woman" ignores the question of virginity which has loomed so large in subsequent interpretation. All the focus in the oracle is on the anticipated baby whose name is Immanuel, "God is with us" (v. 14).

The birth and growth of the baby present a time line to the nations: "Before the child knows how to refuse the evil and choose the good" is commonly reckoned in terms of childhood development as two years. Before two years the threat of Syria and Israel will dissipate (v. 16). That's the good news. The bad news is that with the disappearance of these small kings whom Ahaz so much fears, Yahweh will "bring on you" bad, bad days. Then the prophet utters the phrase, outside today's lection, that completely explodes the fantasy world of the king: "The king of Assyria" (v. 17). The phrase refers to the ominous empire to the north, which is brutal, ruthless, massive, and beyond resistance.

That innocent baby with the odd name, however, is the point of the oracle. The prophet does not seek to adjudicate for the king between little enemies and big enemy, for the king could have done that much on his own. Rather the prophet seeks to gather the entire fearful drama of public life and reorganize it around this baby whose presence and whose name assert the cruciality of Yahweh in the public arena. Because of the baby, public history is not simply a matter of brute power. Public history is working on a different schedule toward a different purpose. The baby is a time bomb in the midst of the great powers, which they can neither stop nor deactivate. The king is called away from his positivistic reckoning of power politics to permit the wondrous gifts and promises and threats of Yahweh to be central in the political process.

The Christian tradition has dared to claim that this "sign" given against the will of the king in fact anticipates the baby Jesus (see Matt. 1:22–23). The Advent question for us is the same one faced by Ahaz. It is the same one faced by Herod and by Pilate. What would happen if life were so reorganized that the baby's presence became the central reality? Everything changes when "God is with us." The time of the baby is fast approaching, and that ticking sensation makes the nations nervous.

Psalm 80:1–7, 17–19

In Advent the church is strongly reminded of the basic posture of human beings before God: helplessness and need. Not only are we vulnerable to those forces which may destroy our happiness—indeed, our very existence—but there is little or nothing that we, when left to ourselves, are capable of doing about our precarious state. And so the Psalm text utters a simple and primal cry: O God, help!

The God whose name is invoked is a special being, and it is on the basis of the psalmist's knowledge of the divine nature that appeal is made. This is a God of compassion who, although specific deeds go unmentioned in that part of the psalm that serves as this day's lection, has a history of salvation in the life of the people (see vs. 8–11). This God is the "Shepherd of Israel," the one who leads "Joseph like a flock." This is distinctive language not used elsewhere, although close parallels exist (cf. Ezek. 34; Ps. 23), and the bold terminology heightens the freshness of the text. (References to "Joseph" in v. 1 and to "Ephraim" and "Manasseh" in v. 2 have suggested to some interpreters a Northern provenance for this psalm.) Tenderness and immediacy are the images here, for God is one who can be trusted and one who is intimately available.

But God is also the being who so far transcends normal human experience that a special theophany is required in the present circumstance. Reference to the One who is "enthroned upon the cherubim" (v. 1) recalls the ecstatic experiences of Ezekiel in Ezek. 1:5–28 and 10:1–22. There, as in the present text, the cherubim suggest—at the same time—distance as well as proximity, "thereness" as well as "hereness." The person of God is so unfathomable that this One must be represented in the likeness of bizarre creatures who possess both human and animal qualities. Thus when this transcendent God engages human life it is with devastating decisiveness.

And so the contrasting images are brought together: tender shepherd and absolute ruler of the universe. And to this paradoxical One is flung the cry "Stir up your might, and . . . save us!" (v. 2; cf. v. 3).

That the distress of the people is not caused by the indifference of God is made clear by vs. 4–6. Indeed, quite the opposite is true: God has intended, or at least permitted, the suffering of the people. Anger at their prayers (v. 4) is the nearest the entire psalm comes to identifying a cause for the present distress, which is characterized by the unusual and cryptic phrases "bread of tears" and "tears to drink" (v. 5). In language more typical of other psalm texts, the anguish of the people is further described as arising in no small part out of their social isolation (v. 6; cf. Pss. 27:2; 31:13). Quite interestingly, nowhere does the psalm link the crisis of the moment to the sinfulness of the people. Perhaps that is because the psalmist felt that the connection would be so obvious it did not demand notation. But more likely is the explanation that, like Job (Job 23:1–7), the psalmist viewed the pain as, in this instance at least, undeserved.

At the heart of the psalm, then, lies a cry for salvation, the urgency of which is conveyed by the repeated cadences of vs. 3, 7, and 19. In this refrain the elements of restoration and illumination are paramount, and both are present as references to salvation. "Restore us, O (LORD) God (of hosts)" employs a verb (*šûb*) which elsewhere carries the clear meaning of a return to an original state, in this case a state of health and wholeness (cf. Ps. 23:3). Even the plea "let your face shine" is a cry for salvation, in that it recalls the presence of God at the exodus and in the wilderness, where the glory of God "lit up the night" (Ex. 14:20) and protected the Israelites from the pursuing Egyptians.

As is evident from the repeated use of the pronouns "us" and "we," this psalm speaks to a crisis involving the whole community of Yahweh's people (see "your people's prayers" of v. 4). Individuals may (and often do) find themselves in threatening situations, either because of their own sinfulness or because of forces over which they have no control, and the Old Testament frequently gives voice to their terror (Ps. 13, as one example among many). But this day's lection is a reminder—if one were needed—that an entire community, even the community of faith, may stand in need of God's intervening love.

An appeal to the office of the king, "the one at your right hand" (v. 17), rounds out the community's petition and anticipates the church's Advent expectation of the coming Messiah, Jesus Christ. In the strength of the king is life for the people (v. 18).

The function of this text as an Advent lesson would seem to serve the purpose of injecting an important element of realism into the new season of the church's life. There is no room here for a sentimental or romantic assessment of the human situation, even of the church's situation before God. The community of faith is not different from humankind at large in terms of our need for divine grace. The distinction is rather that the body of Christ, when it is true to its purpose, acknowledges its inadequacy—both corporately and individually—and throws itself open to the intervention of God's grace. Only when the people of Christ acknowledge their need can we claim the message of anticipation that Advent proclaims. It is only when, with Israel-of-old, the church honestly prays,

> Restore us, O God;
>   let your face shine, that we may be saved

that the redemptive dimensions of Advent and Christmas may become realities.

Romans 1:1–7

The most obvious point of association between these opening lines of Romans and the other texts for this Sunday derives from Paul's reference in v. 3 to the Davidic descent of Jesus. Beyond that narrow connection, however, these verses announce the coming of the gospel of Jesus Christ, so that the assignment of this passage to Advent is far from arbitrary.

Romans 1:1–7 constitutes the most extensive salutation and greeting of any of Paul's letters. Because Paul had not yet been to Rome (see 1:13), he cannot rely on a personal relationship having already been established and needs to provide an introduction of himself (vs. 1, 5–6) and the gospel he proclaims (vs. 2–4). That these two are inseparable is made clear from the way in which they are introduced here.

The three phrases with which he identifies himself reiterate Paul's connection with the gospel. First he says that he is a "servant of Jesus Christ" (NRSV). The Greek word *doulos* is more accurately rendered by the English "slave" rather than "servant," and the more forceful word "slave" appropriately conveys Paul's sense of the compulsion under which he labors (cf. 1 Cor. 9:16). "Called to be an apostle" reinforces the involuntary nature of Paul's labor; that is, he did not choose to be an apostle, but was chosen by God. "Set apart for the gospel of God" both restates Paul's calling and introduces the gospel itself, which becomes the subject of vs. 2–4.

What Paul says first about the gospel is that God promised it "through his prophets in the holy scriptures." This early reference to scripture will seem odd if we think of Roman Christians as primarily Gentile, but there are strong indications that Jewish Christians were also part of the Roman church (e.g., the discussion of the law in Rom. 7). More important, a recurrent issue in Romans is the faithfulness of God, and this early reference to the promises of scripture introduces that issue by insisting on God's having kept God's promise.

In vs. 3–4 the gospel takes on content in the form of two assertions about Jesus Christ. First, he "was descended from David according to the flesh." Second, he "was declared to be Son of God with power according to the spirit of holiness by resurrection from the dead." Formally, the two assertions stand in parallel; the first describes Jesus "according to the flesh" and the second "according to the spirit." There is no indication that the second assertion negates or deemphasizes the first. Both assertions are part of the gospel.

The first assertion locates Jesus firmly within the people of Israel and, indeed, within the royal line itself. Any Christian claim that Jesus was not really a Jew or ceased to be a Jew flounders on this statement that God's Son was from the house of David. This assertion also undermines the perennial Christian temptation to deny or denigrate the humanity of Christ, whom Paul clearly identifies as living "according to the flesh" (cf. Rom. 9:5).

If we read the second assertion as a bit of systematic theology, it poses numerous problems. The suggestion that Jesus becomes "Son of God" only at his resurrection contradicts the Gospels as well as the hymn Paul quotes in Phil. 2:5–11, and consequently commentators scurry to resolve the difficulties. What these attempts sometimes miss is the richness that emerges from the varying early Christian interpretations about the point at which Jesus is the Christ (e.g.: At the baptism in Mark? At the conception in Luke and Matthew? At creation in John?). Attempts to resolve the conflicts also overlook the parallel between the two assertions. Paul's is not a systematic attempt to describe the point at which Jesus *became* the Christ. Verse 4 is, rather, a statement about the triumph of God as it breaks through in the resurrection of Jesus Christ.

Verse 5 moves from this recitation of the gospel *in nuce* back to the apostolic task. It is through Jesus Christ that Paul and his coworkers attempt to bring about the "obedience of faith" among all nations. This peculiar phrase appears again in 16:26 and nowhere else in Paul's letters. It may be a subtle way of forging a compromise between those Christians (both Jew and Gentile) who emphasize the need for obedience to the law and those Christians (both Jew and Gentile) who emphasize the significance of faith alone. To speak of the obedience of faith, or the obedience that stems from faith, is to enable both groups (or the several groups that may have existed) to hear their own claim and also that of their brothers and sisters.

Verses 6 and 7 bring the salutation and greeting to a close in a way customary for Paul. It is important to note, however, that this greeting involves the statement that believers in Rome are called. Not only apostles, but also "ordinary" believers receive their faith as a calling from God.

Matthew 1:18–25

Matthew begins the narrative chosen for this last Sunday in Advent with the declaration, "Now the birth of Jesus the Messiah took place in this way" (1:18). But as the verses unfold, it becomes apparent that Matthew is not so much concerned with Jesus' birth as with his conception and naming. The birth finally is reported in the last verse of the chapter, but simply to signal the termination of the period of sexual abstinence between Mary and Joseph (1:25). The circumstances surrounding the conception of Jesus and the names given this special baby, however, serve to identify who he is and what he is to do.

The *conception* is described from the perspective of Joseph, this righteous man who repeatedly obeys the counsel of the messenger sent by God (1:20, 24; 2:13–15, 19–21, 22). When Mary discovers she is pregnant, who are told nothing of the conversation she had with Joseph, intriguing as that interchange may have been. Instead, we are informed that on hearing the news Joseph determines to handle the matter in as discreet and honorable a manner as possible, until he learns in a dream that the baby is not the result of human activity at all, but of the Holy Spirit.

Through this interesting and somewhat allusive account, two very clear affirmations are made about Jesus. First, the conception is the work of God. Jesus is the product of a fresh, new divine act, startling and heretofore unheard of. While there may have been tales of such unusual births in ancient literature, the long list of characters enumerated in Matthew's genealogy (1:1–17) contains none with a beginning like this. Jesus is not simply one more name like all the rest. From his very conception, this child is distinctive, unique. He is more than the accumulated best of his ancestors. The developing narrative tells how he acts distinctively as the agent of the divine Spirit and how he manifests uniquely the power of God.

Second, the stress on Mary's virginity serves to tie the conception and birth of Jesus to the Septuagint text of Isa. 7:14. Matthew obviously wants to make clear to his readers that neither Joseph nor any other male was Jesus' biological father. Joseph's own suspicions are satisfied by the word of the messenger, and the narrator goes out of his way to remove any suspicions the reader might have about Joseph's part in the conception. "He had no marital relations with her until she had borne a son" (1:25). There may be some attempt here to respond to charges made in or to Matthew's community that Mary was an adulteress and Jesus an illegitimate child (such rumors undoubtedly circulated on other settings; cf. John 8:41). The virginal conception is not to be thought of as disreputable or embarrassing. But more important than this denial, the virginal conception signals the beginning of the fulfillment of God's saving purposes. This fresh, new act of God ushers in an age, long expected and hoped for, yet in a fashion so unusual that it could hardly be anticipated. The sign of Ahaz is finally revealed, but in a way that neither Ahaz nor Isaiah could ever have dreamed.

If the conception calls attention to Jesus' special place in history, so also does his *naming*. Joseph, acting the part of the legal father, is directed by the messenger to call the child Jesus, and in case non-Jewish readers miss the significance of the name, the narrator adds an interpretation, "for he will save his people from their sins" (1:21).

The explanation, together with the title "Messiah" used earlier for Jesus (1:16), alerts us to the peculiar role the infant is to play throughout his ministry and especially in his death and resurrection—the Messiah who heals divided selves and reconciles to God those estranged and alienated (see 9:1–8; 26:28). No ordinary figure this baby is to be, but one who does what only God can do.

This explanation of Jesus' name serves an important function, particularly in light of the narrative Matthew provides us. It is Matthew's Jesus who directs us to turn the other cheek and go the extra mile (5:39–41), to be perfect as the Heavenly Father is perfect (5:48), not to lay up treasures on earth (6:19), to avoid anxiety about basic physical needs and seek the kingdom first (6:25–33). When reading selections of Matthew's account in isolation, it is easy to become overwhelmed by the demands of the gospel and wonder whether one's shortcomings and failures can ever be transcended. But at the outset, before the demands are made, we are told that the Jesus who makes such demands is the one to "save his people from their sins." Wherever the name of Jesus appears, there is the assurance of divine forgiveness.

But the text gives the baby another name—Emmanuel, again given special stress by being translated, "God is with us." It is not so much a name as a title, derived from the citation of Isa. 7:14. But it functions in the narrative as an important description of who Jesus is as he engages in his ministry (Matt. 17:17; 18:20; 26:29). Wherever Jesus is, God is there, present with the people of faith. Of particular significance is the conclusion of the Gospel, where Jesus declares as part of his commission to the disciples, "I am with you always, to the end of the age" (28:20).

Jesus' story is bracketed by these two declarations of the divine presence—Emmanuel. He is no mere figure of the past, contained by the space of three decades, localized in places like Bethlehem, Nazareth, Galilee, and Judea. Jesus is the presence of God, accompanying the church in its mission, energizing its teaching and pioneering its efforts to make disciples of all nations.

Christmas, First Proper

The themes of the rule of God and of the divinely appointed monarch, so prominent in Advent texts, also figure in large measure in these lections for Christmas Eve/Day. In certain ways, these texts are predictable, in that they not only announce the coming of the King, but also project the nature of the divine rule. The two lections from the Old Testament, Isa. 9:2–7 and Ps. 96, are closely related to the political ideology of the Davidic monarch in ancient Israel and, in the view of many scholars, functioned in the life of the people in a political sense, before their transpolitical authority was understood. The Gospel lection is the engaging story from Luke 2:1–20, without a reading of which Christmas could simply not be Christmas at all.

But in other respects these texts are startling and intrusive. In Isa. 9:2–7, the new king is welcomed with all the trumpetry surrounding an important royal birth or coronation, but the text then points not to a triumph of the new king's armies (as one might expect), but to the ascendancy of "justice" and "righteousness." Psalm 96 echoes that expectation, even as it looks beyond any human king to the rule of King Yahweh. Luke 2, for all its familiarity to ears that have heard it over and over again, jolts us by its juxtaposition of the figures of King Jesus, wrapped in swaddling cloths, and the Emperor Augustus, ordering the census of the people. We who have read beyond Luke 2 know which king will truly and ultimately reign, but of that the text itself only hints. And Titus 2:11–14, while perhaps not striking the reader immediately as a royal text, outdistances the other lections for this day, in that it not only celebrates the King who has come, but him who will come again, "our great God and Savior, Jesus Christ" (v. 13).

Thus there are common threads that bind these lections together, but there is also a sense of theological "movement." And together, the texts express that which goes beyond the boundaries of any single one of them. For they urge those who read them and who hear them read not only to celebrate the coming of the King and the dawning of the special qualities of the kingdom, but to prepare for the return of Him whose rule is both "already" and "not yet," both present and still to come.

Isaiah 9:2–7 (A B C)

This well-known oracle is apparently a public decree from the royal palace. It concerns the emergence of a new king in Jerusalem. Two scholarly hypotheses are usual concerning the oracle. First, it may be the *birth announcement* of a new heir to the Davidic throne. Second, the oracle may be a *coronation announcement* when the prince succeeds his father on the throne. In either case, the celebrative rhetoric proclaims the new heir as the fulfillment of all the long-standing hopes and expectations of the realm.

The oracle persists in its "power" voice long after any concrete reference to a specific king has been given up. The oracle has become an announcement of God's faithful gift of newness through a new ruler, in response to sore need in the community. The newness mediated by the oracle is that the realm has come under new governance. That oracle then may have had repeated use in the royal court, as each new king is thought to be at last the one who will establish a right government. Moreover, if the oracle had taken on a life of its own in the political-liturgical rhetoric of ancient Israel, then it is not surprising that the church found the oracle useful and appropriate for its announcement of Jesus.

That indeed is the role of the angels in the Bethlehem story (Luke 2:10–14). They are making an announcement (either birth or coronation) on behalf of the court. A new heir has been designated, who will faithfully inaugurate a new creation. Thus Jesus is not announced in a rhetorical vacuum, but the tradition utilizes the common royal language of newness.

The oracle begins with *a general expression of joy* at the profound transformation that is just under way (Isa. 9:1–2). The joy at the newness is characterized by two references. It is joy as in the time of a good harvest (v. 3). The joy of harvest comes when anxiety about crops is nullified and economic prosperity is assured for another year. Or it is joy as at the end of the battle, when the enemy has been routed (vs. 4–5). The poem anticipates an utter newness, which overcomes all the harsh reality of the recent past.

Future well-being depends on *defeat of the enemy* that has been threatening (vs. 4–5). These verses are commonly skipped over in church reading. They are, however, crucial to the development of the poem. They indicate that the newness is concretely related to the realities of power. The community has lived under the boot of oppression, exploitation, and humiliation. Now, however, in the form of the new king comes rescue!

The anticipated rescue will be brutal and violent. The coming "light" is powerful enough to seize all the boots of the enemy soldiers, all their uniforms, which are soaked in their blood, to burn them in a huge fire (compare Ps. 46:8–9). This is disarmament, but it is disarmament by a victor. The fire is an act of triumph and defiance that nullifies the enemy, to eliminate his threat and to destroy his myth of invincibility. No wonder the folk cheered, for the occupying enemy had generated deep and abiding hatred.

Only now do we learn the cause of the joy (Isa. 9:2–3) and the reason for victory (vs. 4–5). The turn of the future is because *there is an heir,* a son (vs. 6–7)! He will head the government, which has been desolate and irrelevant. In the announcement of birth or of coronation, the new heir is given names that assert Judah's best memories and deepest hopes. The new king will be utterly sagacious in dispensing justice ("Wonderful Counselor"), will have the power, prowess, and potency of a god ("Mighty God"), will be as reassuring and protective as a great tribal leader ("Everlasting Father"), and will be a bringer of peace and prosperity ("Prince of Peace").

The oracle ends with two theological affirmations (v. 7). First, the coming rule is marked by "justice" and "righteousness," by care for people and mercy toward the weak. The new rule is not one of self-aggrandizing power, but it will enact and embody the best hopes of the old Mosaic covenant. Jerusalem had long neglected justice and righteousness (compare 1:21–23; 5:7), but now it will be rehabilitated (compare 56:1). The king will at last do what the prophets had always hoped. Second, the newness embodied by the new heir is the work of Yahweh, wrought by the passion and faithfulness of God. This faithful king is no self-starter. Israel's daily hope is rooted in the reality of this covenant-making, world-transforming, justice-working God!

Psalm 96 (A B C)

This psalm, with its expansive mood of joy and celebration, is an exclamation of praise perfectly appropriate for Christmas Eve or Christmas Day. Like other psalms of praise, Ps. 96 reads as if it were written with an eye toward its use in public worship, the worshiping congregation (v. 7) and the temple of God (v. 6) being almost tangible objects within the poem. Whether, as some scholars argue, it was originally an enthronement psalm for ancient Judean kings or, as others propose, a song in celebration of the ark of the covenant, this psalm has been changed and spoken at festive moments in the life of the people of God over the centuries. Indeed, it is striking that it is the people who are addressed directly throughout this psalm, as Yahweh, the God of Israel, is consistently referred to in the third person.

Perhaps the initial feature of this psalm to attract the reader's attention is the triple imperative that begins the psalm: Sing! (vs. 1–2). The imperative is plural in Hebrew, a feature that, once more, underscores the psalm's interest in the worshiping congregation. Furthermore, this imperative (*šîrû*) is strengthened by the cognate noun "song" (*šîr*), which appears in the very first line of the psalm. An additional note of emphasis is the triple use of the phrase "to the LORD." In other words, the poet has used the very effective devices of repetition and similarity of sound to urge the worshiping people: "Praise the LORD!"

As is often the case in psalms of praise, Ps. 96 soon addresses the reasons for praising God. In the first part of the psalm, these are at least two in number: first, Yahweh is an actual God and not, like the deities of other nations, a nonentity (v. 5a). Second, it is Yahweh, Israel's God, who created the heavens (v. 5b) and who is encountered as a living Reality in the house of worship (v. 6). (It is interesting that 1 Chron. 16, which provides a somewhat different version of Ps. 96, reads for 96:6b, "strength and *joy* are in his [holy] place," 1 Chron. 16:27, emphasis added.)

The structure of Ps. 96:1–6—the imperative to praise Yahweh followed by the reasons for doing so—is repeated in vs. 7–13. Here the imperative is "Give [NRSV "Ascribe"] glory to Yahweh!" a call to worship that is linked with a very specific act of self-giving: "Bring an offering" (v. 8).

In vs. 7–13 the reason for praising Yahweh is as straightforward as it is profound: "The LORD is king!" (v. 10), and here we come to what is perhaps the central affirmation of the psalm. The kingship of God, which was revealed at creation (v. 10b), is further expressed in Yahweh's role as the administrator of justice (vs. 10c, 13). Verse 13, in fact, might be translated, instead of NRSV's "judge," as "bring justice." And v. 13 goes on to detail the means by which Yahweh's justice is to be expressed: "with righteousness" and "with his truth." Thus, as in a number of the psalms that refer to the rule of God or to that of the God-appointed Davidic monarch, the justice of Yahweh the King is linked to the divine expression of other moral values.

And because Yahweh is a king of justice, righteousness, and peace, all creation rejoices (vs. 11–12):

> the heavens,
> the earth,
> the sea and its creatures,
> the field and its creatures,
> the trees of the woods.

All join in praising the coming of the King!

And it is of great significance that the King *is coming* (or has come—the Hebrew is ambiguous). Whatever the original significance of this phrase (v. 13a) within the liturgy of ancient Israel may have been—and we cannot be sure—it deepens our understanding that the psalmist sang not of some distant God, remote and unconcerned. Rather, the God who reigns over Israel and over the world is a God who cares, who insists on justice, righteousness, and peace in the lives of the people, and who is personally present to see that these qualities mold the nature of human life. Thus, the ultimate reason for this song of joy is not simply that the God of justice reigns, but that that God is here. Now.

This is, of course, the story of Christmas: the Babe of Bethlehem and the regnant God are one. That the story is one of mystery and wonder is, of course, a part of its power. Yet the mystery and wonder are not limited to the question of the incarnation: "How in the world could God become a human being?" The mystery and wonder also extend to the prior question, "How could the Maker and Ruler of the universe care whether life is just?" We cannot fathom the answer to either question, of course. But just as the lection from Luke 2 affirms that God assumed human flesh at Bethlehem, so Ps. 96, in lyric tones, insists that God cares how men and women live. When we are seized by the joy of which the psalmist sings, we begin to understand—however dimly—the full meaning of the birth of Mary's Son.

Titus 2:11–14 (A B C)

In common with the other readings assigned for this day, Titus 2:11–14 celebrates the glorious appearance of God's grace. What distinguishes this lesson from the others is the explicit connection the writer makes between that grace and the ethical response it entails.

Warnings about appropriate behavior run throughout this letter. Even the salutation identifies Paul's apostleship with the furtherance of "godliness" (1:1). The bulk of the first chapter concerns qualifications for Christian leadership, and dominating those qualifications is the need for moral and upright behavior. Chapter 2 continues instructions about what Titus is to teach various groups within the community regarding their Christian behavior. While specific admonitions in Titus sharply offend late-twentieth-century Christians (for example, the expectation that women are to be submissive to their husbands and slaves to their masters), the need for discipline and identity within the Christian community emerges as a crucial issue in our own time.

Titus 2:11 shows that the disciplined behavior urged by the author of Titus has a profoundly theological root: "For the grace of God has appeared, bringing salvation to all." In this single verse we find an apt summary of the Christmas story. First, it is about God's grace. In common with other New Testament writings, the event of the birth, death, and resurrection of Jesus Christ is subsumed under the single title "grace."

English translations necessarily obscure the fact that the Greek verb here is *epiphainein,* from the root of which we get our English noun, epiphany. God's grace makes its appearance in Jesus Christ. Notice the way in which what we sometimes think of as an attribute of God—that is, grace—is anthropomorphized by its use with a verb.

The appearance of grace has its purpose in the salvation of all people. It is worth pondering what alternative purpose there might be for the epiphany of God's grace. Perhaps God's grace might find its purpose in self-glorification or in the sheer awe of human acknowledgment of God. The testimony of scripture, however, is that God's intent in the epiphany is to save humankind.

No qualifications limit those who are the object of God's salvation. The noun used in the Greek text, *anthrōpos,* includes both men and women, although it is often translated as "man." "All people" surely includes the well-known categories of human beings Paul uses in Gal. 3:28 (Jew and Greek, slave and free, male and female). It also includes sinner and penitent, persecutor and persecuted, "insiders" and "outsiders" of every type. God's salvific grace knows no limits.

God's grace does, however, have an impact on the way people live their lives. Following v. 11's powerful statement of the Christmas message, vs. 12–14 explain how grace "trains" or, better, "disciplines" human beings in three distinct but related ways. The first discipline of grace is stated in negative terms. Believers are to "renounce impiety and worldly passions," terms that may well reflect the Gentile origins of the writer and his audience. A Gentile who became a Christian was said to have turned away from the worship of idols, things that are not God (Gal. 4:8–9; 1 Thess. 1:9). The same claim would not be made about Jewish Christians, who had always worshiped the true and only God.

It is not enough, of course, merely to renounce things that are bad, although perhaps some early Christians, like some latter-day Christians, regarded Christian behavior simply as a list of prohibitions. The second discipline of grace consists of living "lives that are self-controlled, upright, and godly." This wording has an austere, nearly puritanical connotation that is unnecessarily harsh. To be "self-controlled" (*sōphronōs*) is to show moderation. The word has to do with being reasonable or sensible. "Upright" translates the familiar *dikaiōs,* which pertains to living justly or rightly. To live a "godly" (*eusebōs*) life pertains to devotion or awe that one addresses to God. The first word pertains to the way one deals with oneself (with control), the second to the way one deals with others (justly), and the third to the way one deals with God (with reverence).

While these first two disciplines of grace are confined to life in "this world," that is, in the present, the third discipline results in expectation. Grace teaches believers to wait for "the blessed hope and the manifestation of the glory of our great God and Savior, Jesus Christ. He it is who gave himself for us that he might redeem us from all iniquity and purify for himself a people of his own who are zealous for good deeds" (Titus 2:13–14). This summary of Christian confidence in the future reminds us that our celebration of the first advent of God's grace in Jesus Christ is a celebration of the promised second advent as well.

Luke 2:1–14 (15–20) (A B C)

Luke's account of the birth of Jesus appears as the Gospel lesson for both the First and Second Propers of Christmas. Since the reading for the Second Proper is limited to vs. 8–20, we shall concentrate the commentary on vs. 1–7 for the First Proper and deal with the remainder of the story under the Second Proper.

This passage, so beautifully crafted in Luke's narrative, certainly counts among the most familiar passages in the Bible. Dramatizations of the Christmas story as well as repeated readings make it a well-known text. People in North America who know little or nothing about the Christian faith know about the shepherds and the angelic chorus. For that reason, the text presents a challenge to the preacher to hear and declare a fresh word that probes the familiar and yet moves beyond it.

What immediately emerges from the early portion of this story is the political context in which the birth of Jesus is recounted. We are told that Emperor Augustus had ordered an enrollment and that Quirinius was governor of Syria. Despite the problems surrounding the historical accuracy of this beginning (dealt with in most commentaries), the narrative setting cannot be ignored. It is not against the background of the reign of Herod, the local ruler who is known for his heavy-handed and brutal ways, that the story of Jesus' birth is told (as in Matthew's Gospel), but against the background of the Roman Empire.

The emperor Octavian was a prominent figure, who solidified the somewhat divided loyalties of the various regions of the empire and ushered in the famous Pax Romana. In 27 B.C., the Roman senate gave him the title "the August One." Poets wrote of his peaceful ideals and anticipated that his reign would signal a golden age based on virtue. Ancient monuments even ascribed to him the title "savior." He represented a high and hopeful moment in Roman history.

Luke gives Octavian his familiar title and recognizes his authority by noting that "all the world" (actually the Roman Empire) is encompassed by his decree. Often in ancient times the demand for a census evoked rebellion and opposition, but Luke records a dutiful response: "All went to their own towns to be registered." The mention of Augustus not only provides an indispensable time reference to help readers date the events that are being narrated, but also enables Luke to explain how Mary and Joseph, who lived in Nazareth, had a baby born in Bethlehem.

The introduction, however, provides a much more important function than this. It sets the stage for the birth of one who is Savior, Christ the Lord. Octavian is not pictured as an evil, oppressive tyrant, a bloody beast "uttering haughty and blasphemous words" (Rev. 13:5). The Roman state in Luke's narrative simply does not represent the enemy against which Christians must fight. The backdrop for Jesus' birth is rather a relatively humane and stable structure, the best of ancient governments, which led to dreams of a peaceful era and aspirations of a new and wonderful age. The decades between the time of Jesus' birth and the time of Luke's narrative, however, exposed the failed hopes and the doused aspirations. Octavian is succeeded by caesars who turn the imperial dreams into nightmares.

Against the horizon of disillusionment, we read of the birth of another ruler, from the lineage of David, whose meager beginnings, on the surface, do not compare with the promise and hope of Augustus. All the world obeys the caesar, but Jesus' parents are rejected and relegated to a cattle stall. Yet the birth of Jesus is good news for all the people, ensuring a new and lasting promise of peace and goodwill.

The narrative does not present us with a confrontation between Augustus and Jesus, but with a contrast between vain expectations and true hope, between the disappointment that follows misplaced anticipations and the energy born of a divine promise, between the imposing but short-lived power of Caesar's rule and the humble manifestation of the eternal dominion of God, between the peace of Rome and the peace of Christ. The titles for Jesus, found later in the narrative (Luke 2:11)—Savior, Christ, and Lord—stand out starkly against the claims made for Augustus, and in the ensuing story become titles interpreted in fresh and surprising ways.

The setting for Luke's birth narrative clarifies for us the distinction between false hopes and true ones. Relatively humane, stable structures that contribute to the well-being of others often tend to promise more than they can deliver. Their very positive nature becomes seductive and generates impossible expectations. In contrast, Jesus is the anchor for reliable hope, for dependable promises, for anticipations that are more than fulfilled.

CHRISTMAS, SECOND PROPER

A variety of perspectives characterizes this collection of Christmas lections, and a variety of emotions as well, ranging from hope over what God has promised to do to joy over what God has done. The verses from Isa. 62 express the people's sense of expectation that God will complete that which God has already promised. But this expectation is couched in terms that suggest that God's people—and the hope they cherish—are vulnerable and cannot forever endure God's apparent need to be reminded of what God has promised to do. Psalm 97, on the other hand, knows nothing of vulnerability but is a straightforward celebration of the presence of God, a presence that all creation affirms and that results in righteousness and justice drawn to dimensions that are both cosmic and human.

The tender story of the visitation to the shepherds in Luke 2:8–20 is but an extension of the royal theology of Ps. 97. But what an extension! Here there are no melting mountains giving witness to the rule of God, but a chorus of angels who testify that the King of kings is to be found in a most unkingly milieu—a manger. Finally, the lection from the epistles, Titus 3:4–7, adds to this theological and emotional mix the important element of grace: the good news of God's intervention in human life is a declaration not of that which men and women deserve, but of what God has freely given.

In a significant manner, therefore, the four lections rehearse the drama of redemption, beginning with human need, moving through an acknowledgment of God's concern and power, and culminating in a declaration of God's compassion out of which issues God's saving initiative. They thereby formulate a history of salvation for women and men everywhere who have found in Jesus Christ the expression of all that God is and does.

Christmas is an acknowledgment of that history and, as any meaningful celebration must be, a rehearsal of it. But it is a rehearsal that views the history of salvation, not as chronological increments, but as a progression of events all of which happen simultaneously. Even we who rejoice over a gracious God's gift of the Son and our acceptance of this gift—the latter stages of the drama—must acknowledge that in certain ways we are still mired in the earlier stages in that we are vulnerable and must pray daily for God's presence and affirmation.

That view of Christmas, therefore, which tends to emphasize the triumphalist aspects of the occasion to the exclusion of its statements concerning human weakness and need is only partially on target. The diversity of these four lections helps us to hear the many voices with which Christmas speaks and sings.

Isaiah 62:6–12 (A B C)

This poem is set in the context of exiles who have returned to Jerusalem. They found the city to which they returned less than honored. Indeed, the city, which had been destroyed by the Babylonians, is still pitiful in its desolation, a source of embarrassment. God had promised a transformation, but has not yet worked it. The poem concerns the expectation and insistence of the faithful that God must be moved to act for the sake of the beloved city.

The problem is to compel God to act as God has promised to act. The poet does not reflect on why God has not acted; he only knows that there has been none of the saving action promised by God. For that reason, the poet devises a strategy to secure from God a rescued, restored city (vs. 6–7). "Sentinels" will be stationed on the walls around the city. They will be endlessly diligent in their work; they have only one task, a most peculiar task. They are to speak, not be silent. They are to speak incessantly. Their speech is to remind God of God's promises, to alert God to the needs of the city, to nag God, to invoke God, to move God to act.

The prayer on behalf of the city is an act of passionate hope. The hope is governed by the particle "until" (see v. 1). The city of Jerusalem waits eagerly under the influence of God's "until." The community is in expectation, waiting until God will keep God's promise. Thus the "until" of hoping faith stands between the passionate prayer of Israel and God's own faithful action. It is the conviction of the poet that God can be forced to enact that "until" by persuasive intercession. That, however, can happen only if God is endlessly reminded to be faithful.

The affirmation of these verses is that God has indeed heeded the "reminders" of vs. 6–7, has acted to restore Jerusalem; the city is assured a future of joy and well-being (vs. 10–12). Thus, vs. 6–7 have "worked," and Jerusalem has received its "until" from God.

God's spectacular presence will give the city a new name. The city had appeared to observers to be pitiful and abandoned, called "Forsaken" (see v. 4). Now the ones in the city are a holy people, believing utterly in God. They are Yahweh's redeemed, Yahweh's special project, and recipient of God's staggering care.

As anyone can see, the city is no longer "forsaken," but can be called "Sought Out," cared for, valued, treasured. Thus, what is a hope in vs. 6–7 now has become a reality. The poem asserts that the God who seemed not to care can be mobilized to act.

This poem testifies to God's faithfulness, which transforms Jerusalem. The difficult question is how to treat a Jerusalem text in terms of the rule of Jesus, as the opening of the new age.

It is most plausible to take "Jerusalem" as a metaphor, but as a metaphor for what? We may suggest three ways in which the metaphor might function in rethinking the larger impact of Jesus' birth:

1. Calvin takes "Jerusalem" to be *the church,* God's beloved community, which God shelters and for which God cares. On this reading, the text promises that the church will be healed of its disarray and will become an adequate habitat for the power and ministry of God.

2. "Jerusalem" is no doubt linked to creation in the tradition, so that "new Jerusalem" bespeaks *new creation* (compare Isa. 65:17–18; Rev. 21:1–4). On this reading, the text anticipates the renovation of a needy, distraught world.

3. "Jerusalem" functions in the Gospel narratives in relation to the notion of *kingdom.* Thus the kingdom of David becomes the kingdom of Jesus, which is the kingdom of God (compare Mark 1:14–15). On this reading, "Jerusalem" is a reference to the new society, the new socioeconomic arrangement that makes human, humane life possible.

It is odd that Jerusalem is "invaded" by Jesus in ways that threaten the authorities (Luke 9:51). The same Jesus, however, weeps over and yearns for Jerusalem, waiting with this text for God's promises to be kept (Luke 13:33–35; 19:41–44). Our reading of this text must not be so freely metaphorical that we miss the actual flesh-and-blood reality of the city, a reality enmeshed in dismay, but only "until"—until God acts. When God acts, Jerusalem is "sought out," as is the church, as is every city, as is creation, as is humanity, sought out by God for love, care, healing, forgiveness, and finally newness. The preachable point is God's "until."

Psalm 97 (A B C)

A celebration of the kingship of God, a belief that figures prominently in the faith of ancient Israel, is at the heart of this psalm. The first half of the psalm (vs. 1–6) describes the majesty of the divine King, while the last half (vs. 7–12) raises implications for the life of the people concerning God's rule.

Yahweh's majesty is portrayed primarily by means of figures of speech associated with a thunderstorm: clouds, darkness, fire, and lightning. The presence of Yahweh is so awesome that Yahweh's enemies are reduced to ashes, and even the otherwise solid mountains melt. Hyperbole, to be sure (for similar uses of these figures, see especially Ps. 29). Yet nestled among the metaphors are straightforward statements concerning the personal qualities of Yahweh. Yahweh's rule is based on righteousness and justice (v. 2b), a moral order built into the very fabric of the universe (v. 6).

As to what the rule of God means in the lives of people, the psalm notes that idolatry inevitably leads to despair, whereas Yahweh's presence sustains and supports Yahweh's people (vs. 7–10). Light and joy await those for whom the righteousness of the King has become a personal moral order (v. 11).

The final verse of the psalm (v. 12) is a call to these righteous ones to rejoice and give thanks to the Lord!

The relevance of this text to Christmas lies, first, in its celebration of the royal presence of God. In some ways the fire and lightning of the first half of the psalm may seem out of place in the celebration of the birth of a Babe, the "gentle Jesus, meek and mild" of the familiar hymn. But the church has maintained from its earliest beginnings that the Infant of Bethlehem is but one aspect of the nature of the incarnate Son, that he who "was conceived by the Holy Spirit" and "born of the Virgin Mary" will also "come to judge the living and the dead." And thus this Psalm lection recalls for us that the God who, in the Holy Child, comes to us in vulnerability and weakness is also the One who presides over the affairs of the universe and who insists that justice be done. If the violent language of the thunderstorm seems to the modern mind an unusual means of expressing the nature of God—to say nothing of the concept of the annihilation of God's enemies (v. 3b)—it may be helpful to remember that the language of the biblical poets is often extravagant, in that they frequently used the most intense human experiences to convey the nature of a God whom ordinary words cannot contain (compare Ex. 15:3, "The LORD is a warrior").

Beyond its celebration of the presence of Yahweh the King, this Psalm lection is consistent with other Advent and Christmas texts in its declaration that the rule of God is based on righteousness and justice. The manner in which these qualities are described here makes it clear that they are not incidental to human life, but are part of the tissue that God has woven into the universe. To act unjustly or unrighteously—to be an unjust or unrighteous person or society—is to repudiate the purposes for which all life exists. And it is, of course, to repudiate God.

Thus the value of this psalm as a Christmas lection lies in its ability to project the larger dimensions of the incarnation. It is tempting on this day to be occupied with the image of the helpless child in the manger and, therefore, to orient our festival around the children in our families and around the childishness in us all. To be sure, that is an important quality to be preserved, because it helps us to come to terms with our own weakness and vulnerability. It also brings us nearer to Jesus' teaching that the kingdom of God is a kingdom of children (Mark 9:36–37 and parallels).

But a more comprehensive understanding of Christmas includes the acknowledgment that Jesus' weakness—evident not only at Bethlehem, but at Calvary as well—is complemented by his role as King and divine Lord. At the heart of Christian belief is the affirmation that the infant son of Mary and the crucified Galilean peasant is also the Sovereign of the universe, who was present at the beginning (John 1:1) and who will preside over the end (Rev. 1:4–8). His rule is one of justice, righteousness, and peace, and those who would prepare themselves to be the citizens of his kingdom will dedicate themselves to these qualities now, as they/we try to create of the present time an anticipation of the time yet to come.

To celebrate Christmas without embracing this larger meaning is to sentimentalize and trivialize the festival. Christ's presence in human life is intended to change us, to reshape our commitments and our priorities so that they reflect the values of the kingdom of God. We may meet Christ at this season as the pink and cuddly Babe who reminds us of the innocence with which life begins. But when we follow him from the manger into the harsh and struggling world, we are asked to follow him to a cross. Our Christmas joy, however, derives from our knowing that not even a cross could defeat the just and peaceable kingdom over which he will preside at the end of time.

Titus 3:4–7 (A B C)

This text appropriately stands coupled with the angelic visitation to the shepherds in Luke 2:8–20, for what Luke conveys in narrative, the epistle to Titus asserts in the form of a creed—namely, that the inbreaking of God through Jesus Christ results entirely from God's decision.

In Titus, this assertion begins with a striking contrast between human existence before and after the Christ-event. Verse 3 details a catalog of evils to which human beings are susceptible, in order to show the profound character of God's salvation. Verse 4 introduces the advent of Jesus Christ as an event of radical discontinuity ("But when . . .").

Here the coming of Jesus Christ, the Christmas event, is described as "the goodness and loving kindness of God our Savior." As in Titus 2:11–14 and elsewhere in the New Testament, God's action stems not from self-glorification but from God's profound love of humankind. This attribute of God "appears" in human history, and the verb used here is the same one from which we derive our term "epiphany" (see 2:11).

The verses that follow characterize the meaning of this epiphany for humankind. Titus 3:5 introduces an important contrast, which can best be seen through a somewhat literal translation:

> not from works on the basis of righteousness
>   that *we* did
> but on the basis of *his* mercy
>   he saved *us*.

Several pairs of opposites give emphasis to the contrast here. The first and third lines contrast the means by which salvation has been accomplished—that is, not righteousness but mercy. The second and fourth lines contrast the agents of salvation—not human beings but God alone. The pronouns underscore this contrast, and the result of the whole is a denial of any notion that the salvation of human beings results from their own virtue.

The end of v. 5 amplifies God's salvation. It comes about as a result of his mercy and "by the water of rebirth and renewal by the Holy Spirit." Probably "water" refers to the practice of baptism, which Christians early on associated with renewal and the gift of the Holy Spirit. "Rebirth" (*paliggenesia*), of course, is a concept that many religious traditions associate with conversion. In the context of Titus, rebirth refers specifically to moral rebirth. The gift of God in Jesus

Christ enables human beings to turn from their former lives and to live in conformity with God's will.

At first glance, v. 6 adds little to what has already been said, but it is nevertheless a significant part of the text. First, the statement that God "poured out [this Spirit] on us richly" characterizes God's gift as a generous one. This imagery of pouring out water rather than measuring a minimal amount sufficient for the task conveys the extravagance of God's salvation. Second, the reference to Jesus Christ as the agent of God's salvation tells in concrete terms the means by which God's salvation made its epiphany. Through a human being, God has embraced all of humankind.

Verse 7 recalls the goal of salvation in terms of justification and the eschatological hope. Having been justified by the grace of Christ, believers become heirs "to the hope of eternal life." This statement carefully avoids asserting that believers *already* possess eternal life, for that final gift stands as the culmination of God's acts of salvation. Nevertheless, believers live out of their hope, their confidence, in God's power over death itself.

The opening words of v. 8 ("The saying is sure") suggest that what precedes in vs. 4–7 is taken from an early Christian tradition which the author quotes. These opening words also reinforce the trustworthiness of the claims that have just been made. God may be relied on to complete the salvation begun in Jesus Christ.

As a reading for Christmas Day, this text reminds us of the fact that the birth of Jesus Christ takes place as sheer gift. No human act imagined it, willed it, brought it about. It results solely from the generous, even outrageous, love of God for humankind. This text, with its strong assertions about the salvation accomplished in Jesus Christ, also reminds us that the events of Christmas occur *on our behalf.* The celebration of Christmas as a wonderful story about the lowly birth of a great hero completely misses the point that the Savior who is born is born for us. Here Titus 3:4–7 announces the message of the angels: "To you is born this day in the city of David a Savior. . . ."

Luke 2:(1–7) 8–20 (A B C)

The birth of Jesus is the center of Christmas. What one learns about Jesus from the narratives that relate his birth comes, however, from the actions and words of the other characters of Christmas—in Luke, from the shepherds, the angelic messenger, the heavenly chorus, the mysterious bystanders (2:18), and Mary; in Matthew, from repeated angelic messengers, Joseph, the Wise Men, Herod, the chief priests and scribes. Nowhere is that more evident than in the Lukan story, where a bare statement of the birth of Jesus is followed by the intriguing account of the nameless shepherds. They are traced from their location in the field tending their flock through their visit to Bethlehem and back to where they originated. From their actions and their interactions with the angelic messenger and the heavenly host, we learn about the character and significance of Jesus' birth.

We first meet the shepherds doing what shepherds are supposed to be doing—tending their flocks. They no doubt remind Luke's readers of the shepherding done once in these same regions by Jesus' famous ancestor, David. The routineness of these shepherds' lives is abruptly interrupted by the appearance of the angelic messenger. Their world, circumscribed at night by the wandering of the sheep, is exploded by the awesome presence of this one who brings news of Jesus' birth. The manifestation of the divine glory, the shepherds' fright, the announcement of the messenger disrupt their order and uniformity and set them on a journey to hear and see earth-changing events.

Three things we note about the intrusive announcement of the messenger. First, the good news includes great joy for "all the people." It is not merely the shepherds' small world that is changed by the word of Jesus' birth, but it is Israel's world. While Luke sets the story of the birth in the context of the Roman Empire (2:1–2), he has a primary interest in the destiny of Israel and "the falling and the rising of many" for whom this baby is set (v. 34). Jesus' relevance for the world, in fact, begins in the city of David as the fulfillment of Jewish expectations. It includes the acceptance of Jewish traditions (vs. 21, 22–40, 41–52), and only from this very particular origin does its universal character emerge.

Second, the announcement focuses on three astounding titles this baby is to carry—Savior, Messiah, and Lord. "Savior" has meaning in the narrative because original readers would recognize that such a title the exalted Emperor Augustus had borne. Unfortunately, the eager anticipations for a brighter, more peaceful day stirred by his rule were long since dashed by the brutality and weakness of his successors. Now a true and promise-fulfilling Savior appears. "Messiah" (or "Christ") reminds us of Israel's hope for the anointed figure and God's grand design which he will inaugurate. "Lord," interestingly, occurs four times in our passage, and in the other three instances is used for God (2:9 [twice], 15). It is inescapable in such a context, then, that divine associations be attached to Jesus (in v. 11).

Third, the angelic announcement designates the sign that will assure the shepherds that they have found "a Savior, who is the Messiah, the Lord." But such a strange sign! Hardly fitting for one bearing such honored titles! The babe "wrapped in bands of cloth and lying in a manger," however, is only the beginning of the story of God's unusual ways in accomplishing the divine rule. Not by might or coercive tactics, but in submission and humbleness, Jesus fulfills his vocation.

Perhaps it is the perplexity caused by such a menial sign for such an exalted baby that evokes the immediate confirmation of the heavenly chorus, who join the angelic messenger in a doxology. God is praised for the birth of this child because the birth begins God's reign of peace on earth. The creatures of the heavenly world, in a context of praise, announce God's good plans for this world.

Having heard the heavenly witnesses, the shepherds now decide to go to Bethlehem and "see" this revelation. Like other disciples who abruptly leave fishing boats and tax tables, they go "with haste." We are not told what happened to the flocks, apparently left in the fields. The shepherds' old world has been shattered by the appearance of the messenger, and now they are in search of a new one, one centered in the event that has occurred in Bethlehem.

When the shepherds find Mary, Joseph, and Jesus, the narrator records that they report the message that had been made known to them about the baby. To whom did they give their report? To Mary and Joseph? Perhaps. Perhaps the shepherds in responding to the angelic messenger in fact become a confirmation to Mary and Joseph of the significance of this baby so unusually born. But there must have been a wider audience for the shepherds' report too, since "all who heard it" were astonished—not believing or thoughtful or adoring, just "amazed." Apparently nothing spurred them to ask questions or pursue the matter further. In contrast, Mary clings to what has happened. She continues to ponder the events and the words (the Greek word is inclusive of both) of the shepherds' visit.

Finally, the shepherds go back to where they came from, apparently back to fields and to flocks, but not back to business as usual. What was told them by the angelic messenger has been confirmed. They have heard and seen for themselves. Their old world is gone, replaced by a new world. Whatever the structure and order of life before, their world now is centered in the praise and glorifying of God. The nights in the field will never be the same.

Christmas, Third Proper

Ecstasy over the Christmas miracle is the theme that binds these lections together—unrestrained joy over what God has done and over who God is. Yet it is a clearly focused, informed ecstasy, whose very power is generated by the precision with which events are viewed. The God whom these texts celebrate is a God who, in the royalist imagery of the day, reigns in strength, and whose activity on behalf of humankind is timelessly ancient, coinciding with the initial impulses of creation. Yet the eternal Monarch is not distant and remote, qualities that might be suggested by the terms of majesty in which the king is described. Rather this God is near and immediate, a participant in the human struggle for light and salvation.

The texts begin in a mode of transcendency, but move quickly to one of immediacy. As worshipers, we join in rejoicing over the coming of the messenger "who says to Zion, 'Your God reigns' " (Isa. 52:7). We also celebrate "the Lord, for he is coming to judge the earth . . . with righteousness, and . . . equity" (Ps. 98:9). Then the note of immediacy is struck by the focus on what God has done just now, in these "last days," in which "he has spoken to us by a Son" (Heb. 1:2). The One who was present at creation, the eternal Word, "became flesh and lived among us" (John 1:14).

In reading these texts, one is reminded again of the difficulty that all human wordsmiths—be they preachers or whoever—have in articulating the depth of emotion that accompanies Christmas. For all four of these texts are songs, which rhapsodize rather than explain that which happened at Christmas. Perhaps the one exception is the lection from Heb. 1. Yet even this text, which begins as sober prose, soon breaks into song, as if unable, when faced with the limits of simple narration, to restrain its enthusiasm and joy. Small wonder that worshipers on Christmas Day are more likely to leave the church whistling the anthem sung exuberantly by the choir than repeating to one another phrases from the minister's sermon.

Yet the preacher cannot abdicate the task of proclaiming the Christmas good news to the "musicians" who constitute the church, but must wrestle with the impossible challenge of capturing the meaning of Christ's nativity in the frailty of words. These texts are of incomparable value as she or he attempts to meet the challenge.

Isaiah 52:7–10 (A B C)

This poetic unit is the pivotal statement in "the gospel to exiles" in Isa. 40—55. The poet creates a wondrous scenario in which there are four characters in the dramatic moment of homecoming.

The first character is *"the messenger"* (v. 7). He is the one who hurries across the desert of the Fertile Crescent with news about the titanic battle between Yahweh and the powers of the empire. He has the first news—in a pre-electronic mode—of the outcome of the battle. The term "messenger" is the biblical word for gospel, so that he is the "carrier of the gospel." His way of running already signals that the news is good. Messengers with bad news do not run as well, or as lightly or buoyantly.

The poet piles up words to summarize the message he carries. He announces *"shalom."* He asserts *"good."* He declares *rescue* ("salvation"). Then finally, excited, out of breath, the messenger blurts out the outcome of the contest: "Your God has become king!" The gods have battled for control of the future. The news, the gospel, is the victory of Yahweh. This means for "Zion" a new, joyous, holy governance.

Enter the second voice, *"the sentinel"* (v. 8). On the walls of destroyed Jerusalem, in despair yet still yearning, are sentries. They watch, and they call out what they see. Over the horizon, according to this poetic scenario, they see the runner of v. 7 approaching with a message. They see how he runs. They notice how light and eager are his feet. They conclude immediately that he runs with good news, or he would not run so eagerly. The sentries watch and see only the messenger. They are able, however, to extrapolate from what they see. As they look at the runner and the horizon, they are able to translate both the messenger and the message. What they really see, in a bold act of imagination, is nothing other than victorious Yahweh.

The watchmen sing for joy. They are jubilant because Yahweh is coming. The God long held exile by the empire, the God held as captive as were the Jews, has broken free and is coming home.

The third character in this dramatic scenario is *wounded, defeated, fearful Jerusalem* (v. 9a). The poet imagines that the city, left desolate by the Babylonians, still consists of shattered walls and gates, defeated doors, broken-up streets, all disheveled, despondent, despairing (compare Neh. 1:3).

Then, however, the watchmen on the wall call down into the city. Yahweh is victorious; Yahweh is coming home. The watchmen then invite the broken, forlorn city to change its mood. It is time to sing and dance, because decisive help is on the way. The fate of the city has been broken.

This sequence of messenger (Isa. 52:7), watchmen (v. 8), broken city (v. 9a) is all stage setting for the central character of the plot. The central character, Yahweh, enters the action at this point (vs. 9b–10). There had been anticipation of Yahweh as the messenger announced Yahweh's rule (v. 7), as the sentries see Yahweh's return (v. 8).

Now the poet pays careful attention to Yahweh's dramatic entrance into the poem and into the city. Four statements characterize Yahweh in this moment of triumphal entry.

(*a*) "Yahweh has comforted Yahweh's people" (v. 9b). Since Isa. 40:1, the poet has taken "comfort" as the central yearning of the exiles. "Comfort" does not mean simply resigned consolation, but active intervention, which alters the circumstances of the community.

(*b*) "Yahweh has redeemed Jerusalem." Some texts, instead of "Jerusalem," read "Israel." Either way, Yahweh has gotten the special object of love out of hock, permitted it again to live its own life in freedom.

(*c*) Yahweh has rolled up sleeves as a powerful, strong, intimidating warrior (v. 10). The empires of the world notice Yahweh's power and back off from their dehumanizing policies. In this particular text, the poet finds it necessary to utilize a machismo metaphor to make the claim of power. (Notice elsewhere the use of maternal metaphors to make a very different point: 40:11; 49:14–15.)

(*d*) The culmination of the entire dramatic scenario concerns the salvation and homecoming wrought by Yahweh. God is indeed a God who liberates. Moreover, this is "our God," the God who is "for us," whose whole life is given over to "us." This poem is relentlessly good news for the faithful who are defeated.

Psalm 98 (A B C)

Like the Psalm lections for the first two propers of Christmas, this text is also a psalm of praise to God. Moreover, its primary images are similar to Pss. 96 and 97: God as the victorious warrior and as the creator of the world. The first image is found in vs. 1–3, where the language reminds us of the exodus narrative, especially Ex. 15. Yahweh is portrayed here as the defender of the people of God who, by means of "his right hand and his holy arm" (that is, without human aid), has achieved the people's liberation. In doing this, Yahweh has communicated a basic truth concerning the divine nature in that "he has revealed his vindication." In other words, Yahweh *is* Savior, so that not to have saved the people would have been a fundamental violation of who Yahweh is. And in achieving this liberation, Yahweh has acted in public and demonstrative ways, so that "all the ends of the earth" have witnessed these mighty deeds.

The image of God as reigning creator dominates vs. 4–8, and in the background one detects ancient Israel's memory of the old Creation myths of the ancient Near East in which a hostile primeval ocean was tamed by the power of God (compare Ps. 93:3–4). But if the "sea" once rumbled in anger as Yahweh's enemy, it and all creation (the "world" of v. 7b) now roars its praise of the majestic Lord who rules over it, and it claps its hands in joy (v. 8). Only this cosmological dimension to Israel's understanding of God's activity can account for the universal scope of the imperative in v. 4: All the earth is to sing before the Lord in joy. Israel is to join in this outpouring of praise, of course, with lyre, trumpets, horn, and—needless to say—the human voice.

In all these things, echoes of the Second Isaiah may be detected, since that prophet also compares Yahweh to a warrior and makes frequent use of the Creation as a model for God's other acts of salvation (that is, re-creation). Isaiah 42:10–13 is especially close to our psalm, the first words of Isa. 42:10 and Ps. 98:1 being identical.

But there is a third section to this psalm, and the transition into it is so subtle that it may easily be missed. The One who is Victor-Creator-King is also Judge, and the climax of the text is achieved in the proclamation that the past is but prologue to the coming of this divine Judge (v. 9). Yahweh now comes to judge both creation and those who inhabit it, and to do so by means of righteousness and equity (the Hebrew noun for "equity" is related to an adjective meaning "straight" or "upright"). Verse 9 prevents the psalm from being simply a celebration of what Yahweh *has* done, and decisively shifts the focus of the celebration to what Yahweh *is* doing now.

The relevance of this text to Christmas is obvious, for at Christmastide we reflexively look backward in time, remembering the manger, the Holy Family, the angels and shepherds, and so on. The temptation is to allow our celebration to be lodged there, in the past. To be sure, our joy is motivated by our profession that the Infant is also the risen Christ, through whose death and resurrection we are reconciled to God. And yet, our thoughts tend to remain focused on a scene long ago and far away.

The force of this psalm is to move us away from the past into the present, into the now. And there are at least two words in the psalm that compel this redirection of our attention. The first of these is the word "new" in the first line of v. 1 (compare Ps. 96:1). The implication is that the old songs will no longer do, in that they are incapable of capturing the human response to what God is doing now. (In the mind of the psalmist these "old" songs were likely the laments over Israel's past disasters; see Ps. 74 or the book of Lamentations.) So it seems clear that the Hebrew poet intends to urge the people to adopt fresh expressions of joy commensurate with the present outbreak of Yahweh's activity. God, who is now working in original and primal ways, must be praised in songs similarly cast.

The second term that calls our attention to the contemporary nature of God's activity is the verb "to come," in v. 9. It is true that there is a certain ambiguity in the Hebrew (*bāʾ*), in that the perfect indicative ("he came") and the active participle ("is coming") have the same form. But one may argue for the sense "is now coming" (compare NRSV) because of the parallel verb "will judge" (*yišpōṭ*), which is imperfect (compare Ps. 96:13). Thus God is in the act of coming now to set things right, and God's former acts of creation and re-creation, although fascinating and wonderful, are but preliminary to what God is in the process of doing at the present moment.

Christmas, while commemorating what God did in the long ago at Bethlehem, is in reality the joyful celebration of what God is doing here and now. God is judging creation, specifically the human family, in the sense that God is at work to set things right. Therefore, the contribution of this psalm to the anthology of Christmas lections is to redirect our Christmas wonder. Our carols of great gladness are not just over what God did at Bethlehem, but over what the reigning Christ does today to straighten that which is crooked in human life and to set right that which has fallen.

Hebrews 1:1–4 (5–12) (A B C)

In these opening lines, the author of Hebrews draws upon considerable rhetorical skill to produce one of the most elegant passages in the New Testament. The first four verses, rich in alliteration and imagery, announce the major themes of the book as a whole: Christ is both the exalted Son of God and the one whose sacrifice atoned for human sin. Verses 1–2 introduce the theme of the exalted Son by contrasting him with God's messages to humanity in previous generations, and the contrast between Christ and God's angels runs throughout Heb. 1 and 2. This contrast between Christ and the prophets, or between Christ and the angels, does not cancel out the deep continuity that Hebrews affirms. The God who "spoke to our ancestors . . . by the prophets" is identical with the God who "has spoken to us by a Son." God's action in Jesus Christ is absolutely superior to God's earlier actions on behalf of humankind, but former history is in no way denied or negated, as becomes clear when Hebrews draws on Israel's scripture and history throughout.

Verse 2 identifies God's Son as both the "heir of all things" and the one through whom the world was created. Christ stands at both ends of cosmic history. As the writer of Revelation puts it, he is both Alpha and Omega (Rev. 22:13). The world has its origin and its destiny in Christ. This language bears a striking resemblance to Jewish wisdom literature, in which similar claims appear about the figure of Lady Wisdom. Its use here and elsewhere in early Christianity reflects not only the Jewish "background" to Christian thought but the perennial need to portray Christ in language that people can understand.

With its assertions about Christ reflecting God's glory and his role in purification, Heb. 1:3 introduces the dialectic that is at the heart of Christian faith. Jesus is said to be "the exact imprint" of God's nature—that is, Jesus is in every way like God. And Jesus is simultaneously the one who sacrificed himself as a human being for other human beings.

Verse 4 introduces the motif of Christ's superiority to angels, which continues in the quotations from scripture in vs. 5–12. In common with other New Testament writers, the author of Hebrews displays no concern for the original context of the passages he cites. What matters is that scripture lends itself to the claims being made about Christ. In v. 5, the quotations (Ps. 2:7 and 2 Sam. 7:14) reinforce the assertion of Heb. 1:1–2, that Jesus is indeed the Son of God. Similarly, vs. 6–7 reinforce the contrast between God's Son and God's angels (v. 4) by showing that the angels are instructed to worship God's Son.

God may make "his angels winds, and his servants flames," but the Son is destined to rule forever (v. 8). Verse 9 introduces the notion of the goodness of Christ. He exemplifies faithfulness to God by his righteousness, and thereby demonstrates his fitness for reign. Verses 10–12 continue the contrast with angels by reinforcing the earlier claim that God's Son stands both at the beginning of history and at its end. Christ is God's agent in creation. Christ will always remain the same: "and your years will never end."

The primary thrust of this opening section of Hebrews appears to be doxological. God's eschatological gift of the Son merits human thanks and praise. Within this doxology, the major themes of the book are sounded, and they will be developed in the course of the text. Perhaps there is also a polemical thrust to the contrast between God's Son and God's angels. For example, it could be that some Christians are interpreting Jesus as simply one of God's messengers or that some are actually worshiping angels. Such theories are very difficult to support because of the absence of any explicit polemic.

Whatever the thrust of this text in its own day, the reading of it on Christmas presents several possibilities. With its powerful insistence on Christ as the beginning and end of all things, this text stands as a corrective to any tendency to romanticize the infant Jesus. Just as the theme of Christ's sacrifice stands in tension with his majesty (1:3), so that helplessness of the babe in a manger stands in tension with Christ as the agent and goal of all creation. While the christological language of Hebrews may sound foreign indeed to many contemporary Christians, the proclamation that God's Son stands, unchanging and unchanged, both at the beginning and at the end, may be gospel indeed to people who experience change as the only constant in their lives and who seek frantically for something that abides.

John 1:1–14 (A B C)

The prologue to John's Gospel has perhaps had more influence on the church's doctrine of the incarnation than any other passage. It affirms in carefully stated language the preexistence of the Word, who is identified with and yet distinct from God, who is the divine agent in creation and yet incarnate in the flesh. But when the congregation gathers for worship on Christmas Day, it does not want or need to hear about the precise distinctions of the church's doctrine. The mood of the season hardly calls for a didactic sermon. It is rather the time to celebrate the birth at Bethlehem and to ask about its meaning, its implications for the congregation, for the church, and for the world. Therefore, the question to ask of the Gospel reading for this service is: How does John 1:1–14 interpret Christmas? What can we learn from it about the baby born in the manger and the meaning of that birth for human life?

First and foremost, from the prologue to John's Gospel *we learn that in Jesus Christ we meet nothing less than the revelation of God.* Word (or Logos), the subject of all the verbs in vs. 1–2, has a rich and illustrious heritage in both Hellenistic and Jewish circles. What is most important, however, is the simple notion of communication. When one speaks or writes a word, one is communicating. "The word of the Lord came to the prophet"—and we through the prophet hear God's message. Now we discover that in Jesus Christ the word identified with God from the very beginning (1:1–3) has taken human form (v. 14), and Christmas is the story of the birth of God's self-communication to the world.

Rather than speaking in Johannine terms, it is perhaps more popular today to think of a "Christology from below," that is, to begin with the historical figure who walked the dusty roads of Galilee, who associated with tax collectors and sinners, who was like us in every respect, and then to speak of his special relationship to God. John's "Christology from above," however, still has its place. It provides us with the healthy reminder of God's distance, that we can only know God as God is *given* to us in an act of revelation. Not our best aspirations or fondest longings or even most sincere service can precipitate such an event. Christmas is first of all the celebration of a gracious decision on God's part to become human in the baby of Bethlehem.

Second, from John's prologue *we learn that God's revelation in Jesus Christ is not altogether obvious.* The Word came to a world that should have known him. After all, he had created the world. In particular, he came to a special people chosen from all the nations to be his own and to a land that was his heritage, but he was rejected. Jesus was not universally acclaimed as the revelation of God, nor worshiped as the one in whom we touch ultimate reality. In fact, the rest of John's Gospel relates story after story of how prominent religious people not only did not recognize Jesus but found him offensive, accused him of blasphemy, charged him with being demon-possessed. Those who confidently thought that they saw things rightly in fact turned out to be blind.

John simply will not let his readers off the hook. He confronts us with a divine self-disclosure that does not document itself with foolproof evidence. We are not provided with irrefutable grounds for faith. We are asked to believe that a particular individual, living in a buffer state in the Middle East, powerless before a Roman governor, is the One in whom we meet the Creator of heaven and earth. The fact that the genuinely religious people who should have received him in fact rejected him leaves readers even more uneasy.

But rejection is not the whole story. There are those who received Jesus, who trusted him, who found themselves by a creative act of

God reborn, empowered to be children of God. On the surface they hardly seem potential candidates for the divine family—a Samaritan woman, an unnamed Roman official, a man born blind, an extravagant Mary of Bethany. They are a somewhat unlikely group to become that community called into being and nurtured by the revelation of God in Jesus. But that in itself tells us something about the character of God and God's intentions in Jesus.

Third, from John's prologue *we learn that there is continuity between God's works of creation and revelation.* It begins with language reminiscent of Gen. 1:1, recalling the ancient account of Creation. Then readers are told that the Word enfleshed at Bethlehem is the agent in creation, the one by whom all things were made. There were those in the early church (as there have been those in the modern church) who drove a wedge between nature and grace. The material world for various reasons was thought to be evil, a place from which to escape to a realm of the spirit. Redemption meant freedom from the earthly, the historical, the sensual.

The prologue will have none of this. Salvation is the fulfillment, not the negation, of creation. Jesus does not rescue God's people from a dark and dangerous world. Rather the one who was God's partner in creation has made God concretely known by becoming "flesh." Such a connection between nature and grace certainly underscores the Christian responsibility to care for the earth.

First Sunday After Christmas

The value of Christmas lies not in the fact that it commemorates the birth of a child, for—wondrous as it is—childbirth is a commonplace event, which happens all around us. Rather, the value of Christmas lies in the nature of the new child and in what the child—when grown to adulthood—accomplishes. Thus the lections for this Sunday, while still reverberating to the joys of the holy birth, now begin to look ahead in anticipation of Christ's work as Redeemer.

Christmas joy still resonates in the Old Testament lection from Isa. 63, where the goodness of the Lord results in a celebrative mood among the people. But in the midst of this joy a discordant note is struck, which jolts the reader into the reminder that God's expectation that the divine goodness will be greeted by loyalty from the people is an expectation that is to be disappointed.

The psalm continues the mood of rejoicing over the wonderful activity of God, but the lection from Heb. 2 forcefully redirects our attention to the realization that human sin and the suffering of Christ are inextricably linked—that the Baby whom we happily adore is the One whose identification with humankind leads to a cross. And the reading from Matt. 2, especially when seen in the context of the larger literary unit in which it is placed, describes the violent resistance with which the newly born divine King is greeted on the part of all the sinful powers of the earth.

In other words, these texts initiate the move from the Bethlehem manger out into the larger world of human perniciousness and pain, that world over which the newborn King rules but which he must first claim through his suffering and death. And as the King moves from one venue to another, the worshiping people of God move also. Our hearts still sing over the gleeful news of what has recently transpired, yet the terrible realization of what must yet take place begins to impose a hushed reflection. Our song changes from a simple "The

King has come!" to a more realistic "The King has come to die—and to rise again!"

As it surely must, our Christmas feast begins to incorporate the awful truth of Good Friday, a moment of terror which we may term "Good" only because the God who sent the Babe at Christmas reclaimed the Son at Easter.

Isaiah 63:7–9

These verses are a part of a larger poem which includes an indictment of Israel for disobedience (v. 10), a statement of God's absence (vs. 11–14), and a petition to God for help (vs. 15–19). In that context our verses provide a backdrop for the later elements of the poem. They reiterate past goodness from God as a contrast to present dismay of Israel.

Israel's remembrance of God's past goodness and generosity is saturated with the vocabulary of *God's convenantal faithfulness:*

"gracious deeds" (*ḥesed*) refers to all those specific acts of solidarity which constitute Israel's normative memory
"praiseworthy acts" (*hallôt*), also plural, is here a synonym for *ḥesed*
"great favor" (*ṭôb*) may refer to acts of material blessing—land, food, security, prosperity—but also refers to friendship, so that it is a close parallel to *ḥesed*
"mercy" (*reḥem*), again plural, refers to specific acts of care; the term suggests mothering concern, tenderness, and gentleness
"steadfast love" (*ḥesed*) is repeated so that the last word in v. 7 is the same as the first word

This cluster of words, which comprehends Israel's entire normative memory, witnesses to God's unqualified, massive, transformative fidelity to Israel. This is how God is known in Israel. God is not known primarily in God's power or in God's demands or in God's perfection, but as utterly faithful.

In v. 8, we move beyond Israel's grateful testimony (the voice of the psalmist) to God's own voice. We are taken inside God's intention and God's heart. God's self-resolve was to be one side of a relation of trust and mutual regard. (This yearning anticipation is paralleled in Jer. 3:19.) In both cases the subsequent verses (Isa. 63:10; Jer. 3:20) show that God's anticipated relation of trust is betrayed by Israel and never happens. Thus God sets up God's own self for profound hurt.

Israel lives only because God is faithful. God's faithfulness is distinctive and peculiar to God's own person. There was no other agent of rescue, no intermediary. God had no help from any angel or messenger. (Here NRSV offers a reading that is not only very different from that of the RSV, but in fact moves in a contrary direction. In reading "messenger or angel," NRSV has followed the Septuagint; conversely, the NRSV has kept the word "not" (*lō'*), following the Hebrew text, which RSV had emended to "his" (*lô*). Thus the two translations have opted for different emendations.) It was God's own face, God's own presence, that is, God's own self that rescued Israel from the slavery of Egypt.

Indeed, it is God's "love and pity" that is the driving power of all of Israel's history. In its weakness and weariness, Israel was incapable of making its journey to freedom. When Israel could not travel, God accepted this people as a burden and carried them from slavery through wilderness to freedom (cf. Ex. 19:4; Isa. 46:3–4). Thus the whole of the canonical story of Israel's faith is a story of God's willingness to sponsor and lift Israel, to do for Israel what Israel could not do for itself. God did so in God's great love, even though Israel's characteristic response was rebellion and betrayal.

God's fidelity and *God's deep love* have caused God to act for Israel in extraordinary ways (v. 9). The reality of *God for us* is articulated in two powerful ways.

The first way, however, requires a textual tradition. If one follows NRSV, then the point to be made is that this love and pity that made life possible for Israel are peculiarly the gift of Yahweh. Israel can expect or receive such help from nowhere else (cf. Isa. 40:13–14). The problem with such a rendering (textually preferable as it may be) is that the grouping of this text with the other lectionary readings depends on the positive presence of angels, as the RSV has it. On that reading, "God's angel" is a key actor in these texts, the very actor whom the NRSV reading deliberately eliminates. Thus the two readings from RSV and from NRSV not only read the text differently, but offer theological resources that go in exactly opposite directions. The preacher may decide to follow the older reading of RSV for the sake of the lectionary cluster of readings. Then the "angel" becomes a focal point of proclamation. If the NRSV is followed, this connection will no longer operate.

Second, we are told of God's work which God has done in "love" and in "pity." Calvin observes that God is here compared to a mother who carries in the womb, bears, nurtures, guards, and keeps. Thus the text witnesses to a God who violates all conventional religion, and the preacher dares to speak about God's costly, passionate mother-love.

Psalm 148

The Psalm lection for this day is a typical psalm of praise, with the usual tripartite structure: introduction, body, and conclusion. Indeed, Ps. 148 shares an important characteristic with its neighbors on the final pages of the Psalter in that the introduction and the conclusion are the identical exclamation, Hallelujah! ("Praise the LORD!") (see Pss. 146, 147, 149, 150). These final five psalms, in fact, constitute the crescendo of praise that brings the "hymnbook" of Israel-of-old to an exuberant climax. (Notice the manner in which each of the first four of the five "books" within the Psalter ends on an affirmation of praise [41:13; 72:18–19; 89:52; 106:48]. Is it imagining too much to see in this penchant for the number five a statement concerning the theological centrality of the five books of the Torah, Genesis through Deuteronomy? There are some who point to Ps. 1 as an introduction to the Psalter and who, therefore, see the entire book of Psalms as Torah commentary.)

Yet as predictable as Ps. 148 may be in terms of its structure, it is quite distinctive in content. Most of the psalm is given over to the body, that component in most psalms of praise which describes why Yahweh is to be considered praiseworthy. In this case the body (vs. 1b–14c) is divided into two sections, each of which is announced by an imperative. "Praise Yahweh from the heavens" (v. 1b) is paralleled by "Praise Yahweh from the earth" (v. 7a), and each of these commands determines the direction of the lines that follow. In other words, the heavenly dimensions of creation have reason to praise Israel's God as surely as do the earthly, and it is the clear intention of the text to explicate these reasons.

The first of the two commands is followed by a list of heavenly beings who are under orders to praise Yahweh, even heaven itself (v. 1c) and the "waters above the heavens" (v. 4b). This latter reference clearly has in mind that ancient cosmology which the Israelites shared with many of their neighbors and which conceptualized heaven as a dome resting on a flat earth, both of which were immersed in a primordial and chaotic sea. The waters of this sea are there just as surely under Yahweh's control as they were in the time of Noah, when they reinvaded the cosmos at the divine command (see Gen. 7:11). No less under Yahweh's control are "his angels," "his host," his "sun," "moon," and "stars."

These celestial beings are to praise Yahweh (notice how v. 5a repeats the thought of v. 1b) because they owe their very existence to Yahweh's creative power. The lines 5b and 6a are very nearly parallel, except that 6a prepares the way for 6b as a way of saying not simply that Yahweh brought the celestial world into being, but that Yahweh endowed that world with a place within the larger order of things, and that that place is forever determined. (The NRSV marginal note to v. 6b calls attention to the alternative translation of that line, "he set a law that cannot pass away," which reinforces our sense of the close connection between the theology of the psalms and that of the Torah, referred to above.)

The second of the two major commands within the body of this Psalm text (v. 7a) focuses on the earthly dimensions of creation. The "sea monsters and all deeps" of v. 7b echo the same chaos as that noted in v. 4b, in that the Hebrew word for "deeps" (*tĕhōmôt*) is the plural form of the same noun used in Gen. 1:2. The listing of the nonliving forms of early creation that are to praise Yahweh ("sea monsters" seem to be understood as mythical, not animal realities, at least on the basis of their place in the hierarchy of creation) reaches a conclusion in Ps. 148:9a, and is followed by references to flora (v. 9b) and fauna (v. 10). Finally, human beings are enrolled in the praisers of Yahweh, from rulers to common folk (vs. 11–12). High and low, young and old, individuals and the community at large—all are to lift voice in adoration and worship.

Then, as in vs. 5a–6, the rationale by which these creatures are to praise Yahweh is declared (vs. 13–14c). But here there is a surprise in store! It is not simply that Yahweh has made the "wild animals" and the "kings of the earth," although that affirmation is surely understood. It is rather that *Yahweh is who Yahweh is!* That is to say, there is no other one or no other thing like Yahweh. This God of Israel is absolutely unique; "his name alone is exalted." That alone would be reason enough to affirm "Hallelujah."

Yet there is more to it than even that. This absolutely God-like-no-other-god, who created the heavens and the earth, has also intervened in the life of the people to save them from that from which they could not save themselves. "He was raised up a horn [of salvation] for his people" (v. 14a) is reminiscent of Ps. 18:3, and reminds the community that not only are they the creation of God, but the recreation as well. They are reminded too that the God who made Israel has also saved Israel (cf. Isa. 42:5–9), that the One who constituted the worlds in the first place has reconstituted the people of God as an act of pure grace.

The celebration of Christmas, the sounds of which still ring in our ears and the joy of which is still in our hearts, is an important new beginning in the life of humankind. The Babe of Bethlehem is also to become the crucified Savior and Lord, God's affirmation that that world which was brought into being so long ago will never be allowed to become irredeemably corrupted. In the spirit of that reality, this psalm celebrates the indissoluble link between creation and salvation.

Hebrews 2:10–18

Even as the exultant sounds of Christmas reverberate around us, an ominous note intrudes. The Child who lies in the manger, object of adoration and wonder because he comes from God, is subject to suffering and death because he also comes from humankind. The name "Emmanuel" proclaims not only that *God* is with us but also that God *lives with us* and can fall prey to our sinfulness. While Heb. 2:10–18 does not explicitly have in view the infancy of Jesus, the issues articulated in this text explore the meaning and purpose of Jesus' humanity.

Beginning in 1:5 the author of Hebrews employs a series of quotations from the Hebrew Bible to describe the exaltation of Jesus Christ. Tying this series together is the recurrent comparison between Jesus and the angels who, despite their glory and honor, are as nothing in comparison with God's Son. Into this praise of the exaltation of Jesus, however, the author introduces in 2:9 the notion of Jesus' suffering, which is elaborated in vs. 10–18.

The startling image of Jesus as the "pioneer" dominates v. 10. It is difficult for English translations to capture the subtle wordplay in this verse, where the word "pioneer" (the "chief" or "first" leader, *archēgos*) is closely related to the act of "bringing" or leading (*agein*) God's sons and daughters to glory. Jesus is not a pioneer who strikes out on his own and for his own sake, but one whose action inevitably grasps others.

That God makes Jesus perfect through suffering appears at first glance to conflict with the sinlessness of Jesus proclaimed elsewhere in Hebrews, but the perfection referred to here is not moral perfection. Jesus does not become perfect through suffering, as through a process of purification or refinement. Instead, the perfection or wholeness (*teleioun*) of Jesus is his fitness for the office he holds. If Jesus is worshiped by angels (1:3) and is the occupier of God's throne (1:8), it is because of his suffering (cf. 2:9).

The claim that suffering must be the lot of God's Son was no less offensive in the first century than it is today, and New Testament writers address this issue in a variety of ways. In our text, particularly in vs. 11–13, the claim is made that Jesus' suffering arises from his real identity with human beings. First, the author asserts that Jesus and humanity both come from God: "For the one who sanctifies and those who are sanctified all have one Father" (v. 11). Because of that common origin, Jesus calls human beings his brothers and sisters.

The three scriptural quotations that follow in vs. 12–14, presented here as sayings of Jesus, confirm and elaborate this commonality between Jesus and humankind. The first quotation, taken from Ps. 22:22, reiterates the relationship between Jesus and humankind (that is, they are brothers and sisters) and then further identifies this relationship. Those who are Jesus' brothers and sisters belong to the congregation (*ekklēsia*) or community of God. The second quotation, probably from Isa. 8:17, asserts the confidence in God that is at the root of all Christian faith. Placing this affirmation in the mouth of Jesus demonstrates one of the ways in which he is a "pioneer"—that is, Jesus embodies trust in God. In the final quotation, taken from Isa. 8:18, Jesus announces not only his own presence, but his protection of his brothers and sisters, God's children.

For the writer of Hebrews, this vital commonality as children of the one God provides the explanation of Jesus' suffering. God's children have a common humanity, and Jesus shared that humanity in order to deliver his brothers and sisters from the devil and death (Heb. 2:14–15). To those of us more familiar with Paul's understanding of the relationship between sin and death, the absence of sin from this discussion of Jesus' triumph over death seems odd. Here the enemy of humankind is the devil, whose powerful arsenal includes death, the fear of which enslaves human beings throughout life. Jesus' victory over death, then, becomes the victory of his brothers and sisters, who may live with confidence in God and without fear of either death or devil.

Verses 16–17 bring us full circle, summarizing the claims that have been made about the suffering of Jesus. God's actions in Jesus were on behalf of the "descendants of Abraham." In order to deliver those descendants, Jesus had to become like them. Here the language of Jesus as the "high priest," an image that dominates the Christology of Hebrews, returns to the discussion.

The complexities of the argument in Hebrews may delude us into thinking that the writer's goal is an abstract theory of Christology, but the final verse in our text provides a correction: "Because he himself was tested by what he suffered, he is able to help those who are being tested." Jesus' suffering provides not only deliverance from death, but a model of hope and endurance to Christians who likewise experience suffering and temptation.

Matthew 2:13–23

It is fortunate that the revision of the Common Lectionary has added the heretofore omitted portion of Matt. 2:13–23 (the account of the murder of the Bethlehem children in 2:16–18). The chapter is carefully constructed as a single unit. It is set in a specific geographical structure and exposes Herod as a persistent but unsuccessful opponent of God's purposes. Any treatment of the chapter's segments must take into account its overall unity, including the horror of "the slaughter of the innocents."

The narrator provides two frameworks in which the story of Jesus' early days is set. The first framework is geographical. The birth of Jesus occurs in Bethlehem of Judea, which a citation from Micah 5:2 tells us is the place from which a ruler of Israel is to come. A messenger of the Lord, however, warns Joseph in a dream to leave Bethlehem and flee with Mary and Jesus to Egypt. The reader familiar with Israel's past cannot help recalling the sojourn of an earlier Joseph in Egypt and the strange providence that made Egypt a place of refuge and protection for Joseph's family. But Egypt became also a place of slavery, a place where God's offspring lived under the pharaoh's yoke, a place from which God liberated Israel. And now from Egypt, Jesus, God's son, is called (2:15; Hos. 11:1).

Again, it is a messenger from the Lord who at the death of Herod directs the travels of the holy family from Egypt to "the land of Israel," the land over which this Bethlehem baby is to rule (Matt. 2:5–6). And when the brutality of Archelaus poses a further threat, the family is directed to Nazareth in Galilee. Commentators puzzle over Matthew's pronounced interest in Nazareth (see also 21:11; 26:71), a town not mentioned in the Hebrew scriptures, and over the source and meaning of the quote "He will be called a Nazorean." What does become clear later in the narrative is that Galilee represents the locus of the Gentiles (4:15), and Jesus' ministry there leads to the mission to all nations (28:16–20).

What do we learn from this careful attention to geography? The narrative of Jesus' whereabouts is recounted so that through either direct quotation or pointed allusion the reader recalls decisive moments in Israel's history. Now in the story of Jesus that history reaches a critical point. The history becomes promise, for which Jesus is fulfillment. His journeys are not random or happenstance. In the narrative his associations with Bethlehem, Egypt, Israel, and Nazareth in Galilee disclose him as the accomplishment of Israel's destiny; they relate exactly how Jesus can be thought of as son of David.

The careful geographical structure also serves to show the divine protection of the holy family. Three times within our passage an angel speaks to Joseph to direct the family's travels so as to avoid the threat of Herod and his son (2:13, 19, 22). The reader is keenly aware of the presence of God preserving Mary, Joseph, and Jesus and steering them along a very significant journey.

The other framework of Matt. 2, alongside the geographical one, is the figure of Herod. At the beginning he is the king whom the Magi question about the birth of the "king of the Jews" (2:2). He directs them to Bethlehem and claims that he wants to hear their confirmation of the birth so that he too may worship the king. When the Magi avoid returning to Herod, his anger is aroused, necessitating the detour of Joseph, Mary, and Jesus to Egypt. We then learn of Herod's brutal slaughter of the male babies in and around Bethlehem. Finally the narrator poignantly reports, "Herod died."

The story of the chapter has to do with the birth of one king and the violent opposition of another. The royal power represented by Herod from the very beginning cannot tolerate the presence of Jesus. The first word of his birth leaves Herod troubled, and when he feels helpless to find Jesus his trouble turns to furious rage. In a sense he rightly perceives the threat Jesus represents—Israel's true King, who subverts all claims to absolute authority.

The killing of the male babies has to be understood in the context of the challenge Jesus holds for Herod. We are moved by the weeping of the parents at the senseless murder of their innocent children. The narrator identifies with the pain of Jeremiah (31:15) at the time of the deportation to Babylon, when he remembers tragic moments of the past. And yet we are not surprised at the extent to which Herod goes to get rid of Jesus. The birth of Jesus, when not encased in sentimentality and romance, represents a powerful challenge. The opposition does not sit idly by and take the news of his arrival casually. It understands that the stakes are high, and thus the response is violent and destructive. The story reminds the reader that God's acts of peace and justice inevitably evoke a hostile response.

Herod in a sense represents the enmities that crop up throughout Jesus' ministry, culminating in his violent death. But none of them is able to deter God's plan in Jesus, not Herod nor any other threatened authority. The simple words "Herod died" convey the end of such powers, the end of their plottings and scheming, the end of their pretense and brutality.

SECOND SUNDAY AFTER CHRISTMAS

With a variety of striking images, the readings for the Second Sunday After Christmas invoke praise and thanksgiving to God for God's outrageous generosity in the gift of Jesus Christ. The first three readings all contrast that generosity with the situation of humanity apart from God's intervention. Jeremiah 31:7–14 portrays for us a people in exile, a people for whom despair and grief seem to be the only option. The apparent eternity of winter's grasp dominates Ps. 147:12–20, with its picture of God sending "snow like wool" and "frost like ashes." John's prologue conjures up the hopelessness of life lived out in a dark world, a powerful place in which humans cannot even see how to proceed for themselves.

Common to all these texts is not only the assertion of human helplessness and hopelessness apart from God, but also the proclamation that God has already invaded the world and caused a new world to come into being. God invades and overturns the exile, replacing mourning with exuberant joy. God's gift of spring occurs even without our request for aid, simply because God is one who rescues. The incarnation of Jesus Christ powerfully breaks in as God's Light triumphs over against all darkness. Ephesians 1 asserts the soteriological consequences of God's invasion and proclaims those consequences to have been part of God's will even from the beginning. The gospel is not God's afterthought in response to a problem: it is deeply rooted in God's nature to act on behalf of creation.

Another element common to these texts is their assertion of praise and thanksgiving to God. In response to this proclamation of the gospel, the only right action for human beings is to sing the doxology.

Jeremiah 31:7–14 (A B C)

The exile of Israel smells of defeat, despair, and abandonment. Moreover, it is a place of deadly silence. All the voices of possibility have been crushed and nullified. Our capacity to make this text available depends on making two daring connections.

1.The *deadliness of exile* is the context into which *Jesus is born* and in which Christmas is celebrated. Christmas is an act against exile.

2.The *deadliness of exile* continues to be a metaphor through which to understand *our own social, cultural situation* of defeat, dehumanization, and despair.

Thus all three settings, in the exile of Jer. 31, in the New Testament, and in our time, are closely parallel in their silent hopelessness. Into all three scenes, the gospel flings this strident speech of God.

In the first part of our text, God addresses the exilic community and invites it to a new reality, which is rooted only in God's faithful resolve (vs. 7–9).

1.God issues an invitation to Israel in exile filled with glad imperatives (v. 7). In characteristic hymnic fashion, Israel is invited to sing aloud, raise shouts, proclaim, praise, say. These are all acts of joyous assertion which muted Israel thought it could never voice. The reason for the rejoicing is in the substance of the saying, which might be paraphrased: "Yahweh has *saved* the covenant partner!" God intervenes to liberate and new life begins, new life that was not at all expected. The reason for singing is that the deathly grip of Babylon is broken!

2.Verses 8–9 give the reason for the singing. The introductory "see" invites Israel to notice something utterly new. Now God speaks in the first person. Moreover, God is the willing subject of active verbs that will transform the life of Israel: "I am going to bring, I will gather, I will lead, I will let them walk." The poet conjures a great pilgrimage of people headed home, the ones who thought they would never have a home. In that pilgrimage are included the ones who are vulnerable and dependent, the blind, the lame, the pregnant women. These are the ones who are always at risk. Now, however, that risk is ended; they are safe, kept, and guarded on the way.

Now God addresses the nations (vs. 10–14).

1.The speech of God puts the nations on notice (vs. 10–11). They will have to yield to God's deep resolve. They will have to release their hostages and forgo their supply of cheap labor. God will be the faithful shepherd who values every sheep, even the lost, even the ones in exile. The nations can do nothing to stop God from this daring resolve.

2.The poet then conjures for us what new life will be like when the exiles come home and the power of fear and death is broken (vs. 12–14).

(a) Creation will flourish; there will be extravagant material goods (v. 12). In an arid climate that has only marginal supplies of water, to be by reliable "brooks of water" (see v. 9) is a powerful image of material well-being. Death is fended off.

(b) Social life will resume (v. 13a). Young people can have their loud, boisterous parties. No one will mind; older people will join in, because such noise is a song of confidence, stability, freedom, and well-being.

(c) Restored creation (v. 12) and restored community (v. 13a) are rooted in God's transformative power. It is God, only God, but surely God, who transforms mourning to joy, exile to homecoming, death to life, sorrow to gladness (v. 13b; compare John 16:20).

(d) An ordained religious community will live in utter well-being (v. 14). People will prosper, priests will prosper. Priests and people together will live in well-being, where blessings abound.

In every season, including ours, the oracle of God breaks the dread of exile. Exiles are those who live in resignation, believing no newness is possible. That gripping hopelessness is not explained by the psychology of modernity, but is a deep theological crisis. The only ground for newness is God. Here God speaks unambiguously, against all our presumed death. It is by the power and faithfulness of God that life begins again.

Psalm 147:12–20 (A B C)

The ability of this lection to stand independently of the rest of the psalm of which it is a part is illustrated by the fact that in the Septuagint it is a distinct psalm, Ps. 147 in the Septuagint enumeration (vs. 1–11 of this psalm constituting the Septuagint's Ps. 146). It consists of two basic parts, of which the first is vs. 12–14. These lines urge the people to praise God (v. 12) because God has endowed the nation with peace (the first lines of vs. 13 and 14, respectively) and prosperity (the second lines of these same verses).

The second part of the psalm, vs. 15–20, celebrates the power of God's word. This theme is announced in v. 15, where the Hebrew wordplay goes undetected in most English translations. The Hebrew behind "his command" (NRSV, REB) is *'imĕrātô*, and literally means something like "his utterance," since it is related to the root *'āmar*, "to utter" or "to say." This term is paralleled by "word" (*dĕbārô*) of v. 15b, and the effect of the whole verse is to remind the reader that God is in an ongoing conversation with creation. The action verbs "send out" and "run swiftly" imply incessant dialogue (not monologue, as we shall note below) between God and the people of God (compare v. 19), a continuing hum of communication.

The nature of God's word—that part of the dialogue which originates with the Deity—is described metaphorically in vs. 16–18. It is perhaps coincidental that this description of the wintry blast in ancient Israel is appointed to be read in North American churches at the coldest time of year in the northern temperate zone, and the articulation of these verses will be strengthened in those congregations whose houses of worship lie under blankets of snow on this day. NRSV's "Who can stand before his cold?" in v. 17b is an accurate translation of the Masoretic Text as it stands, but a slight change in the Hebrew letters yields "before his cold the waters stand still," that is, "freeze," perhaps a preferred rendering (see REB).

If vs. 16–17 portray God's deep freeze, v. 18 describes God's thaw. Here is found another wordplay. "Word" of 18a echoes the same term (*dĕbārô*) in 15b, but here it is paralleled not by *'imĕrātô*, but by *rûḥô*, which may mean either "his wind" (NRSV), "his breath," or "his Spirit." The ambiguity is probably not accidental, for another Hebrew poet has written an extended play on this very word in Ezek. 37:1–14, an ingenious creation in which the power of language to speak on several levels at once is remarkably demonstrated. Psalm 147:18 seems to be an intriguing way of saying, "As the warm spring winds blow to melt the ice and snow of winter, so the Spirit of God melts all that is frozen in human life."

As noted above, the statement in v. 15 concerning the presence of God in human life is balanced by a similar statement in v. 19, a pair of "brackets" around the metaphor of vs. 16–18. Yet in v. 19 the application to human life of God's word is given a sharper focus than in v. 15, for here it is applied in a special way to Israel, a thought that is extended into the first two lines of v. 20.

The entire text is climaxed by a final *halĕlû-yāh,* which not only echoes similar imperatives in v. 12, but balances the psalm's opening *halĕlû-yāh,* in v. 1.

The heart of this text is, of course, the metaphor of winter and spring. It limits the power of this passage to see it as a simple statement of God's power over the world of nature, although it does make such a statement. But beyond that it portrays God's role in the movement of the individual person (or human community) from death to life, from desolation to hope, from meaninglessness to purpose. Verses 16–17 may be compared to many of the psalms of lament and of thanksgiving, which describe the human condition of alienation and estrangement in the language of imagery. Psalm 30:9, for example, complains that if the psalmist (or reader of the psalm) is allowed to die, God will be the loser, since the dead are incapable of praise. But "death" is no more the final word in Ps. 30 than is "winter" in Ps. 147:12–20. In vs. 11–12 of Ps. 30 God responds to the human plea for help by restoring the helpless one to life:

> You have turned my mourning into dancing; . . .
> so that my soul may praise you and not be silent.

Yet it is significant that in this lection God intervenes to restore the helpless even though there is no stated plea for help. The warm winds of spring do not thaw the frozen water because of human intercession, but simply because it is God's nature to restore and redeem. The same God who rebukes the ice and snow also rebukes sin and evil, because that's the kind of being God is. Men and women may cry to God for help, but it is God's nature to help whether or not men and women cry.

This reality brings forth the human response of praise, that part of the divine-human dialogue referred to above that originates with men and women. The God of Israel is the Lord of both freezing and thawing, of both death and life, of both alienation and fellowship. And because this God is always at work moving life from the one to the other, the community of faith sings in joyful response: Hallelujah!

Ephesians 1:3–14 (A B C)

Paul customarily opens his letters with an expression of thanksgiving for God's action in the lives of the congregation he addresses. Ephesians, which was probably written by a disciple of Paul rather than by Paul himself, not only continues that practice but expands it. Virtually the whole of chapters 1—3 is taken up with expressions of praise and thanksgiving. Ephesians 1:3 introduces this dominant mood of doxology with an ascription of praise to God for God's gifts to humankind. Since the word "blessing" in Greek can refer both to an act of thanksgiving or praise and to an act of bestowing some gift on another, the play on the word in this verse sets the tone for what follows: God is to be blessed for God's blessings. The extent of these blessings comes to expression in the phrase "every spiritual blessing in the heavenly places." God's goodness takes every conceivable form.

Verses 4–14 detail the form of God's blessings and focus on God's choosing of the elect. First, the author points to the agelessness of

God's election: "He chose us in Christ before the foundation of the world." This bit of eloquence need not be turned into a literal proposition about God's act of election. Instead, the author asserts that God's choosing has no beginning. Just as it is impossible to identify the beginning of God's Christ (John 1:1), so it is impossible to conceive of a time when God did not choose on behalf of humankind.

God's election creates a people who are "holy and blameless before him." Verse 5 elaborates this characterization of God's people. They become God's children through Jesus Christ, but always what happens is "according to the good pleasure of his will." Everything that has occurred comes as a result of God's will and results in "the praise of his glorious grace that he freely bestowed on us in the Beloved." In the face of God's eternal choice on behalf of humankind, in the face of God's revelation of his Son, Jesus Christ, in the face of God's grace, the only appropriate response is one of praise (v. 6).

Verses 7–14 continue the exposition of God's gifts to humankind—redemption, forgiveness, wisdom, faith. The exposition culminates with repeated references to the inheritance believers receive through Christ (vs. 11, 14). That inheritance carries with it the responsibility already articulated in v. 6, which is to praise God's glory. Primary among the Christian's responsibilities is the giving of praise to God. With v. 15, the writer moves from this general expression of thanksgiving for God's actions on behalf of humankind to particular expressions of thanks relevant to his context. He constantly keeps the Ephesians in his prayers, asking for them "a spirit of wisdom and of revelation as you come to know [God]" (v. 17). The prayer continues in v. 18 with the petition that believers might be enlightened so that they know the hope to which they have been called and the riches that are part of God's inheritance. This mood of doxology continues throughout chapter 2 and most of chapter 3, as the author celebrates the nature of God's action in Christ Jesus.

For Christians in the West, particularly for those in North America, these words may have an alien and perhaps even an exotic tone. They run counter to at least two of our most deeply held values. First, these verses insist over and over again that humankind is utterly dependent on God. To assert that God creates, God destines, God wills, God reveals, God accomplishes God's own plan means that human beings, in and of themselves, accomplish nothing. This assault on the Western sense of independence and autonomy poses not only a challenge, but also a significant opportunity for preaching.

The second way in which this text cuts against the grain of Christianity in a North American context derives from its insistence on the obligation to praise God. Our thoroughgoing pragmatism inclines us to respond to the claim that God has acted on our behalf with the question, "What are we to *do?*" If we stand in God's debt, then we understand ourselves to be obliged to pay back the amount owed. The text, however, stipulates no repayment, for the debt can never be paid. Instead, the exhortation is to give God thanks and praise. To our way of thinking, this is no response at all, and yet it is fundamental to our existence as God's creatures. The reading of Ephesians should prompt us to recall the words of the Westminster Larger Catechism, that the chief end of human life is "to glorify God, and fully to enjoy him forever."

John 1:(1–9) 10–18 (A B C)

A portion of the prologue to the Fourth Gospel appeared as the Gospel reading for the Third Proper of Christmas, and the commentary on that lesson focused on Jesus as the revelation of God. Beyond the sentimentality and romance of Christmas, we encounter in the baby born at Bethlehem, so the passage tells us, nothing less than God's decision to become human. The full prologue (if one chooses) now occurs as the reading for the Second Sunday After Christmas, and provides us with the opportunity to reflect on further dimensions of God's incarnation as they emerge from the text.

One notable feature of the prologue is the prominence of visual language (a particularly relevant feature for the Epiphany season). "Light" and "glory" are terms associated with the Word, and "seeing" (alongside "receiving" and "believing") is the verb used for the perception of faith. Even before a statement of the incarnation, we read that the life found in the Word illuminates human experience, that the light continually shines in the darkness, and that the darkness has neither understood nor succeeded in extinguishing the light. (The Greek verb in 1:5 translated in the NRSV as "overcome" has a double meaning: "comprehend" and "seize with hostile intent." Perhaps an appropriate English word retaining the ambiguity would be "grasp," or "apprehend.")

The mention of John the Baptist, who is a kind of lesser luminary or reflected light (5:35) and is contrasted with the true light, signals the movement from a preincarnate lumination to the historic advent of the light in Jesus. It is in this context that we understand that the coming of the light into the world "enlightens everyone" (1:9). This universal reference has sometimes been taken to refer to the ancient notion that every individual possesses a spark of the divine, a measure of a universal conscience. The function of religion (any religion?) is to nurture the inextinguishable spark until it glows with understanding, so the argument goes. But such a reading hardly coheres with the evangelist's use of the image of light throughout the Gospel. Jesus claims in a specific way to be the light of the world (8:12), without whom people grope in the darkness (12:35). The coming of the light entails judgment, because it discloses that people prefer darkness to light (3:19). What seems to be implied in the prologue is that all people, whether they believe it or not, live in a world illuminated by the light just as they live in a world created by the Word. What they are called to do is to trust the light, to walk in it, and thereby to become children of light (12:36).

Whether as a bolt of lightning in a dark sky, or as a distant beam toward which one moves, or as the dawn that chases the night, what light does is to push back darkness. The prologue, however, gives no hint that the light has totally banished the darkness, that life now is a perpetual day. In fact, the story John tells reiterates the powerful opposition of the darkness in the ministry of Jesus and beyond. But the promise of the prologue is that the darkness, despite its best efforts, including even a crucifixion, has not put out the light.

The last paragraph of the prologue has to be understood in terms of the many references to the book of Exodus, which it reflects. In a sense its background is the statement that "no one has ever seen God" (1:18). Though in fact there are places in the Hebrew Bible where people "see" God (for example, Ex. 24:9–11; Isa. 6:1), the statement seems to recall the occasion where Moses, eager to behold the divine glory, is not allowed to view the face of God, only God's backside (Ex. 33:23). In contrast, now God is seen in "the only Son."

Furthermore, the seeing of the divine glory is made possible by the incarnation of the Word, who "tabernacled among us." The Greek verb translated in the NRSV (John 1:14) as "lived" more specifically means "tented" or "tabernacled," and recalls the theme of God's dwelling with Israel, in the tabernacle of the wilderness wanderings and the Temple at Jerusalem. In the humanity of Jesus, the Christian community has beheld the very divine glory Moses wished to see, that unique and specific presence of God that hovered over the tabernacle as a cloud by day and a fire by night.

Terms like "light" and "glory" tend toward abstractions and become very difficult to communicate in concrete language to a contemporary congregation. What, then, does it mean to "see" God, to behold the divine glory? Two other words repeated in the prologue help in the translation: grace and truth. To behold God is to be a recipient of wave after wave of the divine generosity (grace) and to experience God's faithfulness to the ancient promises (truth). "Seeing" includes but goes beyond mere sense perception; it has to do with becoming children of God, with discovering the divine benevolence and reliability. Revelation in the Fourth Gospel has a strongly soteriological cast (17:3).

EPIPHANY

As the reading of Isa. 60:1–6 in the context of the celebration of Epiphany recalls, the coming of God into the world is often understood as the coming of a brilliant light. That light, the gift of God, carries with it the power to transform Israel so that Israel is restored and also those outside Israel are inevitably drawn to the light seen in Israel. While the social context differs dramatically, Eph. 3:1–12 makes a similar point: part of the mystery of the Epiphany is the mysterious inclusion of Gentiles among God's people. Submission to God's gift of light carries with it the obligation to accept and proclaim the inclusion of all outsiders within this mystery.

Psalm 72:1–7, 10–14 and Matt. 2:1–12 draw on imagery of the king and his enthronement, rather than the appearance of light. For the psalmist, the king's power and longevity must serve the purpose of the people's good. Prominent among the king's obligations is his responsibility to protect and liberate those who are not able to protect and liberate themselves. Ironically, Matt. 2:1–12 concerns the birth of an infant king whose power and longevity are severely threatened by another king, who acts only to protect himself. The Magi, outsiders drawn by the light that marks the infant king's birth, mark the beginning of the procession of those outsiders who see in the gospel the mystery of salvation. The juxtaposition of the enthronement psalm and the story of the infant Jesus, already King, dramatically poses the question of where authentic power lies and what constitutes genuine kingship.

Isaiah 60:1–6 (A B C)

Israel has had a long season of darkness (the despair of exile). Now comes its season of light. The light is not self-generated by Israel. It is a gift given by Yahweh. In the liturgical life of Israel, God's powerful coming is often presented as the coming of light, though the word used for such light is "glory." God's glory "shines." And when God's glory (powerful, magisterial presence) "shines," Israel lives in the glow, and is itself a presence of light in the world. Thus the text that moves Israel from darkness to light is a dramatic move from absence to presence, from despair to hope, from dismay to well-being.

God's coming will decisively transform Israel's circumstance of despondency (Isa. 60:1–2). Israel is addressed with an imperative: "Arise." The imperative, however, is in fact an invitation. The imperative is not a burden, but good news. The imperative is an invitation for Israel to return to the land of the living.

The ground for the imperative is introduced by "for" (= because). Israel can arise because "your light has come." The words are wondrously and deliberately ambiguous. "Your light" is in fact Yahweh, who is Israel's only source of hope and possibility. At the same time, however,"your light" refers to Israel's own "glow," which is a gift from Yahweh that changes the very character of Israel. Thus "your light" is both *intrusion from Yahweh* and *restored Israel.*

These poetic lines are constructed so that an affirmation of "God's glory" is stated in v. 1b and reiterated in v. 2d. Between these two affirmations is a statement about darkness and thick darkness, gloom and despair. Thus the "glory" brackets and comprehends, contains and overwhelms, the darkness.

The poet waxes eloquent and extravagant about the magnet of Jerusalem among the nations (vs. 4–7). Something new is happening that Israel could not have expected or believed. When Israel finally lifts its eyes from its despair, it will not believe what it sees! There is a huge procession from all over the known world. Jerusalem had thought itself abandoned; now all the others are making the journey to be in Jerusalem.

On the one hand, "your sons" and "your daughters" will come, cared for, protected, valued (v. 4). These are the exiles that have been scattered far from Jerusalem. They had remained scattered long after the "official return," either because they were restrained by their "hosts" from coming home, or because they had lost their will and desire and resolve to come home. The light ends the exile. The poet imagines a world in which the abused and nearly forgotten now are drawn back to their proper habitat among God's beloved people.

On the other hand, the procession also includes more than the scattered Jewish exiles. It also includes the "wealth of the nations" (v. 5). Israel was rarely if ever one of the affluent nations. Most often Israel, in its disadvantage, stood in awe of its more powerful, prosperous neighbors. The poet plays on Israel's long-established sense of disadvantage, of being a rather second-rate people. Now, in this scenario, realities are reversed. The exotic material of the nations, long coveted from a distance, is given to Israel, who is the locus of the light in the world. The exiles are not coming home empty-handed. The exiles bring all that the nations can offer—camels, gold, frankincense, and flocks. Damaged Jerusalem has become the pivot and possibility for a new world.

The rhetoric of the poem is double-focused, in a quite careful way. On the one hand, there is no doubt that Israel gains as a political, economic power and is assured security and prosperity. On the other hand, that assurance is passionately theological. The exiles bring this much wealth, not to prosper Jerusalem, but to worship Yahweh (v. 7). The passage begins in God's glory (vs. 1–2) and ends in God's glory (v. 7). Israel's new reality of prosperity exists exactly in the envelope of God's glory.

Whenever the nations bring such exotic gifts, they are in fact submitting themselves to God's new future. That is what is happening with the bringing of "gold, frankincense, and myrrh" (Matt. 2:11). When God is thus worshiped, Israel prospers, Jerusalem glows, the nations come to their proper existence, all bask in the glow of God's well-being. God's presence creates newness for the entire world. In this poem, all—Jerusalem, the exiles, the nations—receive the gift of life.

Psalm 72:1–7, 10–14 (A B C)

A widely held scholarly view sees this psalm as a hymn sung at the time of the enthronement of the Davidic king, or if ancient Israel possessed an annual ceremony of reenthronement, as did ancient Babylon, a hymn devoted to that occasion. In either event, there is a sense in which the king is entering (or reentering) the public life of the nation, and the psalm expresses the hopes that the people have vested in this monarch, who is also the representative of God. Therefore it is an appropriate text for the Epiphany observance, a celebration of the entrance of the messianic ruler, Jesus Christ, into the life of humankind.

The opening (vs. 1–4) constitutes a prayer to God that the king will establish a right social order. Prominent in these lines are terms that were often found on the lips of the prophets: righteousness (vs. 1, 2, 3), justice (vs. 1, 2), and peace (v. 3, NRSV "prosperity"). They are also found in certain of the psalms of praise, where they refer not only to qualities characteristic of God, but to the nature of human life before God (Pss. 97:2; 98:9). For the author of Ps. 72, these qualities are not abstractions, but are moral ideals which have become incarnate in the Davidic king. Those qualities which began with God ("*your* justice, . . . *your* righteousness," v. 1, emphasis added) have become the standards by which the human king is to rule. His role is to help those who cannot help themselves (v. 4).

The following section (vs. 5–7) begins as a prayer for the king's long life, the kind of ritualistic formula that has been a part of coronation ceremonies ancient and modern ("Long live the king!"). Yet it is of the nature of this psalm that it will not dwell on the king's good health, but returns to the larger question of the health of the community. As in the first section, "righteousness" and "peace" (v. 7) are the standards by which the well-being of the people is judged, and it is they, not just the heartbeat of the king, that must be preserved past the end of the moon (v. 7, compare v. 5).

The discourse soon turns to the urgent affairs of the society: the well-being (*šālôm* of vs. 3, 7) of the poorest, most helpless citizens. Notice the verbs: "delivers" (v. 12), "has pity" (v. 13), "saves" (v. 13), "redeems" (v. 14). Clearly God's king is to bring the same energies to bear on the quality of the nation's domestic life as on foreign affairs. And—if the literary form means anything—since the king's concern for domestic matters is placed in a climactic position within the psalm, this aspect of his duties is to weigh more heavily upon him than his military adventures.

This lection ends with an affirmation of the value of human life in the king's eyes: "Precious is their blood in his sight" (v. 14).

The most often remarked emphasis of Epiphany is on the appearance of the messianic king, Jesus Christ, and it is in this connection that other lections for this day emphasize light (Isa. 60:1; Matt. 2:2) and the ability of men and women to see God's work (Isa. 60:2; Eph. 1:9, 18). But this Psalm lection contributes an added dimension to the Epiphany observance by celebrating not only the appearance of the king, but the nature of the king's rule as the liberator of those who are unable to liberate themselves. To be sure, the same note is struck in other texts that describe the birth and infancy of Jesus (notably Luke 1:52–53), but few texts draw so tightly the connection between God's act of sending a king and the responsibilities of the king as protector of the poor and the weak.

There is an irony in this theme when it is applied to Epiphany, for Epiphany is the celebration of the visit of the Magi, bearers of precious gifts to the boy-king Jesus. The description of wealth in the traditional Gospel lection for Epiphany (Matt. 2:1–12) is to be found in the gold, frankincense, and myrrh, the treasures of the Magi. In that narrative the messianic King is a weak and vulnerable child, under threat from the tyrannical Herod. His one kingly act is a passive one of receiving the tokens of royalty bestowed by others.

But in the Epiphany Psalm lection, all of that is turned around. Here the royal office itself is that which has been bestowed, not just its tokens. And the giver is not some earthly seer or potentate, but the one true King, Israel's God. As for the theme of wealth in the psalm, while there is some traditional language of empire, the real wealth consists in *šālôm* (vs. 3, 7). This is more than "peace" in the sense of an absence of warfare. It is also more than "prosperity," as the NRSV—with some justification—has it (v. 3). *Šālôm* in this case is the total well-being of the people (compare NEB's "peace and prosperity"), their ability to live free from "oppression and violence" imposed by others (v. 14) and free from the devastating effects of poverty.

Thus the Epiphany celebration is the joyous proclamation of a kingdom like no other. It is the joyous acceptance of a King who has come to set us free.

Ephesians 3:1–12 (A B C)

Following the first two chapters of Ephesians, with their extensive thanksgiving to God, in 3:1 the author takes up Paul's ministry in the context of God's mystery. Verses 1–3 characterize Paul's calling as his "commission." Verses 4–6 elaborate on the nature of God's mystery that is now revealed, and this section provides the most obvious entrance into a discussion of the Epiphany. In vs. 7–9, the focus is once again on Paul's ministry concerning that mystery, and in vs. 10–12 it is on the ministry of the church as a whole.

The opening statement breaks off awkwardly after the identification of Paul as "a prisoner for Christ Jesus for the sake of you Gentiles." Verse 2 verifies Paul's calling as prisoner on behalf of the Gentiles by referring to the gift of God's grace which bestowed on him a "commission" on behalf of Gentiles. Verse 3 makes specific the nature of this gift of grace, in that the mystery became known to Paul through revelation. In common with all believers, Paul's knowledge of God's action comes to him solely through God's own free gift.

Verse 4 returns to the term "mystery," which is initially described only as a "mystery of Christ." The newness of the revelation of this mystery emerges in v. 5, which emphasizes that only in the present time has the mystery been revealed. This assertion stands in tension with statements elsewhere in the Pauline corpus regarding the witness of the prophets to God's action in Jesus Christ (for example, Rom. 1:2; 16:26). What the author celebrates is the present revelation of God's mystery, and the contrast with the past helps to emphasize that fact but should not become a critique or rejection of past generations. Similarly, the second part of v. 5 identifies the "holy apostles and prophets" as recipients of revelation, not because revelation confines itself to those individuals but because of their central role in proclamation.

Verse 6 identifies the "mystery of Christ": "the Gentiles have become fellow heirs, members of the same body, and sharers in the promise in Christ Jesus through the gospel." Given the previous few verses, we might anticipate that the "mystery" refers to the mystery of Jesus' advent. For this letter, however, the "mystery of Christ" has a very specific connotation, namely, the inclusion of the Gentiles. Each word identifying the Gentiles in v. 6 begins with the prefix *syn*, "together," emphasizing the oneness created through the mystery. We might convey this phrase in English as "heirs together, a body together, sharers together." For the writer of Ephesians, central to the "mystery of Christ" is the oneness of Jew and Gentile.

The emphasis here on the social dimension of the gospel, the unification of human beings, needs specific attention. Certainly Ephesians does not limit the mystery to its social component, as if the only characteristic of the gospel is its impact on human relations. The extensive praise of God and of Jesus Christ in chapters 1 and 2 prevents us from reductionism. Nevertheless, here the radical oneness of Jew and Gentile who become one new humanity (2:15) becomes a necessary ingredient in the larger reconciliation of humankind to God (2:16). Any separation between "vertical" and "horizontal" dimensions of faith here stands exposed as inadequate.

Verses 7–9 return us to Paul's role with respect to the gospel. He, despite his own standing as "the very least of all the saints," receives the gift of preaching among the Gentiles and, indeed, among all people (v. 9). Proclamation of the gospel comes not from Paul and his fellow apostles alone, however. Verse 10 identifies the role of the whole church in proclamation. The church, both through its verbal proclamation and through its actions, makes known God's wisdom. Here that wisdom is addressed to "the rulers and authorities in the heavenly places." The gospel addresses not only human beings but all of God's creation.

Verses 11–12 affirm once again the purpose of God in the proclamation of Paul and of the church. God's purpose has its final goal in Christ Jesus our Lord, "in whom we have access to God in boldness and confidence through faith in him." These last terms connote more in Greek than the English translations can convey. To speak "boldly" (*parrēsia*) is to speak without regard for the consequences, and to have "access" (*prosagōgē*) is to have, through Jesus Christ, a means of drawing near to God. In other words, the revelation, or epiphany, of Jesus Christ carries with it both the obligation of proclaiming the gospel and the strength needed for carrying out that obligation.

Matthew 2:1–12 (A B C)

The story of the Magi coming from the East to bring gifts to the infant Jesus is associated in the minds of most churchgoers with Christmas. It is a piece of the scene usually enacted at the Christmas service or pageant. The story, however, with its strong connections with the Hebrew scriptures and its prominent depiction of these non-Jewish worshipers, fits more appropriately the celebration of Epiphany. It telegraphs for the reader of Matthew's narrative the opening of the gospel beyond Jewish boundaries and the reminder of the worldwide mission of the church.

We shall examine the passage in terms of its three primary characters. First are the Magi. The Greek term *magoi* suggests that the "wise men" were priestly sages from Persia, who were experts in astrology and the interpretation of dreams. What distinguishes them in the narrative is *their sincere and persistent search* for the baby "born king of the Jews." While one might suppose them to have been veteran, sophisticated travelers, what is striking is their candor and openness. Almost naive, they seem to anticipate no difficulty in inquiring of Herod the king about the birth of a rival king. Their inquisitiveness forces a troubled Herod to seek help from the chief priests and scribes, who, though aligned with Herod, ironically produce the decisive clue that finally leads to Bethlehem.

Throughout their journeys, the Magi are *patently guided by God.* It is, first, a star in the East and then a text from Micah that lead them to their goal. When the time comes for them to leave Bethlehem, they are warned in a dream to take a different route home to avoid Herod. These strange outsiders do not stumble onto the Messiah as if by accident. They search with purpose and are directed each step of the way by a divine hand.

The Magi's stay in Bethlehem is *marked by great joy, by the worship of the infant Jesus, and by the giving of gifts.* They come prepared and seem to know what to do when they arrive. The narrative is specific about the gifts—gold, frankincense, and myrrh—expensive gifts suitable for royalty. We are not given any clues about the motivations of the Magi, why they came and why they worshiped. The narrator only seems interested in the response they made, the proper response to the King of Israel.

Now the remarkable fact that undergirds the entire portrait of the Magi—their searching, their guidance, their worship—is its character as the fulfillment of scripture. Isaiah 60:1–6 and Ps. 72:1–7, 10–14, two other texts for Epiphany, speak of the time of restoration when

> the wealth of the nations shall come to you. . . .
> They shall bring gold and frankincense,
> and shall proclaim the praise of the LORD.
> (Isa. 60:5–6)

The arrival of the non-Jews at Bethlehem turns out to be a part of the divine plan, an accomplishment of the promises made long ago. The Magi, as representatives of all non-Jews, belong here in the company of those worshiping the infant Messiah. In a sense they pave the way for the command the risen Christ gives to the Eleven at the end of Matthew's narrative: make disciples of all the nations.

A second key figure in our text is Herod the king. He also plays a prominent role in the latter half of Matt. 2, a passage that serves as the Gospel reading for the First Sunday After Christmas in the A cycle. Suffice it here to say that the scheming of the troubled and cruel Herod turns out to be no match for the guileless Magi, guided by the hand of God. Herod's plot to have the Magi search out and identify his rival for him backfires when they are directed in a dream to go home a different way. If the Magi represent the presence of non-Jews who appropriately worship Jesus, Herod represents the imperial powers, imposing and conspiring but threatened and ultimately frustrated by King Jesus.

Third, we turn to the figure of Jesus, who in this narrative says and does nothing, but nevertheless is the chief protagonist. The entire plot revolves around the affirmation that Jesus is King of Israel. The text from Micah that the chief priests and scribes uncover identifies him as "a ruler who is to shepherd my people Israel" (2:6). The Greek verb translated as "shepherd" actually depicts what shepherds do with their flocks—tend, protect, guide, nurture. Jesus' rule is distinguished from Herod's rule by his gentle guardianship, his compassionate care for his people. But it is just this shepherd-king who is finally rejected and mocked by the same chief priests and scribes who, at the crucifixion, say, "He is the King of Israel; let him come down from the cross now" (27:42).

The account of the Magi's visit to Bethlehem and their worship of the King of the Jews becomes a critical episode in the larger story of God's redemptive plan for humankind. Salvation comes through Jesus the Jew, the fulfillment of the prophetic dreams, but it reaches far beyond to strangers from the East, to a Roman centurion, and to a Canaanite woman. At the end of the story it is no longer a matter of non-Jews coming to Bethlehem, but of Jewish disciples going out to all the nations.

First Sunday After Epiphany

(Baptism of the Lord)

Ordinary Time 1

On this Sunday, when many churches commemorate the baptism of Jesus, the lectionary texts recall not only that event but its significance in the context of Israel's scriptures and in the light of Christian baptismal practice. Isaiah 42:1–9 insists on God as the one who alone is able to accomplish "new things" and proclaims the Servant who is God's vehicle for achieving these "new things." While Christians who hear this text read in connection with the baptism of Jesus will necessarily identify him as the servant, the identity of the servant is less significant than is the work of justice and transformation that God enables the servant to accomplish.

Psalm 29 majestically announces the glory of God, who is revealed to be powerful over the turbulence of nature and whose very voice is a transcendent revelation. That God's glory differs from that associated with human kings, however, emerges clearly in the closing lines of the psalm. From this King the people may seek their own strength and their own peace!

Matthew's story of the baptism of Jesus combines these motifs of the servant and the king, although the story itself speaks of Jesus as God's Son. The baptism inaugurates Jesus' ministry, in which he proclaims God's righteousness in terms of the Servant's actions of justice and compassion. As God's Son, Jesus is the true king, whose concern is truly for the strength and peace of his people.

Luke's account of the baptism of Cornelius reminds us that John's baptism of Jesus carries with it the promise of baptism in the Spirit (Matt. 3:11). In Cornelius, the first Gentile convert, that promise finds fulfillment and bursts through the boundaries to include all those who fear God (Acts. 10:35).

Isaiah 42:1–9

This text is an announcement from God to exiles. It asserts two evangelical realities: (a) God has a powerful resolve to do "new things" (vs. 5–9); (b) the Servant is the means whereby God's newness will be implemented (vs. 1–4). While the Servant is surely derived from and in the service of God's purpose, the poem articulates the two themes in inverse sequence, first *Servant,* then *purpose.*

The Servant is announced (vs. 1–4). God says, "Here is my servant," the one who will do my work (v. 1). The figure of the Servant in these poems is left unidentified. Every time we read this poem, we must redecide who this servant is. Characteristically, the church in the season after Epiphany will hear in the poem a reference to Jesus, who mediates the gospel to the world. It is enough for our hearing to let the poetic reference remain open. The Servant, ancient or contemporary, is whoever it is who does God's transformative work in the world. Who the Servant is in any hearing depends on how we hear.

The Servant is powered by God's "wind" (*rûaḥ*), which blows newness into the world (v. 1). The spirit of God equips the Servant to do what the world regards as impossible. The impossible newness the Servant performs is to "bring justice," that is, to make available a world of equitable, trusting, life-giving social relations (v. 1).

The work of justice done by the Servant is a deeply conflicted, high-risk matter. The Servant, however, does not proceed with force or high-handed authority (v. 2). God's justice is wrought gently, carefully, caringly. The Servant is so gentle as to respect "bruised" reeds, so careful as to respect "dim wicks" (v. 3). That is, the Servant has respect for persons who are weak, fragile, and in jeopardy. His way of bringing justice matches the goal of justice which he enacts. The means serves the end.

In v. 4, the NRSV renders "grow faint" and "be crushed." These two words reiterate the key words from the metaphors of v. 3. Thus v. 4 reads, "He will not burn dimly, he will not be bruised." He will honor the weak, but he will be strong to do his work.

The portrait of the Servant now leads to the voice of the God who has sent the Servant (vs. 5–9). The one who intervenes is the same one who has founded and who gave breath to the human creation. The God who gave breath to the Servant (v. 1) has given breath to all (cf. Gen. 1:2). It is God's power over creation that is now at work in the mission of the Servant.

Verse 6 continues four first-person statements, all addressed to the unidentified Servant. The Servant is Yahweh's Servant, set to do

Yahweh's purpose. The purpose of the Servant is the purpose of God. The Servant enacts in the earth the purpose that has been intended from all eternity. God intends that society should be reordered against slavery, oppression, and disability; God now asserts power to enact that transformation. The Creator intends that the creation should be rehabilitated to full, fruitful function.

There is no doubt that as concrete and historical as the work of the Servant is, this liberating work is God's work. Thus the particular words characterizing the Servant (covenant, light, open, bring out, vs. 6b–7), are bracketed by "I am Yahweh" at the beginning (v. 6a) and at the end (v. 8). The Servant is identified by the self-announcement of Yahweh's intention and sovereignty. It is Yahweh, not the Servant, who wills transformed creation. No other voice proposes that transformation. No other devises a way to do it. No other gets credit for it. It is first and last Yahweh, the God of creation, exodus, and homecoming who works and wills a transformed world.

This text thus holds together *the concreteness of the servant,* who works justice, and *the transcendent sovereignty of God,* who wills justice. Concreteness and sovereignty, Servant and God, together lead to the sweeping rhetorical climax of v. 9. What emerges when the spirit-filled Servant does the work of God is newness. It is a word, a vision, an act that exiles were too bruised and dimmed to imagine. These same exiles nonetheless are invited back into powerful hope, rooted in the purpose of God. Now that hope shapes the future concretely through the God of all hope, who intends life in the midst of this history of death.

Psalm 29

One of the most forceful of all the hymns of praise in the Psalter, Ps. 29 has been the subject of much scholarly investigation, especially with regard to its possible connections with Ugaritic literature and with the beginning of the autumn rains. However all of that may be, in the form in which we have received it this Psalm presents Yahweh, the God of Israel, as the Lord of the storm and therefore as the Lord of all of life.

As is typical of many psalms of praise, Ps. 29 is composed of three parts: introduction, body, and conclusion. The introduction (vs. 1–2) calls on the members of the heavenly council, the "heavenly beings" of NRSV, to give glory to the Lord, "glory and strength," "the glory of his name." Since the term "glory" (*kābôd*) is often found in Priestly literature within the Old Testament, where it refers to the theophany of Yahweh (e.g., Ex. 16:7; 24:16; cf. Ezek. 1:28), the repeated use of the term here emphasizes that this psalm is describing not a God who is a distant abstraction, but a God who has appeared in the life of the people.

The second section, the body (vs. 3–10), describes the manner of the Lord's appearing. Here the language, some of the most vivid in the Psalter, evokes images of a violent storm. Especially noteworthy is the repeated phrase "the voice of the LORD," which begins each verse except 6 and 10. At one level this would seem to be a reference to the claps of thunder that accompany the storm, as in Ex. 19:16, but at a deeper level the "voice of the LORD" is synonymous with the "Word of God," or God's self-revelation.

This section lists various aspects of the natural world over which the Lord's glory presides. First, there are the "waters," the "mighty waters," of v. 3. We are not told just which waters the psalmist has in mind (that becomes clearer in a moment), but the presumption of the reader at this point is that these waters are both seas and rivers, as well as lakes and pools. That is to say, all waters are under the rule of the Lord of the storm, the Lord who brings the rains. Next, the forests that grace the land are brought into view (vs. 5–6). The violence of the storm bends and breaks the trees so that even the solid mountains ("Lebanon" and "Sirion"—the latter meaning Mount Hermon) appear to skip like frolicking young animals. The lightning and thunder rattle even the uninhabited spaces.

The final verse of this section (v. 10) forms a climax to the body of the psalm and brings us back to the "waters" of v. 3. The "flood" here is nothing other than the waters of chaos that God pushed back at creation, making place for heaven and earth (Gen. 1:7). These are the same waters, the flood, which invaded creation in the time of Noah (Gen. 7:11), but which God then expelled and over which he promised to rule forever (Gen. 9:11). Now we understand the "waters" of v. 3 and all the other images of this psalm: God is the ruler of all of life. Every aspect of our existence is subject to the divine sovereignty. "The LORD sits enthroned as king forever."

The third section of the psalm (v. 11) is a prayer, which expresses the hope that God will bless the people with strength and peace.

There are at least three elements in the psalm that make it appropriate for use on the Sunday that, in many churches, is observed as a festival to commemorate Jesus' baptism (see the Gospel lection for today). The first is the element of water. The psalm assumes that the reader is aware of the old stories, known by both Hebrews and other ancient peoples, which describe God's conquest of the unruly waters at creation. In the story of Jesus' baptism, not only is the water peaceful and calm, but—by the power and love of God—it has become a medium for the revelation of God's love. It symbolizes the washing away of human sinfulness, God's forgiveness of the dark side of our nature. It also symbolizes a sinless Jesus' identification with this sinful humankind.

A second element in the psalm that makes it appropriate for this day is that of theophany, that is, God's self-manifestation. The recurring use of the word "glory" (vs. 1, 2, 3, 9) reminds the reader of God's continual indwelling in human life in order to lead and save the people. And the almost incessant "voice of the LORD" points to God's nature as one who communicates with the people for their instruction and redemption. This anticipates the "voice from heaven" of Matt. 3:17, which announces to a sinful humankind the Sonship and Kingship of Jesus.

The kingly nature of Jesus connects with a third element within Ps. 29 that renders it appropriate for this day. That is the majestic (v. 4), regal (v. 10) nature of the God of the theophany, the appearing one. This is the Lord of the universe, who rules with strength (v. 1), who bestows strength on the people (v. 11) in order that they may live in safety and peace. Strength is thus seen as one of the qualities of the Son, King Jesus, and his baptism therefore becomes not only a moment of his identification with sinful humankind, but also a moment of his anointing as the Lord and Ruler of life.

Acts 10:34–43

This sermon of Peter's stands near the climax of the story of the conversion of Cornelius. Peter, who has protested against the notion that he might violate the boundaries of the food laws (see 10:9–16), has been summoned to the home of Cornelius. Since God has directly told Peter to cooperate with the summons,he has done so (vs. 19–20). Upon arriving at Cornelius's home, Peter hears Cornelius explain that God had instructed him to send for Peter. In the face of this accumulating evidence that God has accepted Cornelius, Peter can no longer protest. The sermon opens with Peter's proclamation of the impartiality of God: "In every nation anyone who fears him and does what is right is acceptable to him" (v. 35).

Verse 36, then, begins a recitation of the Christian kerygma. The opening words, "You know," seem oddly matched to the story context, since the whole point of the sermon is that Cornelius and his household do *not* know what has happened. Probably these words address Luke's own audience, which would know what was to follow. Peter's first statement summarizes the Christ-event as "the message he sent to the people of Israel, preaching peace by Jesus Christ." Even at this late point in the story, Peter's resistance to the radical inclusion of the gospel shows through, as he identifies the gospel's audience here solely with Israel.

The "message" of this good news was proclaimed throughout Judea, but it started in Galilee "after the baptism that John announced." As in Acts 1:22, Luke carefully refers to the baptism of John, not quite saying that John baptized Jesus. This conforms to the Lukan Gospel, in which John the Baptist is already in prison when Jesus is baptized (Luke 3:18–22). Presumably Luke regarded a direct statement about John's baptizing of Jesus as somehow making him subservient to John. Whatever the reason for this distinction, Luke still ties the beginning of Jesus' ministry firmly with John the Baptist. Indeed, the Lukan infancy narrative couples the two and their work.

Verse 38 summarizes the public ministry of Jesus. First, God anointed him with the Holy Spirit and with power. Jesus does not act of his own accord or out of his own strength. He is God's agent. As such, he "went about doing good and healing all who were oppressed by the devil." Consistent with the Gospels, the healings Jesus carried out are here portrayed as an assault on the power of the devil, not simply errands of mercy.

In the simplest terms, vs. 39–40 summarize the death and resurrection of Jesus. Following his resurrection, Jesus appeared to his disciples, who "ate and drank with him." This bit of information not only recalls the powerful Emmaus road scene in Luke 24 but appropriately refers to Jesus' practice of table fellowship, a practice that is at the heart of the controversy over the inclusion of Gentiles in the fledgling church (see Acts 11:3). The appearance of the risen Lord culminates with his commandment to proclaim the gospel.

Punctuating these terse statements of the Christian kerygma are a second set of statements that have to do with the witness of the apostles. Following the summary of Jesus' ministry comes the first statement that "we are witnesses to all that he did" (v. 39). Jesus' appearances were to those who had been chosen as witnesses (v. 41), and he commanded them to testify (*martyrein,* "witness"). The sermon itself concludes with yet another reference to witness, this time the witness of the prophets.

The theme of witnessing dominates the book of Acts and is in no way limited to this passage. Its function in this passage, however, is important. Peter and his colleagues go to Cornelius as witnesses of the risen Lord, but events that take place in Cornelius's household make them witnesses yet again. Immediately following our passage, while Peter is still speaking, the Holy Spirit comes on Cornelius and his household. Peter, who is forced to pronounce that Cornelius may *also* be baptized with water, becomes now a nearly passive witness of God's intention that the Gentiles become a part of the Christian community.

In one sense, this passage has virtually nothing to do with our commemoration of the baptism of Jesus. Only by stretching v. 37 can we arrive at a reference, however allusive, to the actual baptism of Jesus by John the Baptist. In a deeper sense, however, this passage has everything to do with recalling the baptism of Jesus, for that baptism carries with it the promise of the gift of the Holy Spirit (see Luke 3:16), a promise that is richly fulfilled in the baptism of the Gentile Cornelius.

Matthew 3:13–17

The appearance of Matthew's account of Jesus' baptism in the cycle for Year A of the lectionary presents the opportunity to approach this ancient story in a fashion different from the more familiar Markan and Lukan accounts. The context of the story within Matthew's narrative, the brief dialogue between John and Jesus, and the choice of Isa. 42:1–9 as the Old Testament lesson provide a distinctive slant.

In reading through Matt. 3, one is immediately struck with the sharply contrasting ways in which John receives the Pharisees and Sadducees (3:7–10) and Jesus (vs. 13–14). The former group is rejected. They presumptuously claim Abrahamic descent and ignore the responsibilities of such a heritage. John demands that they "bear fruit worthy of repentance" and warns them of the coming judgment. Likewise, John initially refuses baptism to Jesus. His reluctance, however, is due to his awe of Jesus, to the fact that he perceives in Jesus the "more powerful" one. While the Pharisees and Sadducees apparently lack remorse and a sense of their own sinfulness, Jesus appears to John to have no need for baptism. John needs Jesus' baptism, not vice versa.

Jesus' persistence at being baptized by John has tended to be embarrassing to later interpreters. John's reluctance seems appropriate. Why should Jesus have to receive John's baptism? Why does the eternal Son of God "need" baptism by one lesser than himself?

Jesus responds, "It is proper for us . . . to fulfill all righteousness" (3:15). The term "righteousness" (used seven times in Matthew and with differing connotations) seems here to indicate a divine requirement to be accomplished. The adjective "all" means that it is not simply a special requirement for the Son of God but one that joins him with fellow Christians in carrying out "all that God requires" (NEB). In these first words Jesus speaks, Matthew provides us with a statement that describes Jesus' function throughout the Gospel. He moves about Galilee and later Jerusalem as the obedient Son, who carries out the plan of the Father. He not only teaches but in fact demonstrates the divine will, and in doing so becomes the prototype of all his followers. Here at the beginning of his ministry such a course is set.

The lectionary's choice of Isa. 42:1–9 as the Old Testament lesson to be read alongside Matt. 3:13–17 adds yet another dimension to what Jesus as God's Son fulfills. In the poem describing God's delight in the Servant, four times the root word "justice/righteousness" occurs (Isa. 42:1, 3, 4, 6). The empowerment of the Servant with the Spirit is to the end that he bring forth justice to the nations. The baptism of Jesus in Matthew initiates just that work of the chosen Son. The divine will Jesus performs has a specifically moral dimension in inaugurating a reign where the hungry are fed, the thirsty are given drink, the naked are clothed, and the sick and imprisoned are visited. Early in the Sermon on the Mount Jesus enlists his followers to join him in this mission when he says, "Unless your righteousness exceeds that of the scribes and Pharisees, you will never enter the kingdom of heaven" (5:20).

This "special" Matthean slant on the baptism of Jesus coheres with the rest of the story. The Spirit descends like a dove, and a voice reveals to the readers who Jesus is. The text of v. 17 joins together language about two contrasting images: the royal figure of Ps. 2 and the Servant of Isa. 42. The one evokes the picture of a coronation scene, when kingly rules were initiated with great anticipation. Though repeatedly in Israel's history the expectation exceeded the fulfillment, the people nevertheless had come to hope for a future king who, anointed by God's Spirit, would usher in an era of justice and peace (Isa. 9:1–7; 11:1–9). The other image depicts a patient, faithful servant who despite rejection persists in carrying out the mandate given him to establish justice in the earth. The voice out of heaven announces Jesus as the Son who serves, as the majestic King who rules in meekness, as the royal figure whose concern is not in defeating enemies but in seeing that right prevails.

The voice out of heaven speaks in the third person rather than the second (as in Mark and Luke), indicating that the baptismal story is not to be read simply as Jesus' call. It is not Jesus who must learn who he is, but Matthew's readers. And this understanding becomes foundational for the rest of the Gospel. But just as Jesus lives, dies, and is raised as God's faithful, serving Son, so the Christian community is to follow him. His obedience paves the way for the disciples' obedience, and for them, too, the promise of being called children of God (5:9, 45).

Another way to put this: Matthew's account of Jesus' baptism says something about the nature of Christian baptism. Those who receive it are not only given distinctive names, but by the Spirit are commissioned to obedient, faithful service, to follow the path blazed by the unique Son of God. Their task, like his, has to do with establishing justice in the earth, with being a bonding power to the people and a light to the nations.

Second Sunday After Epiphany

Ordinary Time 2

Two motifs connect these strikingly different passages: the initiative of God in calling forth God's servants, and the communal, even public, character of faith. The prophetic passage employs highly dramatic imagery to describe the character of God's calling. The Servant tells us that God issued the calling "before I was born," "while I was in my mother's womb." The Servant has no right of refusal, no initiative to express. While the psalmist in Psalm 40 speaks of seeking after God, it is God who puts the "new song" in his mouth. Paul, who elsewhere uses the imagery of Isa. 49:1 to describe his own transformation (see Gal. 1:15), identifies both himself and the Corinthians as people who are "called" to be God's people. Both in the prologue to the Fourth Gospel (John 1:6) and in the account of Jesus' baptism, John is identified as one who has been sent for a specific task (1:33). From the greatest figures in the history of Israel and the life of the church to the most anonymous woman and man, God's servants have their role as a result of God's calling.

The callings of God's servants vary as greatly as the contexts in which they find themselves, but the calling is never to a merely private piety. Isaiah 49:1–7 anticipates not simply the restoration of Israel, but the salvation of the "end of the earth"—a limitless arena. Even in the opening lines of his letter to the Corinthians, Paul makes clear that it is not enough for believers to cherish a private faith; their public fellowship with one another must reflect the unity of their faith. John the Baptist proclaims the revelation he has received about Jesus, not in order to enlarge himself as recipient, but to bear witness to God's Son (John 1:34). The psalmist puts the matter rightly: "I have told the glad news of deliverance in the great congregation. . . . I have not hidden your saving help within my heart."

Isaiah 49:1–7

In the midst of the exile, where all futures seemed foreclosed, the poet dares to speak about a servant powered by God. In v. 3, the servant appears to *be Israel*; in v. 6, however, the servant appears to have a mission *to Israel*. It may be that the poem deliberately avoids a specific identity, thus permitting us great freedom in our hearing. The church characteristically utilizes its interpretive freedom in listening, to hear in the poem the servant Jesus.

The speech of the Servant (vs. 1–6) is in two parts. In the first part (vs. 1–4), the Servant narrates how he came to be identified and powered as God's servant. It is as though the Servant needs to establish his authority and the legitimacy of his mission, perhaps in the face of resistance and suspicion. He establishes his authority by the assertion that the mission is not his idea. The initiative for the mission is with God and only with God.

Now God speaks, according to the report of the Servant, to make explicit what the mission is (vs. 5–6). This is the second half of the Servant's speech. This statement of mission from God is in two parts.

First, perhaps predictably, the mission is to return all the exiles to their home. The imagery is daring, for it suggests an incursion into far-flung empires, to force those empires to release and relinquish exiled Jews. The Servant is to win their release, almost as governments now try to secure release of hostages. No wonder the Servant must be "sword" and "arrow," for the kingdoms who first deported the Jews will not easily release them. The God who sends the Servant, however, is a gathering God (cf. Luke 13:34), who wants all the lost ones restored home.

In the process of his mission to the homeless Jews, the Servant discovers a remarkable reality. He had already confessed that his own strength was futile (v. 4). Now, engaged in the mission, God has become his strength (v. 5). God's servant does not have a surplus of strength in advance, but is given strength only in the midst of obedience.

The recovery of the exiles should have been enough. The mandate of the Servant seems to have been completed. Then, however, God holds a demanding surprise in store for the Servant (v. 6). The Servant has already gathered the scattered Jews; but that is too light, too trivial, too insignificant. A whole new enterprise bursts on the horizon of the Servant, for which we had been given no clue. The agenda of God is not only "the tribes of Jacob and . . . the survivors of Israel," the ones the Servant had cared for and gathered. Now the scope of

God's dream is international, "a light to the nations, . . . salvation to the end of the earth," or all the known world.

In a gigantic leap of rhetoric, the poet enlarges the arena of God's concern to include even nonbelievers, who will also be rescued by this same Servant. This is one of the most crucial texts in showing how the Old Testament breaks ethnic limitation and witnesses to the largeness of God's rescue. We may cite two examples of the shift of scope from the one people to the whole world. In the New Testament, the struggle over the "mission to the Gentiles" reflects the dawning awareness that God's mission is for the nations as well as for the Jews (see, e.g., Acts 15). Closer to us, Martin Luther King Jr., at the end of his dangerous mission, recognized that he could not limit his vision to the civil rights of blacks in the United States, important as that was and is, but he addressed the issue of the Vietnam War. He knew that the question of rights is a humanity-embracing question. This poet in our passage already knows that God's powerful will for homecoming has no ethnic limitation.

Only now does God speak directly (v. 7). Heretofore, the speech of God has been quoted in the testimony of the Servant. This single verse is not difficult in its wording, but its intention is not obvious. The address, presumably to the Servant, is to one "despised and abhorred," without any standing, claim, or credential.

This despised, abhorred one shall be honored by kings and princes. Designation by God for God's mission reverses the estimate the nations will make. Nothing gives significance to the Servant except Yahweh's choosing; that act of designation, however, makes this pitiful last one the honored first one. It is no wonder that in this text the church has heard its own most treasured affirmation of humiliation and exaltation (cf. Phil. 2:5–11). In our own time, moreover, we are watching shifts in power and honor, so that some previously rejected and dishonored, tortured and imprisoned, become honored and powerful, for they carry the dreams of God in their daring bodies.

Psalm 40:1–11

Psalm 40 may be composed of two originally independent poems, as some commentators suggest. If so, the first of these, a psalm of thanksgiving for deliverance from some evil, concludes with v. 10, while v. 11 is the initial verse in the second unit, a psalm of distress in which the individual petitions God for help. By including v. 11 in the lection for this day, the passage, while thanking God for deliverance, concludes with a reminder of the weakness of mortal humans and our continuing need for God's sustaining grace.

The psalmist, after acknowledging his own piety before God ("I waited patiently"; cf. Ps. 27:14), summarizes God's saving activity in his life. God heard (v. 1b). God saved (v. 2). God transformed (v. 3). In this final matter, the human subject has been so redirected by God's salvation that the lives of others have also been changed (cf. Ps. 51:13–14). Interestingly, the psalmist here speaks of God in the third person, implying that the words are directed to the worshiping congregation. The description of God's redemptive activity (v. 2) is such that it is applicable to a variety of human situations and experiences.

Verses 4 and 5 pay tribute to God for the multiplicity of God's acts of salvation and love. The word in v. 4 used for "those," *geber*, is a cognate of *gibbôr*, meaning mighty or strong, and may reflect a wordplay on the part of the psalmist by which he intends to emphasize that true human strength rests not in brute force or military power (cf. the deeds of the *gibbōrîm* in 2 Sam. 23:8–39), but in trust in God.

A statement on the nature of true worship and the true law follows in vs. 6–8. The denial of sacrifice as the highest form of worship is consistent with other statements in the Old Testament (1 Sam. 15:22; Ps. 51:16, 17), as is the affirmation that the ultimate law, or Torah, is that which is written not on stone or in scrolls but on the heart (cf. Jer. 31:33). There may be in the reference to the "scroll of the book" a subtle contrast to the usual form in which the law was transmitted, so that the train of thought might run: since the Torah is now written on my heart, it is my faithfulness to God that is left on the divine record (cf. Dan. 12:1).

A description (vs. 9–10) of the psalmist's response to God's saving activity reveals that this person has now become a witness to God's saving deeds. A frequent component of psalms of distress and of thanksgiving is the vow, a statement that says, in effect, that God's redemptive power is such that when it enters the life of a man or woman that life is never the same again (cf. Ps. 30:12). These verses detail the fulfillment of that vow (cf. v. 3b).

A final statement (v. 11) rounds out the lection and, as noted above, injects into the preceding psalm of thanksgiving a note that stresses the continuing need of men and women for the redeeming presence of God.

Lections for this day draw attention to Jesus' fulfillment of his role as servant of God (Isa. 49:1–7) and as the baptized Son of God (John 1:29–34). On one level, the Psalm reading might be understood to be a summary of Jesus' thoughts on his confirmation by God at his baptism. As both Servant and Son, Jesus had been claimed by God for a special purpose. If the idea of redemption that is expressed in the psalm appears a bit forced when applied to Jesus, the theme of witnessing is certainly congruent. Because of the manner in which God touched the life of Jesus—a special endowment of the Spirit of God made evident at Jesus' baptism—Jesus' words and deeds manifest the presence of God in human life as do no other words or deeds (Ps. 40:3, 9–10). And, because the baptism of Jesus is performed—theologically, at least—in the shadow of the cross, v. 11 of the Psalm lection assumes a special poignancy.

But if this psalm is in certain respects the psalm of the newly anointed Servant and Son of God, it is also your and my psalm—if we claim to be the people of the Servant and Son. It is we who have been drawn up out of the miry bog and whose feet have been placed on a secure rock (v. 2). It is we—ideally, at least—who have vested our trust in God's Christ and who thereby gain our strength (v. 4). It is we whose hearts have become the repository of God's instruction and whose names are in the "scroll of the book" (vs. 7–8). It is we who have promised to be the witnesses of Christ's redemptive love and who are committed to speaking and living this love (vs. 9–10). And finally, it is we who live in daily need of the sustaining presence of God (v. 11). Giving thanks, trusting, witnessing, and depending thus become a kind of litany of the Christian life.

John's recognition of Jesus following the baptism results in John's acknowledgment of who he himself is and of who Jesus is. Our experience of the redemptive presence of God has similar results. We affirm our history as the redeemed ones and pledge our continuing intention to speak and live in the light of our redemption. This Psalm lection is the song that celebrates both our affirmation and our pledge.

1 Corinthians 1:1–9

Because Paul follows a standard format in the openings of his letters, the preacher may experience a strong temptation to skip past these lines and into the "meat" of the letter itself. This temptation needs to be resisted, however, since the salutations and thanksgivings reflect some of Paul's most fundamental theological convictions and also provide clues to major topics of the letter.

In the opening lines of 1 Corinthians one theological conviction that emerges is that of calling. The first word with which Paul identifies himself is the word "called." By the will of God, Paul was called as an apostle. Calling belongs not only to what we might term "professional church leaders," however. Already in v. 2 Paul speaks of Christians in Corinth as those who are "called to be saints" and who in turn "call on the name of our Lord Jesus Christ." That this designation is no mere nod in the direction of the laity emerges in 1 Cor. 1:26 and 7:17–24, where Paul uses the language of vocation to describe God's summons of persons to obedience. For Paul each and every Christian is such because of God's calling.

As in other letters, the thanksgiving (vs. 4–9) identifies ways in which Paul is grateful for this particular community of believers. He thanks God for God's grace, specifically for the gift of "speech and knowledge of every kind." The Corinthians lack no "spiritual gift." These words sound odd if we know the discussions that lie ahead in this letter, where it is precisely the Corinthians' knowledge and gifts that provoke Paul's wrath. A suspicious first reading of the thanksgiving might lead us to conclude that these words carry an ironic tone, but they are in fact guarded and carefully chosen. The thanksgiving, after all, addresses God and thanks God for these gifts—not for the accomplishments of the Corinthians. The question that dominates part of the letter is not whether the Corinthians have the gifts, but how they interpret them and how they use them.

Debate about the origin of the difficulties at Corinth continues unabated. Whatever had occurred there, Henry Joel Cadbury's description of the Corinthians as "overconverted" seems apt. Their enthusiasm led at least some of them (perhaps those from the higher social strata) to conclude that they had already arrived at the fullness of Christian life. Nothing more could be added to them (see, for example, 1 Cor. 4:8ff.). Paul responds to this situation throughout the letter, but one element in his response appears already in vs. 7–8, ". . . you are not lacking in any spiritual gift as you wait for the revealing of our Lord Jesus Christ. He will also strengthen you to the end, so that you may be blameless on the day of our Lord Jesus Christ." In common with all Christians, one task of the Corinthians is to *wait*. The ultimate revealing or apocalypse of Jesus Christ lies in the future, not in the past. Only when God has completed that apocalypse can believers expect their own completion, their own "arrival." The reference to a future judgment ("the day of our Lord Jesus Christ") underscores the fact that the Corinthians are not yet to regard themselves as perfected or mature. That decision will come.

Another element in Paul's response to the "overconversion" of the Corinthians comes in v. 9: "You were called into the fellowship of his Son, Jesus Christ our Lord." The vocation of the Christian is a vocation to "fellowship" (Greek, *koinōnia*). In contrast to the factionalism that appears to plague the Christian church in Corinth, Paul asserts the commonality of believers. Over and over in this letter he will insist that considerations about the community as a whole outweigh the prerogatives of individuals or small groups (see, for example, 10:23–30). The reason for this insistence lies not in the inherent good of the group, but in the fact that the fellowship is that of "his son, Jesus Christ our Lord." Because all members of the community belong to the God who has called them in Jesus Christ, the community merits upbuilding.

While it is a kind of table of contents for the remainder of the letter, 1 Cor. 1:1–9 has far more than merely pragmatic significance for contemporary Christians. The insistence on the calling of all Christians challenges our professionalism, which threatens to treat the laity as qualitatively different from the ordained. If all Christians are called, although to differing tasks (as emerges in the body image of 1 Cor. 12), then the gospel's most radical claims intrude into the lives of every believer. Finally, if all Christians are called, they enter alike into a community that requires full participation.

John 1:29–42

The account of the baptism of Jesus in the Fourth Gospel functions in a way different from the accounts of the baptism found in the Synoptic Gospels. In the latter the event confirms for the readers who Jesus really is. In the Fourth Gospel, however, the baptism becomes an incident of revelation to John the Baptist, who in turn relates it as a part of his witness to Jesus.

First, notice the dimension of revelation. As he looks back on the event of Jesus' baptism, John twice says, "I myself did not know him" (John 1:31, 33). Unlike Luke's Gospel, where the kinship of John and Jesus is emphasized, and Matthew's Gospel, where John recognizes Jesus prior to the baptism (Matt. 3:14), the Fourth Gospel presents the baptism itself as an occasion of revelation. John in his ignorance parallels the Jewish community at large (John 1:26). Yet what John does have is a word of promise which enables him to discern that the One on whom he sees the Spirit descending is the One who will usher in the new age of the Spirit.

The knowledge of Christ always comes as an occasion of revelation, as a divine gift, as a manifestation of the Spirit, which produces the change from "I did not know" to "I have seen and borne witness." Whether as a steady progress of illumination like the dawn scattering the shadows of the night or an instantaneous flash like the lightning bolt, it occurs to bring recognition and witness. However and whenever revelation "happens," it results not from the perceptive powers of the human mind nor from the ability some people have to be in touch with reality nor from a keen intuition. It is a sheer gift of grace.

Second, the event of revelation takes on the character of an expanding witness. The narrator of the Gospel momentarily steps aside and lets John the Baptist tell his own story. Since the section beginning at 1:19 states, "This is the testimony given by John," we are not surprised when John says, "I myself have seen and have testified" (v. 34) or again when because of his witness two of his disciples leave to follow Jesus (vs. 35–37). The revelation does not remain the private possession of John only to nurture his own faith and experience, but becomes the opportunity to address others. Furthermore, John's witness reverberates beyond his own control. Andrew, one of the disciples who abandons him, becomes yet another voice to speak to his brother, Simon (vs. 40–42).

In his passion to witness—both in terms of a correct assessment of himself (vs. 19–28) and his positive testimony of Jesus (vs. 29–35)—John serves a paradigmatic role for the church and for individuals within the church. He is remarkably reticent about himself; we are given no elaborate biographical information; we are not informed of the details of his personal experience. What seems to matter is the person of Jesus, not the person of the witness. It is a self-effacing witness, as the narrator tells us: John speaks, and his disciples hear *him* but follow *Jesus* (v. 1:37).

Third, John's witness consists of a confession as to who in fact Jesus is. Two descriptions need special attention.

1. "The Lamb of God who takes away the sin of the world" (vs. 29, 36). Commentators debate the specific Old Testament allusions behind "lamb." Does it refer to the paschal lamb, to the lamb sacrificed in the Temple, to the Suffering Servant, to the lamb of Jewish apocalyptic literature, to a combination of all of these? Who knows? The decisive fact is that Jesus is identified as the One who for the whole world breaks the dominating power of sin, who in the place of bondage, rejection, and disfranchisement brings freedom, acceptance, and belonging. "If the Son makes you free, you will be free indeed" (8:34–36).

It is striking that though Jesus is revealed to Israel (1:31), the scope of his liberating activity is worldwide (1:29). The text echoes the prophetic reading from Isa. 49:6:

It is too light a thing that you should be my servant
    to raise up the tribes of Jacob
    and to restore the survivors of Israel;
I will give you as a light to the nations,
    that my salvation may reach to the end of the earth.

The impression is that the people of God need to know, even if the world does not yet know, that Jesus "takes away the sin of the world." The community of believers cannot act like a privileged enclave, assuming that God loves them and condemns the rest. It is God's redemptive action for the world that becomes the basis and motive for the community's mission to the world.

2. "Son of God" (John 1:34). The way the title Son has already been used in the first chapter suggests that John is confessing Jesus as the unique revelation of God, the only Son, the one in the bosom of the Father who has made him known (1:14, 18). (In light of later uses, the title may also reflect messianic features, the anointed, royal figure, who fulfills the heritage of Israel, 1:41, 49; 11:27.) In the Synoptic accounts of the baptism, this is the confession made by the voice out of heaven, whereas in the Fourth Gospel, John becomes this voice, the first human voice in fact, announcing to the readers of the text the distinctiveness of Jesus.

These two titles belong together. On the one hand, the Son, the decisive revelation of God, is also the Lamb who takes away the world's sin. What he reveals is not a deity aloof and disengaged, apathetic to human bondage, but a saving, liberating presence. We need that because human wisdom is hopelessly ensnared in the clutches of sin's control, and there can be no revelation without freedom. Otherwise, all our gods are merely reflections of our own slavery.

On the other hand, the world's sin cannot be removed by anyone other than the unique Son of God. It takes an action from God's side to break humanity's self-destructive pattern and to bring a liberating knowledge of the true God.

Third Sunday After Epiphany

Ordinary Time 3

The preacher considering the texts for this Sunday is offered a number of options for preaching possibilities, some of which will involve future Sundays as well. The Gospel lection is the beginning of several consecutive readings from Matthew, which would make possible a series of sermons on the early part of the Sermon on the Mount, stretching to the Sunday before the beginning of Lent. The texts highlight the remarkable declarations and demands of the gospel, in this context given a rather distinctive expression. The epistolary readings also provide the opportunity for a series of sermons, from 1 Cor. 1 to 4. In these chapters Paul reflects on the gospel as "the message about the cross," which effects unity, critiques the wisdom of the world, and undergirds the ministry of the church.

As for this Third Sunday After Epiphany, a number of interrelated motifs emerge when the passages are read together. For example, the image of light, characteristic of the Epiphany season, is continued in three of the texts. Two striking associations surface as the image is developed in differing contexts. First, light does not merely illumine, but it brings a changed situation, in which people depressed by the darkness, under assault from known or unknown forces, mired in anguish can experience the new day. It is an image of triumph and conquest. The psalmist's confession of Yahweh links light with salvation. God is the power who can defend God's children and bring to naught the hosts oppressing them. In the Gospel lesson the deliverance is expressed in terms of the nearness of God's reign, overcoming diseases and distortions of every sort. Light permits well-being.

Second, in these texts light becomes personalized. The psalm speaks of God as "my light and my salvation." The text from Isaiah refers to a human agent of vindication, but at the same time anticipates the coming of the Child who exercises supreme authority and brings an era of endless peace, (in the verses following the lection, 9:6–7). In Matthew, Jesus acts powerfully in calling disciples and healing the sick, fulfilling the word spoken by Isaiah. Light is not an amorphous symbol, void of a referent. It is a mode of God's presence, especially to those who sit in the region and shadow of death.

Isaiah 9:1–4

(For more extended comments on this text, see Christmas, First Proper.)

Epiphany is the season of light. "Light" is regularly a mode of God's presence, so that in the epiphany of Jesus, the presence of God is made visible and available in the world. That light (God's presence) is a powerful contrast to the "darkness" of the world. In a world not impressed with technological explanations, the darkness is known to be saturated with the dangerous power of death, and those who walk in the night are vulnerable and exposed.

The coming of God, that is to say, the power of light, dispels the darkness and permits well-being. A world without God, however, leaves one endlessly endangered and under threat. This text, which obviously is a snippet of a larger whole, contrasts darkness and light and celebrates the dramatic transformation wrought by God, from the one to the other.

There was a "former time," which the text still poignantly remembers (v. 1a). It was a time when the northern territory of Israel was held in "contempt," trivialized and treated as unimportant. The context of the eighth-century poet reflects a time when Israel's northern territory was exposed to Assyrian armies, who easily worked their brutal will against this helpless, defenseless territory. Our interpretation, however, need not stay with the concrete situation, but can be extended to include every deliberate humiliation worked against the vulnerable.

There is, however, also a "latter time," quite in contrast to the former time, which is now received in exuberant celebration (v. 1b). The "latter time" is characterized by God's "mak[ing] glorious" the previously occupied, disdained territory. The words "make glorious" also mean to "make heavy," which is a precise contrast to "contempt," which means to "make light." To "make heavy" means to treat with significance, substance, and importance.

Thus the poet constructs a perfect contrast:

former time: contempt, light (*qal*);
latter time: glorious, heavy (*kābôd*)

This contrast is not static; the poet portrays the moment when the light dramatically and powerfully shines in the darkness (vs. 2–4). The light creates possibilities that did not previously exist. Read militarily, this transformation is an act of power by the Jerusalem government, which will end the threat of Assyrian occupation. Read theologically, the transformation occurs because the power of Yahweh is mobilized to create well-being on behalf of the jeopardized. The military and theological dimensions of this transformation are coalesced in the possibility of a new Jerusalem king who will act out Yahweh's good intention against the enemy. In that king, the military purposes of the government and the theological intent of God converge.

It is no wonder that the move from "former time" to "latter time," from light to heavy, from contempt to glory, from occupation to liberation evoked wild, ecstatic joy, joy as in harvest, joy as in victory (v. 3). It is joy released in a context where all hope had been abandoned. There seemed no realistic possibility of newness, for the tyranny and brutality of a destructive social system seemed forever. Now, in this moment of birth or coronation, in this intrusive act of God through a human agent, everything becomes possible. There is newness, because God has moved in decisive, albeit unexpected, ways.

The change wrought by this new initiative (not even entertained heretofore as a possibility) is the end of oppressiveness (v. 4). The "rod of their oppressor" is apparently Assyrian occupation, which is brutal. The poet likens that present oppression to the remembered heavy oppression of the Midianites in the book of Judges (Judg. 6—8). The poem looks back to find an adequate parallel. In that memory, the poem recalls that God ended that oppression through the miracle of a human judge (Gideon); now the poem suggests that again oppression will be ended through a human agent empowered by God.

The text also looks forward. It looks forward to Jesus' power against the oppression of hunger (Mark 6:34–44), blindness (Mark 10:46–52), lameness (Luke 13:10–17), poverty (Luke 16:19–31), and death (Mark 5:35–43). It looks forward to our own time, when God will create (through human agents) new possibilities—for blacks in South Africa, for the despairing in Eastern Europe, for the peasants in Nicaragua, for the underclass in our society, for the brutalized in bad relations, for the denigrated in spirals of poverty, hunger, despair, anxiety, and greed. The light is coming! It cannot be resisted.

Psalm 27:1, 4–9

Psalm 27 is composed of two rather distinct units, vs. 1–6 and 7–14, each of which has a special character. The lectionary passage, by drawing on both of these units, thus captures the flavor of the entire psalm.

The first unit within the psalm is a statement of confidence and trust in God, a God who inspired this confidence by acts of faithfulness in the past and who, therefore, may be depended on to relate to the psalmist in a similar manner in the future. This sense of dependence is declared straightway by the opening line of the psalm, where the metaphor of God as "my light" is seconded by that of God as "my salvation." The first of these phrases is distinctive in that nowhere else in the Old Testament is God referred to as "my light," the nearest parallel, perhaps, being Ps. 18:28: "the LORD my God, lights up my darkness" (cf. Ps. 13:3). The effect of this language is to convey a relationship with God that is intimately familiar, as in Ps. 23, "my shepherd." (For another point of contact between this psalm and Ps. 23, see below).

The quality of God as light is the element that forms the bridge between this text and the Old Testament lection: "the people . . . have seen a great light" (Isa. 9:2). This was a conceptualization that ancient Israel shared with many of its neighbors. But for the psalmist trustingly to designate God as "my light" personalizes the imagery as it was rarely done outside Israel. To add to that the affirmation that God is also "my salvation" simply amplifies this declaration of personal trust, as does the further confession, "the LORD is the stronghold of my life."

After asserting the psalmist's belief that the Lord will defend him or her against all comers (vs. 2–3), the poem gives voice to the psalmist's deepest longing, "to live in the house of the LORD all the days of my life" (v. 4). Although vs. 2–3 are not included in the lectionary passage, they anticipate the petitions of vs. 7–9 and then v. 4 points to the important dimension of worship within the psalm. It may be that the hope expressed in v. 4, which is strikingly similar to that found in Ps. 23:6, should be read eschatologically, that is, that the divine house referred to here is, like the temple of Ezek. 40–48, an edifice that transcends brick and mortar. If so, the psalmist is expressing a universal hope of God's people, which anticipates a new life beyond this one, a life that is lived eternally in God's presence.

But it is also possible that the psalmist has in view here the Jerusalem Temple, and that his or her request is simply for a life oriented around regular seasons of worship and prayer. This interpretation seems to be supported by the last line of v. 4, where the unusual phrase "to inquire in his temple" probably refers to the basic act of petitionary prayer. If prayerful worship is what is intended here, that feature of the human experience before God is balanced by the final line of v. 6, where the psalmist yearns to praise God by means of song and music.

This first section of the psalm ends (vs. 5–6) as it began, with affirmations of trust in the protective and saving power of God. Again the Jerusalem Temple seems to be in the mind of the psalmist, as the words "tent" (vs. 5, 6) and "rock" (v. 5) suggest. The central sanctuary of the nation was a tent before, under Solomon, it became a permanent and lavishly adorned structure, and for a long time after that Hebrew poets recalled the humble origins of the house of God by somewhat surprisingly opting for its earlier designation (cf. Ps. 15:1).

The second section of the psalm (vs. 7–14) contains expressions of heartfelt petition, of which vs. 7–9 are included within the lectionary passage. Verse 8 presents very difficult problems of translation, as a comparison of RSV and NRSV illustrates. Yet the larger meaning is clear. The God whom the psalmist trusts, who has been the light and the salvation of faithful people in the past, is looked to as the only One in whom the psalmist may now hope. The heart of these verses is contained in 7b: "Be gracious to me and answer me!"

The function of this psalm in the midst of the other lections for this day is threefold. First, it continues to remember the Epiphany light, the star that brought the Magi from the East to the side of the Christ-child, and therefore it continues to celebrate the appearance of Christ not just as the King of the Jews, but as the Savior of all humankind. Secondly, it confesses that God's goodness and protection, so crucial in the past, are available now and on into the future. And it expresses this trust in the most intimately personal terms. Finally, it reminds the worshiping community, as well as the faithful individual, of the continuing need for this God of such wonderful grace.

For the psalmist, the medium through which the saving activity of God is comprehended and through which the people of God express their personal trust and commitment is that of worship. Prayer and praise in the house of God, as well as in the temple of the heart, become essential components in the life of God's faithful man or woman.

1 Corinthians 1:10–18

Far from being abstract treatises of systematic theology, Paul's letters provide us with parts of the ongoing conversations between Paul and various early Christian communities. This text, which opens the body of 1 Corinthians, makes the conversational character of the letter apparent. From persons he identifies only as "Chloe's people," Paul has received disturbing news about the behavior of Christians at Corinth. Presumably these agents, perhaps even slaves, of a prominent woman at Corinth have brought Paul a report about the church at Corinth that differs from the report contained in the congregation's own letter (see 1 Cor. 7:1).

The matter reported to Paul by Chloe's people becomes a major pastoral issue in this letter—namely, the presence at Corinth of dissension within the Christian community. The nature of this dissension remains a matter of debate, but Paul's reference to various leaders ("I belong to Paul," "I belong to Apollos," and so forth) suggests that factions have aligned themselves around key personalities and their teachings.

Because it is so easy for us to see the folly of those Corinthians who may have identified themselves with one or another Christian leader, we risk falling into a cheap moralizing of this text by identifying too quickly with Paul's point and distancing ourselves from the actions of the Corinthians. The irony of such a reading of the passage is that we fail to see the extent to which we ourselves participate in, even encourage, similar behavior. Whether in the local congregation or at the denominational level or in our reading of contemporary theology, church leaders especially fall prey to the temptation to identify with a leader or a cause that is penultimate to the gospel itself. Do we see ourselves as aligned with, for example, social activists or the evangelicals, traditionalists or feminists, denominational leaders or local figures?

Paul's response to such dissension and the theological problems behind it constitutes the bulk of the first four chapters of 1 Corinthians, but our text provides clear indications of what the nature of his response will be. The rhetorical questions of v.13 imply a sharp criticism of any devotion to a Christian leader that compromises the central identification of the believer with Jesus Christ. The answer to the question, "Has Christ been divided?" is obviously no, but the behavior of the Corinthians suggests that they believe Christ may indeed be divided into special-interest groups. The seemingly absurd questions, "Was Paul crucified for you? Or were you baptized in the name of Paul?" point up the equal absurdity of identifying oneself with a Christian leader rather than with Christ.

Standing behind these questions is the unspoken assumption that dissension among Christians is inappropriate because they have in common the Lordship of Jesus Christ. It is not Paul or Apollos or Cephas who was crucified or in whose name believers were baptized. The very notion that Christians would identify themselves in terms of their teachers or their favorite preachers rather than in terms of Jesus Christ seems ludicrous on the face of it. The introductory verse in our passage confirms this reading of Paul's response. Paul launches his appeal "by the name of our Lord Jesus Christ." Far from being a mere slogan, this statement grounds all that follows in the single reality of Jesus Christ.

At first glance Paul's point may seem obvious: What else would Christians find to be their unifying center except their faith in Jesus Christ? But there are, always, alternative reasons for urging unity. For example, Paul might have urged unity as a pragmatic good: the evangelistic task of the congregations in Corinth required them to have a "united front," or the stability of the Christian community depended on their unity. Indeed, these very elements emerge later in the letter (see, for example, 1 Cor. 14:16–17), but they are constantly grounded in the theological claim that the church's unity stems from its center, Jesus Christ. The pragmatic need for unity has its origin in the theological unity of the church.

Paul's call for unity may be heard as a threat to diversity of viewpoints and opinions, but that is because we confuse unity with uniformity. Later in this same letter, Paul will defend the plurality of judgments about whether Christians may eat what has been sacrificed to idols (1 Cor. 8) and yet call for care in practice so that the unity of the church and the faith of its members are not damaged. In a similar way, when Paul discusses the gifts of the Spirit and their place in worship, he acknowledges the diversity of gifts, but only as they come from the one Lord, Jesus Christ (1 Cor. 12:4–11). Unity in faith does not mean uniformity in thought and practice.

Matthew 4:12–23

The Gospel reading for this Sunday is an especially important text for those intending to preach from the Sermon on the Mount one or more of the next five Sundays. Chapters 5—7 (or selections from them) cannot be wrenched out of their context, as they so often are, without opening the door to great misunderstanding. The evangelist carefully prepares for the Sermon, and what is said about Jesus and his activity in Matt. 4:12–23 conditions the way the Sermon is heard.

The passage neatly divides itself into four sections.

1. Following the arrest of John the Baptist, Jesus leaves Nazareth and begins to live in Capernaum by the Sea of Galilee. The move has immense significance, the narrator tells us, because the tribal territories of Zebulun and Naphtali (west and north of the Sea of Galilee) recall Isa. 9:1 and the promise that "in the latter time he will make glorious the way of the sea, the land beyond the Jordan, Galilee of the nations." Jesus' journey to Galilee, then, is part and parcel of God's redemptive plan; it is a piece of the fulfillment of the promise expressed centuries earlier by the prophet.

Two related features of the interpreted prophecy of Isaiah need special notice. On the one hand, "the people who sat in darkness" in Matthew's context clearly refers to the Jewish people. (The Greek word *laos*, "people," is consistently employed for the Israelite nation.) The shining of the light, the dawning of the morning, the redemptive brightness is first and foremost for the Jews. The text heralds the ministry of Jesus in Matthew, which is predominantly among and for Jewish people. Such a priority cannot be ignored. On the other hand, the phrase "Galilee of the Gentiles" points to something more, to the mission Jesus gives the disciples from a mountain in Galilee following the resurrection "to make disciples of all nations" (28:16–20). The two belong together in the divine plan.

2. With the move to Galilee, Jesus begins to preach, saying, "Repent, for the kingdom of heaven has come near" (v. 17). The ancient anticipation of the Jewish people that someday God's rule would be universally revealed is reaffirmed by John (3:2) and then by Jesus, both of whom declare that this rule has now come near. So close that it impinges on the present, the reign of God demands repentance. So radical and powerful, its presence calls men and women from their safety and routine to a life of unheard-of newness.

Unlike John, Jesus apparently says little about the sins of those to whom he preaches, and the text says nothing about confession, remorse, and forgiveness. Repentance here means more a change of direction, the gaining of a new set of values, the readiness for life under the reign of God.

3. The demand for change takes on particular force in the story that follows of the call of the two sets of brothers, Simon and Andrew and James and John (vs. 18–22). Clearly the narrator has no interest in providing us with a psychological explanation of how and why

the brothers leave their nets to follow Jesus. Our curiosity that wants to know whether they may have had some experience or knowledge of Jesus prior to this encounter is left unsatisfied. What matters is that Jesus addresses them, and immediately they leave to follow him.

Where the gospel of God's reign is preached, people are called to absolute obedience. The abruptness of the disciples' departure, their break with fishing and family, and their instant acceptance of Jesus' invitation to "fish for people" underscore the sharp demands of discipleship. The message of God's reign is not for the tentative and indecisive, because it necessitates wholehearted allegiance. It brings a severing of old relationships and securities. It puts people to following Jesus, the one whose person and ministry embody God's reign.

4. The passage concludes (v. 23) with a summary statement of Jesus' activity, following the call of the disciples. He teaches, preaches the gospel of the kingdom of God, and heals all sorts of diseases. Two observations need to be made. First, the phrase "in their synagogues" suggests another honoring of the priority of the gospel for Israel (as in v. 16). Jesus begins his public ministry in Galilee not among the Gentiles, but among the Jews. And yet the word "their" also implies a certain distance between the narrator and the Jews. The stance from which the story is being related is clearly outside the bounds of Judaism. The perspective is that of one who is a part of the mission to the nations. Second, the rather extensive description of Jesus' healing ministry involving sick from every corner of the land underscores both the power and scope of the divine rule. Where the reign of God is present, there distortions are straightened, demons are exorcised, the lame walk (cf. Matt. 12:28). God's rule means the exercise of the divine power to make things right. It is not only a spiritual reality touching the hearts of humans, bringing them into obedience. It corrects physical ailments and disabilities, human constitutions that for whatever reason have gone awry.

With the announcement of the nearness of God's reign, the demand for repentance, the call of the four disciples, and the description of Jesus' powerful, redemptive activity the stage is set for the Sermon on the Mount. Readers have a notion of who this Jesus is who teaches in such a radical way and at least some hint of the power and scope of the divine rule. The authority that moves followers to break with the past and their previous loyalties and that miraculously heals broken bodies is the authority that confronts hearers (and readers) in the Sermon (cf. Matt. 7:28–29).

Fourth Sunday After Epiphany

Ordinary Time 4

Life is not to be valued according to appearances. But such a truism is easier to speak than to follow. In our society it is always a temptation to look on the outward expression and take it to be a sign of what's really there. Success comes to those who work hard for it and deserve it the most. Prosperity is a token of blessing. Though we know better, we find it hard to resist such conclusions.

The four texts for this Sunday join in warning the people of God that they should not be confused or intimidated by appearances or by how the larger society values this or that. A faithful hearing and responsiveness to the God of the Bible may not fare so well or look so good in terms of the world's standards of judgment. But what is required and blessed is a community ordered according to the covenantal commitments, shaped by the gracious promises, and attuned to what Paul called the "foolishness" and "weakness" of God.

In the passage from Micah, Israel, when given a chance, presents its case before the divine court. The questions it raises indicate a thorough misunderstanding of Yahweh's demands—burnt offerings, calves, rams, oil, or eldest child. The categories used by the surrounding culture to determine true religion are totally inappropriate to Yahweh. What Yahweh wants is nothing less than a refocusing of life—to do justice, to love covenant loyalty, and to walk humbly with God.

Psalm 15 identifies the elements in true worship. These are not qualities readily apparent to the casual observer, for they involve relationships—relationships with God and relationships with other human beings. Only a life built on those relationships is truly durable.

The Beatitudes describe the direction of God's blessing. Surprisingly, it is the poor in spirit, the meek, those hungering for justice to be accomplished, the merciful, the peacemakers, and those persecuted for righteousness who are the apple of God's eye, singled out for blessing.

Paul in 1 Corinthians eloquently argues that the gospel looks to many like nothing more than weakness and folly. The cross symbolizes defeat, an anathema to a success-oriented society, but is in reality the instrument of power and salvation. It is just God's way to take the low and despised, the weak and the foolish, to confound the wise and mighty.

Micah 6:1–8

The texts of Christmas and Epiphany thus far have concerned God's transformative power and God's gracious intervention. This text marks a new perspective in the sequence of Old Testament texts. The transformative power and gracious intervention of God expect, evoke, and require a response from God's people, a response of trust, gratitude, and obedience. That response, however, has not been deep or serious in Israel.

Israel is called by God into court to adjudicate a fractured relation (vs. 1–2). The summons is marked by stern imperatives: "Rise, plead." "Plead your case" means to bear testimony and give account of your conduct. Behind the metaphor is the recognition that this God-Israel relation which began so generously has not worked. The court must decide who has failed, God or Israel. Israel is summoned to make a case that it has not been remiss in its obligation to God.

Israel is invited to speak in testimony (vs. 1–2), but then is given no chance to answer. Yahweh takes the stand and Yahweh gives testimony (vs. 3–5).

Yahweh begins the argument with a pair of plaintiff questions that imply Yahweh's own innocence and Israel's guilt (v. 3). The first question invites evidence against Yahweh; the tone of the question, however, anticipates that no such evidence will be given. The second question is in fact a rebuke in interrogative form. Asked in one way, the intent is the opposite: "You make me weary" (cf. Isa. 43:22–24). Again there is an imperative that Israel should answer, but then Yahweh keeps talking.

Yahweh first alludes to the long history of generosity and liberation toward Israel that is rooted in the exodus (v. 4). The exodus is a model for all of God's "saving acts" (*ṣidqôt,* v. 5). Yahweh's fidelity and innocence consist in a series of rescues wrought for Israel. The rescue of v. 4 concerns the beginning of Israel's canonical story. Verse 5, in sharp contrast, moves to the end of Israel's canonical story, in Num. 22—25. The reference to Balak and Balaam concerns the odd transaction of Num. 22—24. Balak, the Moabite king, wanted to destroy Israel by curse. Balaam, the prophet, was hired to speak the king's deathly curse. Yahweh, in a powerful preemptive act, precluded such a curse and turned the curse to blessing. Thus to the very end of Israel's sojourn, God has been relentlessly saving Israel from destruction.

Yahweh's testimony thus completely clears Yahweh of guilt. Yahweh has been Israel's faithful savior; Yahweh's testimony decisively indicts Israel as the failed partner.

Finally, only now, Israel speaks (vs. 6–7). Israel, however, offers no self-defense. Instead, Israel utters a series of questions.

The questions make clear that Israel has completely misunderstood its relation to God. Israel thinks in terms of commodities, in categories used by other gods but inappropriate to Yahweh, who has no interest in commodities (cf. Ps. 50:9–13).

The answer of v. 8 shows that Israel has missed the point, even if its motivations were sound. God does not want from Israel any of Israel's "stuff" that would make the relation visible, but completely external. Rather God wants and requires nothing less than the refocus of life in covenantal categories. The poet has God announce this great triad of covenantal possibilities:

Do justice, to be actively engaged in the redistribution of power in the world, to correct the systemic inequalities that marginalize some for the excessive enhancement of others

Love covenant loyalty. The translation of "kindness" is disastrously weak. The word *ḥesed* means to reorder life into a community of enduring relations of fidelity

Walk humbly with God, to abandon all self-sufficiency, to acknowledge in daily attitude and act that life is indeed derived from the reality of God

By the end of the poem, we have left off the abrasive question of guilt. Instead we are given a sharp contrast between *commodity* and *covenant,* and a positive affirmation that covenant is for Israel a choosable alternative way of life.

Psalm 15

Women and men may not truly worship God unless their lives mirror the moral values that God's own life embraces and that God holds up as a pattern for human lives. That, in a nutshell, is the proclamation of Ps. 15.

Scholars tell us that this psalm is an entrance liturgy, similar to Ps. 24, in which a dialogue takes place between a custodian of the house of God (presumably the Jerusalem Temple) and those who have come to worship there. In v. 1 the resident official—the high priest or some other priest acting in the high priest's name—inquires of the congregation that seeks admission to the sanctuary the basis of their intention to enter. Although the question is framed as a prayer ("O LORD, . . ."), it is clearly addressed to the would-be worshipers. The repetition within the two parallel lines, a common poetic device among psalmists, serves to reinforce the importance of the question.

The language of the priest's question is interesting in several respects. To "abide" or "dwell" in Yahweh's house is elsewhere used as a euphemism for worship, as in Ps. 23:6. It includes the understanding that, when one is a genuine worshiper of Israel's God, one's heart is always oriented around the practice of worship, even when one is doing other things. One's heart may "dwell" in Yahweh's house, even when one is far away.

The word "tent" reflects Israel's period in the wilderness, when the shrine of Yahweh was a portable edifice. If this psalm comes from the time of David (note superscription), the reference may literally be to the tent that preceded the Temple on Mount Zion (the "holy hill") of v. 1b (note 2 Sam. 6:17). But even at a later time, "tent" may sometimes have been the word of choice when referring to Solomon's Temple (Ps. 27:5, 6; 61:4).

The response of the worshipers is framed in the balance of the psalm, vs. 2–5. The various articles that they cite echo similar themes in other parts of the Old Testament, especially the Sixth through the Tenth Commandments (Ex. 20:13–17; Deut. 5:17–21). In other words, the reply of the worshipers is strongly biased in favor of community relationships. To be sure, there are some abstractions ("right" and "truth"), but the basic message is: they are worthy to enter the house of the Lord who deal with their neighbors on terms of justice and compassion.

Of course, not all the principles laid out here will resonate in modern hearts. To despise the wicked (v. 4) is to become wicked ourselves, as Jesus taught (Matt. 7:1–5), although to despise wicked*ness* is something else altogether. And the prohibition against lending "money at interest," while it may have served a merciful purpose in ancient Israel (note Ex. 22:25; Lev. 25:35–38), is now a dinosaur. (Again, unreasonable interest is another matter.) But these qualifications aside, the response of the worshipers is the heart of the matter: what God longs for on the part of those who come to worship is not outward show, but changed and redirected lives.

This view is often associated with the prophets of ancient Israel, and with good reason. Amos raised not a few eyebrows when he stood among the throngs of worshipers at Bethel and preached:

> I hate, I despise your festivals,
> and I take no delight in your solemn assemblies. . . .
> But let justice roll down like waters,
> and righteousness like an everflowing stream.
> (Amos 5:21, 24)

And as if to impress on the people of Jerusalem that pseudo-worship could take place there too, Jeremiah said the same thing as Amos, and even went so far as to mock the small talk of the thoughtless crowds who flocked to Solomon's splendid sanctuary:

> This is the temple of Yahweh,
> the temple of Yahweh,
> the temple of Yahweh . . . (Jer. 7:4)

This sermon, in fact, appears so important to Jeremiah's ministry that it is reported twice (Jer. 7:1–15; 26:1–6). It was one of those several terrible occasions when Jeremiah's courage to speak the truth nearly cost him his life (note Jer. 26:7–19).

It does not require a genius to understand that worship must be accompanied by a commitment to social and personal justice if it is to be authentic. What this understanding does require is belief in a God who is motivated by issues of compassion and justice. When that understanding is clear, the business about the nature of true worship cannot help but follow.

Perhaps the really remarkable thing about Ps. 15 is that this concern for commitment to compassion and justice on the part of the true worshiper is framed within a liturgical setting. It is clear that, in the history of worship, liturgy and personal renewal have often been polar opposites. It is so easy to feel that when one has fulfilled the liturgical niceties ("bulls on the altar" or "gone to church"), one has paid one's dues to God. And so a love of formal liturgies and an attachment to the status quo have sometimes been the best of friends. But ancient Israel's prophets knew that should not be so, and so did Israel's priests! (Or at least some of them.) Here, right in the midst of a formal, question-and-answer liturgy about what it takes to enter God's sanctuary, we find a very nonliturgical affirmation: to worship God in an authentic manner, one must first be compassionate and just!

1 Corinthians 1:18–31

In this remarkable passage Paul asserts that the cross of Jesus Christ reveals the power of God. While for Christians some twenty centuries removed from Paul, and accustomed to the cross as a symbol in churches and even in jewelry, this assertion may seem inoffensive, it must have struck some of Paul's contemporaries as the ravings of a madman. The cross was, in fact, the antithesis of power—except as it revealed the power of the Roman Empire to crush those regarded as its opponents. Even so, this humiliating death was reserved for slaves, criminals, social outcasts—those who were deemed to be outside the boundaries of ordinary human society. Only the powerless died on the cross.

Yet Paul, who knew these brutal facts of crucifixion and its victims far better than we do, nevertheless asserts that the cross reveals God's power. God chose this act of foolishness because the world was unable to recognize God's wisdom (vs. 19–21). Instead of meeting the expectations of the world, either Jew or Greek, God offers the good news of "Christ crucified," good news in the form of a scandal. Even so, God's foolishness is wiser than human wisdom. The cross is the point at which the conflict between God's ways and human ways is revealed to be irreconcilable; human wisdom is utterly bankrupt.

Alongside this assertion that the cross is God's power and God's wisdom (v. 24) runs the recognition that not everyone "sees" the cross in this way. It is those "who are being saved," in contrast to "those who are perishing," who are able to see God's power in the crucifixion. The precise expression "who are being saved" is important because it touches on the way in which salvation occurs: human beings do not save themselves, they are the recipients of God's salvation; and salvation is not a past even but a continuous one ("being saved").

Those who are being saved are those whom God has "called," as Paul asserts in vs. 26–31. This passage serves as an extended illustration, based on the experience of the Corinthians, of the point Paul has been making in vs. 18–25. Paul asks the Corinthians to consider their own calling: "Not many of you were wise by human standards, not many were powerful, not many were of noble birth." Interpreters have often understood this verse to mean that early Christians came almost exclusively from the poor and uneducated elements of society, but Paul's statement, as well as the rest of the letter, indicates that indeed *some* of the Corinthians were from the ranks of the well-established. The point Paul is after is not primarily social, but theological: God did not choose you because you deserved to be chosen. God chose those who are undeserving, by the world's logic, in order to confound the logic of the world. The Corinthians, then, may look to their own experience to see that God does not act by human rules.

Later in this letter, Paul hints (not always subtly) that the Corinthians are boasting in their own accomplishments. They have achieved honor because of their wisdom (e.g., 4:8–13); in the gospel they have been freed from restrictive rules and regulations (5:1–3). Throughout the present passage Paul urges a different understanding of boasting, namely, the only boasting that belongs to a Christian is boasting in the cross. The only boasting rightly done is boasting in what God has given believers through Jesus Christ (1:31). Boasting in human wisdom and power is rejected, for it is precisely human wisdom and power that bring about the crucifixion of Jesus Christ and are thereby revealed to be utterly bankrupt.

It may strike us as curious, at first glance, that Paul does not interject in this passage a reference to the resurrection. Surely it is the resurrection rather than the crucifixion that reveals God's true power. In chapter 15, he does explain how the resurrection guarantees God's final triumph over all other powers, but here, in chapter 1, the resurrection is carefully, perhaps even intentionally, omitted. There may be two reasons for this omission. First, Paul understands that the Corinthians, with their emphasis on their own wisdom and their own spiritual gifts, needed to understand that the gospel is not about human accomplishments and being a Christian does not mean that one has already arrived at a life of glory. By issuing this forceful reminder about the centrality of the cross Paul places the entire Christian life in the context of the cross itself. Second, a central theological issue is at stake here—namely, the place of the cross in Christian faith. For Paul this is not merely a persuasive step through which he can bring the Corinthians over to his side. The cross, for Paul, is not a human error that God corrected through the resurrection or an embarrassment to be overcome. It is, instead, the point at which God's own and God's wholly other wisdom and will are revealed.

Matthew 5:1–12

When the preacher prepares to preach from the Beatitudes, the first segment of Matthew's Sermon on the Mount, there are two basic areas to be investigated before considering the content of specific verses: (a) What is a beatitude? (b) What preparation is given the reader to pave the way for the marvelous words of the Sermon? How the two questions are answered (or not answered) will markedly affect the interpretation of the text and the character of the sermon.

First, what is a beatitude? Very often in homiletical treatments the Beatitudes are taken to be moral exhortations. One's actions and attitudes are to be oriented toward the actions and attitudes stated in the text. If the ideal is in some sense achieved, then a reward is granted. God's people should be meek, and if they are meek, then they will be blessed by inheriting the earth. God's people should show mercy toward others, and if they do, then they will be blessed by receiving mercy from God. This ethical stance to the beatitude has a biblical warrant. In the wisdom literature, the beatitude tends to be a statement that clearly carries the force of an exhortation, an ideal to be pursued, a moral maxim.

This approach works with some of Matthew's beatitudes better than it does with others. An exhortation to peacemaking is more plausible than an exhortation to mourn or to be reviled and rejected. But with each beatitude the tendency is toward moralistic preaching, preaching that pitches high standards and then leaves a congregation with a sense of failure because listeners cannot achieve what the text apparently demands. The blessing becomes totally elusive.

There is, however, another approach to the beatitude that recognizes that it is first and foremost a blessing promised by God to those people who already are what the beatitude describes. The meek, the mourning, the merciful hear the text as a word of encouragement and reassurance. In their predicament they are singled out by the blessing of God and are renewed in their hope of the future. Those passionately longing for the establishment of justice in the earth are promised that their longing will be satisfied. The blessings are eschatological, and yet in terms of the eschatological perspective of Matthew, they are not entirely future. They carry a measure of realization in the present. A pattern for this approach to the beatitude can be found in the apocalyptic writings of the intertestamental period.

After addressing the various groups of designated people with a concrete word of good news, the Beatitudes then serve an additional function. They describe the direction of God's blessing. God is a God who cares about the poor in spirit, the humble, those yearning for right to be done, the merciful, the single-minded, the peacemakers, and those persecuted for righteousness' sake. God will not abandon such people or leave them hopeless. This description of God's concern, then, carries ethical implications for all who listen to the text. Their attitudes and consciousness are shaped by the nature of the

God in whom they believe. No strategies are offered; no blueprints are laid out. Instead, imaginations are enlivened and sensitivities are reformed. When the sermon takes seriously the beatitude as an eschatological blessing, it can also provide vision and moral direction.

A second area of investigation involves the context in which the Sermon on the Mount (and of course the Beatitudes) are found. Matthew 5:1 relates the movement of Jesus "up the mountain," reminding the reader that Jesus has carried on previous activity in other locations. Mention of both "the crowds" and "his disciples" pushes the reader back to the earlier section of the narrative, where Jesus' teaching, preaching, and healing have attracted large groups of people and where his authoritative call has drawn two sets of brothers from their fishing businesses to follow him. (The commentary on the Gospel lesson for the past Sunday traces the activity of Jesus in Matt. 4:12–23.)

The point is that the teaching found in the Sermon appears in the context of Jesus' announcement of the imminent rule of God and of his demonstration of God's power. In the narrative Jesus has been established as the Son of God, witnessed to by the voice out of heaven at his baptism (3:17) and validated by his resistance to temptation (4:1–11). A community of disciples has been constituted. The Sermon, then, is not the wise advice and counsel of an ordinary prophet, given to the human race to assist people in coping with life. Nor is it an impossible ideal intended to remind listeners of how far short of God's standards they are. It comes from an authoritative teacher who bears God's imprimatur. It is addressed primarily (though not exclusively) to disciples who have, however uncertainly, begun to follow him. The Sermon is a description of those whom God cares for and how life is to be lived in the coming kingdom. It is a further statement of God's good news.

Not . . .

Fifth Sunday After Epiphany

Ordinary Time 5

As is often the case, three of the lessons for this Sunday have connections out of which a common theme emerges, while the fourth lesson appears to stand somewhat independently of the others. The readings from Isaiah, Psalms, and Matthew are linked by the Epiphany symbol of "light." They call for and celebrate a life of faithfulness in the world, in the public arena where faith functions openly and social injustice is addressed.

Isaiah 58 mocks a worship preoccupied with ritual and blind to human oppression and need. It subverts a religion, no matter how passionate and busy, that ignores the ordinance of God and the social arrangements that leave people dehumanized and enslaved. Authentic worship occurs when the liturgy is joined to a hands-on involvement with the hungry and the homeless. The otherwise absent God then is remarkably available to a seeking community.

Psalm 112 is itself a piece of worship, a song to honor the righteous life, the life marked by the fear of God, generosity, fairness, and a concern for the poor. Such a life endures the test of time and finds enormous resources to remain steadfast and persistent, even amid angry opposition.

These two texts from the Hebrew scriptures undergird the statement of Jesus to the disciples that they are the light of the world and the salt of the earth. "Light" and "salt" are functional metaphors. By their very nature they *do* something, and do it openly. They have an impact on the surrounding environment. No more than the people of Israel of Isaiah's day can the disciples retreat into a private spirituality. Their call is to the marketplace, to the public arena, where discipleship becomes witness and where the same commitments Isaiah demanded are to be practiced (so Matt. 25:31–46).

The reading from 1 Cor. 2 seems independent of the other three. It is crafted in the particular categories of Paul's debate with the divided Corinthians. And yet at the heart of God's hidden and secret wisdom is the figure of the crucified Christ, who for the Christian community has become righteousness (1:30). The vocation of Israel to attend to injustice and oppression, a vocation praised by the psalmist, and given anew to the disciples is both modeled and fulfilled in the cross.

Isaiah 58:3–9a (9b–12)

Israel engages in elaborate and passionate religion; it is, however, piety that completely disregards the character and intention of Yahweh. Such religiosity is in fact an act of self-indulgent rebellion (v. 1) that contradicts the "ordinance of their God" (v. 2). Isaiah 58 reflects a deep conflict in the community of Israel between factions of leadership who hold conflicting views of authentic religion. Such disputes are urgent in the community of faith now, as they were then.

The community is indicted for the wrong kind of religious "busyness" (vs. 3–5). The poet puts in the mouth of busy Israel a cynical, mocking, and shameless self-disclosure (v. 3a): Israel asserts that it has been religiously zealous and scrupulous, but such effort has not produced any of the desired results. God has not noticed all the effort and has not rewarded the people's devotion. Such devotion, says the poet, is calculating and manipulative.

With the double "look" of vs. 3b–4, the poet comments on such blatant, self-serving religion. Such religion is dishonest because it is done only to enhance self and is therefore phony. And it is unrelated to the realities of life. Such religion, because it is phony (even if it is "moral"), does not touch the larger "neighbor questions" of economic exploitation. It easily coexists with "oppression" of workers (v. 3).

Ostentatious efforts at piety, devotion, and morality are not congruent with God (v. 5). Religion is being used to avoid the reality of God. Such religion leaves its practitioners autonomous, apart from God, and therefore, predictably, indifferent to neighbor.

Now comes *the positive counterargument* (vs. 6–7). God does indeed choose a fast, an act of obedience that consists in genuine self-denial. That act of self-denying obedience, however, concerns "yokes." And "yokes," characteristically in the Bible, are power arrangements in economic-political matters that impose excessive burdens on people. Yokes render people dependent and hopeless, denying them dignity and joy. The religious duty of the fast is to break the systemic power arrangements of exploitation and oppression.

The general assertion of v. 6 is made quite explicit in v. 7. The faith here recommended is concrete and daily. There is a hunger for "spirituality" among us; much of that hunger is misguided and misinformed. The presence of this God, so the poet urges, is found in the daily embrace of the neighbor, the hungry, the poor, the naked (cf. Jer. 22:16). Notice how material the new spirituality is; it concerns *bread, home, body, flesh,* engagement with the painful dailiness of human wretchedness and need.

There is a strange interface between v. 6 and v. 7 which permits interpretation. There is no doubt that the "bonds of injustice" alludes to the systemic practice of dehumanization. The response in v. 7, however, is quite local, immediate, and one-on-one. These two verses provide an important linkage between *public issues,* and the systemic character of wickedness, and the *concrete response* of caring people. The response, however, concerns *your* bread, *your* house, *your* self. Thus the commended response which is given freely is neither a complacent amelioration nor a distanced institutional response. What is involved is the direct and immediate engagement of self with neighbor in a clearheaded awareness of systemic issues. In the movement of these verses, the character of *piety* has been completely revamped toward the urgency of *neighbor-engagement.* Risky contact with the needy is a response to systemic wickedness.

This is a piety and a spirituality that yields joy and well-being (vs. 8–9a). The piety critiqued in vs. 3–5 was calculating in its aim of a quid pro quo. This later, recommended piety (vs. 6–7) does not begin with an expected quid pro quo. It is simply done because it is "God's fast." Such a fast, however, inevitably changes those engaged. The poem does not comment on what such acts do for the recipients. The main beneficiaries identified in the poem are the ones who take the initiatives. Engagement in God's chosen fast, of caring for others, does indeed evoke healing. The healing is a by-product of a life lived for the sake of others.

The same "cause-effect" scenario is reiterated in vs. 9b–12, organized around "if . . . if . . . then." The double "if" (vs. 9b–10a) concerns neighbor love. The "then" (vs. 10b–12) envisions well-being and restoration, which are promised as a consequence of neighbor love. There are clues here about rehabilitation of a society in disarray!

Psalm 112:1–9 (10)

The Psalm lection for this day is closely related to the Old Testament text, in that it celebrates the nature of the upright life, a life that is described in the Isaiah passage as rooted not in ritual, but in justice and compassion. Notice the similarities between

> Then your light shall break forth like the dawn,
> and your healing shall spring up quickly;
> your vindicator shall go before you,
> the glory of the LORD shall be your rear guard.
> (Isa. 58:8)

and

> They rise in the darkness as a light for the upright;
> they are gracious, merciful, and righteous.
> (Ps. 112:4)

Structurally, the entirety of Ps. 112 is a perfect alphabetic acrostic, in that, following the initial exclamation "Praise the LORD!" each line begins with the appropriate letter of the Hebrew alphabet (cf. Pss. 111, 119). This feature may help to account for some of the linguistic difficulties in the text, as in v. 4, above, where in the NRSV translation the subject is "those who fear the LORD" of v. 1. Some scholars would argue that the preferred reading of v. 4 is that of the "old" RSV:

> Light rises in the darkness for the upright;
> the LORD is gracious, merciful, and righteous.

In theological terms, Ps. 112 reflects the influences of the wisdom tradition, with its insistence that faithfulness to Yahweh and to Yahweh's moral order brings demonstrable results in the form of prosperity and peace (cf. Prov. 3:5–10). Such a declaration always risks the danger of sounding hollow and mocking, especially to someone who, in spite of a life of faithfulness, experiences defeat or tragedy. This clash of the ideal with the reality is, of course, not unknown to the biblical writers, as it is the stuff of which the book of Job is made. Nevertheless, the easy identification here between faith/goodness, on the one hand, and happiness, on the other, may strike many readers as at best shallow and at worst a lie. Is there anyone anywhere, no matter how great his or her faith, who does not fear evil tidings (v. 7)? Equally problematic is the reference to the anticipated discomfort or destruction of one's enemies (v. 8).

Many of these difficulties may be resolved when the reader of this text remembers the hyperbolic nature of the language with which the wisdom tradition speaks. The strokes on the canvas are made with quite broad brushes, and it is left for others to sketch in the details. Thus, while our psalm would not deny the many inconsistencies and absurdities of the life of faith, it nevertheless stands firm in its assertion that there is a correlation between the orientation of the human heart (our faith commitments) and our strength in confronting the demands that our days bring to us.

It is instructive to notice the qualities of the upright ones. They are compassionate toward their neighbors, and they lend money not with the intention of profiting from the misfortune of others, but in order to help meet human need (v. 5a). Justice characterizes their day-to-day affairs (v. 5b). And they demonstrate liberality and generosity in their giving to those in distress (v. 9a). The motivation that underlies this humanitarian concern is not a simple altruism. The reader of Ps. 112 is informed at the very beginning that the subject of this poem is "those who fear the LORD" (v. 1).

Having described its subject as those who are faithful and compassionate, the text then makes this fundamental declaration: these individuals have obtained a quality of endurance because of their commitments. There is a "light" about them (v. 4a), a metaphor that could have many meanings, but which is probably intended here as a symbol for joy (again, note v. 1: "Happy are those who fear the LORD"). They persist in the face of adversity (v. 6a; cf. 1 Cor. 13:4–7), and they gain the only kind of immortality ancient Israel knew: they are "remembered forever" (vs. 6b, 9b). Moreover, they face danger with resolution (vs. 7–8a).

(As for the troublesome "they will look in triumph on their foes," v. 8b, this element in the psalms [cf. 112:10] must be read in the light of ancient Israel's view—unlike that of modern men and women—that there was no distinction to be found between evil as an abstraction and the men and women who perform evil deeds. Thus to destroy evil one must resort to the destruction of wicked persons. Fortunately, Jesus has led us into a better understanding of the matter; see Luke 23:34).

The psalm is not a description of how this correlation between commitment and inner strength has come about. Indeed, no description is possible, in view of the fact that both of these qualities, as well as the relationship between them, are gifts of God, and thus inexplicable mysteries. Rather, this psalm is a celebration of this correlation, a celebration born of long experience, which recognizes that openness toward God and toward other persons is a trait of personality whose companion is often an inner resilience and peace. This is part of "God's wisdom, secret and hidden," of which the lection from 1 Cor. (2:7) speaks.

And as for the "light" with which the psalm characterizes the life of the upright ones (v. 4a), its most obvious quality is that it should not—indeed, cannot—be hidden (Matt. 5:14–16). Thus our psalm: Hallelujah! Praise the Lord!

1 Corinthians 2:1–12 (13–16)

The art of persuasion surrounds us. From Madison Avenue's slick advertising campaigns to telephone salespersons to political posturing, the tactics of persuasion for a variety of causes and in an expanding array of media are an often unwelcome factor of contemporary life in North America. The question inevitably arises: which of these tactics is appropriate for the promotion of the Christian gospel and how may they be employed with integrity? Is any medium appropriate for the Christian message? What is gained by employing the tactics of Madison Avenue for the church? What is lost by clinging to the media of past generations?

While these questions do not find an easy answer in Paul's comments in 1 Cor. 2, contemporary preachers may take some comfort from the limited correspondence between Paul's situation and their own. In this passage, a central issue is the difference between—the conflict between—human wisdom and divine wisdom. The opening lines, vs. 1–5, have to do with the use of human wisdom as a means of persuasion on behalf of the gospel. Recalling his initial preaching at Corinth, Paul insists that he did not employ "lofty words or wisdom." Rhetoric, the art of persuasion that was highly developed and highly prized in Paul's era, did not become for him a means of proclaiming the gospel.

Since Paul's letters in fact betray his acquaintance with standard rhetorical devices, we may look on his assertions here with considerable skepticism. The point he makes, however, has little to do with whether or not Paul drew on the rhetorical arts. What he is after here is the way in which faith comes into existence. Faith comes, not from elegant speech or from the wisdom of human beings, but from God alone. The right object of belief is not human achievement (in whatever form), but the crucified Christ. This same conviction comes to expression in the notion of the sixteenth-century reformers that faith stems from faith. Faith is not a response to persuasion, whatever form that persuasion might take; it is a gift of God.

Again in this text, as in 1 Cor. 1:18–31, Paul summarizes the content of his preaching as "Jesus Christ, and him crucified." Not only does Paul eschew the effectiveness of ordinary means of persuasion, but he identifies his preaching with that feature of the gospel that most offends and scandalizes human wisdom. Faith in response to this gospel must indeed be based "not on human wisdom but on the power of God" (v. 5).

The second part of this passage, vs. 6–12, appears to contradict the first. While Paul does not preach wisdom, there is a wisdom to be imparted among the more mature in faith. The contradiction, of course, is apparent rather than real, for the wisdom Paul does not employ is "human wisdom," wisdom that stems from the reasoning of human beings who believe themselves to be the sole arbiters of what is wise and good. The wisdom Paul is able to share with the mature stems, on the other hand, from God and concerns God's plan for humankind. Christians come to their awareness of God's wisdom by means of the gift of the Spirit of God (v. 10). The seemingly convoluted discussion about the Spirit in vs. 11–13 is less an analysis of the workings of the Spirit than a confession that only through God's initiative could this insight be granted to human beings. Human beings do not work their way to knowledge of the Spirit or in any other way merit that particular form of wisdom; God's Spirit conveys it as a gift. It would be a serious mistake to read into this passage the existence of a class of special Christians who have earned their access to a secret knowledge about God. Paul's point is that the Spirit gives this wisdom, in the Spirit's own time, to those who are able to understand.

Sometimes Christians see in this passage, together with the end of 1 Cor. 1, the legitimation of a kind of Christian anti-intellectualism. Paul's words about the wrongheadedness of human wisdom serve to endorse the notion that Christians should use their hearts but not their heads. The problems with that sort of reading are several and serious. First, as we have seen, the passage itself is not about reason or wisdom *as such,* but about human wisdom and God's wisdom; or better, about human wisdom as it sets itself over against and independent from God's wisdom. Second, within the text itself as elsewhere in his letters, Paul actively uses his own mental powers in order to make the case that he wants to make; Paul uses his head, in other words. Third, the conclusion Paul draws is not that the brain is a dangerous thing and much to be avoided, but that it, like all other human assets, must be acknowledged as a gift of God. The use of the human intellect is indeed to be commended, with the stipulation only that it be used in service of God's power and God's glory.

Matthew 5:13–20

It is hard to overemphasize the importance of the passage chosen for the Gospel reading for this Sunday. It makes affirmations and issues demands that express the unifying theme not only of the Sermon on the Mount but of the whole of Matthew's Gospel.

First, the passage presents the reader with *two powerful images* for the Christian community: salt and light (with the accompanying pictures of a city situated on the crest of a hill and a lamp hidden under a bushel basket). Though small and common, both images forcefully depict the world-remaking task of the disciples. While they are alike in that both function in relation to a surrounding environment (salt seasons food, and light pushes back the darkness), the two images are developed in differing ways. On the one hand, without offering a detailed explanation, Jesus warns that salt can lose its capacity to season. It can fail to do what it is intended to do; it can become useless; it can be cast aside. Disciples, whether ancient or modern, hear in the image a warning to take seriously the call to mission, to the task of being the church in the world.

On the other hand, the image of light develops more positively the church's place in the wider world. A city built on a hill cannot be hidden. Its very nature is to be visible. Furthermore, it is ludicrous to think of putting a lamp under a basket, since it too is meant to illumine. Following the element of warning developed with the image of salt, the affirmations about light are reassuring to disciples. Echoes of Isa. 60:1–3 reverberate in the passage, suggesting that the listeners have a role in the divine strategy of addressing the nations. They are affirmed as a part of God's plan for bringing light to the world.

Second, the work of discipleship is specified as *good works that are visible but give glory to God.* Readers are here not invited to a secret piety (as in 6:1–18), but to a public ministry, to deeds subject to scrutiny. The antitheses that follow (5:21–48) give some definition to the "good works." But these are deeds which have the character of witness, a missionary function, in that they point beyond themselves and the doers to "your Father in heaven."

The stress on the public dimension of the disciples' lives may seem a bit overdone, until it is recognized that those addressed by the text as "you" are the same "you" mentioned in the concluding beatitude—disciples who have been reviled and persecuted and made the objects of slander (5:11–12). They are followers whose stands for righteousness put them in company with the Hebrew prophets.

But a sustained life of struggle can easily result in retreat to a private world, in withdrawal from conflict to a place of presumed safety. One of those prophets, Elijah, discovered that persistent opposition often proves intimidating and robs the disciple of the initiative for mission. Salt can easily lose its capacity to season and light can be hidden. Thus the renewed call to discipleship and the warning against the temptation of a privatized religion.

Third, the passage asks what relationship do these demands of discipleship have to the law, to the expression of God's will given at Sinai? The text begins an answer by boldly declaring that *Jesus came not to destroy but to fulfill the Hebrew scriptures.* What is radically new in the presence of God's coming rule is not an abrogation but a completion of both the promises and the demands set out in the law and the prophets. To put it another way, Jesus is part on the ongoing story of God's relation to the covenant community, but as such he is the final and decisive chapter in the story. His is the culminating piece of the story that gives meaning to all the rest.

The sharp, absolute character of the statements of 5:17–20 suggests that the text may be aimed at clarifying misunderstandings about Jesus and his ministry (see 26:62; 27:40). In Matthew's community Jesus may have been hailed by some but pointedly criticized by others who understood his ways as a destroying of the law. Here the record is set straight. The law is not to be trifled with; it must be obeyed and taught. Jesus does not deny the Hebrew scriptures, but confirms and establishes them.

Fourth, the relation between the old and the new can be raised not only in terms of Jesus, but also in terms of the disciples. How does the life of the disciples compare with the life of the religious leaders who claim ultimate loyalty to the law and the prophets? "Unless your righteousness exceeds that of the scribes and Pharisees, you will never enter the kingdom of heaven" (5:20). *The demands of discipleship in the new age prove to be more pervasive and radical, calling for a new understanding of the divine will and a higher righteousness.*

It is important to acknowledge that the religious authorities about whom Jesus spoke maintained a vigorous morality, a righteous manner of life, at times even severe and costly. But as the following passage indicates (5:21–48), Jesus' interpretation of the will of God turns out to be more extreme and the depth of obedience more sweeping. He moves beyond a preoccupation with the concrete deed to a consideration of the consistency between inner disposition and specific action. He envisions a different world, marked by unheard-of reconciliation, simple truth-telling, outrageous generosity, and love of one's enemies. The reign of God entails a higher righteousness, a more faithful praxis than the religious authorities of Jesus could possibly imagine.

Sixth Sunday After Epiphany

Proper 1
Ordinary Time 6

How are Christians to understand and be related to the Jewish law? It is an ancient question, debated through the history of the church's life and not always agreed on. Theological traditions that have given birth to particular denominations have been and remain divided on the answer. But the question cannot be relegated to the church's past as if it were one of those issues which has no significance for contemporary Christians, like how many angels can dance on the head of a pin. Modern-day Marcionism is unfortunately alive and well, at least at the point of saying that the ethical codes of Hebrew scriptures are dated and of no value in shaping moral decisions today. The readings for this Sunday address the question and invite the preacher to explore the issue in the sermon.

In the text from Deuteronomy, Israel, standing at the gateway to the Land of Promise, is confronted with a sharp choice. It is a choice between following the commandments of Yahweh or bowing to the gods worshiped by the Canaanites. Choosing the law, however, means something more than legalism. It means choosing a way of life, an understanding of society ordered according to the covenantal commitments, a means of existence different from the surrounding culture.

In Ps. 119 Israel praises the Torah. It is God's gift especially bestowed on Israel to be the authentic guide as to how life should be lived. As such, the Torah distinguishes Israel from the other nations, because it is rooted in God's election and saving activity.

Jesus does not come to abrogate the Torah, but precisely to fulfill it (Matt. 5). The antipathy between Jesus and the Jewish authorities in the Matthew text is not to be read as an antipathy between Jesus and the Torah. Instead, Jesus becomes the authoritative interpreter of the Torah, the one who pushes beyond external behavior to a consistency between disposition and deed. Christians are invited by the text to be different, to obey and teach the covenantal commitments, to be directed in their moral decisions by Jesus' interpretation of the law. In so doing, they become what Paul describes as "spiritual people."

Deuteronomy 30:15–20

Moses is coming to the conclusion of a long, long speech (Deut. 5—30). That speech is placed at the Jordan River, just as Israel is about to enter the Land of Promise. Moses pauses with Israel at the Jordan, because he knows the surge into the new land is a frightened, ominous moment. When Israel arrives in the Land of Promise, it will face alternative ethical options, alternative objects of trust, and alternative modes of power. The prosperity and abundance of the new land may indeed talk Israel out of its faith in Yahweh (cf. Deut. 6:10–15; 8:6–11). Moses alerts Israel to the danger and risk that Israel must now face.

Israel now faces a choice (30: 15–18). The choice is clear and direct in the words of Moses. We are wont to notice only that the choice is "life" or "death." It is, however, also "prosperity" and "adversity"; the good is a material life of abundance. "Death," then, is not physical extermination, but it is existence that lacks joy, well-being, security, and abundance. Death is the negation of shalom. The choice before Israel is expounded by Moses in two daring "if-then" clauses that make astonishing connections. The first "if-then" clause is a positive one (v. 16). The "if," that is, the condition to be embraced, is love of God enacted through obedience to the commandments. The "then" of consequence is life, abundance, prosperity, and blessing in the land. The "connection" is that faithful obedience to the Torah of Sinai will lead to a good life.

The summons to love God and keep God's commandments, however, is not the simple embrace of a set of rules or disciplines. It is an invitation to a covenantal understanding of social relationships. This covenantal obedience includes, according to this tradition:

sharing feasts with the hungry (Deut. 14:27–29)
canceling debts that the poor cannot pay (15:1–11)
organizing government to guard against excessive wealth (17:14–20)
sharing hospitality with runaway slaves (23:15–16)
not charging interest on loans in the covenant community (23:19–20)
paying hired hands promptly what they earn (24:14–15)

leaving the residue of harvest for the disadvantaged (24:19–22)
limiting punishment in order to protect human dignity (25:1–3)

The list could be continued. Obedience issues in specific conduct; it is, however, essentially a different valuing of social reality, refusing to reduce social relations to power, force, greed, and brutality.

From such obedience surely follows the "then" of v. 16. When life is ordered covenantly, there will indeed be well-being. This obedience is a dense social enterprise, which issues in an alternative community. Such density should not be understood as rule-keeping, and the consequence is not an intrusive supernaturalism, but the outcome of genuine social relations.

The negative "if-then" phrasing is to be understood in comparable fashion through the work of social mediation (vs. 17–18). The negative "if" concerns a refusal to "listen" and a readiness to serve "other gods" (v. 17). Obedience to an alien god means the embrace of a world perspective and a practice of social relations that are hostile to covenantal relations.

The alternative gods to which Israel was tempted were variously fertility gods or the gods of the empire. "Fertility gods" are not particularly preoccupied with sexuality. Rather, they are objects of loyalty and trust who reduce the costs of life to manageable technical procedures, so that one can manage the system and thereby secure one's own life on one's own terms. Thus "fertility religion" is a scheme for self-sufficiency.

The "then" (consequence) of such disobedience is to "perish" (v. 18). But such perishing is not wrought through God's supernatural intervention. Rather "perishing" means to be caught in patterns of social relations that generate fear, anger, hate, and diminished human possibility. Thus both the positive and negative "if-then" connections need to be brought very close to concrete social practice. Both Yahweh and the "other gods" are present in the midst of social relations that either *foster caring covenantalism*, or *oppose such covenantalism* in destructive ways.

Psalm 119:1–8

Of the three major psalms in the Old Testament that celebrate the place of Torah in the life of Israel, Ps. 119 is the longest and most complex. (The others are Pss. 1 and 19.) Psalm 119 is an extended alphabetic acrostic, in which eight consecutive lines of the Hebrew text are devoted to a single letter, vs. 1–8 each beginning with the letter *aleph,* vs. 9–16 with *beth,* and so on. In addition to containing a common first letter for each line, each of the twenty-two eight-line units (for the twenty-two letters of the Hebrew alphabet) exhibits another literary feature: with some exceptions, each verse contains a different word meaning "Torah." For example, vs. 1–8 display the following: Torah, or law (v. 1), decrees (v. 2), ways (v. 3), precepts (v. 4), statutes (v. 5), commandments (v. 6), ordinances (v. 7), and, again, statutes (v. 8).

Christian readers of the Old Testament sometimes have difficulty generating the same enthusiasm for celebrating Torah as did faithful people in ancient Israel. We remember Paul's warnings about the shortcomings of the law (Gal. 3:10–11), and we remind ourselves that reconciliation with God comes about not because we keep God's commandments, but in spite of the fact that we do not. Thus, the repeated—some might say, monotonous—statements in praise of God's commandments in Ps. 119 may seem remote and archaic to modern Christians and of little relevance to our lives. After all, we like to remind ourselves, we have been saved by grace!

But the reality is that ancient Israel was under no illusion about the ability of individual men and women, or of the community of faith as a whole, to attain moral perfection. The repeated reminder by the prophets that sin had stained the lives both of the nation (Isa. 5:1–7) and of individuals (2 Sam. 12:1–7) looms too large in the Old Testament to be ignored. Rather, Torah was of crucial importance not because it could be attained, but because it was the only authentic guide available to men and women of faith as to how their lives might be lived. To be sure, the mark was often missed (as it is missed by modern people of the faith community), but the mark remained: the only true guide for worship and conduct in a difficult world.

But that is not all. More than just a reliable guide, Torah, which is best translated "instruction" rather than "law," was considered to be the gift of God. It was that precious endowment bestowed on the men and women of the community of faith as the means by which they might respond to God's saving initiatives in their lives. Notice in Ps. 19 how Torah is elevated to the status of other splendid works of God's creative power (Ps. 19:1–10). How does one express his or her acceptance of God's loving presence in human life? By living one's life according to God's instruction.

The movement in Ps. 119:1–8 takes place in three "steps." Verses 1–3 celebrate the sense of wholeness that comes into the life of the person who makes an effort to live in the light of Torah. "Blessed" or "happy" is the one who walks in the Torah of Yahweh. (Notice the repetition in v. 1b and v. 3b. Verse 3a, which celebrates those who "do no wrong," is hyperbole!)

The second "step," v. 4, is a statement of fact over the place of Torah in the mind of God: it is of crucial importance! Notice that here the language has shifted so that Yahweh, who was referred to in the third person in vs. 1–3, is now addressed directly. "*You* have commanded your precepts to be kept diligently" (emphasis added). This is a significant shift in linguistic direction, in that it is maintained throughout the balance of the psalm.

The third "step," vs. 5–8, is the heart of this unit and the focal point of the Psalm lection for this day. Here the psalmist expresses his or her own resolve to keep Torah and to establish God's instruction as the pole around which life revolves. "My eyes fixed on all your commandments" (v. 6b) and "I will praise you with an upright heart" (v. 7a) express not only the poet's commitment to the teaching of God, but the joy to be found in that commitment. At the same time that the psalmist gives voice to this resolve, however, he or she confesses the power of human ignorance and weakness. In order to keep Torah, it must first be learned (v. 7b). And even when God's instruction has been learned, faithfulness to it is often interrupted by human weakness and sin, so that the petition in v. 5 becomes a necessary one for the poet to raise.

Lastly, in this final step, there is the acknowledgment that when human life is lived in the light of God's teaching, that life is changed. Significantly, the poet, in one breath, expresses this reality with a radiant confidence: "Then I shall not be put to shame" (v. 6a). In the next breath, however, this reality is expressed tremblingly, as a hope and a prayer: "Do not utterly forsake me" (v. 8b). And on this note of prayer, the lection appropriately concludes.

The tentative nature of this climax well illustrates the manner in which this Psalm lection regards God's Torah. All the confident exclamations of our intentions to achieve God's ideal for human life dissolve into a simple but desperate prayer: "O God, do not let go of me, for I simply can't make it on my own."

1 Corinthians 3:1–9

Having just written about the activity of the Spirit of God among believers, and especially about those who are spiritual (1 Cor. 2: 14–16), in this passage Paul uses the distinction between "spiritual people" and "people of the flesh" to illuminate the divisiveness at Corinth. His opposition between the spiritual and the fleshly catches our attention immediately, for we associate that opposition with the extremely negative attitude toward the human body that influenced parts of the church in its early centuries. What Paul articulates, however, is not a rejection of the body for the spirit, but an understanding of what makes for maturity in the Christian community. Very often, in fact, Paul uses the term "flesh" (*sarx* in Greek) in a quite neutral way, simply to refer to human beings in their finite existence. For example, Rom. 1:3 states that Jesus Christ "descended from David according to the flesh," which means simply that Jesus is physically a descendant of David. When Paul writes about being ruled by the flesh or dominated by its way of thinking, however, he refers not to an inherently evil flesh but to the flawed perspectives that characterize human values and human decisions. For example, in 2 Cor. 1:17, Paul asks the rhetorical question, "Do I make my plans according to ordinary human standards?" (literally, "according to the flesh"), a question that suggests that the standards of the flesh are flawed and transient. In our passage, to be "spiritual people" does not mean to ignore or suppress the needs of the body, but to be guided by the Spirit of God as distinct from the standards of the world apart from God.

In his description of the Corinthians as "people of the flesh" or "infants in Christ," Paul employs the image of feeding them with milk, as mothers feed their babies. Paul initially fed the Corinthians with milk, with a form of the gospel they could understand. Even now, when they ought to be ready for more serious nourishment, they are unable to receive it because they remain infants. The evidence Paul produces in order to justify his claim that the Corinthians are still infants is their jealousy and quarreling, especially quarreling over the relative importance of particular Christian leaders, such as Paul and Apollos.

The imagery Paul uses here for his relationship with the Corinthians merits some reflection on Paul's understanding of his apostolic work. Although it is customary to think of Paul in paternal—even paternalistic—terms, language about feeding infants milk is almost necessarily maternal imagery. After all, Paul wrote long before the advent of infant formula and baby bottles, when mothers or wet nurses were the only ones who could feed young babies! This use of maternal imagery, together with other such images in Gal. 4:19 and 1 Thess. 2:7, provokes some reconsideration of the notion that Paul thinks of himself in exclusively paternal terms. Particularly because Paul applies to himself maternal roles that are patently impossible, these passages reflect an understanding that the apostle is also one who nurtures as a mother nurtures.

With the second half of the text (vs. 5–9), the imagery shifts from that of nurturing human life to that of nurturing plants, as Paul develops his objection to divisiveness within the Corinthian church over loyalties to various Christian leaders. Although any form of divisiveness reflects the immaturity of believers, quarrels about the merits of Paul and Apollos reflect a misunderstanding of the nature of Christian growth. Neither Paul's role, that of planting or initiating the church at Corinth, nor Apollos's role, that of watering or watching over the church, makes the church grow. The growth itself comes from God alone. Paul and Apollos are not figures to be regarded with awe or to be compared with each other; they are simply servants of God with a common purpose and a common responsibility.

The final verse in the passage appears, at first glance, to establish a great contrast between Paul and Apollos on the one hand and the Corinthian church on the other: "*We* are God's servants . . . ; *you* are God's field, God's building" (emphases added). Paul does clearly understand that his task sets him apart, although not above, the Corinthians, and he is not afraid of that responsibility. What is more important than the contrast between Paul (and Apollos) and the Corinthians is their common standing before God: "We are *God's* servants . . . ; you are *God's* field, *God's* building" (emphasis added). No matter what the respective roles of Paul, Apollos, and the Corinthians, they all belong to God and derive their importance from that fact alone. Here is an understanding of ministry and the Christian life as a whole that assesses all contributions not as reflections of individual talent or labor, but as part of service to God.

Matthew 5:21–37

Preaching on the Gospel lesson for today presents quite a challenge. On the one hand, the preacher could take one of the issues isolated in the text (anger, adultery, divorce, the swearing of oaths) and make a statement about normative Christian conduct. Even though the texts are sharp and unbending in form, there is perhaps merit in such an option, particularly in a world where the practice of Christians can hardly be distinguished from that of non-Christians.

This approach would be to treat the statements of Jesus not as a new law to be laid on top of or in place of the old law, but as an ethical standard, a standard that goes beyond the boundaries set by civil law. For example, divorce is readily allowed in the courts today for marriages unalterably broken, and generally Protestant churches ask few questions about the courts' judgments. In contrast, and in rather unambiguous language. Matt. 5:31–32 makes the case for lifelong marriages of faithfulness. The statements of such standards, of course, are no more than unfulfillable demands unless the presupposition of the entire Sermon is reiterated: the inbreaking of God's rule and the role of Jesus as God's gracious Messiah.

But most preachers also come to the text out of pastoral experiences and are wary of preaching sermons that may only succeed in creating guilt in the listeners. To say that Jesus forthrightly condemns anger, forbids adultery and lust, leaves no room for divorce or remarriage (except in the case of unchastity), and prohibits the taking of oaths may not advance the relationship with members who are immediately concerned with any of these issues.

On the other hand, the preacher could take a slightly different tack. At the heart of each of the four scenarios lies a broader, more sweeping demand, which addresses every listener and confronts him or her with the distinctive character of life in God's new age. In each case Jesus presses beyond the expressed statement of the law to a deeper question, and the interpreter is invited by the text to do just the same.

For example, the first scenario has to do with the command not to murder. Rather than a casuistic debate of contexts in which killing may or may not be legitimate, *Jesus warns of unresolved anger between family members and calls for a concrete act of reconciliation.* A wonderful picture is painted of a worship service heading toward the climactic presentation of the offering, when suddenly chaos breaks out. This person and that begin to move across the sanctuary to be reconciled with estranged fellow members. It is unclear whether the brother or sister who "has something against you" is justified in being angry or not. Who is right or wrong seems beside the point. At issue is the disrupted relationship and the concrete move toward healing.

Or take Jesus' comments on adultery (5:27–30) and divorce (vs. 31–32). In both instances, *what is called for is a relationship of wholeness between males and females.* Adultery in the biblical world is defined as extramarital sexual intercourse between a man and another man's wife. The prohibition against adultery grows out of the property laws in ancient Israel. The wife "belonged" to her husband, and the extramarital relationship violated the rights of her husband. A man could have such a relationship with an unmarried woman and not be guilty of adultery, but if the woman was married, both he and she were guilty.

Jesus makes no comment about the quoted commandment from the Decalogue, but immediately pushes beyond it to the man who treats a woman as a sexual object. Whether the reference to "woman" in v. 28 designates a married or an unmarried woman is relatively unimportant. The point is that women are persons, and a proper relationship between women and men has to be based on grounds other than implicit or explicit sexual exploitation. The injunction against lust (addressed only to men) provides a certain protection for the disadvantaged woman. The jarring, hyperbolic statements that follow (vs. 29–30) only serve to underscore the importance of the wholesome relationship.

The statement on divorce (vs. 31–32) is more complicated exegetically because of the ambiguity of the word *porneia* in v. 32, translated in the NRSV as "unchastity" (see the discussion in the commentaries), and because of the other references to divorce in the New Testament (see Matt. 19:3–9; Mark 10:2–12; Luke 16:18; 1 Cor. 7:10–12). In any case, the statement is not to be turned into a new restriction that forever keeps broken marriages bound together despite the reality of the brokenness. Instead, the effect of the prohibition is the affirmation of the sanctity of marriage and the encouragement of a reconciled relationship of husband and wife, whose union is characteristic of the new rule of God announced in Jesus' ministry.

The prohibition of oaths (Matt. 5:33–37) presents what seems like an unrealistic demand. Only a few sectarian groups today retain the prohibition as it is given here. But when one moves beyond the prohibition to ask about the positive implication of the text, it has far-reaching significance. The taking of an oath to guarantee one's word implies that otherwise one's word cannot be trusted. *What the text calls for is simple, unabashed honesty in the full range of human relationships.* One's "yes" is to mean "yes" and one's "no" to mean "no."

Christians are not urged by the text to campaign against the use of oaths in the courts and elsewhere, nor are Christians exempt from the legal requirements to take oaths in what is essentially a dishonest society. They are, however, called to truthfulness and faithfulness (whether under oath or not), a rather marked departure from the prevalent practice in the Western world, where for reasons of national security or public relations or personal gain the truth is regularly slanted or distorted. Truthfulness is characteristic of the life lived under the rule of God.

In each of these scenarios Jesus is calling for an entirely new way of viewing human relationships. Behind the prohibitions lies the vision of a restored humanity.

Seventh Sunday After Epiphany

Proper 2
Ordinary Time 7

This set of texts is relentlessly concerned with the moral requirements that belong to life with the God of the Bible. These texts assume, but do not dwell on, the foundation of covenantal law in God's rescuing acts. That foundation is implicit in undergirding these several treatments of God's command.

The psalm in only the most general way celebrates the awareness that life with God is life in an alternative obedience—that is, an obedience that is not just a response to a set of rules, but which is a very different perspective on the whole of existence. The psalm urges not just Torah acts, but a Torah consciousness. The psalmist is aware that the command of God constitutes a radical counterobedience.

The text from Leviticus brings us to the core claims of covenantal law. The rule of the God of Israel leads directly to focus on the neighbor. Indeed, it is in neighbor relations that the life-and-death issues of Yahweh's rule are enacted and made visible in the world. These several commandments affirm that neighbor relations can be reorganized in ways that give healing, health, and well-being. The neighbor is not just an inconvenience or an intrusion, but is the stuff of moral awareness.

Paul's admonitions to the Corinthian Christians do not mention law directly, but they stake the bold claim that Jesus Christ is the central focus of every Christian's commitment. Human wisdom is mere folly with God. The only true wisdom is Christ, and by that wisdom Christ's people are to live.

The Gospel reading lifts demands that are serious, radical, and costly. They require "unnatural responses" that are not "business as usual" according to the ways of the world. They invite the community to reflect on, imagine, and devise extra measures of neighbor love that reflect the character of God.

Life rediscerned in covenantal categories requires a deployment of one's energy and resources in ways that our society does not celebrate or appreciate. The law is not a negative discipline, but a dangerous invitation congruent with the dangerous vision of the biblical God. Another way is possible because of the rule of God. It becomes reality whenever and wherever God's faithful people take the command as the way of life.

Leviticus 19:1–2, 9–18

Israel's narrative of faith portrays the will and character of God. Yahweh is an end and not a means, a person to be honored and not a power to be harnessed. God is not to be reduced to a tradable or usable commodity.

Israel's reflections on faith, however, are always bifocal. Israel never testifies about God without at the same time asking about the character of Israel. Israel embodies holiness by obedience to God's commands. Thus the text articulates a crucial connection between *God's holiness* and *Israel's obedience,* which is the form of human holiness. This text invites reflection on the character of obedient faith as a response to God's rescuing, sovereign holiness.

In this ethical catalog, many of the Ten Commandments are articulated in forms somewhat different from the more familiar versions of Ex. 20 and Deut. 5.

1. Three commandments are voiced, coupled with three statements of God's name and character (vs. 3–4):

(a) Honor (fear) father and mother
(b) Keep my Sabbath
(c) Do not turn to idols

The first two commandments given here enlist Israel in positive acts of obedience. The holiness of Israel is at risk in the most elemental of human relations, parent to child and child to parent. The command on Sabbath affirms that God is sovereign over time, that the time of the neighbor can never be usurped by anyone, and that time cannot be managed against God's will for human well-being (cf. Mark 2:27–28). Concerning both parents and Sabbath, the commandments urge Israel to yield and receive, and not to control and dominate. The move from domination (of parents, of time) to receptiveness is then given a more theological summary, by a contrast between the idols that dominate and Yahweh who invites to an alternative, convenantal relation based on freedom.

2. The provision concerning harvest asserts a major dimension of Israel's ethical tradition (vs. 9–10). The droppings of grain and grapes in harvest shall not be carefully gathered in a second effort. They shall be deliberately left in the field or vineyard for the poor and the sojourner. This economic requirement, which may cost the farmer, is an act of communalism.

3. Now follow three laws that echo the Decalogue: no stealing, no falseness, no swearing in God's name (v. 11). The first two violations are clearly disruptive of neighbor relations. These forbidden practices tend to put the weak at the disposal of the strong, for it is the strong who have capacity to seize what belongs to another, and who are able to control the flow of (false) information. Thus these prohibitions concern not isolated acts, but the capacity to subvert systemic power. The third of these commands is an assertion that God cannot be involved, manipulated, or harnessed for partisan social ends. Thus the law is a warning against the ideological use of God's name (religion) for devious social ends.

4. Two commandments are given that concern the *economically vulnerable* in the community (who are subject to oppression) and the *physically disabled* members of the community (who are subject to abuse) (vs. 13–14). The utterance of God's name identifies Yahweh as the guarantor of life and well-being for the vulnerable and the disabled.

5. Israel's holiness concerns the operation of the courts (vs. 15–16). The courts, under the aegis of Yahweh, are to do justice and to practice righteousness, that is, to administer communal power in ways to make life possible. The two temptations of courtroom manipulation are partiality and slander, both violations of God's will for life. The courts are to be a place where the community acts caringly on behalf of all its members.

6. We are familiar with the final command of v. 18. That command, however, needs to be related to the entire unit of vs. 17–18. Israelites are to "reason" (*ykḥ*, RSV) with other members of the community, that is, to adjudicate differences honestly and openly in an arena that is genuinely just. Adjudication in a reliable context is a responsible alternative to vengeance, which is always destructive.

All the laws in this text concern the neighbor; it is with the neighbor that Israel enacts its holiness. The laws are repeatedly grounded in the assertion of Yahweh, who is holy. Thus the laws link *the reality of neighbor* to *the reality of God.* Holiness in heaven is enacted as justice on earth. Israel has no viable way of holiness except in and through transformed social relations.

Psalm 119:33–40

The Psalm lection for this day is another eight-verse unit from Ps. 119, similar to the Psalm lection for the Sixth Sunday After Epiphany (see commentary for that Sunday). In this instance, however, the verses under consideration begin with the fifth letter of the Hebrew alphabet (*he*). As was true of the previous text (Ps. 119:1–8), this lection is also devoted to a consideration of the central role of God's Torah in the life of Israel. Here, as there, the poet has strung together a series of synonyms for Torah: statutes (v. 33), law (v. 34), commandments (v. 35), decrees (v. 36), ways (v. 37), promise (v. 38), ordinances (v. 39) and precepts (v. 40).

Another interesting linguistic feature of our text is the repeated use of imperatives. The NRSV correctly reflects the Hebrew where, for purposes of emphasis, the imperative verb begins each sentence. Thus the lection communicates a strong sense of urgent prayer: "Teach me, O LORD . . ." (v. 33), "Lead me . . ." (v. 35), "Confirm . . . your promise . . ." (v. 38), and the like. This linguistic device conveys an important belief of the psalmist, namely, that apart from the grace of God, man or woman is helpless in the face of the perils and temptations of life.

In the first two verses (first two lines, in the Hebrew text), there seems to be a statement of the psalmist's resolve to live according to the instruction, the Torah of God. Verse 33b, "I will observe it to the end," is a difficult phrase to interpret, but its parallel in v. 34b, "[I will] observe it with my whole heart," suggests totality of commitment. Taken together, the two verses appear to say something like this: "When I have understood your instruction, O Yahweh, I will not depart from it."

Verses 35–39 heighten the sense of dependence on God, for affirmations concerning the goodness of Torah ("I delight in it," v. 35; "your ordinances are good," v. 39) are interspersed with statements that reflect human weakness and the reality that, left to our own devices, men and women often choose that which maims life and happiness ("Turn my heart . . . not to selfish gain," v. 36; "Turn my eyes from looking at vanities," v. 37; "Turn away the disgrace that I dread," v. 39). These lines state the psalmist's understanding that the instruction of God, a gracious gift to humankind, is the one quality that enables men and women to attain peace with God and with one another. Without Torah there is death. With it there is life. This precious gift thus becomes an object of some reverence to every devoted man and woman of God.

> Oh, how I love your law!
> It is my meditation all day long.
> (Ps. 119:97)

And

> Your word is a lamp to my feet
> and a light to my path.
> (Ps. 119:105)

The life-sustaining nature of the instruction of God is highlighted in the final verse of our lection, where an intensive (piel) imperative of the verb meaning "to live" is used: "in your righteousness give me life!" (Cf. 119:25, where the identical verb form is used, which may be translated "give me life according to your word" [NRSV, "revive me"].) Nothing more clearly portrays the conviction of the poet that the life lived according to the Torah is of supreme importance.

If, by some unfortunate turn of events, the only fragment of ancient Hebrew Torah literature to survive into our time were the verses before us now, we might be permitted the opinion that the law was a narrow and self-serving instrument in ancient Israel. There is, after all, nothing here that moves the focus of our attention away from the relationship between God and the individual (notice the proliferation of first-person pronouns in the text). That the lection concludes with a prayer for the life of the pray-er would do little to dispel that conclusion.

But because of the central place of Torah in the Old Testament it is clear to us that in ancient Israel's eyes the instruction of God was as horizontal in its concern as it was vertical. Along with the (to us) irrelevant formulas concerning the sacrificial system, the law broadcasts its passion for the well-being of men and women and insists that the one who worships God must also care for his or her neighbor. Otherwise that worship becomes a mockery.

Nowhere is this more pointedly illustrated than in the passage from this day's Old Testament lection from Lev. 19:18: "You shall love your neighbor as yourself," a fundamental insight of Torah which Jesus regarded as central to all moral discourse (see Mark 12:31 and parallels; cf. Matt. 5:43, part of this day's Gospel lection).

And so this larger picture of the nature of Torah guards against a cramped and individualistic reading of Ps. 119:33–40. God's instruction is a life-giving element in human affairs, not because it results in some private contract between the Deity and that man or woman who comes to God with all the "right" beliefs or practices. Rather,

Torah brings life precisely because it lifts us out of ourselves and enables us to view our life-before-God in the true social and cosmic context to which it belongs. To cast the matter in the personal terms used by our text: God's sustaining love for me becomes the model for the love by which I work to sustain the neighbor who lives beside me. Only in accepting God's love on those terms may we claim its promise and echo the psalmist's prayer: "In your righteousness give me life!"

1 Corinthians 3:10–11, 16–23

Students of Paul often find his swift changes of metaphor frustrating. In 1 Cor. 3:9, Paul abruptly shifts from a metaphor of planting to one of building—"You are God's field, God's building"—and in our passage he carries that new metaphor through, ignoring the earlier descriptions of himself and his follow workers as tillers of the field. This change does not simply vary the language for the sake of maintaining the reader's interest. Indeed, this particular change allows Paul to introduce the theme of judgment, a theme far easier to explore in the case of a building than in the case of a farmer. The quality of a building depends directly on the work of the laborers, but who can fault the farmer if crops fail for lack of rain?

Whether or not the shift of imagery is intentional, the theme of judgment enters the letter in our passage, a theme that is surprisingly absent from the Pauline letters. In 3:10–15, it is the builders, Paul and his colleagues, who are susceptible to judgment for the quality of their work. In 3:16–18, judgment threatens anyone who might destroy the temple of God, that is, the church. What stands out here is the conviction that the church is itself so important that anyone whose behavior constitutes a threat to it stands in jeopardy of God's own judgment. The language in vs. 13–15 about the "Day" and about "fire" demonstrates the gravity with which this judgment should be regarded.

The metaphor of building also allows Paul to speak of the community as God's temple. Often vs. 16–17 are read in connection with individuals; that is, "Each one of you is God's temple and God's Spirit dwells in you personally." That kind of interpretation leads to an overemphasis on the individual and the individual's personal relationship to God. What that interpretation overlooks is the fact that the "you" in both verses is plural, not singular, so that we might translate "You are together God's temple . . . God's Spirit dwells in you together." Paul and his co-workers have built a building, a temple, out of a *group* of people, and the plural pronoun reflects that fact.

Carrying that plural through the reading of v.17 is equally important. Consistent with the context, in which an individual's actions may either contribute to or threaten the life of the community, the destruction of the temple of God to which Paul refers is some action that threatens the life of the community. Elsewhere in this letter Paul speaks about the human body as belonging to God and about the need to live in conformity with that understanding (1 Cor. 6:12–20), but here it is not the individual but the community that stands in the foreground of discussion. The importance of the community emerges in the threat of destruction against one who would destroy "God's temple."

The theme of boasting, which Paul introduces in v. 18, at first glance appears to be an abrupt intrusion into the theme of building that has dominated vs. 10–17. The unstated premise behind the transition is that boasting in one's own wisdom lies at the root of the threat to the temple, the community. This concern about boasting recalls the discussion in 1 Cor. 1:18–31 about the nature of wisdom and the appropriate and inappropriate bases for boasting.

Paul reintroduces the theme of boasting with a caution about self-deception (v. 18). Like those who evaluate the crucified Jesus by the human standards of power or wisdom (1 Cor. 1:22), those who trust in themselves deceive only themselves. Verses 19–20 of our lection reinforce this point by recalling 1 Cor. 1:20–21 and by the use of quotations from the Hebrew Bible: God's wisdom is such that human wisdom turns into foolishness by contrast. Boasting about human wisdom or about human leaders reveals a shortsightedness about God's own wisdom.

More important, boasting in human leaders demonstrates a lack of confidence in God. Verses 21b–23, with their powerful assertion that "all things" belong to believers, underscore the power of God to care for humankind. Believers may trust that all things belong to them *because* they in turn belong to Christ and Christ to God. Dividing allegiance among various Christian leaders is pointless, because it neglects the obvious fact that all human beings live within, and only within, the grasp of God.

The transitional character of this text may make it a daunting text for preaching. It both summarizes the comments Paul has been making since 1 Cor. 2:5 about the responsibilities of Christian leaders and returns to earlier points about the nature of human and divine wisdom, making it difficult to articulate a single central concern. On the other hand, each of the three themes that emerge—the responsibility of Christian leaders for their work, the necessity of upbuilding the Christian community as a whole, and the need for confidence in God—may prove to be both timely and provocative.

Matthew 5:38–48

The Gospel reading for this Sunday continues the series of consecutive lessons from Matt. 5. Any of the lessons isolated from the context can read like a horrendous burden laid on the backs of disciples, who must exhibit a righteousness that exceeds that of the scribes and Pharisees (5:20). It is critical to keep the lessons firmly anchored in the setting in Matthew shaped by the confirmation of the voice from heaven that Jesus is God's Son (3:17), by Jesus' own announcement of the imminent advent of God's reign (4:17), by the gathering of a community of followers (4:18–22), and by the demonstration of Jesus' power over disease (4:23–24). A radically new era in God's relations with the human community has been inaugurated, and in the Sermon on the Mount Jesus clarifies the nature of the new era, how it entails a reversal of values and undoubtedly evokes opposition. The lesson for today focuses on the final two antitheses established between Jesus' teaching and the teaching of the law, culminating in the command to be perfect "as your heavenly Father is perfect" (5:48).

The fifth antithesis (5:38–42) is concerned with the law of retaliation, which appears several times in the Hebrew scriptures (Ex. 21:24–25; Lev. 24:19–20; Deut. 19:21). Over against the law (which originally seems to have been intended to restrain excessive punishments), Jesus cites four examples of behavior that totally subvert the system of retaliation and depict unheard-of, unrealistic reactions to injustices. The first three involve the forgoing of legal redress—for the insult of a slap in the face, for litigation over a poor person's cloak, for the Roman soldier's demand that his burdens be carried. The fourth example touches on a religious obligation, almsgiving.

Strikingly, Jesus does not adjust the law of retaliation to make it more humane—twenty years in prison instead of capital punishment for brutal murders. It is not the improvement of this world's system he is about, but the vision of a new world, the depicting of human conduct that becomes the sign of God's rule of peace and justice.

As with many of the statements of Jesus in Matt. 5, these are uncompromising and shocking. Misunderstood, they can be easily dismissed as utopian. When taken legalistically and made the standard for community life, they have rarely been productive. They are limited in scope and extreme in their specificity. Though given in the form of legal ordinances, they represent the language of the poet. They describe very unnatural responses, and in effect assail the consciousness of the reader, forcing the contemplation of something other than business as usual in a blemished, defective world where courts of law are demanded and generosity is measured. These statements prod the imagination. Like the Beatitudes, they provoke reflection on a God whose values and commitments seem strange and who promises a brand-new starting point in human relationships.

The sixth and final antithesis (5:43–48) makes an appeal somewhat different from the other five. The statement "and hate your enemy" is not found in the Hebrew scriptures, nor in rabbinic literature. It is apparently a deduction drawn from the command to love one's neighbor, when the neighbor is limited to being a fellow Israelite. In any case, Jesus expands the circle to include specifically one's enemies.

Is this demand of Jesus unreasonable? In one sense, yes. Loving enemies is not the natural thing to do and can hardly be made the crowning expression of human love. It is not immediately translatable into political or social strategy. But the appeal to love one's enemies is not made on the ground that it is the reasonable or expedient thing to do (that is, by doing so, you might convert your enemies or at least create a better world), but rather because it reflects the character of God. The common gifts of divine grace are indiscriminate, and they become both model and stimulus for children of the Heavenly Father. Loving one's enemies may turn out to be of little practical worth and hardly prudent, but it creates signs of God's unconditional love for human beings for their own sake.

The concluding injunction to be perfect as God is perfect is a call to consistency of thought and deed, integrity of word and action, that reflects the divine pattern. Moral perfection that tiptoes around evil and avoids any taint or stain is hardly what is implied. Instead, "perfect" (*teleios*) has to do with wholeness and authenticity of relationships, genuine relationships that manifest the hidden but actual rule of God. Such relationships, which in terms of behavior show themselves in extravagant moves toward reconciliation, new attitudes between males and females, simple truth telling, outrageous expressions of generosity, and the distinctive care of one's foes, begin to flesh out the higher righteousness essential to the rule of God. The very pointedness of the rhetoric jolts the imagination to project unheard-of expressions of obedience to the "perfect" God.

EIGHTH SUNDAY AFTER EPIPHANY

Proper 3
Ordinary Time 8

The assertion of God's rule in the world, the core theme of Epiphany, requires two elemental and familiar responses: "Trust and obey," that is, *acknowledge God* and *live differently.*

The theme of trust is especially evident in the psalm and the Epistle reading. Although the psalm may lend itself to being read as a lament, the dominant theme is that a hopeful trust in God and a life of peace go hand in hand. In its own quiet manner the psalm challenges Israel to a profound "either/or," deciding on ultimate reliance and commitment.

A similar theme is struck, although in a different form, in Paul's letter. The contrast to trust in God is "boasting," self-deception, and self-sufficiency. The invitation of the Gospel is to forswear such human capacity and to trust in God's foolishness, to know that our life belongs not to ourselves, but to God.

This acknowledgment of God, however, does not culminate simply in religious commitment. It issues in a *different life in the world.* Thus the Servant in Isa. 49 has been answered, helped, and kept by God, that is, permitted a whole new life. That Servant is authorized to act and speak differently in the world, in order that the imprisoned and nullified may live freely and well. The indicative assurance issues in demanding imperatives, which derive from belonging to God. Those who trust God act in liberating, transformative ways.

The Gospel lesson is a summons to live differently in the world. Though the Gospel takes up quite concrete human problems, this instruction is not legalism, not a heavy-handed imposition of the law. It is, rather, a guidance toward wholeness, an articulation of the distinctive character of life in God's new age. In more general terms, the Epistle is also a counsel to new obedience, that the faithful community should conduct itself in new and different ways, because it is the building and planting of God. The reality of God's power makes different human relations possible.

What strikes one about this convergence of texts is that they construe the manifestation (epiphany) of God's power quite concretely toward new life in the world. The newly enacted rule of God matters in day-to-day living. Because of the rarity of God's power, and because of genuine reliance on that power, the faithful community is indeed authorized and equipped for alternative existence. The alternative begins in a deep and dangerous resolve of trust. It ends in visible obedience, not to conventional social practice, but to the resolve of God to make all things new.

Isaiah 49:8–16a

The poet celebrates the turn in Israel's situation and the richness of the future that God is about to give. The passage is addressed to the "servant" (note Isa. 42:1–9, esp. vs. 6–7). The identity of the servant, however, is completely elusive. It is enough that God recruits a human agent to intervene, to transform the situation of powerless, hopeless people.

The announcement of God begins in God's declaration of what God has intended and therefore has done (v. 8ab). God addresses the Servant (the "you" of v. 8 is singular). Four powerful verbs voice God's sovereign initiative, which has set in motion new historical possibilities:

1. "I have answered you." Apparently the Servant is one who had prayed and petitioned to God for help; now help is given.
2. "I have helped you." Perhaps the Servant had already resolved to "do good." But the Servant found himself inadequate and incapable of doing what needed to be done. Now the Servant is powerfully supported by God in new ways.
3. "I have kept you." God has guarded and ordered the Servant for the sake of a new future. The Hebrew word is "formed," that is shaped out of clay, but the NRSV follows other versions in reading "kept."
4. "I have . . . given you," that is, commissioned, authorized, and sent. The Servant is the outcome of God's initiative.

The poem turns from God's initiative to the work of the Servant (vs. 8c–9b). God's intention for covenant is now to be enacted by the Servant. The Servant is designated with three tasks, all introduced by infinitives:

1. "to establish the land." This odd phrase suggests that the land has been defeated or diminished, as it might be either by an occupying army, or a drought, or by neglect and abandonment. In light of

the context, presumably the land will be "raised up" when it is again occupied by people who will care for it and treat it as home.

2. "to apportion the desolate heritages." The word "apportion" (*nḥl*) is the standard word used in the book of Joshua for the division of the Land of Promise among the tribes. The rhetoric suggests that the land abandoned through exile will now be reassigned to the returning exiles. It is as though the history of Joshua were being reenacted, so that Israel's history in the land could begin again.

3. "to say." The Servant is to speak to prisoners and the ones in darkness. They are the ones who have been safely locked away. They have been rendered mute, invisible, and therefore absent. The Servant is to go where official persons never go, to be present where folks are almost eliminated. The Servant is authorized to say two things: "Come out." The term is the usual for exodus. Such speech is an act of liberation (cf. John 11:43). The second speech authorized for the Servant is "show yourselves," be visible, which has the force of *be, begin to exist again*, in ways that are visibly present. Thus the Servant acts decisively to restore land that has been abandoned, and to restore people who have been abandoned. The work of the Servant is to reverse the public process of deterioration through which life has become impossible for both land and people.

The poem then describes the future well-being of the ones who are authorized to "show themselves" (vs. 9c–12). As the Servant embodies covenant, so the prisoners are invited to covenantal living. The image of vs. 9c–10 is of grazing sheep who will be led into a safe, pleasant pasture, where they can graze at leisure. The good pasture for the sheep is not automatic, but comes through the caring work of the shepherd.

In v. 11 the rhetoric shifts; now God announces what God (not the shepherd) will do. The language is more like God's direct claim in v. 8. It is God who will build the highway for returning captives (cf. 40:3–4). The announcement evokes exuberant doxology, for God in this promise has *comforted* Israel, and has shown *compassion* to the desperate exiles.

Such assurance and joyous response, however, is not enough. There is yet one more exchange of doubt and assurance (vs. 14–16). Israel's doubt, expressed in v. 14, is likely a liturgical response of grief and abandonment. To this experience of being forsaken and forgotten, the divine oracle of vs. 15–16a voices one of the most poignant of all God's self-presentations. God is like a mother who never forgets God's own nursing baby. No, God is more than such a mother. For such a mother may, on rare occasion, forget the child, but Yahweh will never, never, never forget. God is the rememberer who has the name of beloved Israel written on God's own hand. Even exiles are held safely in God's powerful attentiveness.

Psalm 131

Psalm 131, for all its intense brevity, is a poem of deep emotion, which finely balances itself between two very different casts of mind. It is either a subdued cry of resignation over a life of unrealized ambition or it is a quiet statement of assurance concerning the tranquil life. Or perhaps it is both at once.

Set in the canonical context of a series of "Songs of Ascents" (Pss. 120—134), Ps. 131 is a poem of only four Hebrew lines plus a concluding summary line. Let us first consider the argument that we have here a psalm of lament over the unfulfilled life. Verse 1 (the first two Hebrew lines) is crucial in this regard. NRSV's use (three times) of the adverb "too" is not necessarily supported by the Hebrew text, and if the reader removes this word, the mood of the verse is subtly, but certainly, shifted. Instead of being an affirmation concerning the psalmist's humility, the verse now becomes a statement of regret, if not actual mourning. The psalmist has been beaten down to the extent that the psalmist's head is sunken on his chest, while elevated, purposeful reflection has been abandoned. One remembers Job (Job 3:2–26) and others in the Old Testament (e.g., 2 Sam. 18:31–19:4) who engaged in periods of deep grief over some personal loss. Without the emphatic adverb "too," the addition of which is an interpretive step by NRSV, Ps. 131:1 sounds quite like a statement of deep sadness.

If one wishes to read v. 1 in this manner, then v. 2 becomes a study in irony, or perhaps even sarcasm. To paraphrase: "My soul is as calm and quiet as a two-year-old child"—in other words, not quiet at all! How astonishing that the psalmist should choose a small child as metaphor for tranquility, for unless a recently weaned child in Israel-of-old was very different from a modern "terrible two," quietness and peace are the last qualities one would associate with it.

So perhaps the psalmist is lamenting, "I am beat down, O Lord, by all the forces of life. I have tried to subdue my emotions, but my heart is sobbing like a child." If that is the thrust of this psalm, then the final (Hebrew) line, v. 3, is an affirmation that in spite of having few apparent reasons to do so, the psalmist, whose very invocation of the name of Yahweh (v. 1) is an expression of hope, invites the entire worshiping congregation to join in this hope. It is a hope that is based on the realization that there is nowhere else to turn but to Yahweh.

But if it is possible to read Ps. 131 as a lament, it is equally possible to understand it as a song of quiet confidence and joy. In fact, there is a long tradition of translation and interpretation of this psalm, a tradition that goes back at least to the Septuagint, that "reads" the psalm in this manner. It is in this tradition that the NRSV employs the phrases "too high," "too great," "too marvelous" in v. 1. (One may wish to compare Jerusalem Bible's "Yahweh, my heart is not too haughty," or the Revised English Bible's "Lord, my heart is not proud" for v. 1a.) Considered in this light, v. 1 affirms an absence of hubris in the heart of the psalmist. This is a person who is aware of personal limitations and who has attempted to live a life within those limits. There is no inflated ego here, one that needs constant massaging in order to fend off despair. There is a simple appreciation by the psalmist of the psalmist's own worth before God, an appropriate recognition of his or her humanity and mortality.

And because the psalmist has not tried (and failed!) to be something that God did not intend for him or her to be, there has descended on this person's innermost being a marvelous peace (v. 2). It is not a peace that the psalmist has constructed for her- or himself, in spite of the first-person "I have calmed. . . ." Rather, it is like the peace that naturally ensues when a small child is with its mother. As the inevitable, God-given consequence of a mother's cradling of a child is peace in the child's heart, so God grants quietness and tranquillity to the heart of the one who, without false pride, understands his or her relation to God and to the larger world.

Because peace generates hope, the psalmist now urges the larger community of God's people to learn this hope and to live their lives according to its joyful imperatives (v. 3).

It is quite possible that Ps. 131 may be both an expression of regret over unfulfilled aspirations and a joyful song over a life of tranquil hope. Many of the psalms of lament tie closely together statements of distress and hopeful trust (e.g., Pss. 13:5–6; 22:3–5; 31:3–8, among others), and perhaps there is something of both elements here.

But surely the elements of peace and the joyful hope that surges from that peace are the dominant themes here, and in that sense the ancient tradition has it right. And what word could be more significant than one that sings of the beauty of a quiet life lived in peace and harmony before God! In our social context filled with blaring sounds, with overly aggressive personal aspirations, with greed, and with abuse of others and of ourselves, the psalmist has set an example too often undervalued: "I have calmed and quieted my soul."

1 Corinthians 4:1–5

"Servants of Christ and stewards of God's mysteries"—such language may seem exalted and exotic when read as a part of scripture, but the terms themselves are ordinary, household terms. Moving from his earlier comparisons of apostolic workers with farmers (1 Cor. 3:5–9) and with builders (3:10–15), Paul now compares himself and his colleagues with household workers. A servant (*hypēretēs*) is an assistant who might serve in a variety of contexts; a steward (*oikonomos*) is one who has oversight of a household and is directly accountable to the owner for actions taken. In other words, the apostolic workers are identified less with any power or privileges they might have than with their responsibilities. That is the case throughout Paul's letters, since the terms applied to Paul and his co-workers—slaves (*douloi*), apostles (*apostoloi*)—regularly suggest that they work at the request (or demand!) of and for the will of another.

From 1 Cor. 4:6, it seems clear that Paul has in mind at least Apollos and himself when he employs the first-person plural ("us"). Nevertheless, the point he is after applies to all Christians, not only to a limited number. All believers are responsible for their actions; all labor as "servants of Christ and stewards of God's mysteries," even if their tasks vary. The passage applies both to apostolic workers and to the members of their congregations.

The introduction of the terms "servant" and "steward" leads, not to a discussion of the role of the apostolic worker, but to an enlarged discussion of judgment (cf. 3:10–17). That this is Paul's intent seems clear, because the comment in 4:2 is so obvious as to be gratuitous. Making a point that stewards are required to be trustworthy is a little like insisting that pilots should be impervious to airsickness! The comment serves largely to introduce the issue of judgment, which dominates vs. 3–5.

Since judgment is a topic that appears infrequently in other Pauline letters but frequently in this section of 1 Corinthians, it is important to consider why that is the case. Corinthian Christians, at least as we may infer from Paul's letter, understood themselves to be beyond judgment. By virtue of their superior wisdom and their charismatic gifts, at least *some* Corinthians regarded their new life in Christ as a life of near perfection. As Henry Joel Cadbury described them, the Corinthians were "overconverted." Their own achievements not only placed the Corinthians beyond judgment but enabled them to classify and judge one another, and perhaps even Paul and his fellow workers as well.

Paul responds to the Corinthian "overconversion" in several ways, one of which is by insisting that judgment does indeed lie ahead. When the time of the Lord's return comes (4:5; cf. 3:13), the work of every person will be submitted for inspection. Just as stewards must account to their masters for the way in which property has been handled, so all will give an account before God. The details of such an accounting and its consequences Paul leaves unstated, but he insists on its inevitability. Neither Paul nor the Corinthians nor any other believer has arrived at a point where God's discernment and assessment are unnecessary.

That judgment does belong to God and to God *alone* becomes clear in the passage. Neither the judgment of the Corinthians nor that of any human body impresses Paul (4:3a). He can even assert that he does not bother with judging himself (v. 3b), for "it is the Lord who judges me." Just as it is only God who establishes what is wise and what is foolish (1 Cor. 1:18–25), so it is only God whose criteria for evaluation and judgment have any true merit.

In the middle of this passage, Paul inserts the brief comment, "I am not aware of anything against myself." Over against a conventional portrait of Paul as plagued by guilt and remorse over his persecution of the church, he here and elsewhere (see Phil. 3:6) asserts confidence that his conscience is, in fact, clear.

Although Paul's comments about judgment here have the apostolic workers in view, they speak equally well to all Christians, first-century and contemporary. For those Christians who find even the term "judgment" to be distasteful, Paul's comments stand as a powerful reminder that all human beings are God's servants and stand responsible before God for their behavior. No one escapes that accountability. For those Christians who, on the other hand, savor the prospect of judgment because they have already made judgments of their own, Paul's insistence it is God who judges may cause the tongue to pause mid-accusation. Paul's not-too-subtle point is that God requires no help or recommendations about the judgments of others.

Matthew 6:24–34

The Bible functions in the church primarily to nurture and shape the life of the community and the lives of faithful individuals in the community. It presents a peculiar God, whose character is revealed in Jesus and whose modes of operating are depicted over a long history of engagements with the chosen people. In specific ways the Bible clarifies what life under the reign of God looks like, how faithful disciples think and act, what priorities they set, and what passions control their beings. More often than not, the Bible does this not by prescribing rules, but by prodding the imaginations of the faithful, by offering scenarios, by posing questions about life without giving direct answers, by forcing readers to stop and take stock, by molding intuitions and sensitivities.

Nowhere is this more evident than in the slice of the Sermon on the Mount that is one of the assigned lessons for this Sunday (Matt. 6:24–34). The passage confronts its readers with a series of choices: serving God or pursuing wealth; trusting God or fretting over life's necessities; seeking God's rule or worrying about tomorrow. Parishioners with children to educate and retirement to anticipate are prone to laugh and dismiss Jesus' words as something relevant only to the uncomplicated life of the first century, but far too utopian to serve as practical wisdom for life in a technological world. After all, Jesus couldn't possibly have imagined what incredible pressures modern families face. "Don't worry, be happy" is a counsel of irresponsibility.

But before this text is shelved too quickly, let it work its magic and do its prodding, jostling, questioning, and molding of our sensitivities. Who can measure the ways it can and might address the stressed-out parishioner at his or her wit's end, or the disillusioned member desperately searching for a new way to value life?

There is little a commentator (or preacher) needs to say about the passage. Its images are powerful and the issues it poses are clear. It speaks for itself. Three brief observations are in order, however. First, the passage is directed primarily to disciples. The crowds apparently are meant to overhear the sermon (5:1–2), but this passage contains a specific direct address: "you of little faith" (6:30). It is an expression used often in this Gospel for the disciples in their moments of weakness, when their faith grows timid (8:26; 14:31, 16:8; 17:20). It is never used for curiosity seekers or for the crowds who are not or have not yet become followers of Jesus.

The radical either/or posed in the text and the unusual invitation to trust God's care make no sense at all unless the readers have had some experience with or at least an inkling of the strange God to be trusted. Who is going to abandon the pursuit of wealth or leave the future in God's hands unless that person has confidence that this deity keeps promises and is deeply involved in the lives of people? The persuasiveness of the passage fails completely without the readers' awareness that God's ways are not our ways, God's thoughts are not our thoughts. This is a text for the people of faith, even if only a little faith.

The second observation has to do with the sharp contrast drawn between living according to God's reign and living as the Gentiles live. The text offers no compromises between the two, no easy accommodation, and therein lies its power to probe. Readers simply find no way to escape, no way to get off the hook. For example, it's either the service of God or the service of wealth. Our instinct is to argue and hunt for a middle way, to assure ourselves that we can in fact live with divided loyalties, that our pursuit of wealth can really be a good thing if we spend our money in the right way. But the text exposes our equivocation. It does not solve for us the problem of educating children and planning for retirement. It does not give us specific rules to determine how much we can earn and still be a servant of God. It simply leaves us with the choice: God or wealth.

Or take the counsel not to worry about the necessities of life. The alternative to anxiety is the search for the reign of God (notice the "but" of 6:33). Put another way, the pursuit of God's way (that is, God's reign and righteousness), prayed for in the Lord's prayer (6:10), means breaking with a world of fretting about food and clothing, freedom from the paralyzing worry that cramps human relationships. Pushing and praying for the advent of God's reign entails trusting God for the gifts to sustain life. Again, these are alternatives modern readers naturally find unnecessary, but the text relentlessly pushes a choice.

Finally, the passage at heart issues a profound call to a *lighthearted* service of God, characterized by a reckless trust in the divine provisions. The text resists being turned into a burden to be borne by those who find its choices difficult and into a guilt-promoting device for those prone to fret too much. Instead, it invites disciples whose righteousness is to exceed that of the scribes and Pharisees (5:20) to a wholehearted, joyful pursuit of God's coming reign. The word for God used twice in the passage is "Father," the parent who feeds the birds (6:26) and clothes the fields, who knows "that you need all these things" (6:32) and who promises to provide them (6:33). The text offers gift after gift of divine care to make discipleship carefree.

Last Sunday After Epiphany

(Transfiguration Sunday)

The coming of the power of God into the midst of human reality is no ordinary event. It does not admit of precise description, and the Bible offers no simple, straightforward reportage. Nonetheless, the bible asserts that God's sovereign presence does indeed invade and inhabit the historical process. The Bible, moreover, must find language to witness to this reality, language that is clear enough to show the reality, elusive enough to honor the awe, splendor, hiddenness, and mystery of God's own self.

The Exodus reading is a primal narrative of ancient Israel. In deep deference and careful obedience, Moses enters the zone of God's glory. This odd meeting certifies the authority of Moses: he is the one who has been present before God's own self!

The glory, that is, God's unutterable, sovereign presence, according to biblical faith, is carried by historical persons. In the Old Testament, such a "carrier" is the Israelite king. Psalm 2 resorts to hymnic discourse in order to designate David (and the entire dynasty) as a means of Yahweh's sovereignty in the world. The nations are put on notice that in this human agent, God's own glory is operative in the affairs of the nations.

For Christians, the proclamation and claim of Ps. 2 are taken over in order to make a claim for Jesus as the decisive carrier of God's sovereign glory. The transfiguration story in Matthew replicates the narrative of Ex. 24 in characterizing what is not fully seen or clearly heard. Thus the account of the transfiguration leaves us with a sense that we have seen something of decisive importance, but it is not obvious or easy to say what that is. Jesus is taken up into the zone of God's glory, and so is filled with transcendent authority. Thus, in all three texts, speech about glory points to the assignment of new authority: to Moses, to David, to Jesus. The Epistle reading trades on the story of the transfiguration of Jesus. In a derivative way, the Epistle reading asserts the authority of the true teachers of the church, who rightly present and interpret the scriptural tradition.

The glory asserts that the world is not a place emptied of resilient meaning. It is filled, visited, invaded with a purpose and authority other than ours.

Exodus 24:12–18

The Epiphany season now comes to an end. The church has had a long look at the majesty and glory of God; indeed, that glory has been shown even to the nations. Now it is time to move on. As the church now must move on from Epiphany to Lent, so Israel must move on from Sinai into the wilderness, yet we are here offered one more glimpse of the glory and majesty of God.

This passage begins in *preparation* for Moses meeting with God at the top of the mountain (Ex. 24:12–14). The meeting is initiated by God; it is for the express purpose of receiving the tablets of the law. The meeting is on Yahweh's terms and for Yahweh's purpose. The initial speech of God (v. 12) evidences how fully God is in charge of the meeting.

Moses' response is immediate; he obeys (v. 13). The meeting however, is so crucial and dangerous that attention must be given to the entourage accompanying Moses. Moses takes Joshua with him. Joshua is his heir as leader; his presence draws the next generation into the awesomeness of the meeting. Moses also takes with him the "elders," seventy of them. The elders constitute the influential leaders of the community, perhaps the trusted heads of the several tribes. As the narrative advances, however, neither Joshua nor the elders can accompany all the way to the meeting. Finally Moses must go on alone, to enter the danger zone of God's holiness. (To be sure, in vs. 9–11, in a different tradition, the elders participate fully in the meeting. But not here. This account intensifies the cruciality and distinctiveness of Moses.)

Yahweh, however, is the one who counts. We are led in this narrative to an awesome moment when God makes God's own self available in Israel. God's self-giving, however, is never casual or incidental. We are dealing with a majestic sovereign who must not be infringed on or taken for granted. The splendor of God, even when made available, is kept hidden and inscrutable. There is a cloud. The cloud makes everything about God mysterious, threatening, and beyond reach. Only in the cloud comes the glory. The glory is light, the light of God's sovereign will and presence. Even that light is veiled, because God's holiness is never handed over. Moses is invited to wait in the midst of the hidden glory, in the veiled light. That is all Moses can do—wait. He waits in silence. He waits six days. He waits until God decides to act. Nothing is said. God will not be rushed. The meeting is on God's terms at God's pace for God's purposes.

On the seventh day, after a wait appropriate to God's honor, there is a voice. It is a voice hidden in cloud, mediated as glory. The voice of the Holy One calls to Moses, addresses him and summons him. This speech of God is indeed the center of the text, the center of Moses' experience, the center of Israel's faith. The specificity of what God said is not given us, not until Ex. 25:1ff. When Israel later recalls this confrontation, it remembers that:

> You heard the sound of words, but saw no form;
> There was only a voice. (Deut. 4:12)

That is all. The form would have been for Moses a stable assurance, but there was no form, no firm assurance. There was, however, a voice of sovereign insistence, and that is all. God's self-giving is command, nothing more or less.

We are not told of Moses' response. We know only that he stays in that dangerous place of glory and command for forty days and forty nights. The "forty days and forty nights" is a convention. It means a long time; it is a long, suspended time. For that time Moses was cut off from his community, situated in the awesome, demanding, transformative presence of God. It takes that exposure to God to give energy and authority to the community for its strange way of obedience in the world.

In the older tradition (before the intrusion of Ex. 25—31), the narrative moved directly from the Sinai meeting to the crisis of Ex. 32:1ff. Moses goes down from the mountain into the trouble of the community. In the life of the church year, the community goes from the glory of Epiphany to the threat of Lent.

The text in itself, however, stops short of directing the departure. We only know that Moses waits and is at risk. Moses may move into 25:1ff. and the hard work of hosting God's glory; or Moses may move with the old narrative directly to 32:1ff. and the conflicted realities of social existence. All we know thus far is that Moses has indeed met God. Because of that meeting, nothing will ever be the same.

Psalm 2

Psalm 2 is clearly a royal psalm, which must have been sung on the occasion of the coronation of one or more Davidic kings, or at their reenthronement, if such a celebration was observed in ancient Israel. It is full of militaristic and nationalistic images, and only a few of the Davidic kings could have measured up—even in a quite limited manner—to its expansionist vision of Judah's place in the political scheme of things. Yet the artificial nature of the language of this psalm was not uncommon in the ancient world, a place where priests and scribes praised their monarch in tones that reflected his often unlimited power over them.

Verse 7 suggests that the king himself is the speaker of this poem, and if that is so, it might have been recited or sung by him as a liturgical response to the act of his anointing (v. 2) by priest and/or prophet (cf. 1 Kings 1:38–40; 1 Chron. 29:22). Although the spotlight is on the monarch throughout this psalm, the real subject of the poem is Yahweh, the true King of Israel and of the world (note especially v. 4). In order to heighten the emphasis on the psalmist's conviction that the Davidic king was the representative of Yahweh, Yahweh's own words of enthronement are recited in v. 6 (note the first-person reference to Yahweh).

Verse 7, again employing a direct quote from Yahweh, affirms Yahweh's election of the king and Yahweh's paternal embrace of the new (or reenthroned) human monarch. ("Today" presumably refers to the day of enthronement or reenthronement.) Although the divinity of the ruler became a theological justification for the existence of the state among some peoples in antiquity (notably the Egyptians), the Old Testament is quite clear that no human monarch was to be confused with God. Not even David came near to being accorded that honor (see 1 Sam. 12:1–14). But the psalm insists that there is nevertheless a special relationship between Yahweh and Yahweh's representative, the human king. Yahweh has begotten the king, not as other human beings, but in his (the king's) role as regent, as embodiment of the rule of Yahweh in the life of the nation.

The dependence of the human ruler on Yahweh is stressed again in v. 8, where the monarch's suzerainty over the nations of the earth is realized not by the king himself, but only by Yahweh. In the phrase "Ask of me," the verb is in the imperative mode, implying that the human king has no option but to cast himself on the power of Yahweh, who in turn (notice the use once more of "I") will place the peoples of the earth at the king's disposal.

In the ancient liturgy of entrhonement or reenthronement a sympathetic ritual may have been employed (a not uncommon practice among ancient peoples), perhaps one in which a metal club was used to shatter pieces of earthenware, thus suggesting the manner in which Yahweh would shatter the power of the nations that resisted the Davidic king. If so, the words of v. 9 provided the descriptive commentary to this act.

Verses 10–11 reinforce the message of the Davidic king's authority over all the nations. The phrase "kiss his feet" (v. 12) reminds one of the scene on the so-called Black Obelisk of Shalmaneser III, a basalt stela which commemorates the victories of the Assyrian emperor who ruled 858–824 B.C. and which may today be seen in the British Museum. In one of its panels, the Israelite king Jehu is found with his face on the ground before the feet of the Assyrian ruler, a traditional posture of subservience (cf. Ps. 72:9).

For at least two very important reasons, Ps. 2 came to be understood messianicly by the early church. The first of these has to do with the nature of the language used in the psalm and the universal vision that it projects. No flesh-and-blood Davidic king ever measured up to these hyperbolic images. Not even the greatest of them—Solomon, Hezekiah, Josiah, or David himself—could have done justice to these verses. In the interpretation of the early church, an interpretation that the modern church affirms, only of the ultimate Davidic king may it be truly proclaimed: "The ends of the earth [are] your possession" (v. 8).

The second reason for reading this psalm as a statement about Jesus Christ is the father-son relationship described in v. 7b. "You are my son" echoes not only in the New Testament's description of Jesus' baptism (Mark 1:11 and parallels), but—as observed on this day—in the narrative of Jesus' transfiguration. Again, in the judgment of the early church, a judgment affirmed by Christians ever since, only Jesus could be described, in any essential manner, as the Son of God.

The quite justified use of this psalm as a hymn of praise to Jesus the Messiah, the true Son of God, must be accompanied by some sort of "translation" on the part of the modern Christian worshiper(s), so that language that originally conveyed the politics of imperialism is now made to speak of Christ's rule over those forces which would destroy human life and happiness. Only then may statements like those in vs. 9 and 11 be applied to Jesus Christ, the Prince of Peace. One model for this "translation" may be found in Isa. 11:1–9, where he who "strike[s] the earth with the rod of his mouth" (11:4) presides over the peaceable kingdom where "the wolf shall live with the lamb" (11:6).

2 Peter 1:16–21

Among the most mysterious stories about the life of Jesus, the transfiguration eludes simple description or moralizing. Even if he describes Peter and others as "eyewitnesses" of the transfiguration, the author of 2 Peter refers to it primarily as something that is heard: "He received honor and glory when that voice was conveyed to him. . . . We ourselves heard this voice come from heaven." For this author, the transfiguration gains its significance from what is heard and from those who hear it and become the leaders of the early church. By contrast, the Synoptic Gospels call attention to what is seen—the face of Jesus that shines "like the sun," the whiteness of his clothing, the appearance of Moses and Elijah, the cloud that comes upon them (Matt. 17:1–5).

In the context of 2 Peter, the significance of the transfiguration is christological, eschatological, and ecclesiological. The transfiguration has christological significance, just as it does in the Synoptics, by virtue of the pronouncement "This is my Son, my Beloved, with whom I am well pleased." However, in our passage the transfiguration is further identified as the point at which Jesus "received honor and glory from God the Father when that voice was conveyed to him." It would be a mistake to connect this with the questions that later informed the development of the creeds, such as when Jesus became Christ, concluding that for the author of 2 Peter, Jesus only becomes Christ at the transfiguration. Most New Testament writers are not preoccupied with that kind of question. Instead, the text is a positive assertion about the transfiguration as a moment when Jesus is exalted.

In this passage, the significance of the transfiguration is also eschatological. While the Synoptic accounts of this event connect Jesus with Moses and Elijah, and hence connect it with the fulfillment of past promises to Israel, in 2 Peter the transfiguration points forward. In 1:16 the writer insists that Jesus' coming (*parousia* in the Greek) is not a myth, but a fact. He then demonstrates the reliability of the expectation of Jesus' return by recalling the transfiguration. Just as Jesus was seen then in honor and glory, so his coming is also assured.

The eschatological character of the transfiguration emerges explicitly in 1:19, with the assertion that it is "a lamp shining in a dark place, until the day dawns and the morning star rises in your hearts." The transfiguration here becomes a promise that the glory of Jesus will again be seen when he returns. To a society accustomed to abundant light at any time and at the flick of a switch, the metaphor of light and darkness loses much of its strength. For a first-century audience, however, the metaphor would have been familiar and powerful. To wait through the night for the coming of the morning star (see also Rev. 2:28) is one thing; to wait with the comfort of a lamp—a reminder of the promised light to come and, at the same time, a real help in the darkness—is another altogether. The transfiguration, in this interpretation, is a source of Christian confidence; the glory of Jesus witnessed in the transfiguration promises the glory of all God's creation in the day to come. By virtue of that confidence, Christians live hopefully in the present, by the lamp of the transfiguration.

In addition to its christological and eschatological significance, the author of 2 Peter sees an ecclesiological importance in the transfiguration. Because the letter responds to a situation in which other Christian teachers and preachers have been interpreting the gospel in very different and unacceptable ways ("waterless springs and mists driven by a storm," 2:17), the author seeks to ground the authority of Peter in the life of Jesus. The claim to have witnessed the transfiguration is made in v. 16 and repeated in v. 18. In fact, in v. 18 the personal pronoun "we" (*hymeis*) appears, making the reference to the eyewitnesses emphatic.

In this context, the statements of vs. 20 and 21 regarding prophecy have to do with the authority of the author and his teaching over against the author's opponents. The point being made is that real prophecy (such as the prophecy inherent in the transfiguration) comes from God and not simply from human interpretation. Since Peter witnessed the transfiguration, clearly a divine act, he and his teaching may be regarded as authentic prophecy. Those who attack him, however, are not true prophets, because their message comes from within themselves rather than from God. Taken out of context, of course, vs. 20 and 21 lend themselves to the notion that the interpretation of scripture can itself be somehow divorced from human thought processes and can rely on the direct intervention of God. The apologetic intent of these verses becomes clear at the beginning of chapter 2, which takes up the problem of the "false teachers" directly.

Matthew 17:1–9

The story of the transfiguration of Jesus provides a wealth of theological motifs for preaching—the declaration of Jesus as God's Son, confirmed by the splendor and glory of the divine presence; the apparent confusion of the disciples in the face of such a revelation; the comforting words of Jesus aimed at the disciples' fear; the connection between transfiguration and resurrection. And yet the story is replete with such otherwordly dimensions—glistening faces, clothes dazzling white, the appearance and disappearance of Moses and Elijah, a voice from a bright cloud—that it is not easy to translate. Experiences of confirmation today hardly happen with all the extraordinary trappings of this one. It is no good inviting the congregation to envision themselves there on the mountain with the disciples; it taxes the imagination beyond credulity.

And so the preacher's task is set: to invite reflection on the story, yet without getting bogged down in "explanations"; to take the otherworldly features of the story with utmost seriousness, and yet to avoid a wooden literalness.

The *context of the story* in Matthew's narrative is instructive. It is sandwiched between two words of Jesus' impending suffering at Jerusalem (16:21 and 17:12). The journey beginning at Caesarea Philippi (16:13) and culminating in the triumphal entry into the Holy City (21:1) becomes a setting for Jesus' preparation of the disciples for his destiny at the hands of the religious authorities and for the implications of his suffering and death for their discipleship. At the outset of the journey is this word of confirmation—that the one who is to suffer and die, whose call the disciples have followed, is no less than the glorious, beloved Son of God.

On the last Sunday before the beginning of Lent, when the church prepares for the recollection of Jesus' suffering and death, it is appropriate to hear once again that the journey to the cross is not all shadows and gloom. There is the vision of the transfigured Jesus, stunning in his majesty, mysterious even in his revelation. Paradoxically, with Jesus suffering and glory, darkness and light, death and life belong together.

To be sure, that does *not* imply that we are always able to glimpse the wonder of the divine presence when caught in the midst of pain and rejection. Suffering is not to be romanticized. Rather, the story of the transfiguration is a pledge, God's commitment to resurrection (17:9), to the promise that the various roads to Jerusalem that faithful disciples take are glorious ways to life.

Note also *the content of the affirmation* made about Jesus in the story. First, Moses and Elijah are present on the mountain. They stay only a short time, talk with Jesus, and do nothing. But the simple mention of their names reminds the reader of the connectedness of Jesus with a long history—a history of God's deliverance of Israel from Egypt and the giving of the law at Sinai, of God's sending the prophets to call unfaithful people to grace and obedience. While the transfiguration is a promise of resurrection, it is also a fulfillment of an ancient heritage.

Second, the voice from the cloud confirms what had been announced at Jesus' baptism. Jesus is God's unique offspring. The language of a royal psalm (Ps. 2) and a Suffering Servant's song (Isa. 42) are employed together to declare God's verdict on Jesus. All the details of the story serve to heighten the distinctiveness of the One who alone is transfigured.

Third, the divine injunction to "listen to him" (17:5) evokes memories of Moses (Deut. 18:15), but also alerts the disciples, ancient and modern, to Jesus as teacher, Jesus whose words and ways are to be obeyed. Both his verbal instructions and his path of suffering and death are to shape the identity and life of his followers.

The story of the transfiguration is also a story of *the confusion of the disciples.* Matthew does not include Mark's explanation that Peter spoke as he did because "he did not know what to say, for they were terrified" (Mark 9:6). But it is clear for Matthew that Peter's offer to build three tents is a trivial, ludicrous outburst. His words seem to typify so much religious talk, ill timed and diversionary. He is interrupted in midsentence by the overshadowing cloud and the voice that speaks what is really essential. And yet neither Peter nor his two friends are judged or berated for the useless, perhaps nervous, chatter. When the cloud and the voice terrify them, Jesus does what he has done to the leper, to Peter's mother-in-law, and to the two blind men: he touches them. Then he speaks words of reassurance. It is another of the countless vignettes in the scriptures of incredible grace shown to disoriented, fumbling followers, of divine patience with impatient, confused disciples.

Ash Wednesday

In ancient Israel the symbolism of ashes was understood to be a forceful reminder of the pervasiveness of human sin and of the inevitability of human death. Ashes represented that which, in the human experience, was burned out and wasted, that which once was but is no more. This traditional emblem of grief and mourning has been adopted by the Christian church as a signal of our own sinful mortality; it has also been embraced as a muted trumpet to warn us of the coming dark days in Jesus' life: his passion and death.

The texts for this day are true to the ominous quality the observance is intended to convey. Yet they also point forward—again, in keeping with the character of Ash Wednesday—to the redemptive power of God's grace.

The Joel lection is an alarm bell in the darkness of the night. The crisis is not specified nor is it described in any type of detail, but there is no mistaking its urgency. Those who are caught in this terrible moment cannot hope to save themselves, for they are basically powerless to do anything on their own behalf. They are powerless to do anything, that is, except to repent and to open themselves to God's intervening mercy.

Psalm 51 is a classic (some might say *the* classic) piece of literature that captures the faithful man or woman of God in the act of throwing him- or herself open to God's mercy. The poet is convinced of the personal and profound manner in which he or she has offended God and shattered a relationship that God intended to be warmly intimate. In casting him- or herself on God's grace, the poet not only acknowledges God's role as the unique savior of faithful people, but acknowledges as well the inevitable result of God's intervention: a changed and redirected life.

Paul is acutely aware of the dark power of sin and mortality, as he writes to the Corinthian Christians. Yet the apostle understands that God shares the concern of faithful people over these issues, and he takes pains to point out that it is God, not we, who has taken the initiative to set matters right. Jesus Christ is the one who, by the mercy of God, has been appointed the agent of our reconciliation with God. This present moment is the *kairos* time. "Now is the day of salvation."

The lection from Matthew's record of the Sermon on the Mount is, on its surface, an extended warning against false and manipulative piety. But, at a deeper level, the passage is a declaration that God responds in mercy to the faithfulness of those who attempt to do God's will. Just how the faithful will "receive their reward" is not described, but the strong implication is that a large part of their fulfillment is bound up in their sense of engagement with the ongoing purposes of God.

Joel 2:1–2, 12–17 (A B C)

This text plunges the listener into a crisis. We know almost nothing about the historical setting of Joel. For that reason, it is impossible to identify the historical allusions of the poetry. It is enough to see that this text is a *summons to emergency* that is visible, public, and close at hand. The text is organized around two summonses to "Blow the trumpet in Zion." The first of these identifies the crisis (v. 1). The second requires a response to the crisis (v. 15).

The crisis is announced as urgent (vs. 1–2). The imperative at the beginning invites the sentry to sound a general alarm in Jerusalem. Read theologically, the trouble approaching the city is the "day of Yahweh," which comes as awesome, dreadful, irresistible threat. The crisis is that God has become an enemy attacker against God's own city and God's own people. Read militarily, the attack is a "great and powerful army" (v. 2). That is, the poem describes a military invasion.

We are not told, on the one hand, why God is attacking. On the other hand, we are not told who this great and powerful people is, or why they come. What matters for our reading of the text is that the hostility of God and the reality of human threat are spoken of in the same breath, that is, they are identical. This is not mere human politics, and it is not supernaturalist "scare theology." It is a genuinely human and immediate threat, rooted in and authorized by the will of God.

The poem is an invitation to imagine the city under deep assault. The poem intends to awaken a complacent, unnoticing citizenry to its actual situation, to evoke in it an intentional and urgent response.

The poem drives the listener to ask, "What then shall we do?" (compare Luke 3:10; Acts 2:37). That is the central question of concerned people in the midst of a crisis.

The answer to this implicit question is given: "Blow the trumpet in Zion" (v. 15). This trumpet, unlike that of v. 1, is not a warning. It is, rather, the signal for a response of profound, serious religion: authorize a fast, provide a meeting. The response urged to the military crisis wrought by God is an act of deep religious intentionality, an act of disciplining what is left from a shattered complacency, an act of obedience that breaks off all easy indifference. The community must come to its senses and honestly embrace its true situation. And that can be done only in a meeting that counters all "business as usual."

The "revision of reality" (repentance) urged by the poem is not a set of religious exercises. It is, rather, a deliberate act of re-presenting one's self vis-à-vis God, the same God who is invading the city. The summons to "return" and to "rend" (vs. 12–13) suggests that Jerusalem has forgotten who God is. When God is forgotten or distorted, society is inevitably, commensurately distorted and disordered. Thus the beginning point for rescue is to rediscern God. The rediscernment of God in v. 13 quotes one of Israel's oldest creeds, which voices the distinctiveness of Israel's God (Ex. 34:6–7).

Clearly Jerusalem has forgotten God's utter fidelity. When God's fidelity is jettisoned, human relations become unfaithful and society disintegrates. Thus the purpose of religious discipline is to remember who God really is, what is promised by God, and what is required for God.

This is an odd and suggestive text for Lent. This text plunges Lent (and us) into dangerous public reality. The text does not require dramatic overstatement of crisis, nor "hellfire and damnation."

It is clear to any observer, nonetheless, that our old, trusted, known world is under deep assault. AIDS and "crack" are only surface symptoms of a deathly sickness common to us all. That deep illness may be our counterpart to the invasion pictured in the text.

The "returning" and "rending" to which we are invited is the hard work of rediscerning God, and then making the responses—theological, socioeconomic, political, and personal—that are congruent with God's character. Lent is the reflective occasion out of which fresh discernments of reality may come. When we do not emulate God's mercy and faithfulness in the world, we are invaded by the power of death, which may take many forms. Either we turn in order to live, or we resist the choice and we die. Ash Wednesday is for renoticing our true situation, in the world and before God.

Psalm 51:1–17 (A B C)

Psalm 51 is the classic statement of repentance from the Old Testament Psalter, and so deeply has it shaped the language of confession in both Jewish and Christian communities that its very cadences often echo in synagogue and in church when worshipers address in a corporate fashion their sinfulness before God. The psalm is no less powerful a vehicle for expressing the individual's sense of sin as one makes private confession. Thus its inclusion as an Ash Wednesday lection seems almost mandatory.

The superscription relates the psalm to the terrible incident in which David seduces or rapes (the text is ambiguous) Bathsheba, the wife of Uriah the Hittite, only to be rebuked by the prophet Nathan (2 Sam. 11—12). Yet the text of the psalm itself is lacking any detail that would reinforce that claim. In fact, it is the very universality of the psalm's language about sin that has allowed it to speak to the widest possible variety of human experiences.

The language of the psalm suggests that its author was a priest, well rehearsed in the cultic vocabulary. For example, when the poet prays, "Cleanse me from my sin" (v. 2), the verb that is chosen (*ṭāhēr*) is one that frequently appears in the Priestly literature of the Old Testament to describe cultic or liturgical activity (Lev. 12:7, 8; 14:20). Another example: the reference to hyssop (v. 7) recalls other Old Testament texts in which this plant was used as a liturgical purgative (Lev. 14:4; Num. 19:6). Yet, amazingly, the cultic acts of confession and absolution do not lie at the core of the psalmist's concern, as Ps. 51:15–17 takes great pains to point out. What is of greatest importance is the transformation of the worshiper. A "clean heart," a "right spirit" (v. 10), and a "contrite heart" (v. 17) are qualities most closely associated with God's salvation. What happens to the person is infinitely more important than what happens in the cult.

Psalm 51:1–12 exhibits many of the characteristics common to psalms of individual lament. Verses 1–2 constitute a kind of salutation in which the object of the petition is named ("O God" of v. 1), yet the most urgent phrases are those in which the psalmist pleads for redemption. Notice the four imperatives: "Have mercy," "blot out," "wash me thoroughly," and "cleanse me" (vs. 1–2). The basis on which the psalmist is so bold as to claim God's forgiveness is specifically mentioned: God's "steadfast love" (*ḥesed*) and "mercy" (v. 1).

Having set the agenda, the psalmist lays bare his soul in the subsequent section (vs. 3–5), confessing his sin with profound honesty. Several characteristics of the poet's sinfulness are made evident: (1) The poet's sense of sin is haunting in that he cannot escape it (v. 3). (2) Whatever damage the author's sinful deeds may have done to other human beings, the primary offense is against God (v. 4). Although NRSV correctly reflects the Hebrew text here, "you alone" should not be read as intending to imply that humans do not sin against one another, for there are a number of Old Testament texts that state clearly that they do (see 1 Sam. 26:21). The statement apparently means that, even when other people suffer because of human wrongdoing, all sin is basically an affront to God. (3) Sin is a universal and deeply rooted part of human nature (Ps. 51:5).

In the third section (vs. 6–12), the psalmist returns to the plea for God's redeeming presence that characterized vs. 1–2. (Verse 6 offers special problems in translation and interpretation, for it is not entirely clear to what "inward being" [the Hebrew word is a very rare term—*ṭuḥôt*—apparently related to a verb meaning "to spread over"] and "secret heart" [Hebrew, "that which has been closed"] refer.) Although, as mentioned above, some of the language here is cultic, the primary focus is on the change that takes place within the individual as a result of God's redemptive activity. "Joy and gladness" (vs. 8, 12) characterize the outlook of the forgiven sinner, as do a "clean heart" and a "willing spirit" (vs. 10, 12) and an awareness of God's immediacy (v. 11).

A final section (vs. 13–17) brings the sequence of confession and restoration to an important climax, in that here the promise is made that salvation results in a changed and renewed individual. The psalm is insistent that to be forgiven is not to return to some status quo ante, to some level of consciousness where we resided before our experience of grace. Rather, to be forgiven is to be changed. It is to slough off the old and put on the new—to exchange the heart of despair for a heart of service of God. The climax to our psalm is vs. 13–14, which proclaim, in so many words: "When you have come into my life, O God, that life will never again be the same."

The distinctive place that this psalm has found in the literature of confession is the result not only of its beauty, but also of the relevance of its language, which enables it to speak to and for all varieties of sin-oppressed persons. What is more, it has claimed a home in so many hearts because it recognizes a crucial reality about the task of coming to terms with our sin, and that is, that apart from the grace of God we are absolutely incapable of dealing with the pervasiveness of human evil. It is not until we recognize our own finitude and corruption before God (v. 17) that we receive empowerment from the One who forgives and redeems.

2 Corinthians 5:20b–6:10 (A B C)

Contemporary Christians sometimes look back to the early days in the church's life with rose-tinted glasses. That period seems to have been inhabited by believers who were filled with zeal, who knew the necessity of evangelism, who had the advantages of a new and innocent faith. Read with care, Paul's letters reveal another side to the story, one in which there are conflicts, struggles, and misunderstandings. In the present passage, Paul pleads with baptized Christians, people whom he elsewhere characterizes as being "in Christ" and belonging to the "body of Christ," to become reconciled to God. The need for reconciliation is inherent in the Christian faith—it is not a symptom of degeneracy in the latter days of the church's life.

Set against the other texts assigned for Ash Wednesday (for example, Ps. 51) and other reflections on the need for reconciliation between God and humankind, 2 Cor. 5 sounds a distinctive note. Here human beings do not cry out to God for forgiveness and reconciliation, for it is God who seeks reconciliation. In the sending of Jesus Christ, God acts to reconcile the world to God (5:20a). Paul characterizes the gospel itself as God's making an appeal to human beings to be reconciled to God (5:20; 6:1). Consistent with Paul's comments elsewhere (Rom. 1:18–32), the point he makes here is that it is not God who must be appeased because of human actions; but human beings, who have turned away from God in rebellion, must accept God's appeal and be reconciled. Even in the face of the intransigence of human sin, it is God who takes the initiative to correct the situation; human beings have only to receive God's appeal.

The urgency of the appeal for this reception comes to the fore in 6:1–2. Without accepting God's reconciliation, the Corinthians will have accepted "the grace of God in vain." Moreover, the right time for this reconciliation is now: "Now is the acceptable time; see, now is the day of salvation!" This comment about time lays before the Corinthians the eschatological claim of the gospel. As in 5:16 ("from now on"), Paul insists that the Christ-event makes this appeal urgent. There is also, however, a very specific urgency that affects the Corinthian community. It is time—or past time—for them to lay aside their differences and hear in full the reconciling plea of God made through the apostles. Time is "at hand" (NRSV, near), both for the created order as a whole and for the Corinthians in particular.

Throughout the text, Paul asserts that it is God who brings about this reconciliation, but he also points to the role of Christ. God reconciles the world "in Christ," that is, by means of Christ. Specifically, God "made him to be sin who knew no sin" (5:21). To say that Christ "knew no sin," consistent with Paul's understanding of sin as a state of rebelliousness against God, means that Christ was obedient to God, that Christ submitted to God's will. That God "made him to be sin" suggests, in keeping with Rom. 8:3 and Gal. 3:13, that Christ's death on the cross had redemptive significance. Through it human beings are enabled to "become the righteousness of God" (2 Cor. 5:21b); in Christ's death the reconciling act of God becomes concrete.

Paul's eloquent plea for reconciliation stands connected to comments on the ministry that he and his co-workers are exercising among the Corinthians. Throughout this entire portion of the letter (1:1–7:16), in fact, the focus is on both the nature of the gospel and the nature of the Christian ministry. That dual focus exists not simply because Paul is once more defending himself against his critics (although he certainly is defending himself!), but because the ministry can only be understood rightly where the gospel itself is understood rightly. Paul's ministry, like his gospel, has to do with reconciling human beings to God. In 6:3–10 he expands on that role, insisting that he and his colleagues have taken every measure that might enhance the faith and growth of believers in Corinth. Ironically, he begins his itemization of the things that commend him with a list of things that would certainly not impress many readers of a résumé or letter of recommendation—afflictions, hardships, calamities, beatings, imprisonments. . . . For those who see the gospel as a means of being delivered *from* difficulties rather than *into* difficulties, Paul's commendation of the ministry will have a very negative sound. As earlier in the letter, he insists on the contrast between how the apostles are viewed by the world and how they stand before God. If the world, with its standards of measure, regards them as impostors, unknown, dying, punished, those assessments matter not at all. Before God, the apostles know that they are in fact true, well known, alive, and rejoicing.

This aspect of the passage makes powerful grist for reflection for those engaged in Christian ministry today, but it is equally relevant for all Christians, especially on Ash Wednesday. The reconciliation God brings about in Jesus Christ obliges not only ordained ministers but all Christians to proclaim the outrageous, universal, reconciling love of God.

Matthew 6:1–6, 16–21 (A B C)

The Gospel text for Ash Wednesday provides a formidable context for the self-reflection and piety characteristic of the Lenten season. The text focuses not so much on what Christians should pray for or what acts of service they should perform, as on the manner in which they are to do them. The introductory verse (Matt. 6:1) in a sense says it all, and yet the repetitive parallelism of the three examples cited (almsgiving, prayer, and fasting) carries a powerful effect beyond what a single verse can convey. The language in which the examples are described serves not only to reinforce the point, but to jar the reader a bit, to open the possibility for self-reflection about a matter like hypocrisy, which otherwise could easily be dismissed.

The passage *warns against a manipulative piety that, in effect if not by conscious design, is carried out for an audience other than God.* No one in his or her right mind sets out to be a hypocrite. It is not a planned activity. People are simply drawn into situations or habits whereby their practice of religion is meant to have an impact on others—on children, on fellow church members, on the broader community—until the need for human approval subtly becomes the idol to which worship is offered. The practice often becomes so conventional that the guilty would be surprised by the charge of hypocrisy. Part of the difficulty is this blindness to what is taking place and the fact that the religious establishment tends to thrive on the social pressures that nurture such piety.

The literary structure of the passage and its hyperbolic language, as the commentators note, serve to get the reader's attention. The three examples are given in a parallel pattern, and in each case an antithesis is set up: either sounding a trumpet when giving alms or not letting the left hand know what the right hand is doing; either praying on the street corners or in the closet at home; either parading the fact that one is fasting or disguising it. No doubt most readers would judge their own intentions and actions to be somewhere in between the extremes, but the very sharply stated polarities serve as a lens through which to clarify the ambiguities. The obscure and provisional areas are brought into focus. The alternatives present the opportunity to view one's existence afresh and to detect the dangerous tendency toward hypocrisy.

It is critical that the interpreter recognize the hyperbolic character of the language and not turn the examples into new laws. The passages do not outlaw public prayer or pledging to congregational appeals. Neither do they sanction one's boasting about praying only in the closet. Instead, they function to warn Christians about the natural tendency to use religious exercises for ulterior purposes, to engage in a piety that for whatever reason seeks social approval.

But there is a positive side to the examples cited. They *speak of God's responsiveness to a single-minded piety.* It is intriguing how frequently the notion of "reward" appears in the text. In the introductory verse (6:1), those who practice their piety to be seen by others have no reward from the Father. In the description of the three examples of ostentatious piety, it is conceded that they have a kind of reward, perhaps just the reward they are looking for, namely, that they are seen by others. In the antitheses, however, those engaged in acts of piety with integrity and wholeheartedness, oriented completely to God, will encounter a responsive Father. Three times the statement occurs, ". . . and your Father who sees in secret will reward you" (vs. 4, 6, 18).

We are not told about the nature of the divine reward. From other passages in Matthew one could speculate that the reward is the joy of the presence of God (25:21, 23), but here the issue is simply that God sees the piety practiced "in secret" and responds, in contrast to ignoring the piety done for show. The desperate need for engagement with God is satisfied when God is sought in candor and simplicity.

The concluding verses of the lesson (6:19–21) in a sense initiate a new section of the Sermon on the Mount, a section dealing with one's attitude toward material possessions (vs. 19–34). The antithetical parallelism of vs. 19–20, however, prolongs the sharp either/or choice that so dominates the previous section (vs. 1–6, 16–18). What are we to make of this uncompromising attitude toward money, over against the importance of saving a little for the rainy days? The extreme character of the antithesis leaves the church feeling a bit disquieted with the usual ways wealth is valued and turns a searchlight on the practice of how people earn and spend their money. No concrete answers are offered. The text seems more interested in where the heart is: Is it bound up with a search for security vulnerable to various forms of decay, or is it engaged in a pursuit of God's will?

First Sunday in Lent

For those churches and individuals who do not observe Ash Wednesday in some public manner, this Sunday marks the first opportunity to embrace Lenten themes within the context of corporate worship. And, as the lections for this day make clear, Lent is not the time of "bad news" that precedes the "good news" of Easter. It is a time of grace when the people of Christ reflect on their mortality and sin, as well as on the creative and re-creative power of God by which women and men are saved.

Important events associated with God's activity as Savior are recalled and rehearsed on this Sunday. The original parents of humankind were unable to resist the seductions of the serpent (the first reading), but that tragic narrative is brought to stand beside the story of Jesus' lonely and painful resistance to the power of Satan (the third reading). The old Adam's failure is redeemed by the new Adam's grace (the second reading), a victory celebrated in the psalmist's joy over sin forgiven and in his counsel to "be glad" and "rejoice."

Lent, therefore, presents itself to the worshiper as a time of introspection and confession, but one that is posited on the knowledge that those realities over which we grieve and to which we are, in certain respects, enslaved—that those realities stand condemned by the love and power of Christ. The "one man's obedience" by which "the many will be made righteous" (Rom. 5:19) is the quality that, in the end, endures. Yet there is still a gap between the attainment of that righteousness and the present state of our lives, an emptiness that takes the form of a tension between what is and what is to be. Yet the distance is not so great that it cannot be bridged by hope and trust (Ps. 32:10–11).

To engage Lent and to be engaged by it is to render oneself vulnerable to the reality of who we are as human beings. It is also to open ourselves to the nature of God as Redeemer, the One who will not abide the space that sin has created, and who insists on spanning that abyss with love.

Genesis 2:15–17; 3:1–7

This text leads the community of faith back to basics. It narrates the most foundational memory we have of our true life with God. It articulates in a cunning and understated way the incongruity between our intended life with God and the life we choose in and through other conversations. In popular usage, this text is heavily burdened by a long tradition of theological interpretation, which nearly precludes our hearing the text. Thus the task of the preacher is to move beyond our preconceived theological categories to a fresh hearing of the narrative.

God connected the first creature to the place of the garden, earthling to earth, in a delicate and intentional relation (Gen. 2:15–17). The human creature is not contextless. The garden is not unadministered. The human creature *cares for;* the garden *sustains*. That relation of caring for and being sustained by is ordered by God's decree in a quite precise way.

1. The human creature is given *a task* in the garden (v. 15). The garden cannot exist by itself, any more than can the human creature. The garden requires work, intention, and care. The human task is that of a shepherd who is to "keep" the garden the way a shepherd keeps sheep, gently and attentively. In extreme cases, the shepherd is to give his life for the sheep (see John 10:11), so we imagine the gardener is to give his life for the sake of the garden.

2. The human is given *a permit* in the garden (v. 16). All the trees are available for ease, joy, and well-being. The accent is on freedom in the garden: "Freely eat." There is in the garden a "tree of life." It is offered to humankind. They may eat of the tree of life!

3. The tone of the narrative turns ominous with the adversarial "but" (v. 17). At the center of the narrative comes *a prohibition.* The prohibition focuses on the "other tree," the tree capable of death. In v. 9 there was a second tree, the one offering "knowledge of good and evil." This is a dangerous tree, because it can disrupt the ordered way of the garden. This tree seduces humankind out of its proper role in the garden and energizes humankind beyond its proper way. It empowers humankind toward the things of God (cf. Deut. 29:29), toward a pursuit of what has been withheld from the human creature. The foundational relation of creature and creator is skewed if the "wise fruit" of the tree is pursued.

Now the narrative takes on a more threatening tone (3:1–7). The introduction of "the serpent" is as terse and as abrupt as the initial entry of God into the narrative (cf. 2:7). The introductions of 2:7 and 3:1 permit the characters of God and serpent to operate in the narrative. The two are, however, very different as characters in the plot. God acts with strong and decisive verbs: God formed, God breathed, God planted, God put, God made, God took, God commanded. God is a self-starter, capable of transformative acts. The actions of God are what we know about God. Nothing else is said about God except how God acts.

By contrast, the serpent has no strong verbs, does nothing, has no power to act, is incapable of transformative intervention. The serpent can only talk. Moreover, the narrative warns us in the characterization of the two principals. Whereas God is given no descriptive characterization, the serpent is marked by craftiness. (Notice that the word "crafty" (*'ārûm*) is a play on the word "naked" (*'ārôm*), which may indicate why the word was evoked for the serpent.) Without reference to the wordplay, however, the word "crafty" (RSV "subtle") is important for the character of the serpent. All the serpent does is to speak twice, but the speech is cunning, calculated, and powerfully manipulative:

> "Did God say . . .?" (v. 1)
> "You shall not die." (v. 4)

The first time, the serpent questions what God said. The second time, the serpent contradicts what God says. The purpose of the serpent is to counter the purpose and promise of God, to take humankind out of the zone of God's faithful speech and out of the practice of trust. The serpent makes God's speech in the garden doubtful and negotiable. The wily speech of the serpent creates options for the human creature outside the options God has voiced and authorized.

The woman and the man in turn accept the option proposed by the serpent, and thereby violate God's intention for them (v. 6). The outcome is that they "know" nakedness (v. 7). Their problem is not nakedness: the problem is that their innocence is shattered, deformed, and turned into fear. Fearfulness has entered the garden and the human enterprise. God intends a relationship of innocence; now fear creates a profound tension in relation to God.

The text invites reflection on the gift of innocence and the power of fear. Taken on its own terms, this narrative does not concern the "fall" or "original sin." It is rather a narrative that invites awareness of the contradictions that resist God's good intention and distort human innocence. The serpent disappears from Israel's narrative life, for the terrible work is done. The serpent's killing work is done through speech that is, in fact, without force or authority, but believed by gullible, mistrusting humankind. The narrative sorts out the competing, conflicting voices that seek to define human destiny. Lent is a time to sort out *the voice of life* and the *countervoices of death.* The serpent has no real gift to give, and no real acts to perform. The serpent is a means through which the gift of life is forfeited through a false construal of reality. The woman and the man misperceive their relation to God, and therefore misconstrue their place in the garden. The text is not only an exposé; it is also an invitation back to the single voice that speaks the lean truth of our future.

Psalm 32

Psalm 32 is one of the seven penitential psalms (see Pss. 6, 38, 51, 102, 130, 143), an ecclesiastical grouping that perhaps dates from Augustine. In fact, Augustine is said to have had the words of Ps. 32 written above his bed so that they would be the first thing he saw every morning (see Rowland Prothero, *The Psalms in Human Life and Experience;* New York: E. P. Dutton, 1903, p. 29; cf. Lam. 3:22–23). The psalmist's penitential posture is obviously appropriate for the observance of the season of Lent, but her or his joyful celebration of forgiveness also anticipates Easter and is appropriate for all seasons. Psalm 32 is ultimately a proclamation of the gospel, and it is not surprising that the apostle Paul cites Ps. 32:1–2 in his exposition of justification by faith through grace alone (Rom. 4:6–8).

Verses 1–5. Psalm 32 begins with two beatitudes that recall the beginning of the Psalter (see 1:1, 2:12). In fact, several other items of the vocabulary of Ps. 32 recall Ps. 1 and 2—"sin" (vs. 1, 5; cf. "sinners" in 1:1, 5); "day and night" (v. 4; cf. 1:2); "teach" (v. 8; the root is the same as "law" or "instruction" in 1:2); "way" (v. 8; cf. 1:1 [path], 6; 2:12), "wicked" (v. 10; cf. 1:1, 4, 5, 6); and "righteous" (v. 11; cf. 1:6). By defining "happiness" in terms of forgiveness, Ps. 32 functions as a warning against any tendency to misunderstand Ps. 1. To be righteous is not a matter of being sinless, but rather a matter of being forgiven, of being open to God's instruction (Ps. 1:2; see Ps. 1, Sixth Sunday After Epiphany, Year C), of trusting God rather than trusting self (Ps. 2:10–12). In fact, as Ps. 32 suggests, sin and its effects are pervasive in the life of the righteous.

Words for sin in vs. 1–2 and 5 surround the psalmist's self-description in vs. 3–4—"transgression" (vs. 1, 5), "sin" (vs. 1, 5), "iniquity"/"guilt" (vs. 2, 5). The effects of sin are real, even physical, something to which contemporary persons can also attest. But the reality of forgiveness is even more encompassing than the reality of sin, an affirmation reinforced by the literary structure of the psalm. Whereas sin encompassed the psalmist's life, God's forgiveness encompasses sin (vs. 1a, 5c). Those who do "not hide . . . iniquity" (v. 5) will be the "happy" ones "whose sin is covered" (v. 1; "hide" and "cover" are from the same Hebrew root). Verse 5c is crucial. Its pronoun "you" (God) is emphatic, and it marks the turning point of the psalm. None of the words for sin recurs after v. 5. Things are different for those who acknowledge their sin in reliance on the grace of God.

Verses 6–11. The focus of the psalmist was on herself or himself in vs. 3–5, but the reality of forgiveness apparently directs the psalmist outward. Attention now is focused on others, who are invited to share the palmist's experience (v. 6). And attention is also directed to God, who is addressed in gratitude with a profession of faith (v. 7).The emphatic "you" which opens v. 7 recalls the "you" of v. 5c. The effect is to emphasize God's character and activity. As Robert Jenson suggests, "The psalmist's own stance is that of *witness,* to his experience and to the grace of God" ("Psalm 32," *Interpretation* 33 [1979]: 175). The substance of the psalmist's witness in v. 7c points forward to vs. 10–11, which also highlight God's character and activity. The word "surround" recurs in v. 10 in conjunction with God's "steadfast love," a fundamental attribute of God (see Ex. 34:6–7, where the issue is also forgiveness). The Hebrew root translated "glad cries" in v. 7c underlies "shout for joy" in v. 11. The psalmist can invite others to "shout for joy" because God has already acted to surround her or him with "glad cries." The link between vs. 6–7 and 10–11 is also structural—the function of each verse forms a chiastic pattern as follows: invitation (v. 6), profession of faith (v. 7) . . . profession of faith (v. 10), invitation (v. 11).

The chiastic pattern of vs. 6–7, 10–11 focuses attention on vs. 8–9, which appears to be a further instance of the psalmist's witness. It is possible to understand the "I" of v. 8 as God speaking to the psalmist; however, in view of the psalmist's witness in vs. 6–7 and 10–11, it is more likely that the psalmist is speaking in vs. 8–9. As in Ps. 51, another penitential psalm, the forgiven sinner teaches others God's "way(s)" (see 51:13). This teaching ministry is not presumptuous. The psalmist witnesses not to her or his own righteousness but to God's grace. Thus, "the way you should go" points to the psalmist's example of confession of sin (v. 5) and profession of faith in God's willingness to forgive and restore (vs. 7, 10). The instruction is in essence another invitation—an invitation to others, including the readers of Ps. 32, to entrust their lives to God (v. 10) as the psalmist has done (v. 7).

Psalm 33:1 takes up the invitation with which Ps. 32 ends. A "new song" (33:3) is certainly the appropriate response to God's renewing grace. Psalm 33 also ends the same way as Ps. 32, except that the witness is made in the plural. It seems that a whole congregation has heeded the psalmist's invitation and instruction (32:6–11). The whole congregation is "glad" (33:21; cf. 32:11); they affirm their "trust" (33:21; cf. 32:10) in God's "steadfast love" (33:18, 22; cf. 32:10). Psalms 32 and 33 together demonstrate what always befits sinful human beings—confidence in and praise for God's "steadfast love" (32:10; 33:4–5) and prayer for God's "steadfast love" (33:22).

Romans 5:12–19

The relationship between sin and grace, which comes to the foreground during the season of Lent, dominates Paul's letter to the church at Rome. Beginning with Rom. 1:18, Paul relentlessly asserts both the universality of human sinfulness ("all have sinned and fall short of the glory of God," 3:23) and the universality of grace brought about through the advent of Jesus Christ ("they are now justified by his grace as a gift, through the redemption that is in Christ Jesus," 3:24). In Rom. 5:12–19, he employs the typology of Adam and Christ to explain once more the relationship between sin and grace (cf. 1 Cor. 15:20–22). The passage turns on the profound similarity and profound difference between Adam and Christ. Both act in ways that impact each and every human being, yet their actions have radically different results.

The typology begins with the action of Adam, for it is in Adam that sin and death entered the world. The personifications in Paul's statements that "sin *came into* the world" and that "death *came* through sin" (emphasis added) are not merely poetic expressions that enliven the letter; rather, they reflect Paul's understanding of sin and death as real powers that have (through Adam) invaded human existence. Sin, for Paul, is not a simply "bad" action, as we suggest when prayers refer to "sins of omission and sins of commission." Sin is a power under which humankind has lived since Adam and which causes separation from—even rejection of—God.

Sin's entry into the world is an entry into every human life. Adam is responsible for that entry, and yet Paul's understanding of Adam's responsibility differs from that ascribed to him centuries later in Augustine's view of original sin. Paul does not assert a physical transmission of sin, so that infants inherit it from their parents. For Paul, sin is universal in that it entered the world in Adam *and thereafter every human being sinned* ("because all have sinned," v. 12).

Paul introduces a note here concerning the relationship between sin and the law, a note to which he will return in chapter 7; namely, that the entry of the law only increased the power of sin. Sin already ruled even before the age of Moses and the law (5:13), but without the law there is no reckoning of sin. The law, with its prohibitions, only increases sin (5:20; cf. 7:7–12).

The second member of the typology concerns the advent of grace in the person of Jesus Christ. Paul first asserts the typology negatively, insisting that the workings of grace are not like those of sin. Here he is using a well-established Hellenistic hermeneutical principle by which one argues from the lesser to the greater. An excellent example of the principle appears in Matt. 6:25–33, when Jesus invokes God's clothing of the lilies of the field and providing food for the birds of the air: God's care for these small things means that God will also care for greater things, that is, human life. In Rom. 5, Paul contrasts the workings of a lesser man, Adam, with those of a greater man, Christ. Adam's life brought death; Jesus' life brings grace (5:15). the judgment of Adam brought condemnation, but the gift of Jesus Christ brings justification (5:16). Death's dominion because of Adam is less powerful than the dominion of righteousness because of Christ (5:17).

Despite these contrasts, the typology goes on to compare the two men once again (5:18–19). What connects the two is that each of them sets the course for all of humankind: "Therefore just as one man's trespass led to condemnation for all, so one man's act of righteousness leads to justification and life for all." All of humanity finds itself under the dominion of sin because of Adam. All of humanity likewise finds itself under the dominion of grace because of Jesus Christ.

The Adam-Christ typology rather quickly becomes convoluted, and it is appropriate to ask whether the point Paul is after is worth the trouble of explaining it. What becomes very clear in the passage, and what certainly must be affirmed, is that sin and grace are not mere alternative choices. Paul does not describe a created order in which God lays before individual human beings a choice between sin (and its consequences) and grace (and its consequences). In this sense, Augustine did understand Paul rightly (over against Pelagius), when he insisted on the absolute universality of sin. For Paul, sin and grace are alike in that each is a power and each is ushered in by a single event (the lives of Adam and Christ respectively). The two powers, however, are not to be regarded as equals, for the power of grace is immeasurably greater and more extensive even than the power of sin.

Despite the church's rejection of Pelagius centuries ago, the issues Paul raises in this text need always to be lifted up for believers, many of whom continue to understand sin as an individual act that is morally "bad" and grace as a reward for right belief or right action. Paul's acknowledgment of the universality of sin *and* of what might be called the "superuniversality" of grace comes into such a context as a genuine word of good news.

Matthew 4:1–11

The narrative of Jesus' testing by the devil in the wilderness presents the interpreter with an overabundance of riches. The place of the story in the broader narrative (particularly in conjunction with the account of Jesus' baptism), the profusion of Old Testament citations, the dramatic conflict between Jesus and Satan, the nature of divine Sonship, the role of the Spirit, the refusal of Jesus to perform miracles on demand, the several allusions to previous testings of God's people—all invite careful consideration and reflection. The preacher, facing the beginning of Lent, finds a number of directions in which to move. We mention here only three.

A beginning question might be: What do we learn from the story of Jesus' testing by the devil?

1. We learn the kind of person Jesus as God's Son is. The voice out of heaven declared him to be the beloved Son (Matt. 3:17), and now the clouds part a bit more and we catch a glimpse of Jesus' character, his sense of calling, what his vocation entails. The three testings clarify what is to be expected from the protagonist in Matthew's story.

Is Jesus to use whatever powers he possesses to satisfy his own needs, or does he rely for nurture and support on divine grace? Does he dare to think that God's word will suffice? Does Jesus need to prove to himself (and perhaps to others) that God really does care for him in a special way, or is he willing to settle for no public verification, no demonstrable evidence, to validate his distinctive relationship with the Father? How single-minded is Jesus about the vocation given him? Will he compromise a bit to enjoy the headiness of power and the thrill of control, or is it God alone whom he is to worship and serve?

What emerges from Jesus' response to the tempter's enticements is a clear sense of vocation. In the language and images of Deuteronomy, the picture is painted of who he is and who he is not. As God's Son, he lives out of divine grace. He refuses to take things into his own hands, even to gratify an understandable and basic human hunger. There is no reason to anticipate that his uniqueness will be certified by irrefutable evidence. His own trust in God does not demand a constant show of power. What he is about as the divine Son is obedience to God's will, which is set over against "the kingdoms of the world and their splendor."

2. This clear sense of vocation leads to a second thing to be learned from the narrative: Jesus is a Son to be trusted. Readers of Matthew's narrative have heard of Jesus' unusual birth, his preservation in Egypt, and his baptism by John. They have listened to the divine voice declaring Jesus to be God's Son. Now the Son undergoes severe testing by the devil. He faces challenges that invite him to embrace an easier path, to buy into a worldview that reveres royal power and guarantees certification. He is thrust into a choice between two opposing authorities, two types of existence, two ways of defining himself. Jesus emerges from the encounter as one tested and found genuine, tried and found trustworthy.

Amid the numerous options open to people to which they can orient their lives and from which they can find meaning, Jesus alone has proven worthy of trust. Matthew's narrative offers him as one who has been assaulted at his most critical point and yet has overcome. It is this dependable, reliable Jesus, worthy of confidence and commitment, who is today present to the church and alive in the world.

3. We learn also from this story of Jesus' testing clues that instruct us about our own existence. Jesus' persistence in understanding himself in terms of God's grace, his patient trust, which refuses the presumptuous temptation to force God's hand, his undivided commitment, which frees him to reject enticing alternatives—all become characteristics of faithful disciples. It is interesting that the narrative does not take the testing of Jesus and turn it into a high-priestly Christology, as does the letter to the Hebrews (for example, Heb. 4:14–16). There is no suggestion in the text that Jesus, tempted in every way, has now become an intercessor for his followers who are tempted. Rather, readers are invited to find in his experience an image of what it means to be faithful in their own lives.

The story ends on a positive note. In the final scene, when Jesus rejects the invitation to serve two masters by citing Deut. 6:13, he says, "Away with you, Satan!" And the text reads, "Then the devil left him." In the end it is not Satan who has power over Jesus, but Jesus who issues commands that Satan obeys. To be sure, Satan will return, but the secret in keeping the tempter at bay is out: it is in being faithful to one's vocation to be God's child, clinging tenaciously to the divine calling.

SECOND SUNDAY IN LENT

Faith in God and deliverance by God are themes that dominate this day's lections. The figure of Abraham is presented here as the paradigm of one who casts all baser loyalties aside and who in daring fashion entrusts life and well-being to God's benevolent care. The command in Gen. 12:1 relates not only to geography but to the orientation of Abraham's innermost being, for in leaving "your country and your kindred and your father's house" Abraham follows God's initiatives into new realms of loyalty and purpose. The migration of Israel's "first family" is a model for the movement of any person from despair to hope, from oldness to newness, from death to life. Paul's reflection on the Abraham narratives in Rom. 4 makes explicit that which is implicit in Gen. 12 and elsewhere: although Abraham might be considered to be a model of good works, such a narrow misunderstanding would be tragic. Abraham's deeds are, in reality, the result of his faith, and out of that faith issues Abraham's righteousness. The God who called Abraham and Sarah is the God who "gives life to the dead and calls into existence the things that do not exist" (Rom. 4:17), another way of affirming that the important trek of Abraham and Sarah was a journey not of the body, but of the heart and the spirit.

Another symbolic figure in this day's texts is that of Nicodemus. Although there is no mention of Abraham in John 3, there is a sense in which Nicodemus models an Abraham who has yet to leave Ur of the Chaldees, and who demonstrates little inclination to do so. Nicodemus's comprehension of God's initiatives is shallow and sterile, a misunderstanding typical of literalists who inhabit all of the world's great religions, including Christianity. His questions in John 3:4 betray an ironclad mind, which not even a well-honed figure of speech is able to penetrate. How ironic it is that Jesus' metaphor about being "born anew" (RSV) continues to be misread two millennia after Nicodemus's tragic display of dullness. As Yahweh had earlier invited Abraham to embark on an adventure of trust, Jesus invites Nicodemus to be open to the rush of God's Spirit in such a manner that his very being is renewed. It is the same invitation that is issued to all people in every age, and which the psalm for this day (Ps. 121) greets with joy.

Genesis 12:1–4a

We are told nothing of the personal life of Abraham; of Sarah we know only that she was barren (Gen. 11:30). The text has no interest in anything concerning their personal life. The text focuses clearly, simply, and abruptly on the new life to which God's intrusive speech calls them. Understood theologically, new life is evoked from a single source and requires only a single response.

The source of new life is the speech of God that completely changes the terms of Abraham's existence (12:1–3). The narrative gives us no warning or preparation, nothing about how the voice came or sounded. The new, irresistible fact of Abraham's life is the speech of God which places at the center of his existence a promise, a purpose, and a presence other than his own. God's speech calls into existence for Abraham that which does not exist, until God speaks (cf. Rom. 4:17). Abraham, in his new life, is indeed a new creature, "fresh from the Word" (to use a phrase from Eleanor Farjeon's hymn "Morning Has Broken").

God's speech to Abraham requires Abraham to embrace newness, to go where he has never been, to depart all familiar markings and reference points (v. 1). In this speech, the whole biblical journey to a new Land of Promise is initiated. This speech makes people of faith habitually restless, ready to dare, trusting only in the promise and the One who speaks it. Faith is indeed the capacity to risk what is in hand for what is yet to be given by this intrusive speaker.

Abraham's life before the speech was without a risky imperative. As far as we know, Abraham's "pre-speech" existence was also without the awesome, elusive force of promise. God speaks a massive promise to Abraham, which envisions an existence not yet in hand (vs. 2–3). It invites Abraham to live in hope, to wait for a fulfillment, to trust the promise maker to be a promise keeper. In this moment of speech, a dimension of possibility is introduced into human life that can never be dispelled by ruthless power, by flattened language, or by immobilizing ideology. In this speech, biblical faith sets up a dynamic of a gift yet to be given, a promise yet to be kept, a word yet to be enacted. That gift, promise, and word cannot be resisted by our despair, and cannot be preempted by our ingenuity. It is God's promise, kept only in God's power. The community of Abraham is the beneficiary of this good word, but never its administrator.

The promise is a gesture of well-being for which there is as yet no visible evidence. The promise is the unleashing of blessing in a world of deathly curse. The promise is that all peoples, not only this people, can share in the power of life carried by this family. The claim is that the daring journey of Abraham and Sarah and their progeny is an event of world significance, an act whereby God overrules the deathly power of life without hope.

In this moment of speech, Abraham is transformed into a daring hoper (v. 4a). He trusts the speaker. He believes the speech. He permits a new intent in his life. It is no longer possible for Abraham to live a pre-hope, un-hope existence, either in despair and defeat because of barrenness (=no future), or in pride and power as though he could create his own future.

Abraham goes, as commanded, as promised. He does not hesitate. He does not bargain or probe. He trusts immediately and completely. His immediate response is called "faith." In his moment of hearing, Abraham knows the speech of God—both command and promise—to be utterly true, true enough that he will let his life be reshaped by promise for risk. His faith will be reckoned righteousness (Gen. 15:6). It is his ready acceptance that makes him God's appropriate partner. He can, because of his ready trust, become God's good friend and confidant (cf. Gen. 18:17–18; Isa. 41:8).

Abraham begins a new, daring, dangerous journey. It is a journey all the faithful children of Abraham take as well (cf. Matt. 3:9). It is a journey from old securities to new gifts. The power of the promised blessing permits even departure from what is old and treasured. Our father Abraham heard and went, destined for utter, dangerous, wondrous newness!

Psalm 121

Psalm 121 is part of an anthology of psalms (Pss. 120–134) whose superscriptions label them as "Songs of Ascents." This has usually been interpreted to mean that many (if not all) of these were pilgrim choruses sung by those who made their way to Jerusalem for such important occasions as Passover, Weeks, or Tabernacles.

Psalm 121 shares many of the characteristics typical of this Ascents anthology. Verse 1 directs the eyes of the psalmist upward (cf. 123:1), and has been seen by some commentators as a reflection of the tendency on the part of almost all people, ancient and modern, to think of God or the gods as being elevated, while the forces of death and evil are depressed into the earth (note 1 Sam. 10:5, Prov. 15:24). But if v. 1 contains echoes of some mythological past, in its present setting it is clearly a reference to Mount Zion, the locus of the Jerusalem Temple (note Ps. 125:1–2) and of the people's encounter with Israel's God.

Verse 1 also appears to suggest that the very act of lifting one's vision serves as a reminder of the weakness of the pilgrim, for the declaration in the first line of the verse is followed by the question of the second line: "From where will my help come?" What is its source? The acknowledgment of basic need is an experience of every person, and part of the timeless appeal of the psalms is that they give voice to this and other human universals. It is possible that the question-and-answer formulation of vs. 1–2 reflects an ancient liturgical dialogue or some kind of antiphonal recitation of this text. However that may have been, the question of vs. 1 leads directly to the affirmation of v. 2.

Creation theology, such as that found in many places in the Old Testament, is foundational for biblical thought, because ancient Israel was confident that the creator God was also the compassionate God who had saved the people from their perils in the past. No one makes this connection clearer than the Second Isaiah, who frequently links creation with the liberation from Egypt, as in Isa. 42:5–9 or 51:9–11. Certain psalms also make this connection, such as Pss. 77:16–20 (compare the "deep" of v. 16 with Gen. 1:2) and 136:4–22. Thus present assistance ("My help comes") and past generative power ("who made heaven and earth") are considered as radiating from the same source.

Verses 3–4 surely had in mind the deities of Israel's neighbors, many of whom often behaved little differently from humans. (The shift from the first-person pronouns in vs. 1–2 to third-person pronouns in vs. 3–8 may, as above, reflect the manner of liturgical usage. But the grammatical change does not redirect the theological flow of the psalm.) One remembers Elijah's mocking words to the Baal prophets on Mount Carmel, when their prayers to their master produced no results: "Cry aloud! Surely he is a god; either he is meditating, or he has wandered away, or he is on a journey, or perhaps he is asleep and must be awakened" (1 Kings 18:27). But the God of Israel does not sleep.

Nor does the God of Israel ever suffer from a failure of concentration. It is in Ps. 121:3–4 that we meet the first two occurrences, out of a total of six, of some form of the word "keep." Verse 4, which literally translates as "Israel's keeper will not slumber . . .," anticipates "Yahweh is your keeper" of v. 5. That Israel's keeper and my keeper were and are the same is a source of profound comfort. The necessity for shade in a sun-drenched environment such as Israel-Palestine is a natural analog to the need on the part of weak, sinful humans for God. The reason for the mention of the moon in v. 6 is less clear. It may be a reference to ancient Near Eastern moon worship (both sun and moon were, of course, worshiped in antiquity), or "moon" may be present simply as literary balance for "sun."

The theme of God as "keeper" reaches a climax in vs. 7–8, where the verb "keep" occurs three times. Israel, which has so often been urged to "keep" the ways of Yahweh (note, for example, Deut. 6:2), is reminded that Yahweh will "keep" the people—both corporately and individually—so that the pilgrim who has come with uplifted eyes in v. 1 is reassured that his or her continued going and coming will be preserved by a benevolent Yahweh.

Romans 4:1–5, 13–17

In this, Paul's most extended discussion of the figure of Abraham, he attempts to demonstrate the point he has been developing throughout the letter—the gospel of Jesus Christ reveals God's initiative for the salvation of all people, even in the face of their sinful rebellion against God. Even Abraham, a prime example of *obedience* to God, is not an exception to this claim. Indeed, it is because of Abraham's *faith* that he can become the spiritual father of all believers, both Jew and Gentile.

Two features of Abraham's experience become important for Paul's argument: (a) *how* Abraham is declared to be righteous, and (b) *when* Abraham is declared to be righteous. Paul's discussion of how Abraham is declared righteous (Rom. 4:2–5) turns on a quotation from Gen. 15:6: "Abraham believed God, and it was reckoned to him as righteousness." Paul presses this line to its extreme, arguing as much from the silence of Genesis as from the text: Genesis does not say that Abraham did work that made him righteous, but that Abraham's faith made him righteous. He plays on the term "work," moving from the simple sense of a deed or an act to the "world of work," in which work results in pay. Had Abraham been involved with God in a world of work, God would have been obliged to pay Abraham, and Abraham would have had a cause for boasting in his accomplishments. Of course, that is what Genesis says. Abraham and God are not involved in an equal exchange, work for wages, but in an exchange that is radically different in kind. The question of how Abraham came to be regarded as righteous, then, has its answer: He believed God, and God gave him the designation of "righteous."

The second question, when Abraham was declared righteous, again finds an exegetical answer (4:6–12), although this passage falls outside the lection itself. Beginning with a quotation (from the Septuagint of Ps. 32:1–2) asserting the blessedness of the one who stands before God forgiven, Paul raises the question: Was Abraham regarded as righteous before he was circumcised or only afterward? Since the answer is clear—Abraham is called righteous *before* he is circumcised—then his righteousness depends on his faith and not on his fulfilling of the law. Circumcision, here employed in a metonymy to stand for the law as a whole, comes as a "seal" of righteousness, not as a means for achieving righteousness.

From the answers to these two questions, Paul asserts in vs. 13–17 the priority of faith over the law, an issue that emerges again and again in this portion of Romans. Eventually, the implications of this priority of faith for understanding the law will require Paul's attention (Rom. 7). Here, however, he must conclude his comments regarding Abraham. What is most significant about Abraham, based on the exegetical points Paul has argued in 4:2–12, is that Abraham is the father, not merely of the circumcised, but of all who share in his faith. Because Abraham's righteousness was declared in response to his faith and even before he obeyed the commandment of circumcision, Abraham is the prototype of the believer.

If this conclusion seems to contradict 4:1, with its apparent assertion that Abraham is "our ancestor according to the flesh," that is because the NRSV translates 4:1 wrongly. Much like 3:9 and 6:1, 4:1 actually consists of two questions, and the second clearly expects a negative answer: "What shall we say? Is Abraham our ancestor according to the flesh?" The negative answer comes first in the form of the exegetical arguments of 4:2–12, and then explicitly in vs. 11–12. Abraham is not so much a physical ancestor as he is the ancestor of all who believe.

At the end of Paul's discussion of Abraham, the question that cries out is whether Abraham's faith is work in disguise. Is Paul simply substituting the keeping of the law for a much less clearly defined requirement, namely, that one believe one's way into righteousness? Has the notion of earning salvation gone out the door only to slip in through the window? Although Paul does not explicitly take up this question, there are hints that he has in view a much more radical understanding of righteousness. In 4:5, Paul speaks of Abraham as trusting God "who justifies the ungodly." This assertion, that God justifies the ungodly—not the godly, the good, the repentant—suggests that God's action on Abraham's behalf is God's free and gracious act. Abraham's faith, Abraham's trust in God, reflects the state in which he receives God's declaration, not the condition or requirement for receiving it. Abraham cannot earn righteousness, either through deeds or through believing, for righteousness comes solely as a gift.

This interpretation finds confirmation at the end of the passage, where Paul characterizes God as the one "who gives life to the dead and calls into existence the things that do not exist." In the specific case of Abraham and Sarah, God's gift of a child did almost literally fulfill this characterization. Abraham and Sarah could in no way anticipate the miracle by which their child's life was called into being. Thus, Abraham is not only the prototype of believers but the prototype of all human beings, for whom God's gracious acts have no reason other than God's own good pleasure.

John 3:1–17

The familiarity of the story of Nicodemus and the antipathy some churchgoers feel toward the "born again" language of the passage make preaching on John 3 a challenge. How does one avoid the old ruts and discover a fresh, but still faithful, approach? Two suggestions: First, follow the flow of the story and let the descriptive details and particularly the powerful dialogue carry the sermon. Nicodemus functions as a representative figure ("a leader of the Jews," "a teacher of Israel"), and it doesn't do much good to attempt to get inside his skin and figure out what makes him tick. A psychological analysis of Nicodemus won't work. The conversation, which is highly theological, is the critical thing. Second, pay close attention to the double entendres on which the dialogue is built: anew (RSV)/from above, Spirit/wind, lift up/crucify. The ironic cast of Johannine theology emerges in the powerful wordplays.

The narrative begins at 2:23 with the statement that a faith based on the miracles ("signs") Jesus performs is inadequate. Jesus has little confidence in such a shallow belief. And Nicodemus embodies that perspective. He is impressed with what Jesus is doing and even acknowledges that his miraculous deeds are proof of God's presence with him. Nicodemus represents the curious but cautious person, the one who brings his questions to the right place but hesitantly ("by night"). Faith, he thinks, comes from weighing the evidence and drawing logical, sane conclusions. No hint of commitment or risk.

But Nicodemus puts the issue of faith the wrong way. Something more than a fascination with signs is needed. Amazement at Jesus' healings and exorcisms, at his turning water to wine and multiplication of the loaves, does not lead to the divine rule. "No one can see the kingdom of God without being born from above" (3:3). It takes another miracle, an act of God, an action from above, an event that will reorganize Nicodemus's perspective on life.

Nicodemus trips over the Greek word *anōthen*, which can mean either again, anew, or from above (3:4). As Jesus' reply in vs. 5–8 indicates, Nicodemus's problem is that he lives in a one-dimensional world, a world of "flesh." The term "flesh" denotes human existence lived in terms of its own power, organized according to norms and rewards that seem plausible, but an existence immune to the renewing power of God. There is room for religion in that world, plenty of it; Nicodemus represents it. What is lacking is the divine Spirit. The term "Spirit" denotes an entirely different world, where the blowing of the divine breezes brings a new creation. It is a world vulnerable to the untamed wind of God, a world where the windows and the skylights are open to the incredibly new.

Flesh cannot give birth to Spirit. Nicodemus cannot move from his one-dimensional world to this mysterious world of the Spirit apart from an action from above. His canons of knowledge, religious though they are, cannot grasp the strange ways of God, who persists in making all things new. Notice how Nicodemus begins his encounter with Jesus by making an assertion (v. 2), as religious teachers normally did, and ends by asking a question (v. 9), evoking a comment from Jesus (v. 10). The dynamic of the Spirit thoroughly eludes him.

The clue to the character of God's new world is the action of the Son of Man. No one can know heavenly things, except as one ascends to heaven and then descends. The Son of Man does this, but his "ascent" is really a lifting up, analogous to Moses' lifting up of a bronze serpent on a pole, which brought healing to a stricken Israel (Num. 21:9). Since the Greek word translated to be "lifted up" also means "lifted up on a cross," this "lifting up" is paradoxical. It is both an exaltation and a humiliation (see John 12:32–33). God's giving up of Jesus to death by crucifixion is the event that makes possible the life of the new world.

The passage concludes by speaking of faith again (3:15–16), but it is much different than mere amazement at miracles, without risk, much more than rational conclusions drawn from irrefutable evidence. It is commitment to the One whose death reveals the things of heaven. It is an openness to the uncontrollable wind of God. It is an embracing of the mysterious newness of God.

Third Sunday in Lent

The saving goodness of God and the need for women and men to accept that goodness in trusting and faithful ways are themes in the texts for this Sunday. Common to all the readings is an affirmation of God's benevolent care of those who place their well-being in God's hands, that is, an affirmation of God's unyielding love. Yet, although God's love may be imperishable, it is capable of being frustrated by human pride and faithlessness, so that its intended effects are shunted aside.

An important symbol of God's sustaining grace in these lections is the element of water. Although water is sometimes presented in the Bible as a metaphor for evil or death (e.g., Jonah 2:3), the text from Ex. 17, where the Israelites are wandering through an arid wilderness, portrays water as a life-sustaining substance needed by all. The dependence of the people on this element becomes a statement concerning their dependence on God, and the churlish manner in which they obtain their water stands in the text as commentary on human pride and arrogance. The Psalm lection reflects back on this episode and lifts it out of the tradition as a means of warning the people against the kind of obstinacy that impedes grace.

Water is also central to the symbolism in the passage from John 4. But here the focus is not so much on human arrogance before God as it is on the full actualization of God's love in Jesus Christ. And, in a manner typical of the style of the Fourth Gospel, this symbol is etched in such a manner that its meaning cannot be missed: "Those who drink of the water that I will give . . ." (John 4:14). The Samaritan woman finally comes to the conclusion that the conversation is not about water at all, but about the Messiahship of Jesus, the "living water."

In the text from Rom. 5, there is no reference to water, unless one wishes to include by extension the phrase "God's love has been poured into our hearts" (Rom. 5:5). Yet the reality of God's redemptive grace is as central a feature here as it is in the other passages for this day. Moreover, this grace has been expressed most convincingly in the death and life (note the sequence) of Jesus Christ. The result is a quality of human endurance and joy that, like the miracle of God's grace, may be considered as nothing less than a gift of the Holy Spirit.

Exodus 17:1–7

The exodus liberation promised a new existence for Israel, filled with joy, freedom, and well-being. However, the withdrawal from the imperial system of Egypt brought Israel only to the wilderness, which gave no well-being (Ex. 17:1a). The wilderness is a place of no water (v. 1b). The "wilderness" is a place where the guaranteed life supports of the empire are missing. Thus Israel is plunged into crisis. Such a crisis, predictably, evokes protest and dissatisfaction, which issues in an assault against Moses (v. 2).

The crisis is presented as a crisis of leadership (vs. 3–4). The Egyptian imperial system had not given dignity or freedom; it had, however, offered a steady supply of food and water in exchange for servitude. Now, out of the empire, in the leanness of wilderness faith, Israel's need and thirst and yearning lead to restlessness and an outcry against the leadership of Moses.

Moses, however, is not the real leader. Moses is only an agent for Yahweh, who is the real leader, the one who is responsible for the mismatch between expectation and delivery. For that reason, Moses questions and accuses God. He pushes the question "upstairs." He asks for a new directive from God. Moses is in jeopardy because God has not acted. Moses, along with Israel, is beginning to notice that the God of the exodus is not a great "sugar daddy" who supplies all the desires and yearnings of Israel.

Yahweh's response is abrupt and decisive (vs. 5–6). A command and a promise are issued.

The command requires Moses to act, to act in ways that appear ludicrous. Along with the elders, Moses is to strike a rock. Moses is to seek water from the most unlikely place. The contrast between hard rock and flowing water is complete. God gives no explanation, no supportive argument. The command is terse and nonnegotiable.

The promise concerns God's presiding presence: "I will be standing there in front of you." God will be present in, with, and under the action of Moses. Water will come, Israel will drink. The promise is as lean and unaccommodating as is the command. Yahweh's speech binds Israel to radical action; it also binds Yahweh to radical delivery.

Moses obeys. Yahweh delivers. Water comes; Israel drinks. The crisis is averted. The narrative tells all this in one brief sentence—no trimmings, no commentary, no explanation, no embarrassment. We are given only a simple, bare act for all to see, a lean story for all to hear. It is a situation in which Yahweh sustained life, but in lean, precarious, anxiety-producing ways that require deep trust.

The narrative offers a brief comment on the miracle just witnessed (v. 7). Until now, we have had simple, direct narrative. The narrator, however, is not content with the telling, but offers a first interpretation. The double name with such tendentious meaning indicates that the narrative has no interest in place names, but in the theological transactions in the story. The theological transaction is one of "testing," proving, challenging, and doubting God. The initial challenge to Moses is that Israel wants guarantees. In the end, Israel issues a demanding, defiant question: "Is the LORD among us or not?" (v. 7; cf. Micah 3:11). The question is a harsh insistence that Yahweh must "produce" for Israel on call. Thus if God produces, God is "among us." If God does not produce, God is absent. Thus God becomes a means and not an end, an appendage to Israel's own sense of self. Israel pushes the center of gravity away from God to its own life, an act of idolatry.

In a system devoted only to production and consumption, the role of God *as means* is all that counts. Such a reckoning, however, completely misperceives Yahweh. In this narrative, Yahweh retains all the initiative and does not exist for, or at the summons of, Israel.

Lent concerns the liturgical, spiritual, socioeconomic act of leaving the guarantees of the dominant ordering of social power, and coming to terms with the commands and promises of Yahweh. Compared to the easy gifts of the empire (gifts given with an enormous price tag), Yahweh's way in the world is lean and precarious. Like these narrative voices, we would prefer to challenge God to come to our terms. The response of God in this narrative is only a terse command, a lean promise, and life at the last minute. Israel is led to trust miracles that the empire had judged impossible.

Psalm 95

Psalm 95 is a hymn of praise, one that contains a number of parallels to the thought and phraseology of Ps. 100 (cf. esp. 95:7 and 100:3). Yet Ps. 95 possesses an additional section, vs. 7b–11, which recalls events described in Ex. 17 and which constitutes an obvious link with the Old Testament lection for this day. As in the Psalm lection for the Second Sunday in Lent, we are reminded here that the Lenten season is not exclusively a time for long faces, but is also a period of joyful praise to God. Yet the special feature of Ps. 95 is a warning concerning the implications of a covenant relationship with God.

The theme of God the Creator lies behind, and occasionally at the forefront of, the concerns of this text. This motif is most overtly displayed in the opening section, vs. 1–5, in which the people of Yahweh are urged to praise because of Yahweh's creative activity. In setting the mattering in this way, the psalmist reveals several assumptions.

(a) The mood of praise is that of joy (v. 1) and thanksgiving (v. 2).

(b) Yahweh, who formed the world, stills presides over it as its Lord (vs. 4–5).

(c) This King Yahweh demands the unqualified devotion of those who profess loyalty to him (v. 3).

One may understand, given this interweaving of thematic material with its emphasis on the sovereignty of Yahweh, why some modern scholars have identified Ps. 95 as having originally served as a kind of enthronement liturgy.

But then the focus of concern is narrowed in the second section (vs. 6–7), as the theme of Yahweh the creator of the world is shifted to that of Yahweh the creator of Israel. But the logical flow of these lines is identical to that of vs. 1–5: "Let us praise Yahweh, because he is our Maker!" The One who shaped the mountains and the seas is the One who has called Israel into being. And just as this One sustains the natural order by sovereign and never-failing care, in the same manner does Yahweh sustain Israel. The pastoral image is unavoidable:

> we are the people of his pasture,
> and the sheep of his hand. (v. 7a)

Now comes a change in mood not found in Ps. 100, with the introduction of an admonition to obedience in vs. 7b–11 (cf. a similar shift at Ps. 81:11). This third section allows the entire psalm to conclude on a note of warning, which strongly suggests that it is the primary interest of the poet. The stubbornness of Moses' contemporaries at Meribah and Massah is recalled (see comments on today's Lection from Ex. 17), with the surprising result that "for forty years I loathed that generation" (v. 10). Because of the people's intransigence, they were denied the Land of Promise (v. 11). Thus in outcome the psalm not only enjoins the people to worship the Lord with joy, but then warns them not to be obstuctionist or prideful in their relationship to Yahweh.

The conquest of pride and the subordination of one's self-serving impulses to concerns for God and one's neighbor are, by tradition, important Lenten themes, and the special nuance of Ps. 95, as found in vs. 7b–11, reinforces the importance of these concerns. Yet the force of Ps. 95, when taken in all its wholeness, goes beyond mere self-discipline. It is an affirmation of our creatureliness in the face of God's "otherness." It is an authoritative, joyous reminder that our existence is derivative from God's existence and that we best become who we would be, not when we pretend to be other than we are (the sin of pride), but when we live in a realistic and obedient relationship with God as God is: our loving Creator and King.

In the view of the Old Testament, the irony of an obedient relationship with God is not that it enslaves, as would be the case with a human master (and as was the case in serving the many gods of the ancient world—note v. 3). To serve the living God, the creator of the world and of Israel, was to enter into a relationship that not only liberated the worshiping individual and community (note, for example, Isa. 42:5–9 or Ps. 1), but which also promoted health and creativity on the part of the worshiper(s). This is the reason the psalms always link praise and joy, and in this regard special notice might be taken of Ps. 150, which boils down to something like this: Be as joyful and as creative as you possibly can in expressing loving acceptance of God's will for human life!

With all these assertions Ps. 95 stands in full agreement and, it may be noted, reserves its only negative words for those times when we all are tempted to abandon the freedom and creativity we find in our worshiping obedience of God and turn instead to our own resistive and slavish self-interests—our own Meribah and Massah. Lured by what may seem to be freedom, we abandon trust in God for what may appear to be more immediate gratifications, only to discover that we have enslaved ourselves afresh. In the midst of its joy, Ps. 95 sounds a sober note against that tragedy.

Romans 5:1–11

For many North Americans, the notion of boasting has largely negative connotations. While friends may smilingly indulge the boasting of grandparents or, perhaps, the successful fisherman, boasting more often conjures up the braggart, one who does not recognize that the world at large has little interest in his new car or her annual income. Boasting generally signifies an unacceptable preoccupation with individual accomplishment, often at the expense of others. Given those connotations of the word, it is virtually impossible to imagine a preacher summing up the significance of the gospel with the claim: "Because of God's actions in Jesus Christ we can now make grand boasts!" Of course, in Rom. 5:1–11 that is exactly what Paul does.

Earlier in Romans (2:7), Paul lashes out against those who would boast of their own accomplishments, just as he does in 1 Corinthians (1:29; 5:2). In Rom. 5, however, boasting is not only tolerated; boasting is an accepted and expected part of the response to the gospel. The difference between the two sets of passages, of course, derives from the basis on which boasting is made. Boasting in oneself, apart from an acknowledgment of the life of Jesus Christ, is utterly to be rejected. Boasting in God's actions and in their consequences for human beings, however, is tantamount to proclamation.

In this passage, Paul identifies three ways in which believers may boast: in hope, in suffering, and in God. When Christians boast in hope, it is in their "hope of sharing the glory of God" (v. 2), that is, their hope in God's final triumph as anticipated in Rom. 8. To boast in "hope" will sound very odd if hoping is understood as the equivalent of wishing. When a child "hopes" for chocolate ice cream for dessert, the child expresses a wish—a preference. That wish may or may not find a happy outcome. For Paul, however, hope is not merely wishing or relishing the idea of something that might come to pass; instead, to hope is to expect that which is certain to occur. Because of his absolute confidence in God's glory and his equal confidence in God's justification of "the ungodly," Paul can be certain that human beings will share in God's glory. In such a hope, one may and, indeed, should boast.

If the first reason for boasting lies still in the future, the second lies altogether too close at hand. Believers boast in their suffering—an idea that few would find appealing and that Paul knows will require explanation. He does not glorify suffering in and of itself, as if suffering were itself an act of piety or a reason for boasting. Suffering, however, can lead to endurance, to character, and again to hope. Verse 5 makes it clear that boasting in suffering does not mean boasting in one's own achievements, for those who endure suffering do so as a result of God's love. So understood, even boasting in one's own suffering is boasting in God.

Only at the very end of the passage, in v. 11, does Paul identify the third way in which believers may boast; they may boast in God because of the reconciliation they have received through Jesus Christ. Before he can name that boasting succinctly, he will identify the significance of Jesus' death and its results. Verses 6–10 present a tangled web of assertions to modern readers, unaccustomed to the logical principles with which Paul wrote. What he uses here is the principle or arguing from something lesser to something greater (the same principle appears in Rom. 5:12–21).

The "lesser," in this case, is the death of Christ, in itself an object of amazement, because Christ died for the ungodly. Verses 7–8 elaborate and emphasize this point. *Perhaps* someone might die for a truly good person, but Christ died for sinners! That death resulted in the justification of the ungodly. The "greater," by contrast, is the life of Christ (v. 10). If the lesser thing, Christ's *death,* ushered in the justification of the ungodly, then the greater thing, Christ's *life,* results in much more assurance of salvation and reconciliation.

Another example of arguing from the lesser to the greater runs through this same paragraph. God has already acted to save the "lesser"—the ungodly, the sinful. Now that they have been justified, how much more will God do for the "greater—those who have already been reconciled.

This is more than an enthusiastic celebration of the reconciliation of God and humankind. Paul asserts here *both* that God saves the ungodly, those who merit salvation in no way whatsoever, *and* that God pours out an excessive assurance of that salvation on those who recognize their reconciliation. It is in that reconciliation, accomplished by God alone, that believers may and should boast.

A sermon on the Christian obligation to boast might offer an interesting homiletical approach to this text, which often threatens to become lost in emotionally charged language about the virtues of suffering and endurance and hope. What must be avoided, of course, is the boasting that Christians sometimes do when they proclaim God's goodness and simultaneously draw attention to their own participation in that goodness or their own portion of it. Paul articulates here, not human virtue, but God's gracious salvation of an ungodly world.

John 4:5–42

The preacher who chooses to preach this Sunday from the Gospel reading is faced with a finely crafted story, rich in details and nuanced conversation, and raising several important themes that permeate the larger Johannine narrative. So many sermons with differing foci could be (and have been) preached from the chapter that in moving from text to sermon one is forced to make critical decisions about limits.

The full passage contains five scenes (though we shall focus only on the second one):

(1)	4:1–6	Establishing the setting
(2)	4:7–26	Jesus' conversation with the Samaritan woman
(3)	4:27–30	The return of the disciples and the departure of the woman
(4)	4:31–38	Jesus and the disciples
(5)	4:39–42	The Samaritans and the woman

Two dimensions of the story stand out. First, in a variety of ways the Samaritan woman (like Nicodemus) is confronted with the radical newness present in Jesus. Her religious understanding, her categories of judgment, her whole life are turned upside down by the conversation she has with this strange man at the well. The previous world she has known is called into question by what he says and is. So unusual is his speech that she has great difficulty understanding. She finds one who is not intimidated by the natural barriers of race and gender but addresses her as a human being. She learns from him about the mysterious "living water" that leads to eternal life. He knows the particularities of her personal situation, but does not condemn her. He points her to the new, true worship of God, which transcends the locales of Jerusalem and Gerizim.

These are not minor topics she chats about with Jesus. Their conversation has to do with an alternative way of viewing life, unlike what she has known and experienced. She is faced with "the one who comes from heaven," who "speaks the words of God" and "gives the Spirit without measure" (3:31–36). There is no possibility of business-as-usual for the Samaritan woman after this meeting with Jesus. She may or may not come to draw water again, but the circumstances of her life have been set in a new dimension.

The Samaritan woman (unlike Nicodemus) demonstrates through the conversation a growing understanding of who Jesus is. At the outset Jesus baffles her as he pushes beyond the conventional barriers to ask for a drink. Not only does he persist, however, but she persists in the conversation. She asks for living water. When he points out her personal situation, she does not dismiss him as a meddler, but acknowledges that he is a prophet. She puts to him the question of the proper place to worship and brings up the issue of the Messiah. Whether or not she finally reaches an adequate stage of faith, she certainly engages Jesus at a profound level. She bears the witness ("Come and see a man who told me everything I have ever done! He cannot be the Messiah, can he?" 4:29) that arouses the curiosity of the Samaritans at Sychar and leads to their amazing confession of Jesus (4:42).

The second prominent dimension of the story is the inclusiveness that lies at the heart of the new way present in Jesus. The fact that this incident occurs in Samaria is rather elaborately developed in the introduction (4:1–6). When faced with Jesus' request for a drink, the woman expresses her surprise that a Jewish male should make such a request of a Samaritan female. The aside of the narrator to the reader ("Jews do not share things in common with Samaritans") specifies the problem in terms of the conventions that do not allow them to share the same water dipper. When the disciples return from their trip to buy food, what astonishes them is "that he was speaking with a woman" (4:27).

Repeatedly in the narrative we find details that remind us that the new age fulfilled in the presence of Jesus breaks down barriers. No longer are Jews and Samaritans, males and females, to be thought of in isolated, segregated categories. Salvation comes "from the Jews" (4:22), but something new has occurred in Jesus. Samaritans confess him as "the Savior of the world" (4:42). Worship is centered no longer in places like the Jerusalem Temple of Mount Gerizim. The sweeping, inclusive character of Jesus' mission is a note that needs sounding again and again today. Rebuilding walls seems so much easier than tearing them down. For just that reason, the iconoclasm of this text cannot be ignored.

Fourth Sunday in Lent

This Sunday in the church's year is the occasion for the reading of texts that possess more than ordinary value. The anointing of David to be Israel's king (the first reading), the celebration of the love of Yahweh, The Good Shepherd (the psalm), and the narrative of Jesus' healing of the man born blind (the third reading) are all texts to which the people of God have turned over and over again for their descriptions of seminal events and meanings in the human encounter with God. Even the second reading, while perhaps not chiseled into the church's consciousness as deeply as the other lections, is itself a key text in the manner in which it deals with very foundational issues.

In thematic terms, the two Old Testament texts are nicely paired with each other, as are those from the New Testament. The binding element for the Old Testament texts is, of course, the figure of David. Although three thousand years of tradition have caused us to take for granted the wisdom of David's selection by God, the text from 1 Sam. 16 reminds us of the bold risk that Yahweh, who has just been frustrated in the choice of Saul, took in the anointing of this young and unheralded shepherd. The trembling of the elders and the puzzlement of Samuel over the parade of Jesse's unsuitable sons remind the reader of the vulnerability of all parties to this new undertaking in Israel's—and Yahweh's—experiment in human kingship. Psalm 23, ineradicably linked in the human memory to the person of David, celebrates the mercy and benevolence of God in a manner unsurpassed by any other biblical text. If 1 Sam. 16 causes us to wonder about the adequacy of all human shepherds, Ps. 23 reassures us that one Shepherd never fails.

The most prominent motif in the New Testament texts for this day is the tension between light and darkness as a metaphor for the conflict between goodness and evil. This tension is announced straightway in the passage from Eph. 5, where the mood is festive, as if the struggle has already been resolved: "For once you were darkness, but now in the Lord you are light" (5:8). Yet the text takes quite seriously the continuing problem of sin and the need for the people of Christ to wrestle with its power. But they do so in the knowledge that, by means of the love and presence of Jesus Christ, not even the power of evil can withstand the light. Then, as if to illustrate the power of Christ as a bringer of light, we turn to the rich and intricately told story of Jesus' healing of the man born blind in John 9.

1 Samuel 16:1–13

The Israelite community is in deep crisis. The crisis requires Israel's power and destiny to be reorganized around new leadership in the person of a king. The first effort at kingship is remembered as a miserable failure. Samuel, at the behest of Yahweh, had chosen Saul to be king (1 Sam. 9:17). Both Yahweh and Samuel had erred in that choice. Saul had not worked out. Israel continues in crisis. Samuel still seeks a king. The future depends on finding appropriate public leadership.

God initiates a new possibility for Israel and a new crisis for Samuel, the king maker (1 Sam. 16:1–3). God speaks abruptly, reprimanding Samuel (v. 1). God has "rejected" Saul as king. In enormous freedom, God continues no commitment to leadership or power arrangements that are bankrupt and have failed. God can abandon what does not work (cf. 13:13–14; 15:28).

The rebuke of Samuel by God leads to a command (v. 1). God has found a new king. God has seen (*rā'āh*), foreseen, one whom Samuel does not yet know. Samuel is to take a huge human risk to actualize God's new initiative. Samuel is frightened (v. 2a). There is no vacancy in the leadership of Israel; the throne is not empty, and kings do not look kindly on usurpers, even those who claim religious legitimacy. Yahweh instigates nothing less than a coup. God is more prepared for revolutionary activity than is Samuel.

Samuel undertakes the dangerous mission of newness, albeit fearfully and reluctantly (vs. 4–5). He goes to Bethlehem. It is a little village, largely unnoticed, not likely to be a place in which to find a new king (cf. Micah 5:2–4; Matt. 2:3–6). The elders of Bethlehem, the leaders of the village, are frightened at Samuel's coming (v. 4). Samuel is a part of Saul's entourage. Villagers have learned long ago that the central government only comes to the village to seize something—people, money, produce, or votes. Agents of the government rarely come to give, but to take. The villagers assume Samuel represents Saul. They do not know on what authority he comes to them or for what odd purpose. Either as pro-Saul or anti-Saul, Samuel is a dangerous presence for the villagers. Yahweh's newness is a threat to all parties—to Saul's old guard, to the fearful villagers, and even to Samuel.

Samuel proceeds about his business, though he still keeps his own counsel (vs. 6–11). All the sons of Jesse pass in review. While the sons are reviewed, Yahweh and Samuel carry on a conversation, much like the judges at the Miss America contest, privately conferring in whispers. The quality sought in the new king, says Yahweh, is not appearance. That mistake has already been made with Saul, and is not to be repeated. Yahweh cares not at all about appearances, but is prepared to choose one whom the world (and political bosses) may not regard highly. What counts for this new king is "the heart," the inclination and pattern of loyalty of which the candidate is capable.

The search by Samuel ends without a candidate. Samuel imagines he has made his dangerous trip for naught. Almost as an afterthought, Jesse identifies an eighth son, a little boy, a nobody, no rival to the rejected seven. Samuel is decisive: "Send and bring him" (RSV "Fetch him"). Samuel is obedient to Yahweh and trustful that Yahweh will produce a candidate. Samuel has not abandoned his own, misguided criteria for a king and will follow where Yahweh leads.

The eighth son enters (vs. 12–13). We, along with Samuel, have been told to pay no attention to appearance. The narrator, however, cannot resist what he sees. The little eighth nobody of a boy is "ruddy . . . beautiful . . .handsome." Samuel is open to the option of this nobody. Yahweh is decisive: "This is the one." God has indeed chosen one not powerful to be the shaper of the future (cf. 1 Cor. 1:26). This is the God who makes the last first, who exalts the humble.

Now, only now, very late, we are told the name of the eighth son. The narrative has teasingly withheld the name, much as a presidential nominating speech withholds the name of the candidate until the last syllable. Now we are told: David! David! David! A new name, a new leader, a new future, not as the world expected. The new leader now embodies a vision that is revolutionary and subversive, delegitimating all the old powers.

Psalm 23

There are some biblical texts that appear to the reader so limpid and clear that no commentary is required—indeed, any attempt to explicate only serves to hinder the text's power of self-communication. A number of Jesus' parables are like that, as is Ps. 23. These passages seem to project their distinctive messages so effectively that any attempt to cast additional light on them seems foolish.

Yet the more the perceptive reader opens him- or herself to these texts, the more richly intricate they make themselves to us. We may still understand their message in terms of a basic, fundamental affirmation (Ps. 23: "God is love"), yet as we listen, we grow to a new appreciation of the wondrous complexity by which this primary theme is asserted and if the subtleties by which it is rehearsed.

Much of the charm of Ps. 23 is discovered in its imagery. For many readers this the "shepherd's psalm," an unsurpassed example of the ability of the inspired Hebrew poet to bring to life statements of faith that elsewhere in the scriptures are made more prosaically (cf. Ps. 95:7). That man or woman who connects Ps. 23 with the Shepherd-watching-over-his flock metaphor has claimed a statement of faith without which our understanding of the nature of God would be very different, indeed.

But is that all? Or are there other images working here? Surely, we must add to the shepherd metaphor that of the divine bringer of peace. Verse 5 resonates to the ideal of the peaceable kingdom, which receives attention in other places within the Old Testament, such as Isa. 11:6–9, where it has messianic implications, and Zech. 8, where Jerusalem has become the New Jerusalem.

And so the shepherd of the people or, as Ps. 23 has it, the shepherd of the individual, has become the maker of peace. But still we have only begun to explicate the imagery. A close reading of the Hebrew text of v. 6 reveals an interesting fact. Virtually every English translation, from at least King James onward, has chosen to translate not the Masoretic text, but the Septuagint. That translation reads *kai to katoikein me . . .*, "and my dwelling . . . ," from which most English versions arrive at "And I shall dwell . . . ." But the Masoretic text actually reads *wěšabtî*, "and I shall return. . . ." If one translates the Greek text back into Hebrew, the difference with the Masoretic Text is quite slight, meaning that the Greek text may have it quite right. But it is equally possible that the Hebrew text has it right, and that v. 6 actually proclaims: "I shall return to the house of the Lord for the rest of my days."

The interpretive implications of this difference in translation are not earthshaking, but are nevertheless worth pondering. If the psalm begins (vs. 1–3) on a note of supervised wandering (in many English translations the verb "lead" appears twice, vs. 2 and 3—although different Hebrew verbs are involved), and if it continues with that same theme through v. 4, where the wanderer passes through the "darkest valley," is it not possible that the same image is intact in the concluding verse, where the psalmist "returns" (led by Yahweh, of course) to the house of the Lord? Or to put all of this differently, although a number of distinct metaphors for Yahweh appear in this psalm—shepherd, warrior (the "rod" and "staff" of v. 4 could be understood to be weapons of war), maker of peace—the one pervasive metaphor seems to be that of Yahweh the guide. Yahweh the fierce yet gentle companion who, though we stray, never lets us out of his benevolent keeping, giving us rest and sure direction (vs. 1–3), protecting us in the extremities of life (v. 4), and brining us home again to a reconciliation with those from whom we are alienated and to a reunion with the very Guide who has never left us.

When seen in this manner, Ps. 23 is an earlier version of the parable of the prodigal son, except that in this account the Father actually went out with the son in order to bring him home. This manner of "reading" Ps. 23 has the obvious connection with Lent in that Lent too is a story of pilgrimage. Its model is Jesus' forty days in the wilderness, a time of trial and testing in which, during much loneliness and suffering, he accepted himself and his mission—but not before considering and rejecting other options. In Lent we are also called to come to terms with who we are as Jesus' disciples, not in some nominal sense, but in terms of our visceral commitments. And these commitments, like Jesus' commitment, must be made in the process of considering and rejecting all other options—*our* temptations. In the forty days of our Lenten wilderness, we too confront the valley of extremity and other sources of suffering and loneliness with which the desert abounds.

But the promise of Ps. 23 is that, even in the desert, there are green pastures and still waters—that even in "the darkest valley" (NRSV), our benevolent Guide is there to defend us. At the conclusion of our journey, our Guide arranges a reconciliation with our enemies, even the enemy of death, as on Easter day. And finally there is the experience of our "return" to the Guide who, ironically, has never left our side.

Ephesians 5:8–14

While the advertising wizards of Madison Avenue would find the language of Ephesians hard to sell, the "before" and "after" imagery of this letter would be right at home in the league of the hard sell. Ephesians 5:8–14 begins with the before-and-after imagery that dominates the letter ("For once you were darkness, but now in the Lord you are light"). The writer has already spoken of the audience as those who had been dead but now live (2:1–10), as Gentiles before but now brought near to Christ (2:11–22), as children before but now matured (4:14–16). In this section of the letter the before-and-after imagery becomes ethical in its thrust, as the focus changes from what God has done for believers to what is expected of them as a result of God's action.

The stark contrast stated in v. 5:8 warrants attention. English translation can scarcely do justice to the simple but eloquent juxtaposition here, which could be rendered somewhat literally as: "You were then darkness, but now light in the Lord." The contrast between darkness and light, a proverbial means of referring to conversion in many religious traditions, reflects the universal human experience of the powerlessness of life in the darkness, whether induced by a modern power failure or the simple onset of night in an age before electricity. When the darkness of night comes, the eyes cannot see.

Of course, the before-and-after contrast this text envisions arises not on Madison Avenue's terms, by individual achievement or acquisition, but "in the Lord." The juxtaposition in v. 8 is uneven, since the Lord stands on one side of the contrast only. Indeed, what makes the darkness hopeless and helpless is the fact that the Lord is *not* there; life within the darkness is utterly alone. The closing line of the passage reinforces this point, as it is Christ who brings, who embodies, the light in which believers dwell. Those who awake from sleep do so entirely because of Christ's light.

That believers exist within the light of Christ here becomes the basis for ethical admonition: "Live as children of light" (v. 8). The implications of this admonition are several. First, it means that the children of light will associate themselves with the good. They will actively seek to determine that which pleases God (v. 10). Second, they will not only avoid the darkness, but expose it (v. 11). Verse 12, with its delicate reluctance even to mention the actions associated with darkness, causes the imagination to speculate on specific persons and actions the writer may have had in mind, but the point of the verse is rather that the "works of darkness" are too terrible even to discuss. What is important is that those works be exposed by the light so that the light may redeem them. The third implication of the admonition to live as children of the light, then, is that the light has the power to rescue those who are in darkness.

This sort of ethical dualism, which pits the members of a religious community over against those who are outside that community, appears in many places in the New Testament. Many Pauline texts, for example, reflect such dualism, as do the Gospel of John and the Johannine epistles. While the language is familiar, the problems of the language need to be frankly acknowledged. A cursory reading of this passage might reinforce a kind of self-righteous division between those who are "churched" and those who are "unchurched." Members of various Christian traditions, and even members within Christian communities, sometimes adopt the notion that they alone may legitimately claim to be the "children of light." In addition to his highly divisive way of reading such passages, ethical dualism can be used in a self-congratulatory manner, as if an individual or community managed to move itself from darkness into the light. The temptation to replace God with human achievement is universal, and that temptation finds in the language of "light" and "darkness" altogether too easy a resource. Discussing this passage apart from the strong doxological character of Ephesians can produce the assumption that believers can simply *will* to live in the light and need little or no help to do that.

The pitfalls of ethical dualism are many, but it also presents numerous possibilities for Christian proclamation and education. In Ephesians, more clearly even than elsewhere in the New Testament, the children of light know that they exist in the light because and only because God "has blessed us in Christ with every spiritual blessing in the heavenly places" (1:3). The light is theirs as God's gift, and the language of ethical dualism clearly identifies it as such. To say that believers exist in the light, in other words, is to say a word about God—not about human beings. At the same time, to claim that the gift of light comes from God is also to claim that God stands behind and empowers God's people. The light strengthens and enables those who live within it. They are no longer helpless and alone. Finally, while the identification of light and darkness has the potential for being used in harmful and divisive ways, it can also be, as it most often is in the New Testament, a way of creating community where none exists. Those who live in the light do so *together*.

John 9:1–41

Few stories in the New Testament are told as well as the story of the healing of the blind man. Scenes are smoothly connected; characters unfold before our eyes; questions are employed in a timely fashion; and above all, the crisp dialogue, ironic at almost every point, unveils the satire of a blind man who comes to see and sees people who prove themselves blind. It is a story of high drama, staged in seven scenes.

1. Jesus, the disciples, and the blind man (9:1–7)
2. The blind man and his neighbors (9:8–12)
3. The blind man and the Pharisees (9:13–17)
4. The Pharisees and the parents (9:18–23)
5. The Pharisees and the blind man (9:24–34)
6. Jesus and the blind man (9:35–38)
7. Jesus and the Pharisees (9:39–41)

While the story is a work of art to be admired, it also raises powerful questions with readers who identify with this or that character and find themselves exposed by their identifications: with the blind man who gains his sight and, amid pressures and rejection, also faith; with curious but meddling neighbors; with accusing Pharisees who seem to know it all; with intimidated parents who fear the truth and its consequences. In a sense, the story needs only to be told, not preached on. It makes its own theological claims.

Here are four observations on the narrative (though a dozen more could be made). First, the beginning and end of the story are concerned with the matter of sin. The disciples ask, "Who sinned, this man or his parents?" (9:2). The religious authorities have an answer (v. 34) and so does Jesus (v. 3). The religious authorities also are certain that Jesus is a sinner (v. 24), but in the end it is they, quick in their judgment and rigid in their theological analysis, who bear the label "sinners" (v. 41). The narrative is about their false certitude, their claims to see while they live in deep darkness. "I came into this world for judgment so that those who do not see may see, and those who do see may become blind" (v. 39).

Second, the frequency of the verb "know" in the story is remarkable (vs. 12, 20, 21, 24, 25, 29, 30). *Who* knows and *how* one knows are at issue in the text. The blind man initially admits his lack of knowledge (v. 12), and under questioning by the Pharisees continues in his agnosticism about Jesus but clings to his experience, the one thing he does know (v. 25). Jesus reorients the issue of knowledge for him by raising the question of faith (v. 35), and faith leads to worship (v. 38). The progression is instructive. The parents of the blind man, however, cannot claim what they do know. The threat of rejection frightens them into silence. The Pharisees are certain in their knowledge (9:24), but that very certainty prevents their openness to Jesus and where his authority comes from (v. 29).

Throughout the story, the blind man makes significant steps in his knowledge of Jesus—seeing him as a prophet (v. 17), then as a man from God (v. 33)—but only when Jesus discloses himself is there faith and worship. In a sense, the blind man, though miraculously healed, can get no farther than the miracle until the revelation occurs (v. 37).

A third observation that the Pharisees, with their demanding questions, paradoxically push the blind man toward faith. Initially, they ask him to retell the story of his healing, and in doing so he concludes that Jesus must be a prophet (v. 17). Then they demand that he give glory to God by denouncing Jesus as a sinner (v. 24). At this point, the blind man takes the initiative in the conversation by teasingly accusing the Pharisees of wanting to become Jesus' disciples (v. 27) and then by using their own theological stance to argue that Jesus must be God's messenger (vs. 30–33). His argument runs: God listens only to obedient people. God has obviously heard Jesus, since Jesus miraculously opened my eyes. Jesus, therefore, must be an agent of God. The Pharisees cannot argue with the sound logic of his argument. They can only act angrily at the conclusion he draws.

Fourth, Jesus is physically absent from the action during much of this story. As soon as the blind man goes to wash in the pool of Siloam, Jesus disappears and does not reappear until the blind man is cast out of the synagogue. And yet in his absence Jesus is the main issue at stake. How do characters respond to him? With honesty and increasing knowledge? With curiosity? With fear? With anger and threats? He is still the main issue at stake in human life.

Not surprisingly, Jesus reappears in the story just at the moment when the blind man is cast out of the synagogue. Cut off from family and religion, from heritage and home, the blind man is sought out by Jesus and offered the possibility of faith. No doubt many of the initial readers of John's Gospel found in Jesus' reappearance a great sense of hope. Many of them had also been ostracized from the synagogue. They were likely a community who had found faith outside the regular bounds of religion. And there on the outside they could anticipate the presence of Jesus.

Fifth Sunday in Lent

Lent proves difficult for many Christians, perhaps especially North American Christians, for it recalls not only the intractable reality of human alienation and sin, but also the inability of human beings to save themselves from that reality. Confronted with the multiple problems of contemporary society, whether of health, economics, social justice, or the environment, a conventional response is to ask, "What do we do?"

By contrast, the readings for this Sunday forcefully claim that it is not within human power to "solve" the problem of sin. All four readings present some profound human problem for which the response might well be, "What do I do?" The prophet surveys the valley of dry bones, symbolic of an unrepentant Israel, and asks God how to bring about their enfleshment. Paul's contrast between life in the flesh and life in the spirit provokes the question of how one moves from the realm of the flesh to that of the spirit. Even the psalm and the story of Lazarus prompt a parallel question, for death itself leaves many of us asking what we can do, and what we should do, how we can alter the situation so that it proves less devastating.

Strikingly, none of the texts answers that question, for these are instances in which human beings can do nothing. The dry bones in Ezek. 37 cannot find flesh for themselves; they cannot even cry out to God for help. Only God can breathe renewal into human life, send the Spirit, raise the dead. Humans can do nothing to "solve" the problem of human sinfulness apart from the God who can raise even dry bones. The psalmist rightly concludes that only God can "redeem Israel from all its iniquities."

The difficulty Lent poses, then, is that it recalls not only the depth of human sin, but also the inability of human beings to "solve" their own problems. Rather than wallow in this powerlessness, however, the texts call for recognition that God, who alone holds the power of life and death, can and does bring about the triumph over what Paul would call the realm of the flesh. Of course, that triumph does not always find welcome, as the story of Lazarus dramatically reveals.

Ezekiel 37:1–14

The prophet is led to the valley by the hand and spirit of God. In that valley the prophet experiences two stunning newnesses—first a vision of God's utter sovereignty, and second the newness of life created by God's sovereignty. Both God's sovereignty and newness of life are impossibilities as judged by the conditions of the valley, which is filled only with dry bones.

The initial conversation between God and the prophet poses the most urgent question of Israel's faith (Ezek. 37:1–3). Ezekiel is shown the valley. It is full of bones. They are dry, very dry which means they have nothing of the power of life about them. The question is, "Can these bones live?" (v. 3). This is always the question for Israel. Can a rescue be worked? Can the blind see, can the lame walk, can the poor rejoice? (cf. Luke 7:22). Can the power for life override the reality of death? Asked in many ways, the urgent question is: Is there a future for those who are in the power of death?

Ezekiel's response to the question is prudent but exactly right: "Lord GOD, you know." Only God can answer. This is not a question permitting human response, because the power for life is held only by God. Only God knows, not because God has "information," but because only God has the power to make life happen.

God accepts the verdict of the prophet (vs. 4–10). God does indeed know the future of the bones. And God will give an affirmative answer. Yes, God knows. Yes, the bones can live. Yes, newness is possible.

1. God makes a self-announcement that is a powerful promise (vs. 4–6). The promise is cast in a series of first-person, powerful verbs: I will cause breath, I will lay sinews, I will cause flesh, I will cover, I will put breath. The text gives no hint about how this happens. It is in the power of God. God intends it, and clearly will do it.

Two outcomes are anticipated from God's sovereign action. The bones will live; the bones will know that it is Yahweh who causes newness. The two statements belong together. Living and knowing Yahweh are practically synonymous. That is how we live, by knowing who Yahweh is.

2. The promise is kept (vs. 7–8). In the very speaking of the words, life comes. This is life "fresh from the word." The bones rattle with vitality. There is sinew and flesh. However, God has not yet kept the

full promise of vs. 5–6. There is still no breath. The task is unfinished. The difficult part remains. One can assemble a working body; it is the inscrutable power of life that is still withheld.

3. The breath (wind, spirit) is given (vs. 9–10). The prophet is invited to summon the wind, the wind that breathes life and newness and possibility. At the command of God, at the speech of the prophet, breath comes (cf. John 3:8).Wind invades. There is life. The bones can function again.

This detailed, sequenced narrative enacts four affirmations, which converge: (a) It is God, only God, who creates new life. (b) The speech of the prophet is the means whereby God's newness comes. This speech is concrete, human speech. (c) The command of God and the speech of the prophet evoke a resurrection to new life. This is indeed a resurrection event. (d) The narrative account of the resurrection is cast as a retelling of the creation story—first the forming of the body, then the breath of life (cf. Gen. 2:4b–7). This is a powerful moment of creation, when God's sovereign purpose for life overrides the threat of nullity.

Thus far the vision narrative keeps us in suspense. We do not know what the valley or the bones are. The vision narrative concludes with interpretive comments that tie the prophetic experience to the reality of Israel's life (vs. 11–14). The connection to public reality is made quickly and directly (v. 11). The bones are the house of Israel. The valley refers to exile, where the bones of Israel are dry, cut off, and without hope. Thus the initial question, "Can these bones live?" is in fact, "Do the exiles have a future? Can a community that is displaced prosper in its home again?"

After the interpretive comment of v. 11, the sovereign power of God is reasserted:

I will open your graves,
I will raise you,
I will bring you home,
I will open your graves,
I will raise you,
I will put my spirit within you,
I will place you in your own land.

The text is about homecoming. The announcement concerns the resumption of free, functioning historical existence. "Resurrection" is in fact a metaphor for God's capacity to work a newness in the historical process. Because the metaphor of resurrection serves the reality of exile and homecoming, faith claims about resurrection can be understood afresh in public, historical ways.

The preacher must take care that this text is kept focused on historical possibility, on the power of communities to function, and not reduce the text to "spiritual," private matters. The issue posed in the text is whether powerless communities can again participate in the power of public life. The answer is, "Yes!"

The text continues to pose questions about communities of oppressed, defeated peoples. In our time we watch while the dry bones of oppressed peasant communities and enslaved black communities are permitted (by the power of God) reentry into public history. There are indeed "dry seasons" of defeat and despair. (On the phrase, see André Brink, *A Dry White Season;* New York: Penguin Books, 1984). God, however, is restless and intent. When a community is permitted a homecoming to its own proper place, it notices that there is new life, joy, and vitality. It also dares to confess, whenever there is such homecoming and restoration, that God's sovereignty is visible. In the end, the text concludes not by celebrating Israel's new life, but by asserting Yahweh's faithful, powerful sovereignty, which works newness. The claim made for God stands outside and over against the closed reality of the empire, which intends that the dry bones should never live again. God keeps doing what the empire has precluded. Lent is learning to reject the conclusion of the empire, and to trust the stunning freedom and power of the God who gives life.

Psalm 130

This well-known and beloved psalm has been read mostly through the Pauline-Lutheran notion of the wretchedness of "the human condition." And, indeed, "the human condition" of iniquity is present in Ps. 130:3, 8. The intention of the psalm, however, is not to comment on that wretchedness, but to speak about, and to enact, a transformation that liberates those in the depths into new freedom.

The psalm begins a passionate, pathos-filled petition. This is Israel's primal address to God, characteristically voiced from a situation of deep need and impotence. This petition is "out of the depths," from a deep valley where one can hardly muster a prayer. The noteworthy matter is that a faithful Israelite is not a mute Israelite. Even in such a situation of deep need, the Israelite still speaks, still names God, still voices a petition, still makes an insistence, still sounds needy, and in so doing, still hopes.

The petition is not specified, beyond wanting to be heard by God. Perhaps wanting to be heard at all is the first urging of any Israelite, for Israel knows that the conversation with God itself is a saving, liberating transaction. Israel wants to be heard, for being heard means being honored, taken seriously, and thereby empowered.

It is conventional to say that the core petition of this psalm is a prayer for forgiveness. One is inclined, however, to take vs. 3–4 not as the core petition, but as a quite subordinate clause which serves to support the petition of vs. 1–2. The speaker does not ask for forgiveness. The speaker acknowledges a large measure of iniquity, which on its own terms would preclude petition and disqualify the petitioner. The speaker knows and trusts, however, that God's forgiveness has long since overridden any disqualifying iniquity or guilt. Thus forgiveness is not sought, but is assumed as the basis of the conversation. This taken-as-certain forgiveness is not an outcome of devotion to Yahweh (fearing God = "revere"), but is the premise of revering God. Thus the speaker does not grovel in guilt, but accepts as a premise for petition that forgiveness has already been granted, even before the petition. The speaker is, then, revering God, that is, taking God with utmost seriousness, but is doing so on the basis of a life long since pardoned. This is the prayer of a forgiven, untroubled speaker, not any longer looking back in guilt but willing to leave iniquity in the sure hands of God. The overriding tone of the psalm is one of glad liberation. The prayer is the voice of a genuinely free person.

The speaker thus looks forward in eager longing and expectation, watching for what God will do, confident that God's promises are reliable and that their newness will create great good and well-being. This is not a poem of groveling guilt, but of liberated expectation. In vs. 5–6, the sequence "wait/hope/wait" is the Hebrew trial *qûh, qûh, yḥl,* so that the initial term *qûh* is in the NRSV rendered both as "wait" and "hope," and is a synonym for *yḥl,* "wait." Thus "wait" and "hope" are complete synonyms. They both bespeak active, eager anticipation that God will bring a newness that is well beyond anything known in the present tense.

The triad of hope is reinforced by the double use of the verb "watch" *šmr,* which refers to the night watchman, vigil, or sentry who stands alertly on guard to anticipate any intrusion that will disrupt or disturb. The watching of a sentry can be defensive, but it can also be anticipatory, as in waiting for a messenger with an order or with a battle report, or the arrival of much-needed supplies. This petition waits for God's future, and welcomes it with eagerness.

Only now, in vs. 7–8, are the petition of vs. 1–2 and the watchful hope of vs. 5–6 given any substance. The verb "hope" (*yḥl*) in v. 7 picks up on the verbs of v. 5. But now we learn the reality of that hope. It is expected that God's *ḥesed,* God's steadfast, abiding loyalty will now act for Israel, for the depths have been the place where God's *ḥesed* has been absent. The psalm voices Erik Erikson's "basic trust," in which buoyant Israel hopes for that which it does not have in hand, because it trusts fully in God's faithfulness.

The content of that hope from God, the outcome of that *ḥesed,* is voiced in the double use of the verb "redeem." While, the last phrase reduces "redeem" to the problem of sin (see vs. 3–4), in fact the term "redeem" in Israel carries all the liberating potential of God's acts related to every social condition, that renders one powerless. Israel is redeemed from bondage, but individual persons are liberated as well from loneliness, sickness, and prison as well as from sin. Thus this psalm enacts, in anticipation, the entire drama of the gospel. The petitioner is in the depths, but the waiting and reliance upon God's *ḥesed* anticipate a whole new life of freedom, dignity, and well-being. The past acts of God wrought in *ḥesed* make present-tense confidence possible, even in a miserable circumstance.

Romans 8:6–11

The opening lines of Rom. 8 provide a needed transition from chapters 6 and 7, with their discussion of the relationship between the gospel of Jesus Christ, on the one hand, and the present order dominated by sin and even by the law, on the other. Chapter 8 looks forward to God's final triumph and assures believers that no struggle can separate them from God. In 8:1–11, Paul reviews what he has said earlier in the letter: the gospel of Jesus Christ has freed human beings from sin and death.

In this paragraph, Paul also introduces some new terms that will play a prominent role in this chapter. He talks about two kinds of people, those who "live according to the flesh" and those who "live according to the Spirit." Since the dichotomy between flesh and spirit later in the church's life results in a very negative assessment of the human body, and since some Christian ascetics and Gnostics did see Paul as a champion of their viewpoints, it is only natural that Paul has been held responsible for introducing that negative view of the body into Christian thought. The words "flesh" and "spirit" cause some to think that Paul is talking about two different parts of a human being, the flesh and the spirit, an unseen part that has to do with feeling and perceiving. What makes the problem of interpretation more complex is that sometimes Paul does use these words in just these ways. In Rom. 9:5, for example, he speaks of the Messiah coming from Israel "according to the flesh," referring to Jesus' physical origins, and 1 Cor. 2:11 speaks of the spirit that knows what is within a person.

When Paul refers to "liv[ing] according to the flesh" and "liv[ing] according to the Spirit," however, he juxtaposes not two parts of the person but *two ways of living*. Living according to the flesh, then, does not necessarily mean living a life of gluttony or indolence or vanity—a life subservient to the demands of the body. Instead, it means living in a way that is shaped by, controlled by, the values and standards of the world in rebellion against God. What Paul refers to here is not a list of bad behaviors, but what we would call a mind-set, and it is a mind-set that daily makes its way in the world apart from the recognition of its Creator.

Paul contrasts this way of living with living according to the Spirit. Paul's comments about this manner of living are brief and elusive. As elsewhere when he describes the Christian life, Paul avoids offering the kind of strict guidelines that can too readily be subverted into rules and regulations. Here he simply says that living according to the Spirit is to have one's mind set on the Spirit; it means life and peace.

Having read this contrast between living in the flesh and living in the Spirit, heirs of American pragmatism will inevitably begin to assess themselves and cast a sideways glance at the neighbors: Who stands where? What yardstick will allow an accurate evaluation of where people are? Another response, again shaped by the concern for practical action, is to conclude that Paul wants his readers to choose. He offers the proverbial fork in the road.

A careful rereading of the passage reveals the shortsightedness of these questions. Paul both challenges premature conclusions about life in the Spirit and offers a positive statement of the Spirit's work. First, the Spirit does not belong to any human being. The Spirit is always *God's* spirit, never a possession to be acquired. God *gives* the Spirit. If even Jesus did not raise himself from the dead but was raised by the Spirit of God, then no human being can earn the Spirit or even choose it. It is always and forever a gift of the one sovereign and powerful God. To those Christians who would assert their own authority or correctness by means of their spiritual gifts, Paul sounds a powerful word of correction.

Second, the gift of the Spirit is a gift of empowerment. Paul does not have in view here the public and flashy spiritual gifts of speaking in tongues or performing healing, but the power of the Spirit to give life itself. It is the Spirit, after all, who enables human beings to leave behind the reign of the flesh—the reign that answers all questions by means of the world's answers—and to freely live in conformity to Christ. It is the Spirit who enables human beings to see the world's riches and power as mere entrapment and to see the foolishness of a crucified Messiah as life-giving power. For those Christians who find even the word "Spirit" distasteful and slightly embarrassing, this passage forces the awareness that the gifts of the Spirit are not optional to the Christian faith.

Third, the Spirit's gifts belong not only to the present but to the future, as v. 11 makes abundantly clear: "If the Spirit of him who raised Jesus from the dead dwells in you, he who raised Christ from the dead will give life to your mortal bodies also through his Spirit that dwells in you." The Spirit of God secures the promise that life in the Spirit belongs not to this age alone. God's resurrection of Jesus from the dead means that God will grant that same life to human beings, to their "mortal bodies." Even the power of death cannot ultimately defeat God's Spirit.

John 11:1–45

For the fourth Sunday in a row, the Gospel lesson comes from the great dramatic narratives of John—the stories of Jesus' encounters with Nicodemus, the Samaritan woman, the man born blind, and now Lazarus and his family. It may be a bit surprising to find this last story as a reading for a Sunday in Lent. The raising of Lazarus is often associated with the resurrection of Jesus and might seem to come in the lectionary cycle more appropriately after Easter. To contemplate preaching from it before Easter, so close to Holy Week, however, provides the opportunity to read the text with new glasses.

For instance, an analysis of the structure of the story reveals an extensive set of circumstances and conversations between the time Lazarus is first introduced (11:1) and the time when Jesus calls him from the tomb (vs. 43–44). A lengthy introduction reports Jesus' conversation with the disciples about Lazarus and the trip back across the Jordan to Bethany (vs. 1–16). When Jesus arrives at Bethany, we learn of an extended conversation with Martha (vs. 17–27) and then another with Mary and the Jewish mourners (v. 28–37). Even at the tomb, the raising is delayed by Martha's protests and Jesus' prayer (vs. 38–42). The miracle is followed by an interesting account of responses to the event (vs. 45–53). There is certainly more here than a bare account of the raising of Lazarus.

As the story unfolds, with the usual touches of Johannine irony and wordplay, *Jesus persists in the face of a number of deterrents to bring life to the dead.* First, when the word comes of Lazarus's illness, the disciples urge him not to go back to Judea because of the hostile reaction to him there (v. 8). Misunderstanding Jesus' metaphorical use of "sleep," they argue that if Lazarus is resting then he should be alright (v. 12). When Jesus arrives at Bethany, Martha is unable to grasp what he says and what he is about to do. Her traditional language exposes her bafflement (vs. 24, 27). The Jewish mourners cannot share in the anticipation. They are irritated that Jesus did nothing to prevent Lazarus's dying (v. 37). At the tomb Martha worries about opening the grave because of the smell of a body dead four days (v. 39). No one understands. No one expects that life can come out of death. No one grasps that Jesus is the life-giving power of God.

But Jesus persists. To Martha's conventional Jewish theology, Jesus declares, "I am the resurrection and the life." The dynamic life of the age to come is no longer a future expectation, but a present reality. "Those who believe in me, even though they die, will live, and everyone who lives and believes in me will never die" (vs. 25–26). To be united to Jesus means to be a recipient of eternal life. The unheard-of claim of God's renewing power in Jesus is then acted on, as Jesus calls Lazarus from the tomb. Deed follows word. Amid the symbols of death—intense grief, a skeptical and somewhat impatient audience, the odor of a decaying body, the tightly wrapped grave clothes—Jesus speaks and acts, and there is life.

It is surprising that the text indicates little rejoicing at the resurrection of Lazarus. Some of the Jews believed in Jesus because of the incident (v. 45), but others, in the verses that follow today's lection, feeling threatened by his awesome power to give life, go to the religious authorities and precipitate a plot to crucify him (vs. 46–53). *This story of the giving of life then leads to a story of death.*

Throughout the narrating of the events at Bethany we are given clues that point forward to Jesus' passion. Mary is introduced as "the one who anointed the Lord with perfume and wiped his feet with her hair" (v. 2), anticipating the incident in 12:1–8 where Jesus responds to Judas's complaint by saying, "She bought it so that she might keep it for the day of my burial" (12:7). Jesus' question to the mourners about Lazarus's body, "Where have you laid him?" (11:34) is later paralleled by Mary's request of "the gardener" at Jesus' tomb (20:15).

But more important than these clues is Jesus' own somber demeanor at Bethany. He "was greatly disturbed in spirit and deeply moved" (11:33, 38). The Greek terms carry the notion of anger and distress. It is more than a statement of Jesus' empathy with grieving friends. He is troubled. He perceives the evidences of death all about and knows that its power is still very much in place. He sees the sharp opposition that cannot tolerate the giving of life, the religious authorities who are threatened by his transforming deeds. Like the moment in Gethsemane, he confronts the forces set against him as well as his own vocation, put so eloquently in the ironic statement of Caiaphas (11:50–52).

There is not much rejoicing at the raising of Lazarus. Since the giving of life projects a future full of surprises, it turns out to be a menace to those who think they control the future. They respond the only way they know, with violence. They even plot to do away with Lazarus (12:9–10). But the larger story confirms that life will not be overcome by death. What remains beyond the raising of Lazarus is not only Jesus' death, but his resurrection and his persistent giving of life.

Sixth Sunday in Lent

(Palm Sunday or Passion Sunday)

Palm Sunday is customarily referred to as the "triumphal entry" of Jesus into Jerusalem, and, indeed, the Gospels describe Jesus' enthusiastic reception by crowds of people. That he comes on a little-respected beast, with a pitiful retinue, and without a military victory to celebrate can be overlooked by virtue of the number of people who welcome him to the city that stands at the center of Israel's life. Jesus does triumph, if only in the hearts and imaginations of the people of Jerusalem.

Each of the texts assigned for Palm Sunday interprets this triumph by raising profound questions about who truly welcomes Jesus and under what circumstances. Isaiah 50:4–9a, with its reflection on the genuine Servant of God, recalls the hostility that inevitably follows upon servanthood. A moment of acceptance, even welcome, will not hide from the Servant the fact of the rejection to come, although the Servant's confidence in God's power to sustain and vindicate will prepare the way for that rejection.

As is also the case with the passage from Isaiah, Ps. 118 again and again asserts that the city and the victory and the "one who comes" all belong to God. In that overwhelmingly theocentric context, any victory declared by human beings is bound to vanish as quickly as the day itself. The fickle greeting of the crowds stands as less than nothing beside "the gate of the LORD" and the "day that the LORD has made." Similarly, the Philippians hymn asserts Jesus' own determination to be obedient even to death and God's consequent exaltation of Jesus above all creation. That triumph mocks the presumption that the inhabitants of ancient Jerusalem or any human city in any time can declare a victory or celebrate a triumph.

Even in the Gospel accounts of Jesus' "triumphal entry," the triumph is one of meekness and humility rather than of power and pride: "Look, your king is coming to you, humble . . ." (Matt. 21:5). The greetings of the crowds signal the importance of this newcomer to Jerusalem and cause readers to anticipate Jesus' victory in coming days. But when the crowds return, it is not to declare Jesus victorious but to demand his death (Matt. 27:15–23). Even as it celebrates Jesus' arrival in Jerusalem, Palm Sunday reveals the bankruptcy of humanity's notions of power and victory and the true power of God.

Isaiah 50:4–9a

This text is the voice of God's Servant, who acknowledges deep trouble and who confesses bold confidence. We are not told who the Servant is, or why there is such trouble. It is clear that every faithful servant of God has life placed in jeopardy, because the truth of God does not easily mesh with our dominant illusions about reality. As this poem concerns the deep jeopardy of the Servant, so the church knows that Jesus' conflict will lead to suffering and death. In that deep conflict, however, he continues to be God's trusting, faithful, obedient servant.

This text is dominated by the fourfold "The Lord GOD." Thus the statement of the Servant is passionately theocentric. The Servant is focused utterly on God.

The Servant acknowledges his particular ministry as given by God (v. 4). His ear must be receptive to a very odd message from God, and his tongue must be skillful in speaking that same oddity.

This ministry of hearing and speaking has a specific intention. His work is to "sustain the weary." The weary ones are the ones who are in exile, who have their life shaped and crushed by the power of the empire, and who daily live close to despair. To "sustain" does not mean simply to speak a gentle word of consolation. It means, so we gather from the context of the poetry, to speak a reality that counters the weariness, to mediate to the exhausted an alternative reality which creates space, freedom, and energy. Thus the speech that can sustain the weary in exile is the word that Yahweh has defeated the power of the empire, that it is Yahweh who governs and not the debilitating power an ideology of the empire (cf. 40:9; 52:7). Thus sustenance to the weary is the bold theological assertion that reshapes the world, that voices new possibilities outside the assumed realities that dominate, and that invites the weary to change their self-perception and therefore their action.

Such a daring theological assertion is sure to evoke resistance and hostility (vs. 5–6). Hostility to this prophetic message might come from the empire itself, which when threatened seeks to silence such a dangerous alternative. Or resistance might come from the religious community of exiles who had become acclimated to the empire and did not want such demanding good news.

The hostility enacted against the Servant suggests physical abuse, social exclusion, and harassment (v. 6). This Servant, however, neither breaks off nor strikes back. This Servant is free to make a more effective and peaceable response of nonresistance, because "the Lord GOD has opened my ear." Perhaps this means that the Lord God has spoken to the servant assurances and consolation.

The theme of confidence in the face of hostility is explicated in vs. 7–9a. The language and tone of these verses is disputatious. Perhaps the servant has been called into court, accused of speaking treasonable words in asserting Yahweh's sovereignty over the empire. Or perhaps the courtroom language is only a metaphor for a messenger under social pressure. Either way, as a literal courtroom or as a metaphor for a trial, the Servant is called to hostile account for his speech and for his faith.

The language of vs. 8–9 offers a courtroom scene. The brief unit is built around two contrasting figures, but the sharp contrast is lost in translation. At the beginning of v. 8, the "vindicator" is the *one who declares innocent (saddîq).* At the beginning of v. 9, the alternative is the *one "who will declare me guilty (rāšā').* The two words, "declare innocent" and "declare guilty" make a perfect contrast in the two words *saddîq* and *rāšā'*, which we usually translate "righteous" and "wicked." The Servant is sure he will be declared innocent, and so has no fear of those who want to see him pronounced guilty. He has utter confidence in the outcome of the court proceeding, because his message is true.

There may be a temptation, because the text is elusive, to treat it on rather formal grounds concerning the office of the Servant, without attending to the hard-nosed substance of the Servant's claim. The Servant's business is to assert that Yahweh is indeed the one who governs. The Servant is sustained because he himself believes the message he asserts. That same message, which puts the messenger in jeopardy, is the one that will sustain. Opposition to the claim of this God does not detract from the truth of the claim, its validity for the weary, or its power to guard and keep the messenger.

Psalm 118:1–2, 19–29 (A B C)

Palm Sunday is a juncture at which two conflicting emotions collide. On the one hand, there is the festal jubilation over the entry of the King into his royal city, a procession of majesty that dwarfs all other such ceremonial entrances, as this King dwarfs all other kings. This note of celebration is struck, in the Gospel account, by the shouts of the crowd:

> Hosanna!
> Blessed is the one who comes in the name of the Lord!
> Blessed is the coming kingdom of our ancestor David!
> (Mark 11:9–10)

On the other hand, however, there is a strong sense of foreboding, which tempers the joy of the moment. All perceptive persons who come to the Palm Sunday festival (including modern worshipers) are aware that the exaltation of the King which is shortly to occur, and of which the Palm Sunday entrance is the prelude, will be deeply scarred by pain and death.

This amalgam of sensations—anticipation, thanksgiving, supplication—is evidenced of the Psalm lection, where the various emotions are juxtaposed so strikingly that one most raise questions about the psalm's logical coherence. After the initial formulaic thanksgiving (vs. 1–2), the psalmist's song of gratitude over having been saved by Yahweh's power (v. 21) is soon matched by his petition to Yahweh for action (v. 25). The psalmist speaks now to the gatekeepers (v. 19), then to Yahweh (v. 21), and ultimately to the people (v. 29). Yet through the whole there is a consistent motif: we, the people, have arrived to celebrate God's wonderful presence. Fling open the gates that we may enter!

Thus, of the two principal moods of Palm Sunday, Ps. 118:1–2, 19–29 is clearly weighted in favor of joyous celebration. Yet even here the shadow of the cross cannot be blotted out entirely. The stone that Yahweh has chosen as the "chief cornerstone" has been rejected by others, and all who have read the story through to its conclusion know that these evil forces still lurk nearby in their attempt to make this rejection permanent.

In its entirety, Ps. 118 is a psalm of thanksgiving sung by one who has been to the edge of the abyss and who has been delivered by God (see especially vs. 10–14). But only in the verses that form this day's lection do we encounter the theme of pilgrimage to the Holy Place. In its original setting, this was most likely Jerusalem at a time of special significance—the autumn festival, perhaps—the "day that Yahweh has made" (v. 24). In that setting, the "gate of Yahweh" (v. 20) is the gate of the city or of the Temple. "The one who comes in the name of Yahweh" (v. 26) is the pious pilgrim.

In its Palm Sunday application, however, much of this meaning is transformed. The procession is not that of a band of devout worshipers, but of a king and his court. (Some scholars would insist that this "reading" of the text is consistent with its original setting, in that the hymnic literature of ancient Israel's autumn festival, including this psalm, celebrated the reenthronement of the Davidic monarch. If that much-debated interpretation is correct, the Davidic king, or King, is the subject of the psalm both in its Old Testament and its New Testament understandings.) The "blessed . . . one" is no representative pilgrim, but the King of kings. The "day that Yahweh has made" (v. 24) is not an annually repeated occasion, but a once-and-for-all moment leading up to the humiliation and exaltation of this Messiah-King.

Striking in its singularity in this text is v. 22, which juts quite unexpectedly above the surrounding context. Nothing has been said to this point in the entire psalm about a building stone, nor is the matter broached again. The thought appears as an exclamation mark in the middle of a sentence:

> The stone that the builders rejected
> has become the chief cornerstone.

And the question naturally arises: To what or whom is the psalmist referring? To declare that this is some preexisting proverb which has been incorporated into the psalm may be quite true, for the lines do have a certain axiomatic ring to them. But what flow of logic within the mind of the psalmist called forth their use, and of what building has this rejected stone become the chief corner? Various answers have been proposed, but one thing seems perfectly clear. The writers of the New Testament could think of no one to whom these lines applied more appropriately than the about-to-be-rejected Jesus, who becomes the adored and reigning risen Christ (Mark 12:10 and elsewhere).

> This is the LORD's doing;
> it is marvelous in our eyes.
> (Ps. 118:23)

Indeed, it is the power of God in the events of Christ's passion and resurrection that Christians celebrate when we use this text as a Palm Sunday lection. The power of God is at the text's heart and core. For that which occurred at Calvary and the open tomb shattered all human expectations, even those—especially those—of the men and women who were eyewitnesses of the events. More than logic or "nature" were on display here. The One who entered the city as a ridiculous-looking, donkey-riding King destroyed the bonds of sin and death. And he did so by the strength of a loving and redeeming God.

Thus the climax of the lection, which in v. 1 appears to be an overly familiar refrain (compare Pss. 107:1; 136), here becomes a surge of thanksgiving from hearts that have been touched by a God whose saving love extends to the grave and beyond.

> O given thinks to the LORD, for he is good,
> for his steadfast love endures forever.
> (Ps. 118:29)

Philippians 2:5–11

The Gospel accounts of what we call "Palm Sunday" highlight the joyous reception of Jesus when he enters Jerusalem. With hosannas, the crowds greet him as the Son of David, elevating him to a position of majesty and royalty. Readers unfamiliar with the Gospel story might conclude that this triumph represents the final stage in the world's response to Jesus, rather than a prelude to the final rejection. It appears that human beings indeed possess both the ability to discern who is "Son of David" and the will to elevate that one to his rightful place. Over against the apparent optimism of the Gospel accounts stands the passage from Phil. 2.

While the precise origins of this hymn remain unknown, it seems highly unlikely that Paul composed it. In its broad contours, the story of a god who descends to earth in human form and later ascends to his heavenly home might come from a variety of sources. Paul probably knew the hymn and found that it suited the point he wished to make, much as a contemporary preachers employ hymns of popular music or even slogans drawn from advertising.

In the first half of the hymn, the action derives entirely from Christ, who "regard[ed] . . . , emptied . . . , taking . . . , being born . . . , being found . . . , humbled . . . , became obedient." Paul elsewhere makes assertions that conflict with this apparent claim of preexistence (see Rom. 1:3–4), but what matters here is less the precise character of the preexisting Christ or the consistency of Paul's thought than the intentional self-effacement and humility of Jesus Christ. What the hymn relentlessly affirms is the obedience of one who might have asserted himself but chose instead to submit to God's will. Not only did Jesus yield up his own identity with God but he submitted to becoming human, even to being a slave. Not only did he submit to being merely human, but his obedience led to his death. That death was not a normal human death, a death with honor and dignity. Jesus' death was "even death on a cross," the most debased and shameful public death imaginable in the ancient world. If, as many scholars think, the phrase "even death on a cross" is a Pauline addition to the earlier hymn, it reflects Paul's characteristic emphasis on the importance of Jesus' death. Jesus is a downwardly mobile savior.

At v. 9 the hymn radically shifts as the initiative now comes from God, and the action is "upward" rather than "downward." God's action, in response to the obedience of Jesus ("therefore"), exalts him and, indeed, makes him again to be identified with God, since "the name that is above every name" is surely a circumlocution for the divine name. God's exaltation of Jesus ultimately results in the subjection of all creation to Jesus and the naming of him as Lord. The entire action described by the hymn is ultimately for "the glory of God the Father."

Paul introduces the hymn with the exhortation: "Let the same mind be in you that was in Christ Jesus." For Paul, the important christological claims of the hymn exist side by side with the anthropological implications. This does not mean, of course, that Christians may enter into obedience with the expectation that they too will be glorified by God. No such bargain is being offered. It is the "mind" of Christ, or Christ's way of thinking, that Paul presents as a model to be imitated. Christ's obedience, Christ's willingness to regard others as more important than himself, Christ's rejection of his own status—these are the aspects of Christ's "mind" that Paul urges on the Philippians. The opening lines of chapter 2, where Paul urges these very same virtues on his readers, confirm this reading of the hymn.

In its Pauline setting, of course, the hymn says nothing about Palm Sunday and Jesus' reception in Jerusalem. Nevertheless, by assigning this passage to Palm Sunday, the lectionary introduces a quiet protest of the notion that *humanity* exalts Jesus. First, the hymn recalls for a church caught up in the pageantry of Palm Sunday that the same Jesus who today enters in triumph will, within the week, die on a cross. Neither Jesus' contemporaries nor their heirs within the church are able or willing to exalt him. They only appear to do so, the reality being that fickle human opinion will turn when the powers that be threaten.

Second, the hymn recalls for a humanity ever beguiled by its own power that only God is able to exalt. The human "power" that seems to exalt Jesus on Palm Sunday is a sham, just as the human "power" that condemns Jesus on Good Friday is shown to be a sham. The only one who can truly exalt or condemn is also the one who gives and sustains life, namely, God. At God's final triumph, all of creation will indeed bend the knee to Jesus Christ, but that submission occurs only as part of a final triumph willed and brought about by God. Palm Sunday reveals, not the good judgment of humankind, but its utter folly.

Matthew 21:1–11

Palm Sunday comes around once a year, and it taxes the minister to find a fresh word to say. Accounts of the entry into Jerusalem are found in all four Gospels, but the differences between them are not great. After one gets beyond describing the parade—the branches and cloaks on the road, the excitement, the hosannas—what is significant and life-changing in the event?

Let's examine two pieces of the story. First, it is not just an old city to which Jesus is moving; it is Jerusalem. As early as Matt. 16:21 Jesus announces his intention to go to Jerusalem. It is the Holy City, about which great promises are made, and Jesus, the promised Messiah, enters the gates amid pomp and circumstance. The one thing said in the passage about Jerusalem is that "the whole city was in turmoil" (21:10). Were the citizens expectant, or afraid, or dizzy with excitement? The greek verb used in 21:10 is normally used for storms, earthquakes, and violent shakings of the earth, apocalyptic events that accompany momentous happenings (8:24, 24:7, 27:51; 28:2). Here it is not the ground that trembles, but the city, a city face-to-face with its Messiah. The question the city asks, "Who is this?" is answered by the crowds, "This is the prophet Jesus from Nazareth in Galilee" (21:11).

Jerusalem is a city confronted with a decision. What will it do with a Messiah who ushers in a reign of peace, not warfare? What will the city do with a prophet who cares deeply for it, as a mother hen cares for her brood (23:37–39)? How will it respond? We the readers view the scene with apprehension, because we have already been told that Jerusalem is the place of rejection, suffering, and death (16:21; 20: 18–19). But for the moment Jerusalem has a chance. Will the killing and stoning of the prophets cease?

Second, consider the one who comes to Jerusalem. The portrait of Jesus is painted here in the colorful words of the Old Testament. Verse 5 comes primarily from Zech. 9:9, with an allusion to Isa. 62:11 (quoted also in John, but omitted in Mark and Luke). Two things stand out about the way the citation is handled in the Matthean text. In the first instance, two animals are mentioned—a donkey and the foal of a donkey. In Zechariah they are a hendiadys, a figure of speech in which two nouns hooked together by a conjunction (in Hebrew; see KJV) are used to express a single notion. The terms are paralleled for effect, but clearly only one animal is intended. Matthew, however, takes the poetry literally and goes out of the way to describe for us an impossible scene, with Jesus riding two animals! Matthew's literalness stresses the fulfillment of scripture. There is to be no mistaking the fact that the individual entering the city is "your king" of Zech. 9:9, who will command peace to the nations and whose dominion will reach to the ends of the earth. This is a royal scene, and the king comes as the long-awaited completion of Israel's hopes.

In the second instance, the text of Matthew abbreviates the text of Zechariah in that the line "triumphant and victorious is he" is omitted. The effect of the omission is to highlight Jesus as the *humble* king. Despite all the pomp and circumstance, the branches and cloaks, the hosannas, this king differs from other kings. He is marked by meekness, a characteristic that distinguishes the way of Jesus and those who follow him (see Matt. 5:5; 11:28–30).

The description "humble" is not easily pinned down. The location of the word here at the beginning of the passion story, however, is critical. What happens in the days ahead—what Jesus teaches and how he conducts himself in the face of arrest, betrayal, denial, trial, mocking, and finally death—provides the appropriate definition of "humble." He gives the quality its meaning. He resolutely lives out his vocation to be the Son of God, refusing to come down from the cross, saving others and not himself, trusting only in God (27:40–44).

For Jesus being "your king" then, means not chauvinistic claims about control and domination, about grinding enemies into the dust and building monuments of battle. Instead, it means obedience to a divine calling, acceptance of the role as God's suffering Son. A *triumphal* entry? Only as the triumph of the meek, the victory of the humble.

Holy Thursday

With its multiple historical connections—the betrayal and arrest of Jesus, the Last Supper, the Passover—Maundy Thursday becomes an occasion on which Christians recall these important events in the life of Jesus and the history of Israel. But merely remembering does not do justice to these events, which have ongoing, present significance for believers. The passages assigned for Maundy Thursday press beyond recollection of what happened to re-presenting (in the sense of presenting again) them to Christians today.

The notion of re-presenting Passover comes to expression in the text's instructions to Israel. Elaborate instructions regarding the celebration of Passover serve not simply to remind Israel of a past event but to present, even to create, that event afresh in each generation. In that sense, the exodus is not a faint memory of something that happened to distant relations, but an experience that is shared by each new generation.

Paul's instructions regarding the Lord's Supper urge a similar connection between present community and past event. As Paul saw it, the Corinthians ate the Lord's Supper in a way that failed to acknowledge its connection with the death of Jesus, but the meal itself was a proclamation of that death. In the meal, believers stand between the death of Jesus and his parousia, living with the reality of both those events.

Although the Fourth Gospel's story of Jesus washing the feet of his disciples finds scant place in the church's liturgy, it too urges representation rather than mere recollection. Not a simple tale about Jesus' humility and service, the story foreshadows the death of Jesus and thus represents his ultimate act of servanthood. By virtue of his service to his disciples and the service of his death, Jesus radically challenges conventional, hierarchical notions about leaders and followers. Small wonder that the story of Jesus' betrayal immediately follows this disturbing scene.

In one sense, the psalm stands apart from these stories or instructions about specific events in the life of Israel or the church. The psalmist's gratitude, however, expresses itself in a public way, "in the presence of all his people." By virtue of this public display of thanksgiving, and indeed by means of the psalm itself, the psalmist presents again to believers of every age the present need for thanksgiving and praise.

Exodus 12:1–4 (5–10) 11–14 (A B C)

Jesus' last supper with his disciples before his death is linked to the celebration of the Passover. For that reason, the Old Testament reading concerns Israel's provision for Passover. The Passover regularly needs to be understood on its own terms as a commonality shared by Christians and as a genuinely Jewish practice. When understood on its own Jewish terms, it is then possible, as a second interpretive move, to incorporate into this festival the story of Jesus. Obviously such a Christian appropriation of the story and the festival must take care not to intrude on the intrinsically Jewish character of the festival.

The larger part of this text is a Priestly instruction for the careful liturgical management of the festival (Ex. 12:1–10). Liturgical rites, especially those which are precious and crucial, take on a life of their own. As a result, some of the detailed observances continue to be honored and taken seriously even though the original reasons for them may have been lost. These verses may be understood as analogous to a manual of instruction for Christian priests in a high sacramental tradition, concerning the particular gestures of celebrating the Eucharist. Every gesture counts and must be performed with precision.

This festival marks a beginning point in Israel's life (v. 2). It is as though life begins again in this moment of remembering and reenactment. The focus is the lamb. The lamb is both good food and costly commodity. A whole lamb may be too much meat and too much expense for a small household (v. 4). Careful attention is paid to the economic factors in the festival requirement. The lamb must be a good one, not a cull, for it must be worthy of its holy function (v. 5). The lamb provides blood as a sign on the doorposts and roasted meat for the meal. Israel's religious act consists in replicating a memory of eating together.

After the actual guidelines for proper celebration, we are offered theological interpretation of the act (v. 11). The meal with the lamb could be simply a meal. In the community of memory, however, the meal takes on peculiar signification. This is not an ordinary meal, and it must not be eaten in an ordinary way. Israel is to dress for the occasion in its travel clothes, with shoes (sandals) and weapons on (girded loins), with a staff in the hand, ready for leave-taking. The meal must be eaten quickly, with a sense of urgency. This "street theater" will be reenacted as though it were the moment before the exodus departure. In each new generation, the boys and girls participate in the drama of leave-taking from Egypt. They gulp the food, lean toward the door, watch in eagerness, and wait in anxiety, for they are at the brink of dangerous freedom. At the edge of freedom, nobody wants to linger with Pharaoh. This is a quick meal, not fancy or decorous, just provision for the long, hard trek to newness.

The passage concludes with a more formidable connection to the exodus memory (vs. 12–14). The term "Passover" now becomes a routinized festival, originated (so Israel remembers) in an awesome, dread-filled political act of violence wrought by God. The meal refers, as Israel tells it, to a powerfully partisan act. God acts against the Egyptian empire, on behalf of the shamelessly abused slaves who became Israel.

The text is a liturgical memory, but it is cast as a present-tense happening. God is the key actor: "I will pass through. . . . I will strike down. . . . I will execute judgments." The act of justice (judgment) that God performs is to crush the oppressive power of the empire. In that act of justice, it is clear that "our story" revolves around Yahweh, the God of freedom and justice.

Psalm 116:1–2, 12–19 (A B C)

Psalm 116 is, in its entirety, a song of thanksgiving on the part of one who has been delivered by God from some distress, probably physical illness. As is typical of both psalms of thanksgiving and psalms of lament, attention is here given to the psalmist's vow to Yahweh. While such an element may seem to modern readers an offensive sentiment, in that it smacks of an attempt to bribe God, the interest of the poet lay in quite a different direction. The vow was an effort to say, in essence, "In response to your saving love in my life, O Yahweh, I confess that I will never again be the same person that I was before." Psalm 51, a model psalm of confession, contains this realization by the psalmist:

[In response to your love, O Yahweh,]
. . . I will teach transgressors your ways,
and sinners will return to you.
[When you have delivered me, O God,]
O God of my salvation,
. . . my tongue will sing aloud of your deliverance.
(Ps. 51:13–14)

The Psalm lection for Holy Thursday, after an introduction that affirms the grace of Yahweh (Ps. 116:1–2), turns to that part of the psalm which comprises the vow. Having thanked Yahweh for saving him, the poet now describes the change this salvation has brought to his life.

Structurally, this passage is composed of two quite similar parts, vs. 12–14 and vs. 16–19, separated by a verse (15) which, because it seems to break the logical flow of the text, may be a later insertion.

The first section, and thus the entire lection, is introduced by a question in v. 12 that reminds one of Micah 6:6. Yet the concern here is not, "How may I please God?" but, "How may my life more adequately express the redemptive power of God within me?" The response (Ps. 116:13) is in terms of drinking the cup of salvation and of openness to the reality ("the name") of God. The brief section closes (v. 14) with a promise, the major theme of the passage: "I will pay my vows to Yahweh."

The second section (vs. 16–19) is closely parallel to the first except in two respects. In place of the question of v. 12, v. 16 insists on the low status of the pray-er. The description of the psalmist as the child of a serving girl may suggest to Christian readers the figure of Jesus Christ, son of Mary, but to ancient readers the phrase would have been evocative of Ishmael, the son of Abraham's (Sarah's) servant Hagar (Gen. 16). Although a son of the patriarch Abraham, Ishmael was cut off from the promise because of his mother's inferior status. And so the psalmist is calling attention to his own weakness and alienation at the same time that he celebrates God's intervention, which has overruled these realities. The force of Ps. 116:16 is strikingly captured by the REB:

Indeed, LORD, I am your slave,
I am your slave, your slave-girl's son;
you have loosed my bonds.

The other important manner in which the second section differs from the first is in the substitution of v. 17a for 13a, identifying a "thanksgiving sacrifice" as an appropriate vehicle for expressing God's redemptive presence instead of "the cup of salvation."

The balance of the second section replicates the first, in that vs. 17b–18 are identical to vs. 13b–14. Verse 19, which has no precise equivalent in the first section, is merely a poetic extension of v. 18b (14b).

The result of viewing the lection as two parallel sections, divided by the "foreign" (?) v. 15, is that we may identify three specific acts as the psalmist's means of expressing the reality of what God has done in his life:

1. Because of the goodness of Yahweh (vs. 1–2), I will lift the cup of salvation (v. 13a).
2. [I will] call on the name of Yahweh (v. 13b).
3. I will offer to [Yahweh] a thanksgiving sacrifice (v. 17a).

The relevance of this lection to the Last Supper and to Maundy Thursday observances through the ages may be found in all three of the psalmist's affirmations. (It is not entirely clear what the psalmist had in mind by the phrase "the cup of salvation," although a liturgical setting is likely, as in Num. 28:7.) Not only are these themes present in the narrative descriptions of Jesus' final meal with the disciples before the crucifixion (see Mark 14:22–25), but they permeate all celebrations of the Christian Eucharist. And by one of those hermeneutical "leaps" that transform many Old Testament texts, the subject of the psalm, the one who prays it and who experiences that which the text describes, is not just any human being, but Jesus Christ, that quintessential human being who is also God's representative to humankind. It is Jesus Christ who both lifts the cup of salvation and, through his shed blood, fills that cup. It is Jesus Christ who not only calls on the name of the Lord, but provides us with that unique name by which we approach God. It is Jesus Christ who not only offers a thanksgiving sacrifice, but himself becomes that sacrifice.

Even the "intruding" (?) v. 15 of Ps. 116 assumes new meaning when this text is read christologically.

> Precious in the sight of the LORD
> is the death of his faithful ones.

Of all the Lord's faithful ones, who was more faithful than He? Of all the deaths, whose is more precious than His?

1 Corinthians 11:23–26 (A B C)

These lines concerning the sharing of bread and wine are so familiar to most Christian ministers that the act of reading the text may seem superfluous. As the "words of institution" they are known by heart and can be recited verbatim. And, indeed, that intimate knowledge of this passage is consistent with the way in which Paul introduces it. When he writes, "For I received from the Lord what I also handed on to you," he uses technical language for the transmission of tradition, and the church's intimate knowledge of this passage continues that understanding of it.

The tradition itself contains the simple and direct words that connect the ordinary sharing of bread and wine with the death of Jesus and its significance for humankind. The bread signifies the body of Jesus, broken in death. The cup signifies the blood of Jesus, poured out in death. Through that death comes a new covenant, and through participation in the meal comes the remembrance of Jesus. The word remembrance (*anamnēsis*) appears in both the statement regarding the bread and the statement regarding the wine, suggesting that the Lord's Supper is vitally connected with the church's memory of Jesus. What the exact nature of that remembrance is becomes clearer in 1 Cor. 11:26.

With v. 26 Paul no longer cites the traditional words of Jesus, but offers his own interpretation of the Supper: "For as often as you eat this bread and drink the cup, you proclaim the Lord's death until he comes." Two crucial points emerge here. First, Paul asserts that the very act of the meal *is* an act of proclamation. In the celebration of the Lord's Supper itself, the church engages in the preaching of the gospel. Protestant exegetes, uncomfortable with the omission of the verbal act of proclamation in this passage, long rejected this point by attempting to argue that Paul means that preaching *accompanies* every celebration of the Supper. If understood that way, however, the verse simply tells the Corinthians what they already know (preaching accompanies the meal) and adds nothing at all to the passage. Verse 26, in fact, culminates Paul's discussion of the meal by explaining its significance. The Lord's Supper is not just another meal, the eating of which is a matter of indifference; this celebration is itself a proclamation of the gospel of Jesus Christ.

The second point Paul makes in this verse comes in the final words, "You proclaim the Lord's death until he comes." The Lord's Supper is a very particular kind of proclamation—a proclamation of Jesus' death. A different kind of celebration, perhaps a celebration of

Jesus' miracle of multiplying the bread and the fish, might proclaim Jesus' life and teaching. Even the Lord's Supper might be understood as a celebration of the person of Jesus as a divine messenger. Building on the words of institution with their emphasis on the coming death of Jesus, Paul forcefully articulates his view that the Lord's Supper proclaims Jesus' death. Unless the final phrase, "until he comes," merely denotes the time at which celebration of the Lord's Supper will come to an end ("you keep proclaiming in this way until Jesus returns"), what it does is to convey the eschatological context in which the church lives and works. The church proclaims Jesus' *death* within the context of a confident expectation that he will come again in God's final triumph.

In this passage Paul has a very sharp point to make with Christians at Corinth, who are preoccupied with factions, with competing claims about the gospel, and with what appear to be class struggles. Paul's comments about their celebration of the Lord's Supper do not make the situation entirely clear to us, but it appears that they have followed the customs of the day, according to which the hosts of the meal served the choicer foods to their social peers and the less desirable foods to Christians of lower social or economic status. The activity of eating and drinking, and the struggle over that activity, have dominated the celebration of the meal. Paul's response to that situation is to recall forcefully the nature of the Lord's Supper. This is not another social occasion. It is *in and of itself* the proclamation of Jesus' death. Because it is a proclamation, Christians must treat it as such. Whatever conflicts there are about eating and drinking, they belong outside and apart from this occasion.

As earlier in the letter, Paul emphasizes the proclamation of Jesus' death as central to the gospel itself (see 1 Cor. 1:18–25; 2:1–2). Over against the Corinthians' apparent conviction of their own triumph over death, their own accomplishments and spiritual power, Paul asserts the weakness of Jesus, whose faithfulness to God led to his death, and Paul insists that the church lives in the tension between that death and the ultimate triumph of the resurrection.

In the context of the church's observance of Maundy Thursday, this passage recalls again the death of Jesus. That recollection is no mere commemoration, as occurs with the recollection of an anniversary or a birthday. The remembrance, especially in the Lord's Supper, serves to proclaim the death of Jesus Christ once again, as the church continues to live between that death and God's final triumph.

John 13:1–17, 31b–35 (A B C)

Thursday of Holy Week is often a time for congregations to celebrate the Lord's Supper. The four texts listed in the lectionary for the day in varying ways provide interpretations appropriate to the observance. Of the four, the reading from John's Gospel is unique. Jesus' washing of the disciples' feet is found in no other Gospel, and in the Johannine narrative it takes the place of the institution of the Supper. In doing so, it provides an interpretation of Jesus' death, just as the traditional words of institution in the Synoptic Gospels and in the Pauline letters do.

Before considering the foot washing as an example of service given to the disciples, we must first see it as *a dramatic commentary on Jesus' death.* The introductory verses (13:1–3) set an unusual context for the action Jesus performs—he knows that the time for departure has come; he loves his disciples to the uttermost; he anticipates a return to the Father. Before Jesus takes the towel and the basin, we the readers are reminded of what is to occur immediately beyond the incident. Further, the language that says he "took off his outer robe," "tied a towel around himself" (v. 4), and "put on his robe" again (v. 12) is reminiscent of the good shepherd who lays down his life in order to take it again (10:17–18).

The dialogue with Peter occupies most of the story and provides the essential explanation of Jesus' action (13:6–10). Peter is not chided for his misunderstanding, but is told, "You do not know now what I am doing, but later you will understand." After Jesus' death and resurrection, Peter will be in a position to grasp what has happened to him. When Peter vehemently resists, Jesus warns him, "Unless I wash you, you have no share with me." The only way to belong to Jesus is to receive his cleansing service, to let him do what he came to do. Peter apparently prefers a different kind of Savior, one whose journey to God takes him by another route than the cross. He might have been happier washing Jesus' feet than letting Jesus wash his. The thought of Jesus on his hands and knees at Peter's feet is too threatening. Only with great reluctance does he yield to a serving Lord.

The shorter reading of 13:10 (see the margins of RSV and NRSV) is probably to be preferred over the longer reading ("except for the feet"). "One who has bathed" *is* the one whose feet have been washed. Nothing further is needed. The humiliating death of Jesus is sufficient to provide thorough cleansing.

After seeing in Jesus' washing of feet an interpretation of his serving, saving death, the reader is in a position to view the washing as *a drama of what Jesus' followers are to be and do.* He has given "an example" which the disciples are to emulate, and what a radical example it is! More than simply kindly deeds to the neighbor, more than a cherry pie in a time of crisis, more than money donated to a worthy cause.

The precise wording of the challenge in vs. 13–14 is critical. It is "your Lord and Teacher" who washes feet. While it might not have been so unusual for the pupil to wash the feet of the teacher, in this incident the roles are reversed. The One who had come from God and was going to God performs the menial chore for reluctant disciples. The action of Jesus subverts the regular hierarchical structure. The accepted patterns of authority are undermined, or, better said, authority is redefined in new and vivid images—a towel and a basin.

Following Jesus' example ("You also ought to wash one another's feet") means creating a community of equals, where the status of superior/inferior is reversed in the act of service. The world demands a pecking order in which everyone knows his or her place and in which power is carefully protected. Jesus' deed and his subsequent challenge to the disciples reject such a structure in favor of a new kind of parity. The Lord takes on the role of the slave. When people have a share with Jesus and respond to his cleansing death, they constitute a community where such reversal of roles is the norm and not the exception. The church is "blessed" when it follows Jesus' example (v. 17).

It is instructive that at two points in the narrative there is mention of the presence among the disciples of one who will betray Jesus (vs. 10b–11, 18–19). The church should not be surprised that it is a mixed body, that it includes both the faithful and the unfaithful, both the washers of feet and the betrayers. Yet Judas is not mentioned by name. He is not singled out. The other disciples do not know who the guilty one is until after the fact. They are not told to wash only the feet of those they think are faithful and to ignore the rest. In fact, they expect to serve the betrayer in their midst—just as Jesus does.

The incident provides real depth for understanding the new commandment Jesus gives (vs. 34–35). Love is defined as more than feelings, more than liking, more than compassion-from-a-distance. "Just as I have loved you, you also should love one another."

GOOD FRIDAY

The Gospel writers often frustrate modern readers, whose preoccupation with human emotion wishes to know not just what happened and why, but how those involved *felt* about things. Readers of the stories of Jesus' passion and death may wonder why the Gospels give so little detail about the crucifixion itself, especially about the emotional state of those present. John, the only Gospel writer who includes Jesus' mother among those present at the cross, ascribes to her not a single thought or word. Perhaps the utter shame of crucifixion prompted the evangelists to move with some dispatch through this scene. More likely, the horrors of crucifixion were too well known to require rehearsal for a contemporary audience.

In the Synoptic Gospels, the dominant emotional tone of the story stems from the dying Jesus, who cries out his despair and forsakenness. This connection between Jesus' death and his sense of being abandoned by God probably stems from the reading of Ps. 22 and, in turn, prompts Christians to see in this psalm, as in Isa. 52:13–53:12, reflections of the abandonment of Jesus. The passage from Heb. 4 and 5 likewise emphasizes Jesus' suffering, a suffering that makes him fully human.

At the same time, it is not appropriate to conclude that God disappears at the cross and only emerges again in the event of Easter. Christian proclamation of the cross begins with the understanding that *even* in Jesus' utter abandonment, God was nevertheless present. John's narrative displays that presence through the sign that proclaims Jesus "King of the Jews" and through Jesus' own declaration that all is fulfilled (19:30). The revelation to Mark's centurion, who proclaims Jesus to be "God's Son" when Jesus breathes his last breath, likewise shows God's presence in and through the cross.

The passages from Isaiah and from the Psalms continue to aid Christians who struggle to articulate the profound mystery of this event. It displays the profound despair of God's Son. It prompts human despair at the utterly corrupt ways of a world in which the innocent suffer, too often alone. And yet it simultaneously asserts God's presence, even within that final aloneness. If the promise of God's final triumph reveals itself only in Easter, it nevertheless presses to be seen even in the noon hour of Good Friday, for even there God does not abandon the world.

Isaiah 52:13–53:12 (A B C)

This well-known text is notoriously elusive and elliptical. The text is far from clear, and the historical reference is completely obscure. Indeed, David Clines (*I, He, We, & They: A Literary Approach to Isaiah 53*; Sheffield: JSOT Press, 1976) has urged that the poem deliberately avoids concrete historical reference. That poetic strategy, among other things, has permitted the church to hear in "my servant" an allusion to the suffering and death of Jesus as a saving event willed by God.

The poem (the part chosen for today's lection) begins with a resounding, triumphant assertion (Isa. 52:13). This nearly defiant enunciation becomes more astonishing as we hear the subsequent poem, which reads like a contradiction of this buoyant verse. Thus, from the outset, the poem voices a remarkable dissonance. This one who "had no form or majesty," this one "despised and rejected . . . held [to be] of no account . . . struck down . . . wounded . . . oppressed . . . afflicted," this one will prosper. We know from the beginning what the abusers of the servant never discern. The servant will be "lifted up . . . very high."

The servant may prosper. For now, however, the servant is lowly, unattractive, and without commanding presence (52:14–53:3). We are not told his precise condition; it is enough that he is "marred." His condition "startles." He has the sort of defect that causes people to look away in repulsion and yet to look glancingly back in fascination. He is a loser, an outsider from whom no one expects anything. He reminds nobody of authority, or of the power to transform or save.

Nonetheless, the servant carries in his body the capacity to heal and restore (53:4–9)! Verses 4–6 make some of the most remarkable statements in all of scripture. These claims are so familiar to us that we almost miss their power and daring. This unattractive loser has embraced and appropriated "our" infirmities, diseases, transgressions, and iniquities. It is *his* suffering embrace that has caused *us* to be healed, forgiven, and restored.

We are here at the central mystery of the gospel, and the miracle voiced by this poem. We are face to face with the deepest issue of biblical faith: How can one in suffering appropriate the hurt and guilt of another? This is not a question that is ever resolved by conventional logic. It rests only on a poetic affirmation that lives very close to honest human experience. It is the case, for example, that the suffering of a parent does indeed transform a child. It is the case that a "wounded healer" can profoundly heal. Here that same inscrutable power of transformation (which defies conventional logic) is embraced by the servant with overwhelming force. This servant gives self over to the hurts and guilts that he could have shunned. He does not shun, but embraces. And "we" are made whole, that is, "given shalom."

The appropriation of hurt and guilt could not happen boisterously, aggressively, or violently. It is done, rather, silently, peacefully, with no violence, with not even an outcry (vs. 7–9). The servant acts vulnerably, in the only way hurt can be healed or sin assuaged. Thus the poem not only witnesses to the agent but also radically asserts the only kind of act that can heal and make whole. In his staggering appearance and in his more staggering action, the servant has indeed changed the world, tilting it (and us) toward wholeness and well-being.

Now the promise of 52:13 will be kept (53:10–12). We return to the word "prosper" (see 52:13). This utterly obedient one will have long life and prosperity. The one who gave his life will receive back an abundant life. He will be exalted and lifted up, because he carried the burdens that were unbearable for the others.

On this holy day, the poem helps the church in rediscerning what Jesus has done and is doing. Jesus' entry into the hurt and guilt of the world has indeed changed the world toward wholeness. We must not exult and expostulate too much. The poem, and its evangelical enactment in the cross, do not warrant loud claims. They call rather for stunned, awed silence in the face of a mystery too deep for speculation or explanation. The miracle here characterized calls for a long, quiet, grateful pause. We watch while God acts vulnerably to do what could only be done vulnerably, caringly, at enormous risk, hurt, and pain. We watch while a healed world is birthed out of the wretchedness.

Psalm 22 (A B C)

The power of Ps. 22 lies in the fact that it is a statement by one who has felt utterly cut off from both God and the human community, yet who, in the end, achieves a remarkable level of peace and lifts to God moving affirmations of thanksgiving and praise. The manner in which the poet initially (vs. 1–21) alternates between expressions of despair and self-reminders of God's goodness in the past strengthens the forcefulness of the text, as if to portray the emotions of one who is utterly at the end of life's rope. The text thus becomes the vehicle for expressing the hopelessness of anyone who feels cut off from all the sources of support so necessary for happiness and well-being. And because of later echoes of this psalm in the narratives of Jesus' passion (especially vs. 1, 7–8, 18), it has a particular relevance for the Good Friday observance.

The "movement" in vs. 1–21 is that of one who tries without success to raise his head, only to sink again into despair and frustration. After having complained to God that God is not to be found in spite of all the poet's efforts (vs. 1–2), the thought of the poor mortal turns to the history of God's people (vs. 3–5). Yet the promises of old,

> To you [our ancestors] cried, and were saved;
> in you they trusted, and were not put to shame,

become a bitter mockery to the psalmist for the very reason that God's saving activity of yesteryear seems not to be available here and now.

Again the cycle is repeated, but this time the psalmist complains of total alienation from the human community. With the bitterness of one who has taken life's social relationships for granted, only to discover how vital they are now that they are gone, the poet laments the loneliness of isolation. Those other human beings who should be sources of comfort and strength have turned their backs, so that in v. 6 the very humanity of the psalmist is brought into question:

> I am a worm, and not human.

Once more a remembrance of the past goodness of God is raised by the poet (vs. 9–11), with special emphasis on one of the strongest of all human bonds, that of the mother and the child. But in despair, the poet must acknowledge that the God who created and sustained him is now nowhere to be found.

Having vainly tried twice to lift his spirits through references to the past goodness of God, the psalmist now attempts to describe his total desolation (vs. 12–21). Most of the metaphors employed here have counterparts elsewhere in the Psalter (compare Pss. 31:9–10;

32:3–4), but the manner in which they are piled on one another imparts an unusually heavy mood of melancholy and resignation.

In a general sense, vs. 1–21 give tongue to the unutterable despair felt by one whom circumstance has cast completely adrift from all the reference points of life and from all other persons who lend joy and hope. There is no glimmer of divine grace, except that which the memory can borrow from the past. Only the act of prayer itself, which implies that someone must be listening, betrays any hope on the part of the poet. God is gone, and God's only presence is a distant flame, whose glimmer can be seen faintly across the years. The entire substance of vs. 1–21 is summed up in v. 1.

Yet there are two features that prevent these stanzas from becoming, like Ps. 88, an almost completely negative statement. The first is that vs. 1–21 are balanced by vs. 22–31, where the saving deeds of God are celebrated with thanksgiving and joy. (For comments on vs. 22–31, see the Second Sunday in Lent, Year B.) The other—and far more important—feature of this text is to be found in its association with the sufferings of Jesus Christ. As noted above, this includes direct connections with the passion narratives in the New Testament, but it is an association that extends beyond these verbal links. For whoever the original psalmist may have been or whatever human figure that inspired writer may have had in mind, Christians have understood that this psalm describes in a special way that human being who, because of the weight of sin attached to his suffering and death, stood in greatest isolation from God—Jesus Christ!

Thus, one cannot read v. 1 as an expression of one's own sense of apartness from God without remembering the utter despair with which these same words fell from the lips of the Crucified (Mark 15:34). One cannot consider vs. 7–8 as relevant to whatever betrayal and isolation one has experienced from those who were supposed to be friends without remembering the betrayal and mockery of Jesus (John 18). And one cannot find in v. 18 a statement concerning injustice suffered at the hands of others without recalling the terrible miscarriage of justice at Calvary (John 19:23–24).

But if despair, betrayal, and injustice had been the only realities at Calvary, we would today remember the execution of the Galilean peasant in a very different way, if we remembered it at all. However, in the end, despair was overturned by hope, betrayal gave way to trust, and injustice was conquered by the righteousness of God. For Good Friday was subordinated to Easter, and joy returned: the God who seemed to have forsaken Jesus raised him from the dead. And in Jesus' place, God crucified the despair of those who were convinced that they could never find God again.

Hebrews 4:14–16; 5:7–9 (A B C)

In its opening chapters, the Christology of Hebrews strikes a tone of exaltation. Jesus is the "heir of all things" (1:2), an agent of creation (v. 2), superior even to the angels (vs. 5–14). Even if the subjection of Jesus to the weakness of human life is mentioned (for example, 2:14–18), that subjection pales in comparison with the language that celebrates the "apostle and high priest of our confession" (3:1). In its characterization of Jesus as the "great high priest who has passed through the heavens" (4:14) and as "without sin" (v. 15), the passage assigned for Good Friday continues this theme of the exaltation of Jesus. Alongside the exaltation of Jesus, however, this passage sounds a different note. Jesus is able to "sympathize with our weaknesses" (4:15), and Jesus "offered up prayers and supplications, with loud cries and tears" (5:7). Like human beings who serve as priests, Jesus' priesthood results from God's will, rather than his own (5:1–6).

At the heart of the passage is a comparison of Jesus' priesthood with that of human beings. This comparison allows the author of Hebrews to say something important about Jesus and, at the same time, to offer comfort and encouragement to the audience. In 5:1–4, Hebrews describes three aspects of the priesthood of human beings. Human priests have a particular function (they are "put in charge of things pertaining to God"); they have certain personal characteristics (they are themselves "subject to weakness" and "must offer sacrifice" for their sins); and they are designated by God ("And one does not presume to take this honor, but takes it only when called by God").

Hebrews 5:5–10 demonstrates that the priesthood of Jesus shares in these same three aspects, taking the three in an order that is the reverse of vs. 1–4. First Jesus, like human priests, serves at the appointment of God (vs. 5–6). Second, again like human priests, Jesus has the characteristic of being subject to weakness. Jesus' weakness is not sin—a statement that seems unimaginable to Hebrews (4:15)—but nevertheless Jesus participates in the human vulnerability of feelings and needs. As evidence of Jesus' human feelings, the author refers to Jesus' act of offering "prayers and supplications, with loud cries and tears" (5:7). Read in the context of Good Friday, these "loud cries and tears" appear to refer to the agony of Jesus on the cross. In the context of Hebrews, however, where Jesus' supplication addresses "the one who was able to save him from death," Jesus' cries seem to be a plea for deliverance from *out of death.* That is, the author envisions the already crucified and dead Jesus calling to God for deliverance from death. The overarching point, however, remains that Jesus' priesthood is one characterized by sympathy with human anguish. Third, like human priests, Jesus' priesthood has a function. He learned obedience through his suffering (5:8), and he initiated not just forgiveness of sins but eternal salvation for humankind (vs. 8–9). In v. 10, the author places Jesus within the priestly order of Melchizedek, essentially repeating the opening verse of the passage with its designation of Jesus as the "great high priest."

In an attempt to make real the familiar story of Jesus' death as a criminal, Christian preachers and teachers sometimes emphasize the details of physical and emotional suffering produced by crucifixion. And, indeed, the cruelty and shame attached to this particular form of execution, reserved largely for the outcasts of society, can serve to counter the romanticism signified by the wearing of the cross as jewelry. Sometimes, however, rehearsal of the horrifying details of crucifixion has the effect of suggesting that the significance of Jesus' death arises from the extent of his suffering; that is, Jesus suffered extreme physical pain and, as a result, brought about a glorious form of salvation for humankind. The flaw in this way of thinking about the crucifixion can be seen when other deaths, arguably even more cruel and inhumane, enter the conversation. Many of those who died in the Holocaust, with no shred of human respect or decency, as a result of an unbelievable process of cruelty and torture, surely endured more sheer physical pain and emotional grief than did Jesus or other victims of crucifixion. Does that mean that their deaths are somehow salvific or that their pain purchased the eternal life of others? In common with other New Testament writers, the author of Hebrews would answer that question negatively. Hebrews does not elaborate the details of Jesus' pain because that pain is not itself salvific. Jesus' priesthood derives, not from the quantity of his suffering, but from God and from Jesus' own obedience. It is God's sacrifice of Jesus, God's Son, that makes Jesus appropriate as "great high priest."

This reflection on the priesthood of Jesus, here as elsewhere in Hebrews, has a pastoral thrust to it. *Because* of Jesus' priesthood, believers may and should "hold fast" to their confession (4:14), confident that what they say together about God is reliable. Believers may and should "approach the throne of grace with boldness" (4:16), for Jesus has taught them that God hears their prayers. Believers need not be afraid of God, who wants them to approach and who intends to help them.

John 18:1–19:42 (A B C)

John's narrative of Jesus' arrest, trials, crucifixion, and burial is made up of numerous individual scenes, each of which is appropriate for a Good Friday sermon. And yet the two chapters are themselves a literary gem, relating the events with sophistication and subtlety. The preacher's task is to isolate a piece of the broader story for preaching, but at the same time (as with all the Johannine narratives) not to lose sight of the whole and the powerful impact it makes on the careful reader. The skillfully fashioned narrative presents a portrait of Jesus as King of the Jews, who is in complete charge of his own destiny, in the presence of religious authorities who lose faith and governmental officials who lose power.

In reading the narrative, it is critical to notice the strategy of staging that gives individual scenes enormous force. Two examples (though there are many): (*a*) Jesus is questioned before Annas and Caiaphas in scenes that in themselves carry little significance (18:12–14, 19–24, 28). The scenes serve, however, an important purpose in that the narrator interrupts the questioning to tell about the denials of Peter (vs. 15–18, 25–27) happening simultaneously. The readers are faced then with two trials, one in which Jesus affirms his consistent testimony and is punished with a slap on the face by a guard and another in which Peter rejects his real relationships and goes free. (*b*) When Jesus is brought to Pilate, we are told that the Jewish authorities do not enter the praetorium, so as to maintain their ritual purity (v. 28). Pilate moves back and forth from talking to the Jews on the outside to talking to Jesus on the inside. The careful staging highlights the ludicrous behavior of the religious people, preoccupied with eating the Passover lamb, but all the while preparing for the death of the Lamb of God. A universal hazard of religious people!

Almost every scene in the narrative exhibits at least some element of irony, incongruities that expose the true nature of Jesus and the feeble, often pretentious schemes of other characters. For example, before Jesus is sentenced Pilate has him flogged by the soldiers, who turn the scene into a mock coronation of the King of the Jews (19:1–3). Interestingly, the narrator never uses the word "mock" (as do the Synoptic accounts), nor is it suggested that this is a charade. The soldiers see and speak the truth when they say, "Hail, King of the Jews!" He is in fact a rejected, maligned King.

Perhaps the most telling irony in the story occurs when Pilate brings Jesus outside the praetorium face to face with the Jews and announces him as "your King." When the people persist in demanding that Jesus be crucified, they justify their actions to Pilate by declaring, "We have no king but the emperor" (19:13–15). Within hours they would recite in their Passover liturgy that their only king is God, but here, in order to reject Jesus, they have to reject God. They unwittingly testify to the fact that Jesus and the Father are one.

Pilate is a key player in the narrative, occupying center stage with Jesus from 18:28 to 19:22. From early on, the reader gets the clear impression that Pilate, representing the power of political authority, is on trial, not Jesus. Jesus asks the pertinent question (18:34) and points out that Pilate inadvertently acknowledges his kingship (v. 37). "Do you not know that I have power to release you, and power to crucify you?" Pilate asks rhetorically (19:10), but as the trial progresses it becomes increasingly clear that Pilate has no power at all. The religious authorities play the stronger hand. Where once Pilate offered the authorities the choice of Jesus or Barabbas, now the tables are turned, and the authorities offer Pilate the choice of Jesus or Caesar (v. 12). Inside the praetorium Pilate is impressed with Jesus, but outside he is at the mercy of his subjects.

But ultimately it is neither Pilate nor the religious authorities who hold the power at the trial and crucifixion. The narrator includes three fulfillment scenes (vs. 23–24, 28, 36–37), whereby details of the story are viewed in light of the Hebrew scriptures, as the fulfillment of divine predictions. The effect is to remind the reader that what is happening is part of the greater plan of God. Jesus confronts Pilate's pretense of power: "You would have no power over me unless it had been given you from above" (v. 11). At his death Jesus utters a word not of distress or God-forsakenness, but of completion: "It is finished" (v. 30). The purpose of God has been fulfilled.

Easter

Perhaps on no other Sunday of the Christian year are the lections so nicely focused as they are for Easter Day. The common themes of the reality of death, the powerful intrusion of the delivering God, and the manifold responses to resurrection run prominently through the texts—themes needing to be rehearsed in every congregation.

The readings from Ps. 118 and from John 20 honestly face *the reality of death.* In the former, as the psalmist rejoices at an occasion of divine deliverance, death is remembered as the threat, the power opposed to God, from whose clutches God has provided rescue. In the latter, Mary acknowledges the devastation of death and begins to come to grips in a reasonable way with her grief and consternation. In neither case is there any covering over of the fierce and destructive fashion in which death separates and threatens the vitality of life.

Prominent in the texts is the announcement of *God's deliverance from death,* the divine "power play" that brings life not only for "the one ordained by God as judge of the living and the dead" (Acts 10:42), but also for God's people (Col. 3:1–4). The resurrection of Jesus is more than a miracle; it is an eschatological event that makes possible a radical style of new life. Closed worlds are broken open, and old perceptions of what is plausible and possible are shattered. The future becomes a promise of sharing in the resurrection (Col. 3:1–4).

Finally, in varying ways, the Easter texts enumerate *several responses to God's deliverance.* The psalmist offers a prayer of thanksgiving for the Lord, "my strength and my might," who "has become my salvation" (118:14). Mary becomes a witness to declare, "I have seen the Lord" (John 20:18). The text of Peter's sermon alludes to eucharistic fellowship and puts the hearers under a mandate to preach and testify to the risen Jesus (Acts 10:41–42). First Corinthians 15 is a reminder that Jesus' resurrection is a critical chapter in a larger story, reaching back to Adam and forward to the Second Advent. In the meantime, the call is to steadfastness and growth in the work of the Lord. In both worship and everyday human relationships, responses are made to the gracious word of the empty tomb, the word of divine deliverance.

Acts 10:34–43 (A B C)

The Easter celebration is the central event of the Christian year, the center around which all else revolves. In recognition of its special character, the lectionary provides during the entire Easter season (including Pentecost) a reading from Acts as a first lesson. The emphasis in these texts is on the kerygmatic proclamation of the early church and on the work of the Holy Spirit in the response of women and men to that proclamation. The death and resurrection of Christ are viewed by these texts as God's acts of grace, by which women and men are saved and reconciled to God and to one another. In certain respects, many of these texts are the gospel *in nuce,* and that is certainly the case with the passage at hand.

Acts 10:34–43 is one of several sermons by Peter reported in Acts, this one directed to a godly Roman centurion, Cornelius. It is evident to the reader of this text that the presence of the Roman is not incidental to the narrative, inasmuch as the author of Acts wishes to use this occasion to stress the universality of the gospel. Not only has the Spirit spoken to the Roman in a dream commanding him to seek out the preached word (10:1–8, 30–33), but Peter has likewise received a special visitation, which declares, in effect, God's inclusion of Gentiles in the church (vs. 9–16). Yet, even though we have been prepared by these elements for the inclusive nature of Peter's sermon, the force of Peter's universalism is as refreshing as it is energetic. Twice in a single breath the inclusiveness of the gospel is stressed: "In every nation anyone who fears [God] and does what is right is acceptable to him" (v. 35) and "Jesus Christ—he is Lord of all" (v. 36). No matter that the first of these assertions lays emphasis on the oneness of the human family before God, while the second is primarily focused on the unlimited nature of Christ's dominion. In the final analysis, they boil down to a basic affirmation: neither race nor any other quality that marks some as different from others may separate a person from the love of Christ. Neither ought these qualities to separate persons from one another.

Then Peter turns to the Word itself (notice how the declaration of "the message"—or, "the word" [NRSV]—in v. 36 is repeated in v. 37

and made the focus of the balance of the passage). Verses 37–42 recount the events that, in greater detail, are recorded by the four evangelists. Jesus, who had been empowered by God from the beginning (v. 38a), lived a life of remarkable good works, which were intended to thwart the power of the devil (v. 38b) and which were experienced by many people (v. 39a). (Notice that no mention is here made of what Jesus taught.) The outcome of this good life was Jesus' execution (v. 39b). But God did not allow this evil to carry the day, for God both raised Jesus from the dead on the third day and demonstrated his resurrection to those whom God chose as witnesses (vs. 40–41a). These witnesses joined Jesus in eating and drinking—a remark (v. 41b) with clear eucharistic overtones—and they have been charged with the responsibility of spreading the word about the risen Christ (v. 42). Then, almost as an afterthought, the role of the Old Testament prophets is recalled (v. 43).

Two considerations. The first is that this passage, which began by striking such a strong chord of inclusiveness, defines the human family more narrowly only at one point: those who were/are witnesses to the resurrection of Jesus do not include everyone, only those "chosen by God" (v. 41). At first blush this seems a contradiction of the bright note of universalism with which the lection opens. If God "shows no partiality" (v. 34), why are only some chosen? If Jesus Christ is "Lord of all" (v. 36), why are not all persons his witnesses?

The text has, of course, confronted one of those imponderable paradoxes of the gospel. Although the arms of the risen Christ are stretched wide to receive all persons, only some exhibit evidence of the work of the Spirit within them. And since their testimony is that it is not they, but God, who has initiated this saving relationship, we cannot help but wonder about others. Yet of one thing we may be sure: God has not abandoned them or ceased to yearn for them. But the limits of human understanding prevent us from saying more.

A second consideration: the unambiguous turning point in the text is v. 40. All that goes before and all that comes after hinges on the resurrection of Christ. It is the resurrection that demonstrates in a unique manner God's vindication of Jesus and that overturns the work of those who plotted evil. (Notice how, in the text, the murderers of Jesus are not singled out for God's wrath. These people are simply referred to by the innocuous pronoun "they" in v. 39b.) It is also the resurrection that makes it possible for those "chosen by God" to be witnesses to the risen Christ, to eat and drink with him, and to preach and to testify that God raised him from the dead.

In its spare and economical language, Acts 10:34–43 reminds us of that central affirmation of the Christian faith that is repeated in countless ways on Easter Day: "Jesus Christ is risen today. Alleluia!" Let us keep the feast!

Psalm 118:1–2, 14–24 (A B C)

(See Palm Sunday for vs. 1–2, 19–24.)

The speaker of these verses (14–24) has just been rescued by God from the assaulting nations (vs. 10–13). A seemingly hopeless situation has been transformed by the radical intrusion of God: "The LORD helped me" (v. 13). For that reason, the speaker gives thanks to God. In the context of Easter, the church reads this psalm as the voice of Jesus, who has been beset by the powers of death. It is only by the greater power of God that the life of Jesus is wrenched out of the grip of death. For that reason, thanksgiving is an appropriate tone and posture for Easter.

Our reading begins with a powerful assertion (v. 14). "[Yahweh] is my strength . . . my might . . . my salvation." The psalm echoes the language of Moses, who celebrates God's massive defeat of the Egyptian empire (Ex. 15:1–3). This verdict is, on the one hand, a conclusion in the psalm, derived from the recent rescue. On the other hand, it is a premise for what follows in the psalm. God's recent rescue of the speaker becomes the ground for the hope and buoyancy that follow.

The voice of the psalm is one of grateful righteousness (Ps. 118: 15–20). The "righteous" are not necessarily the good or the obedient or the pious. They are, rather, the ones who are rescued and vindicated by God. The text speaks of the "tents of the righteous," where the rescued live (v. 15), the "gates of righteousness" through which the obedient enter to worship (v. 19), and the entry of the righteous, the willingness of Yahweh's rescued to come to worship (v. 20). This community consists of those who have known God's massive action on their behalf and who live their lives in glad response to that action. While there is a moral dimension to righteousness, this psalm concerns those who are glad benefactors of God's powerful love. They are righteous not because of what they have done, but because of what they have received from God.

The righteous are not self-congratulatory. Rather, they are exuberantly grateful. They shift all attention away from themselves to the rescuing power of God. Thus the grateful rescued sing three times, "The right hand . . . the right hand . . . the right hand" (vs. 15–16), an allusion to God's powerful, continuing purpose and presence. The church knows at Easter, as this psalm knows, that Easter would not have happened, and new life would not have been given, except by God's powerful intrusion.

It is because of that "right hand" of power that the speaker draws the conclusion, "I shall not die" (vs. 17–19). I was about to; I could have, but I did not, because God moved against death. Death is a formidable power, which wants to take control; but God will not let it happen. Thus death is not simply a state of negativity, but is an active force for evil. Evil, however, is no match for the power and resolve of God, and so singing is appropriate. Note well that the entire structure of these verses depends on understanding death as an active force, which cannot withstand the authority of God. Neither this text nor the claim of Easter makes sense unless God and the power of death are seen to be in profound conflict.

The utterance of the word "death" is decisive for this psalm. In the world of modernity, it is exceedingly difficult to voice "death" as a hostile power that threatens to undo our lives. That, however, is what the psalm is about. And that is what Jesus knows between Friday and Sunday. Jesus is being undone by the power of death, and the world is being undone with him. But Yahweh "did not give me over to [the power of] death" (v. 18), because God has kept me for the power and prospect of life.

The reading ends in boundless gratitude (vs. 21–24). God has answered. God has heard the need. God has rushed to intervene. God has changed death to life. God has overpowered Friday for the sake of Sunday. The rejected one, left for dead, is the valued one (v. 22).

What a day (v. 24)! The day of rescue is a day for joy. What a day—Easter Day—life day—new day—beginning day. It is a special day. For those saturated with the claims of this psalm, every day is a day of new life. This is the day of God's power for life, and therefore our day of singing and gratitude. On this day, God's people are at a beginning, not an ending.

Colossians 3:1–4

In the joyous festival of Easter, Christians proclaim that God triumphs even over death itself. Easter celebrates not the regular renewal of the earth in spring, not even the astounding event of the resuscitation of an individual, but the faithfulness of God, whose promises are secure. As Paul insists in 1 Cor. 15, the importance of Jesus' resurrection for Christian faith is paramount, because it is in Jesus' resurrection that we see the power of God most clearly.

Christians understand the consequences of Easter for believers in terms of this "power play" on God's part. Jesus' resurrection guarantees God's power and faithfulness not only to Jesus himself, but to every human being. Jesus is the "first fruits" (1 Cor. 15:20) of the harvest, which will be God's final triumph and the eternal life of God's people.

In Col. 3:1–4, the resurrection takes on ethical consequences by virtue of the connectedness between the believer and the resurrection of Christ: "If you have been raised with Christ, seek the things that are above, where Christ is, seated at the right hand of God." The connection appears in a more explicit fashion earlier in the letter: "You were also raised with him through faith in the power of God, who raised him from the dead" (2:12). Already, even in the present time, believers somehow participate in the resurrected life of Jesus Christ. Their understandings and behavior take their cues from God's triumph over death in Jesus.

This identification of the believer with the resurrected Jesus seems, at first glance, to contradict Paul's words in Rom. 6, where he carefully distinguishes the believer's present participation in the death of Christ through baptism from future participation in the resurrection of Christ (Rom. 6:5–11). Perhaps Corinthian enthusiasm led Paul to be cautious about asserting the present identification of believers with the resurrection. In Colossians, we do find a caution, although it comes to expression in a slightly different way. Even if the believer already shares in the resurrection, a final revelation of Christ's future glory awaits, and that revelation will also contain the glory of believers (Col. 3:4)

More important than this distinction between the present and the future is the fact that the identification between believers and the resurrected Christ is not an identification that glorifies the believer. Instead, it is an identification that empowers the believer to live in a certain way: "Set your minds on things that are above, not on things that are on earth." What this means, of course, requires careful exploration, especially since Christians have often used such language to justify a negative view of the human body and, indeed, life itself. This language has also served to justify the status quo. If slaves could be made to believe that life in the present does not really matter, then they might tolerate their oppression passively.

What does the author mean by "things that are above" and "things that are on earth"? Colossians 3:5–10 indicates that "earthly" things are not synonymous with everything on earth but with thoughts and actions that abuse the self and others: sexual immorality, greed, evil desires, deceitful practices of all sorts. "Things that are above," by contrast, refer to a life that is determined by the "new self" (3:10). This renewal recognizes no divisions between peoples but only a oneness in Christ (3:11). It lives out of the peace and love of Jesus Christ, and is ruled by the indwelling of the word of Christ (3:16). The things "above," then, consist of the mind-set and life conformed to the life of Christ.

The language of Col. 3 sounds to the ears of contemporary American Christians a bit quaint and even moralistic. Behind the moralisms, however, stands a profound understanding of the difference between a life controlled by a finite, even warped, human understanding of what is right and wrong and a life controlled by the renewal of humanity brought about through the death and resurrection of Jesus Christ. In Jesus Christ, God enables believers not only to glimpse but to embody an alternative perspective on the world, one shaped by the knowledge that God indeed creates, that God's power indeed triumphs over all other powers, and that, in Jesus Christ, God signals the redemption of humankind.

Our passage functions as a kind of pivot in the letter as a whole. Up to this point, Colossians is largely preoccupied with explaining God's action in Jesus Christ and the church—what is conventionally referred to as the indicative. From Col. 3:1 on, however, the focus of the letter turns to the imperative—what believers are to do in response to God's action. The resurrection of Jesus connects these two parts of the letter. It is the specific act of God in raising Jesus Christ from the dead, and the believer's connection with that resurrection, that both authorizes and enables believers to live a radically different kind of life. To have the mind-set of "things that are above," then, is to be shaped and motivated by the Christ who sits at God's right hand.

If 1 Cor. 15 portrays the resurrection of Jesus as a "power play" on God's part, a demonstration of God's power in advance of God's final triumph, then Col. 3 portrays the way in which that power play empowers believers in the present time.

John 20:1–18 (A B C)

At the heart of the Gospel reading for Easter is the resurrection appearance of Jesus to Mary Magdalene, leading to her confession, "I have seen the Lord." The narrative tells a wonderful story of a seeking woman, who is surprised by what she finds, or better, by the One who finds her. Hearing her name spoken by Jesus' familiar voice brings a transformation of her grief and the opening of a new world. A number of exegetical puzzles in the text remain to be solved, but, fortunately, they do not hinder our grasp of the basic story.

The actual encounter between Mary and Jesus occupies only four of the eighteen verses. We need, therefore, to pay special attention to what occurs prior to the encounter, in order to be able to understand what is at stake in Jesus' disclosure to Mary, and we need to take note of the brief account of Mary's response to Jesus in the closing verse.

Mary's participation in the story is marked by three parallel statements she makes—to the two disciples (John 20:2), to the two angels at the tomb (v. 13), and to Jesus, alias the gardener (v. 15). Her preoccupation is with the body of Jesus. The empty tomb does not prod her to faith, but rather makes her worry about what has become of the corpse. Who might the "they" be who "have taken the Lord out of the tomb" (v. 2)? The Jews? Joseph of Arimathea and Nicodemus? Grave robbers? The gardener?

Mary's anxiety and consternation are natural. She comes to the tomb early, perhaps for a time of private grieving, for beginning the slow, painful process of coming to grips with the absence of one she deeply loves. Her tears are right on the surface. The cemetery is an appropriate place to grieve. But the removal of the stone and the empty tomb disrupt what she is about and only create fear and frustration. Her mind moves logically to the conclusion that someone has taken Jesus' body. What other possibility might there be?

When faced with the open tomb, Mary functions as a reasonable, sane character. Her grief does not cloud her rational faculties. She arrives at the only conclusion a person in her (and our) right mind can arrive at. Dead bodies do not simply "disappear." Someone has to move them. In a world of cause and effect, of established rules as to what can happen and how, in a closed structure that allows only for the old and familiar to recur, Mary's logic is right on target. Find the body, wherever it has been taken, and get on with grieving.

Apparently, the two disciples (at least, "the other disciple") share Mary's predicament. On hearing the news of the empty tomb, they go to the site and confirm things for themselves. The grave clothes are there, all neatly folded. The text reports that "the other disciple . . . saw and believed" (v. 8). But believed what? Clearly *not* that Jesus was risen from the dead, since the text goes on to explain that the disciples did not yet understand the scripture and that they "returned to their homes." Their experience of the resurrected Jesus comes later (vs. 19–29). For now, what "the other disciple" believed was evidently Mary's report that the tomb was empty. His investigations confirm her statement. He sees no more than she sees, but he is less inquisitive.

Mary's closed world (and ours) is broken open when Jesus calls her name. Something illogical, impossible, and unnatural takes place. The One who was certified as dead (19:33) greets Mary. The established rules as to what can happen and how are overthrown. The old plausibility structure is left in shambles. It is a new day.

The part of the dialogue between Mary and Jesus, though not entirely transparent, is critical. Mary says to the gardener, "Tell me where you have laid him, and *I will take him away*" (20:15, emphasis added). Mary wants the body of Jesus; she wants to do for him what is conventional and proper. She cannot accept the prospect that the corpse has been stolen or hidden. He deserves a decent burial. Jesus responds, *"Do not hold on to me,* because I have not yet ascended to the Father" (20:17, emphasis added). The risen Jesus cannot be controlled, even by Mary's loving concern for him. Her logical and kindly pursuit of his deceased body simply does not leave room for the miracle that has happened, for resurrection, for ascension. The voice of Jesus calling her name shatters her customary world, reasonable though it may be, and opens up a brand-new future. What she is to do is to grieve no longer, but to go to the disciples with the word of Jesus' impending ascension.

Mary's reaction includes an obedient response to Jesus' command and an amazing statement, "I have seen the Lord" (v. 18). Her preoccupation with the corpse is made irrelevant by her encounter with the risen Jesus. Her logical language of cause and effect is replaced by the language of confession. It is a confession to sustain her in the new era without the historical Jesus, an era, nonetheless, in which Jesus' God and Father is the God and Father of the church (the word "your," where used in v. 17, is plural).

SECOND SUNDAY OF EASTER

Often called "Low Sunday," this Second Sunday of Easter provides an opportunity to explore various dimensions of Jesus' resurrection and the implications for human community. Though each text has its own peculiar perspective on the delivering power of God, in a remarkable way the texts group themselves.

The readings from Ps. 16 and Acts 2 naturally fit together, since the latter quotes the former. Both celebrate the presence of God in human life and the powerful expression of that presence. The psalmist trusts in Yahweh's protecting hand in the face of Sheol, and gives thanks that he has not only been spared the "Pit" but has been given direction by God for "the path of life" (Ps. 16:11). In his Pentecost sermon Peter sees a messianic application of the psalm to the resurrection of Jesus. God is not absent from the crucifixion, but is expressly present in raising Jesus, in not abandoning him to Hades or letting him suffer corruption.

By quoting Ps. 16, Peter's sermon also takes seriously the power of death that has been overcome by the power of God. In the resurrection, Jesus is "freed . . . from death," delivered from a power that could not hold him (Acts 2:24). The citation of the psalm serves as a reminder that death and resurrection are broader than the issues of physical death and immortality. They connote the various forces that hinder life's full expression and the promise of God's presence to overcome their intimidation and paralysis.

Just as the readings from Ps. 16 and Acts 2 exhibit parallel concerns, so the passages from John 20 and 1 Peter 1 demonstrate similarities. Two common and even interrelated features are prominent. First, both texts affirm that resurrection creates community. The image of "new birth" (1 Peter 1:3) implies a new family, a new relatedness for mutual support in a time of various trials. John 20:19–23 stresses the close continuity between the risen Jesus and the emerging church.

Second, both 1 Peter and John stress the faith and love of Christians that arise without the experience of physical contact with Jesus. Instead, for later generations belief and commitment are born out of the witness of others, out of the repeated declarations of forgiveness, out of the nurture and support of the very community that Jesus' resurrection created.

Acts 2:14a, 22–32

The report in Acts 2 of Peter's Pentecost sermon and of the impact the sermon had on its hearers provides the lectionary texts (first reading) for the three Sundays following Easter. As in the Acts 10 lection for Easter, the focus is on the centrality of the resurrection of Christ.

Luke has shaped Peter's sermon to the Pentecost multitude in order that the resurrection theme may be emphasized in different ways. In vs. 22–32, appeal is made to the Old Testament and to the model Old Testament king, David. Before that appeal is made, however, the kerygma is proclaimed (vs. 22–24): Jesus, in spite of performing the wonderful deeds of God, was murdered by evil persons. But God raised Jesus from the dead!

Several elements are noteworthy in this proclamation, the first being the contrast between the good works that God accomplished through Jesus and the evil deed performed by those who crucified Jesus. Nothing in Jesus' death was merited or deserved. It came about solely as a result of human sin.

A second interesting feature in vs. 22–24 is the inevitability of the resurrection, given the nature of God. Nowhere in the New Testament is there the slightest hint that Jesus' resurrection was the outcome of a struggle between God and Satan that resulted in God's triumph. Rather, God magisterially acts to resurrect the dead Jesus, much as God magisterially spoke the words at Creation. "God raised [Jesus] up . . . because"—since God is who God is—"it was impossible for [Jesus] to be held in [death's] power" (v. 24).

A third important element in this brief proclamation is the reference to the continuing activity of God. It is God who worked through Jesus—the "deeds of power, wonders, and signs" of v. 22—and it is God who raised Jesus from the dead. This assertion rules out any effort to understand Jesus as just another good man. It also denies that Jesus is some superman who, through his own toughness, has cheated death. God was the operative force in what Jesus did for others (v. 22) and God is the power behind the resurrection (v. 24).

Peter's appeal to the Old Testament, as Luke has recorded it, occurs in a reference to Ps. 16:8–11, quoted here in a form somewhat different from that which occurs in the Hebrew Bible. Verses 27–28 (Ps. 16:10–11) are clearly that part of the psalm which appeals to Peter's interest in the resurrection, the apostle's logic (in vs. 29–32) running like this: The psalm describes salvation from death and restoration to life. Since it is obvious that David is dead, he could not have been referring to himself. Thus, he must have been referring to Jesus. Of the resurrection, Peter and others are witnesses (v. 32).

Much has been said elsewhere about the numerous speeches that occur in Acts and the extent to which these represent a tendency among many Hellenistic writers to allow an interpretation of important events to be made by influential characters in the narrative. While the use of this artistic device may shape our understanding of the nature of Acts as literature and our understanding of the methods of Luke, it does serve to remind the reader (and preacher) that Peter's sermon in Acts 2 (like similar sermons elsewhere in Acts) is more than just padding to the narrative. To the contrary, the sermon interprets the events described by the narrative. It introduces us to the grand scheme of what is afoot.

What is afoot here, of course, is that God is at work in the world in profoundly decisive ways. God established the monarchy of old and, in Luke's view, inspired the quintessential Old Testament king to point beyond himself to Jesus, in ways that would have perhaps surprised even David himself. God was at work in Jesus throughout his earthly life, but supremely so at the resurrection, that moment which reveals God more clearly than any other. And, as future lections from Acts 2 point out, it is God who is at work in the life of the church and in the lives of individual Christians.

All of this reminds us that Easter is a celebration of the vulnerability of God in becoming open to the needs of sinful men and women, and of the power of God in meeting those needs. God's vulnerability is to be recognized in Jesus' being placed within the reach of "those outside the law" (v. 23). God's power is evident in the resurrection (vs. 24, 32). In both of these aspects of the Easter festival women and men encounter a God in touch with their lives, whose vulnerability is a corollary of our own weakness and mortality, and whose strength is our salvation. Without vulnerability, God would be distant and unreachable; without power, irrelevant. But through the vulnerability and power of God, our weakness is made strength.

The central locus of the resurrection in Luke's theology is of crucial importance for the Christian life. That which anchors our hope is confidence that the God who became vulnerable in Jesus Christ and who also demonstrated unique power over those things which threaten all human health and happiness—that this same God is actively at work in human life today, on both individual and societal levels. Because of the Easter story, all of life is fundamentally transformed. As the second reading of the lectionary for this day proclaims: "By [God's] great mercy he has given us a new birth into a living hope through the resurrection of Jesus Christ from the dead" (1 Peter 1:3—see comments in that section).

Psalm 16

This psalm of trust is quoted in part in Peter's sermon as a witness to the resurrection (Acts 2:25–28). The psalm must be read in double focus, on its own terms as a voice of Israel's faith, and as a witness to the resurrection of Jesus.

The psalm begins in a way characteristic of Israel's petitionary prayer (vs. 1–2). The petition is a single imperative verb, "Protect." This is followed by three reasons offered to God in order to motivate God to act: (a) "I take refuge"; (b) "You are my Lord"; and (c) there is no other "good," that is, source of prosperity. While this is a petition, it is clear that there is no anxiety or impatience in the prayer. The petitioner is fully confident of God's attentiveness.

Verses 3–4 provide a reflective interlude, contrasting the two ways of the "holy ones," that is to say, the ones completely devoted to Yahweh's Torah and the choosers of other gods who bring trouble on themselves. The speaker clearly identifies with the first group. The purpose of such an identity is to establish the speaker's covenantal fidelity, and therefore qualification to deserve and receive God's blessing. Thus the need for protection is situated in a life of loyalty and trust. The speaker is fully devoted to God's commands and seeks help from no other source, for this single source is completely adequate.

This affirmation of trust knows that life and well-being are gifts from God. The lines are nearly symmetrical, and we may consider in turn each of the brief poetic units.

1. The psalmist has received from God a goodly inheritance (vs. 5–6). The language of "portion," "lot," and "heritage" recalls Israel's enduring preoccupation with land. Land as free space and as safe place is an overriding concern of ancient Israel and the memory that stands behind the psalm. The speaker is grateful that God has given a pleasant, serene place, a place free from threat, which makes shalom possible.

2. The speaker is preoccupied with God's goodness and lives in happy communion with God (vs. 7–8). This communion with God gives direction to life. A heart attuned to God endlessly instructs, disciplines, enlivens, and illuminates the speaker. A life lived wholly from God and for God and to God has staying power. There will be no threat, no destabilization, no anxiety that can seriously intrude. This psalm voices sweet, gentle, innocent Torah piety as not yet unnerved by questions of injustice.

3. The speaker counts completely on God, without doubt, anxiety, or misgiving (vs. 9–10). "Therefore"! The poem looks back to vs. 7–8. Because the speaker lives in such utter commitment to Yahweh, for that reason there is complete well-being. That well-being is enacted as "glad," "rejoic[ing]," "secure." The well-being here offered concerns all parts of the speaker's life, "heart," "soul," "body." The rhetoric moves from a general (though personal) affirmation to a concrete reference (v. 10).

The speaker remembers a specific time of acute trouble. The trouble is the threat of Sheol, the pressure of nonbeing, the power of the Pit, which will render one helpless. The language is concrete, but it is not specific. We do not know and are not told what the trouble is. We only know that the threat was larger than the resources of the speaker. The threat, however, is more than countered by the affirmation made to God: You did not abandon my life (v. 10). I have been trusting, that is why I am faithful (*ḥāsîd*); now your faithfulness responds with decisive power. Thus the speaker asserts his own fidelity and celebrates God's responding fidelity.

4. The psalm concludes with a happy affirmation (v. 11). After the rescue, life has resumed. Thus the psalm walks us deep into trouble and confidently out again. At the center of the trouble, the speaker has come face-to-face not with death, but with the faithful, powerful presence of God—who does not abandon.

It is easy and obvious to see why this psalm was taken up into the church's preaching of Easter (Acts 2:25–28; 13:35). The quotation of the psalm in the sermon of Peter (Acts 2) is remarkable for its extensiveness and its appropriateness in its new, christological context. It is Jesus who lives at God's right hand of power, and who is able to rejoice; it is Jesus who will not see corruption and will live in God's promise, because God did not abandon Jesus to Hades.

The use of this psalm in Peter's sermon no doubt escalates the intent of the psalm. Most probably the psalm does not address physical death. Rather "death" in the psalm is a metaphor for every threat that diminishes our capacity for the full humanness that God intends. By incorporating the psalm into the story of Jesus, the claims of the psalm are pushed to their theological limit. Even the power of death is not powerful in the face of God's faithful resolve.

There is a great temptation in Easter preaching to focus on "life after death." In the rhetoric of the psalm, it is important that the language of death not be reduced to issues of mortality. The poem refers to the power for life given by God, which overrides every threat to our humanness and every diminishment of our full creaturely existence. That is, the *power of death* may meet us as hunger, poverty, and homelessness, or it may confront us as despair, greed, and anxiety. Christians take Jesus as the classic case where the threat of death is real but the power of life is more powerful.

1 Peter 1:3–9

In the Gospel reading for this week, the risen Jesus responds to the confession of Thomas ("My Lord and my God!") with the words, "Have you believed because you have seen me? Blessed are those who have not seen and yet have come to believe" (John 20:29). That blessing appears to prompt the selection of this passage from 1 Peter, in which the author says that the "exiles," his audience, love and believe in Jesus Christ although they have not seen him (v. 8). Both texts acknowledge the difference between the experience of those who came into contact with Jesus during his ministry and those whose faith comes as a response to proclamation *about* Jesus. Thomas has the opportunity to examine the risen Jesus, an opportunity not offered to later believers. (The importance of this difference should not be exaggerated, of course, since clearly many of Jesus' contemporaries both *saw* and chose *not* to believe.)

If the readings from John and from Acts address the christological implications of the resurrection, this reading approaches it largely in anthropological terms. What is at stake here is not what the resurrection implies about Jesus, but what it accomplishes for human beings: a new birth, an inheritance, and salvation.

The audience of 1 Peter consisted entirely of people who had never seen Jesus, but their faith has created for them such a disruption of the ordinary that the author speaks of it in terms of a new birth: "By his great mercy he has given us a new birth into a living hope through the resurrection of Jesus Christ." (1 Peter 1:3; cf. 2:2). The resurrection of Jesus somehow brings about the "new birth" of human beings. This imagery of new birth, of course, occurs elsewhere in the New Testament, as it does in a variety of religious and philosophical traditions, usually in connection with conversion to a different faith or a radically changed viewpoint. First Peter uses the imagery of new birth to undergird the social cohesion of the community. All those who are reborn through the resurrection of Jesus together belong to a family that nurtures them and sustains them from the menaces of the outside world. The resurrection has, therefore, as its first anthropological implication the creation of a new community constituted of the newly born, or reborn.

The resurrection grants to those who are newly born a "living hope." Taken by itself, this phrase seems to be redundant; how could there be a "dead hope"? Hope that does not live can scarcely be thought of as hope! The significance of the adjective "living" emerges from the context. The "new birth" to this "living hope" comes through resurrection, Jesus' resurrection from the dead. Death stands vanquished by Jesus' resurrection and contrasted with the language of birth and the vibrancy of hope. The resurrection brings life to Jesus and newness of life for humankind.

The new life given to humankind by virtue of the resurrection consists not only of an extended or enhanced biological life, but also of "an inheritance that is imperishable, undefiled, and unfading." Because this inheritance is being "kept in heaven," it clearly refers to some future expectation, although the language itself is highly elusive. Since most things that are inherited—a parcel of land, a sum of money—clearly do perish, become defiled, or fade away, the notion of an inheritance that cannot be diminished recalls the contrast between death and "living hope." More important, inheritance normally occurs within the structure of a family. Those who have been newly born through the resurrection belong together both in the present and in the future. Whatever may be their situation in the present, and vs. 6–7 indicate that they undergo sufferings of some kind, they belong together and have assurance that they will continue to be bound together into the future.

The future will reveal the salvation of believers (v. 5), which constitutes the outcome of faith (v. 9). At first glance, this salvation appears to refer exclusively to the future disposition of the soul, especially as the NRSV translates the end of v. 9 as "the salvation of your souls." The Greek word *psychē*, however, refers not to some abstract piece of the human being, but to the very core of life itself. The outcome (*telos*) of faith, or its fulfillment, ultimately results in the salvation of those who are reborn. While that salvation will appear fully only in the future, Christian confidence in that salvation empowers life in the present and changes it qualitatively, so that salvation can be thought of both as present and as future.

Because Christian proclamation of the resurrection of Jesus Christ involves a flagrant contradiction of the ordinary and observable laws of nature, reflection on the resurrection can easily lapse into regarding it as a trick that serves largely to demonstrate the power of the wonder-worker. Certainly the resurrection does, as 1 Cor. 15 indicates, demonstrate that God's power extends even to death itself, and, as Acts 2 and John 20 indicate, the resurrection poses radical questions about the identity of Jesus. In addition, however, 1 Peter shows that the resurrection of Jesus Christ demonstrably changes the character of human life both in the present and into the future.

John 20:19–31

The calendar on which the lectionary is built follows the sequence of events found in the Gospel of Luke and in Acts—Easter, then forty days to Ascension Day, then ten more days to Pentecost Sunday. The Gospel of John, however, views Jesus' resurrection and ascension and the giving of the Spirit from a different perspective. The statement made to Mary Magdalene, "I am ascending to my Father and your Father" (20:17) turns the appearance to the disciples behind locked doors (20:19–23) and the appearance to the disciples with Thomas present (20:24–29) into post-ascension appearances. In the former of those appearances Jesus gives the gift of the Holy Spirit (20:22). Easter, Ascension, and Pentecost, therefore, are drawn tightly together in John's narrative; in a chronological sense, one might say they are merged. John wants to clarify that Jesus must depart to the Father so that he can send "another Advocate" (14:16), but that the other Advocate will come after only "a little while" (16: 16–20). It all happens on Easter.

The two appearances to the gathered disciples with and without Thomas parallel each other in several ways: Jesus comes despite closed doors on the first day of the week and offers the same greeting. And yet the accounts of the two appearances play differing roles in John's narrative.

1. The first appearance (20:19–23) describes the beginning of the church. All the ingredients are here in the text: a company of disciples; the presence of the crucified, now risen, Christ; the sending of the church into the world; the giving of the Holy Spirit; the message of the forgiveness of sins. With the coalescing of Easter, Ascension, and Pentecost and the particulars of this appearance, the passage stresses the close continuity between Jesus and the church. Just as Jesus is sent by the Father with a mission, so the church is sent by Jesus with a mission. Just as Jesus has been the bearer of the Spirit,

so the church is the bearer of the Spirit. Just as Jesus has declared the forgiveness of sins, so the church declares forgiveness of sins. Though the word "church" (*ekklēsia*) does not appear in the Fourth Gospel, from beginning to end the narrative makes clear that the Christian community finds its model and mandate in Jesus himself. The church is to be hated as Jesus is hated (15:18); it is to be one as Jesus and the Father are one (17:20–23).

The text reminds the contemporary church as well as John's community that it is rooted in and continues the ministry of Jesus. Despite the realistic pressures of voluntarism that constantly plague the local congregation (for example, attracting new members, keeping old ones, motivating people to participate), the church is different from other social groups. It has a divine origin and discovers its reason for being not in its apparent successes or failures, in its growth or influence, but in the call and commission of Christ.

2. The second appearance of Jesus in the passage (20:26–29) concerns the grounds of faith. The narrator goes into detail to recognize Thomas's absence from the first appearance and his doubting of the testimony of the other disciples (20:24–25). When Jesus comes, Thomas has his doubt removed. The One present in the midst of the disciples is none other than the One who was crucified and who continues to bear the scars. Thomas's disbelief is turned into a profound confession of faith.

The concluding statement of Jesus (20:29) does not depreciate Thomas's experience of seeing and believing, but pronounces a blessing on those who believe without the confirming experience Thomas has had. It anticipates generations ahead (at least one generation between the time of Jesus' resurrection and the writing of the Gospel) who cannot "see" in the same way that Thomas has seen. Somewhat ironically, it will be Thomas's testimony, united with the testimony of Mary Magdalene and the other disciples, that leads future followers to faith. The author now has his rationale for writing. This Gospel records a selection of the deeds of Jesus that become the medium to generate and sustain faith in the crucified and risen Messiah. The Word-become-flesh is to be discovered in the written words that testify to his transforming presence. Later generations who believe the written words and are transformed are in no way inferior to Thomas and his first-century colleagues.

THIRD SUNDAY OF EASTER

What does Easter mean? Beyond the startling declaration that "Christ is risen," beyond the empty tomb and the astonished disciples, what is the Easter message and what are we to do with it? Is it simply part of the upbeat mood of the season, when flowers burst into bloom, the weather warms, and the heavy clothes of winter give way to the lighter, brighter garb of spring? How does Easter touch human lives and make a difference? Is the resurrection only an event in Jesus' career and nothing more? How does this story that understandably seemed "an idle tale" actually make sense?

The texts for this Sunday address just these questions as they focus on the various human responses to the news of God's deliverance. Easter becomes more than an anniversary celebration. It intrudes into the lives of real people, evoking worship, confession, repentance, communion, transformation, obedience, and mutual love.

Two dimensions of the responses to God's act of raising Jesus stand out. First, repeatedly the texts speak of public worship. Songs of thanksgiving, reverence, open affirmations of faith, the reading and interpretation of scripture, baptism, the sharing of Communion—all characterize the responses of the people touched by Easter. The resurrection faith is not one about which believers can keep silent. It spurs praise to God and public acknowledgment.

Second, the texts speak also of changed lives. The audience for Peter's sermon at Pentecost was "cut to the heart," resulting in repentance, baptism, and a new orientation. They attended to the means of grace, which became means of growth. In 1 Peter 1 the resurrection effects a new birth, marked by obedience to the truth and mutual love.

The two responses—public worship and transformed lives—are not separated from each other in the texts. One leads to the other, and back again. They belong together as interrelated pieces of the Easter experience, dimensions of the rhythmic response to the mighty act of God in the resurrection of Jesus.

Acts 2:14a, 36–41

This text has been crafted so that it includes both the introduction to Peter's Pentecost sermon (Acts 2:14a) and the sermon's conclusion (v. 36), with the intervening material omitted. Yet these verses serve as brackets to imply that those who hear and interpret this lection will have heard and internalized the message of the sermon (see the reading from Acts for the Second Sunday of Easter). This "frees" the present lection to concentrate on the effects of Peter's preaching (vs. 37–41).

Still, the sermon itself should not be dismissed as incidental to the text. Verse 36, while not mentioning the resurrection directly, clearly has the Easter event in mind. It is because of Jesus' resurrection that one is able to affirm that the crucified Nazarene peasant is no simple victim of a miscarriage of justice. Rather, he is "both Lord and Messiah" (RSV Christ), an absolutely unique expression of the love and presence of God. Furthermore, as is the case throughout Peter's sermon (for example, vs. 22, 24) it is made clear the the Easter event and its consequences are the work of none other than God. We are dealing with no historical accident here, nor with some outsized human strength on the part of Jesus. "*God* has made him both Lord and Christ, this Jesus whom you crucified" (emphasis added).

This unusual doubling of divine titles is an emphatic expression, one that not only serves as an exclamation mark to punctuate the finale of Peter's sermon, but also prepares the reader for the extraordinary response to the sermon, about which we are shortly to be told. The reference to Jesus as Lord (*kyrios* in Greek) is, of course, an affirmation of his deity, as this is precisely the term the Greek Bible of the early Christians, the Septuagint, uses to translate the divine name of Israel's God, *yhwh.* In Paul's view, the confession that Jesus is *kyrios* is the result of the activity of the Spirit of God (1 Cor. 12:3), a connection with which Luke is very much in agreement (Acts 2:37–41, esp. v. 38). *Christos,* or *māšîaḥ,* is the Anointed One of God, the Davidic embodiment of the inbreaking of the kingdom. Thus, to claim that Jesus is "both Lord and Christ" is to claim that the crucified, resurrected One is both God and the bringer of the kingdom of God.

The response to Peter's kerygmatic message is as electric as the sermon itself. The audience, being "cut to the heart," is instructed by Peter first to repent, an act of submission which, in this context, refers not only to their sinfulness in general terms, but specifically in terms that are christological. The failure of Peter's hearers is that of not previously recognizing that Jesus is "both Lord and Christ," and their repentance is of such a nature as to lead to confession of his deity and his messiahship.

Thus Peter's second instruction to his audience is that they be baptized, "every one of you in the name of Jesus Christ" (v. 38), for in Luke's theology, indeed in that of the entire New Testament, confession of faith leads to baptism and to identification with the church, the body of Christian believers. But baptism here is not a liturgical act only; it is the act of becoming open to the presence in one's life of the Holy Spirit of God. Each in its own way, this day's lections lay stress on the connection between openness to God and the change in human life that results from such openness (see esp. Ps. 116:12–13, 17; 1 Peter 1:21–23; Luke 24:32, 35). But only Acts places such emphasis on baptism (mentioned twice) and on the corporate life of the church (compare the eucharistic overtones in the Acts lection for next Sunday). They are the visible evidence of that which the Holy Spirit has done and continues to do within the heart of the believer.

The contextual reality that Peter's sermon is directed at the Jewish community may not be overlooked, yet that should not obscure the universalism of the text. While "all who are far away" (v. 39) is a somewhat obscure phrase, Luke's concern for the Gentile world which is evidenced over and over again both in the Gospel and in Acts seems to imply that Peter's message is really intended for both Jew and non-Jew. "The entire house of Israel" (v. 36) may be the immediate objects of Peter's appeal, but beyond them it is directed to "everyone whom the Lord our God calls" (v. 39). Here, well before Peter's celebrated statements concerning the universality of the gospel in Caesarea (Acts 10:34–35) and in Jerusalem (15:7–11), we find Luke subtly pointing at the direction in which this apostle would lead the church. And although too much weight may be placed on such a brief phrase as "all who are far away," the stand that Peter, Paul, and others took in favor of inclusiveness within the life and work of the church must not be lost on modern readers and interpreters of this text.

The issues before modern churchmen and churchwomen may not relate to Jewishness and Gentileness of persons, but in ways too numerous and painful to recall the church has discriminated against individuals and groups down through the ages, viewing some as second-class Christians. Denying full participation in the life of the church to any group of Christians on the basis of their race, sex, or other characteristics is a denial of the universalism of the gospel, a universalism toward which Peter's words—here merely a hint—are later in Acts directed with full force.

Psalm 116:1–4, 12–19

The faithful must respond when God has acted on their behalf. The rescue wrought by God is an inscrutable act from heaven; our response, however, must be made on earth. This psalm reflects on how to make adequate response to the good news of God.

The psalm begins with a song of thanksgiving (vs. 1–4). This form of prayer is the counterpoint to a psalm of lament. In the lament, the speaker states a description of present trouble, and then petitions for help from God. In a song of thanksgiving, the speaker reviews the previous trouble and acknowledges that God has heard, acted, and overcome the trouble.

The trouble is here described in v. 3. The speaker was in sore straits and experienced life under threat. The speaker prayed to God and asked for deliverance from trouble (v. 4). God heard and acted (vs. 1–2).

In addition to expressing a tone of joy, the speaker is resolved to trust God with all future life. To "love Yahweh" (v. 1) means to acknowledge God's sovereignty and to submit to God's rule, or commandments. To "call on him" means to entrust all future life, all future need and trouble to God. Thus the speaker, in a reflection on a past miracle of deliverance, resolves to maintain a long-term, profound loyalty into the future, come what may.

You may find it useful to read vs. 12–19 from their center in vs. 15–16. The poet enunciates a theological conviction (v. 15), followed by a much more intimate articulation of self-identity (v. 16).

The theological conviction is a generalizing statement (v. 15). The speaker is clear that God pays great attention to the "faithful ones" (*ḥăsîdîm*). They are the ones who diligently keep covenant; God pays daily attention to them because God values them. God notices when the faithful are under threat of death. God engages the power of death, intervening to save the faithful from the power of death.

Then the speaker gives us the specifics that support the preceding verdict (v. 16). The speaker engages in a remarkable act of self-disclosure, announcing who he is. It is as though he has discerned, in this dangerous crisis, who he is and whose he is. His life is identified by reference to God. He addresses God: "O LORD." Then he says twice, "I am your servant." Behind the assertion of self-identity lies the simple confession, "You have loosed my bonds." Who "I" am depends on what has been done by "You."

The news confessed is in the verb of v. 16. You have "loosed" (*pātaḥ*). God has opened and released. God has acted for me, to end my powerlessness and give power, to end the helplessness and permit life. God has done for me what I could not do for myself. God "protects," "deals bountifully," and "delivers" (vs. 6, 7, 8). The verbs are those which portray God acting decisively against every bondage. Because of the power and fidelity of God, the speaker is free of death and is in "the land of the living" (v. 9).

Arrival in the land of the living by the power of God requires a response. The speaker asks, "What shall I return?" (v. 12), literally, "What shall I give back (*šûb*)?" The question is given two answers by the speaker.

1. The first answer is a statement of resolve in three first-person assertions (vs. 13–14): "I will lift . . . , [I will] call . . . , I will pay." The speaker's resolve is to act decisively in response to Yahweh's decisive saving action. The three promised actions are all public "religious acts" in the presence of all Yahweh's people. The speaker proposes to "go public" with gratitude. The "cup of salvation" must have been a ritual act of acknowledgment and celebration for God's rescue. "To call on the name" is to acknowledge loyalty to and reliance on. To pay vows indicates that the speaker had previously made a vow of money or offering, conditional on God's rescue. All three acts are ways of announcing that God has acted and that life is changed.

2. A second answer to the question of v. 12 is offered (vs. 17–19). Again the resolve of the speaker is threefold, with the latter two elements being the same as in vs. 13–14. The only changed element in this response is the first. Instead of "I will raise the cup of salvation," the resolve, again in inverted word order, is:

> To you I will offer a thanksgiving offering.

The term "thanksgiving" (*tôdāh*) means to give a visible offering, which constitutes a public acknowledgment and confession of loyalty. Thus the intent of this second answer echoes the first. The speaker is filled with resolve to confess Yahweh as the God who has saved, and to confess Yahweh as the God who will be praised and obeyed. Life is now completely given over in gratitude to the God who gives life and overrides death. The rescue from death and the gift of life permit this psalm to serve the church at Easter. It is worth noting that in eight verses of thanksgiving (vs. 12–19, the name of

Yahweh is named nine times. Life has been utterly transformed by Yahweh. The strong name of Yahweh is an alternative to death. The poem cannot sound the name too often. No wonder the psalm ends in praise to Yahweh and thanksgiving for new life.

1 Peter 1:17–23

The dramatic stories in the early chapters of Acts give the impression that joining up with the Christian community in its formative stages was an easy matter. Even if the authorities in Jerusalem did interfere occasionally, they posed little real danger. By contrast, becoming a Christian meant an enthusiastic welcome, the sharing of property, and the joyous confidence in the resurrected Lord. This romantic picture does not work for much of Acts, however, and it fades quickly when we read other parts of the New Testament.

The author of 1 Peter describes the Christians to whom he writes as "exiles," a word that is often understood to refer in an entirely metaphorical sense to the fact that believers are no longer at home in this world. They are exiles who really have their home in heaven. Recent study of 1 Peter, however, raises up another dimension of its language of exile. John Elliott (*A Home for the Homeless;* Philadelphia: Fortress Press, 1981, 21–58) contends that the audience of this text consists of people who actually occupy the social and political fringes of their society, and who have found that the Christian faith has caused them more social tension rather than less. The letter seeks to offer them a new community as a social and religious center, and the language of the household occupies a central place in that strategy.

In this particular passage, these exiles are admonished to "live in reverent fear." A wide variety of biblical texts present fear as an appropriate response to human awareness of divine activity. The fear encouraged here corresponds more nearly to awe than to terror, as is evidenced by the comments that surround this admonition. The God whom believers are to "fear" is the one who judges all people impartially (1 Peter 1:17); that is, this God may be relied on to do justice to every human being. Moreover, this God has already acted to save human beings from their own futile lives, has raised Jesus from the dead, and has given human beings every reason for trust. This God merits awe and reverence.

As the writer describes, in vs. 18–21, the actions of God through Christ, the implication is that these actions took place on behalf of the Christian community: "You were ransomed," "for your sake," "you have come to trust in God." If the original audience of this letter in fact consisted of people who were socially and politically marginalized, these assertions offer them confidence and hope. While they may have no place in the world around them as it is ordinarily understood, they know that God has already acted on their behalf and that their real place is secure. Without an awareness of that particular historical context, of course, Christians have felt justified in reading such passages as indicating that God acted exclusively for their own benefit. In that way, the text becomes a license for asserting a kind of Christian possession of God rather than a word of assurance to the displaced and dispossessed.

The final lines of this passage introduce once more the notion that Christians have been born again. Because this language occupies an important place not only in 1 Peter but also in some segments of contemporary Christianity, it merits further attention. To some Christians, being "born again" is a personal, even private, experience. It becomes a way of talking about an individual's relationship with God, or even about a particular incident of conversion. The phrase is also associated largely with the realm of spiritual experience more than with ethical behavior.

What comes through clearly in this text, as elsewhere in the New Testament, is that being "born again" means far more than simply having a private religious experience. Verse 22 admonishes believers to "love one another deeply from the heart." This notion of mutual love within the community is closely related to the household imagery that comes to the fore again in 1 Peter 2. Here, however, the emphasis is on living in a manner consistent with the gospel itself. New birth necessarily involves more than new mental processes or new spiritual awareness—it means new life, new action.

While this new birth is intensely personal, in that it involves individual human beings who find their lives radically changed by the gospel, it also involves an intensely social dimension. Those who experience the new birth *belong* to one another in a profound and unrelenting way. These newborns are not members of disparate family units, each of which may take its own infant and go home. They belong to one another, as surely as they belong to the God who grants them this new birth.

That it is God who grants this new birth is obvious, yet often overlooked: "You have been born anew, not of perishable but of imperishable seed, through the living and enduring word of God." Understandable and justified enthusiasm about being "born again" occasionally leads to the impression that those who are "born again" somehow accomplished this deed on their own, or at least that they had a significant role to play. Here, as elsewhere, the biblical word is that, as God alone creates life, God alone can claim responsibility for newness of life. The only word human beings may appropriately offer is one of doxology.

Luke 24:13–35

This story of Jesus' journey with the two disciples on their way to Emmaus is told with consummate skill. It deftly recapitulates Luke's narrative of Jesus (24:19–24), draws together a number of prominent themes developed in the Gospel, and announces that the self-revelation of the risen Messiah comes through the interpretation of the scriptures and the breaking of bread. In essence the story relates how the church encounters Jesus and learns to see him as someone other than merely a strange fellow traveler.

Readers come to this passage as people who already know that Jesus is risen. There is no secret about the resurrection to be disclosed to them. Instead, what they discover is a story of how disbelief is dispelled, how two deeply involved disciples are able to move beyond the tradition about Jesus to an experience of personal recognition. Early in the passage we learn that the two fail to perceive that it is Jesus who comes to walk with them because "their eyes were kept from recognizing him" (24:16). God apparently has temporarily blinded them. Toward the end of the account we read that "their eyes were opened, and they recognized him" (24:31). The story relates what happens in moving from blindness to sight, from disbelief to confession, from sadness to delight.

Two actions of Jesus lead Cleopas and his companion to recognize him. First, Jesus interprets for them the Jewish scriptures. Though they can recount the story of the empty tomb from the women and from the disciples who confirm the women's statement, this is not enough. The tradition must be viewed through the lens of scripture. In Jesus' death and resurrection the long story of God's purpose for Israel finds its culmination. The resurrection is not just a miracle of a revived corpse. In it the plan and reign of God are fulfilled.

What emerges in the story is a paradoxical relationship between the risen Jesus and the Jewish scriptures. On the one hand, it takes the risen Jesus to explain the meaning of the text. He is the critical interpreter, who teaches the church how to read the scriptures and how to discern there God's intentions. Only in light of Easter does the divine story make sense. On the other hand, an understanding of the scriptures is critical to recognizing who Jesus is and to grasping the import of what he has done. His death and resurrection are to be seen in a perspective broader than trials before Pilate and Herod, Roman gallows, and the empty tomb. One has to go back to Moses and the prophets to get the full picture.

Second, Jesus breaks bread with the two companions. The language of 24:30 recalls the account of the feeding of the multitudes (9:16) and the last supper with the disciples (22:19), making the allusion to the Lord's Supper inescapable (especially since the day is Sunday; see 24:13). The experience of eating precipitates recognition. In both 24:31 ("their eyes were opened") and 24:35 ("he had been made known to them"), however, the passive voice is used. Recognition does not come mechanically, nor is it the end product of an intellectual or existential search by the seeker. It is the gift of God, a self-revelation by which God honors promises made long ago to the covenant people.

The interpretation of the scriptures and the breaking of bread appropriately go together. The rhythm of 24:30–32 (table fellowship, recognition, remembrance of Jesus' opening the text) indicates the interrelatedness of the two. In both, Jesus is understood as Messiah (24:26) and confessed as Lord (24:34).

The concluding scene at Jerusalem pictures a gathering of the Eleven and their friends and the two who had walked to Emmaus, each confessing the risen Jesus and relating their experiences of recognition. The church is composed of those who have been led beyond disbelief to faith by the gracious revelation of God. Their repeated telling of and listening to the foundational story empowers them in anticipation of their mission to all the nations, a mission to begin here at Jerusalem (24:47).

In addition to being an account of recognition, this story also reflects several other themes important to Luke's telling of the story of Jesus: (a) the necessity of Jesus' death (9:22; 18:31–33; 24:44–46); (b) the confirmation of the women's witness (24:1–11, 22–24); (c) Jesus as the great prophet (7:16, 39; 9:8, 19; Acts 3:22); (d) the importance of hospitality to strangers (Gen. 18:1–15; Heb. 13:2).

FOURTH SUNDAY OF EASTER

Three of the readings for this Sunday evidence a common theme that might be profitably exploited in a single sermon—the image of shepherd and sheep. The other passage, from Acts 2, continues the sequential reading of Acts, which is maintained from Easter through the Day of Pentecost.

Psalm 23 and John 10 picture the marvelous and familiar relationship of trust that sheep exhibit toward the shepherd. Helpless and vulnerable, they depend on the shepherd for nourishment, protection, and guidance. In moments of threat, it is the shepherd who places himself between the dependent sheep and the aggressive enemy to ward off destruction and exploitation. The psalmist puts words in the mouth of the sheep, "You are with me; your rod and your staff—they comfort me."

John 10 and 1 Peter 2, however, interrupt this rather idyllic picture by introducing the costly price paid for protection. The shepherd is abused, suffers intensely, and finally has to lay down his life on behalf of the sheep. Their safety comes not without immense and undeserved sacrifice. The opposition is violent.

Then 1 Peter 2 gives yet another twist to the sheep-shepherd imagery. The shepherd's sacrifice makes possible the return of wayward sheep, who have mindlessly wandered away from the protection of "the shepherd and guardian of your souls" (2:25). But this is all in the context of the bold proposal that the suffering of the shepherd is paradigmatic. Not only slaves, but the entire community (4:12–19) are vulnerable to violent opposition and are to find in Jesus' redemptive suffering a model for life. They are not finally abandoned in their plight (Ps. 23 is still true), for they can continue to trust, as Jesus did, in "the one who judges justly." Nevertheless, readers are faced with the paradox of human suffering and eternal safety, of human pain and divine protection.

Acts 2:42–47

The Acts passage for this day continues the series of readings having to do with Peter's Pentecost sermon and its effects. Readers/interpreters who have followed the previous two lections from Acts 2 will be familiar with the content of Peter's sermon and its proclamation of the kerygma (Second Sunday of Easter) and with the initial reaction on the part of Peter's audience (Third Sunday of Easter). The present passage continues a description of that reaction, but pursues the activity of the young church over a more extended period of time.

The Acts passage for the Third Sunday of Easter (Acts 2:14a, 36–41) placed a great deal of importance on baptism as a sign of the activity of the Spirit of God, going so far as to mention baptism twice (vs. 38, 41). The present passage places a somewhat more subtle, yet nonetheless significant, emphasis on the Eucharist, also mentioning twice the operative words, in this case the phrase "breaking of bread" (vs. 42, 46). In v. 42 of our text "the breaking of bread" is listed with "the apostles' teaching and fellowship" and "the prayers" as auspicious activities within the life of the new church. To be sure, it may be argued that "the breaking of bread" is primarily a reference to the disciples' habit of eating their meals together, an activity in which our text asserts that they engaged. Yet as is clear from other passages within the New Testament, references to ordinary meals often contain thinly veiled statements concerning the Christian Eucharist (cf. Luke 24:35), and there is no compelling reason to doubt that such is the case here. Thus, the Eucharist joins baptism as two of the several observances that characterize the distinctive nature of the life of the church.

The second reference to breaking bread (v. 46) casts this special activity in a different light. Each day the new disciples worshiped in the Jerusalem Temple (since they were all—or perhaps almost all—Jews), and in doing so they reaffirmed their sense of continuity with God's saving role in the life of Israel-of-old and their sense of respect for the written record of God's redemptive activity, the Old Testament. But also each day they worshiped in their homes in a specifically Christian sense by means of the eucharistic celebration. And celebration it was, in that their mood was one of thanksgiving and joy (vs. 46–47a). Having accepted the old, they also embraced the new, and the transformation of their lives was expressed in their worship as well as in their relationships with their neighbors.

Yet an interest in the Eucharist is not the only noteworthy element in this passage. The sense of awe that permeated the lives of the first disciples (v. 43) not only bound them to the object of their awe, the God who raised Jesus from the dead, but bound them also to one another. This awe is the same "fear of the LORD" that is the beginning of wisdom (Prov. 1:7) and that is also the beginning of a true understanding of oneself in relation to the rest of creation (Ps. 33:8). But in this text it is linked in a special manner to an appreciation of the ability of God to change human life in lasting and decisive ways. The "wonders and signs . . . being done by the apostles" are mentioned by Luke not to elevate these persons to a greater importance than they deserve, but to remind the reader of the sense of immediacy to the life-transforming power of God's Spirit, which the earliest Christians possessed. That their experiment in communalism did not last (cf. Acts 5) should be understood more as a commentary on the deviousness of human nature than on any wrongheadedness in the part of the early Christians. Their overflowing love of God resulted in an irresistible urge to express affection among themselves.

The currents of mutual love and concern to which the text bears witness could not be contained within the bounds of the Christian fellowship itself, but lapped outside, catching up other persons in their appeal. The amazing growth of the young church (v. 47) is seen by Luke not as an end in itself, but as a result of the combined energies of God's Spirit and of the affection of the members of the young church for one another and for those outside their fellowship. And it was an auspicious time for the church to grow, evangelism flowing out of the church's ardent sharing of the story of the resurrected Christ, as in Peter's Pentecost sermon. But as the text makes quite clear, this successful evangelistic effort was a by-product of their energies. An important by-product, to be sure, but not the primary focus of the early Christians' concern. They did not "devote" themselves to evangelism (v. 42), but to teaching and fellowship, to worship and to acts of caring. And the growth of the church was generated out of these activities by the Spirit of God (v. 47). There are undoubtedly lessons in this matter for the church to ponder in this and every age.

Psalm 23

Life in faith is a gift we receive. Our life begins in God, in God's good intent and God's utter reliability. Our role is to receive, accept, trust, and respond. Among the more complete and poignant metaphors for this peculiar notion of life is the image of shepherd and sheep. The metaphor is adequate and powerful because the shepherd is always primary in the relation; the sheep is derivative and dependent.

The speaker characterizes a life of well-being under the serene protection of the Good Shepherd who is indeed "shepherd and guardian of [our] souls" (1 Peter 2:25; cf. Ps. 23:1–3). The psalm opens with a concise articulation of this life of trust and confidence. "Yahweh is my shepherd" (v. 1). The relation of sheep and shepherd in a pastoral economy is one of intimacy, trust, harmony, and well-being (see 2 Sam. 12:3). The sheep knows the voice of the shepherd and heeds it gladly; the shepherd knows the names of the sheep and values them, each for itself. The outcome of this life of trust is that the sheep lacks nothing.

The speaker plays out in detail the metaphor of trust (vs. 2–3). These verses explicate the large claim of v. 1. Sheep need three things for well-being: good pasture land, adequate water, and safe paths. These are needed in a land of inadequate rain and untamed beasts. The sheep is incapable of finding grassland and water, unable to defend itself under attack. The sheep is utterly needful and dependent.

The shepherd does for the sheep what the sheep cannot do for itself. The shepherd is alert, always planning, looking ahead, making provision. The sheep is amazed and grateful for the attentiveness of the shepherd. There is always adequate grass, always clear, refreshing water, always safe ("right") paths on which to walk and from which to graze. The sheep lives a good, full life, only because of the shepherd. Yahweh is the quintessential shepherd, making possible life that we cannot find for ourselves.

This idyllic picture of calm grazing (vs. 1–3) is interrupted by a second scene, now much more ominous (vs. 4–5). The flock is not always a safe place. There are dangerous, threatening places to be traversed, dangerous paths, lively enemies. The "darkest valley" is terrain that has lots of hiding places, suitable for attack and ambush. Those places cannot be avoided, and they are fraught with threats.

The sheep moves into and through such places, not because it is stupid or impervious, but because of its utter trust and confidence in the shepherd. The sheep is unfrightened because the sheep is not alone, not autonomous, not required to fend for itself. "You are with me." For the first time, the sheep addresses the shepherd directly. It is a statement of simple confidence and affirmation: "I know you will not leave me." The sheep is realistic about the danger, but even more realistic about the shepherd. The trust of the shepherd overrides the danger of the pastureland.

The imagery changes slightly in v. 5. Now the shepherd has become a host serving a meal. That image is not, however, far removed from our dominant metaphor. The sheep eats serenely, while the enemies (robbers, thieves, wild animals) stand and watch. They dare not intrude or attack, because between the vulnerable sheep and the aggressive enemy stands the shepherd. Under threat, the sheep is profoundly safe and grazes casually, almost defiantly. Thus the dangerous valley of vs. 4–5 becomes as safe as the righteous paths of vs. 2–3. The shepherd reshapes and recharacterizes all of life.

The final verse returns to the sweeping thesis of the beginning (v. 6). The speaker exults in well-being. Notice that Yahweh is mentioned only in v. 1 and in v. 6. The psalm, like the life of this speaker, is bracketed by the reality of this utterly faithful God. With this God is the place of well-being.

It takes little imagination to see why the early church, in its deep jeopardy, found the metaphor of Good Shepherd poignant in its witness to Jesus (John 10:1–10). Like the sheep, the early church had to live under threat from enemies, in a valley of jeopardy. Like the sheep, the church trusts the One to whom it belongs, and finds itself safe. The Shepherd stands between the church and the enemies that threaten. With this Shepherd, the church is utterly safe, utterly trusting, utterly at peace. It need only trust fully and know the voice of the faithful Shepherd.

1 Peter 2:19–25

Although this reading begins with 1 Peter 2:19, even a glance at the context reveals that it addresses slaves and that complementary admonitions to wives and to husbands follow in 3:1–7. The seemingly innocuous claim that believers should follow Christ's example of suffering and patience takes on an entirely different tone in view of the fact that the particular group being called to suffering and patience consists of slaves (2:18). Since one knows the way in which these ethical injunctions have been employed in the church's life, this text may promote acute embarrassment, shame, and outrage. The temptation to select another text for preaching lies near at hand.

A closer examination of this entire section of the letter may cast a different and, indeed, racial light on the admonitions in vs. 18–25. Certain anomalies about this household code (the set of admonitions to members of a household) call for attention. Unlike other New Testament examples of the household code, this one *begins* with admonitions to slaves. In Eph. 5—6, for example, the code addresses first wives and husbands, then children and parents, and finally slaves and their masters (cf. Col. 3:18–4:1; 1 Tim. 5:1–6:2; Titus 2:1–10). First Peter does not include the admonition to owners that normally stands in parallel to the admonition to slaves.

The substance of the ethical admonition in this passage is striking, because what slaves are encouraged to do here duplicates what all believers are called to do elsewhere in 1 Peter. If slaves suffer unjustly, so apparently does the entire audience of the letter (1:6–7; 2:12). Chapter 3:13–22 repeats the claim of 2:19–25 that believers are to be willing to suffer on behalf of the good and that Christ provides an example of just such suffering. The substance of this admonition, then, is in no way unique to slaves or incumbent on them alone.

Another unusual feature of this admonition is that the word "slaves" in v. 18 translates the Greek word *oiketai,* rather than the more usual *doulos.* While *doulos* refers to slaves in a general sense, *oiketai,* used only rarely in the New Testament, specifically refers to slaves within the household. Given 1 Peter's emphasis on the household of God, the appearance of *oiketai* rather than *doulos* can scarcely be accidental, and surely recalls the household motif. If all believers are part of God's new household, a household that offers protection from a threatening world and solidarity within, the *oiketai* occupy an important place within that household.

The best explanation of the various anomalies in this household code comes from John Elliott, who argues that the *oiketai* in 1 Peter stand as paradigms for the way in which all members of the household should conduct themselves (*A Home for the Homeless;* Philadelphia: Fortress Press, 1981). In fact, all believers are slaves, in that they belong to God (2:16) and to the new household created through the gospel of Jesus Christ (2:2–10). In this new household, there are no "masters" or "owners" to address, since all alike are slaves. All believers are liable to suffer unjustly and may endure that suffering because they know that they follow Christ in so doing. The "example" of Jesus provides a model for all believers (2:21–24). All believers have been returned to their Shepherd (2:25).

By reversing the usual order of the household code, placing the admonition to slaves before that to wives and husbands, 1 Peter also demonstrates the way in which the gospel overturns the hierarchy of the conventional household. Slaves are not, in this new household, the last and the least, to be treated merely as an afterthought. They occupy first place, because their *involuntary* submission to human masters has been transformed into a *paradigmatic* submission to God,who is the only appropriate master of the new household.

There is no easy way for contemporary preachers to employ the language of this passage, since it is imperative to avoid anything that even appears to soften or legitimate or romanticize the brutal facts of human slavery. On the other hand, particularly in a North American context, which understands faith to be an option among a vast array of options, this lection's reminder that the gospel involves real submission carries a potent, and highly unpopular, message.

The relentless christological appeal of the passage bears home the message that Christians are always to be the obedient slaves of God, just as was Christ. The passage drives away at the unjust suffering of Christ. Verse 21 introduces this motif and the notion that Christ provides an example for believers. The example becomes very specific in the lines that follow. Verse 22 applies to Christ a quotation from Isa. 53:9 about the Suffering Servant, who is accused without reason. Verse 23 expands the motif by insisting that Christ did not repay the evil done to him. Verses 24–25 recall the result of Christ's suffering for humanity. This repetition serves to make the nature of Christ's suffering undeniably clear.

Throughout this passage, Christ becomes the example in whose steps believers are called to follow. Here the example of Christ is urged, not in the sometimes trivial way that asks what Jesus would say or what Jesus would do, but as the first and foremost among the slaves of God's household.

John 10:1–10

The imagery of the shepherd and the sheep is a familiar one to both ancient and modern readers of John. The Jewish scriptures are filled with examples, employed in a variety of ways (e.g., Pss. 23; 100; Ezek. 34; Num. 27:15–17), and the picture of the Good Shepherd laying down his life for his flock (John 10:11–18) is a vivid expression of Jesus' love for the church.

The language of John 10, however, is at times confusing. When the passage is treated as an allegory and the symbols are pressed for precise referents, the results are not always clear. At one point, Jesus is the gate (vs. 7, 9); at another point, he is the shepherd (v. 11). At one point, the thieves and bandits try to enter the sheepfold not by the gate, but by climbing the wall (v. 1); at another point, they come to the gate and call the sheep, but their voice is not heeded (v. 8). The interpreter does well to acknowledge these inconsistencies and yet not allow them to blunt the force of the text. They are probably due to an uneven uniting of sources, but such a powerful array of symbols is nevertheless effective, despite its inexactness.

The passage is divided into two sections (which might lead to two separate sermons). In 10:1–6 a contrast is established between thieves and bandits, on the one hand, who surreptitiously try to gain control of the flock, and the rightful shepherd, on the other hand. Since the passage is loosely connected to its context, the identification of a precise historical group of thieves and bandits is hard to come by. They are, rather, characterized by their actions—an individual or group who attempt to "fleece" the flock, who seek to manipulate the sheep for personal gain. When they are later described as coming to steal, kill, and destroy (v. 10), presumably their violent intentions are in the interest of acquisition. A whole host of candidates, both ancient and modern, come to mind as referents. The flock seems perpetually an easy target for exploitation.

At this point in the passage, the shepherd is not specifically identified either, though it seems clear that Jesus is intended (as in v. 11). What marks the shepherd is the close relationship he has established with the sheep, a relationship born of experience. The sheep hear and recognize his voice. He has a name for each of them. They follow his leadership.

Strikingly, the close relationship between shepherd and sheep is not so much encouraged as assumed. The possibility is not even entertained that the sheep, in moments of perplexity or uncertainty, might confuse the voices and follow the thieves and bandits rather than the shepherd, a phenomenon that according to church history has frequently occurred. Instead, the sheep are familiar with the shepherd's voice. The positive statement is meant to reassure. Amid the welter of conflicting appeals, the sheep are able to recognize and follow the single voice that can be trusted.

In the second section (vs. 7–10) the imagery shifts, and the focus falls on Jesus as the gate of the sheepfold. On the one hand, a warning is given about the thieves and bandits who appear before the gate, but whom the sheep do not heed. On the other hand, an invitation is issued, promising salvation, nurture, and abundant life to all who pass through the Jesus-gate. Jesus has come not as the thief to kill the sheep and leave the flock in disarray—he has come to give fullness of life.

The repetition of the phrase "I am the gate" (10:7, 9) places emphasis on the exclusiveness of Jesus as the way to eternal life. It is a prominent motif in the Fourth Gospel, and no doubt helped to establish the peculiar identity of the Johannine community in distinction from the synagogue. They were a people who saw no hope apart from the Good Shepherd, whose voice they had come to know.

Despite the emphasis on the exclusiveness of Jesus, the ultimate impact of the sheep-shepherd imagery of John 10 is to encourage and embolden readers. There is no threat of division between good sheep and bad sheep, no suggestion that thieves and bandits will succeed in destroying part of the flock. Instead, the sheep are the shepherd's "own." Their familiarity with the shepherd guarantees their safety and security. The language is reminiscent of the Twenty-third Psalm. What is eloquently sung there about the Lord's care, guidance, and protection of the flock is here reaffirmed in terms of Jesus.

Fifth Sunday of Easter

Since the beginning, Israel's faith has turned to God in situations of acute trouble. In such turning, Israel has found God utterly reliable, and able to rescue. Today's psalm reading sounds those ancient cadences of reliability. On the one hand, the psalm acknowledges deep trouble and danger. On the other hand, God is able, powerful, and willing to rescue and to lead Israel to a safe place, a rock, a fortress, a refuge.

The sermon in Acts 7 takes up those ancient cadences of confidence, and places them on the lips and in the mouth of Stephen. Stephen talks the way Israel has characteristically talked. In his Easter proclamation, it is evident that the early church celebrates realities and trusts in affirmations that the world could neither understand nor tolerate. The preaching of Stephen evokes powerful hostility in his listeners. In the end, however, it is Stephen (and not his opponents) who knows the joy and well-being of life as a gift from God. His trusting innocence is sharply contrasted with the hate-poisoned lives that are spent in the service of death. The one whom the world sees as killed is the one who in the end knows God's rescue.

Both the Gospel and Epistle readings turn the faith of the psalm and the drama of Stephen's ending toward the concrete reality of the church. Both readings are here tilted toward the need of a domesticated church to reengage its peculiar identity and its odd mode of being. The Gospel concerns a safe, guaranteed "place," a place of safety and well-being in which it can practice its peculiar life, unafraid and unintimidated. The Epistle reading concerns a household, an intentionally alternative household. Because of its peculiar faith and its identity formed in hurt, the church is a unified community capable of a risking hospitality. In speaking of a place with the Father (in the Gospel) and in a "house" (in the Epistle), these readings return to the language of the Psalms, which seek from God a safe place. This is a community emboldened by the God of refuge, rock, and fortress, not fearful of its enemies, not seduced by other places. Stephen turns out to be a buoyant believer, who in his crisis is the only one who is not "displaced." The language of "place" serves the practice of risky, confident obedience.

Acts 7:55–60

The first reading for the previous three Sundays has centered on Peter's Pentecost sermon and on the effects that that proclamation of the kerygma had on the apostle's hearers. The present lection deals with effects on its auditors of another sermon delivered by a different preacher. While the results of Stephen's message are quite different from those of Peter's, the contrast is intentional and probing. The proclamation of the gospel may win many hearts to an allegiance to Jesus Christ, but it also has the potential to arouse the deepest hostility on the part of others.

Stephen's lengthy sermon (Acts 7:2–53) is basically a recitation of the saving activity of God in the life of Israel, with emphasis on the manner in which God fulfilled the divine promises again and again. Yet also brought clearly into focus in Stephen's message is the continued intransigence of the people in the face of God's gracious overtures. The people rejected the prophet Moses (vs. 35–39), and they denied their dependence on God by worshiping idols crafted by their own hands (vs. 40–41). The flash point of Stephen's sermon is reached when he accuses his hearers of being of the same obstinate and rebellious stock as Moses' generation (vs. 51–53). Just as they denied the prophet Moses, so they have denied the latter and greater prophet, Jesus, whose office Moses has foretold (v. 37).

The narrative of Stephen's murder, today's lection, is terse and violent. The contrast the lectionary draws between the attitude of Peter's hearers and that of Stephen's audience is sharpened by the details of the text itself. Stephen's executioners are infuriated (v. 54) and deaf to all reason (v. 57), exhibiting the kind of rabid violence that thirsts only for blood. On the other hand, Stephen's vision is of beauty and joy (v. 55) and his spirit forgiving (v. 60), his prayer for mercy on his attackers being reminiscent of that of Jesus on the cross (Luke 23:34). The manner in which Luke has set these polar attitudes is striking, in that the mind of the reader is concentrated, first, on the hatred of the murderers (v. 54), then on Stephen's holiness (v. 55), then back to the killers (v. 57), and so on.

During the account of Stephen's stoning, the stage is set for the next major section in Acts by the mention of Saul/Paul (v. 58; cf. 8:1), the soon-to-be missionary apostle who at this time is still in the camp of the persecutors of the church. (See the first reading for the Sixth Sunday of Easter.)

The celebration of Easter and its aftermath almost always concentrates on the victory that Christ has won over the forces of sin and death, and that is as it should be. "Where, O death, is your victory?" (1 Cor. 15:55), Paul asks near the end of his extended invitation to the Corinthian Christians to celebrate the resurrection. His mood is almost taunting, as if he *dares* death so much as to raise its ugly head in response. But death is not dead yet, neither is evil or pain. They may be doomed, but they are still very pervasive realities, with which men and women must deal daily. And as if to remind Christians of the persistence of the enemy, Luke balances the positive response of Peter's hearers in Acts 2—a response that leads to the explosive growth of the church—with the negative reaction of Stephen's auditors, one that leads to the disciple's death. Not all good works result in benefits to those who do them. Not all fidelity to the truth of God brings immediate blessing on those who are faithful. Commitment to the Messiah of God may just as easily result in pain as in joy, in death—as it does here for Stephen—as in life.

Yet while acknowledging the continuing reality of evil, the text makes it quite clear that those who are really dead are not Stephen, but the disciple's killers. His pain may be the most immediate, but his joy is ultimate and final, while their twisted and hate-poisoned hearts show no inclination to be open to any good news of what God has done and is doing. And so the Easter victory is genuine and enduring, but in important respects it is a victory whose final consummation is still held in anticipation.

What medieval theologians referred to as the "beatific vision" is, in certain important ways, the crux of the passage (v. 56). The words call to mind Jesus' baptism in the Jordan (Luke 3:21–22 and parallels), a feature of the text that is possibly quite deliberate and by which Luke intends to stress Stephen's "rite of passage"—not from life to death, as it must have appeared to the murderers, but from life to life. Whereas Jesus' baptism and accompanying experience of the Holy Spirit marked the beginning of a new phase in his faithfulness to God, Stephen's vision identifies his full entrance into the kingdom and the consummation (for him!) of the Easter hope. It is this sense of the sureness of God's promises (detailed in Stephen's sermon) and of the certainty of the victory of God over all those ancient wrongs that distort human life and rob it of its joy—it is this sense and only this sense that can effect a joy so serene that it prays for the well-being of those who wish to do it to death.

Psalm 31:1–5, 15–16

The speaker of this psalm is under profound threat from enemies that endanger life. The psalm is candid in its voice of danger, knowing that even the faithful are in jeopardy. The threat drives the speaker to God, so that the prayer of petition for rescue is prayed boldly and in great confidence.

The psalm begins with a passionate address and an urgent petition (vs. 1–2). The psalm opens with direct address that inverts normal word order: "In thee, Yahweh." The petition is focused on Yahweh; only after the address to God, comes along the speaker.

The petition is a collage of powerful verbs and graphic nouns. The nouns offer a scenario in which the speaker is eagerly seeking a safe place in which to hide: "refuge . . . rock . . . refuge . . . fortress." The speaker is vulnerable, exposed, and without defense. In addition to the verb "incline," the petition employs three of Israel's standard verbs for deliverance: "deliver . . . rescue . . . save" (*pālaṭ, nāṣal, yāša'*). The speaker is utterly needful and dependent, and mobilizes Israel's best speech tradition in making an appeal to God.

The middle portion of our reading reiterates the same rhetorical pattern (vs. 3–5). Again there are the nouns of protection: "rock . . . fortress . . . refuge," and the strong verbs; "lead . . . guide . . . take out . . . redeem." This second section of the psalm not only repeats the accents of the first, but adds a more graphic metaphor, namely, the "net" (v. 4).

The psalm does not dwell, however, on the predicament of the speaker, but on the fidelity of God. The psalm uses the word "you" (*'attāh*) twice' in these verses to assert who God is, and perhaps to insist on God being so. Moreover, the appeal is "for your name's sake," that is, for the sake of maintaining God's reputation. The suppliant has no claim to make, except to trust in the character and intention of God.

Special interest may focus on v. 5, for the language anticipates the familiar statement of Jesus from the cross (Luke 23:46), and is paralleled by Stephen (Acts 7:59). As in Ps. 23:1, the language is inverted, so that the sentence begins with God: "Into your hands," that is, into God's utterly reliable, trusting power. The speaker cedes his jeopardized life over to God, over to God's safekeeping. The speaker can no longer sustain his own "spirit." His life can, however, be entrusted to God, and that is enough.

The final two verses of our reading divide nicely into two parts (vs. 15–16). The first part, the first line of v. 15, is a sweeping act of trust, submissiveness, and confidence. The plural "times" recognizes that persons and communities face many different seasons and circumstances, troubling as well as wondrous. Ancient Israel characteristically avoids absolute statements of timelessness, and experiences life as "time-full." That is, every passing moment, day, and year bring newness and variation and risk. All these variations here are entrusted to and willingly handed over to Yahweh in confidence and serenity. The speaker has no doubt that Yahweh presides over and brings a good outcome to every circumstance of life.

On the basis of that affirmation, vs. 15b–16 address God with three imperatives:

1. "Deliver me." The prayer, like many in the Psalter, is uttered by one in an exposed, vulnerable situation. The speaker is not strong or resourceful enough to cope with adversaries—but Yahweh is.

2. "Let your face shine." The phrase is reminiscent of the familiar priestly benediction of Num. 6:22–26. The strong face of God bespeaks God's presence and beneficence, appealing to the image of light (as the coming of the sun), which brings with it well-being, healing, and safety.

3. "Save me." The verb is parallel to "deliver" in the preceding verse. Here it is further identified by "steadfast love," that is, God's abiding resolve of covenant.

These three petitions are spoken in confidence and expectation. In speaking in this way, the prayer invites into a life of danger this Third Party, who will refocus all of life, that is, every time and circumstance, toward well-being. Confidence arises in the context of submissive trust.

1 Peter 2:2–10

This passage usually appears in discussions of the priesthood of all believers, or the spiritual priesthood. Within the context of First Peter, however, as John Elliott has demonstrated, this passage serves to introduce the notion of the "household of God," which v. 5 signals with the unusual expression "spiritual house," or "spiritual household (*A Home for the Homeless;* Philadelphia: Fortress Press, 1981, 23, 75). The household code of 2:18–3:7 underscores the importance of this motif, as does the use of the "household of God" in 4:17. Recurring language that describes believers as "newly born" or "reborn" and that seeks the unity of believers within the community further enhances this motif.

Chapter 2:4–5 introduces the household language, which vs. 6–10 develop through a variety of biblical quotations and editorial comments. Indeed, the profusion of biblical quotations and allusions in vs. 6–10 seems bewildering apart from the underlying theme of the unity of believers in a single household. Understanding Jesus as the living stone, believers are also to see themselves as living stones, whom God builds into a single, spiritual house (vs. 4–6). Again, like Jesus, these stones will be rejected by unbelievers, by the world at large, but will be affirmed by God (vs. 7–8). The various descriptions of vs. 9–10 serve to reinforce this notion that the community of believers is *one* community. Together it constitutes "a chosen race, a royal priesthood, a holy nation, God's own people." These expressions, like that of the "household," underscore the collective nature of the community.

The imagery in this passage may seem exotic, and perhaps even exclusivistic ("a chosen race, a royal priesthood"), until the author's specific pastoral goals become clear. First, the insistence on the unity of believers in *one* body—household, race, priesthood, nation—serves to create and maintain a social identity. If recent research is correct in its understanding that the audience of this letter consists of persons who are displaced and dispossessed, not only spiritually or religiously but socially, economically, and politically, then what the author does here asserts that in Christ, God creates a new place for those who have none. The language of the household erects boundaries that provide place, purpose, and community for those who "have tasted that the Lord is good" (v. 3).

Second, the passage links this particular community with Jesus Christ. Commentators have often ignored the concrete social dimensions of this passage, but correcting that misreading should not lead to the conclusion that the social dimension constitutes the whole of the passage. This "spiritual house" is not a social club, which exists solely for the needs of its members. It is, rather, a household of which the head is God and the cornerstone Jesus Christ. As much as believers belong to one another within this household, they also belong to God. God builds the house (v. 5), God lays the cornerstone (v. 6), the house is known (and accepted or rejected) by its cornerstone (vs. 7–8). By virtue of God's own mercy and nothing else, this household has come into being (vs. 9–10).

Third, as a result of their identification with one another and as members of God's household, believers within this new household have a new standing. No longer outcasts, marginalized by their social condition, believers may be described in powerful and positive terms. Like the prototypical "living stone," Jesus, believers are "chosen and precious in God's sight" (v. 4). The language of v. 9 exalts the community and implies its privileges before God. Even if the household was once "not a people" and "had not received mercy" (v. 10), it now can rightfully claim to be the people of God's own possession.

Given the historical setting in which the author of 1 Peter wrote, the language of this passage serves an important pastoral need. That need continues in every Christian generation, for the church constantly requires the recollection that God created it to be a single household, taking its identity from Jesus Christ and set apart from the world. Given the intractable human temptation to convert a gift into a possession, however, Christians have too often read passages such as this one to mean that *their* standing before God came as a result of their own goodness and permitted them to exclude others from membership in the same household. The text grants no such license for exclusivity or condescension. The householder, God, has sole authority over admission at the doorway.

For North American Christians, perhaps especially in the present crisis of the "mainline" churches, the challenge of this text lies in its assertion that the household does have boundaries. Identification of Christianity with the larger society and its social and political and economic structures makes it difficult to understand the church as an alternative household. The perceived need to seek new members and retain current members creates a climate in which congregations try to make themselves attractive by means of programs that only duplicate the structures and values of the larger society. Tragically, at a time when people seek the very boundaries of identification and meaning offered by the Christian faith, its churches fear making those boundaries clear.

John 14:1–14

This familiar section of Jesus' farewell speech in John's Gospel offers at least three significant themes for preaching. The nature of the topics enables the preacher to think of separate sermons, and the context allows for this. At the same time, the themes are connected by a common logic and are not simply isolated theological reflections. If nothing else, the setting in which Jesus talks to the disciples about their life following his death offers a unifying thread.

First, Jesus promises the disciples a permanent existence lived in fellowship with him. Admittedly, 14:2–3 are notoriously difficult verses. The language describes Jesus' departure to the Father's house, then Jesus' return, at which time he gathers his disciples to take them to a permanent dwelling place (not unlike 1 Thess.

4:13–18). Commentators fret about this apocalyptic scenario, because the rest of the farewell discourse speaks of Jesus' coming in terms of his fellowship with the disciples in this life and not a departure to another realm (e.g., 14:23). Does the realized eschatology of the rest of the farewell discourse (and most of the entire Gospel) neutralize or reinterpret this mention of preparing a place and a future parousia?

The picturesque language of 14:2–3 unambiguously speaks of a location ("a place," "my Father's house," "many dwelling places") and expresses movement—a here and a there, a going and a coming—making it difficult to reduce these verses to purely realized or spiritualized eschatology. John makes no obvious effort to harmonize this apocalyptic scenario with the realized eschatology. A clue, however, to their connection may be found in the Greek word translated "dwelling places" (14:2). It is the noun of the characteristically Johannine verb "abide." The "abiding" in Christ that now marks the Christian experience (15:1–11) reaches its culmination in the permanent abiding place, which Jesus had prepared. What distinguishes such a "place" is the security of the divine presence ("that where I am, there you may be also"). It remains appropriate, therefore, to hear in John 14 a word of promise regarding an established and unfading fellowship with Jesus, even beyond death.

Second, the language about going to prepare dwelling places in the Father's house raises the issue of the journey and leads to the affirmation that Jesus is the exclusive way to the Father. The question of Thomas (14:5) and the request of Philip (v. 8) evoke the strong statements of v. 6 and vs. 9–11. The knowledge of Jesus *is* the knowledge of the Father; the seeing of Jesus *is* the seeing of the Father. Nothing is more characteristic of John than this.

What often creates uneasiness among many interpreters is the exclusiveness of Jesus' revelation of the Father. "No one comes to the Father except through me" (14:6). Does this imply that only those who deliberately embrace the Christian faith can be related to God or be saved? The usual way to deal with the issue is to ask at what or at whom the statement might have been aimed in the evangelist's day, and either to leave it there or to find a modern analogy. The problem with this approach is the uncertainty as to whether the statement is polemical in the first place, and if so, who the target is.

Another approach is to recognize that this exclusive Christology and soteriology are integral to the Johannine community's understanding of itself. Its distinctiveness lies not in its sense of moral superiority over its environment or in the influential position it can assume in the culture, but in its confession of and commitment to Jesus as the only way to the Father. The question to ask is: Could this dimension of John's perspective in any way be instructive to the modern church as it struggles with its identity? The Christian community of North America has so bought into the world's economics, its psychology, its standards of morality that visitors from outer space would have a difficult time discerning the difference between the social and political culture of the day, with its civil religion, and the church. Maybe the real issue is not whether people outside the church are saved, but whether people inside the church have any sense of their distinctiveness. Could the confessions of the Johannine church help the contemporary church begin to reclaim its unique identity?

Third, Jesus makes the pledge to the disciples (repeatedly) that their prayers will be answered (14:13–14; 15:7, 16; 16:23–24). The text makes clear, however, that this pledge is not a willy-nilly commitment to give to overly indulgent children whatever their hearts fancy. Prayers are to be made "in [Jesus'] name" (14:13–14), that is, they are to be made out of the disciples' relationship established with and by Jesus. The answering of the requests does not serve those who pray, but is to the end "that the Father may be glorified in the Son." These are prayers offered in behalf of the community and the community's mission. They undergird the "greater works" that the church is to perform.

Perhaps it does not need to be said, but the promise of a permanent fellowship with Jesus, the confession of Jesus as the only way to the Father, and the pledge that the community's prayers will be answered are all made to comfort troubled hearts. The opening verse (14:1) sets the tone and direction for the entire passage.

Sixth Sunday of Easter

These readings, powerfully focused on the reality of God, move in two quite distinct directions. On the one hand, the Psalm lection and the reading in Acts address the ways in which the concrete faith claims of the community have credence outside that community. That is, these texts undertake something of an apologetic task, making the faith credible to outsiders. The psalm is rooted in quite concrete, personal experience and passion. It is nonetheless addressed as a summons to the nations, inviting them on the basis of this personal testimony to come share in this new life given by the God who has saved. In the sermon of Acts 17:22–31, Paul also makes concrete confessional claims about Jesus in response to the vague, amorphous religious inclination of his Hellenistic listeners. Paul's strategy is to make his appeal as broadly as possible, thus withholding the name of the "man," so as not to offend more general sensitivities. In both cases, in the end the appeal to the nations makes no accommodation to the "wisdom of this age," but depends on primal communal testimony, which has no compelling warrants beyond its own convinced experience and passion.

On the other hand, the Gospel and Epistle readings focus on the needs of the church community and seek to offer pastoral consolation. The Gospel invites the believing community to place confidence in the presence of God, because it knows what the world does not know and cannot see. More explicitly, the Epistle addresses the pervasive, inescapable issues of suffering and death. The believing community experiences the burdens of life, even though it makes this claim about God's triumph and governance. The Epistle affirms that in all such troubles, it is the power, fidelity, and presence of God that finally enable believers to persist in the present through hope.

This configuration of texts sets up a noticeable tension. The Psalm and Acts readings are like a "journey out," to the nations and to attentive nonbelievers. The Gospel and Epistle readings are a "journey in," to the life and needs of the church. This "out-in" tension is inescapable in the church, whenever it seeks at one and the same time to take the world seriously and to acknowledge honestly its own evangelical distinctiveness. The twin accents are held together by a single affirmation of the Gospel: It is God whose presence and power matter decisively. This presence and power can make a decisive difference in the nations who will accept this testimony. This presence and power give the church staying power and resilience in its struggles. This presence and power are known peculiarly and decisively in Jesus, but they are operative anywhere and everywhere. For anyone inside or outside who confesses this faith and names this name, all of life is reconstrued, both in fresh assurance and in new obedience.

Acts 17:22–31

The series of texts from Acts relating to the proclamation of the gospel on the part of the early church is continued in this passage, an account of Paul's sermon to the assembly of Athenian philosophers. Stylistic and conceptual differences between this sermon and Paul's letters have resulted in a protracted discussion among commentators as to the authenticity of this text, that is, whether it is the sort of message Paul is likely to have composed, even in view of the distinctive nature of his audience. However that debate may be decided, it remains clear that this is a formulation of the Christian message on the part of some important spokesperson for the early church, be that individual Paul, Luke, or whoever. Furthermore, its most distinctive element involves not some alternative understanding of the essential Christian message, but an accommodation of method to the prevailing interests among the community of Greek philosophers, principally the Stoics.

There is a smooth progression of thought in the passage, which suggests either that a period of time was involved in its composition, thus allowing the author opportunity to rewrite and polish the material, or that the sermon is the product of a mind that was accustomed to arguing in logical and coherent fashion. The initial section, Acts 17:22–23, acknowledges the religious (and not just philosophical) orientation of the audience. Most notable in this regard is Paul's reference to the altar dedicated "To an unknown god," but that citation is anticipated by the preceding reference to the "extremely religious" views of the assembled philosophers. The reality, of course, was that, although few Greek thinkers—including the Stoics—actually denied the traditional objects of religious devotion, these deities were often relegated to the sidelines of philosophical inquiry as being all but irrelevant. Thus, while the characterization given to Paul's audience in vs. 22–23 is not incorrect, it probably employs a certain hyperbole. One thinks of our own society, in which belief in God always ranks high in the polls, but appears to be less important in the living of daily life.

The second section, vs. 24–28, is introduced by the final sentence of v. 23, which says in effect, "I am now going to tell you about the God of whom you are only vaguely aware." There are several qualities to this God, according to Paul. First, this God is the creator of the cosmos. Second, this God so transcends human life that (unlike certain of the Greek deities) this Deity is independent of any need for human support. Third, this Deity is the Lord of all life, not only as creator, but also as the giver, shaper and sustainer of human existence. Fourth, the human dependence on this Deity has resulted in a universal quest for God (the implication being that the Greeks' altar is evidence of this quest), a God who is nearer to us than we sometimes suppose. The conclusion to this rather elaborate syllogism is: As humans, we relate to this Deity as children to a parent, a fact that some Greek thinkers have already acknowledged. "In him we live and move and have our being" (v. 28) is perhaps (but not certainly) a quotation from the sixth-century B.C. writer Epimenides of Crete (to whom is also attributed the quotation in Titus 1:12). "For we too are his offspring" is from the pen of Aratus of Soli (in Cilicia, the native region of Paul), who was active in the third century B.C. In the introduction to his popular poem on astronomy and meteorology entitled *Phaenomena,* Aratus, who often reflected Stoic influences, wrote: "Everywhere we all need Zeus, for we are also his offspring."

As the final sentence of the first section introduces the second section, so the final sentence of the second section introduces the third (vs. 29–31). "Since we are God's offspring, . . ." certain things may be deduced. First, we cannot make God into some idolatrous form, in light of the fact that God has made us. Furthermore, while there may have existed a season in which God turned a blind eye to the ignorance of humankind, that period is no more. It is at this point that the message becomes specifically Christian: God now demands repentance (v. 30), because the time of judgment is at hand, a righteous time presided over by a "man" whom God has designated (v. 31a). The event that symbolizes the truth of this present and coming reality is the resurrection of this "man" from the dead, a resurrection brought about by God (v. 31b).

The skill of the writer of this text is demonstrated by the manner in which, having worked within Greek philosophical and literary contexts through the brief sermon, he turns to unreservedly Christian statements for the conclusion to the passage. And although the name of Jesus never appears, it is quite clear that Jesus is the centerpiece of the preacher's thought and that the Easter event is, in his view, the central fact of human history. The postscript to the sermon (vs. 32–33), although not included in the lection, leaves no doubt about that.

Jesus Christ and his resurrection, the primary event of human life, to Jew and to Greek, to man and to woman (note v. 34), to ancient and to modern! Thus, Acts 17:22–31, while dressed in Greek attire, is the same essential proclamation as Acts 10:34–43 and 2:14a, 22–32, 36–41, the other texts from Acts on which the lectionary has, to date, focused during this Easter season.

Psalm 66:8–20

The psalmist has an intimate memory of God and makes a repeated self-announcement, "I, I, I." The psalmist also has a communal experience of Israel's life with God and dares to say "us" without embarrassment. The intimate "I" and the daring "us" are not, however, enough. The psalmist wants to share this "I" and "us" with the nations, wants other peoples to participate in this concrete witness. It is this move from *concrete confession* to *comprehensive witness* that is the work of this text.

The Psalm reading is organized around two sweeping invitations addressed to those outside the community of faith (vs. 8, 16). In the first, the address is "O peoples," presumably the nations. The God the nations are to bless, that is, praise and trust, is "our God," the God of Israel who has kept "us" alive. In the second address, the appeal is to "all you who fear God," that is, those who have serious religious passion (v. 16). They are invited to the testimony that concerns God. Thus the nations are invited to take seriously the concrete testimony of Israel, which is quite specific and removed from the nations. This pattern of rhetoric suggests this movement:

Universal appeal ⟶ concrete base
O peoples ⟶ *our* God
all who fear ⟶ for *me*.

That the testimony concerns "me" and "us" is perceived as no barrier in the nations receiving the good news of God. The other peoples, however, will have to appropriate this faith from "our/my" confession. That is all that is said about the nations. The rest of the reading concerns our/my testimony of a most specific kind.

The remainder of the reading makes its testimony in three rhetorical patterns:

1. The nations are invited to this awesome *you* who has been decisive for Israel's life and memory (vs. 10–12). The substance of these verses is in fact another recital of Israel's memory, which moves from testing (v. 10) to "a spacious place" (v. 12), that is, from the furnace of slavery in Egypt to the well-being of the Promised Land. Every step of the way has been a hard and demanding one, every facet has been dominated by "you." This tale of suffering and trouble is in fact a story of life relentlessly given and guarded by God; the nations can join in blessing this God of life.

2. The recital now becomes more personal with a sequence of "I" statements (vs. 13–15). The speaker tells in detail of a passionate resolve to worship the God of life, to offer burnt offerings, to pay vows, to keep promises, and to give generous offerings. The drama of worship, sacrifice, and offering is a powerful certification that, in the midst of trouble, there has been rescue. The act of worship itself is an act of testimony to nonbelievers that devotion, generosity, and gratitude to God are a response to deliverance.

3. The glad worship of vs. 13–15 is rooted in a remembered act of deliverance (vs. 16–20). That remembered act of God, however, is necessarily a two-way conversation: "I cried, I cried aloud," passionately, desperately. Surely God heard! That is the miracle, the wonder, the source of power, the rootage of new life, the trigger for joy. It is this pivotal affirmation of v. 19 on which everything turns. The news about God is interactive, concrete, and personal.

In v. 8 the nations are urged to "bless" our God. Now, in v. 20, the speaker goes ahead to bless, with or without the nations. This is a clear reason for which to bless God. This God has listened. This God has heard. This God has received and attended to my prayer. The reason for that attentiveness, stated in the parallelism, is that God has acted out of God's *ḥesed.* This is the bottom line, the last word. The psalmist has saved the best claim about God until now. Everything in Israel's memory and in the speaker's experience depends on God's fidelity.

The nations can know this *ḥesed.* The nations can share in it. The reality of intense personal fidelity from God is Israel's offer to the nations. The nations are invited to re-perceive their own life and the life of the whole world in new categories, categories of elemental fidelity and care. The large theological claim depends on the concrete testimony: God listened.

1 Peter 3:13–22

To read 1 Peter is to enter a struggle to understand Christian suffering. Even the opening lines concede that those who have been newly born in Christ are, at present, undergoing suffering (1:6). Outsiders slander them (2:12). Those who are slaves remain especially vulnerable to the harsh treatment of their masters (2:18–20). The bulk of chapters 3—4 addresses the way in which Christians should understand and face the suffering that is their lot.

Clearly the suffering that plagues the author arises from human action, not from physical or other natural causes. Unlike 1 Thess. 4:13, which reflects the dilemma posed for Christians by deaths within their ranks, here the plague is of human origin. For reasons that were presumably too well known to require explanation, Christians suffered at the hands of outsiders. The nature of that suffering is likewise uncertain, beyond the references to verbal harassment (2:12) and "various trials" (1:6).

The historical situation behind this suffering probably does not arise from widespread, organized Roman persecution of Christians. Unlike Revelation, with its thinly veiled polemic against Rome, 1 Peter's positive assessment of the role of human institutions, including the emperor and governors (2:13–15), reflects a general sense of confidence in the government. The suffering noted here more probably arises in the form of sporadic and localized incidents of harassment against a group of marginalized zealots.

In this particular passage, 3:13–22, the author undertakes to offer, first, ethical guidelines for dealing with suffering (vs. 13–17) and, second, a christological grounding for those same guidelines (vs. 18,21b–22; see below on vs. 19–21a). The passage opens with a question, the apparent naïveté of which startles contemporary readers: "Now who will harm you if you are eager to do what is good?" Since some people manifestly *will* harm even the innocent (cf. 2:19, 22), the question serves a rhetorical function by making a transition from the biblical quotation back to concrete advice for those who suffer.

First, the author insists that those who suffer are blessed. In the face of those who might suggest that Christian suffering demonstrates that God has turned away from Christians or that suffering somehow calls their faith into question, here suffering for the good is equated with being blessed. The second statement ("Do not fear what they fear") may bear a surface resemblance to popular psychological wisdom, but it actually comes from Isa. 8:12–13:

> Do not call conspiracy all that this people calls conspiracy, and do not fear what it fears, or be in dread. But the LORD of hosts, him you shall regard as holy; let him be your fear, and let him be your dread.

Christians are to distinguish their fears (their values) from the fears of the surrounding world. Only God is to be their "fear," their value. Third, Christians should respond to suffering, not with silence, but with gentle, reverent witness. As in Luke's story of the early Christian community praying for boldness to proclaim the gospel whatever the context (Acts 4:23–31), persecution should not lead to silence. Fourth, Christians must see that their behavior in no way justifies slander against them, so that their accusers appear merely ridiculous (1 Peter 3:16–17).

Apart from the fourth admonition, which stems largely from pragmatism, this council relies on the theological conviction that those who inflict suffering have only a relative and limited kind of power. Christians, who know that God ultimately holds and protects them, can endure any human suffering and, in some cases, make it an occasion for proclaiming the gospel.

The strongest evidence for this point comes in the appeal to Christ's own suffering in vs. 18, 21b–22. As recalled earlier in the letter (2:21–25), Christ himself suffered and died as a righteous person on behalf of an unrighteous and sinful humanity. His death did not, however, give to his enemies the final victory. The resurrection reveals their "power" for what it is—a sham. His present life with God and God's court (v. 22) vindicates him and all who belong to him.

Because of its role in the creedal tradition of the church, the reference in v. 19 to Christ's preaching to the spirits of the dead dominates interpretation of this text in a way that distorts its actual importance within the argument. Worrying about the particulars of this tradition interferes with understanding what is at stake here theologically. By asserting that Christ preached to those who died in the Flood, 1 Peter insists that no one exists beyond God's power for redemption. Even those who died in the flood in Noah's day (v. 20), guilty and "in prison," remain within God's grasp. Those who survived the flood with Noah anticipate Christian salvation, which also comes through water, although this time the water of baptism.

If 1 Peter's struggle to speak a word of encouragement and consolation to fellow Christians who suffer unjustly does not fully satisfy their questions, contemporary Christian preachers may empathize. In the face of any suffering, whether caused by human inhumanity, by disease, or by nature, the available answers always fall short. What Christians can assert with 1 Peter, as with Christians of every time and place, is that God stands with those who suffer and that God ultimately triumphs over that suffering.

John 14:15–21

The Gospel reading for this Sunday continues that of last Sunday. The disciples are gathered with Jesus at the Table, listening to his farewell words. Their occasional question reveals their own confusion and uncertainty (John 14:5, 8, 22). What are they to think in light of Jesus' prediction not only of his own death, but that one of them would betray him and another deny him? The tone of Jesus' words is reassuring and encouraging, but the content is profoundly theological. It is remarkable how the pastoral needs of the disciples are addressed not by analyzing their shaky situation, but by promising the permanence of the divine presence.

The first thing to observe about the text is that it begins and ends with *the correlation between love and obedience* (14:15, 21). (The same is true if the reading is continued through v. 24.) The relationship between disciples and Teacher is not to degenerate into sentimentality or into a wistful nostalgia once he has gone, about "how wonderful things were when Jesus was with us." Love expresses itself in obedience, in keeping Jesus' words. The disciples have a clear directive about life and relationships from Jesus' teaching, about washing feet and loving one another. Ignoring or disobeying that directive exposes a lack of love.

But this demand for obedience is delivered from legalism by *the accompanying promise of the divine presence* to be with those who love Jesus and obey his word. A question might be raised whether obedience is a precondition for receiving the divine presence, whether the Spirit and the risen Christ come only to those who convincingly demonstrate by their actions that they really love Jesus. Taken in isolation, some verses in the passage could be read this way, except that the entire context is affirmative and not provisional. Jesus wishes to relieve troubled hearts. To be sure, the passage does draw a very sharp line between the world and the disciples (to which we shall turn shortly), but the line is not intended to create in the disciples an anxious concern as to whether they have loved and obeyed sufficiently. Obedience and presence are better thought of as a chicken-

and-egg proposition. Those to whom the Spirit comes live in love and obedience, and those who live in love and obedience are persons in whom the Spirit dwells.

The language about the divine presence expresses the coming of the Paraclete (14:16–17), the coming of the risen Jesus (v. 18), and, beyond our selection, the coming of Jesus and the Father together (v. 23). It is frankly impossible on the basis of the text to draw distinctions between these comings as if they represented different experiences, three separate advents of God. Instead, the text makes the single point that after his return to the Father, Jesus remains in communion with the disciples through the presence of the Paraclete.

Two critical statements are made about the divine presence. On the one hand, the world does not know or recognize the divine presence. On the other hand, the disciples do know and recognize the divine presence. A sharp difference between the world and the disciples is established, and apparently the disciples need to understand exactly the nature of the difference (since the statements are repeated: 14:17, 19–21). What the disciples cherish, what sustains them and undergirds their life together, what keeps them from being orphaned is a reality that the world cannot discern.

We do well to reflect on this sharp difference drawn by the text between the world and the disciples. The church cannot expect the world to appreciate or participate in its reason for being, its mandate for mission, its source of strength. The one who guides the church into all truth remains a secret to the world. The world's ways of knowing and its criteria for evaluating what is real and important do not allow for such a divine presence as this. This suggests that the church, particularly in its moments of uncertainty and confusion, cannot look complacent about what it is doing. It cannot expect that its way of loving Jesus and obeying his commandments will necessarily be highly valued, that it will receive plaudits when it is most faithful to Jesus' directive.

At the same time, the church is prevented from an arrogant aloofness from the world, because it knows that the divine presence is a gift. Jesus looks on a potentially orphaned community and asks the Father to send the Paraclete to be present with them. It is not a reward for the church's good behavior or its sincere piety, but an expression of God's grace that the people of God enjoy the presence and direction of God.

Ascension

The festival of the Ascension is endlessly problematic and admits of no simple or single "explanation." It is clear in these texts that the church struggled to voice a reality that ran beyond all its explanatory categories. We must take care that we do not engage in domestication that curbs the wonder and wildness of these texts.

The presenting problem is, on the one hand, the disposal of the body of Jesus, what happened to Jesus after Easter. That, however, is a small agenda. On the other hand, the continuation of the church when Jesus is no longer present is an acute issue. Thus the issue in the narrative is much more a church question than it is a Jesus question. That presenting problem, however, only provides "cover" for the larger story. That story is that this fearful, waiting community, which is anxious and bewildered, has no power of its own. It possesses none and it can generate none for itself. It has no claim and no cause for self-congratulation. And yet, oddly, power is given that causes this fragile little community to have energy, courage, imagination, and resources completely disproportionate to its size. How can one speak about this changed situation that can only be attributed to the inscrutable generosity of God? How is it that this church with no claim becomes a powerful force in the larger scheme of public life?

The church has no special language of its own through which to utter the unutterable. For that reason, it must rely on its ancient doxological tradition (in the Psalms), which breaks out beyond reasoned explanation into wonder, awe, amazement, and gratitude. Worship is the arena in which the new power given the church by God is voiced. And that lyrical worship leads to glad witness, asserting that the world is oddly open to new governance.

The preacher will profit from noticing that these stories are cast in odd modes of discourse. There is nothing here that is conventional, controlled, or predictable. The nature of the story requires a peculiar mode of utterance. The narrative lets us see in wonderment glimpses and hints, but not more. God's new rule is beyond our logic. We see only its residue and effect in a transformed community. That community is not certain what has happened, but is sure enough to affirm its identity and embrace its proper work.

Acts 1:1–11 (A B C)

In the Lukan narrative of God's saving activity in Jesus Christ (the Gospel) and in the Holy Spirit (Acts), the story of Jesus' ascension marks the end of Jesus' postresurrection appearances to his disciples and the prelude to the sending of the Spirit, thereby marking a transition point from Easter to Pentecost. In the liturgical tradition of the church, Ascension is all of that and more, for it also has become a festival of the exaltation of the risen Christ.

The Acts lection for this day consists of two main components. The first (Acts 1:1–5) serves not only as an introduction to the entire book of Acts and thus to the work of the Holy Spirit in the life of the young church, but also—in a more immediate sense—as an introduction to the Ascension miracle. The second part (vs. 6–11) is the account of the miracle itself. In both these sections, however, the primary emphasis is on the coming of the Holy Spirit.

Verses 1–5, after a brief statement of purpose (vs. 1–2) which parallels Luke 1:1–4, set forth a terse summary of the events of the forty days following Easter, a time when Jesus "presented himself alive to [the disciples] by many convincing proofs" (v. 3). It is perhaps assumed by Luke that "Theophilus" has heard of these appearances of the risen Christ, since no effort is expended to provide the details of these encounters, other than what is offered in Luke 24. Following Jesus' order to the band of his faithful followers to remain in Jerusalem (Acts 1:4), he delivers the promise of God, namely, that God's Spirit is soon to be made evident in fresh ways. This coming of the Spirit is explained in baptismal terms: whereas water was the baptismal medium of old, "you will be baptized with the Holy Spirit not many days from now" (v. 5).

The second part of our text (vs. 6–11) repeats this emphasis on the coming of the Spirit, but in a different context. Here this gracious and decisive gift of God's Spirit is compared to the political hopes the disciples had vested in the Messiah. Their question about the restoration of the kingdom to Israel (v. 6) betrays that not even the events of Easter and the succeeding forty days had disabused them of a comfortable stereotype, that is, that God's Messiah would reinstitute the political fortunes of the old Davidic monarchy. Jesus deflects their question (v. 7) and refocuses their attention on the marvelous display of God's power and love that they are soon to see. It is not the restoration of the kingdom of Israel that will energize you, Jesus says in effect. Rather, "You will receive power when the Holy Spirit has come upon you" (v. 8a). Thus vs. 5 and 8 lift before the reader an announcement from God that is not to be overlooked: the age of the Spirit is about to dawn.

Then Jesus is elevated beyond the limits of their physical senses, and "two men in white robes" (compare Luke 24:4) gently chide the disciples for vacant gazing, even as they promise Jesus' Second Coming (Acts 1:9–11).

While the liturgical tradition of the church has tended to make the ascension of Jesus into a festival to his glory and power, the emphasis in the biblical tradition is elsewhere. Not only is the ascension rarely mentioned in the New Testament (compare Luke 24:51 and Mark 16:19), but the interest in Acts 1 appears to be less in what is happening to Jesus than in what is about to happen in the lives of the earliest Christians. Twice in this brief passage the declaration is made that the Holy Spirit is about to infuse the life of the church in new ways. Not that the Spirit was unknown before this. The "Spirit of God" was the phrase that from very early times had been applied to special expressions of God's guiding and redemptive presence in human life (note, for example, 1 Sam. 11:6, and compare it to 1 Sam. 16:14). But the import of Acts 1:5 and 8 is that a new dimension to the Spirit's work is about to become evident. It is as different from what has gone before as the Spirit is different from the ordinary water of baptism. It is as different from what has gone before as the transcendent kingdom of God (v. 3) is different from the political kingdom of David and his descendants.

Just how the Spirit finds expression the disciples are not told. That is a matter of suspense, which will not be resolved until Pentecost (Acts 2). In the interim, they (and the disciples in every age) are to "be my witnesses in Jerusalem, in all Judea and Samaria, and to the ends of the earth" (1:8). It will become clear only later that in this very activity of witnessing they will provide the channels for the Spirit's power and grace.

So in the New Testament perspective, Ascension is an interim time, a period—not unlike Advent—between promise and fulfillment. The disciples of Christ are called to live faithful and obedient lives and to remember that the wonder of God's love and presence revealed so radically in the cross and the open tomb still has in store fresh surprises of joy. The disciples of Christ are called to witness, little realizing how the Spirit lurks to transform all that they do into magnificent occasions for the outpouring of God's love. In this manner Ascension points to Pentecost and to all the marvelous ways of the Holy Spirit of God.

Psalm 47 (A B C)

The festival of Ascension is not about the physical ascent of a body (the body of Jesus) into heaven. It is, rather, a liturgical celebration whereby Jesus "ascends to the throne," that is, is dramatically elevated to a position of sovereign authority. In enacting this ritual of enthronement, the church's liturgy draws heavily on the liturgy of ancient Israel, whereby Yahweh was elevated and enthroned as a powerful sovereign. Our psalm reflects such a liturgical enactment.

The initial hymnic unit celebrates the power, authority, and sovereignty of Yahweh (Ps. 47:1–4). The hymnic summons is addressed to "all you peoples" (v. 1). The liturgy of the Jerusalem Temple dares to imagine that its worship is an act concerning all nations and peoples. This inclusive horizon is advanced by reference to Yahweh as "Most High" (*'Elyôn,* v. 2). The title is not an Israelite name for God, but is a generic name for the great god, a name to which all peoples could subscribe.

The reason for such praise is the kingship of Yahweh, the establishment of Yahweh's sovereign rule (vs. 2–4). The ground of praise is twofold. On the one hand, this God is "Elyon," the God of all peoples, who presides over all the earth, who has subdued peoples and nations and drawn them under a new aegis. On the other hand, the actual speakers in the liturgy and in the psalm are Israelites, who know this universal God by the exodus name of Yahweh, and who confess that God chose land "for us" and loves us (v. 4). Thus the hymn holds together the sweeping notion of universal sovereignty and the concreteness of the experience of the Israelite community.

The first characterization of enthronement in this psalm is a splendid liturgical act (v. 5). "God has gone up"! The language portrays an act of coronation or enthronement whereby the candidate (like the winner of the Miss America contest) ceremoniously, magnificently, and ostentatiously ascends the throne and dramatically claims power and receives obeisance. The kingship of Yahweh is enacted and implemented liturgically, as is every political ascent to power. When we say of Jesus in the creed, "He ascended into heaven," in the first instance this is the language of ritual enthronement and coronation. What is claimed substantively, politically, and theologically is first asserted dramatically and liturgically.

The second hymnic element reiterates the main themes of the initial verses (vs. 6–7). Four times the congregation is urged to "sing praises" (*zāmar,* v. 6). The identity of Yahweh in this summons is "God," a universal title, which is matched by "our King," the governor and guarantor of the Jerusalem political-religious establishment.

The second reflective statement describes the new world situation in light of this act of coronation (vs. 8–9). We are taken into the throne room. Around the throne sit all the obedient, glad subjects (v. 9). There is among them no conflict, dispute, or challenge to the authority of Yahweh. "The princes of the peoples," that is, all the other kings and rulers whose gods have been defeated by Yahweh and who now submit to Yahweh, all are present. The wonder of our phrasing is that they are gathered together "as the people of the God of Abraham" (v. 9). This does not say that they have entered into the Mosaic covenant and have become adherents to the Torah. It is affirmed, however, that they have embraced the promises God has made to Abraham and Sarah, and have agreed to live under the power of God's promise.

This psalm invites us to understand the festival of Ascension anew. The festival is not about getting the body of Jesus off the earth, and it is therefore not marginal and incidental to the life of the church. The festival is a dramatic moment whereby the presence of Jesus in the church is converted into a large, cosmic rule. Rooted in liturgical rhetoric, this claim for God (and subsequently for Jesus) envisions important political spin-offs. All kings are indeed under God's feet (see Eph. 1:22). God's promise, we know very well, is a rule of mercy, compassion, forgiveness, and caring. The new enthronement changes the climate of the earth and the modes of power now permitted in the affairs of princes and kings. The kingship of God revamps all other forms of governance.

Ephesians 1:15–23 (A B C)

Since it separates him from his followers—at least in a physical, visible sense—the ascension of Jesus might have been recalled by the church as a time of grief and confusion. How would the straggly group of Jesus' followers continue in his absence? What meaning could his absence from them have, other than their own isolation and aimlessness?

Luke, alone among the Gospels, not only describes the ascension but portrays it as a time of empowerment. Both in the Gospel and in Acts, Jesus tells his disciples to wait for the Spirit, a Spirit that comes only after Jesus himself has departed. At the ascension itself (Luke 24:44–53; Acts 1:1–11) Jesus' final instructions immediately precede his ascension and the repeated instructions of two men in white robes. By this means, and by virtue of the narrative connection, Luke depicts the ascension of Jesus as the empowerment of the church itself.

The brief reference to the ascension in Eph. 1:15–23 stands out in contrast to the accounts in Luke and in Acts. Here we find no references to Jesus' postresurrection stay with his disciples, to his mysterious ascension, to the return to Jerusalem. Instead, the ascension functions as part of the author's general doxology about God's actions in Christ on behalf of humankind. A closer examination, however, will show that in Eph. 1, as in Luke-Acts, the ascension of Jesus signals the empowerment of the church.

While the passage is a single unit, the content of which is a prayer, it moves from thanksgiving to intercession to doxology. Verses 15–16 first recall the faith of the Ephesians and their love toward all believers. This faithfulness on their part prompts the writer to an exuberance of thanksgiving. As elsewhere in New Testament letters, the response to the gospel in itself provides a reason for gratitude to God.

That thanksgiving does not mean that the church now stands alone or can operate autonomously. The intercession of vs. 17–19 specifies that the church needs wisdom, revelation, and hope. Believers need to know God's power "for us who believe, according to the working of his great power."

At first glance, the remaining verses of the prayer appear to be only a kind of christological footnote. The content is familiar, perhaps so familiar that it slips out of the reader's awareness, dismissed as so much theological "filler" without any substantive connection to the issue at hand, the needs of the community. Several aspects of the passage, however, connect it firmly with the intercessory prayer of vs. 17–19.

Most clearly, both the intercession and the doxology revolve around the writer's confidence in the power of God. Verse 19 refers to the "immeasurable greatness" of God's power and the working of God's "great power." Verse 20, which begins the section on the ascension, begins with "God put this power to work in Christ." In Greek, vs. 19 and 20 are connected by the repetition of "working" (*energeia*) at the end of v. 19 and "put to work" (*energeō*) at the beginning of v. 20. The power already at work in the community and invoked by the author for "wisdom and revelation" is none other than the power that raised Jesus from the dead and exalted him to heavenly places.

What follows in vs. 20–23, then, serves to tie the empowerment of the community to the power of God more than it does to describe in precise detail the present whereabouts and activity of the risen Lord. The statements about Christ's ascension are nevertheless important, particularly for the way in which they underscore this notion of God's power. For the writer of Ephesians, reference to the resurrection alone does not suffice, but must be expanded by a glimpse of the further exaltation of Christ in the ascension. Christ sits at the right hand (v. 20), above every form of "rule and authority and power and dominion," and "above every name" of every age. All things are already subjected to him (v. 21).

These same motifs occur elsewhere in the New Testament, of course, but here Christ's complete triumph has already taken place. The Philippians hymn *anticipates* the exaltation of Christ above every name, but that event has not yet occurred (Phil. 2:5–11). In 1 Cor. 15, Paul confidently asserts that God will finally triumph over "every ruler and every authority and power" (15:24), but that triumph also lies in the future. The apparent conflict among these texts perhaps arises because the author of Ephesians wants to ground the power of the church in this overwhelming demonstration of the power of God. That Christ has already triumphed means that the church itself will surely be sustained by God's power.

The connection between the ascended Christ and the church becomes explicit, of course, in Eph. 1:22–23. Here the metaphor of the church as a body *in Christ,* found already in 1 Corinthians, changes so that the church itself *is the body of Christ.* In 1 Corinthians, that metaphor serves to underscore the unity necessary for the church, even within its diversity. In Ephesians, the transformed metaphor serves to ground the church itself in the power of God. The church may act with confidence, because it knows itself to *be* Christ's own body, the body of the one whose exaltation derives directly from God's own power.

Luke 24:44–53 (A B C)

In the conclusion of Luke's Gospel, the narrator draws the story to a close by sounding again several notes that the careful reader has heard in earlier chapters. They come appropriately now as the final message of the risen Jesus to his disciples and, together with the account of Jesus' departure, serve as the connecting link to the beginning of the book of Acts, Luke's second volume.

What are those repeated themes? First, the Jewish scriptures provide an understanding of the Messiah and his destiny. This concern emerges early in the chapter, as Jesus walks with the two travelers to Emmaus (Luke 24:25–27, 32). Now, as he meets with a group of disciples, he again speaks of the scriptures and their witness to him, to the gospel, and to the mission to the nations. It is not important what specific passages Jesus (or the narrator) might have had in mind. The point to be made is that what happens to Jesus and what the disciples are to do in the days ahead are consistent with God's intentions from the beginning. The suffering and resurrection of the Messiah and the mission to the nations are not accidents of history, but fulfill the divine plan. One has to look to the scriptures to discern God's strategy in inaugurating the anticipated reign of justice and peace.

While the Jewish scriptures provide an understanding of the risen Jesus, it is the risen Jesus who rightly interprets the scriptures. A veil of mystery hangs over the text, leaving it enigmatic and inscrutable, until the resurrection. "Then he opened their minds to understand the scriptures" (v. 45). Neither the intellectual acumen of the scholars nor the spiritual capacity of the mystics grasps the intent of God in the ancient writings, apart from the presence of the one to whom the writings point.

Second, the declaration is made, "You are witnesses of these things" (v. 48). What (or who) is the antecedent of "you"? At the historical level, the answer is presumably "the disciples," though one has to go all the way back to v. 33 to find a specific referent. At another level, one might answer "the Jewish community," since this commission reconstitutes the people of God and gives them the particular responsibility to begin at Jerusalem and proclaim the gospel to the non-Jewish world (see Isa. 49:6). Not surprisingly, the group returns to the Temple as the place of worship and waiting.

At still another level, the "you" is directed to a broader company of readers, ancient and modern, who at the end of the narrative are drawn in as participants in the story. They (we) are witnesses, who are not allowed to put the book down like a good novel and return to business as usual, but are mandated to proclaim the story, to call for repentance, to declare divine forgiveness. They (we), like the original hearers, are to be recipients of the power that the Father promises, an indication that God intends for the plans to be completed and the divine strategy to work.

Third, the narrative ends in a remarkable outburst of worship. Rather than being depressed that Jesus has withdrawn and left them with a heavy responsibility, the disciples are ecstatic and worship Jesus. And their joy seems more than a temporary high, since they are "continually in the temple blessing God" (Luke 24:53). Just as Jesus' entry into the world evoked songs of praise from Mary, Zechariah, Simeon, Anna, and the angelic choir, so Jesus' departure to the Father sets the community again to singing.

Worship and witness belong together. Like the bud that will not bloom without regular watering, the church's mission dries up without the renewal of worship. The singing of hymns, the prayers of thanksgiving and intercession, the reading and exposition of scripture, and the breaking of bread keep the church in touch with the promised power of the Father and make possible the glorifying and enjoying of God that is done outside the sanctuary. Worship becomes the occasion when the story that must be told and retold among the nations is heard afresh, when the witness to the world is reenvisioned. At the same time, worship divorced from witness is empty. The church merely turns in on itself, loses its reason for being, and finds its singing, praying, and reading of scripture bland and impotent.

Ascension Day is an appropriate time to reflect on the church's mission in the world, on the importance of worship as a partner to mission, and on the critical role of the scriptures in providing direction.

Seventh Sunday of Easter

The church strains imaginatively in these texts to find language adequate to the newness that swirls around the terminating events of the life of Jesus. These events shatter all conventional categories of discernment, so the church has recourse to liturgical, lyrical, doxological speech. Thus speech matches the newness that is beyond any usual experience or explanation. The church can only practice stunned receptivity, which shakes the church out of all its self-control.

The oddity of these events around Jesus concerns the new rule of God and the in-breaking of a new age on earth. Focus in the entire Easter season is on that new governance which breaks the grip of all that is old, tired, deathly, and enslaving. To voice this newness, the Psalm lection shows the church using the ancient language of enthronement. That language originally was "sanctuary drama," and now it is Jesus through whom the drama of God's power is brought to fruition. Jesus becomes the key player in God's large drama.

This new rule of God, however, is not in these texts preoccupied primarily with God or with the ascended Jesus. These staggering events are given a poignant *churchly* tilt. The new rule concerns the community of believers; the texts rethink how this community can be formed in response to Jesus' new governance. What difference does it make for day-to-day faith and practice?

In the Acts text, the community accepting the new governance is to be a bold witness in the world, sustained by a disciplined life of prayer. This text starts the church of Acts on an astonishing career of unfettered freedom and daring in the world.

The other two New Testament readings are even more pastoral in their presentation of the authority of Jesus. The Epistle reading addresses people who are in the midst of suffering, hurt, and need. On the one hand, they are enjoined to powerful hope for the time of

God's eventual and full triumph. Someday it will all be made right, and the church counts heavily on that assurance. On the other hand, however, the reading concerns the present in its freighted significance and in the need to practice discipline. That is, those who are believers are not to give in, or to quit, but are to hold to an evangelical discernment of the present as the place where faith is to be given and to be lived.

The Gospel reading portrays the church under the power of God's resolve, being given a wholly new identity and vocation in the world. Being "prayed for" completely repositions and redefines the church. It is no longer a body of helpless, frightened folk who are confused about the future. Rather, it is a community that belongs to God and is freed for God's massive purposes in the world.

All these texts show the church at work, seeking to embrace, embody, and enact its convictions in the world. The new rule of God permits new human life in the world. Such new human life is not easy, but it is possible. That new life requires discipline, but it is also marked by a relentless buoyancy that refuses the despair of the world and the seduction of the world. The ground of such a bold refusal is God's own powerful resolve, which permeates the character of the church. Because of Easter, this community is indeed an Easter-powered community!

Acts 1:6–14

(Because some prefer to celebrate Ascension on this Sunday rather than on Ascension Day, the preacher may wish to substitute for the above reading from Acts the first lesson for Ascension, Acts 1:1–11. In any event, he or she may wish to consider the comments on that lection, as that text contains much of the same material as the first reading for this Sunday.)

The present passage begins with Luke's account of the ascension of the risen Christ (Acts 1:6–11) and concludes with the immediate response of the disciples (vs. 12–14). The text makes clear that in the understanding of Jesus' followers the Lord's resurrection, an event affirmed by his repeated appearances (Acts 1:3), marks a fresh break with the past. What is not clear, however, is the nature of the new beginning, and the disciples speak to this uncertainty as they wonder, "Lord, is this the time when you will restore the kingdom to Israel?" (v. 6). This may be the expression of a type of narrow nationalism with which the messianic hope was sometimes associated, but it may also be nothing more than the disciples' effort to probe the ultimate meaning of their experiences of the resurrected Christ. *Something* new impends! Could it be the restoration of the Davidic throne?

Jesus' reply is unambiguous, at least to the extent that political expectations are dashed (v. 7). Yet when Jesus speaks of the personal empowerment of the disciples (v. 8) he does so in a manner not calculated to satisfy their curiosity completely. The emphasis here is on the coming presence of the Spirit as the reality of the new age, the reality that will transform them. This, not some reinstitution of a long-defunct monarchy, will be the signal that nothing can ever again be the same. It is to be a very personal transformation, for it will happen to *them.* (Notice the repeated use of the pronoun "you" in v. 8—the English of NRSV accurately reflects the Greek text.) Yet precisely what is to happen they are not told, and the effect is to hold them—and the reader—in suspension, a suspension that will not be resolved until the narrative of Acts 2 (see the first reading for Pentecost).

Yet their role in the coming new age is not a matter left completely in the dark, for they are instructed to be witnesses (v. 8), a role which, as good Jews, they would have at least partly understood. For in the Hebrew legal tradition a witness was one who, because of experience and observation, was in a unique position to tell the truth in some deeply important matter. Certain obligations were placed on witnesses, as well as sanctions in the event they failed their obligations (Deut. 19:15–21). Thus, the disciples' participation in the coming new age was to involve their truth-telling in connection with the most significant event in human history, the resurrection of Jesus Christ from the dead. If there is any doubt that this is precisely what Luke has in mind, one only need read the sermons of the early disciples in Acts 2, 17, and elsewhere. "This Jesus God raised up, and of that all of us are witnesses," Peter is recorded as preaching to the Pentecost assembly (Acts 2:32). Yet the full import of Jesus' promise, as well as of the demands he is placing on them, would become apparent only with the passage of time and the transpiring of certain crucial events.

According to our text, this is the final deed of the earthly Jesus, the ultimate act—at least in the Lukan sequence—of a drama that began long before with the annunciation to Elizabeth (Luke 1:5–25). Jesus ascends into heaven (Acts 1:9), while the earthbound disciples are left gazing upward and doubtless wondering about the significance of it all. Jarred out of their reverie by "two men in white robes" (v. 10; cf. Luke 24:4) they are promised that the Jesus who has left them so miraculously will, in no less wondrous fashion, come again (v. 11).

The second part of the text (vs. 12–14) marks a period of retreat and reflection. The disciples (who are named in v. 13) return to Jerusalem and there enter a season of prayer in the company of other followers of the Master, including members of Jesus' own family. In the entirety of Acts 1, these verses mark a period of preparation for the naming of Judas's successor (vs. 15–26), but within the confines of today's lection they may be understood as indicating a time of retreat and personal renewal before the wonderfully shocking events recorded in Acts 2, the miracle of Pentecost. The disciples have not yet begun to witness as the Lord has commanded, but they are keeping their faith with the Risen One and with one another by "constantly devoting themselves to prayer" (v. 14).

Taking its cue from the text, the church on this day remembers God's mighty acts in Jesus, specifically in his resurrection and ascension. Yet the eye of the people of God is on the future, for just ahead lies the challenge of bearing the truth of what God has done to a world that will respond to this good news sometimes in joy, sometimes in anger, but rarely in indifference. And so the people of God pause, in prayer, and gather their strength for the days shortly to come.

Psalm 68:1–10, 32–35

The festival of the Ascension continues to exercise its influence in this set of readings. In this festival, the church plays on the imagery of "going up." In the liturgy, "going up" refers to the ascent of the king to the throne; Jesus assumes the place of honor and power "at the right hand" on the throne.

This psalm pleads for this "going up" to power and authority: "Let God rise up" (Ps. 68:1). Let God rouse God's self, let God assume and show power, let God be the powerful agent of change that God is capable of being. Everything can and will be changed when God is roused to power.

The fundamental petition (vs. 1–3) is that the God who has been asleep should awaken to power (cf. Ps. 121:4; Isa. 51:9–11). That is, this rhetoric does not assume that God is constant in attentiveness and power, but that God moves in and out on God's proper business. Later in the psalm we shall see the reason for such a view of God.

The psalm does not doubt that when God is awakened to action there will be a decisive sorting out, a decision made between those who are God's friends and those who are God's enemies (vs. 1–2). God's power is not in doubt, but God's attentiveness must always be secured anew. The main reason to seek God's intrusive action is that God needs to act against those who oppose God's purpose. These opponents of God are variously named as God's "enemies," as "those who hate" God, and as the "wicked." They are not said to be the enemies of the one who prays, but the enemies of the God to whom the prayer is addressed. That is, the speaker suggests to God, these are not my enemies, but yours. That which finally opposes God cannot continue to exist in God's presence.

The positive counterpoint in the prayer is less developed (v. 3). The righteous, antithetical to the wicked, are those who will benefit from God's arousal. They will welcome God's intrusion, because they regard themselves as properly aligned with God's intention.

The poet explicates the reason for the doxology of v. 4 (vs. 5–6). The reason for praise is that this God characteristically does what enhances the righteous. Thus this God is the guardian, legitimator, and guarantor for the socially disfranchised, widows, and orphans. Moreover, this God is a custodian for the homeless, the ones without community, and an advocate for prisoners, who characteristically are the poor. Thus the righteous (v. 3) who celebrate (v. 4) are likely to be those without conventional social power, the widows, orphans, homeless, and imprisoned. They are the ones who need God to be aroused, who turn to God because they are otherwise helpless, and who anticipate a good life when God acts. Thus the petition of vs. 1–2 and the entire urging that God should rise up makes most sense when the petition and urging are on the lips of the helpless and powerless.

The reference in v. 6 to "parched land" prepares us for the final section of the main part of our assigned reading (vs. 7–10). Now, for the first time in the poem, God is addressed directly. In these verses, rain is part of the theophany that bespeaks God's terrible power and presence. In this historical recall, rain is simply one aspect of God's dramatic, cataclysmic coming to be present in Israel with sovereign power.

The significance of the image of rain changes, however, in vs. 9–10. Now rain is not an element of theophany, but is simply God's gift to the land which lets the earth flourish; from theophany, the poem has moved to the reliability of creation, guaranteed by God's attentiveness.

The conclusion of these verses uses the term "thy living ones" (Hebrew; NRSV and RSV "flock"). The verse indicates that the needy (i.e., afflicted, oppressed) ones now have found the rain-soaked land to be a place of goodness, a safe home. The reference to the needy (v.

10) recalls the needy in vs. 5–6. The coming of rain is a rich gift to those who have no other resources for life.

Thus the psalm juxtaposes two very different motifs. First, Yahweh is the rain God who gives rain and causes life. With this image, we can understand how it is that God waxes and wanes and is not constant. God's absence is because the deathly gods of drought have their day of preeminence; this God of life returns when the rains come.

Second, rain becomes a way of speaking about caring social relations that let the needy share in the good life. Thus rain comes to mean all the showers of blessing, justice, righteousness, equity, shalom. The two themes together, rain and care for the needy, that is, a motif or *creation* and a theme of *covenant,* converge in this theological affirmation. It is the rule of God over creation and through covenant that makes new life possible, because this God overrides the power of death.

The conclusion of the psalm is a doxology and acclamation of the God of life, who reappears in power in order to replenish the earth and to renew the covenant (vs. 32–35). The God who is praised is the "rider in the heavens," the one who comes in power on a cloud, in a rainstorm (v. 33). The great God of power (v. 34) is to be praised both by the "kingdoms of the earth" (v. 32) and by Israel, to whom this God is peculiarly committed (v. 35). Israel joins all the earth in singing to and celebrating the God of creation and life, who has decisively defeated the power of death.

1 Peter 4:12–14; 5:6–11

In this passage, 1 Peter's preoccupation with the suffering of Christians comes to its conclusion. The letter makes frequent reference to the suffering of the faithful and its prototype in the suffering of Christ (1:6; 2:18–25; 3:8–4:6). Although the exact nature of the suffering remains hidden from modern readers, it clearly includes verbal abuse and harassment (2:12; 3:15). By means of the motifs of the new birth and the household of God, the author works to draw together a community that can withstand suffering inflicted by external forces. The occasional reminder that believers should be subject to suffering only for a good cause and never as a result of actual wrongdoing (4:15) serves to recall the weakness that can enter the community from within its own ranks.

The language of this lection reveals that the sufferings of believers derive from real and powerful sources. First Peter 4:12 conjures up a "fiery ordeal" that comes to test the faithful. Chapter 5:8b dramatically portrays the devil—"like a roaring lion"—as the adversary of the faithful, which "prowls around, looking for someone to devour." In this striking personification, evil emerges as the enemy that actively and intentionally seeks to destroy those who belong to God. By contrast with contemporary tendencies to abstract or even to deny the existence of evil by reducing it to social or political or psychological factors, this writer knows that evil wills itself to happen, that evil engages in battle with God and with God's own creatures.

Alongside this acknowledgment that believers suffer and this vivid portrait of the cause of suffering, 1 Peter places Christian confidence in God. Believers may rejoice, not just in spite of but *in* their suffering, "because the spirit of glory, which is the Spirit of God, is resting on you" (4:14). The humiliation of believers is a prelude to God's exaltation of them "in due time" (5:6). God will care for Christians and take on their anxieties (5:7). The temporary suffering of Christians will find its end when God will "restore, support, strengthen, and establish" them.

This emphasis on God's future reward for the sufferings of the present smacks of what is often referred to as "pie in the sky by and by." For those who will endure the present, putting up with the humiliation and suffering to which believers are subject, God holds out the promise of a future reward. One difficulty with this position is that it calls for certain groups (e.g., African American slaves in this country) to endure the status quo without confronting and overturning it. Another difficulty is that it views the present as meaningless, reducing human physical life to a mere threshhold for "real life" with God after death.

Such attitudes undeniably exist among Christians, some of them based no doubt on texts such as this one. The text itself, however, at least *implies* that the present has meaning in and of itself. The author does not exhort the audience to exit the world by denying the reality of physical suffering or by passively acquiescing to the circumstances. Instead, the author depicts an active and realistic response. First, believers humble themselves before God. An admonition to humility only *seems* to invoke the "pie in the sky" attitude mentioned above. To humble oneself before God, "the mighty hand of God," is to insist that God will finally triumph, even over the undeniable power of the devil. Out of this confidence in God comes a related admonition: "Cast all your anxiety on him, because he cares for you" (5:7). God's strength is accompanied by a compassion that enables God to take on the cares and concerns of God's people.

The second kind of response believers can make to evil and suffering is to resist it: "Discipline yourselves, keep alert. . . . Resist him. . . ." (5:8–9). In a sense, the whole of 1 Peter concerns the making of protective boundaries around a community made up of believers who have no clear social or political identity. These marginalized persons, part of a new household that God has created in Christ, together inhabit a new home whose walls are invisible to the naked, untransformed eye. Language about discipline, alertness, resistance invokes the need for such actions if the new household is to be maintained. Only the household that stays ready can face the intruder with confidence. (Here the "intruder" is identified entirely with evil, never with yet another marginalized human being who might simply be led to join with the household.)

A final—and seemingly bizarre—response to evil is rejoicing. Suffering puts Christians in direct contact with the life of Christ, who suffered on their behalf. That connection, together with the expectation that Christ's glory will finally be revealed (4:13) prompts believers to the apparent absurdity of rejoicing even in the face of suffering. To the world outside God's household, of course, such laughter in the face of torment will go by the name of madness or weakness or cowardice. Apart from an understanding that Christ's own suffering was salvific, the "normal" rules hold, and suffering signifies failure and loss. Christians, however, know both the reality of evil and, somewhere down the road, its ultimate defeat.

John 17:1–11

The so-called "high-priestly prayer" in John 17 comes at the conclusion of the farewell discourses. The narrative pictures a confused group of disciples, unable to comprehend the significance of what is being said or what is about to happen. The air is heavy with the prospect of Jesus' impending departure, and, appropriately, Jesus prays for the disciples—for their protection, their solidarity, their steadfast future after he is gone. The prayer is addressed to God, but the disciples, both ancient and modern, are invited to sit in and be comforted by the words Jesus speaks in their behalf.

1. Before the prayer takes on its intercessory qualities, however, Jesus asks that the Father glorify the Son so that the Son in turn may glorify the Father. The verbs are the language of revelation. Jesus has made visible the Father's presence and power throughout his ministry, and now he prays that God will reveal the divine majesty specifically in the events of death, resurrection, and departure.

The disciples, then, are not left to their own devices and desires. In the future they fear so much the divine veil is pulled back, and the face of God is seen in the face of Jesus. The disciples are not to be left with the best of human possibilities, but with the very reality of God. They have a name and a basis for confronting the riddles of human existence, even though they live without the physical companionship of Jesus.

2. Something earth-shaking, life-changing is at stake in this act of glorifying, this revelation of the Father. It is not merely the datum for another religion, but the giving of life—not just breathing, eating, moving, but the life of the age to come. More sharply than any other writer in the New Testament, the writer of the Fourth Gospel sees in the coming of Jesus a change in the aeons, a movement in the world's clock, the dawning of a new day, so that the life of eternity can be experienced now. Jesus, as the revelation of God, has the authority "to give eternal life to all whom you have given him" (John 17:2).

"And this is eternal life, that they may know you, the only true God, and Jesus Christ whom you have sent" (17:3). Of course, the verb "know" in the Fourth Gospel carries the notion of something more than intellectual acceptance, something different from mystical meditation. It does not imply a solution to all the intricacies of Trinitarian theology nor does it mean that the knower is transformed into a model of piety. Rather, knowing God means being related to a revelation that has happened in history, confessing a person named Jesus, crucified and risen, as Son of God. Knowing God entails obeying the commandments of God, and especially the new commandment to live in a loving relationship with other "knowers" of God.

3. In addition to this amazing revelation of God and giving of new life, Jesus pointedly prays for the disciples (17:6–11). Somewhat to the surprise of the readers of the text, they are now depicted not as helpless, frightened followers who are confused about the future, but as God's possession, given to Jesus, people who have kept the word taught them and have understood that Jesus has come from God. They belong to God, and God is enjoined to protect them as they live out their calling in the world, to enable them to maintain their unity. Jesus' stance toward his followers is not one of condescension or pity. He describes them as they are seen by God.

What are we to make of v. 9, where Jesus declares that he is not praying for the world but only for the disciples? Some interpreters find here a Gnostic-like attitude toward the world and the fostering of a dangerous elitism among Christians. But there need be no suggestion that God (or Jesus) has abandoned humanity in general or lost interest in the world's welfare. John 3:16 should lay such a thought to rest. Rather, the Fourth Gospel takes a sober and realistic position toward the church's situation in the world. The hostility generated against the gospel means that those who preach and live it will be hated (15:18–25; 17:14–16). In such a context, the lines are clearly drawn between church and world. Jesus simply expresses in his prayer the petition that the Father protect the church in its responsibility of being a distinctive, called-out community.

The contemporary church may be in a different place from the initial readers of the Fourth Gospel. Certainly the text challenges any notion of an easy peace between the church and the world. Having and keeping the divine word creates a unique community, which does not belong to the world, but is sustained and protected by God, appropriately addressed as "Holy Father" (17:11).

PENTECOST

The scope of the texts for this special festival in the life of the church is both narrow and broad. It is narrow in the sense that a single theme predominates: the gift of the Spirit of God is new life. Yet it is broad in that the nature of this life is understood in the most expansive ways.

The foundation of the Pentecost festival is that series of events recorded in Acts 2; the lectionary focuses on vs. 1–21 of the chapter as its special object of attention. Here is to be found a decisive proclamation that links new life in Christ to the activity of the Spirit of God (2:4). This new life is quite distinctive, for it not only reanimates that which has seemed defeated (the young church), but it also impels the body of believers in new directions, using the transformed words of an ancient prophet to do so (2:17–21). At the heart of the church's new life is its experience of the crucified, risen Lord, a reality emphasized not only by the context of the passage from Acts 2 (especially what precedes it in Acts 1:1–14), but also recalled—by means of a "flashback"—in the Gospel lection from John 7.

But if the lections for Pentecost make clear the links between the gift of new life and the activity of the Spirit of God, they also describe this new life in the most wide-ranging terms. Psalm 104:24–34, 35b is, on one level, a celebration of the power of God in endowing the heavens and the earth with life, an endowment which, as in Acts 2, is linked to the work of God's Spirit (Ps. 104:30). On another level, however, the life that is celebrated here is not just physical, but transcendent. Men and women live because of a relationship with Yahweh that elicits praise (vs. 33–34). Thus we stand reminded that the gift of the Spirit has been life from the very beginning of God's creative activity. While, at the other end of the chronological spectrum, 1 Cor. 12:3b–13 points the reader to the reality that the gift of life, having once been made, remains with the Spirit-led person in the form of a heart reoriented to new and marvelous deeds of witness.

Acts 2:1–21 (A B C)

New life—sudden, unmerited, irresistible new life! That is the reality the Pentecost narrative in Acts 2 broadcasts, and the text transmits the story in the most expansive way imaginable. All the stops on this great literary organ are employed: a heavenly sound like a rushing wind, descending fire, patterns of transformed speech, and the like. It is as if not even the most lavish use of human language is capable of capturing the experiences of the day, and that is undoubtedly one of the emotions the text wishes to convey.

It is not accidental, of course, that the birth of the church, this great "harvest" of souls, should occur on this important festival. The Feast of Pentecost, or Weeks, as it is known in the Old Testament, marked the end of the celebration of the spring harvest, a liturgical cycle that began at Passover and during which devout Israelite families praised God for God's grace and bounty. It also was the beginning of a period, lasting until the autumnal Festival of Booths (or Tabernacles), in which the first fruits of the field were sacrificed to Yahweh. And among at least some Jews the Feast of Weeks was a time of covenant renewal, as the following text from the Book of Jubilees (c. 150 B.C.) makes clear:

> Therefore, it is ordained and written in the heavenly tablets that they should observe the feast of Shebuot (Weeks) in this month, once per year, in order to renew the covenant in all (respects), year by year. (*Jub.* 1:17; trans. O. S. Wintermute in James H. Charlesworth, ed., *The Old Testament Pseudepigrapha;* Garden City, N.Y.: Doubleday & Co., 1985, vol. 2, p. 67.)

Pentecost/Weeks is thus a pregnant moment in the life of the people of God and in the relationship between that people and God. Or to put the matter more graphically, but also more accurately, Pentecost is the moment when gestation ceases and birthing occurs. Thus, it is both an end and a beginning, the leaving behind of that which is past, the launching forth into that which is only now beginning to be. Pentecost therefore is not a time of completion. It is moving forward into new dimensions of being, whose basic forms are clear, but whose fulfillment has yet to be realized.

Those who follow the cycle of lectionary texts (or, for that matter, those who simply read the book of Acts) have been prepared for this moment. Twice, in connection with Jesus' ascension, the coming of the Spirit has been promised: "You will receive power when the Holy Spirit has come upon you" (Acts 1:8; compare 1:5). That promise is now realized in a manner far surpassing the expectations of even the most faithful disciples. New life for the church! New life for individuals within the church! New life through the Spirit of God! That is the meaning of Pentecost.

No one present is excluded from this display of God's grace. Unlike other important moments in the history of God's mighty acts of salvation—the transfiguration (Mark 9:2–13), for example, where only the inner few are witnesses to the work of God's Spirit—everyone is included at Pentecost. The tongues of fire rest upon "each" (Acts 2:3) of the disciples, and a moment later the crowd comes surging forward because "each one" (v. 6) has heard the disciples speaking in his or her native tongue. In order that not even the least astute reader may miss the inclusiveness of the moment, the list of place names that begins in v. 9 traces a wide sweep through the world of the Greco-Roman Diaspora. That which happens at Pentecost is thus no inner mystical experience, but an outpouring of God's energy that touches every life present.

Yet not everyone responded to the winds and fires of new life, at least not in positive ways. Some mocked (v. 13) and, in their unwillingness to believe the freshness of God's initiatives, reacted with stale words (compare 1 Sam. 1:14) as they confused Spirit-induced joy with alcohol-induced inebriation. Perhaps it was the very extravagant expression of the Spirit's presence that drove them to conclude: "This cannot be what it seems to be!" Yet what it seemed to be is precisely what it was. God's Spirit unleashed! New life—sudden, unmerited, irresistible new life! We may hope that those who mocked were among those who, on hearing Peter's sermon, were "cut to the heart" (v. 37).

Peter's sermon begins—and this day's lection ends—with a quotation (vs. 17–21) from the prophet Joel (Joel 2:28–32a), and nothing could be more symptomatic of the nature of Pentecost than the transmutation of this text. That which in the prophet's discourse appears prominently as a forecast of destruction and death has become on Peter's tongue a declaration of new life. For Joel the signs of the outpouring of the Spirit are a prelude to disaster (see especially Joel 2:32b, c), but for Peter these wonders have been fulfilled in Jesus Christ, himself the greatest of God's wonders (Acts 2:22), and their purpose, *Christ's* purpose, is nothing less than the redemption of humankind. Again the Spirit has invaded human life in ways that shatter old expectations. It is not death that is the aim of the Spirit's visitation, but new life—sudden, unmerited, irresistible new life! "Everyone who calls on the name of the Lord shall be saved" (v. 21).

Psalm 104:24–34, 35b (A B C)

The singular event of Pentecost concerns God's gift of Spirit, which gives life to a defeated church. This psalm reading pushes our horizon of Pentecost into larger spheres of faith and reality. God's gift of Spirit concerns not only the community of faith, but the life and well-being of the whole creation. The church lives only because of the gift of God's Spirit; so also creation lives only because of the gift of God's Spirit.

The world belongs utterly to God (Ps. 104:24–26). The first twenty-three verses of this psalm have provided a doxological inventory of creation; each part of creation is named as a product of Yahweh's inimitable power and resolve. Now, in v. 24, the psalm draws a conclusion from the long preceding recital. The psalmist speaks in astonishment and delight: How many are your creatures! We did not know there were so many creatures until we made a comprehensive list. Special attention is given to the seas, sea creatures, ships, and even Leviathan, the sea monster. In the rhetoric of ancient Israel, the sea is ominous and foreboding, a relentless threat of chaos and embodiment of evil. This psalm, however, makes the daring, massive claim that even Leviathan is a pet of Yahweh, Yahweh's "rubber duck." God utterly rules the sea; the threat of chaos is completely eliminated. All of creation is unqualifiedly and gladly Yahweh's.

All creatures are gladly dependent on Yahweh's life-giving power (vs. 27–30). These verses, closely paralleling Ps. 145:15–16, provide a wonderful "table grace." Such an incidental prayer is not causal or trivial. It is a confession of dependence on God lodged in the most elemental act of eating. All creatures depend on God's generosity and live by a ration of God's daily bread. No creature has private resources for life, and none, not even humans, can store up power for life. Such power must be regularly and faithfully given by God's generosity, and regularly received in creaturely gratitude.

Abruptly the images shift from *food* to life-giving *presence* (vs. 29–30). Having made the point concretely with food, now the poem speaks more elementally about God's power for life. These verses are arranged as negative (v. 29) and positive (v. 30). The key elements are arranged chiastically: "face . . . spirit . . . spirit . . . face." In each verse, the first member of the set refers to God's life-giving presence and the second member refers to the creature's capacity to live:

v. 29 negatively: your face . . . their spirit (breath)
v. 30 positively: your spirit . . . face of the ground

The terms "face" and "spirit" (or "breath") are roughly synonymous, both referring to God's life-giving presence. The negative affirmation is that the absence of God's face carries a loss of human spirit and therefore death. The positive affirmation is that God's spirit causes newness on the face of the earth. The language is exceedingly personal and primitive. God's presence lets life live. God's absence causes life to terminate. The theological claim expressed in this language is enormous. The world is not autonomous. Creation is not a self-starter. It depends always, daily, and immediately on God's attentive self-giving.

Because the poem uses the term "spirit" twice, God's breath/world's breath, we can see that Pentecost is here writ cosmically. The world depends on God's breath and God's food for viable functioning. The text stands as a massive protest against all modernity, all mistaken autonomy, all the seductions of technical thinking that imagine we can have life on our own terms. Even as the church cannot have its life in its own terms, without reference to God's life-giving Spirit, no more can the world ever be self-sufficient. The "greenhouse effect," the disruption of the rain forests, and death by agricultural chemicals all are evidence that the world cannot be made self-sufficient according to human desire, ideology, or technology. Against our powerful technological self-confidence, the primal claim of this text invites us to theological realism about our world, about the ways in which the creation finally lives from the Creator.

The psalm culminates in an exultant doxology (vs. 31–34). What else can we do in light of the preceding affirmations except to praise! The doxology is a prayer that Yahweh will continue to delight in God's works, for without God's delight the earth dies. The earth is as immediately dependent on God as a young child is on its mother. Yahweh only looks and the earth trembles (v. 32); Yahweh only touches and the mountains smoke (v. 32). Yahweh holds all the initiatives. The only adequate human response to this wonder of creation is to sing, to sing praise, to meditate, to rejoice (vs. 33–34, 35b).

1 Corinthians 12:3b–13

When Christians recall the gift of the Holy Spirit to the early church, Luke's account of the events of Pentecost inevitably comes to center stage. The dramatic story should not, however, create the impression that the gift of the Spirit to the church was a one-time-only event. Because the outpouring of the Holy Spirit at Pentecost is associated with the beginning of the church's life in Jerusalem, it may be tempting to conclude that the Spirit functions somewhat as God's initial "capital investment" in the church: whatever happens after the initial investment depends on the labor of the church itself. The Pauline reading for this Sunday can help to correct any notion that the gift of the Spirit is such an unrepeatable act.

This lection is part of an extended discussion of problems related to worship, and that fact needs to be taken into account. Beginning in 1 Cor. 11:2, with the discussion of the appropriate appearance for women who participate in worship, and running through the end of chap. 14, Paul addresses a variety of issues concerning *corporate* worship. What Paul says about the Spirit within this context, therefore, pertains to the corporate life of the community of believers, as the "body" metaphor of this passage illustrates. Indeed, Paul seldom refers to the Holy Spirit as a way of talking about God's action in relation to the private faith of individual believers.

In the context of the Corinthian church, Paul's reference to "spiritual gifts" is already a mild act of pastoral confrontation. At least some of the Corinthians appear to have excelled in wisdom and have been speaking in tongues, activities they understood to reflect *their own* spiritual superiority and authority. By casting this discussion in terms of the Spirit's role, Paul makes a powerful theological claim that whatever their accomplishments, the Corinthians have only the Spirit (not themselves) to thank. These "spiritual gifts" range from the exotic and dramatic (speaking in tongues, working miracles) to the less dramatic (interpretation). They begin with the gift of faith itself, the confession that Jesus is Lord (1 Cor. 12:3). Throughout Paul's comments runs again and again the reminder that these gifts, whatever they are, come from the Spirit alone. Because they are gifts, not achievements, they reflect on the Giver rather than on the recipient.

Apart from this underlying insistence that all spiritual gifts are indeed gifts, two inseparable issues dominate the passage: the variety of spiritual gifts and their place in the upbuilding of the one Christian community. While it may seem obvious that there is a diversity of gifts, that diversity regularly causes great trouble in the church's life. At Corinth, the diversity threatened to become a hierarchy, in which the more dramatic gifts reigned over those that seemed to be more ordinary. Paul attacks this problem by means of several general observations about diversity. First, as noted earlier, he insists that each of the spiritual gifts comes from the same God (vs. 4–6). He then elaborates on the diversity by itemizing some of the gifts, especially those relevant for the worship setting (vs. 8–10). Within this listing, however, he repeats the phrase "to one is given" or "to another," thereby drawing attention to the fact that no individual receives every spiritual gift. Verse 11 makes the point explicit: "All these are activated by one and the same Spirit, who allots to *each one individually* just as the Spirit chooses" (emphasis added). The one Spirit of God grants all these diverse and multiple gifts, but the Spirit grants them to individuals according to the Spirit's own plan.

Alongside this emphasis on the diverse distribution of gifts and, indeed, completely inextricable from it, stands Paul's insistence that the diversity exists solely for the upbuilding of the one Christian community. This concern enters the passage in v. 7, with the comment that "to each is given the manifestation of the Spirit for the common good." The "common good" is a central issue in 1 Corinthians, where the pluralism of viewpoints seems strikingly akin to modern individualism and even relativism. Paul insists, over against the notion that individuals or small groups are free to employ their gifts as they please, that the spiritual gifts exist to serve the good of the whole community. In 1 Cor. 14 Paul explores the exact implications of this principle, insisting that speaking in tongues and prophesying without interpretation does not aid the community.

Following the itemization of various gifts, the issue of the common good emerges again in 1 Cor. 12:12–13 in the form of the image of the one body. Because believers, however different their gifts and even their social origins, are part of the one body, their gifts must be exercised within and for that one body. To think otherwise is to imagine that the hand can act independently of the arm!

The tension in this passage between the diversity and the unity of believers is well worn, but ever in need of proclamation. Whether discussing gifts related to worship or gifts related to education, service, or fellowship, the concern for diversity and the concern for unity must be held together. To call for unity without acknowledging the fact, even the grace, of diversity is to confuse unity with uniformity. To celebrate diversity without seeking unity is to misunderstand what goal diversity serves.

John 7:37–39

The lectionary provides alternative Gospel readings for Pentecost Sunday–John 7:37–39 or John 20:19–23. Since the latter passage is also listed (and commented on) for the Second Sunday of Easter, attention here is given to the former passage.

(The Greek text contains in 7:37–38 a problem of ambiguous punctuation, which influences the translation and in some cases the interpretation of the passage. To illustrate, the translators of the NRSV made a rather substantial change in the rendering from the RSV. The NRSV is being followed here, though interpreters would do well to consult the major commentaries on the Gospel of John for the particulars of the problem.)

The setting for Jesus' words is the Festival of the Booths (or Tabernacles), which is a harvest celebration rooted in the memory of Israel's wilderness wanderings. It re-creates the nomadic experience of the desert and the transient character of life on the move. Part of the ritual of the festival is the daily libation of water brought to the Temple from the Pool of Siloam. Against such a backdrop, Jesus speaks of the gift of abundant water, living water that flows from the center of the believer's being. The narrator clarifies that Jesus has reference to the coming of the Spirit, not yet given at this moment in Jesus' ministry.

Three paradoxical observations help us to grasp the character of Jesus' words about the Spirit. First, the gift of living water is set in contrast to the water of the Jewish festival and comes as a radically new and different experience. What Jesus promises is not more of the same—more religion, more piety, more ritual—but something unique, a transforming gift of the Spirit which produces life. The language connotes the notion of excessiveness and abundance. No more frantic searching in the desert in hopes of finding an oasis or a wadi not yet dried up, but instead rivers of living water.

And yet, despite its astonishing newness, the gift of the Spirit is the fulfillment of a promise made long ago. Exactly which text from the scriptures the narrator has in mind in John 7:38 is impossible to tell, but there are many in which the promise is made that God will do a new thing like this.

> I will pour water on the thirsty land,
>   and streams on the dry ground;
> I will pour my spirit upon your descendants,
>   and my blessing on your offspring. (Isa. 44:3)

(Cf. 43:19–20; 58:11; Zech. 14:8; Ps. 78:15–16.) The gift of the Spirit, so renewing and transformative, confirms that God is faithful to commitments made and carries out purposes long ago inaugurated.

The second observation has to do with the relationship between Jesus and the Spirit. On the one hand, there is a close connection, evidenced by the fact that the thirsty come to Jesus, but the water they are given is the Spirit. It is typical of the Fourth Gospel to insist that the Spirit comes from Jesus and does not operate independently of Jesus. The connectedness of the two is a healthy reminder that there is no religion of the Holy Spirit apart from the historical Jesus, no cozy togetherness that can ignore the hard teachings of Jesus or the reality of his death.

On the other hand, the passage clearly affirms a distinction between Jesus and the Spirit. The Spirit does not come to the believing community until Jesus is glorified. When the Spirit does come, a divine vitality and presence is let loose in the church, producing the renewal and empowerment of the people of God. Believers actually become bearers of the Spirit. Out of their hearts flow rivers of living water.

Third, we observe that Jesus' words at the Festival of the Booths (following the lectionary passage) evoke from the people both confession and rejection (John 7:40–44). It is not patently obvious to all that the promise of the Spirit means good news or that Jesus is to be received as the Messiah. Repeatedly the Fourth Gospel presents a realistic picture of the reception of the gospel. Time and again groups of hearers are divided.

It is striking that the issue that separates the crowd is by no means trivial. The rejecters don't just say, "This is not for me," and walk quietly away. They want to arrest Jesus. Even in their denial they perceive the threatening potential in his message and determine that he must be done away with. What is at stake—the presence of Jesus and the promise of the Spirit—is of momentous significance. It evokes hostility and commitment, rejection and faith. Pentecost is a matter of life or death.

Trinity Sunday

The character of God is endlessly urgent in the church, and enduringly the subject of reflection and articulation. Trinity Sunday is an appropriate time for the church to reflect on the dynamic tension between what we know of God and our mumbling attempts to formulate and articulate what we know. One danger is to imagine that we do not know about God at all, as though nothing has been disclosed. The other danger is to imagine that we have the inscrutable character of God fully captured and domesticated in our familiar formulations.

The text from Genesis demonstrates that the God of Israel, the creator of heaven and earth, is unlike other gods and must be served and worshiped exclusively. The Psalm lection asserts the same power of God, but is more explicit about the implications for human life of God's governance. The Gospel reading reflects on the gift of God's presence in the church, a presence marked by moral expectation and demand, as well as assurance. The Epistle reading voices the strange convergence of God's authority and God's remarkable grace known through the presence of Christ.

These texts may suggest that (a) the God to be trusted is not the one the world conventionally articulates; (b) the gracious God is the one to be obeyed; (c) the Trinitarian formula is a treasured breakthrough in the church's thinking; but, in the end, (d) it is not our theological formulation but our embrace of God's gracious majesty that counts in our life. All these texts assert that the community of faith must endlessly struggle to know more fully the God both disclosed and profoundly inaccessible.

Genesis 1:1–2:4a

The Priestly creation poem in its final form is more than 2,500 years old, yet it continues to evoke not only wonder but deeply emotional debate. Although scholars are now able to reconstruct much of the literary and theological context of this skillfully crafted mini-epic, thereby permitting us to understand more adequately certain of its referents and allusions, many in our time insist that it be read, not as theological reflection on God's creative activity, but as reportage. "Creationism" (variously defined) is thus alive and well, as many public school science teachers will attest. Therefore, the need is as great as ever to move beyond a reading of this majestic song to the creator God as narrative, and to understand it as an exclamation of praise.

The polished symmetry of this hymn is one clue to its character, for each "stanza" is carefully balanced by a companion, until the climactic seventh "stanza" is reached, which, because it stands alone, lays emphasis on the human response to God's creative activity.

Brief Introduction: 1:1–2

First Stanza: 1:3–5 God creates day and night	*Fourth Stanza:* 1:14–19 God creates celestial bodies, which "rule" day and night
Second Stanza: 1:6–8 God creates the dome of the sky, which separates the waters	*Fifth Stanza:* 1:20–23 God creates beings that inhabit the waters and the sky
Third Stanza: 1:9–13 God creates the seas and the dry land, permitting the dry land to produce vegetation	*Sixth Stanza:* 1:24–31 God creates creatures who live off the vegetation, supreme among which are humans, who "have dominion"

Seventh Stanza: 2:1–3
God rests and "hallows" the seventh day

A Final Concluding Formula: 2:4a

The possibilities of a choral recital will present (and have presented) themselves to those who are musically or theatrically oriented.

But a more profound clue to the nature of this literature as celebration lies in its exultant, almost defiant tone. The preacher who consults a good critical commentary on Genesis will be rewarded by being invited to view the parallels between Gen. 1:1–2:4a and important examples of ancient Near Eastern mythology. When read in this context, the Priestly creation hymn appears to call into question the views concerning the origin of the world that prevailed among Israel's neighbors, especially the Babylonians, in whose captive service the Jews found themselves at the time this hymn was composed. "It was not Marduk (or some other god) who created the heavens and the earth," our text insists, "but Yahweh, the God of Israel!" If the authors of this hymn borrow the language of ancient Near Eastern mythology to make their affirmation, it is only to challenge the pretensions of that mythology.

The heart of Gen. 1:1–2:4a lies in its opening phrases, vs. 1–2. The NRSV, in rendering v. 1 as a dependent clause, has provided the reader with a less familiar, but perfectly legitimate translation. Instead of functioning as a declaration ("In the beginning God . . ."), v. 1 here provides an introduction to v. 2, so that the whole of vs.1–2a describes the state of chaos at the time God initiated the creative acts.

The translation of v. 2b is perhaps less felicitous. The Hebrew *rûaḥ* has a range of meanings, which include "breath," "spirit," and "wind." But the accompanying verb, *rāḥap* (used only here and in Deut. 32:11), appears to mean something like "to hover watchfully." Thus, a hovering spirit from God (or Spirit of God) seems nearer the mark in Gen. 1:2 then a sweeping wind. Therefore, in addition to challenging prevailing mythological views regarding the nature of the world, the text seems to assert that the God of Israel bears a relation to the natural order similar to that of a vigilant mother bird. In Deut. 32:10–12, the subject is God's watchful care for Jacob; here, employing the same verb in a crucial location, the subject is God's watchful care for creation.

Gerard Manley Hopkins caught something of the power of v. 2 in his poem "God's Grandeur."*

> The world is charged with the grandeur of God.
> It will flame out, like shining from shook foil;
> It gathers to a greatness, like the ooze of oil
> Crushed. Why do men then now not reck his rod?
> Generations have trod, have trod, have trod;
> And all is seared with trade; bleared, smeared with toil;
> And wears man's smudge and shares man's smell: the soil
> Is bare now, nor can foot feel, being shod.

*From *Poems and Prose of Gerard Manley Hopkins*, ed. W. H. Gardner; London: Penguin Books, 1953, p. 27.

And for all this, nature is never spent;
There lives the dearest freshness deep down things;
And though the last lights off the black West went
Oh, morning, at the brown brink eastward, springs—
Because the Holy Ghost over the bent
World broods with warm breast and with ah! bright wings.

Psalm 8

This familiar and lyrical psalm holds together the wondrous sovereignty of God and the glorious dignity of humankind. It asserts that God's sovereignty and human dignity are intimately linked to each other.

The psalm is bracketed by a sweeping doxology in praise of Yahweh (vs. 1a, 9). At the beginning and end of the psalm, it is confessed that Yahweh is LORD of all the earth and is everywhere in the earth honored, worshiped, and obeyed. Everything else that happens in this psalm is derived from and contingent on this massive affirmation of Yahweh.

The next element in the psalm is unclear and problematic (vs. 1b–2). The statement of God's glory in v. 1b seems incongruously followed by v. 2. That verse suggests that all is not as serene and settled under God's rule as the initial doxology has suggested. In God's world there are "foes," "enemy," and "avenger," that is to say, a host of recalcitrant citizens of the earth who resist the rule of God.

How shall the sovereign rule of Yahweh deal with these resisters? Not in a great show of power, but in a way we least expect. The response of Yahweh to such opposition is to have "babes," or suckling children, sing their innocent, simple songs of praise, and out of the materials and expressions of these songs comes a powerful "bulwork," which will withstand the resistance. Thus the unequal content between "babes and infants" and "foes . . . enemy . . . avenger" is effective for Yahweh, because the "babes and infants" are allied with God's majestic sovereignty. God's mode or means of sovereignty thus appears to be modest, weak, and unlikely to succeed; it does succeed, however, for this God of strength and majesty acts in ways the world takes to be weak, and yet prevails.

This contrast between God's power and human weakness is continued in vs. 3–4, only now in a clearer, more focused way. The poet reflects on God's wondrous creation—heaven, moon, stars, all works of God's artistry—and then ponders God's sovereign power.

Contrasted with such impressive power, the human being is seen as a feeble agent in the midst of creation. The poet is astonished that this great Creator should invest so much and risk so much on the human person. Nonetheless, the poet does not doubt that God remembers (is "mindful of") the human person and cares for that special creature.

Indeed, God not only remembers and cares for humankind, but gives to the human person status, honor, dignity, and authority (vs. 5–8). Now the poem turns from God's majestic power to reflect on this most enigmatic of all creatures, the human person.

The human person is unimpressive when compared with the sun, moon, and stars. And yet the human person is elevated by God above all creatures, and stands next to and close to God and God's angels in dignity and authority. Astonishingly this one, of all creatures, is given dominion and authority to command all other creatures, all elements of the creation. The poet provides an inventory of those other creatures: sheep, oxen, beasts of the field, birds of the air, fish of the sea—all beloved creatures of God, all creatures under human governance! The last three phrases of this list conventionally are used to refer to "all living things." And then the poet returns to a sweeping doxology in praise of Yahweh (v. 9).

In this psalm we arrive at a central claim and oddity of biblical faith. At the beginning and end of the psalm, all "sovereignty" belongs only to God. In between these doxologies, all "dominion" belongs to human agents. The two affirmations of "sovereignty" and "dominion," however, are not in conflict or in competition. Human dominion derives from and is authorized by divine sovereignty. Divine sovereignty is the warrant for human dignity, which is authorized to care for the earth so that the whole of the earth may become its true, productive self.

This psalm unmistakably comes together with Gen. 1, and is a lyrical reflection of the same affirmations made there. The psalm is peculiarly appropriate to Trinity Sunday, for as Heb. 2:6–8 makes clear, the "human being" who is understood in the psalm is none other than Jesus, whose dominion is linked to God's sovereignty. Thus in a quite inchoate way, this connection anticipates the Trinitarian formula of the relation of "Father-Son." It is Jesus who is "a little while lower" (Heb. 2:7), and who is "subjecting all things" to him. The psalm is transposed in Hebrews into an affirmation of the governance of Jesus.

But the governance of Jesus is not a thing held only for himself, but is a dignity and honor for all those who serve him and all those who live gladly under his rule. The confession used for Jesus is also a manifesto for the peculiar preciousness of the human creature who is "servant of God" and "Lord of all."

2 Corinthians 13:11–13

An initial reading of the closing section of 2 Corinthians, especially 13:5–13, may cause us to wonder what has become of Paul's emphasis on God's grace. The exhortation with which this section begins, "Examine yourselves to see whether you are living in the faith," can be read in a moralistic fashion, meaning that believers must prove their faith through their actions. The lection proper, vs. 11–13, reinforces this impression, for here it appears that God's presence with the community depends on their way of living out the gospel. Only a closer examination of the larger context and the text itself will show that the text cuts in a different direction.

Second Corinthians 10–13, which may well be a fragment from a letter distinct from the letter (or letters) represented in chaps. 1–9, addresses the nature of apostolic authority. Far from compiling an abstract thesis about such matters, Paul writes here a heated response to what is apparently severe criticism. Some "super-apostles" (see 2 Cor. 11:5; 12:11) have questioned Paul's authority, charging that he does not display the signs of an apostle. Paul's biting response consists of his own apostolic boasting, not a boasting in his great miracles and visions, but in his suffering (11:21–29), in visions that are *not* to be described (12:1–6), and in his bodily affliction, which God declines to heal (12:7–10). Underlying this bitter irony is the theological claim that faith in Jesus Christ measures weakness and strength by criteria other than those used by the "super-apostles." Throughout 2 Cor. 10–13, Paul refers time and again to varying assessments of what makes for weakness and strength (10:1; 11:21; 11:29–30; 12:9), culminating in 13:3–4, where he speaks of Christ's crucifixion in weakness and resurrected life in power. When we turn to 2 Cor. 13:5–13 (NRSV), the admonition to "examine *yourselves*" (emphasis added) takes on a different meaning. Because so much of what precedes has to do with the way in which Paul and his co-workers are being evaluated, what 13:5 does is to turn the tables: "Examine yourselves [rather than examining us]." This interpretation finds confirmation not just from the context, but also in the fact that, in the Greek, the pronoun translated "yourselves" stands first in the sentence: "*Yourselves* examine!"

The chapter continues to focus on the relationship between the Corinthians and the apostles. Verse 6 expresses the hope that the Corinthians will not determine that the apostles are "unexamined," and v. 7 the hope that the Corinthians will pass the test, *even* if that means that the apostles themselves will have failed. Paul can even affirm that he is pleased when the Corinthians are strong and the apostles weak.

What is at stake here is not, of course, simply a social relationship. Paul desperately wants an improved relationship with the Corinthians, and he wants them again to acknowledge his authority, but that authority is not an end in itself. Instead, the relationship among believers has a christological warrant (see v. 5b); it is based directly on God's action in Jesus Christ. Believers do not belong to themselves, that they may do as they wish; believers belong to Christ, and the relationships among believers must reflect the One to whom they belong.

Belonging to Christ exerts an absolute claim over the life of the believer. The act of God in Jesus Christ (what we often call the "indicative") and the called response of human beings (the "imperative") are integrally related for Paul. God's gracious and unconditional gift is simultaneously a calling to "what is right" (13:7). Doing "what is right" also evidences itself in a life of peace and love within the community, as is clear in the closing lines of the letter, the lection proper (vs. 11–13). Prominent in these admonitions is the plea that the Corinthians attend to Paul's words ("listen to my appeal") and that they restore harmony within the community ("agree with one another, live in peace").

Because of its threefold nature the benediction in v. 13 is associated with Trinity Sunday, but the order (Christ, God, Spirit) distinguishes this benediction from that of later Trinitarian formulas. Neither does this benediction focus on the relationships among the three members of the Trinity. The questions about the nature of the Trinity, over which the church later struggled (and still struggles), were not a pressing concern for Paul, and attempts to find a doctrine of the Trinity in Paul's letters are exceedingly hazardous.

As important as it is to offer instruction about the Trinity, then, this passage may be of little direct use in that instruction. Here, the focus is not on the Trinity but on its gifts to human beings, the gifts of grace and love and fellowship. These very gifts are the ones that ensure that believers are not required to prove their faith, for their faith itself comes as God's grace.

Matthew 28:16–20

This familiar conclusion to the Gospel of Matthew is loaded with significance for the church. In it many elements that have appeared and reappeared throughout the narrative are brought to a head, and the reader's attention is drawn to the import of the story of Jesus and what is to be done in response.

It is easy to identify with the eleven disciples. At the sight of the risen Jesus, they worshiped, just as they had done when he walked on the water (Matt. 14:33) and as the women had done when Jesus met them (28:9). But their worship was mingled with doubt. The sight of him did not remove all the uncertainties and questions. The Eleven wavered between adoration and indecision, between prayer and puzzlement. What is striking, however, is that the disciples are not excluded because of their questions. In fact, it is precisely to these followers, who are worshiping *and* doubting, that the Great Commission is given.

Jesus is the protagonist in this final scene, and it is to his words to the disciples that we must attend. First, *Jesus announces the premise on which the Great Commission rests.* Behind the imperative stands the divine authority. Jesus has the right to command the Eleven to "make disciples" because "all authority in heaven and on earth" has been given to him. It is not a surprising word for the reader, who has heard repeatedly through the narrative of Jesus' authority (7:29; 9:6, 8; 11:27; 21:23–27) and is reminded of it once again.

Though not surprising, this statement of authority is nevertheless a welcomed word when coupled with the commission. The word "authority" carries not only the notion of warrant, but also the notion of power. To be sure, the disciples are given the credentials for their mission, but more, they are promised the potency to carry it out. They are invited to take part in an activity by a Commissioner whose power they have seen in action, a power exceeding their wildest dreams. The mission to which they are called, then, is not jeopardized by their weaknesses nor limited by their uncertainties.

Second, *Jesus confronts the disciples with an awesome commission.* They are to "make disciples of all nations." (The "go" is actually in Greek a participle and therefore subordinate to the imperative "make disciples.") Though earlier in the ministry of Jesus the charge was to avoid the Gentiles and Samaritans and to go only "to the lost sheep of the house of Israel" (10:6), now, in light of the death and resurrection, the scope of the mission is universalized. Without rejecting Israel's pride of place, the *gôyim* are included among those to be made disciples.

Two significant activities are mentioned as ingredients of the commission. (a) "Baptizing" highlights the priestly function, which introduces people to life in God's reign. The triadic formula no doubt accounts for the selection of this passage as the Gospel lesson for

Trinity Sunday. It goes without saying that the formula is not to be interpreted as if it came from the creeds of the fourth and fifth centuries, and yet its presence here should not be ignored. The "in the name of" (occurring five times in Matthew and nowhere else in the other Synoptic Gospels) signifies "with reference to" and implies a new belonging. Beyond repentance, those who are baptized confess that they now belong to the Father, Son, and Holy Spirit. A relationship is established that marks them as a peculiar people. But this confession implies, too, that the baptized are claimed by no one less than the tribune God. Disciples remember baptism as a certification of this mutual commitment. It sustains them in times of puzzlement and confusion.

(b) "Teaching them to obey everything that I have commanded you" adds a further dimension in the calling of the nations. The Eleven are commissioned not only to instruct the baptized about what Jesus has said about the kingdom of God, to transmit his interpretations of the law, but also to teach them to *obey* Jesus. The didactic task is only completed when the nations in fact perform the teaching of Jesus.

This stress on teaching and obeying Jesus' words protects the Christian message from being reduced either to cheap grace or to a private faith. The intent is to nurture a community that does not take God's goodness lightly, but lives out in the world the discipleship to which it is called.

Third, *Jesus promises the divine presence to the church as it responds to the commission.* At the beginning of Matthew's narrative readers are told that Jesus' name is Emmanuel, God is with us (1:23). Along the way, they overhear the promise to the disciples that when they gather for worship, Jesus will be present (18:20). And now, at the end of the story, they read of this commitment of Jesus to accompany his disciples.

This means, on the one hand, that the church must always beware of claiming too much for itself. It always baptizes, teaches, serves, speaks, makes disciples of the nations in the awareness of the presence of the risen Jesus. Its authority remains a derived authority, dependent on the One who possesses all authority. On the other hand, the church after Easter is not abandoned. Though sent "like sheep into the midst of wolves" (10:16), it can count on the attendance of the crucified and living Christ, even in its darkest hours.

Proper 4

Ordinary Time 9

Sunday between May 29 and June 4 inclusive (if after Trinity Sunday)

A brief glance at the lections for this day reveals that a common theme is that of a trustworthy God and the faith that that God inspires. The text from Gen. 6–8 recalls the reality that, although sin may threaten the very existence of God's creation, the God who stands behind that creation will ultimately act to save. Psalm 46 sings of a God whose people have no need to fear, whatever the circumstances, for the basic reason that "the LORD of hosts is with us" (vs. 7, 11). The passage from Rom. 1 and 3 connects the "righteousness of God" with the "faith/faithfulness of Jesus Christ" (3: 22), while Matt. 7:21–29, in words that mark the conclusion to the Sermon on the Mount, distinguishes the mere appearance of faith from its reality. Such themes are appropriate since the time from Trinity Sunday until Advent (the former Trinity season) celebrates the church's joyful task of daily witnessing—by word and deed—to the reality and truth of the gospel, a mission motivated and impelled by the church's faith.

Yet surprises abound that remind the reader and preacher of these texts that, while faith may sometimes be "simple," it is rarely easy or uncomplicated. The Genesis lection, which emerges from the "world history" of Gen. 1—11, points, among other things, to the larger human implications of God's soon-to-be-revealed promise to Abraham and Sarah (Gen. 12:1–9; see Proper 5), and thus thwarts any temptation to interpret God's deeds of salvation in narrow or provincial terms. The Psalm for this day, although couched in triumphalist tones, nevertheless reminds the reader that certain initiatives on the part of men and women of faith are necessary in order to apprehend God. The passage from Romans echoes the themes of the Genesis lection by focusing on the activity of God in the salvation of all humankind. And Matt. 7:21–29 forces the reader to confront the issue of the true nature of faith.

Thus, if there is one image that emerges from the convergence of these texts, it is that faith is less a state of being than an ongoing conversation in which, in response to God's continued faithful love, men and women live out the dimensions of their trust in God, the One who has spoken and acted in their lives as has no other.

Genesis 6:9–22; 7:24; 8:14–19

The Old Testament lection for this day, although it may at first appear to be somewhat disjointed, provides a fine synopsis of the rather lengthy story of the Flood. It enables a worshiping congregation to read a comprehensive précis of Gen. 6—9 without becoming bogged down in an impossibly protracted reading of the entire story. (The lection may be further pared by the omission of 6:9–10, 15.) Genesis 6:9–22 represents the beginning of the story and 8:14–19 its conclusion, with 7:24 serving as the modulation, or bridge, between the two major parts.

We must accept at face value the text's affirmation that "the earth was corrupt" (6:11), although we are given few specifics. To be sure, the abduction by the "sons of God" of human women (6:1–4) has just been adduced as evidence of moral decay within God's good creation, yet it strains the reader's sense of justice for God to condemn all creation for the violations perpetrated only by these divine beings (6:5–8). The text instead is calling on the reader's own knowledge of human nature when it asserts the corruption of God's good handiwork. The reader does not have to be convinced that sin has invested creation—he or she knows that fact firsthand, so that the function of the story about the "sons of God" serves to remind the reader of something of which he or she is already deeply aware. It is much like the single chair onstage in Thornton Wilder's play *Our Town,* which represents an entire village; it is one prop that stands in for many, many more.

And notice that it is not just men and women who are corrupt, but "all flesh," so that God intends to destroy all creation (vs. 13). Unlike the Yahwist's account (7:1), the Priestly story provides no immediate announcement to Noah that he and his family are to be saved, and even less any rationale as to why they are to be spared. Instead, a simple command is given that Noah is to construct an ark according to certain specifications. It is only after the directions for the ark are completed that what has been implicit in those directions is made plain (6:18).

The use of the word "covenant" here suggests a fresh start in the relationship between God and creation. It is more than a simple matter of wiping the slate clean and starting over again; that which will postdate the flood is to be a new order of creation, in that creation will have a newly ordered relationship with God. Sin has not been eradicated—no reader ancient or modern should be confused about that—but God's relationship with sin-corrupted creation will never again admit of its complete destruction in vengeance. The use of "covenant" in 6:18 anticipates 9:11 (not included in the lection for this day) and the rainbow that seals this new order of the universe.

Noah's acceptance of God's initiative is summed up in 6:22. In other words, by his obedience Noah renders God's covenant operative.

Moving through the transition passage, 7:24, the reader arrives at the climax of the narrative (8:14–19). The fact that "earth was dry" contrasts strongly with the "flood of waters" which are both promised (6:17) and delivered (7:24). "Go out" (8:16) bears echoes of "come into" (6:18), in that this command represents the completion of the ordeal begun earlier. Both its beginning and its ending come about as the result of the word of God. In the same way that "all flesh" (6:12) had become corrupt and thus had been destroyed, except for the saved remnant, so now that remnant emerges from the boat of life—not just Noah and his family, but "all flesh" (8:17). Their purpose is the same as that originally vested in their ancestors at creation: "be fruitful and multiply on the earth" (8:17; compare Gen. 1:28). And as Noah and his family had obeyed God's earlier command to build and enter the ark (6:22), they now obey God and leave it (8:19), thus extending their act of accepting God's covenant.

And so the covenant is now in place, although the narrative of its final declaration must wait for another day (9:1–17; note First Sunday in Lent, Year B). Yet the stage for that final declaration is set. The rainbow *will* arc the sky!

Psalm 46

This much-used psalm is a statement of confidence and trust, which especially counts on God's protective presence in the city of Jerusalem. Thus it is probable that it was used in the liturgy of the Temple. One of its spin-off effects is that it served to legitimate the Jerusalem political-liturgical establishment, with the Davidic dynasty understood both as the protector and the beneficiary of this place of God's sure presence.

Psalm 46 begins with an affirmation of God's protective presence, though without explicit reference to the Temple (vs. 1–3). We may take v. 1 as the thesis sentence of the entire poem. God is a reliable presence and help in every trouble. Such an assertion may in part be based on the experience of the city, such as the astonishing deliverance of Jerusalem from the Assyrians in 701 B.C.E. (Isa. 37:33–38). And no doubt the assertion is in part based on the theological-ideological claim of God's abiding presence in the Temple, which is much older than the reports of deliverance. (On the theological-ideological claim, see especially 1 Kings 8:12–13.) Everything in the psalm follows from this initial affirmation.

The consequence is that worshipers in the Temple are free of anxiety, unafraid even when life becomes disordered and unstable. In this the first example of the city under threat, the anticipated assault on the city is cosmic and geological, for the Temple is understood as not only a historical but a cosmic reality (vs. 2–3). The fourfold threat (the earth changing, the mountains shaking, the waters roaring, and the mountains trembling) portrays a destablizied earth. It is indeed an awesome account of the palpable threat of chaos when the creation is undone. These images may be understood literally or metaphorically and liturgically. In any case, those who trust in God's presence are unflappable. They find God's reliability more compelling than the threat that can undermine all else, all of creation, but cannot impinge on the faithfulness of God. The text is a profound assurance when life becomes unglued!

The first unit of the psalm has focused on the large picture of creation and chaos (vs. 2–3). The second focuses on a military-political threat, for the fortress city of Jerusalem was endlessly exposed to such assault (vs. 4–9). Verse 5 is an affirmation not unlike v. 1. God is in the midst of Jerusalem, that is, in the Temple, so the city is safe. The city has an adequate water supply, a stream that makes the city "glad," a stream that has special significance for God's presence and for the sacred dimension of royal power (cf. 1 Kings 1:33–45). Notice that while there is a reference to God's presence, the focus here shifts away to the reliability of the city itself, because of God's presence (vs. 4–5).

This time it is the raging nations that threaten. They are in fact, however, no more threat than the chaos of vs. 2–3, because God's sovereign word is more than adequate to command the nations, to ensure a decree that overwhelms armies and compels the earth to obey. The Lord of creation is also the Lord of history and the nations that occupy it.

Verse 7 is a responsive refrain that is reiterated in v. 11. It may indeed be a liturgical cliché, assenting to the promise of protective presence. Up until this point in the psalm, God has been referred to only generically (vs. 1, 4, 5), suggesting this may be a generic psalm borrowed from a non-Yahwistic religious tradition. In the refrain, "Yahweh" is specified. The God featured here is "the LORD of hosts," that is, the commander of the armies, with massive political authority and military capacity, which may be mobilized to overcome every assault that jeopardizes the city.

The military metaphor of v. 7 is extended in the next unit of the poem (vs. 8–11). Yahweh does extraordinary acts of power ("works"). These acts serve to savage any enemy of Jerusalem. Thus the Lord of the troops has a capacity of halting wars (v. 9). The way of stopping wars, however, is not peaceable or benign, or simply by decree. Rather, the graphic image is of requiring a surrender, confiscating all enemy weapons (bow, spear, shield) and burning them all, so that the threatening enemy is completely disarmed (cf. Isa. 9:5). Conflict ends because Yahweh prevails, and the enemy is rendered helpless and impotent.

At the conclusion, Yahweh now speaks in a solemn, sovereign, first-person voice, the first time in the psalm (v. 10). Yahweh now addresses the enemy nations and orders them to desist ("Be still!"). This phrase is not a pious, romantic, or spiritual utterance, as it is often construed. It is rather a harsh, imperative command, which tells the attacking enemies and the forces of chaos to stop their foolish, inappropriate, and ineffective assault on God's city and God's people. Yahweh here asserts that Yahweh's governance will be obeyed, acknowledged, and exalted by the very nations that must stop their misguided resistance to God's rule. (See the more directly political reference to the same matter in Ps. 2:4–11.) As long ago as the Pharaoh in the book of Exodus, the nations have refused to "know" Yahweh (see Ex. 5:1–2). Now, however, they will come to acknowledge Yahweh as ruler; Yahweh will prevail and defeat every threat.

This first-person oracle of God is answered by worshiping Israel, by the refrain repeated from v. 7. God's power and resolve evoke profound trust and confidence on the part of the Jerusalem worshiping community.

This psalm is a crucial one, given our cultural situation of dismay and anxiety. The disappearance of old structures and signals of cultural order causes us to experience the world as falling apart. A keen sense of God's powerful protective presence (of whatever constitutes our precious "Jerusalem") permits us to experience and embrace even that disorder with freedom and equanimity. Much may fall apart, but we are not finally in jeopardy (cf. Rom. 8:37–39). God is faithful, God is present, God is powerful. Nothing else matters in the face of that sure reality.

Romans 1:16–17; 3:22b–28 (29–31)

A text such as this one, well known from the history of Christian thought and well worn in the pulpit, poses a difficult challenge for the preacher. How is it possible to break through the heavy cushion of familiarity to hear once again a fresh word from this text? One strategy is to pay close attention to the role this particular text plays within the conversation of the letter itself, looking for the cutting edge of the text.

Romans 3:22b–31 brings to a climax the point Paul introduces in 1:16–17, that the gospel is God's power for salvation to all people, Jew first and also Greek; the gospel reveals God's righteousness. In the very next verse (1:18) Paul parallels that revelation with the revelation of God's wrath. That statement initiates a discussion of the universality of human sin (1:18–3:20). All human beings have rebelled against God *as God,* by denying their own creatureliness. The forms of this rebellion have varied, but the result is the same. This line of argument comes to a head in 3:22–23: "For there is no distinction, since all have sinned and fall short of the glory of God." But 3:21–28 also returns to the revelation of God's righteousness, announced in 1:16–17 and here dominating the conversation: "But now, apart from law, the righteousness of God has been disclosed." (Even if the 3:22a is not part of the lection proper, it cannot be omitted from consideration here.)

But what does Paul mean by the "the righteousness of God"? God's righteousness is not simply a quality comparable to God's goodness or God's immutability. Although God's righteousness is never severed from God, God's righteousness is a gift graciously bestowed on human beings. To glimpse Paul's meaning here we need to use active verbs, for God's righteousness is a way of talking about God's actions of reclaiming the world for God (to paraphrase Ernst Käsemann).

While God's righteousness is not a new thing, at the present time (vs. 21, 26) that righteousness has acted in a new way—"through faith/faithfulness of Jesus Christ." This somewhat more literal translation of *pistis Iēsou Christou* than that found in the NRSV demonstrates the ambiguity of v. 22. Most contemporary translations take v. 22 to mean that the righteousness of God is "through faith in Jesus Christ" (NRSV), but a growing number of exegetes argue that the translation should be "through the faith/faithfulness of Jesus Christ." That is, it is Jesus' faithful act of obedience that reveals God's righteousness, which encompasses all people.

This interpretation of the "faith of Jesus Christ" (*pistis Iēsou Chris-*

tou) helps to unravel v. 25, which may be translated: "whom God put forward as a redemption through faith/faithfulness in his blood." Here faith is once again the faithful obedience of Jesus Christ, which extends to the shedding of blood. What is striking about Paul's reference to Jesus in this text is that he links the revelation of God's righteousness directly to Jesus' death—not to his teachings, his exemplary life, or even his resurrection.

Of course, even if "faith of Jesus Christ" means the faithful obedience of Jesus rather than the believer's faith *in* Jesus, the text still refers to human faith. Verse 22 refers to those who believe and v. 26 to those who live out of Jesus' faithfulness. This does not mean, however, that human beings now achieve their salvation by means of their faith. Not only would that claim make faith a matter of boasting (vs. 27–28), a work, but such a reading makes the text into a statement centered on the consequences of God's righteousness for human beings.

This is a difficult point for most Protestants to grasp, since we customarily read Romans through the filter of Luther's question, "How can I find a loving God?" When read in that way, this passage yields the answer, "You must have faith, and you will find a loving God." But the focus of the text, as we see when we trace the argument from 1:16 on, is not on the human quest for a gracious and loving God. Instead, Paul's focus is on the radical act of God in reclaiming *all* humankind.

What Paul says about God here is precisely the cutting edge of this text, for Paul insists that God has, in Jesus Christ, shown grace and mercy to all human beings, each and every one of whom rebels against God. In the following chapter, Paul will refer to God as the one who justifies not the good or even the repentant, but the "ungodly." This, of course, sounds an unacceptable, even threatening, note to those of us who want to earn God's love. It sounds an even more unwelcome note when we want to be assured that God has forgiven us, but not those whom we identify as sinful. Paul's words place many of us in the role of the elder brother in the parable of the prodigal son; we may be glad to see our brother, but we want what we assume to be rightfully ours. Once again, we want to dictate terms to God, and this is precisely where Romans calls us up short.

Matthew 7:21–29

It is disturbing to read the Gospel of Matthew. Its anticipation of the coming judgment and its sharp words of warning to one group or another who live hypocritically or lawlessly create an uneasiness. They become particularly unsettling words when the group being judged is clearly a group of insiders, active followers, who might be expected to be commended for their piety or for their extraordinary accomplishments. Readers are repeatedly forced to ask questions about themselves.

Such is the case with the concluding words of the Sermon on the Mount. The text speaks of those who confess the highest Christology ("Lord, Lord"), who utter profound prophecies, who demonstrate control over demonic powers, who even work miracles, but who fail to do "the will of my Father in heaven." With the devastating words "I never knew you," such workers of lawlessness will be rejected.

Three observations about Matt. 7:21–23. First, the description of the group condemned has to be taken at face value. They *really do* affirm the basic creed of the church ("Jesus is Lord"); they *really do* preach powerful sermons; they *really do* extraordinary deeds of exorcisms and healing—and all in Jesus' name! By all rights, they are not only in the church—they are its leaders. They have accomplished amazing feats as a part of their involvement. They are clearly not the Jewish leadership against which harsh judgments are later brought (23:1–36), nor can they be dismissed too quickly as the bad guys, the outsiders. The words of the text leave the reader perplexed and a bit disturbed that such religiously active people can be so decisively renounced by Jesus, and their accomplishments labeled as lawless. It is clear that judgment begins with the people of God, not with the remote corners of the world where the gospel has never been heard. Hardly a balm for the reader's anxiety!

Second, the judge, who pronounces such a harsh verdict, is Jesus himself (7:23). The one who eats with tax collectors and sinners (9:10–11), who frets over Jerusalem as a mother hen cares for her brood (23:37), and who comes to save the people from their sins (1:21) utters the condemning words. Judgment and grace are not separated in Matthew's narrative, as if one comes from an angry God and the other from a loving Jesus. Rather, judgment and grace are both dimensions of God's movement toward the world. Jesus, the Savior-Judge, graciously claims people for a life of obedience and relentlessly will not let them presume on the divine generosity. The words of judgment in the text are aimed at those who take that generosity lightly, who want acceptance without change, forgiveness without repentance, grace without discipleship.

Third, the problem with those judged is their failure to do God's will. Their downfall derives not from a faulty theology or an inadequate church life, but from the avoidance of the divine demands. The shocking reality in the text is that these are religiously active people. They have prophesied, exorcised demons, and worked miracles. Only, the life of faith is not measured in terms of religious activity (which can be equated with lawlessness), but in terms of obedience and faithfulness.

But how is one to know God's will? The simple parable in 7:24–27 about the two builders takes the reader a step farther. The wise builder who constructs his house on a solid foundation is described as one who hears and does "these words of mine." The divine will is opened up by the teaching of Jesus, who in three chapters of the Sermon on the Mount has turned out to be the authoritative interpreter of the law (5:21–48).

But it is not simply a matter of hearing Jesus' words, of knowing God's will. What separates the wise from the foolish builder is the *doing* of "these words of mine." The words are not there to be toyed with or debated over or played off one against the other. They are to be obeyed. Or to put it another way, Jesus' words are not really "heard" until they begin to work within the hearer to transform life and direct behavior. Only in the changed action of the hearer is it clear that a proper "hearing" has taken place.

The Sermon is concluded with the report that "the crowds were astounded at his teaching, for he taught them as one having authority, and not as their scribes." The scribes could only assume a form of derived authority. "Rabbi X said such and such. And on the basis of this, I say this further word." But here was one who needed to cite no precedent, who confronted people with the very presence of God. Jesus' words conveyed an unmediated reality. They announced decisions beyond which there was no appeal.

Furthermore, Jesus' words have the power to accomplish something. He spoke and things happened. "Your sins are forgiven you." "Take up your bed and walk." "Stretch out your hand." The linguistic analysts label it "performative discourse." It is language that does not merely describe or command, but that creates and recreates—and with such an unheard-of ultimacy. In reality, to hear Jesus' words is to be grasped and reshaped by them, to be activated to obey them, to be set by them on a journey of discipleship. Thus, in these unsettling passages of Matthew's story are words of power and hope, speech that effects change, language that mediates the very presence of God.

PROPER 5

Ordinary Time 10

Sunday between
June 5 and 11 inclusive
(if after Trinity Sunday)

The four lessons for this Sunday from various perspectives confront us with the character of the human response to the gracious initiative of a promise-making and promise-keeping God. Each response (or reflection on a response) has its own peculiar dynamic, and yet the four are linked in the extraordinary way in which the promise and demand of God are met and confirmed in the midst of real human experience.

Genesis 12:1–9 describes the faithful obedience of Abraham, who responds to God's call to leave the ancestral homeland and to venture to a new country. It is a journey of considerable risk, yet a risk that makes possible a future rich with promise and hope. Paul reflects on the faith of Abraham in Rom. 4:13–25 and understands it as more than the solitary response of a single individual, more than the extraordinary achievement of an unusual saint. Abraham is a paradigmatic figure. His descendants become all those who share his faith, are linked with him to the divine promise, and are drawn into a special family composed of many nations. Abraham's faith is a model for Christian faith. At heart both share the conviction that God gives life to the dead and calls into existence things that do not exist.

Psalm 33:1–12 is an expression of great joy over the reality of a God who both creates and sustains. The "word" by which God acts is characterized by covenant fidelity as well as by great power. Thus God's people respond with an overwhelming gladness, which others, who do not know this God, can never appropriate. The text from Matt. 9 in blunt and direct language relates Matthew's obedient response to the call of Jesus. In marked contrast to the religious people who grumble at Jesus' association with tax collectors and sinners, Matthew follows, no questions asked. The move from the tax table to the table in Jesus' house is the move of faith in response to a gracious call, but in Matthew's case a move always bound to elicit conflicting reactions.

Genesis 12:1–9

After eleven chapters of "world history," we are plunged abruptly and unexpectedly into the life and faith of Israel. The entry of Abraham and Sarah into the biblical story has no antecedents. They are new characters in the story. This is a new beginning, wrought only by the free speech of Yahweh, which summons new partners into speech and faith.

1. *Israel's life and Abraham's sojourn of faith begin in God's speech.* In Yahweh's first utterance, Israel knows everything it is to know of God (vs. 1–3). On the one hand, God's speech is *a terse command* (v. 1). God's first utterance is an imperative, "Go." On the other hand, God's speech is an *extravagant promise* (vs. 2–3). The promise, with no visible guarantees, is to govern and determine the categories of Israel's life for all time to come.

The second part of the promise places Abraham intentionally among the nations whose sorry story we know in Gen. 1–11. "The nations" have been characterized in those chapters by trouble and curse. Now Abraham is made crucial for the status of other peoples, who will have to come to terms with Abraham. Nations will be dealt with according to the way they deal with Abraham. God pledges to guarantee that odd connection. Abraham is made the determinative factor for the future of world history.

The final line of the promise in v. 3 is even more stunning. Other nations will have a blessing "in you." The existence of Israel is the clue to the power for life that is available among other peoples. This remarkable promise is taken by both Jews and Christians as a warrant for the cruciality of the community of faith. For Jews, the promise surely anticipates the historical community of Israel and the rise of David. For Christians the promise foreshadows the presence of the church in the midst of the world. Both readings stress that the concreteness of a particular community is decisive for the future well-being of the world.

2. *Abraham responds* to the address of God: "So Abram went" (vs. 4–5). Abraham speaks not a word. He acts silently and immediately. He trusts the promise. He honors the command. At the word of God, Abraham uproots his life and is on his way in obedience. No wonder that Abraham is reckoned as the father of faith. His exemplary trust in God is that he took the promise at face value; he decisively

reordered his life in immediate response to the word of God. He did not linger, hesitate, or bargain. He simply went.

3. *The goal of Abraham's journey is another land,* a land promised by God but not specified (vs. 1, 7). In this first journey, the narrative places Abraham in Canaan, Shechem, Bethel, Al, and finally toward the Negeb. It is as though the story provides us an orienting map for the Genesis narratives that are to follow. We are given an overview of the territory in which the life and faith of Israel will be staged.

Three items are important about Abraham's journey into the land. First, the Bible is relentlessly concerned with land, with historical concreteness, with materiality. The story is a foundational protest against any escapist spiritualizing tendency. Biblical faith concerns real people in real places with real estate. Second, the land is for the future and is not claimed in the present. Thus far the land is only trusted promise, not controlled possession. Third, when Abraham arrives in the land he is to possess, it is already occupied: "Canaanites were in the land" (v. 6). The Land of Promise is not empty space; it is already claimed and occupied. This means that the promise immediately and endlessly places Abraham in crisis. Life in the real world is restlessly ambiguous; faith never permits the people of Abraham to escape the ambiguity. This ambiguity is decisive for biblical faith. Faith, as Abraham embraces it, is a decision to live the promise precisely where the promise is in question and at risk.

4. Our narrative is concluded as *Abraham undertakes two explicitly religious acts.* First, Abraham builds an altar to acknowledge Yahweh (v. 7). The erection of an altar is a dramatic, public declaration that Yahweh is the acknowledged ruler of the territory, and that the territory has come under the aegis of Yahweh's powerful promise. The altar is a political assertion that denies suzerainty to the Canaanite gods and delegitimates the land rights of the Canaanites. Building the altar is a highly partisan, political act.

Second, Abraham "invoke[s] the name of the LORD" (v. 8). The phrasing suggests that Abraham intentionally and explicitly acknowledged that Yahweh is his God, and thereby acknowledged that Abraham is subject to the purposes of Yahweh. More precisely, Abraham acknowledges the power of the promise in his life, and his readiness to trust the promise.

These two acts should not be understood as "generic" acts of piety. They embody, rather, a concrete decision about the central loyalty of Abraham's life, the central power of promise for his future, and the central subject of Israel's story that follows. It is on that basis that Abraham "journeyed on" (v. 9).

Psalm 33:1–12

This psalm is a hymn of praise, with a horizon as large as all creation. In our verses, the pattern of a hymn is twice enacted, vs. 1–7 and vs. 8–12.

The first standard rendition of praise is in two characteristic parts, the summons to praise (vs. 1–3) and the reasons for praise (vs. 4–7). The summons consists of six words evidencing great exuberance: rejoice, praise, praise, make melody, sing, play skillfully. The speaker intends to mobilize all of the choir and the sanctuary orchestra to join in celebration of Yahweh.

We may notice two special items in these verses. First, v. 1 identifies the "righteous" and "upright" as the ones who may properly praise. Those who have not kept Torah obedience are not invited to praise, and their praise is not fitting; it is incongruous with the character of Yahweh, who is "upright." Thus even in the initial summons to praise, Torah piety prevails. Second, the last term, "loud shouts," does not mean simply boisterousness, but a cry of victory, which celebrates God's sovereignty.

The reason given for praise is regularly introduced by "for" ("because" = *kî*) (v. 4). Two reasons are here given for praise of God. First, God's word, work, and love are marked by covenant fidelity (vs. 4–5). This vocabulary (upright, faithfulness, righteousness, justice, steadfast love) constitutes Israel's preferred and recurring phrasing for Yahweh, as seen in Ex. 34:6–7a. God's word is utterly pure, and God's work is completely reliable. It is because Yahweh's speech and action are marked by faithfulness that Yahweh should be praised.

The second reason for praise is that "the word" mentioned in v. 4 is effective and powerful (vs. 6–7). God's speech is the means whereby God has created the world. God has powerfully uttered the world into existence, like the commanding utterance of a royal ruler.

By this royal decree out of the mouth of Yahweh, there came to be the heavens and the "host of heaven," that is, the stars. The parallel to "word" as agent of creation is God's "breath," which translates the Hebrew *rûaḥ* or God's spirit, on which see Gen. 1:2. With this combination of agents, "word" and *rûaḥ*, the psalm parallels Gen. 1:1–3, which includes the same two agents. By speech God gathers the seas together, in order to create dry life for living things, and God has placed the dangerous, life-threatening "waters" in safe storage, so that they may be appropriately managed and distributed; see Job 38:11, 16, 22. In Job 38:22, the same term is used twice that is in our verse translated as "storehouses." All these actions by God create living space in the midst of chaos and make the world safe for life. No wonder Yahweh should be praised!

In the second rendition of a hymn, the same sequence of summons and reason is reiterated (vs. 8–11). The summons is stated in two jussive verbs, "fear . . . stand in awe" (v. 8). This summons is not as direct as in vs. 1–3 or as is customary in this form. The content and intent are nonetheless the same. The world is to be amazed, astonished, and obedient to this great God.

The reason (introduced by "for") is that the word of God as command, the same word characterized in v. 4, is indeed powerful and effective (vs. 9–11). In addition to the large claim of v. 9 for creation in general, the poet becomes quite specific in vs. 10–11. Negatively, Yahweh nullifies the intention of the nations and prohibits their plans (v. 10). As in Ps. 2:2–3, the plans and counsel of the nations are a conspiracy whereby the nations (and their gods) seek to take over the rule of the earth and preempt the sovereignty of Yahweh. Thus the conspiracy is both theological and political. Yahweh, however, will not permit such a conspiracy to succeed, and is powerful enough to resist such a bald and unrealistic challenge to the proper ordering of the world.

Positively, Yahweh's "counsel" is utterly reliable and beyond challenge. Yahweh's "plans" endure for all time. The NRSV "plans" in v. 10 and "thoughts" in v. 11 are the same Hebrew term *ḥšb* (cf. Gen. 50:20; Jer. 29:11; Isa. 55:8–9). Thus it is counsel versus counsel and plan versus plan. Yahweh's intention (plan, counsel) will prevail and can be relied on against every threat, challenge, and conspiracy. Moreover, we know from vs. 4–5 what Yahweh's plan and counsel are: that the world be shaped according to faithfulness, justice, righteousness, and enduring love. Israel in its praise counts on the well-being of God's world, the friendliness, fruitfulness, and faithfulness of creation as a given for life, over which Israel need have no anxiety. No alternative power will be able to jeopardize God's good intention. No alternative that intends ill can possibly prevail in a world where God is Lord.

Our reading culminates in v. 12 with a didactic conclusion that follows from the doxological affirmations of the preceding verses. The conclusion is that God's chosen people will be made "happy" ("blessed") by this steadfastness and reliability of creation. Certainly this verse speaks of the people Israel, the "righteous" and "upright" of v. 1. Israel is here taken to be a faithful Torah keeper, and so a trusted creation means to live by the rules that will make creation flourish and Israel joyous.

While the linkage between creation and Israel's covenant of trust and obedience is clearly the intention of this verse, we may in our reading extrapolate, to affirm that every living community has the potential of taking Yahweh as God along with Yahweh's Torah, and so of living faithful to the nature of creation, and so a happy, blessed life. Thus the doxology to the Creator has quite practical implications. Those who conspire against this life-giving order in recalcitrant ways, in the end will not be "happy."

Romans 4:13–25

The biblical story of Abraham figures prominently in a number of early Jewish and Christian texts. The diversity of this reflection about Abraham is evident even within the New Testament, since the author of the letter of James can use the story of Abraham to draw conclusions that appear to be diametrically opposed to Paul's own (James 2:21).

In Rom. 4, Paul makes three points about Abraham by way of underscoring his argument about the manner in which God deals with humankind. First, Paul insists that not even Abraham was justified by his deeds; he was justified because of his trust in God (4:1–9). Second, Abraham's justification came about before he had been circumcised, that he might be father both to the circumcised and to the uncircumcised (4:10–12).

The third point Paul makes about Abraham comes in our text, 4:13–25, and has to do with the promise that was made through Abraham to all his descendants. Verse 13 introduces the issue of the promise, insisting that it came about through the "righteousness of faith" and not through the law. Verses 14–15 put the matter more negatively by juxtaposing the law with faith. Paul comments on the negative impact of the law: "The law brings wrath; but where there is no law, neither is there violation" (v. 15). Eventually, in Rom. 7, Paul will address the law in a more sustained fashion, because he needs to explain the comments he has made along the way. In the context of chapter 4, however, these are tangential comments and should not be overemphasized to the detriment of the positive claim being made about God's dealings with Abraham.

Paul returns to those dealings in v. 16, which can be translated: "For this reason [the promise comes] from faith, in order that [it might be] according to grace, so that the promise might be confirmed to every seed, not to the [seed] that is from the law only but also to the [seed] that is from the faith of Abraham, who is the father of all of us." Dominating this statement about the promise to Abraham is the word "faith." Initially, Paul does not specify whose faith (or faithfulness) is in view, although v. 13 causes us to think the faith is that associated with Abraham. The end of the verse makes it clear that the promise is associated with Abraham's faith.

But the phrase "in order that [it might be] according to grace" prevents us from concluding that Abraham *earned* the promise by means of his faith, that God rewarded Abraham's faith. Instead, faith relies on grace. In other words, faith itself is a gift from God, never an achievement—not even for a person as exemplary as Abraham.

The question that cries out to be answered here is, What is Abraham's faith? Despite Paul's claim here and in v. 12, it is clear that neither he nor other early Christians operated with Abraham's faith, if by that phrase we mean the content of Abraham's faith. While early Christians varied in their beliefs, common—indeed central—to their faith was the notion that God had acted in Jesus Christ, and that central element is nowhere part of the Abraham story. Does this mean that Paul is simply confusing his own faith (that is, its content) with that of Abraham? Does he impute to Abraham belief in Jesus Christ as the Son of God, as would some later Christian thinkers? In what sense do first-century Christians have a share in Abraham's faith?

Verses 17–18 provide an answer to the question. Verse 17 affirms that the promise was made to Abraham "in the presence of the God in whom he believed, who gives life to the dead and calls into existence the things that do not exist." What Paul and his contemporaries have in common with Abraham is not a belief in Jesus as the Christ nor a belief that "faith" is the way to find God, but the conviction that God is powerful even over death and nonexistence.

In Abraham's case, this conviction took a specific form, as vs. 18–21 indicate. Abraham trusted that God was able to deliver on the promise made to him and to Sarah concerning their offspring. Despite the clear evidence to the contrary, his own advanced age and Sarah's previous barrenness, Abraham was "fully convinced" (v. 21) that God would do as God had said.

It is this faith that Paul offers as exemplary for Christians, as becomes evident at the end of the chapter. The story of Abraham was written not for Abraham's sake, "but for ours also. It will be reckoned to us who believe in him who raised Jesus our Lord from the dead" (v. 24). The common claim is that God is able to deliver on God's promise, whether that promise regards a childless couple or the resurrection of the dead.

It would be a mistake to read this text simply as a call to "more" or "better" human faith in God. The point Paul is after is primarily about God. Underlying Paul's discussion of Abraham's faith is the utter conviction that God has not changed. While the advent of Jesus Christ is an apocalypse, an in-breaking of God in the world, God nevertheless continues to deal with human beings in the same way God dealt with Abraham. God may be trusted to justify human beings out of God's own grace and not based on their achievements or shortcomings.

Matthew 9:9–13, 18–26

The wealth of possibilities in the Gospel lesson for this Sunday will likely force the preacher to make some choices. The reading consists of the story of the call of Matthew (9:9), the account of Jesus' table fellowship with tax collectors and sinners (vs. 10–13), and the sandwiched stories of the restoration of the synagogue leader's daughter (vs. 18–19, 23–26) and the woman with persistent hemorrhaging (vs. 20–22). Each of the four incidents invites serious reflection.

First, Jesus sees Matthew "sitting at the tax booth" and confronts him with the abrupt command, "Follow me." And Matthew follows. It is not unlike the call earlier in the narrative of the two sets of brothers, who leave their boats and nets to follow Jesus (4:18–22). There are no windows that let the readers see the psychological dynamics at work in those confronted by Jesus. We are given the bare story. The point is that discipleship has to do with divine calls and human responses, with drastic changes of direction and radical transformation of commitments. Disciples are those who risk a break with the familiar in order to follow Jesus.

In one important feature, however, Matthew's call differs from the call of the two sets of brothers. Matthew is a tax collector, and collecting taxes is not the same as fishing. Already we have learned from the Sermon on the Mount that tax collectors can be singled out as people who act always in their own self-interest (5:46). They are prototype sinners. Here such a person responds to Jesus' call and follows. The immediateness of his obedience is striking. What a contrast he presents to the scribes who think evil in their hearts and grumble among themselves at Jesus' authority to forgive sins (9:3–4)! The consummate sinner obeys Jesus' word, while the religious are offended by the expression of his transcendent grace.

The second story follows immediately on the first. Not only Matthew but *many* tax collectors and sinners come and dine with Jesus. It is not clearly stated in the text in whose house the gathering took place, but there is sufficient evidence in Matthew's narrative to assume that it was Jesus' house in Capernaum (see 4:13; 9:28; 13:1, 36; 17:25). Jesus is not only present but the host of the occasion, the one who invites known sinners to join him and his disciples and to eat at his table. The situation can be blamed solely on Jesus. This becomes clear in the Pharisees' question to the disciples: "Why does *your teacher* eat with tax collectors and sinners?" (emphasis added). Apparently, he does it often enough to gain the reputation of being "a friend of tax collectors and sinners" (11:19).

The Pharisees' question is inevitably one for those whose world is tidily organized according to the religious and the irreligious. Many Pharisees held that ritual purity was not to be practiced by Temple priests alone, but was an imperative for all Jews. Such an arrangement, however, has the effect of separating the good guys from the bad guys, and enables those who maintain the purity laws to be secure in their own situation. The boundary lines are distinct. There is a certain comfort in knowing where one stands and who are the insiders and the outsiders. Not surprisingly, Jesus' behavior disturbs and threatens such a world. His association with sinners blurs the lines and uncovers a grace so amazing that religious people, otherwise snug in the security of their religious identities, are left unsettled.

From the perspective of the tax collectors and sinners, however, Jesus' hospitality is welcomed. There is no threat, no menace, no intimidation in Jesus' house. Accustomed to living on the fringes of the religious community at best, they are not invited to dine at the table of One who has authority on earth to forgive sins (9:6). They are accepted by the One who is the ultimate judge (7:22–23).

The two miracle stories, so neatly interwoven in the way they advance the timing of the narrative, present an intriguing parallelism (9:18–26). Both characters are called "daughter" (9:18, 22). Both are restored after an approach is made to Jesus, the one publicly by the girl's father, the other secretly by the woman herself.

But the two stories also contain remarkable contrasts. The leader of the synagogue is a prominent figure, and the raising of his daughter is an astounding event that is reported throughout the region (9:26). The hemorrhaging woman, on the other hand, is unclean, and in Matthew's abbreviated account her healing goes unnoticed by anyone but herself and Jesus. For twelve years her physical condition would not allow her to enter the synagogue over which the leader presided. Yet, in her desperate act of reaching for the hem of Jesus' robe, she becomes a model of faith. Three times in the narrative, the verb "made well" (*sōzō*) is repeated, the same verb elsewhere translated "save." What happens to the woman is both a physical and a spiritual healing.

PROPER 6

Ordinary Time 11

Sunday between
June 12 and 18 inclusive
(if after Trinity Sunday)

While the lessons for this Sunday differ from one another dramatically, two threads run through all of them. One of these threads is the claim that God is powerful over all things. Psalm 116 makes this claim most eloquently with its assertion that God "has heard my voice and my supplications." No less forcefully the story of the promise of Isaac's birth demonstrates that it is God and God alone who gives life, even under circumstances that would seem laughable. Matthew situates the call of the disciples within the larger context of Jesus' mission and understands their work to be the consequence of God's decision to send workers. Paul's elaboration of the accomplishment of Jesus' death and resurrection emphasizes the power of God by recalling that God's act of reconciliation comes within the context of human alienation and hostility ("while we still were sinners," Rom. 5:8).

The second thread in these passages is that of the unworthiness of those whom God chooses. Paul is most explicit about this fact, insisting that Christ died for the ungodly, not for some group of people who could claim a share in Christ by virtue of their goodness. The theme of unworthiness is also present in Matthew's Gospel, which identifies a tax collector, a Zealot, and a betrayer among the disciples of Jesus. The story of Isaac dramatically conveys this point, for no sooner does Sarah laugh than she attempts to conceal her skepticism by denying her laughter. With its reminder that women and men are dependent on God's "cup of salvation" (Ps. 116:13), the psalm conjures up images of human need and dependence on God.

Genesis 18:1–15 (21:1–7)

It seems clear that this engaging story was once told (and retold) for the purpose of explaining the origin of the name Isaac, meaning "he laughs" (for another account, see Gen. 17:17). Yet by virtue of its place within the canonical form of the book of Genesis, this narrative assumes a theological importance that outreaches its earlier function as etiology. It is one example among several of the means by which God has reclaimed the divine promise of Gen. 12:1–3 at just the moment when the promise appeared to be in great peril.

Much about the narrative seems ordinary. The nomad Abraham is resting in the shade of his tent on a blistering afternoon, and in typical nomadic fashion he extends hospitality to three strangers who suddenly appear. His offer of food and drink is accompanied by the observation that he is aware that they cannot stay with him, but that they must continue their journey after their repast (v. 5). Abraham is not puzzled by their unexpected arrival, nor is he curious about their destination. Travelers were a common sight, and the fact that they undertook their journey in the heat of the day meant only that their mission was of some importance.

But at the turn of v. 9 the text begins to assume the properties of the extraordinary. Their question, "Where is your wife Sarah?" is quite strange on two counts. First, it seems odd that they would know Sarah's name, because they were, after all, strangers. But secondly, even if they had inquired down the road, let us say, about the identity of the couple living in the tent at Mamre, it is unlikely that they would have asked by name about the wife while leaving Abraham's name unmentioned. Thus their question hints at supernatural knowledge.

More mysterious still is the fact that it now becomes apparent that the three strangers (v. 2) include Yahweh. (The association of the three beings in this story with the three Persons of the Trinity has been too tempting for many Christian interpreters over the years to pass by, but there is nothing in the text to suggest that the "three men" [v. 2] are the Father, Son, and Holy Spirit. That idea is best avoided.) The aura of the divine is enhanced by the fact that Yahweh knows of Sarah's skeptical attitude toward the promise of v. 10, even though Sarah's laughter has been "to herself" (v. 12). And so it is not out of ignorance that Yahweh asks, "Why did Sarah laugh?" (v. 13); rather, the question becomes a rhetorical rebuke of the woman's incredulity. Nothing is too wonderful for Yahweh (v. 14)!

The promise of v. 10 is repeated in v. 14, and Sarah—speaking openly now—denies to Yahweh that she laughed; denies, in fact, that she doubted. But Yahweh insists that she did, and the repeated verb "laugh" simply emphasizes the connection between this incident and the name of Isaac. Isaac! Isaac! Like the ringing of a bell: laughter! laughter!

Once more, the promise of Gen. 12:1–3 has been in danger, and once more Yahweh has stepped forward to rescue it. The promise had been in peril from Abraham's and Sarah's faithlessness in Egypt, but had been saved by the intervention of Yahweh (12:10–20). It had likewise been endangered by Abraham's doubt, but had been safeguarded by Yahweh's reaffirmation of the covenant (Gen. 15). So now the promise is reaffirmed in the face of Abraham's and Sarah's advanced age, and in spite of Sarah's doubt. We now know that a son is to be born and, on the basis of the wordplay, we know his name is to be Isaac.

Genesis 21:1–7 is optional for the lectionary, but of great importance in understanding the full force of 18:1–15. The promise is fulfilled in the birth of Isaac and the skeptical laughter of Sarah in 18:12 now becomes the confident and celebrative laughter of 21:6. The equating of what Yahweh says and what Yahweh does in 21:1 is of crucial significance. God's word is true. In spite of threats to that word posed by human sinfulness (e.g., Sarah's doubt) and by human weakness (Abraham's and Sarah's old age), God protects the word, God sustains the word and brings the word to fruition.

Psalm 116:1–2, 12–19

See the discussion of this passage under the Third Sunday of Easter.

Romans 5:1–8

The opening lines of Rom. 5 mark a transition from Paul's discussion of Abraham to an elaboration of the nature of life in Christ. Verses 1–5 speak about the peace inaugurated through Jesus Christ, a peace that brings about boasting—even in suffering—and also brings about hope. These themes reemerge in a more prominent way in Rom. 8, but here in chapter 5 they yield to a discussion of the role Jesus Christ plays in this new life.

Verses 6–11 (which take us beyond the lectionary text) consider the role played by the death of Christ and the role anticipated by his resurrection. Although Paul makes a single point in these verses, two distinct moves are made within the argument, one in vs. 6–8 and the other in vs. 9–11. Verses 6–8 lift up the fact of Jesus' death on behalf of human beings. The repetition of this statement throughout the passage signals its importance for Paul: "Christ died for the ungodly" (v. 6); "Christ died for us" (v. 8); "justified by his blood" (v. 9); "the death of his Son" (v. 10). And vs. 9–11 continue this line of argument by means of a common exegetical strategy, by which what is said to be true for a "smaller" thing is also true for a "greater" thing (as, for example, in Matt. 6:26).

Among the striking features of this lection is the way in which Paul repeatedly refers to hope: "We boast in our hope of sharing the glory of God" (v. 2); "character produces hope," (v. 4); "and hope does not disappoint us" (v. 5). Here, as elsewhere in Paul, hope has little or nothing to do with the pallid expressions of hope in contemporary conversation, as in hoping for good weather or hoping for victory in a baseball game. Instead, in v. 2, hope seems to be almost an abbreviation for the eschatological future; that is, Christians boast in the conviction they have about their future life with God. In vs. 4–5, hope is both the conviction itself (produced by suffering and endurance and character) and the future, which will not prove to be a disappointment. Hope may be strengthened by these human experiences, but it remains a gift of God, as the end of v. 5 makes clear.

Another striking feature of this passage is its straightforward talk about Christians boasting "in our hope of sharing the glory of God." Although v. 11 falls outside the lection proper, it is important to notice that Paul returns to this theme at that point, with the claim that believers "boast in God through our Lord Jesus Christ." Here the NRSV has improved the RSV's use of "rejoice," a word that may have been more palatable to modern taste, but which obscured the Greek use of the verb *kauchasthai*.

Precisely because the NRSV now translates "boast," however, readers may wonder whether Paul is now contradicting himself. After all, in Rom. 2:17 Paul castigates those who boast of their relationship to God, and in 2:23 those who boast in their knowledge of law. Those passages could prompt the conclusion that Paul has targeted boasting in and of itself. But the fact that he encourages boasting in the present passage means that boasting as such is not the problem; it is the object of boasting (or that in which one boasts) that reveals difficulties. To boast in one's relationship with God (2:17) is to boast in one's own achievements. It is, even though the boasting is religious, to act as if there is no God, for it is boasting of one's own actions. To boast in Christian hope (5:2) or in God (5:11), by contrast, is to acknowledge God and rely on God (cf. 1 Cor. 1:30), the author of reconciliation.

With vs. 6–8, Paul turns to the specific means by which "God's love has been poured into our hearts," namely, the death of Christ. Along with the simple reiteration of this event of Christ's death for human beings, vs. 6–8 emphasize that Christ's death was for those who were unworthy. Here again notice the repetition: "while we were still weak" (v. 6), "for the ungodly" (v. 6), "while we still were sinners" (v. 8). Verse 7 bears down on this point by noting that someone (for example, a hero) might choose to die on behalf of *good* people, but no one would choose to die on behalf of the undeserving! Various theories of the atonement may build on this text, but Paul himself is silent about the workings of Christ's death, except to insist that it is for those who are unworthy.

Verse 8 connects Christ's death for sinners back to the love of God introduced in v. 5. Precisely in Christ's death for the undeserving, humanity sees the truth of God's love. As the first three chapters of this letter relentlessly demonstrate, of course, the category of those who are undeserving includes all human beings, without exception (see, for example, 3:23).

So many important theological terms make an appearance in this passage that preachers may be tempted to extract one and build a sermon on the "concept" of hope or suffering or character. If that is done, it should be with the full awareness that Paul is not writing here about hope or suffering or character *in the abstract*. He is talking about the love of God demonstrated in the death of Jesus Christ and the consequences of that love for humankind.

Matthew 9:35–10:8 (9–23)

A prominent section of Matthew's Gospel is devoted to the commissioning of the disciples for a journey. One gets the distinct impression that the commissioning process in the text is really aimed at the readers of Matthew's story more than the original disciples, at those who hear the Great Commission (28:19–20) and who have an assignment to "make disciples of all nations."

First, notice how the task of the disciples is rooted in the activity of Jesus. Before any commission is announced, we are provided with a summary of what Jesus has been doing in and around Galilee—teaching in the synagogues, preaching the gospel of the kingdom, and healing every disease and infirmity (9:35; cf. 4:23). It is out of *his* primary mission that the mandate for the disciples develops. Theirs is not the lonely task of spiritual entrepreneurs who blaze their own trail. Rather they are invited to engage in a mission established and undergirded by Jesus himself.

Second, notice Jesus' attitude toward and insight into the plight of the crowds (9:36). He has compassion on them, because they are distraught and helpless. The comparison of the crowds to "sheep without a shepherd" evokes a picture of bewilderment, lostness, and vulnerability. The image often appears in the Hebrew scriptures to depict God's people at times when they are leaderless and subject to manipulation and attack (Num. 27:17; 1 Kings 22:17; 2 Chron. 18:16; Jer. 23:1–6; Ezek. 34:5–6). Throughout Matthew's narrative, the "crowds" are not portrayed as enemies of Jesus, as those who are hostile and violent. On the whole, they are sympathetic and at times amazed at Jesus' words and deeds, but they remain without faith, no more than curious observers. In Jesus' eyes they are not to be rejected or attacked, but are the object of divine compassion.

Third, notice that Jesus' vision of the crowds leads to the rightness of the moment for mission. It comes as a surprise. The crowds, who have been pictured as a flock harassed and thoroughly exhausted, are now envisioned by Jesus as a bounteous harvest. In his compassion Jesus sees beyond their obvious aimlessness and confusion and declares that they are ready for the message of the kingdom. A very desperate situation becomes the appropriate occasion for mission, the time for harvest.

The dilemma, Jesus acknowledges, is that the laborers are few. Again we are met with a surprise. One might have anticipated that Jesus would then say, "You disciples must go into the fields and gather the harvest." Instead they are told to pray to the Lord of the harvest that *he* will send the necessary laborers. Indeed, the disciples will be commissioned, but first comes the pointed reminder that the mission is God's, not the disciples'. The rightness of the moment and the choice of the messengers are not just human decisions. Prayers of intercession and supplication become essential, since God alone assures the faithfulness and productivity of the proclamation.

Fourth, notice the commission itself and the names of those commissioned. The very authority with which Jesus has healed the sick and exorcised the demons is now given to the disciples. Not only is their activity rooted in Jesus' activity, but his energy is theirs as well. We are reminded that the word "authority" carries with it not only the connotations of right and warrant, but also power and impetus. The disciples are not expected to work wonders on their own, but are to be empowered by the divine gift, so that the irruption of the reign of God happens time and again in their ministry.

The whole commissioning takes on a remarkable quality when we finally reach the list of names of those commissioned and discover who is included. Some members of the group are singled out by their family associations ("his brother" and "son of . . ."), but three carry unusual distinctions that force us to ponder the character of this band. Matthew "the tax collector" is among the despised, partly because his profession is noted for fleecing the people and partly because it has meant collaboration with the Romans. Whatever Matthew may have done since leaving his tax booth to follow Jesus, he still carries the distinction of being "the tax collector." Then there is Simon the Cananaean, whose distinction is not that he comes from the town of Cana or is a Canaanite, but that he is or was a Zealot, a political enthusiast, probably a member or former member of the Zealot party. Think what it must have been to have a collaborator with the Romans side by side with a Zealot, dedicated to the ousting of the Romans! And finally, there is Judas Iscariot, "who betrayed him." His presence among the disciples is a constant and sober reminder that those included in the mission carry the potential to oppose the very Christ who commissions them.

Fifth, Jesus' speech (10:5–23) depicts a mission fraught with rejection and opposition, hardly a grand success story. The image of "sheep [in] the midst of wolves" carries a variety of connotations, few of them positive. But the promise is the coming Son of Man (10:23), whose presence symbolizes vindication and restoration for the people of God.

PROPER 7

Ordinary Time 12

Sunday between
June 19 and 25 inclusive
(if after Trinity Sunday)

An essential biblical dynamic of threat and promise characterizes the readings for this Sunday. Implicit in the story of Hagar and Ishmael is the threat—here relieved—to Isaac and to God's promises to Abraham and Sarah. The psalmist vividly captures the terror by unnamed forms of destruction that may threaten an individual or people (note v. 16, which forms a link to the Genesis lection). More systematically, Paul raises the specter of that most universal threat—death—but does so within the context of the new life won by Christ's resurrection. Matthew describes various ways in which the enemies of Jesus threaten his disciples because of their association with him.

Despite the reality and power of each of these situations, God's intervention proves to be more powerful still. The dynamic of God's threatened people always carries with it the assurance of God's presence. Matthew 10, with its familiar words of assurance concerning God's care even for the sparrows—even for the hairs on the head of a single human being!—promises God's continual connection with humanity. Paul's elaborate logic in Rom. 6:1b–11 labors to assert that life in Christ is even more powerful, even more pervasive, than the power and pervasiveness of death. The psalmist displays a faith in God's protection for those who trust in God. Isaac is redeemed by Abraham's harsh treatment of Hagar and Ishmael, but they in turn are redeemed by the promised protection of God.

God's presence in all these situations in turn makes a claim for faithfulness and loyalty. Faithfulness and loyalty are not preconditions for God's presence; nevertheless, the presence and promise of God assert God's claim in human life. In the terms of Matt. 10, the disciple and the teacher are profoundly connected. The disciple cannot rightly seek the protection of the teacher without also living in the light of that connection.

Genesis 21:8–21

This story is a difficult text from which to preach, for it appears to approve of the harsh treatment of Hagar and her son, Ishmael, a treatment many modern readers would consider unjust. The ancient writer (the Elohist, in the view of many Old Testament scholars), however, had a different perspective and seems to have recounted the story as an example of God's mercy.

There can be little doubt that the narrative reflects ethnic and geographical distinctions of which most (if not all) ancient Israelites would have been conscious. A group of nomads, who probably spoke in a Semitic tongue closely skin to Hebrew, roamed the southern deserts. These "Ishmaelites" were traders (note Gen. 37:25), but because they were closely associated with another group, the Midianites (Judg. 8:24), it may be that they, like the Midianites, also lived as predators and raiders. In Ps. 83:6, Ishmaelites are listed among the enemies of God and of Israel.

Yet the Old Testament lectionary passage for this day is aware of a deep kinship between the Israelites and the Ishmaelites. And it affirms that, just as Isaac—and thus Israel—received life as a result of God's mercy, the same is true for Ishmael and his descendants.

The narrative rings with authenticity as a portrait of the patriarchal society that existed in the ancient Near East during the early second millennium B.C. Abraham, as the senior male figure, exercises life-and-death authority over the members of his family. Sarah, for her part, is queen of the harem and is thus able to wield influence over Abraham as Hagar cannot. Jealousy over Hagar and fear that the older child, Ishmael, might someday lay claim to his patrimony in such a manner as to exclude Isaac—these are the compelling reasons why Sarah demands their expulsion from the family. Yet even as God consents to the plan, God assures Abraham that Ishmael, too, will be the ancestor of a "nation" (Gen. 21:13).

The emotions of the reader are intensified as the sufferings of the mother and child increase. With their water and food exhausted, Hagar and Ishmael face a certain death, and the mother cannot bear to watch her child's final moments. But God responds to their peril and opens Hagar's eyes so that she can see the nearby well. (Interestingly, the narrative describes *Hagar's* weeping in v. 16, but in v. 17 reports that God heard the voice of the *boy*.)

The saving of Ishmael's life and his subsequent marriage to an Egyptian woman fulfill God's promise to Abraham recorded in v. 13. And so Abraham is on the way to becoming the father of not one, but two nations, an understanding reflected in the modern Arab view that Abraham is the father of both Jews and Arabs.

Psalm 86:1–10, 16–17

This rich psalm is a characteristic song of complaint, composed of a series of imperative petitions addressed to God, supported by a set of motivations introduced by the preposition "for," which might be rendered "because." The petitions ask (demand?) that Yahweh should reverse the present, unspecified threat and trouble. The reasons offer God motivations for acting in positive response to the imperative prayer.

The first set of petition and reason is stated in vs. 1–4. The series of imperatives—"incline . . . answer . . . preserve . . . save . . . be gracious . . . gladden"—all are the yearning, hopeful, insistent speech of someone in deep trouble who prays with urgency and confidence and with a sense that one has the right to ask for God's intervention. The petitions are supported with a series of reasons:

> for I am poor and needy
> for I am devoted to you
> [Your servant] trusts in you
> You are my God
> for to you I cry all day long
> for to you I lift up my soul

This series suggests *great trouble,* with which God should be mightily impressed. It also affirms *deep trust* in God and honest, complete dependence on God.

These two elements, petition and reason, constitute Israel's most elemental prayer. Beyond the rhetoric, we may notice that this is a powerful act of faith. The speaker is completely confident that as God intervenes the trouble will be overcome. God is indeed interested in the troubles, and God is fully competent to overcome them.

Verse 5 is a momentary intrusion into the recital of petition and reason. This verse is a doxology which serves to remind God who God is, and how God characteristically and faithfully acts. This verse and the fuller version in v. 15 quote or at least allude to Ex. 34:6–7a, one of Israel's most preferred phrasings of faith, which is often and regularly reiterated. It asserts that the primary qualities of God are fidelity, forgiveness, and generosity. The prayer voices the hope that

God will bring precisely fidelity, forgiveness, and generosity to this particular circumstance of crisis, as God has done characteristically. In its present context, the doxology functions as a sweeping motivation offered to God, derived from Israel's primary confession of faith (cf. Num. 14:17–20). God is asked to be the same God here as God has been in the past.

Verses 6 and 7 resume the standard pattern of prayer we have already witnessed in vs. 1–4, a series of petitions followed by a motivation. The petitions are "give ear . . . listen . . . I call," all seeking to get God's helpful attentiveness. The reason, "for you will answer," is a statement of great confidence, which is based on the affirmation of v. 5. God will answer because God is "good and forgiving, abounding in steadfast love." God will act in God's characteristic way, it is affirmed, and overcome the problem.

After this second set of petitions, the psalm moves to a second lyrical doxology, something of a counterpart to v. 5. The doxology begins with a statement of God's incomparability. There is no other God and no other source of help that is as sure and reliable and powerful as is Yahweh (v. 8). There is no other God who is so ready to forgive and intervene.

Because of this doxological certitude, the speaker anticipates that all nations will eventually come to trust in and serve this God. Thus the psalm moves from the quite particular to a very large vista of adherence to Yahweh. The reason the nations will trust and serve this God is that the nations will, sooner or later, notice that their other gods, by contrast, are neither powerful nor faithful. Eventually all will recognize the splendor of Yahweh, about which this speaker already knows. The ground on which the nations shall come to faith in Yahweh are Yahweh's glorious deeds of creation, liberation, and transformation, which no other god can do.

The final verses now offer a third group of petitions plus reason (vs. 16–17), thus paralleling vs. 1–4 and 6–7. This series of petitions now provides descriptive references to the needful speaker, moving progressively from "me" to "your servant" to "the child of your serving girl." Thus the speaker is one without social standing or power, and therefore utterly needful and dependent. The final lines of the psalm seek a complete inversion of circumstance, whereby the powerful shall be shamed and the little one helped and comforted. This assertion of the last becoming first and the humbled becoming exalted includes important echoes of the song of Hannah (1 Sam. 2:5–8) and the song of Mary (Luke 1:51–53).

This prayer breathes a piety of great confidence in Yahweh, utter trust that Yahweh has the capacity and authority to make life whole, no matter what the problem in the life of the pray-er may be.

Romans 6:1b–11

In Rom. 3:21–5:21, Paul had developed the theme of God's gracious gift of righteousness. Human beings, who are universally under the power of sin, are also the object of God's actions in Jesus Christ, actions that reveal the extent of God's grace. The claim that righteousness comes to humanity as a genuinely "free gift," to use a contemporary redundancy, inevitably prompts some questions. Surely some in Paul's Roman audience found these remarks offensive, for they blur the cherished distinction between "good" people, who are thought to have "earned" God's favor, and those who are understood not to be good, to have "earned" God's displeasure. If none of Paul's contemporaries accused him of espousing"cheap grace," that is only because the phrase was not yet familiar. The facetious question he himself imagines someone asking in 6:1b reflects the response that Christians have made throughout the centuries to the radical notion of grace: "Does that mean that it doesn't matter what I do?"

The answer to that question carries Paul throughout Rom. 6, but it begins with the emphatic "By no means!" of 6:2. Paul's response has two major foci: the believer's union with Jesus Christ, and the believer's freedom from sin. At first glance, Paul's reference to baptism in 6:3 appears to be abrupt. Not only has he not spoken of baptism earlier in the letter, but this is the only place in which Romans refers to baptism. The reference here is essential, however, since Paul sees baptism as incorporating believers "into Christ" (see Gal. 3:27) and bringing about the union with Christ that serves as the basis for Paul's comments in vs. 3–11.

Because baptism connects the believer's life with that of Jesus, it also connects the believer with Jesus' death. "Do you not know that all of us who have been baptized into Christ Jesus were baptized into his death?" (v. 3). However, the death of a believer is not physical; it is instead a death to the "old self" (v. 6), a death to sin (v. 11). Just as death can no longer have power over Christ, so sin no longer has power over the life of the believer. As is often the case in Paul's letters, the imagery here is physical in nature. The believer, by virtue of baptism, is *moved* from one arena of power to another. Baptism brings about a real and concrete change of location, so that the believer is no longer in the arena that belongs to sin. For that reason, to say that one can be in the arena of grace, the arena of Jesus Christ, and at the same time in the arena of sin is for Paul an impossibility. Paul operates with a theological version of the physical law that the same object cannot occupy two places at once.

Baptism not only incorporates the believer in the death of Christ but also in Christ's resurrection. Here Paul chooses his language with very great care, perhaps because at least some believers at Corinth had concluded that their baptism meant that they had already been resurrected. The first half of v. 5 ("For if we have been united with him in a death like his") leads one to expect that the second half will affirm that "we have also been united with him in a resurrection like his." Since the death of the believer is not a physical death, Paul might also refer to a kind of resurrection that has already taken place in the life of the believer. He carefully avoids making that statement, however, by anticipating the resurrection of the believer at some future time. Nevertheless, baptism already inaugurates a new or renewed life (vs. 4, 11). If believers are not yet resurrected, they are already "alive to God in Christ Jesus" (v. 11). Having been removed from the arena of sin, the power of sin, believers now inhabit the arena that belongs to God.

Within the context of the believer's dying and rising with Christ, Paul refers to slavery and freedom. The one who is crucified in baptism is no longer enslaved to sin but has been given freedom from sin (v. 7). Perhaps because of modern preoccupation with and understanding of freedom as a kind of license to do whatever one wishes, it is easy to read Paul's discussion of freedom as simply a freedom *from* the power of sin. But looking at the text that follows today's lection, we see that Paul's comments on freedom in 6:15–23 make it clear that Paul has in mind both freedom *from* the power of sin and freedom *for* obedience (see, for example, v. 17). In fact, v. 22 refers to Christians as having been "freed from sin and enslaved to God." The notion of enslavement, even enslavement to God, falls harshly on modern ears, but Paul does not operate with a generalized notion of freedom, in which human beings achieve a kind of independence from all powers and authorities. For Paul, humankind is always and inevitably enslaved to something or someone. The decisive question is not whether one is enslaved, but what form that slavery will take. The appropriate answer, in Paul's view, is that slavery to God stems from creation itself. God as the creator and redeemer of humankind rightly claims that humankind for God. At the same time, that profound enslavement means a profound liberation for genuine life and for service.

Matthew 10:24–39

Some scriptural texts are harder to handle than others. None, however, may be more difficult than the texts that depict a dire role for the followers of Jesus—trials, sufferings, betrayals, threats, and even death. What are modern readers to do with such words? Most of the time, I suppose, we try to keep the texts at a great distance. Their words of warning about opposition and danger may have had significance for one group of disciples at a particular moment in time, we reason, but they are really not relevant to life in the world of North America at the end of the twentieth century. In a condensed version of the Bible, they would be the parts we would eliminate. They have historical value to tell us how dangerous it must have been to follow Jesus in the environment of the first century, but we do not live in the first century, and we sense an enormous gap between the readers Matthew addresses and ourselves. We find it hard to imagine ourselves as "sheep [sent] into the midst of wolves" (Matt. 10:16).

At the same time we dare not dismiss a text like Matt. 10 too quickly. It speaks a pointed message to the particular readers the evangelist projects; we do well to listen in on that conversation, to eavesdrop as Matthew conveys Jesus' charge to the disciples. The text says a lot about fidelity and fear, about the present and the future. In the particularity of the text may be a needed word for modern disciples.

The assigned reading for Proper 7 (Matt. 10:24–39) breaks down into four distinct movements. First, there is the close connection drawn between the disciple and the teacher, the slave and the master (10:24–25). Already, in the charge, the authority and mission of Jesus have been transmitted to the disciples (9:35–10:1); now the consequences are also transmitted. "If they have called the master of the house Beelzebul, how much more will they malign those of his household!" (10:25; cf. 9:34). There is an understated "logic" here. Why should disciples who have heard the words "Follow me" expect a different reception from the one Jesus receives? The details spelled out in 10:16–23 should not come as a big surprise for people who are "coming after" Jesus.

The second move in the text reassures the perplexed reader who begins to understand what being "like the master" implies. Three times in the paragraph (10:26–31) the command is given "Do not fear." (a) Do not fear, because the meager beginnings of the message of the kingdom will have grand consequences. What has been quietly spoken as a secret will be shouted from the housetops. A reality, powerful and conclusive, has been launched, and there is no turning back the clock. (b) Do not fear those whose power is limited to the body. They can wreak their havoc, but they cannot ultimately destroy. Instead, be in awe of God, who finally controls the destinies of body and soul. The old adage finds scriptural warrant here: "Fear God, and fear no human authority." (c) Do not fear, because as heavenly Father, God knows and cares about every family member. If the sparrows get the divine attention, how much more will daughters and sons?

The third move in the passage is from reassurance to the reminder that human behavior ultimately matters (10:32–33). What is done or not done today in the project of being "like the master" has eternal consequences. There is no evading responsibility or claiming exemption because the issues were cloudy or the context uncertain. Matthew's Gospel in one sense is a long commentary on what it means to acknowledge or deny Jesus. From the call of the disciples to the Great Commission, the text confronts readers with characters who say yes or say no, with vignettes of faithfulness or unfaithfulness, with parables exposing devotion or defiance.

The fourth move in the passage is to the jagged words of Jesus, "I have not come to bring peace, but a sword" (10:34). The advent of the new order Jesus brings, so radical in its message of love and freedom, challenges the structures and arrangements of the old order. The old wineskins cannot contain the dynamic of the new wine (9:17). The result is conflict ("a sword").

To change the image, when a blast of cold, arctic air moves south from Canada and meets the hot, humid air from the Gulf of Mexico, along the edge of the encounter a front forms, usually marked by storms and volatile weather. Jesus' word states that there is no encounter between the new order and the old that will not at some level be fraught with conflict, division, and pain. It is not simply that the old is threatened and resistive to the new; the new challenges the old and precipitates the strife.

The citation of Micah 7:6 (in Matt. 10:35–36) is a startling move by the narrator. In its context in the Hebrew scriptures, the passage describes the corrupt predicament in Judah when all the righteous people have perished and all productive social relationships have come to an end. The words in the Matthean context are now employed to depict what happens when the gospel is preached. The sacred institution of the family is singled out as the place where the conflict rages most severely, an area where loyalties run deep. In the text from Matthew the first commandment of the Decalogue is applied here as in other arenas of human life.

Jesus' message, then, does not provide an unequivocal reinforcement of family cohesiveness. It does not suggest that the sticking together of families necessarily reflects faithfulness or that by family solidarity society's ills will be remedied. Instead, Jesus calls into question an idolatry of the family and warns that the gospel may divide rather than unite the home. The sharp either/or of 10:37–38 is supported by the paradox of 10:39. The losing of life for the sake of Christ (and in Matthew's context, explicitly including vulnerability to martyrdom) is how life is experienced and truly discovered.

Proper 8

Ordinary Time 13

Sunday between June 26 and July 2 inclusive

No unifying perspective characterizes these four lections, although each deals in some sense with the perennial and difficult issue of human identity in relationship to God. The passage from Gen. 22 is one of the most challenging in all scripture. Not only does the urging of God call on Abraham to do the unthinkable—offer his only son on the altar of sacrifice—but it places in greatest jeopardy the long-delayed, but now realized, promise. Yet in the end it is Abraham's faith and God's grace that prevail. God does provide! It is to Abraham's credit that he perceives that reality, so that Isaac lives. And the promise lives, as well.

Psalm 13 is a classic lament, the prayer of one who is deeply troubled over some crisis. The anxiety that churns in the psalmist's soul results in expressions toward God that are confrontational and hostile. God has neglected the psalmist, with the result that he or she is in intense pain. The urgent imperatives that burst from the psalmist's lips—"consider . . . answer . . . give light"—are an appeal for release from that pain, and at the same time are intended to offer relief from the distress of alienation from fellow human beings. In the end, there is a distinct shift in mood, in that God has responded to the cries of distress, and the prayer-er is thus transformed.

In the passage from Rom. 6, Paul juxtaposes three pairs of opposites: sin versus righteousness, freedom versus slavery, and wages versus gifts. The seriousness with which Paul takes sin quickly leads the reader away from the view that sin is simply that which one does or fails to do. For Paul, sin is a power that exceeds the abilities of human beings to contest with their own strength. Only God is a match for the power of sin, which means that freedom from sin is the result of liberation by God. It also means that one does not earn or achieve eternal life, for that is a free gift bestowed only by God.

As for the Gospel lesson from Matt. 10, to say that "whoever welcomes you welcomes me, and whoever welcomes me welcomes the one who sent me" is to make a powerful claim about the identification of believers with Jesus and, in turn, with God. While that profound connection between disciples and Jesus implies the ultimate vindication of disciples (see the reward language in Matt. 10:41–42), the immediate result of that connection will be disruption of the world, even of its most precious family relationships. Identity as "child of God" preempts even identity within the family.

Genesis 22:1–14

This narrative is among the most odd and most compelling in the Bible. Much of its oddness and power comes from its strategic location in the larger Abraham-Sarah story. At the beginning of that story (Gen. 12:7), God had assured Abraham there would be descendants for his family, so that the promise would persist. For a very long time, however, there had been no child given by God to the aging couple. The narrative makes us wait until the last moment for the birth. Finally, in 21:1–7, the son is given, in very old age. Sarah laughs the laugh of the blessed (21:6). The promise is kept. God is faithful. The future is open.

Only kept, faithful and open, however, until the next chapter! In our narrative that follows close upon the birth, Abraham is again sent into crisis, over the same issue. The theme is testing (22:1). God will discern whether Abraham trusts and obeys the Giver, or whether Abraham only cherishes and covets the gift. Abraham's question in this narrative is the same as Job's question: "Does Job fear God for nothing?" (Job 1:9). Or does Job (Abraham) fear God for a reward?

1. In the first scene (vs. 1–5), Abraham is addressed by the abrupt voice of God, *a voice of savage sovereignty* (v. 1). The voice utters only the name, "Abraham!" (v. 1). Abraham, with his identity now at risk, answers readily and firmly, "Here I am." Without any trimmings, Abraham receives an awesome, unthinkable demand: "Take your son, your only son Isaac, whom you love" (v. 2). Take the gift, the one you have hoped for so long, the sign of your faith, the only source of your laughter, and surrender him. The episode begins only because the God of Abraham is a God of such authority who dares require of Abraham whatever God wills.

As soon as the voice finishes, Abraham acts in obedience (vs. 3–5). He acts promptly and readily, as promptly and readily as he had first responded (12:4). He is to "worship" (22:5). He tells his servant, "We [the boy and I] will come back to you." Does he believe in a miracle?

Is he lying to his servant? Does he deceive himself? Does he recognize he will return alone if he fully obeys the voice? None of our questions is answered.

2. In the second scene (vs. 6–8), the plot reaches close to its center. Abraham is about to obey. He is addressed by a second voice. Isaac, his cherished, long-awaited son, speaks, *a voice of innocent pathos*. Isaac addresses his father in bewilderment. The father answers his son the same way he answered his God: "Here I am . . ." (v. 7); he adds: "my son." The father discerns the pathos in the conversation. The boy asks the obvious question, not comprehending that he himself is the proposed and intended answer. He is the intended lamb of slaughter. The father answers quickly (v. 8). His is the measured answer, telling us everything, except what we most want to know. Is the answer a loving deception of the boy? Is it a direct lie by the father? Is it a brute reference to bloody obedience? Is it an act of outrageous hope? We have no clue, but the pathos of the father and the son is now heavy in the narrative.

3. In the third scene (vs. 9–14), Abraham's obedient offering is about to be made. The blade lingers in the air, against his son, his only son, whom he loves. Just then, at the last moment, Abraham is addressed one more time. This address is urgent, as though the speaker may have waited an instant too long before making an intervention. This is a second voice from God, a different voice, now cast as an angel. This is *a voice of stunning generosity*. Again Abraham answers. He answers the angel's generosity the way he answers God's sovereignty and Isaac's innocence: "Here I am" (v. 11).

The angel grants a reprieve to the son, who will live. Indeed, the angel grants a reprieve to the father, who need not obey. Now God knows (v. 12)! God knows that Abraham not only covets the gift of the son, Abraham trusts God the giver. Abraham does indeed fear God for naught—not for reward, but because he is formed for faith. Abraham's enigmatic response to Isaac in v. 8 turned out to be true, more than Abraham knew. God does indeed provide. Abraham's faith is decisive; what Abraham's faith wrought gives a name to the place of the generous miracle (v. 14). The name of the place is not a tribute to the faith of Abraham, however. Rather the name remembers and mediates God's generosity. God continues to provide!

The narrative skillfully links his poignant crisis to the larger story of faith. Everything for the larger story hinges on this moment. In this moment, Abraham must answer all the voices that put him at risk. Faith comes in such small, frightened moments. Abraham's response permits the journey of faith begun in Gen. 12 to continue.

Psalm 13

This psalm divides into three distinct parts, and is the classic example of a psalm of complaint. As is characteristic of this genre, this psalm shows that a prayer of complaint is a vigorous, active form of hope in God. Thus the psalm moves from a situation of need to a resolution in joy and confidence. It is the tracing of this movement that is most important to the psalm.

At the outset, the speaker voices a complaint in four questions (vs. 1–2). The opening "How long?" indicates insistence and impatience, and here, as often, contains a scolding accusation against God. These lines assert not only that the speaker is desperate, but that in fact God is responsible for that desperate situation. It is God who has forgotten the petitioner, the same God who swore to remember and pay attention. It is God, the one to whom Israel prays that God may "make his face to shine upon us," who has hidden God's life-giving face. The root of trouble is God's absence and God's indifference, because life requires the presence of God in order to have joy and well-being.

The result of God's neglect is that the speaker experiences pain and sorrow (vs. 2ab). Notice that the pain and sorrow are not specified, so that the poem is available and useful for folk in many different circumstances. The last line of v. 2 perhaps provides a clue to the trouble. The enemy of the speaker has gained the upper hand and prevails. Thus it may be that the trouble is one of humiliation and shame for believing in and betting on a god who is absent and has abandoned the one who trusts. The power of such abandonment is enormous in a "shame"-based community.

On the basis of the complaint that portrays for God a circumstance of profound needfulness, the speaker now utters to God a threefold imperative of petition (vs. 3ab). The verbs are "consider . . . answer . . . give light." The first two imperatives summon God to pay attention and to take the situation seriously. The third petition asks for the gift of life, for "light in the eyes" indicates vitality which for this speaker is almost exhausted. Thus the prayer is from one who feels close to death, and who asks the Giver of life to intervene, in order to restore the fullness of life. Notice, incidentally, that such an intervention by God would not only restore vitality, but would also vindicate the speaker before all mockers.

As we have seen in other psalms, here the petition is characteristically followed by "motivations" (vs. 3c–4). The speaker gives three reasons why God should intervene: (a) If there is no intervention, the speaker will die, and the life of the speaker is presumably precious to God. (b) If there is no intervention from God, the enemy will gloat, thus shaming not only the speaker, but also the God of the speaker. (c) If there is no intervention, the foe will rejoice. It is clear that the speaker wants to establish for God that God has an important stake in this problem and its resolution. For if the enemy and the foe gloat and rejoice, it is because the enemy prevails not only over the human speaker, but also over the speaker's God. The enemy will conclude that God is weak and irrelevant (cf. Num. 14:16), and so God will be shamed. Therefore God must act to save in order to make manifest God's own sovereign power (cf. Ezek. 36:22, 32).

When we come to vs. 5–6, the mood of the psalm is entirely different. It is as though God has intervened and rescued the speaker. On the basis of the radically changed tone, we are justified in concluding that the prayer has indeed been answered. The God who forgot has remembered. The God who "hid" has now shone. God is vindicated, and the speaker has prevailed over gloaters.

The concluding affirmation is a threefold, first-person acknowledgment of God's decisive intervention.Thus "I/my heart/I" affirm God's "steadfast love/salvation," which has "dealt bountifully." It is important that the last verb is one of "completed action." It has been done! The rescue is completed, even as the speaker utters the word. The prayer is answered. Life has moved into the space that death almost occupied.

The psalm that began in suffering ends in exuberance. The speaker has passed from pain to joy, made possible by the God who hears and answers in powerful, transformative ways.

Romans 6:12–23

When charting the sometimes troubled waters of Paul's argumentation, preachers and teachers often take their bearings from his use of opposites. Already in Romans, Paul has juxtaposed the figure of Adam with that of Christ (chapter 5). In Rom. 8, he will juxtapose life in the spirit with life in the flesh. In this lection, three such pairs come into play: sin versus righteousness (or sin versus God), freedom versus slavery, and wages versus gifts.

As Paul sets in opposition sin and righteousness (or sin and God), he continues the argument from the earlier part of the chapter (see the discussion on Proper 7) about Christian freedom from sin. Readers who persist in the notion that sin means failing to do something "good" or the commission of something "bad" will find themselves utterly bewildered by Paul's talk about presenting oneself "to sin"

(v. 13) and the dominion of sin (v. 14). Sin cannot, at least in the Pauline letters, be equated with transgression or trespass.

By sharp contrast, Paul understands sin as a realm of power, more than capable of ensnaring and enslaving human beings. As is clear when he anthropomorphizes sin in Rom. 6–7, Paul views sin as virtually a personal power, set up in competition with the power of God. To speak of sin's exercising "dominion in your mortal bodies" (v. 12), of being "slaves of sin" (v. 17), is to understand sin as a force of vast proportions. To speak of being freed from sin, then, does not conjure up an individual's moral victory over the inclination to do bad things. Freedom from sin, instead, is being liberated from a real and dangerous force.

The large canvas on which Paul paints Rom. 6 contains portraits of two competing powers, God and sin. Human beings exist in a relationship of freedom and enslavement to those powers. With the second pair of opposites, this dynamic comes into view. Human beings are slaves of either God or sin, and human beings are free from either God (or the demands of righteousness, which stem from God) or sin. Verses 17 and 18 set out this assumption, as Paul gives thanks for the move of Roman Christians from slavery to sin toward obedience "from the heart to the form of teaching to which you were entrusted," having become "slaves of righteousness."

With the legacy of a century of depth psychology, contemporary readers may rush to protest Paul's thought here. His assumption that one is *either* under the power of sin or free from sin, *either* obedient to righteousness or disobedient, strikes modern sensibilities as wildly naive. Again, it is necessary to recall that Paul has his eye on a competition of what we might call superpowers, God and sin. The topic here is not spiritual growth or personal development, but the power of the gospel of Jesus Christ over against the power of sin.

What is at stake for human beings comes into view with the third pair of opposites, which enters the lection only at the very end. If it is true, as Paul assumes, that every human being is free from something and every human being is enslaved to something, then one might ask whether it actually matters whether one is freed from sin. No absolute freedom lies around the corner. No autonomous life has been promised. With the third pair of opposites, however, Paul makes it quite clear that this is not a matter of indifference.

"For the wages of sin is death, but the free gift of God is eternal life in Christ Jesus our Lord" (v. 23). A first reading of this statement might anticipate that Paul would juxtapose the "wages" of sin with the "wages" of God. Instead, this clinching assertion actually transforms the language of "wage" into "gift." Sin does pay out a wage to its slaves, but the wage is death itself. God, however, pays no wages. Instead, God grants the gift of life. That is to say, no one earns anything from this obedience.

For many contemporary readers, Paul's use of slavery language will constitute a profound offense. Particularly in contexts where systems of human slavery lie in the not sufficiently distant past, every use of the terminology risks anger and pain. Although the workings of the slave systems of Greece and Rome were different from those of North America, they constituted a real and present factor in the regions of Paul's mission (as his letter to Philemon makes clear). It is presumably because Paul knows what slavery is that he elects such a forceful way of insisting that all human beings are, rightfully, slaves of the God who made them.

Equally offensive to modern sensibilities will be Paul's insistence that God pays no wages (v. 23). Even if no one utters a protest or enters into dispute with the text, readers of Paul again and again manage to diminish the force of his argument here. The perennial desire to believe that obedience to God somehow achieves salvation or deserves the reward of eternal life successfully silences the text. And yet it stands: eternal life is God's free gift!

Matthew 10:40–42

For three Sundays the lectionary has directed us to Jesus' missionary charge to the Twelve in Matt. 9–10. Unlike Luke, Matthew makes no mention of the actual mission itself, whether the Twelve ever went or what their mission experience was. The effect of the omission is to highlight the speech as a direct address to the readers. The audience is left not so much with a historical report of what occurred in the ministry of Jesus as with a description of its own ministry. Many of the features of the charge fit better a later period in the first century (see 10:17–23). The warnings and promises of the text, then, are warnings and promises to those long after the time of the Twelve who find themselves commissioned by 10:7–8 and who discover that the announcement of the dawn of a new age is forever risky business.

The final paragraph (10:40–42) should not in fact be separated from the rest of the speech. In a sense it responds to the sharp words of vs. 34–39 and the recognition that the gospel can and does split families, setting one member over against another. These were no less harsh words in the first century than they are today. What is offered, however, is a more binding relationship than even the natural family.

In the carrying out of their mission, the disciples are rejected by some but received by others. In the welcoming process, a connection is forged between hosts ("whoever welcomes you"), disciples, Jesus ("me"), and God ("the one who sent me"). By means of the principle of identification, the four parties are joined in a profound solidarity. A new family is created of those who faithfully carry out the mission and those who openly receive the mission, and a fellowship is established that includes the divine presence. The message is not unlike that of Matt. 12:46–50, where Jesus relativizes the natural family relations and establishes a new family bound together by a common commitment to do God's will.

The new family does not *automatically* emerge to replace the support of the old family ties. It is born in the context of mission. The community "on the road" is the community needing to be welcomed and needing to receive a cup of cold water. They are the ones bonded together with the divine presence.

But attention in the text is focused not only on those bearing the message but also on those who receive the messengers. In connection with them, the word "reward" is used three times in today's paragraph. We are not told the nature of the reward. Maybe hospitality to God's messengers carries its own reward; maybe the new fellowship that emerges is the reward. In any case, the notion of reward suggests that the act of welcoming does not go unnoticed by God. God is intimately involved in the mission, both in sustaining the messengers (10:31) and in rewarding those showing hospitality.

Proper 9

Ordinary Time 14

Sunday between
July 3 and 9 inclusive

The Old Testament lection for this week if the familiar story of Abraham's quest to find a bride for Isaac from among his own people. Narrative beauty and emotional drama are combined in this story, and the reader is touched by Abraham's need and by the sensitive response of Rebekah as well. Rebekah chooses to return with the servant, and in opting for Isaac she makes of herself the instrument for the preservation of the promise (Gen. 12:1–3). That which has been in danger is now saved, and the reader is reminded that God's declared intentions are sure.

Psalm 45, a hymn in honor of the marriage of the king, is apparently placed in the lectionary to match the passage from Gen. 24. Implicit in that text is the future birth of Jacob and the sustaining of the family and nation. In the psalm, reference is made to the sons who will become "princes in all the earth" (45:16). In both cases the marriage union is a special blessing, which gives the community a future and which evidences God's attentive blessing to this particular people.

Romans 7 depicts a battle, not of the nation Israel, but of human life. Here it is the strong desire to do good, to serve God rightly, that finds itself threatened by the enemy, sin, an enemy capable of perverting even the best of human motives and actions. On its own, humanity has not the strength to resist the overwhelming power of sin. Even the law of God can be used by sin for the destruction of humanity. Only God, here known through the death and resurrection of Jesus Christ, can bring victory.

Of course, these "victories" are not always visible to the unassisted human eye. Who can see the defeat of sin? The prayer of Jesus in Matthew recalls that knowledge of such things comes, not to those who are intelligent by ordinary, human standards, but to those "infants" to whom God has granted revelation. Those who do enter into

Jesus' discipleship will find in their relationship to him a new understanding of power and of service.

Genesis 24:34–38, 42–49, 58–67

Genesis 24 is the story of Abraham's successful quest to find a wife for Isaac from among the ancestral family near Haran (note Gen. 11:31–32). It is an extended narrative, but the lectionary has pared it down to manageable size by a careful selection of verses.

In the portion of the story that precedes the verses chosen for the lectionary, Abraham has sent his servant (probably Eliezer mentioned in Gen. 15:2) to the homeland of his family in search of a bride for his heir. The seriousness of the mission is symbolized by the oath the servant takes (24:9), in which the loins of Abraham represent the reproductive power of the patriarch. In other words, this story is about the fulfillment of God's promise concerning the future of Abraham's family (Gen. 12:1–3).

The sheer beauty of the encounter at the well between the servant and Rebekah is matchless (24:10–27). The description of Rebekah's lovely appearance and her cooperative spirit is designed to elicit the hope within the reader that this is, indeed, the one who is to be Isaac's bride. And the manner in which the servant's prayer (vs. 12–14) is answered by the young woman's behavior serves as a strong signal that God is directing the course of events to their divinely intended purpose. The prayer of vs. 12–14 is balanced by the servant's second prayer (vs. 27), this time an expression of deep thanksgiving to Abraham's God.

Brother Laban's warm response to Rebekah's report of her encounter with Abraham's servant (vs. 28–33) sets the stage for the first section of Gen. 24 designated by the lectionary: vs. 34–38. Here the servant recapitulates what the reader has learned from vs. 1–9. The man emphasizes that Abraham's vast wealth has now become Isaac's, and that that fact is a blessing from Yahweh. But Yahweh's blessing also extends to Isaac's remarkable birth (v. 36). The logical consequence of these things is that the heir now needs a wife, in order that both wealth and family may be prolonged. Yet the servant is not innocent of the ways of the world. Neither extravagant wealth nor the wondrous power of God in giving Sarah a son in advanced age is proof that the woman whom the servant finds will cooperate with the purposes of his visit. It is a commentary on the text's high regard for women that unlike brides in some societies, both ancient and modern, Rebekah cannot be coerced. If she will not accompany the servant back to Abraham in order to marry Isaac, then the servant is to leave her at home and to be free from his oath (v. 41).

That portion of the text chosen by the lectionary is joined again at v. 42. Here (vs. 42–49) the servant rehearses those events previously described in vs. 12–27. (It is this frequent repetition within the text that makes the selective method of the lectionary feasible.) The section concludes with an appeal by the servant that brother Laban and the father, Bethuel, may deal honorably with cousin Abraham. There is a sense in which v. 49 may seem to repeat a time-honored formula that often accompanied business transactions in the ancient world. Yet it is a formula often *dis*honored in practice, and thus there is a certain sincerity about it.

In vs. 50–51 Laban and Bethuel defer the matter to Rebekah herself. The men's view that "the thing comes from Yahweh" may seem to steal the issue, yet Rebekah is nonetheless allowed to speak for herself.

Verses 58–67 form the climax to the story. Rebekah chooses for Isaac, and preparations are made for the trip back to Canaan. The blessing of v. 60 may seem stereotypical, yet the reader knows that more is involved here than the perpetuation of a family dynasty. The "thousands of myriads" again sends our minds back to Gen. 12:1–3, and we, the readers, are assured that God's promises will be kept.

The final section, vs. 62–67, is appropriately touching. Isaac, who is walking outside in the cool of the day, sees the caravan approaching, while, for her part, Rebekah veils herself until the time appropriate for her to reveal her face. Isaac not only takes Rebekah for his wife, but "he loved her," a reference to not just a sexual union between the two, but a union of the "soul," as well. Rebekah's place in Isaac's heart is so great, in fact, that the blow occasioned by the death of Sarah is softened.

And so the promise is kept alive. It had been in danger through the barrenness of Sarah, but was redeemed by the birth of Isaac in Sarah's and Abraham's advanced age. It was in danger through Isaac's bacherlorhood, but has now been renewed by God's gift of Rebekah. God's promises will not fail.

Psalm 45:10–17

Psalm 45 is commonly classified as a royal psalm. Moreover, it is commonly thought to be a poem concerning the pageantry of a royal wedding, the marriage of the king. The early part of the psalm (vs.

1–9) uses extravagant language to praise the king and to celebrate what is sure to be a successful, prosperous future.

As our reading begins at v. 10, "daughter" is addressed. It is not clear who this person is, except that she is the one whom the king "will desire," who will be the bride of the king. And because she is chosen by the king, she must decide to become a part of the king's household and entourage. She must leave her own family and enact loyalty to this regime. The last line of v. 10 uses words not unlike those spoken to Abraham in Gen. 12:1. Her departure and entrance are at the command of the king, and so are presented as the will of the royal God. In one of our own traditional wedding formulations, the bride is to "forsake all else" and "cleave to him only." Behind this formulation is likely the drama of a foreign princess making the drastic move of loyalty to a new royal regime.

Because she is the king's desire, two things are clear and sure. First, she is to be utterly obedient to the king, to regard him not first as husband, but as "lord" (v. 11b). Second, because she is the king's desire, the richest peoples, even of foreign lands like Tyre, will bring gifts of all kinds (vs. 12–13a). Clearly the wedding has important political dimensions, and so the gifts to the bride are homage to the king or part of royal bargaining and negotiation.

Now the poem breaks out in a lyrical description of the queen's procession as she enters the palace of the king with her own retinue (vs. 13b–14). She is dressed in rich robes of many colors. She leads a procession of attendant maids, who care for her and are her companions. The luxury of the scene, plus the mention of Tyre, leads one to imagine that this is a spectacular that might belong to the prestigious days of Solomon, and that the new queen is the daughter of a foreign king, indicating the preeminence of the king in Israel (cf. 1 Kings 3:1–2; 11:3). However, we are given no specific historical location for the event.

It is obvious that the real point of interest is the king, so in vs. 16–17 the poem returns to the king. It is clear that "the princess" exists in order to enhance the king. More specifically, "the princess" exists solely for the purpose of bearing children to the king, in order to guarantee the dynasty into the next generation. (Thus the "queen mother" is a dominant figure in the royal life of Israel, on which see, for example, 2 Kings 23:31, 36; 24:8, 18.) Because of the lovely, pedigreed princess, the king will have sons, and the king's name will be celebrated for a very long time to come.

This psalm is much neglected in church usage, and not without reason. Surely the psalm will be difficult to use in a social context like ours, which is attentive to issues of sexual discrimination and sexual equity. It will, on the face of it, be offensive, first because the "daughter-princess" exists as a function for the well-being of the king and the dynasty and has no purpose of her own, but is to "bow to him" in obedience. Second, in that royal patriarchal society, only sons are valued, so that women exist to produce sons, a reality still operative in too much of the world.

Interpretation of this psalm will need to be done with great sensitivity to these issues. I suggest that the psalm might best be treated in relation to the Old Testament reading. The role of the woman and the significance of sons is that God's power for blessing is operative in the life of Israel, as the promise of God is thus kept intact and transmitted to the next generation. Even if such a theological affirmation is remote from royal intentionality in its "original usage," the outcome is that the community receives as God's gift well-being and life-power into the next generation. The decisive value of such a gift from God is no small matter in a society that either doubts the future or imagines its own control of that future. In this poem, the man and woman play their essential roles, but finally the birth of newness is an awesome gift of God's generosity.

Romans 7:15–25a

If preaching from texts that are unfamiliar and alien to congregations has its difficulties, preaching from highly familiar passages such as this one offers its own challenges. A survey of the great variety of interpretations of this passage, both scholarly and popular, would reveal that it functions for readers much like a Rorschach test: readers see in it what they bring to it. The reasons for this vast array of interpretations lie ready to hand. On the one hand, the passage itself contains a number of problems that make for conflicting readings of it: the identity of the speaker (the "I") of the passage, Paul's varying uses of the term "law," the relationship between the passage and the larger context. On the other hand, the passage stimulates a powerful sense of identification among many readers, and that sense of identification prompts interpretations that are highly individualistic.

Given this situation, clarity about Paul's intention will probably remain elusive. Is Paul speaking autobiographically, or is the "I" here the equivalent of "one," as seems to be the case in 1 Cor. 13? Does he refer to the period of his life prior to his own conversion, the time of his conversion, his life as a Christian, the time in human history before the coming of Jesus Christ? In all likelihood the answers to these questions will remain obscure, although the context makes it unlikely that the "I" refers simply to Paul's own personal experience. Even if he includes himself within the "I," he refers to the experience of humankind.

Whatever the concrete autobiographical or historical details of the situation Paul has in mind, the passage stems from his prior remarks about the relationship between the law and sin. Given Paul's comments about the law earlier in this letter, readers or hearers of Paul's letter might conclude that the law itself is sinful (7:4). Paul strenuously objects to this possible conclusion, but he does concede that sin uses the law. Sin is capable of "seizing an opportunity in the commandment" (7:8, 11). Even if the law is "holy and just and good," sin is nevertheless able to employ that law to bring about its own evil ends.

Taking that observation as a starting point, Paul's primary concern in vs. 14–15 comes into view (though the actual lection text does not begin until v. 15). If sin can use God's law, twisting even God's law so that it leads to death, then sin's power can surely prevail over any human being, even one whose intentions and motives are good. If sin can use the law, which is spiritual, sin can even more readily invade the human being (7:14). The conflict Paul described in vs. 15–20 is a fundamental human conflict between willing and doing. Despite every good intention, every healthy resolution, every excellent desire, human beings find that they do not follow through on those plans: "I can will what is right, but I cannot do it." This state results, in Paul's analysis, not from some defect of character or some psychological burden, but from the omnipresence of sin ("sin that dwells within me," v. 20).

This description pertains not simply to all humanity, in that all have failed to acknowledge the existence and power of God (see, for example, Rom. 1:21), but especially to those who desire the good. Paul has in view here the religious person, the responsible member of the human community, the one who wants to be a contributing member of society. Despite every attempt to accomplish good for others and for self, the efforts of the religious person come to nothing. Ernst Käsemann succinctly summarized Paul's point in this passage: "What a person wants is salvation. What he creates is disaster" (*Commentary on Romans*; Grand Rapids: Wm. B. Eerdmans Publishing Co., 1980, p. 203). Sin's power is such that it corrupts even the best instincts of the most faithful and religious person.

In contemporary North American Christianity, proclaiming this passage as a profound psychological insight would be relatively innocuous and even comforting ("How marvelous that Paul understood our problems!"). Acknowledging the power of sin to corrupt human life, even religious human life, will prove to be more difficult—even offensive. Few faithful Christians relish the thought that their resolve to be good people nevertheless leads them into sin. To complicate matters further, as has often been pointed out, the topic of sin is itself offensive. Failures and shortcomings may be attributed to psychological problems or social contexts, but seldom if ever to the power of sin. Nevertheless, Romans relentlessly insists, not only in this passage but throughout the letter, that sin powerfully invades and controls human existence.

What is the remedy for this problem, if not more human resolve to do good, more human will? God has acted in Jesus Christ to free humanity from the power of sin. For those who are in Christ, there is "no condemnation" (8:1). No human initiative, no matter how good or forceful, can overcome the power of sin, but only God, who has already acted in Jesus Christ. That initiative of God's enables human beings to live free of the paralyzing conflict Paul describes in Rom. 7, because they are confident that God has already acted to deliver them. They know that God can take their motives and actions, however flawed, and turn them into service of the good.

Matthew 11:16–19, 25–30

The designated Gospel reading for Proper 9 includes two slices of Matt. 11 that on the surface appear unrelated. The first slice is a parable about children who cannot agree on the games they play, and the stated application has to do with the reception given John the Baptist and Jesus (11:16–19). The second contains Jesus' prayer reflecting on the mystery of divine revelation and an invitation to the tired and disillusioned to come to Jesus (vs. 25–30). But a probing of the two slices vindicates the decision of the lectionary committee to bring the two together for a single Sunday.

The parable depicts a generation that cannot come to grips with either John or Jesus. Children pipe happy songs and their friends refuse to dance; they play mournful tunes and their friends refuse to weep. The friends are totally unresponsive. They apparently have no intention of joining the music. John came as a sober figure, a teetotaler who ate a strange diet, and he was labeled demon-possessed. Jesus came as a convivial character, eating and drinking with all sorts of people, and he was dismissed as a glutton and a drunkard.

"This generation" has been given every opportunity to hear, but they refuse. Take the cities of Chorazin, Bethsaida, and Capernaum (11:20–23). They are the privileged sites, where Jesus has done many mighty works. Citizens have more than enough evidence to discern who he is. But instead of being moved by what they see, the citizens have remained blasé. Their resistance leaves them in a worse state than the pagan cities of Tyre, Sidon, and Sodom.

Jesus' prayer of thanksgiving stands in sharp contrast to the deafness and blindness of "this generation." He thanks God for having revealed the truth to infants, meaning the unprivileged, tax collectors and sinners, the poor. By the context as well as vs. 25–26, the point is driven home that IQ and privileged education are no avenues to the knowledge of God. Revelation is God's decision, and the divine preference is for the "infants." But why?

The next verse (v. 27), with its complex Christology, provides an answer. Jesus, who is questioned by John the Baptist (11:2–3) and is rejected by the people from his own home territory (11:20–24; 13:54–58), is only known by the Father. The verb "know" in both Old and New Testaments, of course, means more than the act of intellectual perception; it includes the notions of choice and intimacy. The Father, in love, has "elected" the Son, and on the basis of this choice the Son "knows" the Father and can thus disclose the Father to whomever he chooses.

The exclusiveness of the relation of Father to Son reminds the readers that humans have no capacity of their own to fathom the knowledge of God. Neither the Father nor the Son is a genie to be controlled by human brilliance. God is known only as a gift of incredible grace. Even our efforts to know the Son only end up in images fashioned after ourselves. God simply eludes the human grasp.

Now this is precisely why the "infants" assume the place of divine favor. They make no pretense to knowledge. Whatever they have is given them. They are those who do not judge God by some preconceived criterion, those who (in Paul's language) do not find the crucified Christ either a stumbling block or foolishness (cf. 1 Cor. 1:18–25). The "infants" are those who let God be God on God's own terms.

The invitation (Matt. 11:28–30) appropriately brings the passage to a climax. Rather than make demands or lay ponderous loads on followers, the text summons readers to a discipleship that is easy and a burden that is light. (The Greek word rendered as "easy" carries also the connotation of "suitable, appropriate, easy to wear.") The invited are, no less than the "infants," now described as "you that are weary and are carrying heavy burdens." Like the people of the street who are gathered at the last minute for the wedding feast (Matt. 22:9–10), these folk find the welcome almost too good to be true.

The offer is "rest," the divine Sabbath—not, however, to be construed as sheer passivity. In fact, the text is another call to discipleship. This schooling, however, is distinguished by the fact that it is not obedience to a code of external rules, but loyalty to a leader. "Learn from me" (the verb sharing the same root as the noun "disciple"), Jesus says. The weary are summoned to a new form of learning, in which the teacher is "gentle" (or "meek," as in 5:5; 21:5) and "humble in heart."

Alongside the warnings described in Matt. 10 of the costliness of following Jesus and the eventuality of conflict with the powers of this age, this passage needs to be set as a counterpoint, a reminder of the gracious Lord to be followed and the gentleness of his call.

Proper 10

Ordinary Time 15

Sunday between
July 10 and 16 inclusive

How wonderful and mysterious are the ways of God!

If there is one theme that might be said to characterize the four lections for this day, this might be it. The Old Testament lection from Gen. 25 marks the beginning of the narrative of Jacob's life. The passage is at one and the same time a story about Jacob and about Esau, but primarily it is a story about Jacob. Previously rehearsed themes are raised again (for example, the barrenness of the mother, the redemption by God of the promise to Abraham and Sarah, and the like), but perhaps that which stands out in sharpest relief is the election of Jacob to be the heir to the promise—Jacob, who has no claim to be the heir except that which the grace of God bestows on him.

The text from Ps. 119 represents one of the twenty-two sections from that psalm, each of which is devoted to one letter of the Hebrew alphabet, in this case the letter *nun*. Because of the literary constraints placed on the author (each of the eight lines in a section must begin with the same Hebrew letter), there is little room for theological or literary development. Rather, a single motif is announced: the result of trust in God is a life of joy and gladness.

Paul sets two polarities in Rom. 8:1–11: those who "live according to the flesh" and those who "live according to the Spirit." "Flesh" and "spirit" are not to be understood as two parts of the same person, but as a cosmic duality having to do with the rule of sin and the rule of God. In the end, those who would deny sin (the "flesh") and live for God (the "spirit") are able to do so only because the spirit (or the Spirit) is the free gift of God.

The parable of the sower and the seeds in Matt. 13 is an object lesson in the mysterious grace of God. The human heart may be stony or thorny or receptive, and will respond to the grace of God accordingly. But the seed has within it the power of new and rejuvenating life, so in the end the harvest is assured.

Genesis 25:19–34

It is now Jacob's time in the ancestral story. Everything is ready for Jacob and his story, but the story does not begin as intended. In Genesis, Israel regularly has difficulty beginning the story of the next generation because the well-pedigreed mother is barren (v. 21; cf. 11:30; 29:31).

1. *The crisis of barrenness* is the beginning of Jacob's story (25:19–21). Everything is ready, but nothing works. The crisis turns out to be not a biological, but a theological crisis. Isaac is driven to prayer (v. 21). Isaac and Rebekah do not between them have the resources or the capability to generate their own future. They are required to assume a position of need and a voice of urgent petition.

The narrative is terse. Isaac prayed: Yahweh heard; Rebekah conceived. The prayer of Isaac is answered. Yahweh does for them what they cannot do for themselves. It is Yahweh who opens their future. The new narrative concerning Jacob is possible only because Yahweh gives good gifts in answer to petition.

2. *The gift of pregnancy is freighted with trouble and danger* (vs. 22–26). In v. 22 the narrative makes a leap. We know only of the conception. Now, without warning, it is "the children." There are two of them in the mother's womb. They "struggle." The verb is a strong one. They "crush" each other. There is violent conflict between the two already, before birth. Rebekah is troubled. She knows her condition is not as it should be. As did Isaac in v. 21, now Rebekah prays. She turns to the God whose pregnancy this is (cf. Num. 11:12). We are not told what she prayed. We are told only God's answer.

In response to her "inquiry," Yahweh now speaks (v. 23). Yahweh's answer in the form of a poetic oracle is the rhetorical center of our passage. Yahweh speaks ominous words. The two sons in the womb are in fact two nations, two peoples. They will be "divided," at odds, in tension. There will be an inversion: "The elder shall serve the younger"! The boys are not yet named or known. Even before birth, however, we know that Rebekah will bring into the world a scandalous, unnatural conflict, sure to be troublesome and fraught with unending vexation.

The oracle is laconic about the tension and the inversion. That tension could be one between two cultural inclinations, reflecting the victory of the tent dweller over the hunter (see v. 27). Perhaps the verdict reflects an ethnic agenda, that Israel will prevail over Edom, whose progenitor Esau is. Beyond the cultural and ethnic accents, the verdict in God's mouth has an important sociopolitical dimension. The oracle overturns the practice of primogeniture, the privilege and entitlement of the firstborn. This oracle, however, subverts that social convention and opens the way for the "last one" to become the "first one." The old, settled entitlements are questioned; new opportunity is legitimated for those conventionally unentitled.

Beyond the cultural, ethnic, and sociopolitical aspects of the oracle, however, we are confronted by a theological verdict in the mouth of God. The poem is a decree of Yahweh concerning the coming supremacy of Jacob, that is, of Israel. No reason is given and no justification is offered for Jacob's anticipated preeminence. On the one hand, the assertion concerns Yahweh's utter freedom to make and break. The new outcome is wrought by Yahweh's unfettered power. On the other hand, the oracle is an anticipation of what is to come later for Jacob. What Rebekah inquires about with God is now decreed as the shape and destiny of Jacob's life.

3. *We move quickly away from the birth* (vs. 27–34). Esau is hungry and wants to eat (vs. 29–30). Jacob has food and will share it with his brother, but only after he bargains. Jacob's demand is rigorous: "Sell me your birthright" (v. 31). The oracle of v. 23 had destined Jacob to preeminence, but it was only an oracle. In this episode, what has been decreed is *now given societal, legal embodiment.* The trade is made; Jacob is now entitled, and Esau is fed. Jacob has long-term entitlement, Esau has short-term satisfaction. The conclusion of the narrative is brusque. Jacob "went his way." He is on the move, in a hurry. Esau is not as easily disposed of by the narrative. Esau lingers in the last line, having given away his future.

The juxtaposition of oracle (v. 23) and narrative (vs. 29–34) is poignant. On the one hand, Jacob is given his singular destiny. On the other hand, Jacob acts by his own nerve to acquire what is not his. In the latter account, God is not visible or even mentioned. Jacob is on his own in his cunning. Except that Jacob is never on his own. He is a creature of his free, powerful, decisive God, the one who ended barrenness and caused birth, the one who ended primogeniture and entitled "the younger," the one who anticipates the narrative of barter.

Psalm 119:105–112

Psalm 119 is the longest in the Psalter and serves as a joyous affirmation of God's Torah. The psalm is an eightfold acrostic. That is, in Hebrew the first eight lines all begin with the first letter of the alphabet, the second begin with the second letter, and so on. Our particular verses are the eight lines that begin with *nun* (=*n*). It is likely that the psalm is written in this tightly disciplined fashion so that the "medium" is a match for the "message." The message is that a Torah-obeying life is a *rightly ordered* life, and so the acrostic expresses a psalm that is *rightly ordered.* Unfortunately, that acrostic order is completely lost in English translation.

As with much of this psalm, our verses begin with a readiness to trust in and to obey God's command. The two words used here for the Torah are "word" and "ordinance." While "word" may elsewhere be more dynamic, this psalm reflects on the written word, in the world of the scribes. The "word" is the written set of commands. The written command, it is asserted, gives light and guidance for the journey of faith. It shows one what is safe, what is wise, where to stop—that is, how to act and what to do. The alternative to a Torah-governed life is a life "in the dark," without any guidance, so that one steps into all kinds of danger without having a clue. Moreover, these ordinances are "righteous," which means not only are they aimed at something "true," but they are active agents in providing a rightly ordered life, that is, ordered in tune with the intention of Yahweh and with the structure of God's created world.

In the midst of praise for the commands, vs. 107–108a break into a different pattern of rhetoric. First, in v. 107, there is a petitionary prayer that refers to affliction and then seeks to motivate God to action, the saving action that only God can do. That is, God is the giver of life and is asked to give life as God has promised.

The petition is promptly followed by an act of praise and a resolve to learn the commands (v. 108). This verse suggests that the prayer of v. 107 has been answered, and so the speaker moves toward a new life, new joy, and new resolve.

This prayer and praise is now followed by a second sequence of verses, which promise to obey (vs. 109–112). The speaker begins with an acknowledgment of having control of and responsibility for his own life. He is indeed a free agent, who can dispose of his own life as he chooses.

But as soon as the truth of autonomy is uttered, it is checked and corrected by remembering the Torah. The Torah gives anchor and shape to life beyond one's self, because one is in fact not free, and one is not capable of holding together one's own life.

This speaker does know about the temptation to reject the commands. Indeed, there are social pressures and social options that are persuasive and seductive. The "wicked" are those who have departed Torah obedience, and who believe that life is more effectively lived without submitting to command. In Ps. 1, another Torah psalm closely linked to this one, the wicked give other advice and are said to be "scoffers and sinners," that is, those who ridicule a life of disciplined, intentional obedience. This psalmist, however, refuses such a snare and opts for obedience. As an alternative to such autonomy, this psalmist is deeply resolved to value God's decrees, to rejoice in them, and to take them with active seriousness all his life long.

This is not a terribly interesting psalm, as there is not much in it of drama or development. In fact, it is a "one idea" reading. But what an idea: that a life of joy comes from a ready trust in God's commands, which accepts God's commands as a covenantal shaping of reality!

One must take care that the use of this psalm does not collapse into easy or quarrelsome legalism. For there is nothing legalistic in this Torah faith. Without such hardening of God's will into harsh, self-serving absolutes, there is an urgent word here for us. There is among us in the U.S. church an anti-command notion that confuses Christian "grace alone" with the autonomy of Enlightenment modernity. The latter asserts that the self is the ultimate unit of meaning. Against such a mistaken conviction, the Torah psalms affirm that one is always connected and accountable, and cannot escape the demands of the holy God.

There is, in the judgment of this writer, an emergency need to show that God's commands are a reliable "lamp" for life, a gift of grace. The commands no doubt require endless interpretation and reapplication. Nonetheless, they stand over time, unflinching, setting boundaries against both self-indulgence and self-hate.

Romans 8:1–11

Certain portions of Rom. 8 are among the most familiar parts of Paul's letters. Verses 31–39 appear often in funeral liturgies, where they serve as an appropriate reminder of the faithfulness of God to God's people. Less happily, v. 28 has a tendency to appear when Christians attempt to make sense of tragic events. Three consecutive readings covering all of this chapter give the preacher an opportunity to show the way in which these passages serve a larger argument.

This first lection begins by recalling some major themes of the earlier sections of Romans. Accustomed to written texts, we forget that the earliest audience for this letter would have *heard* it read. Without the printing press, much less the techniques of photocopying, Christians could not rely on individual copies of texts. Paul had to provide ways in which listeners could follow what he was saying. Thus, the chapter begins by recalling God's action in Jesus Christ, an action that means that there is no condemnation for those who are in Christ Jesus. God has done what human beings could not do because of their sinful state (see Rom. 3:21–31).

Even as Paul reviews what he has said earlier in the letter, he also introduces some new terms that will play a prominent role in this discussion. He talks about two kinds of people, those who "live according to the flesh" and those who "live according to the Spirit." The words "flesh" and "Spirit" may cause us to think that Paul is talking about two different parts of a human being—the flesh, the stuff that covers up your bones and the spirit, an unseen part that has to do with feeling and perceiving.

In this particular text, however, when he talks about living "according to the flesh" and living "according to the Spirit" Paul juxtaposes not two parts of the person but *two ways of living.* As in Rom. 6 and elsewhere, Paul describes the Christian situation by means of opposing powers or arenas of power. In Rom. 8:1–17 he opposes the Spirit of God to flesh. People either walk "according to the flesh" or "according to the Spirit." If their minds are "set . . . on the flesh," they are set on "death." Believers are not "in the flesh," but "in the Spirit." Notice that one cannot be in both arenas at the same time; neither can both Spirit and flesh influence a person. These are mutually exclusive categories.

Despite the first impression this flesh-Spirit opposition leaves, Paul is not simply invoking a moral dualism between the flesh as evil and the Spirit as good. The dualism reflected in this passage is cosmic or transcendent rather than moral, since the realm of the flesh refers to the realm ruled by sin, while the realm of the Spirit refers to the realm ruled by God. In this passage, Paul employs the terms "flesh" and "Spirit" in a metonymy, a figure of speech in which one feature of an entity serves to refer to the entire entity (for example, "counting heads" for counting persons, "the hand of God" for God). "Flesh" then refers to the rule of sin, in which human flesh, while in itself neutral rather than evil, is held hostage and is subject to corruption (along with the rest of creation). "Spirit," by contrast, refers to the realm ruled by God, in which the Spirit of God exerts its powerful role.

"Liv[ing] according to the flesh," then, does not necessarily mean living a life of gluttony, or indolence, or vanity. It means living in a way that is shaped by, controlled by, the values and standards of the world in rebellion against God. What Paul refers to here is not a list of bad behaviors but what we would call a "mind-set"—a mind-set that daily makes its way in the world apart from its Creator. Paul contrasts this way of living with living "according to the Spirit." Paul's comments about this manner of living are a bit elusive. Here he simply says that living according to the Spirit is to have one's mind set on the Spirit; it is life and peace.

Having read this contrast between living in the Spirit and living in the flesh, the immediate response of many will be to look at ourselves and around at our neighbors: Who stands where? We are pleased to find ourselves living in the Spirit, although we may have some concerns about various of our friends and neighbors. And we being to congratulate ourselves on our good judgment. Or we may simply conclude that Paul wants us to choose: the proverbial fork in the road is before us. Which path will we select?

Reading v. 11 should correct this response: "If the Spirit of him who raised Jesus from the dead dwells in you, he who raised Jesus from the dead will give life to your mortal bodies also through his Spirit that dwells in you." By a simple reassertion of the Easter event, Paul teaches us a most important lesson. First, the Spirit does not belong to human beings. The Spirit is always God's Spirit, never a human possession. Second, God *gives* the Spirit. If even Jesus did not raise himself from the dead but was raised by the Spirit of God, then human beings cannot earn the Spirit. We cannot choose or obtain the Spirit. The Spirit is always and forever a gift of the one sovereign and powerful God.

Matthew 13:1–9, 18–23

The Christian church has always been faced with the mystery of the gospel: why some people hear and eagerly respond and others hear and remain either indifferent or openly hostile. What explains the varying responses? Does God choose for some to be open and receptive and others to be deaf? Or are humans totally responsible for their own "hearing"? The mystery perplexed the disciples during the ministry of Jesus, and perplexed even more the early communities during the time of the writing of the Gospels.

Matthew's narrative reflects such a struggle, particularly in the section from 11:2 to 13:58. From the questions put to Jesus by an uncertain John (11:2–3) to the rejection of Jesus in his hometown synagogue (13:54–58), the text ponders the reality of divided reactions to the message of the rule of God. The Gospel reading for last Sunday (Matt. 11:16–19, 25–30) stressed that the knowledge of God is a gift of grace, fitting for infants who make no pretense to wisdom. "No one knows the Father except the Son and anyone to whom the Son chooses to reveal him" (11:27). The parable and its interpretation assigned for this Sunday, however, focus more pointedly on the audiences to whom the gospel is declared—their outright rejection, their short-lived acceptance, or their enthusiastic and fruitful response. The readings for the two Sundays, taken together, present the paradox of divine election and personal responsibility, the unrelieved tension between God's gracious gift of revelation and the need for human response.

Two dimensions of the text need to be underscored. First, the way in which the interpretation is linked to the parable stresses its impact particularly on the disciples. The audience for the parable itself is "the whole crowd" (13:2), and its closing words embrace a wide group: "Let anyone with ears listen!" (13:9). With 13:10 the immediate audience is narrowed. While the disciples don't ask for an explanation to this particular parable but for a rationale as to why Jesus speaks in parables at all, nevertheless what they get is an allegorical interpretation of the parable aimed pointedly at them. (Whether the interpretation of the parable historically comes from Jesus himself is not important for preaching.) Verse 18 can be paraphrased, "You disciples, listen to the parable of the sower." The "you" is emphatic.

The effect of directing the interpretation toward the disciples is to take the mystery of hearing the gospel out of the arena of speculation and to make it an existential issue. As hearers, the disciples are not allowed the luxury of armchair quarterbacking, of deliberating over someone else's positive or negative response as to who gets the credit or the blame. The text bluntly asks: How do *you* hear? What type of soil are *you*? Does your hearing lead to understanding? Those included within the circle of followers are face-to-face with their own quality of hearing. There is no place for smugness. Rather than judging the reactions of others, the disciples are forced to examine their own responsiveness to the gospel and whether or not they have exhibited the staying power that eventuates in a fruitful harvest.

The second element of the text that sticks out is the extraordinary proportions of the harvest. The three types of bad soil are paralleled by three levels of prosperity. Historians suggest that a seven-to-tenfold harvest would have been considered average. Here the talk is of a thirtyfold, sixtyfold, and even hundredfold harvest.

While the disciples may have to ask themselves questions about their own hearing of the gospel, there is nevertheless assurance about the ultimate outcome of the sowing of the word. The final scene is a picture not of the birds' snatching away the seed sown on the path, nor of the rootless plants on the rocky ground wilting in the blistering heat, nor of the spindly stalks crowded out by the weeds, but of a full and bountiful harvest. To the original disciples, who were so few among so many, and Matthew's community, dwarfed by its surroundings, the final scene engenders great confidence in God's purposes. Though the numbers are small, the opposition painful, and the rejections many, the remarkable size of the harvest is a reminder of God's blessing, the assurance of a grand and glorious conclusion.

PROPER 11

Ordinary Time 16

Sunday between
July 17 and 23 inclusive

At first reading the four passages assigned for this Sunday seem to have very little in common with one another. Genesis 28 is the narrative of Jacob's encounter with God in a dream at Bethel, while Ps. 139 is a moving statement on the ubiquitous nature of God's presence, but beyond this specific reference not many connections are apparent. Romans 8 relates Paul's poetic reflection on a groaning world, and Matt. 13 relates the parable of the wheat and the weeds, or tares, and the injunction to patience about the presence of evil in the community.

And yet a careful consideration of the texts yields a certain common rhythm among three of them, providing a story of God's activity in deliverance, with the psalm offering a marvelously contemplative piece about the ever-present love of God.

First, the texts start with depictions of the social setting of God's activity. In Gen. 28 it is the loneliness of the bedouin Jacob who, in his solitude, experiences an unexpected encounter with God. In Rom. 8 it is the broader context of creation itself, animate and inanimate, groaning in travail out of a sense of incompleteness and bondage. God listens.

Second, the text tells of God's commission of human agents, weak and inadequate, to carry out the divine tasks. Jacob may not be totally aware of the plans God has in store for him, but the reader knows. Paul declares that the people in whom the Spirit of God dwells are very much in tune with the pain of creation. They experience its frustration and slavery, and they too long for God's final deliverance. Just at the point of the reluctance of God's agents to carry out the tasks, the parable from Matthew about the wheat and weeds gives hope. The main reason for hesitancy is the sense of one's own impurity, unfitness, and mixed motives. Such a weakness cannot be overlooked, but at the level of the community it is not to be a cause for paralysis. God will take care of the weeds in God's own time.

Meanwhile, the present is a moment for risk, for venturing, for boldness (as the two adjoining parables in Matthew suggest).

Next, the texts call for a future that is hope-filled. But hope is not shallow optimism, nor is it only to be claimed in the fourth quarter when your side has built up a massive lead. "Hope that is seen is not hope. For who hopes for what is seen?" (Rom. 8:24). The unknown beckons Jacob. Only God can effect deliverance. Yet hope is vested in God.

Finally, we hear the introspective rejoicing of the psalmist, who praises God for the revelation of God as a merciful and gracious deity.

Genesis 28:10–19a

Fear and assurance, ignorance and certainty, isolation and community—these are among the polarities that are set against each other in this text, in each case the first, negative condition being resolved in favor of the second, positive one. Jacob leaves the family home in Beer-sheba after having skillfully and maliciously maneuvered his older brother out of the birthright and the blessing that were rightfully Esau's. The resulting estrangement causes Esau to plot Jacob's death (Gen. 27:41), which, in turn, leads Rebekah to arrange for her favored son's hasty departure. But Jacob's fear is, if not entirely quenched, at least diminished by his vision of the ascending and descending angels of God. Esau's hand may be against him, but at least God is accessible, and that is no small comfort to the fugitive's spirit.

Up to this point in the story of Isaac's two sons, the young men are presented by the text in quite secular terms. Unlike Abraham, who frequently prayed and worshiped, and even Isaac—a shadowy figure—who at least knew how and when to invoke the name of the Deity (Gen. 27:27–28), Esau and Jacob have betrayed little sense of the role of God in their or their family's lives. Jacob's motivation, sly fox that he is, is basically greed, while poor, fumbling Esau is portrayed as a foil for his sibling's schemes. But at Bethel Jacob encounters the living God and life begins to assume a different perspective. Ignorant Jacob has found the gateway to God's dwelling, of that he is certain, and his new assurance is reflected in the name that he confers on the spot: Bethel, the House of God (28:19a). The use of this proper name, in fact, has been anticipated in vs. 16–17, where the newly enlightened Jacob cries, "Surely Yahweh is in this place—and I did not know it! . . . This is none other than the house of God (*bêt 'ĕlōhîm*), and this is the gate of heaven."

But more important than either of these resolutions of polarities is that which involves the movement from isolation to community. The text implies that, were it not for the intervention of Rebekah (Gen. 27:42–45), Esau, the skillful hunter, would by now have murdered the wily introvert Jacob (25:27). Jacob is not only a fugitive, but, like many fugitives, he is a "loner." There is no other family member, not even a servant, in attendance as he makes his way across the countryside. How totally unexpected, then, are Yahweh's opening words to the outcast, pointing as they do in both genealogical directions: "I am Yahweh. I am the God of your ancestors and I am the God of your descendants." Suddenly the solitary Jacob, a refugee from his own community, is not only described in communal terms, but is portrayed as being the focus of that community, the interface between his community's past and its future.

And it is in the context of affirming this community that the text makes its boldest claim. The promise to Abraham, expressed in Gen. 12:3, is here renewed and vested in Jacob. "All the families of the earth shall be blessed in you and in your offspring" (v. 14). He who contrived to gain an undeserved birthright and blessing is now described as the one through whom the entire human family will receive blessing! Yet this is no accident, no "fluke" of history. It is the unfolding intention of God who, Jacob's unsavory character notwithstanding, promises to accompany the fugitive in order to ensure his safety and well-being. The solitary Jacob is solitary no more: "Know that I am with you and will keep you wherever you go" (v. 15).

This turning point in Jacob's life thus becomes a moment of renewal in the history of God's dealings with all humankind. For his part, Jacob never renounces his crafty ways, cleverly repaying Laban's trickery in the matter of the older man's daughters (29:21–30) with some skullduggery of his own (30:37–43). But his life is never again lived apart from God's claims, and he will later demand of his family the same devotion to the God of Bethel that he learned at that sacred spot (35:1–4). All of which is a cogent reminder of the power of the Spirit of God to reshape and reorient human life. Jacob was not an entirely new person, but neither was he the same old Jacob. The change of his name to Israel (32:28; 35:10) signifies a deeper, more profound recasting of his values, a reordering rooted in the Bethel experience.

But the vision of God at Bethel also represents a reaffirmation of God's commitment to all humankind and stands as a model of the manner in which God may work. It has been often observed of this text that it illustrates a repeated motif in Genesis, that of the renewal of God's imperiled promise, a promise that is often endangered from a number of quarters, in this instance the sinfulness of the heir to the promise. Beyond that, however, the text also affirms that in the matter of God's saving interaction with people, the initiative lies with God, our faithfulness (even when it is partial, as was Jacob's) being a response occasioned by God's compassionate intrusion into our sinful ways. Jacob contributes little to the Bethel experience, except (and what an enormous "except" it is) to say yes to the living God. Not only did Jacob not contribute to God's presence at Bethel, he was not even aware of what was about to happen (28:16).

Psalm 139:1–12, 23–24

This most remarkable psalm offers some of the most intense communion with God that is found anywhere in the Psalter. It is a prayer that does not ask for anything, as do the petitionary prayers, but is itself an act of engagement in which the speaker ponders aloud the presence of God, the mystery and miracle of being a subject of God's attention.

The psalm begins (vs. 1–6) aware of the reality that this is a God "from whom no secrets are hid." The psalm employs a vocative address to Yahweh, to whom the whole of the psalm is addressed. It is Yahweh, the one who acts in history, who cuts through all pretense and deception to see the true character of the one who prays. The first four verses are dominated by the verb "know" (vs. 1, 2, 4), reinforced by a series of active verbs: "search . . . discern . . . search . . . [be] acquainted with." The description of God's penetrating awareness utilizes three verbs: "when I sit down . . . when I rise up . . . my lying down." The verbs "sit," "rise," "lie down" intend to portray all human actions, all times and places (on which see also Deut. 6:7 and Judg. 5:10). There is nothing that can be hidden from God, and therefore there is nothing that we need try to hide. The speaker is not resistant or petulant about this reality, but simply ponders what is taken to be true and awesome.

In v. 5, the knowledge that God has is moved to more physical imagery: "hem in . . . lay hand upon." That is, the speaker is completely surrounded by God and held in God's firm grasp. This life is dominated by the reality of God, perhaps wishing for but eschewing every dimension of independence or autonomy from God.

The response of the speaker to this inescapable redefinition of reality again uses a form of "know" (v. 6). The speaker is dazzled by the awareness that life is saturated with God. (In Job 7:11–21, the same reality is acknowledged, but with hostility.)

From knowledge of the inescapability of this God, the reflection of the psalmist now focuses on God's presence (vs. 7–12). This is not God's presence that is mystically available by intentional human seeking. This is rather a presence that is active and intrusive. Now the rhetoric employs spatial imagery: God is present in heaven, in Sheol, and in the sea (vs. 8–9). Sheol is not hell, but refers to the hidden places in the core of the earth. The three terms voice the physical extremities of creation. This is not a God who is "present everywhere," in some indwelling sense, but one who is actively in pursuit of the speaker and turns up wherever the speaker goes.

It is not clear why the speaker wants to flee from God (v. 7). Perhaps it is fear of God's demanding way, but there is no hint of that. More likely, it is a yearning for independence, not wanting life to be crowded by and dominated by the reality of God.

It turns out, however, that God's presence is friendly and positive. The speaker discovers that the God who cannot be escaped is a God who "leads" and who "holds me fast" (v. 10). The verb "lead" most often means to guide safely in order to protect and to bring to well-being (cf. Deut. 8:2–4; Ps. 23:2–3). To "hold fast" (or grasp) often means to hold in order to keep from falling or straying into danger or being vulnerable (cf. Ps. 73:23–24). Thus, in every and all places, the inescapable God is protective, and therefore the speaker is safe. The speaker cannot get beyond God's protective presence.

And even if the speaker tries to hide from God in the darkness, a fleeing into the disorder that seems to be beyond God's good governance, this is no adequate hiding. The God who goes to heaven, Sheol, and the sea is not put off even by the darkness, which seems beyond God's rule. This God is perfectly capable of operating effectively in the darkness, unencumbered. Indeed, God's decisive presence makes darkness undark, and night becomes as day (cf. John 1:5). It is all the same to God. All of life is under this relentless sovereign and subject to the God who holds sway over all of creation.

In the final verses of the psalm, the speaker, after this sweeping reflection, utters a first petitionary prayer (vs. 23–24). But it is a different kind of petition than those found in most of the psalms. The words return to the initial verses of the psalm. What was a declaration in vs. 1–2 now becomes an imperative:

> You have searched me . . . search me;
> [You have] known me . . . know my heart;
> You discern my thoughts . . . test me;
> You know it completely . . . know my thoughts.

The speaker now submits to the sovereign rule of God. But this is not a submission accepted because it is inevitable. Rather, the speaker appeals to God to conduct a complete investigation, confident that God will declare the speaker innocent (v. 24). Innocence is anticipated, without "any wicked way in me." The speaker is confident in self and is glad to be examined by God and acquitted. The outcome of such innocence is to be led in an "everlasting" (=continually reliable) path, that is, on a safe, protected journey, which constitutes life. One can see that what dazzled the speaker at the beginning now becomes a source of comfort, reassurance, and well-being (v. 24).

This psalm is an amazing statement of the power, certitude, and confidence that come in a God-centered life. The God who is inescapable becomes a profound source of strength and well-being. Such a God is an amazing possibility in a time like ours. We are beset with the temptation to autonomy, to going it alone.As counter to that option, many are tempted to embrace a god who is either maudlin or coercive. The God of this psalm, however, is neither of these. This God offers sure life and well-being, even in the face of threat and danger. Now life begins anew, in honest, submissive, dazzling, trusting communion. No need to try to hide from God what in any case is known by God.

Romans 8:12–25

Paul opens today's passage from Rom. 8 with the powerful imagery of indebtedness, with its connotation of being under obligation to another person or group, which helps him amplify his understanding of the conflicting arenas of flesh and Spirit. Verse 13 states the consequences of that indebtedness, since those who live in the realm of the flesh inevitably die.

Although Paul never returns to the logic of v. 12 to complete the statement, the implication is clear: those who live by the Spirit are debtors of the Spirit, debtors of God. Since he elsewhere speaks of his own obligation to God (1 Cor. 9:16) and of himself and others as slaves of God (Rom. 6:22; 1 Cor. 7:22), there can be little doubt that he would use the strong language of indebtedness to apply to believers. Nevertheless, this particular passage extols with soaring language God's rich gifts to believers and their hope for the future, and for that reason Paul may have avoided the obvious conclusion that believers are debtors of the Spirit.

Instead of using the language of debt, v. 14 shifts to imagery of childhood and adoption. Those "who are led by the Spirit of God are children of God." The Spirit they have received is not a "spirit of slavery" but a "spirit of adoption" (v. 15). This contrast imagines believers as children who have been adopted into a household. Even if they did not originally belong within the household, adoption assures them continued standing and ongoing nurture. Whatever belongs to the household will eventually be theirs.

The brief statement about the believers' cry to God (vs. 15–16) warrants close examination: "When we cry, 'Abba! Father!' it is that very Spirit bearing witness with our spirit that we are children of God." What Paul offers in this passage is not simply an abstract, logical analysis in which believers *function* like children of God. He addresses, instead, a kind of intuitive knowledge that comes to expression in the heart's longing for God. The cry to God as one's parent, the desire for God that can only be conveyed as a plea—these subjective experiences confirm the theological argument Paul is making.

By virtue of their adoption as God's children, believers become both "heirs of God and joint heirs with Christ" (v. 17). This relationship with Christ appears earlier in the passage, when Paul compares Jesus' resurrection from the dead with that which awaits believers (v. 11). Here, the believers' co-heirship with Christ requires that believers suffer with Christ (v. 17). To share in Christ's sonship means that one is subject to the sufferings of Christ. To share in Christ's sonship also means, as the end of v. 17 indicates, that eventually believers will be glorified with Christ.

For Paul, suffering is real and present among believers, as it is in creation as a whole. While human beings themselves cause much suffering and can challenge and overturn those forms of suffering, acting on the basis of confidence in God and solidarity with one another, there is also suffering that arises from death itself, a power that no human being can overthrow or escape.

Paul knows full well the power of death and the suffering it can inflict, but he nevertheless asserts in this passage that the glory that awaits in God's final triumph is so magnificent that it cannot even be compared with present suffering. The two are of different orders: "The sufferings of this present time are not worth comparing with the glory about to be revealed to us."

Is this reference to the glory to be revealed in the future simply a strategy of denial? Is Paul offering "pie in the sky by and by," in order to encourage people to live for the future and ignore the present? While it is true that Paul insists on *both* the reality of suffering *and* God's final triumph over that suffering, his understanding of the future is not an escape hatch from the present. Indeed, he emphasizes the reality of suffering by connecting human suffering with that of creation itself.

What does Paul mean when he refers to "the creation"? The Greek word *ktisis*, like the English word "creation," refers to that which has been made. That is, Paul refers here to everything that is made, everything that is not God. Humanity does not exist on its own, set apart from nature, but the two exist in some interconnected relationship with each other.

As he works to express the situation of creation at present, Paul uses the powerful imagery of labor pains (v. 22). He probably comes to this imagery by means of other Jewish literature of this period, which frequently compares times of tribulation and trial with the anguish of a woman who is in childbirth. In Rom. 8, however, it is not the mother ("creation") who will bring the new babe into existence. Instead, all of creation waits together for God to free it, to reveal God's children, to bring about redemption.

If all of creation waits to "be set free from its bondage to decay" and longs for redemption, the question that naturally arises is whether that longing is simply an empty fantasy. Paul here returns to the problem introduced by v. 18: how is it possible to be confident about the future? The answer to that question occupies most of the remainder of Rom. 8, but Paul begins to address it in this particular passage by means of a reflection on the meaning of hope.

Matthew 13:24–30, 36–43

Perhaps more than any other Gospel, Matthew deals with practical, human problems, the kinds of problems confronted every day by individual Christians and by local communities. Matters like anger, sexual behavior, divorce, hypocrisy, taxes, church discipline, and the power of possessions figure prominently in the narrative. Readers might not like what the text says, but they cannot argue that Matthew is abstract or that the Gospel avoids routine, down-to-earth issues.

Such is the case with today's reading—Jesus' parable of the weeds among the wheat (13:24–30) and the resulting interpretation (13:36–43). Who has not wrestled with the paradoxical character of a congregation, where committed members with perceptive visions about what the church ought to be and to do exist side by side with those who are indifferent or who apparently are motivated only by self-interest? It is not an idle matter, because often the opinions of the latter prevail over the opinions of the former, and the whole congregation is affected. Who has not wanted to be rid of the bad apples that spoil the barrel?

The parable, which so eloquently addresses the mixture of the good and not-so-good in the church, operates with the same language and imagery as the parable of the sower and the seed, which precedes it. Only now, a new character has entered the picture—an enemy who alongside the good seed sows weeds. The parable does not debate the role of the enemy or contest his presence, but rather focuses on two responses to the effects of his work. First, the workers become alarmed at the sight of weeds sprouting among the wheat. They are edgy. They are perplexed as to where the weeds came from. They seem even to harbor doubts about the householder and whether the seed he sowed was really "good" seed. When the workers are told that an enemy is responsible for the weeds, they want to take matters into their own hands and pull up the weeds to maintain a pure crop. Their response is understandable.

Second, there is the householder, who doesn't seem surprised or agitated about the weeds, but urges the workers to be patient. It is not that the householder is indifferent to the weeds or doesn't care. Rather, he knows what to do with weeds—turn them over to the reapers at harvesttime, who can properly separate them from the wheat. Any premature "weeding" is bound to damage the wheat as well.

Even without the allegorical glossary with which to interpret the parable (13:37–39), readers are confronted with its double-edged impact. On the one hand, the nervousness that makes us want to banish recalcitrant members from the church is exposed as foolhardy, if not arrogant. Church discipline has its place (and Matthew is not opposed to church discipline; see 18:15–20), but it has to be tempered with the long look, which leaves ultimate judgment in the hands of the ultimate Judge. A zealousness to purify the church, even when some purification might yield a stronger community, is called into question. It too easily presumes that the purifiers have perfect vision and neglects the fact that they will likely uproot wheat along with weeds.

On the other hand, the parable, in the imagery of the apocalyptic tradition, confronts the readers with the final judgment, and the mention of judgment invariably evokes existential uncertainty. Where do I stand in terms of the coming separation? Matthew's story persistently calls not just for talk, but also for deed (for example, 7:21–27). At the same time, deeds by themselves can be pure hypocrisy unless they cohere with an inner commitment (for example,

7:17–20). There has to be a consistency between thought and deed, between motivation and action. The final judgment exposes that critical relationship and brings to light what otherwise is easily concealed.

Without entirely dissolving the anxiety created by the expectation of judgment, the parable, located where it is, nevertheless pushes beyond mere worry. The parable of the wheat and weeds and its parallel, the parable of the net (13:47–50), function as brackets around two other parables (vs. 44–46). One of those parables describes the joyful pursuit of treasure hidden in a field; the other tells of a merchant who sells all he has to purchase "one pearl of great value."

In light of the coming judgment, the present is not a time of paralyzing nail-biting, but a time of risk, of joyful ventures taken, of discovering what is really valuable, of a boldness not intimidated by the fear of failure, of a persistence in pursuit of the coming reign of God. And the Son of man who sends his angels to effect judgment (13:41) is the Son of man who on earth forgave sins freely, who suffered at the hands of betrayers, and who confirms for us that God's gracious promises can be trusted.

Proper 12

Ordinary Time 17

Sunday between
July 24 and 30 inclusive

One of the major tasks of preaching is the discovery of speech that renders the presence of the biblical God available, confronting, and nurturing to a contemporary congregation. It is not just how one talks *about* God, but how one talks so that the speech of God is heard, so that God's voice speaks afresh, so that people encounter the reality of the God of Jacob and of Jesus. God's speaking and human hearing reorient the present and open up for the people of God a new and hopeful future. Of course, talking about God and talking in such a way that God's speech is heard are not unrelated. Our texts for this Sunday make that abundantly clear. They bring together the remembrance of God past with the reality of God present.

At first glance the story in Gen. 29 of how Jacob won Rachel would seem to have little to do with God. Jacob, who has so cleverly duped his older brother, Esau, out of what was rightfully his, is the object of a similar ruse, for he awakens to discover that he has married not the beloved Rachel, but the less desired Leah. The trickster has been tricked, and readers of this story—both ancient and modern—have gained wonderful entertainment over Jacob's predicament. But Jacob is no fool. Through a combination of patience and perseverance he ultimately wins Rachel, thus setting the stage for all that is to follow in the story of Abraham's family. Yet the insightful reader senses that the real reason Jacob has prevailed is because God has chosen him.

Psalm 105 addresses a forgetful community, which has lost touch with the God of the exodus. Israel is invited to seek its God by remembering the wonderful works God has done and by declaring those works among the people. Remembering turns out to be a powerful experience when it focuses on both God's actions and God's judgments. Recalling that God has not forgotten the covenant made with Israel enables Israel to remember the promise of the land given as its inheritance. The present and the future are reenvisioned in light of the recollection of the authorized past.

Romans 8 is also a reminder of God's way ("We know . . . ," 8:28), of God's movements from knowledge to action, from saving grace to promised glory. Weakness is not the final description of the human condition, because the God who once acted still acts. Through the Spirit, God hears the prayers of the saints, just as the cries of the Israelites were heard in Egypt.

The scribe of Matthew's short parable (Matt. 13:52), who is being schooled for God's future reign, brings out of the storehouse both what is new and what is old. There is no true future without a remembrance of the past. The rehearsal of God's promised reign enables the community to understand the decisively new action of God in Jesus, the confirmation of the promise, and the claim of the future.

Genesis 29:15–28

The trickster tricked! Such a heading might be placed over this bitter- (for Jacob) sweet (for the reader) narrative.

Jacob is in Haran, in part at least because he has fled the wrath of his elder twin, Esau, from whom he has skillfully extracted his birthright and whose blessing he had tricked from his father, Isaac. These two hereditary benefits seem to have been foreign to ancient Israelite society generally, and may have been borrowed from the Hurrians who inhabited the region around Haran. In any event, the manner in which Jacob takes advantage of Esau's vulnerability to coax from him the birthright (Gen. 25:29–34) and then takes advantage of their father's infirmity to steal the blessing that rightfully belonged to Esau (27:1–40)—these events have resulted in a deep rupture between the brothers. Because his life is in danger, Jacob flees from Esau and heads for the homeland of Uncle Laban and other relatives (27:41–45).

Yet Jacob's journey to Haran is also occasioned, in part, by Rebekah's wish that her favorite Jacob should marry "from the family" and not from among the local women, a sentiment that reminds the reader of a similar attitude on the part of Abraham (Gen. 24:3–4; see Proper 9).

Once Jacob has arrived at Laban's home, it may not have taken long for him to fall in love with Rachel. The text is not specific about that (but note 29:9–11), but it did take a long time for him to claim Rachel as his wife. Seven years is the period of indenture that Jacob promises to serve his uncle for the prize, and his ability to claim Rachel at all is a result of their kinship (29:15). Not just any bedouin showing up at the oasis could hope to labor for the sheik's daughter.

The characterization of Leah's eyes (v. 17) is uncertain. The adjective (*rakôth*) may mean "tender," as in the case of the flesh of the calf Abraham prepared for his guests (Gen. 18:7), or it may signify "incompetent," as in David's rhetorical question concerning himself in 2 Sam. 3:39. Thus, while NRSV reads that Leah's eyes were "lovely," other translations opt for "dull-eyed" (REB) or "weak" (RSV). Probably some negative quality is intended, since the contrast is with the beloved Rachel, who was "graceful and beautiful."

Laban's statement in v. 19 is self-serving, in that the reason the deal is "better" is not because of some superior quality in Jacob, but because of the fact that no other young man would be foolish enough to serve so long (fourteen years, as it turned out) in order to gain a wife, no matter how beautiful. There were quicker methods in the ancient world of claiming the girl of one's dreams! Perhaps a large part of the reason Jacob did not object to the unconscionable demands placed on him was that he was in no hurry to return home to angry Esau. That sober reality, in addition to "the love he had for [Rachel]" (v. 20) helped to shorten the days.

How delicious Laban's joke must have seemed to the older man! A veiled bride in the dark of night, a shared bed, and—with the coming of daybreak—surprise! Surprise, indeed! It was not Rachel at all whose warm embraces had transported Jacob all the night long, but unloved Leah! The father had managed a marriage for the daughter who could boast no suitor. (The reader can only speculate on Leah's mood. Did she enjoy this wonderful joke also? If this subterfuge had failed, would she have lost her only chance ever to claim a husband? But it didn't fail. The trap was sprung—on Jacob!)

When Jacob complains of his deception, Laban's excuse is lame. "Oh, yes," he says in effect, "I neglected to tell you. There is this custom among us: elder daughters first! After your weeklong honeymoon, begin another seven-year indenture and, on its completion, Rachel will be yours."

If Jacob has any recourse (contest at arms, appeal to the tribal elders, or whatever), he does not pursue it. He simply complies, and only after working another seven years is he able to lead Rachel under the bridal canopy. (The "week" of wedding festivities mentioned in v. 27 appears to have been confused in v. 28 with the "week" of years for which Jacob must work. The final sentence in v. 30 makes it clear that Jacob worked an additional seven years for Rachel.)

And thus the one who had created so much anger and mistrust at home by his cunning and deception is himself deceived. Yet in the end he prevails because his persistence is as great as his perfidy. Subtly woven in as a subtext to this story is the crucial realization that Jacob also prevails because God has chosen him (Gen. 28:13–15).

Psalm 105:1–11, 45b

Psalm 105 is an act of passionate remembering. The remembering, however, is not an act of nostalgia, but a way of defining the present in a specific way, and inviting the community to a future that is given only by this remembered God. Israel's faith is an endless process of making the past contemporary as an angle from which a very different future is possible.

The psalm begins in an exuberant summons to thank and praise (vs. 1–6). These verses do not develop or advance an argument, but simply repeat and reiterate in various ways the central act of Israel's life, praise and gratitude. The psalm is clearly an antidote to a community infected with amnesia, which cannot remember anything important. Such an act of exuberant remembrance is crucial in a community like the biblical community of faith (synagogue and church), which suffers from systemic amnesia, which knows little of its past, and which lacks the patience, language, and energy to receive and appropriate the past. A community that is indifferent to and illiterate about its past gifts and miracles will surely misunderstand, misread, and misconstrue the present. This psalm is at the same time a battle for a concrete past and an advocacy for a different present. The present, however, is not available without a reappropriation of this past.

The subject of this past now recovered and recited is not us in our power and self-sufficiency. The subject is Yahweh, who was so central and prevalent in the past, but who now appears to be irrelevant. Israel has always known that when Yahweh's name and deeds are forgotten we will be seduced into imagined self-sufficiency, which will end in destruction (Deut. 8:11–20). In the lyrical verses of this psalm, the summons to remember is at the same time the very act of remembering. The act of remembrance is constituted in a gesture of praise, which reshapes the past as a gift from Yahweh. Thus the psalmist speaks of "deeds . . . works . . . wonderful works . . . miracles . . . judgments."

The psalm now becomes specific (vs. 7–10). The thesis is stated:

Yahweh is our God (v. 7). That is who God is, the one who has done miracles. That is who we are, partners with God in covenant, recipients of God's goodness. God's life and our life are inalienably linked. Moreover, our present-tense life with God is rooted in God's uttered "judgments" (vs. 5, 7a), which persist everywhere. The "judgments" are God's self-announcements, which have ordained in our present life purposes, resolves, and intentions other than our own that operate with enormous authority. Our life is shaped and bound by God's uttered resolves, of which we are the bonded recipients.

Again the recital becomes more specific. God has made covenant, an abiding, persistent, definitional relation, which is the overriding reality of our life (vs. 8–9). A larger purpose is at work on our behalf. We are bound in a covenant not devised by us, a promise of fidelity, a promise of care and governance, an oath to fend off every seductive fickleness. The psalm invites the community to reread its present existence through categories derived from this precious, powerful, authorized past.

The poet names the futures that emerge from the old promise: "land . . . portion . . . inheritance" (v. 11). The memories of Genesis push out beyond our mothers and fathers, beyond wilderness to land, beyond exile to homecoming, beyond death to life, beyond marginality to well-being. The promise of God intends that none shall live as displaced persons, none shall live without life supports and social guarantees, none shall live without belonging in full membership. Moses invokes that powerful promise, names the ancestors, and envisions the land (Ex. 3:15, 17). Moreover, the Gospel reading is about the "kingdom of heaven," about the Promised Land of well-being which exists only in God's resolve and in the evangelical imagination of the church. Life pushes toward well-being intended by God. Israel remembers in order to hope. Israel praises in order to imagine. In this doxological recital, Israel learns that the truth of its life consists not in security and achievement and power, but in miracles remembered, in promises trusted, and in futures given beyond our own invention. Israel rereads its past and its future, and is liberated for a different present tense.

Romans 8:26–39

The conclusion of Rom. 8 begins with an astonishing assertion of weakness and concludes with an even more astonishing claim about the future. Far from having escaped the world, believers do not even know how to pray as they should. The language of v. 26 leaves it unclear exactly what Paul means by "We do not know how to pray as we ought." Although often taken as a reference to the subjective stance of those who pray (for example, who do not know what words to use or how to express their petitions), little elsewhere in early Christian writings indicates a feeling of inadequacy in prayer. Paul may have in mind a more theological weakness in Christian prayer; that is, even believers do not know what the will of God is that they should be seeking in their prayer.

Verse 27 reinforces this reading of the passage, recalling that God knows what is in the mind of the Spirit and that the Spirit intercedes according to God's will. Despite the weakness of humankind and its sense of isolation from God and longing for God, what Paul conveys here is a deep interconnectedness between God, God's Spirit, and God's creatures.

In vs. 28–30 Paul turns from this direct consideration of the suffering, longing, and weakness of humanity to explicit and powerful words of comfort. The first statement of comfort has often emerged from interpreters' hands as a word of law or a litmus test of faith: "We know that all things work together for good for those who love God, who are called according to his purpose." However, to say that everything works together for good means, *in this context,* that the longing of creation, the activity of the Spirit, even humanity's inarticulate cries do not exist apart from God's will. God is able to use even those things which reflect the depth of human weakness and turn them for the good.

The lines that follow reinforce this seemingly outrageous claim: God foreknew, God predestined, God called, God justified, God glorified (vs. 29–30). The point here is not to figure out who belongs within the circle of the justified and who does not. As is generally the case in Romans, Paul has in view the action of God and only very subordinately its implications about human standing. The insistence here, then, is not that some people are predestined to be among God's family and others are not. Instead, Paul insists that *God* is the one who designs, desires, and brings about the good. Everything that God has put in place has been for the salvation of humankind. No human act can secure this salvation, and no human act can jeopardize this salvation. It belongs to God alone.

The opening question in the third section of the lection signals that what follows is to be important (cf., for example, 3:9; 4:1; 6:1). The words that immediately follow this question tip Paul's hand by revealing what the paragraph itself will say: "If God is for us . . . ." For Paul, the "if" does not indicate that he has a question about God's allegiance. Instead, "if" signals the presupposition from which other questions are to be answered. God *is* on humanity's side.

The dominant question throughout the passage is, "Who?" First it appears in the form of "Who is against us?" If God has already given up his only Son on behalf of God's people, will God not also give them everything else? This form of logic strikes modern ears as strange, since God might conclude that the gift of the Son was sufficient and more. Paul is using a method of reasoning that was well established in his day, in which it was regarded as logical to reason from something greater to something lesser.

The second "who" question comes in v. 33: "Who will bring any charge against God's elect?" and is followed immediately by a restatement: "It is God who justifies. Who is to condemn?" The language recalls that of a courtroom, and Paul pauses to suggest one who might be imagined as prosecutor: Jesus Christ. But since Jesus died and was raised and, indeed, intercedes for God's people, Jesus will certainly not prosecute God's own.

The third "who" question comes in v. 35: "Who will separate us from the love of Christ?" This question moves away from the courtroom scene of vs. 33–34, and so it may seem formally different from the ones that have preceded. In a sense, however, this question not only restates the preceding questions, but pulls them together. This indeed is the underlying question: Who or what can effect a separation between God and humankind?

Having arrived at the heart of the matter, Paul offers a sustained and emphatic response. First, he asks yet another question about what can separate humankind from God, and then he provides a list of threatening events or experiences that have in common the fact that human beings themselves can and do bring them about. Second, Paul quotes a psalm to interpret these experiences as happening for the sake of Christ. Finally, not content to let the audience deduce his answer from the questions he has asked, Paul asserts emphatically: "No, in all these things we are more than conquerors through him who loved us." Now the horizon expands dramatically. Not only are human actions unable to bring about separation from the love of Christ, but even those powers which go beyond the merely human (death itself, angels, powers that rule this world) cannot separate humanity from Christ's love.

Matthew 13:31–33, 44–52

Though the Gospel reading is composed of five separate units of material found in the latter half of the parable chapter of Matthew's Gospel, the units together provide an occasion for reflecting on dimensions of discipleship—its prospects, its discovery, its urgency, and its discipline. The vividness of the imagery and the contrast between this-worldly language and otherworldly language have immense evocative power, perhaps suggesting that the sermon on the passage should be one that allows the images the freedom to function, to stimulate the imagination of modern disciples in their efforts to be faithful.

1. The parable of the mustard seed (13:31–33) in some ways images the primary theme of the entire chapter. It offers a word of encouragement to those who puzzle about their investment in the Christian mission. The reign of God may seem like sheer weakness, no more than an insignificant mustard seed. But take heart. The tiny mustard seed ultimately produces a huge shrub, and God's reign is like that. Don't be deceived by its modest beginnings. Its final consummation will be great.

2. The parables of the treasure in the field (13:44) and the pearl of great value (vs. 45–46) belong together. They share a common pattern, in that when the treasure or the pearl is found, the discoverer sells all he has and buys it. One thinks of the demands of discipleship, the costliness of life under the rule of God, the theme usually developed from the text. And yet the two parables are also different, and in their differences other ideas are sparked.

The protagonist in the first parable is presumably a worker, who perhaps in plowing the field comes across the valuable treasure. His discovery is an unexpected surprise. He is overcome by his good fortune and joyfully goes about selling what he has to purchase the field in order to secure the treasure against any other claimant.

The protagonist of the second parable, however, is a pearl merchant, likely a person of means, who sets out on a quest to locate the "one pearl of great value." His discovery is not a totally unexpected event. It is the result of persistent searching. But he, like the first man, liquidates all his assets to buy the sought-after gem.

The experience of discovery differs for each of the two characters, the result of entirely different backgrounds and circumstances. In both cases, however, the object found becomes the overriding concern, the concern that crowds out all other concerns. Neither protagonist considers the possibility of passing up the chance to purchase the field or the pearl. The discovery takes precedence over prudence or caution. Living under the reign of God entails discoveries like these, which reshape priorities and result in single-minded devotion.

3. The parable of the net (13:47–50) presents a dramatic contrast to the previous parables, because an interpretation is attached that gives it an apocalyptic reading. The dragnet collects all sorts of fish, both edible and nonedible. When the net is dragged to shore, fishermen put the good fish into baskets and throw out the bad fish. "So it will be at the end of the age." Evil people and righteous people in the world will be separated, and the evil will be punished. The parable with its interpretation recalls the earlier parable of the wheat and the weeds and its explanation (13:24–30, 36–43).

This parabolic depiction of the final judgment adds a dimension to the understanding of discipleship. The discovery of treasures and pearls is not a trivial pursuit; it carries ultimate significance. Selling all one has and buying the desired objects are not just admirable options; they have eternal consequences. Mention of the final judgment reminds the hearers and readers of the parables that discipleship is not a game of "let's pretend"; it is a matter of life and death.

4. The section of Matt. 13 relating the parables comes to a close with Jesus' question to the disciples, "Have you understood all this?" How are we to take their bold answer, "Yes"? Is this an arrogant statement later to be exposed when their ignorance comes to the fore? Is it an honest misunderstanding on their part to claim that they understand? Or do they really understand? The narrator leaves us dangling, since Jesus passes no verdict one way or another on their answer. Hereafter in the story, they both understand and misunderstand.

What readers do learn is that understanding is critical—not so much intellectual perceptiveness, but an understanding of the heart (13:15; Isa. 6:9–10). The scribe who has undergone training for the kingdom of heaven is a lively image. It conjures up the specter of disciplined learning, of committed engagement to prepare for life under the divine rule. The disciplined learning involves things both old and new. There is the old story to be rehearsed, of God's promise to establish a reign of peace and justice in the world and of God's working in the history of an ancient people to bring about that reign. There is also the new fact—Jesus' entry into the story, confirming the promise and demonstrating, albeit in a hidden way, the nature of God's reign. In the disciple's training the two belong together.

Proper 13

Ordinary Time 18

Sunday between July 31 and August 6 inclusive

On any given Sunday in any given congregation are heavyhearted people. One may be the person whose business has turned sour and who is wondering what the future holds. His failure leaves behind wrenching feelings of worthlessness. And there is the middle-aged woman with gaping wounds of grief, newly facing life without a spouse, scared to death of how she will cope. And the socially marginalized may be there, perplexed and angry because obstacles are constantly put in their way. Whatever their circumstances, these people are among the many asking, "Does God care? Can God do anything about my situation?" They may not speak so clearly as the psalmist, but his words are in fact their words: "Hear a just cause, O LORD; attend to my cry" (Ps. 17:1).

Of course the preacher can't offer these burdened people immediate and particular assurance, even from God. There is no divine guarantee that the business will turn around for the troubled businessperson, or that the middle-aged woman will not ache in her loneliness, or that the marginalized persons will suddenly find the barriers removed. But the texts assigned for this Sunday in one way or another do take seriously both the anguish and distortions of human life and the divine concern for human needs. The God of the Bible is a God who cares and whose history with the community of faith is a long story of suffering love and caring provision.

The narrative of Jacob's wrestling with the "man" at the Jabbok in Gen. 32 is one of the Bible's archetypical stories of struggle. At one level, this is a story of the human struggle with God, but at another level it is a story of a human being's struggle with himself. Yet what emerges from the tale—in a most cryptic and imperfectly understood manner—is the reality that, even in the midst of our struggles with God and with self, the most enduring word is a word of God's grace. In the end the "man" blesses Jacob and bestows on him a new name.

Romans 9 also deals with suffering, in this case that of Paul over the failure of Israel to receive God's Messiah, the Christ. It is clear that this anguish is very personal, for it involves the dilemma of how God's own people could reject God's Messiah without rendering invalid the Word of God. Yet not even so difficult a dilemma can obscure the fundamental mercy of God, and it is on that emphatic note that the lection ends.

The story of the feeding of the multitudes in Matt. 14 is also a reminder that God's mercy is real. Obedient disciples become agents through whom God's provisions are served to hungry people. In the unusual language of the text readers also discern overtones of the Sacrament, where the presence of Christ is made available for God's people.

The readings provide dramatic instances to declare that God does care and that God never abandons people of faith.

Genesis 32:22–31

These verses, which constitute the last of three consecutive lections having to do with Jacob/Israel, form one of the more celebrated stories from Genesis. Part of the fascination with this text is that it purports to explain the name Israel in terms of the verb *śārāh,* meaning "to strive" (but cf. Gen. 35:9–15, where no such explanation is given), while somewhat incidentally it also provides a rationale for the name of a place (v. 30) and (in the verse that follows, v. 32) for a certain dietetic practice.

But another part of the power of the text lies in its unanswered questions. Who is the "man" with whom Jacob struggles? Why will he not tell Jacob his name? From what source does he derive his authority to bless Jacob and to change Jacob's name? And why does the new name of the schemer Jacob, and not that of the less controversial Abraham or Isaac, become the name of the special family of God?

Even the causes of the struggle between Jacob and the "man" are unclear. Is Jacob the aggressor, having violated the domain of some river genie? Or is the "man" to be understood as some bedouin thief, a desert criminal who violates the ancient laws of hospitality by preying in the darkness on unsuspecting travelers and who fears above all the revealing light of day? In either event, Jacob and his adversary are an equal match, and the "man" succeeds in disentangling himself from the fray only at the cost of conferring a blessing on Jacob. Yet Jacob, for all his strength and skill at self-defense, is not able to wrest from the "man" his name, the key to his identity and an important source of power over him.

In the midst of the array of unanswered questions, at least two things stand clear. The first is that Jacob's new name, Israel, reveals his character: he is a fighter. The NRSV marginal reading of v. 28 is perhaps the best rendering of the Hebrew text: "You have striven with divine and human beings, and have prevailed." Or to paraphrase, "You, Jacob, have slugged it out with nature and with your neighbor, and you have succeeded at every turn. And so your new name will reflect your character: Scrapper-with-God." When one remembers the earlier stories of how the second-born Jacob overcomes the disadvantage of his birth by outwitting his elder brother and his father, it becomes apparent how appropriate the new name is. And when one also recalls how the vulnerable son-in-law, although temporarily duped by the rich father of the bride, ultimately succeeds in winning the favorite daughter and the favorite livestock alike, the impression is strengthened.

Another reality is that, whoever the "man" may have been (perhaps in some precanonical version of the story), in the text we have received there is no doubt in Jacob's mind that he is *'ĕlōhîm,* either God or a representative of God. A large part of the appeal of this passage has to do with the manner in which this insight is achieved by Jacob, who seems ignorant of the "man's" character until v. 30. One possibility is that the being's superior strength proved his superhuman nature. But Jacob is elsewhere frightfully aware of his own limited strength (32:7) and, what is more, the power of the "man" is simply not that overwhelming. Another possibility is that Jacob recognized the divine character of his opponent in the authority with which the "man" blessed him. But Isaac also blessed Jacob (27:27–29), and in far more lucrative terms than did the "man."

Although the text is not explicit in the matter, Jacob seems to understand the "man" to be *'ĕlōhîm* by virtue of the new name the "man" confers. Who else but God would have understood so fundamentally the mind and heart of Jacob as to call him Israel? Who else but God would fathom the intricacies of Jacob's being and boldly designate him Scrapper-with-God? And who else but God would be so audacious as to bestow a blessing on Scrapper-with-God, a blessing that implied a special and continuing relationship between deity and human individual (cf. 35:11)? Thus an ultimate irony: being confronted with the mirror that God held before beleaguered Jacob, a mirror that reflected a flawed and sinful Jacob, Jacob saw also Peniel, the face of God.

Of great importance, then, is the connection that the text draws between our understanding of ourselves as we truly are and our recognition of God as God truly is. There is a great deal in the biblical tradition that draws attention to the movement from an awareness of God's good character to a constructive awareness of our own sinful character. Isaiah 6:1–8, where the prophet is impressed, first, with God's holiness and, subsequently, with his own flawed morality, is a classic case in point. But the present text seems to move in a somewhat different direction. Jacob could not have helped but understand his own conniving ways. The less-than-amicable leave-taking from Laban (31:1–17) and his fear of encountering Esau (32:3–8) could not entirely be put down to persecution by others. And so what he learns in the struggle at the Jabbok is not that he is a schemer, but that God knows who he is and accepts him anyway. The "miracle" of the Jabbok is in reality the good news, the gospel, that God engages us as we are and, having named our name, preserves us (v. 30) in order to transform us.

Psalm 17:1–7, 15

Israel's faith permits it to voice all its reality directly to God. In Psalm 17, the speaker cries out to God in the midst of danger. The very act of crying out is itself an act of enormous trust and confidence in God. The speaker is unjustly accused, and seeks acquittal from God.

The speaker is a just, righteous, obedient, good person who states his innocence (vs. 1–5). The petition is not frivolous, but just. That is, the speaker has a legitimate claim on God. The speaker does not ask for mercy or a free gift of grace. Rather the speaker has upheld his side of the covenant with God, and now warrants a good hearing from God.

The statement of innocence includes "lips free of deceit" (v. 1). This speaker has not lied or borne false witness or committed slander. The speaker is willing to be tested and closely examined, for there will be no evidence of wickedness (v. 3). The speaker has avoided the ways of violence, either by the way he talks (v. 4), or by the way he walks (v. 5).

It is remarkable that this entire claim of innocence has to do with lips and words. The speaker knows that among the powerful, speech is the most powerful and dangerous tool, for speech can create a false reality through propaganda, ideology, and dishonest policy, which can distort social reality. This speaker has done none of that (cf. Isa. 5:20 for a contrast). The voice of this psalm has named things by their right names, and has lived in honest recognition of social reality as it in fact is.

For all his discipline and innocence, however, the speaker is nonetheless in a situation of tribulation, perhaps is unjustly accused of having skewed social reality. The prayer appeals to juridical metaphors. Thus "just cause . . . vindication . . . try." He has his rights before God and expects them to be honored. Conversely, God has obligations to honor. Thus the prayer is offered in boldness.

The speaker asks for vindication, the right, that is, acquittal (v. 2). We now learn what acquittal would look like (vs. 6–7). God is expected to hear and answer. The speech proceeds as though God is the presiding officer of a court. The petition is only that the testimony of the speaker should be taken seriously, for if taken seriously, there is no doubt that the verdict will be acquittal.

On the basis of hearing and answering, God will exhibit steadfast love (*ḥesed*) (v. 7). In this word (*ḥesed*) we come to the theological center of the psalm. The petitioner asks only that God would show appropriate convenantal fidelity. We now see why the psalmist has used so much energy stating his own innocence and fidelity. It is his fidelity to covenant that gains the right to insist on God's fidelity in response. Everything depends on God's *ḥesed,* and the mobilization of God's *ḥesed* depends on the *ḥesed* and passionate urging of the petitioner. Notice that this model of prayer is quite at variance from our usual notions of deference and submissiveness. This is not the voice of an empty-handed suppliant, but of one who has a place to stand vis-à-vis God, who insists on some rights in the presence of God. The psalm intends to put God on the spot, to see if God will intrude, that is, extend *ḥesed* to such a needy, passionate, deserving subject.

Predictably, the lectionary reading skips over the hard critique of the adversary and the passionate hope for the downfall of the adversary (vs. 13–14). To that extent, the reading reneges on the mutuality of fidelity on which the prayer is promised. The absence of these verses permits the psalm to be read as empty-handed submissiveness, which it manifestly is not.

In the end, the psalmist anticipates full entry into the promise and presence of God (v. 15). Astonishingly, the psalm anticipates "beholding your likeness," that is, actually seeing God. The language is usually taken to be either metaphorical or referring to cultic communion. Whatever its words may suggest, the psalmist anticipates an occasion of full, open communion in which the cause of trouble is overcome and God is fully, freely available. God's "righteousness" (v. 15) means the happy correction of all injustice. The petitioner speaks his prayer with passion and urgency, but not in despair. The prayer is an act of convinced hope, utterly sure of God's power and God's responsiveness to human fidelity. All that remains for the speaker is to mobilize God to act in *ḥesed*; then the world will become an area for full covenantal communion.

Romans 9:1–5

Standing at the outset of Rom. 9–11, in which Paul discusses the relationship between Israel's vocation and Israel's rejection of the messiahship of Jesus, this passage must be considered in its larger context. Paul, having just concluded an exalted affirmation of God's power to overcome anything that threatens God's people (8:31–39), here takes up a threat that is specific and grave. The vast majority of Jews do not understand that Jesus is the Messiah of Israel, and Paul, a Jew proud of his heritage, experiences in that contradiction both existential grief and a severe theological problem.

What comes to expression most clearly in 9:1–5 is the personal anguish this situation causes for Paul. With three separate affirmations ("I am speaking the truth in Christ," "I am not lying," "my conscience confirms it by the Holy Spirit"), he paves the way for the serious topic at hand. Verse 2 speaks of the "great sorrow and unceasing anguish," still without revealing what causes this pain. Only in v. 3 does the topic itself emerge—"for the sake of my own people"—and here with an assertion of frightening magnitude. For the sake of these people, Paul could wish himself to be "accursed and cut off from Christ." In order to effect the salvation of Israel, Paul would take on himself the anathema of Christ!

What drives the discussion that follows in chapters 9–11 is not only this personal grief. Already in 9:6, Paul moves from his own private anguish to the profound theological question: Has God's word failed? Does the fact that most of Israel rejects the messiahship of Jesus mean that God has failed? Does it mean that God has rejected God's own people? Throughout this section of the letter, Paul will struggle to hold together two seemingly contradictory assertions. He will insist *both* that Israel's calling is irrevocable *and* that God's word has not failed. Israel's calling remains intact, because God is faithful and has perennially elected God's own chosen from within Israel. God's word has not failed, because the temporary exclusion of Israel takes place within God's larger plan for the salvation of all human beings.

In this larger context, Rom. 9:1–5 serves primarily to introduce the topic at hand. Verses 4–5, however, contain some specific assertions to which Christians need to pay close attention. Here Paul itemizes those things which belong to Israel: "the adoption, the glory, the covenants, the giving of the law, the worship, and the promises; to them belong the patriarchs, and from them, according to the flesh, comes the Messiah, who is over all, God blessed forever." Three observations need to be kept in mind regarding this list. First, Paul at least implicitly, if not explicitly, designates these characteristics of Israel as *gifts* of God. The phrase, "God blessed forever," at the culmination of the list, along with the overall context, confirms that God has freely granted Israel these privileges. Among them, notice, is the law, which Paul explicitly terms a gift. Contrary to much in Christian, especially Protestant, interpretation, the law is not a burden, but first of all a gift.

Second, these gifts continue to belong to Israel. The NRSV puts this list in the present tense ("They *are* Israelites, and to them *belong* . . .," emphases added). The Greek list contains no verbs, but the implication of the Greek is, nevertheless, that the gifts are ongoing in nature. Indeed, if that were not the case, then both Paul's grief and the tortured logic of Rom. 9–11 would be unnecessary. God's gifts to Israel, primarily indications of God's relationship to Israel, continue. This is not, of course, simply an item of historical interest, but a crucial theological point, since Christian history frequently reflects the attempt to claim Israel's gifts for the church. Supersessionism, however, flounders on the ongoing nature of God's relationship with Israel. The predominantly Gentile church does not replace Israel or strip Israel of its favor with God.

Third, the list of Israel's gifts culminates with the gift of the Messiah. The Messiah comes from the house of Israel. That simple historical assertion, acknowledging that Jesus is born as a Jew, secures the particularity of the Christian gospel. In that gospel, God becomes incarnate in the particular form of a Jewish male. Attempts to separate Christ from that history by claiming, for example, that Jesus' Jewishness is merely accidental or that Jesus' Jewishness no longer matters following the resurrection, amount to attempts to separate Jesus from history. They are a kind of Docetism, seeking to separate the risen Lord from the history of Israel and the life of humankind. This passage, as much else in the New Testament, affirms the connection between the Messiah and the people of Israel. Given the fact that Paul generally shows little interest in the events of Jesus' life, the assertion of this connection with Israel is significant indeed.

Preaching any part of Rom. 9–11 proves difficult because of the historical situation that stands behind it, the complexity of Paul's argument, and the tragic history of Christian-Jewish relations since the first century. Nevertheless, these chapters warrant frequent reflection, not least because of their reminder of the ongoing nature of God's faithfulness.

Matthew 14:13–21

We have learned in recent years that there are various ways of approaching a text, various avenues of investigation, various questions to be asked. Familiar passages often yield fresh meanings when more than one line of approach is followed. So it is with Matthew's story of the feeding of the five thousand.

First, consider the context. The story occurs in the narrative immediately following the account of the beheading of John the Baptist (Matt. 14:1–12), an incident that is a flashback to an earlier time in order to explain why Herod (actually Herod Antipas, son of King Herod) is anxious about Jesus. He thinks Jesus may be John risen from the dead, and his anxiety leads Jesus to attempt a withdrawal to a "deserted place."

The context then confronts us with two contrasting meals—Herod's birthday party and Jesus' feeding of the crowds. In the former story, amid a context of plenty, we encounter the gruesome details of Herodias's scheming. The account becomes a tale of rancor and revenge, even to the point that Herod himself grieves when he awakes to the diabolical web in which he is caught. A prophet of God is murdered by a threatened authority. In the second story, amid a situation of need, we see Jesus moved by great compassion, curing the sick and providing a bountiful meal for the crowds. Though apparently under threat himself and unable to make a successful withdrawal (14:13), he becomes the host for a hungry multitude. The compassion of the one meal stands in sharp contrast to the vindictiveness of the other.

Second, consider within the text itself the dynamics between Jesus and the disciples. Jesus' compassion for the crowds rubs off on the disciples. They become concerned about the lateness of the hour and the lack of available food for the multitudes. When they suggest that Jesus send them to the surrounding villages to purchase supplies, he clearly has other plans. His instructions are decisive: "They need not go away; *you* give them something to eat" (emphasis added); "Bring them here to me." (The omission of the boy from the story [cf. John 6:9] leads to a more concentrated focus on the relationship between Jesus and the disciples.) The resources the disciples can muster are meager, but Jesus helps them to discover that such resources are sufficient. In his hands they become more than enough.

The story provides a description of the miraculous power of Jesus in the face of a difficult situation, but integral to the exercise of power is the role of the disciples. They are indispensable—from the diagnosis of the need to the gathering up of the leftovers. They act on the orders of Jesus, orders that seem preposterous and beyond credulity. And yet the crispness of their response and their unquestioning obedience make them model figures. They here symbolize what it means to participate in the compassionate ministry of Jesus. Furthermore, the disciples learn about the divine concern for the hungry precisely by doing what they are told. They are not given any prior briefing about how it will all work out. Rather, in the act of carrying out Jesus' directions, they discover one whose compassion goes beyond their wildest dreams.

Third, consider the broader context. A number of details in the story itself lead us to recognize in the feeding a eucharistic meaning. Strikingly, it is only the loaves (and not the fish) that are specifically given to the disciples for distribution (14:19). The orderly arrangement of the people, the prayer of invocation and the blessing, the liturgical act of breaking the bread, the immediate parallel to the death of John the Baptist—all are unmistakable clues that point to the celebration of the Lord's Supper. The initial readers of the Gospel who already gather regularly for sacramental observances are bound to draw connections between the feeding in Galilee and the feeding in the upper room in Jerusalem.

But what can we learn by acknowledging the connections between the accounts of the two events? For one thing, Jesus here is clearly the compassionate provider, who not only gives a morsel of bread and a sip of wine, but heals sicknesses and feeds the body. His ministry is physical as well as spiritual. At Communion, we are reminded that Jesus takes seriously all the dimensions of human brokenness and need. For another thing, this feeding, as well as the last supper, occurs in the face of fierce opposition. As the psalmist put it, "You prepare a table before me in the presence of my enemies" (Ps. 23:5). The eucharistic meal has a special significance for those whose faithfulness has placed them in a precarious position. Finally, the disciples obviously are under the mandate to feed the hungry. To be sure, they are not left alone to perform the miracle, but they function as essential agents to carry out Jesus' ministry to the multitudes.

PROPER 14

Ordinary Time 19

Sunday between
August 7 and 13 inclusive

The beginning of the story of Joseph from Gen. 37 is the Old Testament lection for this Sunday, a narrative so rich in color and imagery that it remains one of the most vivid in the Old Testament. The theology of the passage is hidden, in the sense that there are not immediate moral conclusions placed before the reader, and God is not even named. But those who read the story to its conclusion will be impressed that things would have turned out very differently for Joseph (and for Israel) had it not been for the watchful care of the One who called Israel into being (note the Old Testament text for Proper 15).

Psalm 105 is a brief recital of the saving events in Israel's life, and that part which is included in this day's texts remembers the story of Joseph and, like the Genesis narrative itself, stresses both the hiddenness and the crucial significance of the mercy of God. The God of Israel both tested and saved Joseph and the nation Israel. And in the final exaltation of the psalm (v. 45c) one discovers that urgent response to the mercy of God: "Hallelujah! Praise the LORD!"

The passage from Romans 10 is notoriously difficult for the exegete and the preacher, in that Paul's argument is susceptible, at a number of points, to widely divergent interpretations. Yet one possible approach for the preacher is to note the apostle's high regard for scripture, even if modern exegetes might not always want to use the Old Testament in the same manner as Paul. Another possibility is to note the manner in which Paul brings the past to bear on the present, in terms of the saving activity of God. Still another hermeneutical opportunity is to note Paul's insistence on the universal availability of salvation. When all has been said, however, one of the challenging things about so formidable a text is the reality that passing generations of preachers will never exhaust its riches.

The Gospel reading from Matt. 14 has Jesus stilling the storm. Like the other texts, this one points to the inexplicable wonder of God's redeeming love, which can be appropriated and answered only in doxology. At its core, biblical faith emerges from a miracle of salvation, wrought by the faithful power of God.

Genesis 37:1–4, 12–28

This interesting and important narrative marks the beginning of the cycle of Joseph stories, surely one of the most-often-read parts of the book of Genesis. Evidence within the text may suggest that two or more different versions of the story have been combined to form the present narrative. For example, it is first Reuben (v. 21), then Judah (v. 26) who steps forward to prevent the taking of Joseph's life. Again, Ishmaelites are initially identified as the group that carries Joseph to Egypt (vs. 25, 27), but then responsibility for that deed is subsequently laid to the Midianites (vs. 28, 36). Be that as it may, the story as we have received it constitutes an essential narrative unity in which the various elements cohere without difficulty.

Verses 1–4 lay the foundation on which the structure of the dramatic action is built. That the Joseph stories are, in reality, a part of the larger cycle of stories about the patriarch Jacob is evident from the opening sentence. (Also note v. 2a). The Jacob narratives will end in Gen. 50 with the conclusion of the material relating to Joseph.

One cause of the friction between Joseph and his brothers is suggested through the reference to Bilhah and Zilpah. As a son of Jacob's favorite wife Rachel (Gen. 35:24), Joseph would have been a natural target of animosity on the part of the sons of Jacob's other wives. Harem intrigue was a familiar fact of life in the ancient Near East (and other parts of the world, as well), and the Israelites were not immune to it. For example, Bathsheba's intervention on behalf of her son Solomon in the question of the Davidic succession is a celebrated case in point (1 Kings 1:11–31). There seems to be little reason for mentioning the genealogical relationships among Jacob's sons in v. 2 unless it is to point to this element in the half brothers' animosity toward Joseph.

(Incidentally, from the reference in v. 3 it would appear that Benjamin had not yet been born at the time of this incident.)

Jacob's favoritism toward Joseph is in evidence in the gift of the "long robe with sleeves." (The celebrated "coat of many colors" of the King James Version is actually based on a misreading of this passage on the part of the Septuagint translators.) It is difficult to know exactly what is meant by this phrase, which in the Hebrew appears to mean something like "a tunic reaching to the palms of the hands and the soles of the feet." But 2 Sam. 13:18, where reference to a similar garment is made, suggests that it was a very fine garment, the wearing of which bestowed certain honors on the wearer. It is little wonder that Joseph's half brothers hated him (v. 4).

(In order to avoid too extended a reading, the lectionary wisely omits vs. 5–11, but most worshipers will be familiar with Joseph's insensitivity to his half brothers' feelings which is described here—an insensitivity that understandably came across to Jacob's other sons and to Jacob himself [v. 10] as sheer arrogance. There is therefore no reason for the preacher to avoid mention of Joseph's dreams in interpreting the larger passage. In fact, v. 19 almost demands some reference to vs. 5–11.)

Verses 12–17 describe how it is that Joseph travels to find his half brothers near Shechem. It may be that Joseph was kept at home when Jacob's other sons left with the sheep because of his tender age. Yet the text makes no mention of that (other than v. 3), and the implication thus is that Joseph is once more the object of preferential treatment.

Verses 18–28 describe the plot and its execution, although in modified form. The other sons can stand Joseph's special status no longer, and the wicked scheme is hatched that, if successful, will culminate in Joseph's death and the absence of any suspicion regarding the half brothers. Reuben's intervention saves Joseph's life (assuming, as we must, that the other sons of Jacob—with the possible exception of Judah—actually intended to murder Joseph). Joseph's life is spared, but only for the moment, for the conditions under which Joseph is confined (v. 24) would soon have resulted in his death.

It is with Joseph's ominous circumstances—a waterless pit in the desert—in mind that Judah steps forward (v. 26) with the suggestion that Joseph be sold to the Ishmaelites/Midianites. When Joseph is hauled out of the pit and carried off to Egypt, his life is spared. And the reader is aware of a delicious irony: the lives of Jacob and his eleven other sons have been spared also—as subsequent events are to prove.

Interestingly, there is no mention of God in this passage. (No angel appears to Joseph to strengthen him, for example.) The story unfolds much as any other story of human adventure might. But the reader will be alert to a reality that Joseph is later to affirm, and that is that this frightening episode would have turned out quite differently had it not been for the loving will of God (Gen. 45:5, 7, 8; note Proper 15).

Psalm 105:1–6, 16–22, 45b

Our reading in Ps. 105 has an introduction inviting to *praise and wonder* (vs. 1–6), and a conclusion summoning to *obedience* (v. 45b). The substantive narrative part of the psalm concerns the Joseph narrative, and so is an appropriate psalm to go along with the Old Testament reading.

On the introductory verses (vs. 1–6), see the exposition of the psalm in Proper 12.

This psalm retells in lyrical fashion the normative narrative memory of Israel, from the ancestors in the book of Genesis (Abraham, Isaac, and Jacob; vs. 7–15) to the story of Moses, the exodus, and the entry into the land (vs. 23–44). The story line is closely paralleled to the narrative account in the Pentateuch.

Sandwiched between the ancestral narrative and the Moses story is the account of Joseph with which we are concerned today, matching the narrative of Gen. 37—50. In the Pentateuch, the Joseph narrative seems to function as a transition item between the two more definitional narratives, and so perhaps is something of a transitional piece in the psalm as well.

Nonetheless, the Joseph story both in Genesis and in the psalm makes a theological point all its own. The point is that the experience and destiny of Israel are guided and presided over by Yahweh, who in hidden ways shapes the decisive moves in the life of Joseph. Specifically we may notice three (perhaps two) occasions for such inscrutable governance in the wording of the psalm. First, Yahweh called ("summoned") the famine (Ps. 105:16). Second, Yahweh "sent a man" (v. 17). Third, Yahweh sent a king (v. 20). This third usage is ambiguous in the Hebrew. The NRSV takes "the king" (=Pharaoh) as subject of the verb. It is possible, however, to take Yahweh as the subject of the verb, as in v. 17, making the king the object of the verb, as is the man in v. 17. (Notice the same verb in Gen. 45:5, 7, 8.) Thus Joseph's life and all of life around him is permeated with God's hidden but decisive purpose, God's firm but hidden dispatch of God's agents.

The outcome of God's governance concerns Joseph's life. At the outset he is "sold as a slave" and is in fetters (vs. 17–18). He is weak, powerless, and without authority or any prospect of authority. His fate turns abruptly to well-being, because his interpretations of dreams come true. His capacity to so interpret dreams comes from his God-given gift of discernment. As a result of that capacity, he is released and elevated to power as the king's top adviser and de facto ruler. This is a tale of the humiliated become exalted, the last becoming first. Joseph is a case study of the way in which God acts characteristically in Israel's life to work good from evil (e.g., Gen. 50:20).

The concluding verse of the psalm (v. 45) shows that Israel's act of remembering, which dominates this psalm, is in order to evoke obedience to God's Torah, on which see Proper 12.

Thus the Joseph story concerns God's *providential care,* which transforms human prospects. The human correlation to God's providence is *obedience.* In this psalm Israel resolves to practice obedience to the providential (hidden) purpose of God in its life, which is decisive and works good in every circumstance. While the conclusion to the psalm invites obedience to statutes and ordinances (on which see Proper 12), the remembering in the middle verses of today's text invites to an obedience less precise, but more overwhelming in its claims. Israel, like Joseph, acts in the conviction that God is with him for prosperity, working in ways that are not easily noticed.

Romans 10:5–15

Of all the lectionary readings taken from Romans, this one may deserve to be labeled as the most challenging for the preacher. To begin with, the reading seems to have no concrete setting at all. It appears in the middle of what is already a digression about how it is that Israel "did not succeed in fulfilling that law" (Rom. 9:31). As a whole, of course, Rom. 9–11 considers whether Israel's rejection of Jesus as Messiah compromises God's faithfulness to God's promises. In 9:31–10:21, Paul departs from that larger topic to give an account of Israel's situation. The present lection comes within that digression, but, as it stands, nothing in the lection concretely refers to Israel, making it easy to speak in abstract and vague terms that ignore the context. On the other hand, explaining the context could involve the preacher in a lengthy excursus.

Even without these problems of context, the passage presents an array of difficulties. Is Paul contrasting the "righteousness that comes from the law" with the "righteousness that comes from faith," as most commentators insist? Or is he engaging in a scriptural argument to demonstrate that the two are in fact the same? Does he draw on preexisting Christian tradition, on Jewish interpretive practices, or on Jewish wisdom reflection? A review of the standard commentaries will show just how contested is virtually every inch of this exegetical turf.

How might the preacher approach this passage without becoming sidetracked by either these internal exegetical questions or the complicated relationship between this passage and its context? One approach might be to attend here to the way in which Paul engages in a lively reading of scripture. (For an extremely suggestive discussion of Paul's exegesis, see Richard Hays, *Echoes of Scripture in the Letters of Paul;* New Haven, Conn.: Yale University Press, 1989.) Although a recital of the technical discussion about Paul's use of scripture here would be deadly, stepping back from that debate to notice Paul's profound engagement with scripture might be very illuminating. The passage opens with a quotation from Lev. 18:5, and then takes up lines from Deut. 30:11–14, which Paul reads through the lens of Christian proclamation; it is Christ who is in heaven and Christ who comes up from death. Deuteronomy 30:14 becomes, for Paul, a summation of what it means to confess faith in Jesus Christ with the mouth and with the heart. Quotations from Isa. 28:16 and Joel 2:32 reinforce Paul's ongoing argument about the gospel's inclusion of all, both Jew and Greek.

Even the most cursory study shows that Paul blatantly ignores the historical context of these passages. That, of course, is to be expected; he follows the exegetical conventions of the first century rather than the twentieth. What is more important, however, is that here we see Paul's sense of engagement with scripture. He is not so much reading scripture here and interpreting it (an action by Paul on a passive object), or even turning to it as an authoritative source of information, as he is in lively and enlivening conversation with it. He seeks in scripture language that will enable him to address the needs of the present.

Another possibility for preaching from this passage is to focus on its articulation of continuity between God's actions in the past and those in the present. This issue certainly is directly connected with the way in which Paul reads scripture, for he sees in scripture evidence that, even in Israel's past, what God wanted was "the righteousness that comes from faith" (10:6). To say that Deuteronomy refers to Christ (vs. 6–7) is, historically speaking, absurd and can promote a supersessionist mentality. What Paul is after, however, is a way of asserting that God's dealings with Israel have remained faithful and fair. After all, one way of responding to the anguish of Rom. 9:1–5 is to say that God is the guilty party, that God has proven to be fickle (see the denial of this claim as early as 9:6 and throughout Rom. 9–11).

Yet another aspect of this passage that might lend itself to preaching occurs in vs. 11–13, with its insistence on the universal availability of God's salvation. When Paul quotes from Isa. 28:16 in v. 11, he inserts "no one," making the way for the inclusive claims of vs. 12 and 13. There is "no distinction between Jew and Greek," God is "Lord of all" and generous "to all," and "everyone" who calls on God will be saved. This prominent theme from the early chapters of Romans returns as Paul recalls that God's salvation knows no boundaries. Just as all stand condemned of sin, so all may live within God's salvation.

The final verses of this lection (vs. 14–15) are intimately connected with the passage that follows (through 10:21), about Israel's unwillingness to hear the word that has been preached. Read in connection with vs. 5–13 and apart from the conclusion of the chapter, they add little to the passage. Nevertheless, they constitute a powerful reminder to preachers about the importance of their task. With the plethora of expectations and responsibilities most pastors carry, it is altogether too easy to demote preaching into one more routine task of the week. Paul's words here, surely a reflection of his own sense of vocation (see also Rom. 15:14–21), forcefully recall for contemporary preachers the place of Christian proclamation in the mission of God and God's church.

Matthew 14:22–33

The story of Jesus' walking on the water is found in three of the Gospels—Matthew, Mark, and John—but Matthew provides by far the fullest account, the only one to include the information about Peter's walking on the water to meet Jesus. The care with which the story is told, from its initial setting through to the disciples' confession, means that it is rich in details and offers a mine of possibilities for the preacher.

For example, we discover that Jesus amid the pressure of his ministry finds the time and place to pray. He makes deliberate plans to escape both the disciples and the crowds in order to be alone (Matt. 14:22–23). This comes after a previous effort to do so was foiled (v. 13). But alongside the praying of Jesus, the narrator juxtaposes the situation of the disciples, struggling through the night against a stormy sea. The bifocal picture is remarkable in its realism.

Then there are the comforting words Jesus speaks to the frightened disciples, who are terrified by the figure coming to them on the sea: "Take heart, it is I; do not be afraid" (v. 27). The whole gospel is wrapped up in such a reassurance. Again, at the end of the story, there is the response of the disciples, who have watched and listened to all that has taken place and can do nothing but worship and confess Jesus as the Son of God (a remarkable confession, since it occurs two chapters ahead of Peter's confession at Caesarea Philippi).

But the heart of the incident for Matthew is the interchange with Peter and his walking, sinking, and rescue (vs. 28–32). It intrudes into the story between the initial disclosure of Jesus and the dying down of the winds and thereby becomes the climax of this unit of material.

First, notice Peter's unusual request: "Lord, if it is you, command me to come to you on the water" (v. 28). He addresses Jesus as believers or serious seekers do in Matthew's narrative ("Lord"), and predicates his petition on the truth of Jesus' presence. There may be a tinge of uncertainty in Peter's words (the clause translated "if it is you" could just as easily be rendered "since it is you"), but what is most striking is the recognition that this extraordinary request has no validity apart from the command of Jesus. Peter does not so much ask for supernatural powers as he asks to recognize that whatever Jesus commands, Jesus makes possible. The commands of Jesus, taken seriously, create miracles; they open an incredible reservoir of divine resources. Apart from such commands, not much unusual is going to happen.

Second, when the command is spoken, Peter gets out of the boat and begins to walk toward Jesus. Dietrich Bonhoeffer's classic analysis of Peter's response is worth citing.

> Peter had to leave the ship and risk his life on the sea, in order to learn both his own weakness and the almighty power of his Lord. If Peter had not taken the risk, he would never have learned the meaning of faith . . . . The road to faith passes through obedience to the call of Jesus. Unless a definite step is demanded, the call vanishes into thin air, and if [people] imagine that they can follow Jesus without taking this step, they are deluding themselves like fanatics.

Bonhoeffer goes on to draw the theological paradox that emerges from this scene: only the one who believes is obedient, and only the one who is obedient believes. "Faith is only real where there is obedience, never without it, and faith only becomes faith in the act of obedience" (*The Cost of Discipleship;* New York: Macmillan Co., 1960, pp. 53–60). Had Peter remained in the boat and not taken the first step, his faith would have been worthless.

Third, Peter walks, becomes frightened by the wind, begins to sink, cries out to Jesus, and is rescued. This familiar sequence of actions needs to be understood in light of the obedient act that put Peter on the water in the first place. It is not the story of the skeptic who habitually doubts, but the story of the faithful follower who becomes overwhelmed by the circumstances surrounding him, who begins to lose his nerve when he discovers the odds stacked against him, but who from Jesus finds a steadying, delivering hand. The phrase "you of little faith" occurs in two other places in Matthew—for those anxious about clothing (6:30) and for the disciples in the boat anxious about the storm (8:26).

In this story Peter becomes a mirror in which disciples, ancient and modern, are able to see themselves and to take heart. They find courage from his daring response to Jesus' command and from Jesus' gracious move to secure his faltering faith.

PROPER 15

Ordinary Time 20

Sunday between
August 14 and 20 inclusive

There is no indication that the various texts appointed by the lectionary for this day were chosen for congruity of themes. And yet a close reading of these passages discloses that, in one fashion or another, they all speak to the issue of the mercy of God. In addition, several of them also speak of the manner in which God's mercy promotes human reconciliation.

The text from Gen. 45 is part of the climax of the cycle of Joseph stories. How intriguing from a purely literary standpoint is this passage, for it portrays Joseph in a moment of triumph. The trials of the past are over, and his trembling brothers—whose evil intentions sent him to Egypt in the fist place—are now in his power. But instead of venting on them a wrathful spirit, Joseph acknowledges God's hand in the events of his life and—in a powerful emotional scene—is reconciled to those who attempted to do him harm.

Psalm 133 is a brief but exuberant song to the spirit of unity and fellowship that can (and should!) exist among the members of the family of God. Community harmony is like precious oil, like mountain dew. It is a blessing from none other than the God of Israel.

Paul, who sharply felt the irony of the rejection of God's Messiah by God's chosen people, in Rom. 11 delivers a resounding "no" to the idea that God has now rejected Israel. One of the results of human disobedience is an outpouring of the mercy of God, and such will surely be the case in the present instance. God's election is irrevocable. In fact, Paul uses daring language which affirms that "all" are the recipients of God's mercy.

The wide umbrella of God's mercy is surely illustrated by the story of Jesus and the Canaanite woman in Matt. 15. The woman's faith and persistence, in a situation where she might easily have been intimidated, serves in a curious manner to minister to Jesus. As she becomes a means of God's grace to Jesus, Jesus extends God's mercy to her.

Genesis 45:1–15

Avarice and greed, jealousy and sibling rivalry, sex, politics, and palace intrigue—such are the ingredients of the story of Joseph! Small wonder that this section of the book of Genesis (chaps. 37–47) has been favorite reading for Jews and Christians over the centuries, for it mirrors human nature in every age. Yet to concentrate on these characteristics exclusively is to lose sight of the central thrust of the cycle of Joseph stories, namely, that in and through all the events of Joseph's life God was at work to save the people. Most immediately the people who benefit from God's grace are old Jacob and his family, but the ultimate object of God's loving intervention in Joseph's life is all humankind.

In terms of the development of the plot of the Joseph stories, this lection from Gen. 45 is crucial. Joseph has now become the virtual ruler of all Egypt, having survived threats to his life and well-being that are familiar to everyone who knows this tale, including a murderous plot by his brothers, attempted seduction by the wife of a powerful Egyptian, and the forgetfulness of the royal cupbearer. The famine that has ravaged Egypt has also desolated Palestine, so that Joseph's brothers, in their efforts to find food, have come face-to-face with the brother whom they earlier had sold into slavery. Yet, in an ironic twist, while Joseph recognizes them, they are ignorant of the identity of this powerful official with whom they have been negotiating and before whom they now stand condemned of theft. In purely literary terms, what could be a juicier turn of events: Joseph, with one wave of his hand, may now avenge the terrible wrong done to him so long ago by snuffing out the life or the liberty of these trembling sons of Jacob.

But that is not Joseph's way, because that is not God's way, and Joseph is—first, last, and always—God's man (notice v. 8). Joseph's virtual collapse in the presence of his brothers reveals his awareness of God's role in his life as much as it reveals his humanity. Only the Egyptians are meant to be excluded from this catharsis, lest they misinterpret Joseph's tears for weakness.

The emotional energy displayed by Joseph is countered by the awestruck dumbness of the eleven. Are they unable to speak simply because they find this revelation hard to believe, or is it out of terror over what might soon happen to them at the hands of their long-lost but now powerful brother? Probably both, but it is their terror-for-their-lives that Joseph addresses by attempting to calm them (v. 5). The reason for comfort that Joseph extends has nothing directly to do with his own emotions, although his concern for his father (v. 3) would doubtless have ruled out any violence against his brothers, even if Joseph had been so inclined. His brothers are to be at peace because "God sent me before you to preserve life" (v. 5). Notice that the phrase "God sent me" (or its equivalent) is repeated in vs. 7 and 8. (Compare v. 8: "God . . . made me a father to Pharaoh" and v. 9: "God has made me lord of all Egypt.") Not only does Joseph want to reassure his astonished brothers, but those who are responsible for the text, in the shape that it has reached us, want to be sure that we, the readers, do not miss the whole point of the narrative: behind all the events of Joseph's life, God was at work to bring good out of evil.

The arrangements for the family's comfort that Joseph outlines in vs. 10–11 provide a kind of denouement to the drama. The blood still races with excitement over Joseph's startling self-disclosure, but Joseph pushes forward to other things. After urging the inclusion of their father in this new life, Joseph outlines to the eleven what kind of life it will be. In spite of the five years the famine has still to run, theirs will be a time of peace and plenty under Joseph's personal protection. Their families, including children and grandchildren, will be secure, even their flocks and herds. Only then, after Joseph has hugged and kissed them all, are the brothers' tongues unlocked and they begin to talk to him (v. 15).

It is as difficult for modern people as it was for ancient people to believe that God is at work even in the dark and destructive moments of life. One of the great obstacles to faith is that, no matter how hard one tries, it simply is not possible to identify grace or redemption in so many human experiences. And it is easy—some would say, compelling—to extrapolate from that that God is *never* present in human suffering and defeat. But the Joseph stories lead us to a different conclusion, which is that, in spite of the awful tragedies from which God seems irretrievably absent, the Ruler of the universe is a caring friend and will ultimately have a friend's way.

So, in the Joseph stories, Joseph is a paradigm of what the grace of God can do in human life: transform a curse into a blessing. But Joseph is himself a metaphor for God: the One who has every reason to reject a wayward human family, but who instead loves them even to the point of the One's own participation in their suffering.

(Note the discussion of most of this lection text at the Seventh Sunday After Epiphany, year C.)

Psalm 133

This brief psalm is now placed in a larger group of "Songs of Ascents" (Pss. 120–134), presumably grouped together to be used in pilgrimage toward the Jerusalem Temple. The entire group tends to be buoyant and somewhat celebrative, the kind we might expect in a group of joyous, exuberant pilgrims on their way to Jerusalem. Such a literary-liturgical context, however, does not tell us much about the psalm itself.

Psalm 133:1. The theme of the psalm is clear and succinct in the first verse. To have members of an extended family (tribe) living together in harmony and unity is a wondrous thing, "good and pleasant." The alternative, which this poem wants to reject, is that a family should be at cross-purposes, quarrelsome, inclined to hostility, and, in the case of a tribe, given to internecine vengeance. Thus the poem affirms and celebrates a community that functions in a healthy, reconciling way.

This vision of communal harmony may be rooted in a quite concrete social experience. The imagery of vs. 2–3a suggests that this may be a specific agricultural community, one most likely to dispute over land and property (see Luke 12:13).

Verses 2–3a. These lines, focused in two metaphors, are subservient to the theme of v. 1. The poet characterizes the goodness and loveliness of communal harmony in two ways. First, such communal harmony is like precious oil, in which a community may luxuriate when it is festive, secure, and prosperous. Oil was a scarce and precious commodity in a local community, and was to be used only for the essentials of life, such as light and heat. But on festive occasions oil might be "wasted" in extravagance, when one could be showered with it as a sign of peculiar well-being. One can imagine a community without any surplus of riches on occasion permitting itself extravagance that is economically wasteful—life is so good that it must be marked by luxury (cf. Mark 14:3–9). Communal harmony is as good as extravagant oil, overflowing in joy and delight, turning life into a celebration of well-being that is unguarded, careless, and generous. A community at peace is one with more than enough.

Second, communal harmony is like mountain dew. This image may be peculiarly poignant in an arid climate, where any hint of moisture is a special gift and a cause for joy. The two images of oil and dew reinforce each other, and together present a picture of extravagant well-being—that is what harmony is like!

Verse 3b. The incidental reference to Zion in v. 3a permits what appears to be the add-on line of v. 3b. This line seems to have no direct relation to the rest of the poem. Indeed, it has been suggested that the Songs of Ascents have been systemically transformed by additional reference to Zion. This could be the case if older songs have been reused by pilgrims to Jerusalem. In any case, the incidental reference to Zion in v. 3a in the next line is taken as the main subject. Now Zion is "there." Jerusalem is the place wherein the blessing of God, life forever, is located. But even if this line is somewhat extraneous to the poem, the motif of "blessing" nicely returns to the images of oil and dew, for "blessing" refers to all that enhances and affirms life.

The bold affirmation of our psalm is that shared human community is itself an experience of the life that God intends. Such an equation of shared community with life is a warning against religious individualism, which imagines one can have gospel blessings all alone, one at a time, and against a religious community that may be serious about faith but is contentious and fractious, thereby contradicting its very reason for being. This equation of shared community and life is most poignantly asserted in 1 John 3:14:

> We know that we have passed from death to life because we love one another. Whoever does not love abides in death.

In quite concrete and practical ways, our psalm anticipates the Johannine transposition of resurrection into genuine community.

Romans 11:1–2a, 29–32

As the reading for Proper 13 identifies God's gifts to Israel, this reading begins with the unavoidable question about the present standing of Israel: "Has God rejected his people?" The resounding "no" of Rom. 11:1 is quickly followed by a variety of arguments (omitted from the lection). First, Paul insists that a remnant does believe (vs. 2–5). Then, he argues that Israel's rejection has served for the inclusion of the Gentiles (vs. 7–12). Third, he turns to Gentile Christians with the claim that the Gentiles have a role to play in the salvation of Israel (vs. 13–16). So Paul reasons in this chapter, characterizing his ministry as that of making Israel jealous of the Gentiles so that the final inclusion of Israel will be great indeed.

The lectionary omits vs. 2b–28, presumably because of the lengthy nature of the point Paul is making here. It is difficult to address any part of this section of the letter in isolation from the whole, so awkward decisions about passages are inevitable. Nevertheless, the reading as presently defined omits a crucial part of Paul's address to the Gentiles: Gentile Christians have no right to boast about their election by God and to exalt themselves above Jews. "If you do boast, remember that it is not you that support the root, but the root that supports you" (v. 18). Gentiles have entered into the community by means of the root of Israel and cannot turn around and boast of their place as if it were their own accomplishment.

Much of Rom. 11 involves Paul in speculation about the way in which events will unfold. Israel will be grafted in again (v. 23). God has hardened Israel temporarily, for the sake of the Gentile mission. At the completion of that mission, Israel will again return (v. 25). Paul here stretches to envision the time when both Gentiles and Jews will fully participate in the blessings inaugurated by Jesus Christ. The details of the future Paul imagines matter far less than the ultimate outcome: the salvation of all God's people. For Paul, the rejection of the Messiah cannot mean that Israel is cut off from God; therefore, it must mean that these events are occurring as part of God's will.

In the second part of the passage as defined by the lectionary, 11:29–32, Paul moves beyond this attempt to explain God's actions and returns to the theological convictions that form the foundation of this section. First, "the gifts and the calling of God are irrevocable." To say that Israel was called by God in the past requires, with absolute certainty, the conclusion that Israel is called by God in the present and the future. Regardless of Israel's actions or inactions, the call of God remains in force. This conclusion comes, not because Israel has somehow earned the right to keep God's calling, quite apart from faithfulness or unfaithfulness. This conclusion comes solely because any other conclusion implies that God cannot be counted on, that God is faithless. Romans 9–11 begins with the question, Has God's word failed? and ends with a resounding, No! As often in this letter, what motivates Paul is less the need to explain the human situation (in this instance, Israel's standing before God) than the need to explain the fidelity of God. Regardless of Israel, regardless of the Gentiles, God's word holds secure.

In vs. 30–31 Paul moves to a second point. If God's calling is irrevocable, and yet Israel manifestly does not accept Jesus as Messiah, then there must be a reason for Israel's rejection. Paul locates that reason in the mission to the Gentiles; that is, the disobedience of the Jews has brought about the Gentile mission, and the mercy shown to Gentiles will eventually bring about the inclusion of Jews. Jews have played an unwitting role in the Gentile mission, and Gentiles will play a role in the Jewish mission. That mutuality of Jew and Gentile reflects the fundamental point that they hold in common. Despite their many differences, both Jew and Gentile have been disobedient; God has acted and will act to redeem both. Here the letter circles back to the point made in 1:18–3:21. As surely as all human beings,

Jew and Gentile, have rebelled against God, just as surely God has acted in Jesus Christ to show them mercy.

The final statement of the passage makes explicit Paul's point about the universality of God's grace: "For God has imprisoned all in disobedience so that he may be merciful to all." Taken in isolation, this statement suggests that God has been playing a kind of game with humanity, first casting all humanity into prison, and then setting them free. In the context of Paul's reflection on the ways in which Jew and Gentile have interacted, however, a different reading emerges. God "has imprisoned all in disobedience" means not only that God allowed God's creatures the freedom to rebel, as Rom. 1 makes clear, but also that God has used the rebellion of the Jews for the sake of the inclusion of the Gentiles.

Finally, however, God's goal is that of mercy for all human beings. The universalism of this statement often provokes objections that God's mercy is for all who repent or for all who call on God's name. Often it is those who faithfully serve the church and strive to do good who especially protest this assertion of the breadth of God's mercy. The assertion, however, stands. God's mercy extends to all people, none of whom can claim it by virtue of their own goodness.

Matthew 15:(10–20) 21–28

This marvelous story of Jesus' engagement with the Canaanite woman, her ministry to him, and his ministry to her offers rich resources for preaching, but the story needs to be treated with great care. Interpreters are often scared away by Jesus' use of a rather harsh metaphor for the woman as a non-Jew, a feature of the narrative that simply cannot be ignored or easily dismissed. Any sermon on the text today has to confront honestly the epithet of "dogs" and what it may imply about the relation of Jesus and the woman.

It helps to recognize that this is a story told from a Jewish point of view. Most of us who read it are non-Jews, and it takes an imaginative leap to appreciate its original impact. The woman, of course, is a Canaanite, but she acknowledges Jesus' Jewish status by addressing him as "Son of David." Jesus does not answer her, but when the disciples, annoyed by her persistence, want him to send her away, he says to them, "I was sent only to the lost sheep of the house of Israel." We hear in these words echoes of Jesus' earlier charge to the disciples (10:5–6, 23) and the recurring theme of Matthew's narrative that the gospel belongs first to Israel.

Though the Jewish religious authorities repeatedly come in for scathing judgment, the narrator of this Gospel wants to make absolutely clear that God has not abandoned the Jews, God's faithfulness to the covenant remains, and Jesus' ministry is first and foremost to Israel. There is no equivocating on that point. Only *after* the crucifixion and resurrection is the door thrown wide open to the non-Jewish world (28:16–20). Before that time only here and there in the story—the Magi (2:1–12), the centurion (8:5–13), the Canaanite woman—do we catch glimpses of God's all-inclusive intentions. Thus Jesus' apparent reluctance in responding to the petitions of the Canaanite woman serves to underscore the priority of the Jews in the divine economy.

This gets us to the heart of the story. The Canaanite woman wrenches from Jesus the blessing that she, as a non-Jewish mother, needs. First, she is persistent. She refuses to be deterred either by Jesus' reluctance or by the disciples' irritation. She perseveres in her conviction that Jesus can do for her what she desperately needs. Jesus finally comments, "Woman, great is your faith!" In her single-minded pursuit of Jesus, she presents a remarkable contrast to the scribes and Pharisees with their legal entanglements (15:1–9) and the disciples with their lack of understanding (15:10–20).

But the Canaanite woman is not only persistent; she is free of pretension. Though she comes and kneels before him, Jesus, whose focus is on the primary mission to Israel, addresses to her a severe parable (v. 26). The use of the term "dogs," even though metaphorical and possibly to be translated as "puppies," is hardly a label of endearment. It was regularly applied, with some condescension, to Gentiles. The woman has every right to take offense. But her response, certainly to be read as more than a witty retort, indicates that she is beyond recrimination: "Yet even the dogs eat the crumbs that fall from their masters' table" (v. 27). She is willing to wear the label as long as she can get food from the table. In effect, she accepts her secondary status as an outsider, a Gentile, but takes the risk of remaining a petitioner.

The woman with her persistence and lack of pretension in a sense performs a ministry for Jesus. She becomes the spokesperson to him to bring about the release of divine grace in a dramatic event of healing. She becomes the model voice from beyond the boundaries who stakes her claim on the mercy and generosity of God. Just as others minister to Jesus by providing food or housing, she ministers by facilitating his movement across ethnic borders, an action that anticipates the wider mission to the world.

But just as the woman ministers to Jesus, Jesus ministers to the woman. Her demon-possessed child is healed. The Son of David renders wholeness to a Gentile daughter. As in the case of the healing of the centurion's son (8:5–13), there is no touching or dramatic action. The spoken word effects the cure. The miracle of faith is confirmed by the miracle of healing.

If the preacher chooses to include the section 15:10–20, then a remarkable contrast is established between the failure to understand on the part of the crowds, the disciples, and Peter, and the profound understanding of the Canaanite woman. As an outsider, she grasps what they as Jews cannot perceive—that the good news belongs also to the outsiders.

PROPER 16

Ordinary Time 21

Sunday between
August 21 and 27 inclusive

These texts have no common theme. They all do bear witness to the rich and powerful sovereignty of God, who generously gives life.

In the Old Testament narrative from Ex. 1 and 2, both the future of Israel and the future of God's plans for all humanity are imperiled. "A new king arose over Egypt" (1:8) was a reality that boded ominously for God's chosen, but captive, people. The circumstances surrounding the birth of Moses are reflective of this danger, and, at one level, the infant is saved only by the cunning of his mother and sister and by the compassion of the Egyptian princess. Yet the reader is alert to the truth that, in the end, Moses is saved only by the grace of God.

Psalm 124 looks beyond the birth of Moses to the moment of the exodus, and celebrates with great joy God's redemption of the people. In daring syntax the poet first poses the question of God's absence, but quickly rejects that possibility in favor of the gleeful realization that the Lord was present at the exodus in a mighty and saving way. The imagery of the trapped bird, now liberated from its confinement, describes the condition of God's saved people, and the vivid impression is made that only by the help of God can humans find life and freedom.

The familiar words of Rom. 12 have struck many readers as a moment when Paul turns from a "theological" to an "ethical" discussion. Yet such a characterization overlooks the essentially theological nature of all of Romans. Paul is, in reality, calling for the transformation of the person through the power of God. The imperative is "be transformed," not "transform yourselves," thus placing primary emphasis on the activity of God in the life of the Christian.

The Gospel reading from Matt. 16 is a confession of Jesus' identity as the Messiah, "Son of the living God." Although this incident is recorded in each of the four Gospels, Matthew's distinctive emphasis is on the rootedness of the church in the disciples' recognition of the messianic nature of Jesus. Certain burdens (notably conflict and suffering) and certain opportunities ("the keys of the kingdom") flow from this confessional foundation.

Exodus 1:8–2:10

In this first of a series of lections whose subject is Moses, a wide panorama is spread before the reader and interpreter, an expansive sweep both in time and in the experience of the special people of God. "A new king arose over Egypt" (Ex. 1:8) are words that toll ominously for the Israelites and that warn of oppressive times ahead. The enforced servitude that ensues was to be terrible to remember, for the narrative (vs. 9–14) bristles with such emotive words as "dread," "ruthless," and "bitter." Pharaoh's decree that every Hebrew male child is to be killed (v. 22) forms a brutal climax to the effort to contain the Israelites.

But the text moves on to include the tender and redemptive story of the birth of Moses (2:1–10). The unnamed mother of Moses (how tragic that her courage is not rewarded by the mention of her name!; but see Ex. 6:20) stands as typical of the Israelites' bravery and resourcefulness, as does the young sister, presumably Miriam, who watches the watery crib from afar and steps forward at just the right moment. Moses' mother is blessed in being allowed to nurse the child, but cursed in subsequently having to surrender the boy to the royal princess. (The role of the princess is only sketchily told, but her dim portrait is painted with great sympathy. She would have been an idiot not to guess that the Hebrew woman, her breasts bursting with milk, was Moses' mother. Yet she treats with great kindness both mother and child.)

However, if Moses' mother receives a limited blessing in giving suck to the child, the ultimate blessing is to be on all Israel and, through Israel, on all humankind, for Moses is to live. All who have read the story to its completion know that Red Sea and Sinai and successful journey through the wilderness are made possible because Moses is to live. These great paradigms of freedom and deliverance will now come to pass because of the compassion of the royal princess and the tortured courage of Moses' mother.

And also because of the faithfulness of God! *Fundamentally* because of the faithfulness and compassion of God! Not only is God's role made clear in the brief pericope concerning the courage of the

Hebrew midwives (Ex. 1:15–21), but the book of Exodus as a whole leaves no doubt that events are moving toward a redemptive climax, not accidentally or haphazardly, but because of the involvement of God in the life of the people (cf. Gen. 3:7–12). The oppressive hand of Pharaoh may be strong, but the redemptive hand of God is stronger still.

Thus the text conveys a decided sense of momentum. The passage of time (of unspecified duration in the text, yet clearly involving some years) is the setting for a movement from oppression toward freedom, from despair toward hope. The redemption that God is to bring to the lives of the people is not yet a reality. Much suffering is still to be endured, much patience called for, yet the birth of Moses unambiguously signals that God is at work in the life of Israel and that the evil represented by Pharaoh's schemes will not prevail.

Of special significance is the nature of God's redemptive activity, unlike that which is portrayed in other parts of the Old Testament. Often God is described as responding to the cries of the people when they are in need, cries that reflect the people's sense of sin and their recognition that only in God's strength can they obtain protection and salvation. The book of Judges, for example, plays on this theme repeatedly as when, in response to the people's realization of their waywardness and their appeals for help (Judg. 4:1–3), Yahweh raises Deborah to free the people from the oppression of the Canaanites.

But notable by their absence from the story of Moses' birth are any indictment of the people and any pleas from the people for God's assistance in their time of distress. The people are imperiled through no fault of their own, and while God understands their need and responds to it, God has not as yet been invited by the people to do so. These are qualities of the narrative that strongly suggest a multidimensional character to God's compassion. The mercy of God is not simply reactive, returning love for love. It is proactive—seeing human need even more profoundly than they who endure that need, and benevolently intruding into their lives even when unbidden.

The generations of ancient Israel yet unborn would come, in time, to celebrate this strange and paradoxical grace of God, a grace that is responsive, in different ways, to both human sin and human faithfulness. Yet it is a grace that is constantly there, even when women and men have not formed their lips to speak its name. It is little wonder that the psalmist would joyfully proclaim, in the words of this day's psalm text (Ps. 124:1, 4):

> If it had not been [Yahweh] who was on our side . . .
> then the flood would have swept us away.

And it is little wonder that the early church, having discovered God's mercy in Jesus of Nazareth, would sing:

> Thanks be to God through Jesus Christ our Lord! (Rom. 7:25)

Psalm 124

This poem is utterly realistic about the vulnerability of faithful living. Evil is powerful, and we are helpless in the face of it. The poem juxtaposes two different scenarios of human destiny. On the one hand, imagine life as a two-membered conflict between "us" and the "enemy." In that unequal contest, the speaker is hopeless, unable to compete or withstand (Ps. 124:1–5). On the other hand, however, imagine life as a three-membered conflict (vs. 6–7). There is again us and the enemy. There is now, however, a third party, Yahweh, present and vigorous. That third party changes everything and reshapes the unequal contest. Faith, so deeply settled in this psalm, is the profound affirmation that this third party is decisively present in the serious conflicts of life.

The psalm begins with a dependent clause (repeated, vs. 1–2). It entertains a negative possibility: "If Yahweh were not on our side . . ." That negative possibility is stated only theoretically, because exactly the opposite is true: Yahweh is indeed *for us,* decisively, insistently, relentlessly. This is the premise of the psalm, and indeed the premise of Israel's faith. This alliance of Yahweh "with us" changes the psalm as it changes reality. God "for us" is the most foundational claim of evangelical faith, here expressed in a military metaphor (cf. Rom. 8:37 for another military metaphor).

Only now do we reach the main clause (vs. 3–5). Verses 1–2 are governed by a double "if," which has turned out to be a condition contrary to fact. In fact Yahweh *is* and *was* on our side. The main clause continues from the "if" of vs. 1–2. The main clause tells, with a threefold "then," the consequences of the double "if" of vs. 1–2. If Yahweh had not been on our side, "then . . . then . . . then." The poet uses the metaphors of "flood . . . torrent . . . raging waters" to characterize the deathly disorder that would occur without the protective alliance of God.

Verses 1–5 create a scenario of threat, danger, and destruction. The entire if-then proposal, however, is false; it fails to reckon with the crucial role of Yahweh in the midst of such human threat. Thus vs. 1–5 are voiced as a foil to prepare us for the affirmation that follows in the remainder of the psalm.

The poet now offers an alternative vision of reality, which has Yahweh at its center (vs. 6–8). The result is that we have been kept from the devouring teeth that could chew us to bits. Verse 7 is constructed as a chiasmus: "escape . . . snare . . . snare . . . escape." The threat is a snare; the image is that of a basket in which birds are trapped. The snare, however, is resisted. At the beginning and end of the verse, "we have escaped." We have remained free and unfettered, because God "has not given us as prey." Thus, in vs. 6–7, God has been faithful and therefore we are safe.

The concluding statement is a sweeping doxology which connects this rescue to a cosmic affirmation (v. 8). The God concerned for us is the creator of all things (cf. Ps. 146:6–9 for the same linkage of cosmic sovereignty and immediate help). The power sustaining heaven and earth is mobilized on behalf of us in our particular crisis. This ultimately powerful God is concretely faithful and engaged, and therefore we are safe.

The rhetoric of this psalm is relentlessly about *us.* It abounds in first-person-plural pronouns—we, our, us. This is the voice of a community remembering deep danger and noticing miraculous deliverance. This is indeed a poem about *us.* Our life, however, is imaginatively positioned vis-à-vis the reality of Yahweh. At the beginning, God is hypothetically eliminated from the psalm (vs. 1–2). In the center, God is blessed for being present, for cosmic power and for concrete fidelity (v. 6). The fabric of the poem embeds us in God's life, entwines God in our life, and thereby permits us to affirm "God with us" when life is under threat.

Israel's life is incessantly in danger. Faith is the capacity to read, discern, and live that life under threat, always in solidarity with God. The psalm is the voice of trust, confident about a counterlife with God, beyond threat, utterly liberated and confident.

Romans 12:1–8

In Rom. 12 Paul turns from what is usually designated the "theological" section of the letter to the task of offering "ethical" instruction. This careful distinction between theology and ethics is artificial and alien to Paul, for it ignores the ethical implications in Rom. 1–11, just as it ignores the theological framework for Rom. 12–15. Paul's appeal in 12:1 to "the mercies of God" firmly connects the two parts of the letter. The ethical admonitions that follow have as their motivation neither anticipation of a reward nor fear of punishment, but "the mercies of God." That phrase refers back to the whole of Rom.

1–11. Because of all that God has already done on behalf of human beings, Paul urges Christians to respond appropriately.

An appropriate response consists of presenting "your bodies as a living sacrifice, holy and acceptable to God, which is your spiritual worship." Here Paul joins the language of worship to the demand for the giving over the whole person, for "body" (*sōma*) means not simply the physical body, but the entire person. Only the gift of the entire person constitutes "spiritual" or, better, "reasonable" worship. What Paul is after here is much more radical than a contrast between the sacrificial system of Judaism and some spiritual Christian worship. He calls for the presentation of the whole self as the only acceptable offering.

Verse 2 elaborates that point with its call for transformation. As is clear elsewhere in this letter, Paul understands that the gospel brings about transformation in the lives of human beings. The Christian faith is not simply another religious practice to be taken up and carried out alongside other commitments. The gospel shatters the lives of those whom it touches, whatever their background or starting point. Being "conformed to this world," then, is assessing oneself and all of creation through the eyes of the world. Believers, by contrast, are to be transformed.

Paul gives few concrete details about transformation, but several features of v. 2 help to shape an understanding of it. First, the injunction is to "be transformed," not to "transform yourselves." That is, transformation comes about as the gift of God and not as the accomplishment of human beings. Second, transformation involves the mind: "be transformed by the renewing of your minds." Here the Greek word is *nous,* which comes close to the contemporary English notion of "mind-set." Transformation comes about not simply by having the right thoughts or the appropriate intellectual framework, but by a change in the way in which people think. This passage recalls other passages in Paul's letters in which he characterizes the differences between believers and nonbelievers as a difference of perception (for example, 1 Cor. 1:18; 2 Cor. 4:3–4).

One result of this transformation is that believers are enabled to "discern what is the will of God." The relationship between God and believers is such that believers have a glimpse of the divine will. The prospect of such discernment will fill some Christians with awe and others with eagerness. What it demonstrates is the extent to which Paul is convinced that the gospel has real power to bring about change—dramatic change—in human lives. It can even empower people to discern God's will. Contemporary Christians, who see both in history and in themselves the continual failings of believers, may suspect that Paul is naive about human nature, but there is ample evidence that Paul knew the limitations of Christians. Nevertheless, he *expected* the gospel to transform human lives, an expectation that much of the Christian church has ceased to share and needs to rediscover.

The call to present the self and the call for transformation form the basis for all the ethical instructions that follow in chapters 12–15. The Christian belongs to God and operates with a mind-set that has been formed by the gospel; what she or he does must conform to that fundamental understanding. The specific section contained in this lectionary reading, vs. 1–8, pertains largely to life within the Christian community. Here Paul takes up an issue that acutely influenced the Corinthian church, that of the relationship between the life of the community and the gifts of individuals. Asserting neither the individualism beloved of North Americans nor a tyranny of the group, Paul's approach is somewhat dialectical. Individual believers have received varying gifts and must exercise those gifts, but without claiming them as personal achievements. These varying gifts should not become places for competition among individuals or objects of envy. The gifts, which differ both in kind and in quantity, exist for the service of the community as a whole and need to be exercised within it. Twice in this passage Paul recalls the God-given nature of the spiritual gifts. Christians are to act "according to the measure of faith that God has assigned" (v. 3), and these gifts "differ according to the grace given to us" (v. 6). Boasting and envy are completely out of place in a Christian community, because Christians know that the skills and talents they bring to that community come from the one God and not from any human accomplishment or intentionality.

Matthew 16:13–20

To preach on the story of Peter's confession at Caesarea Philippi in Matthew's Gospel necessarily means to make some choices of what will and what will not be dealt with in the sermon. The dramatic power of Jesus' questioning the disciples, the variety of nuanced titles for Jesus that appear in the text, the special blessing of Peter, not to mention the words that following the lection about Jesus' suffering and death and about the disciples' bearing the cross, are too much for one Sunday. Attempting too much is often a recipe for confusion.

Since the incident occurs in each of the Synoptic Gospels (and in John too—John 6:66–69), one way to achieve a clear focus is to ask what is distinctive about Matthew's report. What is the peculiar cutting edge of the account here in comparison to the accounts in the other Gospels? The answer is clear. Matthew alone includes 16:17–19, verses that connect Peter's confession of Jesus as Messiah and Son of God to the reality of the church. In Matthew's narrative the declaration of who Jesus is has special significance for who the church is. (The only appearances of the word "church" in any of the Gospels are in Matt. 16:18 and 18:17.) Since (unlike Mark) prior to this incident all the disciples have confessed Jesus to be the Son of God (14:33), the way Peter emerges in 16:17–19 as the recipient of revelation and the "rock" on which the church is built stands out. A sermon with an ecclesial focus is thus appropriate.

But what can be said about the church from this text? First, *the church is rooted in the confession of Jesus as Messiah, Son of God.* What makes Peter and the church so special is nothing inherent to either, not their brilliance or their faithfulness, not their cunning or their courage. Peter immediately will show himself guilty of such gross misunderstanding that Jesus calls him "Satan" (16:22–23), and the church proves no more insightful than Peter. And yet both remain special. They draw their distinctiveness from the confession that claims them.

What's more, the insight about Jesus comes as an event of divine revelation.The passage makes it very clear that Peter does not reason his way to the acknowledgment of who Jesus is. Sound logic could never arrive at the conclusion that this one destined for the cross was acting out his proper role as Son of God. Such knowledge comes only as a divine gift. The text does not so much argue for a correct Christology, getting the titles for Jesus in just the right alignment, as it affirms that the confessing church lives out sheer grace. Its uniqueness derives from a God who graciously initiates a self-revelation and who even now through this ancient text keeps disclosing to the church who Jesus is.

Second, *this passage clearly sets the church in a context of conflict.* The privileged place it occupies is as the designated opponent of "the gates of Hades" (not inappropriately rendered in the RSV as "the powers of death"). The imagery is both vivid and ambiguous. On the one hand, the word translated "prevail" suggests that death takes the offensive, laying siege to a beleaguered community, dug in and determined. Despite the onslaughts, the church hangs on and ultimately emerges victorious. On the other hand, the image of "gates" connotes a stationary, defensive posture, implying that the church is the aggressor, the invading army that storms the powers of death and liberates Hades' captives.

In either case, the church is not a place of repose, but a community engaged in mortal conflict. It anticipates, even prepares itself for, vigorous opposition. Its clear confession of the crucified and risen Jesus threatens those who choose a more palatable creed and capitulate to the apparent finality of death.

Third, *the church is entrusted with the keys to God's reign, symbolizing the ultimate victory over death.* The graphic verbs "bind" and "loose" (16:19) tantalize. Whatever their origin, they conjure up the notions of restraining this person or freeing that person, of forbidding this action or permitting that action. They describe the functions of "keys" in excluding or admitting people to God's reign. Since they are backed with the authority of heaven, they are not functions to be taken lightly. Peter initially carries the "keys," but in light of Matt. 18:18 they are democratized and given to the whole church.

What a power to have in the midst of conflict! The "keys" become weapons of war in the struggle with the forces of death. Death is a powerful antagonist, with an array of tactics, mocking and intimidating the reality of life—only death fights with one hand tied behind its back. It has no access to the rule of God. Whatever the church binds, death cannot loosen, and whatever the church loosens, death cannot bind. Death is destined to lose, because its opponent has been given the decisive weapon.

PROPER 17

Ordinary Time 22

Sunday between August 28 and September 3 inclusive

The readings for this Sunday invite the listening church into the fullness of covenantal existence. That pecular way of life is marked by celebrative gratitude and willing obedience. These are the only two matters that count for the church, gratitude and obedience.

The familiarity of the story of the burning bush in Ex. 3 should not be permitted to obscure the terrifying, yet liberating, event it remembers. Moses is attracted to inspect the bush because it is an oddity, but the real miracle he encounters is the presence of the living God, the God of Israel's ancestors. Not even Moses, however, could be prepared for the challenge that ensues: that he must return to Egypt to liberate his people, God's people. That Moses shrinks before such a chilling prospect is understandable; but the God-of-the-bush will not take "no" for an answer.

Psalm 105 is an exuberant recital of God's great acts of mercy in Israel's life (note Propers 12 and 14), in this instance focusing on Moses and Aaron (note v. 26). The key verb here is "sent" and its subject is, of course, God. There should be no mistaking the source of Israel's salvation, and in recognizing that source Israel sings the ultimate word of praise (v. 45c).

In the text from Rom. 12, Paul has taken the notion of covenant demand and has expounded it with daring and imagination. Obedience in covenant is not merely a matter of keeping rules. It is an act of being massively and completely transformed, readied for a new life in the world, which is marked by liberality and hospitality. Paul provides an inventory of new life for those who are changed and renewed by the gospel.

The Gospel reading from Matt. 16 is one of Jesus' most acute reflections on the obedience expected of the faithful. On the one hand, Jesus announces his own destiny of suffering obedience. On the other hand, Jesus invites his disciples to share in that radical destiny of obedience to death, promising that such willing and total obedience is the door to new life.

It is clear in all these readings that there is for the faithful no "business as usual" permitted. The genuinely liberated are mandated to a new, costly way of life in the world. All of life is reshaped in response to the God who liberates and who continues to preside over that liberation with definitive and uncompromising demands. The required move from liberation to demand anticipates the Gospel announcement that obedience is a mode of freedom, that death is the way to real life.

Exodus 3:1–15

First, the miracle. The bush that is being burned but not consumed is one of those seminal emblems in the Bible for the presence of God. It is symbol of an irresistible Being, whose energies cannot be contained but who Itself/Himself/Herself (no pronoun is adequate) is not subject to decay or deterioration. This is the God whose self-description, "I AM WHO I AM" (v. 14), suggests a God who is so completely unlike all other existing persons and things as to make comparisons meaningless. This is the God who generates, but who also stands outside, the spheres of generation and degeneration.

Moses, whose eye is caught by the visible miracle, moves in for a closer inspection only to be seized by the larger miracle of the nature of this Diety. The command to Moses that he remove his sandals serves to remind him (and to remind us, as well) that the real wonder here is not that of a shrub that refuses to be burned up, but that of a God unlike any other. Yet a new surprise follows: Moses' awe is immediately brought up short by a second declaration from the God-of-the-bush. This is no mountain jinni, no spirit of the rocks and sand. The terrible God-of-the-bush is also the familiar God of the Hebrews' ancestors. The Unknown One is none other than that One who clearly showed abundant compassion to the generations of Abraham, Isaac, and Jacob.

Second, the declaration. This God-of-the-incredible-bush, this God of Abraham, Isaac, and Jacob is a God who cares about the sufferings of people (vs. 7–9). Moses, who himself knew what it meant to protect and defend others, would resonate to this aspect of God's personality, because Moses, of all people, knew that caring for others was expensive and hurtful (note Ex. 2:11–22). And so it would have been with great joy that Moses heard God's declaration, "I have observed the misery of my people . . .; I have heard their cry . . . . I have come down to deliver them." If the promise of a land of milk and honey seemed too good to be true, that would have been beside the point. The God-of-the-incredible-bush cared about Israel, and about justice, and about protecting those who couldn't protect themselves. And that made all the difference.

But then, the challenge! Moses is openly astonished that what this compassionate, justice-loving God-of-the-bush intends to do is to be done by none other than Moses himself. "So come, I will send *you* to Pharaoh to bring my people, the Israelites, out of Egypt" (v. 10, emphasis added). To Moses' mind, such a plan of action must have presented at least two difficulties, but he verbalizes only one of them. If you are a consuming-God-who-is-not-consumed, why not take care of this yourself? Moses must have wondered. Still, he gives voice only to the more uncomfortable question: "Who am I that I should go to Pharaoh, and bring the Israelites out of Egypt?" (v. 11). God's response to Moses' understandable reservation is, of course, to say that Moses will not be alone. The awesome God-of-the-bush will be with him, so that not even Pharaoh need be feared.

This seems to be the force of the puzzling statement, "This shall be the sign for you that it is I who sent you" (v. 12). Although NRSV and other translations render the English in such a manner as to cause the demonstrative pronoun "this" to refer to the people's act of worship on the mountain at a future time, "this" almost certainly is a reference to the burning bush. A different translation might be:

> He said, "I will be with you, and this [experience of the burning bush] will be the sign for you that it is I who have sent you. [Thus,] when you have brought the people out of Egypt, you shall worship God on this mountain [in commemoration of the encounter with God here in the burning bush].

No one is a witness to this sign but the solitary Moses, yet its meaning will be in his heart in the days to come when he stands before Pharaoh. He has been commissioned to lead his people out of bondage by none other than the terrible God-of-the-bush, the faithful God of Abraham, Isaac, and Jacob, I AM WHO I AM. When faced with such a commission from such a Being, not even the trembling Moses could say no. Like many faithful people since (cf. Jer. 20:9), Moses' instincts for comfort and safety are brushed aside by the terrible presence of the living God, a God whose call to service he could not bring himself to ignore.

Psalm 105:1–6, 23–26, 45c

As in Propers 12 and 14, this Psalm reading is a recital of Israel's normative memory, this time focusing on the experience of Israel in the abuse of Egypt, the house of bondage.

On the hymnic introduction of Ps. 105:1–6, see Proper 12. Israel is invited to awe and wonder at God's transformative interventions.

The brief portion of the body of the psalm that is our reading concerns the transition of Israel in Egypt, from welcomed guest to exploited labor (vs. 23–26). The beginning point for Israel in Egypt, as this psalm reckons it, is not the coerced arrival of Joseph sold as a slave, but his father, Jacob, drawn to the food of Egypt by the famine of Canaan (Gen. 45:9–47:4). Thus, "Israel" in v. 23 is parallel to "Jacob" and refers to this man who is father of a large, extended network of tribes represented by his sons. Jacob and his family came to Egypt ("land and Ham") as fugitives from famine. Though Jacob was received by Pharaoh and welcomed with great pomp and proper protocol befitting a chieftain (Gen. 47:7–12), he was nonetheless an outsider without property or political rights. The term "alien" (which is often translated as "sojourner") is a legal classification that means that one lives at the behest (whim) of those in power, thus always in a position of vulnerability and political and economic jeopardy (cf. Gen. 47:4).

Two things happen to this man and his family, finally recognized as happening at the behest of Yahweh, whose "guests" they turn out to be (cf. Ps. 39:12). First, Yahweh, the Lord of all lands and Lord of creation, made the people of Jacob fruitful, numerous and strong. The narrative telling of Ex. 1:7 uses the phrasing of the Creation narrative (Gen. 1:28), suggesting that all the power of blessing in the process of creation is here assigned to his singular family. This family is the carrier of blessing with enormous potential, which turns out to be a threat to Pharaoh.

Second, the subject "he" in Ps. 105:25 is also Yahweh. It is Yahweh who caused the foe to hate Jacob and his people, so that they become the object of rage and resentment, which issues in imperial policies of exploitation. In the larger narrative of Exodus, two reasons are given for the hostility of official Egypt: Israel is so numerous as a result of God's blessing that they constitute a population threat to the settled population (see Ex. 1:9–10).The second reason for abuse is that the Israelites are a supply of cheap labor and must not be permitted to escape (see Ex. 5:4–9). Thus, the two reasons are mutually exclusive. Because too numerous, it would be better if they left; but as cheap labor, they must not leave. It is noteworthy, however, that the version of this emergence of hatred in the psalm is credited to neither of these reasons. Rather, it is Yahweh who turned (inverted) the hearts of the Egyptians (Ps. 105:25). The same sentiment is elsewhere expressed, that Yahweh "hardened" their hearts (cf., e.g., Ex. 7:13; 8:32). The same God who makes prosperous is the God who sponsors anger and an adversarial relationship. Because of Yahweh's inscrutable negative activity, Egypt deals deceptively with Israel, rendering Israel ever more helpless and dependent.

But then, in v. 26, Yahweh intervenes once again, with the decisive word "sent," as in vs. 17 and 20, on which see Proper 14. Moses and Aaron, servants of Yahweh, are chosen for a special work, namely to extricate Jacob's family from their enslavement. Our reading is terse concerning Israel's future opened by Moses and Aaron, on which see vs. 27–44, part of which appears in Proper 20.

These verses of the psalm thus witness to three actions of Yahweh:

(1) positive: Yahweh made Israel fruitful;
(2) negative: Yahweh turned hearts to hate;
(3) positive: Yahweh sent Moses and Aaron.

Israel, in telling its tale of faith, finds it necessary to tailor God's story to the intractable realities of experience. God governs, but in no single, clean line of success. All is in God's good hands. The outcome is glorious, but the "road is stoney."

On v. 45 and the conclusion of obedience, see Propers 12 and 14. This leads to the ultimate response of praise: "Praise the LORD!"

Romans 12:9–21

This lection consists of a series of loosely connected exhortations, each of which provides a glimpse into what is meant by presenting the body "as a living sacrifice" (12:1; see the comments for Proper 16). Those who have been transformed in this way are enabled to discern God's will (12:2) and to act on behalf of the larger community (vs. 3–8). These specific instructions, then, serve to illustrate what has been identified already as the nature of Christian life.

The particulars of vs. 9–21 derive from a variety of sources. Several come from the Jewish wisdom tradition. Verse 15, for example, echoes Sir. 7:34: "Do not avoid those who weep, but mourn with those who mourn." When Paul warns, "Do not claim to be wiser than you are. Do not repay anyone evil for evil," he clearly recalls Prov. 3:7: "Do not be wise in your own eyes; fear the LORD, and turn away from evil." Romans 12:20 directly quotes from the Septuagint of Prov. 25:21.

Some of these admonitions have close parallels elsewhere in the letters of Paul. For example, Rom 12:9 closely follows the sense of 1 Thess. 5:21–22, though not the actual wording. Second Corinthians 8:21 is echoed in v. 17; and 2 Cor. 13:11 in v. 18. Perhaps most surprisingly, given how seldom Paul appeals to the teachings of Jesus, at least one of these instructions (v. 14) recalls a saying of Jesus (Luke 6:28).

Identifying these various sources and parallels does not clarify the task of preaching from this passage, of course. If anything, it increases the sense that the passage is a disjointed hodgepodge of ethical instructions, which overwhelms the reader by its lack of focus. The temptation may be to domesticate it by appealing to a vague and sentimentalized form of love.

One alternative approach might be to explore the connection made here between the believer's love of God and service in the human community. The opening of the chapter has already made clear, at least implicitly, that the proper response to "the mercies of God" is one that serves both God (12:1–2) and other human beings (vs. 3–8). The link between the two continues in this lection, where being ardent in spirit and serving the Lord (v. 11) stand alongside mutual affection and contributions for the saints (vs. 10, 13). Over against the tension in contemporary Christianity between those who would emphasize one side of that imperative to the exclusion (or apparent exclusion) of the other, Paul sees them as intimately connected.

Another alternative might be to focus on what Paul says here about dealing with evil, since that concern appears in several of the exhortations. Initially, Paul admonishes that Christians should "hate what is evil" and "hold fast to what is good" (v. 9). No expansion explains the directive or justifies it. Evil is simply to be avoided or rejected.

Paul returns to the topic, although this time in a more specific form, in v. 14: "Bless those who persecute you; bless and do not curse them." Here he addresses not evil in a general sense, but the particular instance of those who persecute the faithful. Consistent with the teaching of Jesus (see Luke 6:28), the persecutor is to be blessed rather than hated. As in the first instance, however, no elaboration justifies or explains this directive. Verse 17, while lacking the positive note about "blessing" of v. 14, again simply instructs that evil is not to be exchanged for evil.

With vs. 19–21, however, explanations enter the picture. One of these explanations is entirely theological; the other might be termed "pragmatic." The reason that Christians are not to "repay anyone evil for evil" or avenge themselves is that God alone has the right to vengeance. Consistent with Paul's notion that judgment is reserved for God (see, for example, Rom. 14:10–12), he here insists that vengeance also is reserved for God. In other words, Christians have no need to seek revenge or repayment of wrong. That is God's prerogative, and God's alone!

With the use of Prov. 25:21–22 in Rom. 12:20, however, Paul does offer a solution for the short term: "If your enemies are hungry, feed them; if they are thirsty, give them something to drink; for by doing this you will heap burning coals on their heads." Rather than seeking revenge, Paul sagely encourages the doing of good to the enemy, for the impact of that good promises to be far more humiliating—far more effective!—than sheer repayment of evil. Verse 21 seems to make it clear that this is his understanding. To "overcome evil with good" is not to lie down before evil so that it simply has its way, but to conquer it by the skillful use of good.

So familiar is the "doormat" version of Christianity, in which Christians are taught that their duty is to accept whatever evil comes their way, that the craftiness of Paul's words here slips by. Evil *need not* be passively accepted, nor need it be avenged, when we understand that, finally, God is the one who judges all humankind. In many forms, evil can also be thwarted in the meantime by those who understand the capacity of good to humiliate and expose evil for what it truly is.

Matthew 16:21–28

This Sunday's reading from the Gospel can hardly be separated from the reading for last Sunday. The two belong very much together. For example, Jesus' anticipation of his suffering, death, and resurrection in Jerusalem (Matt. 16:21) is particularly important because it follows Peter's confession of Jesus as Messiah and Son of God in 16:16. The sayings about self-denial and cross bearing become critical in light of Jesus' earlier conversation with the disciples in vs. 13–20. And perhaps most of all, Peter's exchange with Jesus in vs. 22–23 cannot be severed from Peter's previous confession of and commendation from Jesus (vs. 16–19).

Peter's conduct throughout the passage is intriguing. We are not surprised in v. 16 when Peter is the one to respond to Jesus' question. After all, he is the first disciple to be called (4:18), and his name heads the list of the Twelve when they are commissioned (10:2). He alone of the disciples walks on the sea to meet Jesus, if only a few fearful steps (15:28–31). In one sense, in responding to Jesus, Peter acts as spokesperson for the other disciples, but in another sense he speaks for himself. It is he alone to whom the divine revelation has been given; he is the only one about whom the special beatitude is spoken. He is singled out as distinctive, honored by being the peculiar recipient of a heavenly gift.

Then something drastic happens in the narrative. Jesus begins to talk to the disciples about the immediate future, the journey to Jerusalem, his suffering, death, and resurrection. Peter again becomes a participant in the conversation, in fact an aggressive participant. He feels strongly that he must dissuade Jesus from going to Jerusalem and meeting such a dire fate. "This must never happen to you!"

In an instant, Jesus and Peter are on opposite sides of a conflict. Colleagues have become opponents. "You are a stumbling block to me," Jesus says. "You are setting your mind not on divine things but on human things." The prophet who has received the special revelation from God becomes immediately mired in a human way of thinking. The one especially blessed by Jesus is now called "Satan." The rock on which the church is to be built turns out to be a stumbling block for Jesus.

What precipitates Peter's change? He *does* nothing wrong. According to Jesus' verdict, Peter simply begins to think the wrong thoughts. The imagination that once was attuned to the divine revelation becomes domesticated. He cannot bring himself to contemplate that suffering and death are a part of the vocation of the Messiah. Peter's rebuke of Jesus might be rendered, "Certainly God will be gracious to you, Lord, and will not let this happen!" His human viewpoint wants to exclude vulnerability, to pull down the blinds on the distasteful, and to see Jesus through to a successful Messiahship. Setting the mind on earthly things hardly seems a dastardly deed, but it proves ultimately decisive.

The dramatic shift in Peter's place in the narrative makes a powerful impact on the careful reader. Nothing in the text attributes the shift to a defective trait, to a fickle or impulsive personality. To dismiss Peter as a wishy-washy type who speaks before he thinks misses the point. It fails to take seriously both Jesus' commendation of Peter (16:17–19) and his rebuke of Peter (v. 23). Peter really does occupy a special spot as the recipient of divine revelation, but it is just this privileged place that fails to grasp the reality of Jesus' suffering and death. Peter has his followers in every generation, religious people who give the right answers (and genuinely so) but who find a crucified Christ offensive.

Jesus' sayings about denying self and bearing the cross hit home in light of Peter's domesticated mind-set. What is true for the Messiah is also true for the Messiah's disciples. The language sounds almost too radical to be realistic, too sharp and demanding to be taken seriously. The coopted imagination assumes that there is a way to gain life other than by losing it, a way to Easter other than through Good Friday, an avenue to messiahship other than through suffering and death. But the rhetorical questions of v. 26 powerfully expose the presumptuousness of any other alternative to the cross.

The two final verses set the whole passage into an eschatological context. The Son of Man, about whom the disciples were initially queried (v. 13), turns out to be both the judge who calls to account all God's people and the inaugurator of God's sovereign rule (vs. 27–28). What disciples think and how actions and thoughts cohere, then, are not trivial matters. They are the concern of the returning Son of Man, who himself resisted the allures of the tempter Peter and fulfilled his vocation at Jerusalem.

PROPER 18

Ordinary Time 23

Sunday between
September 4 and 10 inclusive

Issues of trust and of the joy that trust inspires lie at the heart of human life. It is not simply a question of "Whom can I trust?" but the matter, as well, of how the faithfulness of the one who elicits trust from the other may be recognized. In various ways the lections for this day address these concerns.

At one level the passage from Ex. 12, which provides instructions for keeping the Passover, presents daunting problems, for it seems to celebrate the activity of Yahweh, bringer of death. Yet while the difficulties in this text should not be lightly dismissed, they should not blind the interpreter to the deeper insight, namely, that Yahweh is one who may be trusted, for Yahweh defends those who seek Yahweh's shelter. In the end, the people stand liberated not just from Pharaoh, but from Egypt's gods as well. That is to say, the people stand liberated *from* all false loyalties and allegiance, *to* an allegiance to Yahweh alone.

Psalm 149 is one of those several songs of great joy with which the Psalter closes, yet this psalm is different from the others in its strong note of realism. The rule of Yahweh brings Israel to an understanding that the social order must reflect the moral integrity of the world's ultimate King. Injustice must be denied; the oppressed must be delivered. And all of this is done in a spirit of celebration because of the sovereignty of Yahweh.

The Epistle reading from Rom. 13 marks a point of transition within Paul's letter. Paul's ethical instruction, begun in chapter 12, will give way in chapter 14 to a concern for Jewish-Gentile tensions within the church. Basically, Paul is here urging his readers to trust the fact that faith in Christ makes a difference. It makes a difference in one's ability to "love your neighbor as yourself." It makes a difference in the joyful urgency with which life is lived.

The Gospel lection from Matt. 18 speaks to the importance of trustworthiness in the life of the believing community and provides measures for the restoration of confidence and for reconciliation among members of the community in the face of injury and dispute. The trust exhibited among members of Christ's family is an important expression of the trust that characterizes the kingdom of heaven.

Exodus 12:1–14

The series of Old Testament texts relating to Moses and the exodus continues with this passage, which provides instruction for the keeping of the Passover festival. For Israel, ancient and modern, Passover is an unparalleled time of celebration of God's activity as Redeemer—an Old Testament "Easter," as some commentators have observed. And yet this text is marked less by a mood of gaiety than by one of sobriety, for the Passover event itself, accompanied by the death of all of Egypt's firstborn, is to transpire within a context of great suffering. Israel will be spared God's judgment, it is true, but the avenging Yahweh will move among the Egyptians in terrible proximity to the people of Israel. Not only that, but the moment of liberation will give way to new and, as yet, unfathomed experiences in the wilderness. Therefore, the mood of this text is muted, recognizing Yahweh's terrible power and justice but trembling at the cost in human life and security (false security, as it turns out) that must be paid.

Any honest hermeneutical treatment of this passage must face up to the terror within the text and to the God of death who is portrayed here. What kind of God would achieve some purpose—no matter how justified and benevolent—by bringing about the deaths of so many, most of whom we may assume are so young as to be innocent of the sins of oppression for which their nation is being judged (v. 12)? Does Yahweh not love the Egyptians too?

There are no completely satisfactory answers to these questions, and the morally sensitive interpreter of this text is left with an uncomfortable feeling. One may, of course, rehearse the usual explanations. The passage comes from a time when women and men, including Israel, were accustomed to think of supernatural activity in more warlike terms than is the case today. Thus, while the Passover texts are accurate in portraying the redemptive activity of God in Israel's life, they also reflect the thought patterns of the world in which their authors lived and worked. Another explanation is that, since ancient Israel conceptualized evil not in abstract but in personal terms, the only way in which God could be understood to be combating evil was if God brought judgment on evil persons or, as in this case, persons who were members of evil societies. And these explanations point to important realities which must be taken into account in any effort to wrestle with such a text as this.

Yet not even these or similar explanations resolve the problem of Yahweh, the bringer of death. And the only valid means of moving beyond this difficulty into the genuine values of this text is to admit that the understanding of Yahweh as the Deity who slaughters the firstborn is partial and, therefore, distorted. One may understand why the ancient writers conceptualized God as they did, but, in the light of other biblical insights into the nature of God, one must also deny the portrait of Yahweh as the killer of the innocent. For example, that other great collection of liberation texts within the Old Testament, that of the Second Isaiah, viewed Israel's redemption not in terms of the destruction of Israel's captors, but in terms of the captors' *enlightenment* into the ways of Yahweh (Isa. 42:6–7). The prophet Jonah reluctantly bore witness to the God who loves all people passionately, even those oppressors who have earned the wrath of the oppressed, while Jesus demonstrated the love of God even for those who crucified him (Luke 23:34).

The error in identifying God as the slayer of the wicked or, worse, as the slayer of those innocent people who are kin to the wicked, is that it is so easy for a nation or a group to put on God's mantle and to begin to do God's work for God. The weapons of mass destruction have brought home to the human race more forcefully than ever before the folly of such thought and behavior.

But having said what one must deny in this text, the interpreter is bound to emphasize with equal vigor that which must be affirmed. As mentioned above, the grounds for this distinction are not subjective, but are based on the ability of other biblical texts to inform our reading of this one. That motif which stands forth as being of paramount significance in this regard is, of course, that of God as Redeemer. Thus, the symbol of the slaughtered lamb in this passage is crucial, as it gives substance to the New Testament image of Jesus as the "Lamb of God who takes away the sin of the world!" (John 1:29).

Not only does Yahweh intend to save the Israelites in a physical sense, but Yahweh intends to redeem that special relationship which binds them to Yahweh and Yahweh to them. The struggle with Egypt is not only with its people and its government, but also with its gods (v. 12). Yahweh's liberation of the Israelites is understood by the text to be a liberation of the people from the power of that which pretends to stand in God's place. Again, this theme resonates within the prophetic word of the Second Isaiah, who, while valuing the worth of Israel's oppressors, ridicules their idols, declaring that any freedom granted by Yahweh is rooted in liberation from false worship and devotion (Isa. 44:9–20). Thus the institution of the Passover is not only a proclamation of that *from* which God redeems us, but of that *to* which God redeems us, as well.

Psalm 149

Psalm 149 stands among the marvelous grouping of Pss. 145–150 as a lyrical, doxological conclusion to the Psalter. Unlike every other psalm in this group, however, this psalm interjects a note of political realism and even military conflict.

The psalm begins with a repeated imperative summons to praise, a standard form in hymnic style (vs. 1–5). After the initial ejaculation of praise (v. 1a—matched by the conclusion of v. 9c), the psalm offers a series of imperatives and jussives, anticipating praise (vs. 1b–3). The whole of the song of praise is a "new song," that is, a liturgical action indicating a marvelous *novum* in God's life with Israel. The "assembly of the faithful" (*ḥăsîdîm*), the committed Torah keepers, are to meet for praise of God. The praise is invited by the jussive verbs of vs. 2, 3, and 5. The praise is to be enthusiastic (v. 3) and is to be done both in public (v. 1) and in private (v. 5).

The reason for the praise is that God is peculiarly favorable to the Israelite people, who here are understood to be exploited. Israel is not exploited in every season of its life, but this psalm reflects such a condition. Abused Israel, perhaps nearly driven to despair, is invited to liturgical celebration that is not primarily informed by circumstance. The reason for such praise in such circumstance is that Israel *with Yahweh* is so completely different from Israel *without Yahweh.* With Yahweh, Israel is assured of a protector and guarantor, who is the enforcer of Israel's rights and the enactor of Israel's well-being. The hymn gives full play to Israel's dependence on Yahweh, and the decisive difference made by the power and reality of Yahweh.

An important transition is marked in the psalm at v. 6. The first line of the verse is in substance and style a continuation of the praise of vs. 1–5. The second line departs from that substance and style, and goes in a quite unexpected direction. The people of Israel are to have "two-edged swords" in their hands, to take power into their own hands, and to act as enforcers themselves. The peculiar combination of exuberant praise and armed power is not unlike "Praise the Lord and pass the ammunition." The second line is in deep tension with the first line, for the first line turns life over to God's wondrous rule, whereas the second line legitimates human acts of a vigorous, even violent kind. In the latter case, Yahweh becomes the legitimator of such self-protective action.

The authorization of v. 6b is now further explored (vs. 7–9a). The purpose of such words is that Israel is to "do" (*'śh*; NRSV "execute") vengeance and punishment, to imprison kings and nobles, and to "do" justice. The verb "do" might be noticed, because in v. 2 the term "Maker," applied to Yahweh, presents God as the "doer" (*'śh*). Thus what Yahweh has done decisively, Israel is now to do.

What Israel is to do with its legitimated weapons is to impose social order (vengeance) on a disordered social scene, apparently disordered not by mobs and thugs, but by exploitative rulers who appear to be legitimate but in fact are not. There is, then, in this psalm a tone of "class conflict" between powerful lords of legitimate rule and needful Israelites who are victimized in a situation to which Israel is often subjected. In such a situation, the rule of Yahweh permits forcible action in order to overthrow exploitative power, for the citizenry has an obligation to oppose forcibly the practice of injustice, even if done by allegedly authorized government. Note well that such an authorization here is only for the sake of the oppressed. It is not a broader sanction for organized violence.

In v. 9b, this exercise of human responsibility for public justice against oppression is said to be the "adornment" (NRSV "glory") of Israel, a point of pride and beauty. In this verse, as in vs. 1 and 5, the subject is "the faithful" (*ḥăsîdîm*), the serious Torah keepers. Thus the move from God's wondrous rule to human action is not undertaken or authorized in a self-serving interest, with only a facade of ideological support. Such use of power in the public process is here legitimated only for those who understand their lives in terms of obedience to Yahweh, an obedience that entails attentiveness to the holiness of God and the neighborliness of social order. In our own time, of course, we have ample evidence of the ideological use of such religious warrants. The psalm affirms a Yahwistic base for military action against craven or ambitious exploiters. The psalm betrays no awareness of the ideological temptation in such an authorization.

Romans 13:8–14

This lection stands at an important juncture in Romans. Ever since Rom. 12:1 Paul has been engaged in ethical instruction. In 14:1 he will turn to specific problems that grow from tensions between Jews and Gentiles within the Christian community. Today's passage, then, brings the general ethical instructions to a close and sets the framework for what follows.

In 13:8–10 Paul moves from the statement of obligation in 13:1–3 to a positive assertion about the need for love: "Owe no one anything, except to love one another." The lines that follow explain that love fulfills all the commandments, because love would never be involved in the adulterous act, in murder, in theft, or in covetousness. The difficulty with this injunction to love, of course, is that it becomes a new burden for those who feel that they must love everyone, for those who constantly measure themselves by their ability to love everyone. Others, rather than experiencing this demand as a burden, fulfill this call for love with a superficial and saccharine profession of love for the entire world, a love that never manages to find its way into the nitty-gritty of everyday life.

Two aspects of the text may guard against these problems. First, the injunction of v. 9 is to the love of the *neighbor,* not to some universal love. Even if the category of neighbor includes those usually regarded as enemies (see, for example, Luke 10:29–37), it nevertheless concerns those with whom one comes in contact. Paul calls for the difficult task of real love for real people who are met in everyday life, not theoretical love for humanity as a whole.

Second, the injunction is to the love of neighbor "as yourself." Only a healthy, whole person—one who is capable of loving herself or himself—is capable of loving another. Love of the other does not require self-deprecation or self-hatred, emotions that in fact inhibit the ability to love others. Love of the other begins with a self-love that is able to acknowledge and enjoy the handiwork of God in every creature.

The final verses of the lection, vs. 11–14, may seem an alien intrusion into all that has preceded. With its ethical dualism and eschatological urgency, this section admittedly does differ from what has preceded. The urgency does, however, rightfully appear in close proximity to the ethical demands of this part of the letter. What makes it imperative that Christians behave in a worthy manner, both within the community and toward the outside, is that the time itself has grown short. There is no slack time, no cushion that allows for future correction. What happens now genuinely matters.

A second important feature of these closing lines is their utter confidence that Christian faith makes a difference. Just as Christians are transferred from one realm of belief to another ("we became believers," v. 11), so they are transferred from one realm of behavior to another. Paul cannot imagine one movement without the other.

(For additional comments on Rom. 13:11–14, see the First Sunday of Advent.)

Matthew 18:15–20

The passage for this Sunday reminds us that Matthew's story was written initially for a small community, living in a hostile environment, that took its corporate life very seriously. The text in isolation reads like a legal manual on how to deal with someone else's sin, what steps to take en route to a member's excommunication. The cut-and-dried character of the process leaves us somewhat uncomfortable. We are not at all sure we want to deal with grudges and grievances the way this passage suggests, much less make it the basis of a sermon. But before we dismiss it out of hand, the passage at least deserves a careful reading.

First, we discover the remarkable context of Matt. 18. From beginning to end it points in quite a different direction from that of self-righteousness and harsh judgment. When the disciples ask, "Who is the greatest in the kingdom of heaven?" a child is placed in their midst, and Jesus says, "Whoever becomes humble like this child is the greatest in the kingdom of heaven" (18:4). Then the disciples are warned against putting stumbling blocks in the way of others and are invited to be self-conscious about their own manner of life (vs. 6–9). They are not to disdain fellow members ("little ones"). God cares about straying sheep and rejoices when one is restored. "It is not the will of your Father in heaven that one of these little ones should be lost" (v. 14).

Following 18:15–20, today's reading, comes the word to Peter that forgiveness cannot be calculated. God does not keep a scorecard of rights and wrongs, and neither can we. Finally, the chapter concludes with the memorable parable of the servant who accepts from the king the generous release of indebtedness, but cannot forgive one of his fellow servants a relatively paltry amount (18:23–35). Withholding forgiveness to a fellow human being raises questions as to whether one has really discovered God's forgiveness.

The powerful images of pardon and mercy found in the context color the reading of 18:15–20. Forgiveness and restoration are the topics of the day. God forgives freely, and those forgiven evidence their reception of forgiveness by forgiving others. Thus, when we are the injured party, we are to seek out the person who we think has done the injuring and initiate reconciliation. We have no right to nurse our grudges, whine about our wounds, and resist efforts at healing. We are to take the first step, to risk the engagement that can lead to a restored relationship. That surely is easier said than done, and the parable of 18:23–35 (to be dealt with next Sunday) addresses the difficulty.

The second thing we discover in today's passage is that situations of alienation are to be taken very seriously. Breaches between members cannot be simply glossed over or treated as unimportant. Nothing is gained by overlooking the injury, by not talking about it in hopes that it will soon go away. Forgiveness never happens by default. It occurs in the risky encounter between the alienated parties.

While the threefold process of dealing with the alienated party outlined in 18:15–17 may not always be an advisable process to follow today, it acknowledges the reality that not every participant will immediately own up to his or her part in the broken relationship. What if we take the initiative and are rebuffed—what then? The matter is not merely ours alone. The Christian community has a stake in brokenness and reconciliation—not only in the liturgical declaration of pardon every week, but in the actual relationships among its members. The church is under the same mandate of forgiveness as the alienated parties and therefore joins in the search for a resolution. One is reminded of Jesus' words in the Sermon on the Mount: "When you are offering your gift at the altar, if you remember that your brother or sister has something against you, leave your gift there before the altar and go; first be reconciled to your brother or sister, and then come and offer your gift" (5:23–24).

Briefly, the third thing we discover in the passage is the personal element. While a rather elaborate process is established, which reads like a manual of discipline, the first step comes in the face-to-face encounter of the two involved persons. The text makes no effort to probe that personal exchange, to indicate what words must be spoken or deeds must be done to effect restoration. "If the member listens to you, you have regained that one [literally, your brother]" (18:15). There is a certain reticence to go beyond the verb "listen," because every such encounter has its own peculiar dynamics. No rules can be drawn to describe what can or should take place.

The three concluding verses of the passage (vs. 18–20) underscore the critical importance of reconciliation in the Christian community. Precisely who "the two" are who agree is not clear. It is "the two" who visit the alienated member and who concur in excommunication, or is it the warring parties who have discovered healing? In either case, the agreement of two regarding a common request unleashes a powerful force: Jesus promises his presence.

PROPER 19

Ordinary Time 24

Sunday between
September 11 and 17 inclusive

The Bible keeps returning to the primal saving event of the exodus. In that miraculous liberation, Israel receives its identity and its clearest disclosure of God. The Old Testament reading from Ex. 14, in stylized liturgical statement, narrates the exodus event. It tells of the massive power of God, and the decisive defeat of Pharaoh and his armies. It tells of the utter commitment of God to Israel, and of Israel's fearful doubt. As the story is crafted in this reading, it is a narrative "toward faith." It culminates with Israel's faith not only in God, but also in the leadership of Moses.

Psalm 114 is a buoyant, almost defiant celebration of the exodus, in which all the enemies of Yahweh are put to embarrassing flight. Israel enjoys immensely the humiliation of all who resist God. It is recalled that Yahweh's sovereign power to liberate is decisive for the world, as it is for Israel.

In the passage from Rom. 14, Paul struggles with the issue of freedom within obedience, and moves us beyond the letter of the law to its spirit. What is at issue for the apostle is not legal detail, but the attitude of faith which shapes human conduct. Not only are the members of the community of Christ led away from needless bickering, but they are led to faithfulness to one another and to the living Lord.

The parable of the unforgiving servant, which lies at the heart of the Gospel lection (Matt. 18:21–35), reminds all would-be disciples that law must be tempered with mercy in their dealings with one another if they expect to receive mercy from God.

Exodus 14:19–31

Many of the same questions that trouble the modern interpreter of Ex. 12:1–14 (Proper 18) are present in this lection, with its graphic portrayal of the drowning of the army of Pharaoh. But the emphasis here falls more strongly on Yahweh's rescue of Israel than on the decimation of the oppressors, with the result that the proclamation of great good news resonates through this text.

The crossing of the sea is Israel's rite of passage by which the people became a nation. Behind lay Egypt and bondage, ahead lay the wilderness and freedom. Israel entered the channel, which Yahweh had carved by the strong east wind (v. 21), as a group of refugees, terrified and in panic. The people emerged on the other shore in awe and in an attitude of faith in Yahweh for this great miracle of salvation (v. 31). Although some commentators through the years have attempted to explain the parting of the waters by means of various natural phenomena, such attempts are irrelevant and distract one from the main thrust of the text. *Yahweh* saved Israel, not some fluke of nature. That which Yahweh promised Moses after the theophany at the burning bush (Ex. 3:20) has now been realized. Yahweh is their savior and redeemer!

Thus part of the emphasis of this passage lies on the weakness of Israel. As the climactic moment approaches, the Israelites are struck with terror over their own helplessness. They cry out to Yahweh (Ex. 14:10) and they reproach Moses for leading them into this predicament. "Weren't there enough graves in Egypt for us to be buried there and not in this terrible place?" they taunt Moses (v. 11). And then, like the naysayers that they are, they remind Moses that if he had just listened to them, their advice would have saved them. Better a slave in Egypt than a corpse in the wilderness (vs. 12–13).

The salvation of Israel, then, has nothing to do with the people's strength or cleverness, for if left to their own devices, they would never have emerged from slavery. The salvation of Israel was nothing other than the work of God, the same God whose revelations to Moses had been characterized by a concern for the oppressed and by a passion to bring to them justice and mercy. The walls of water that hold the sea at bay are emblematic of Yahweh's grace, which protects and shelters the people.

Thus, in addition to calling attention to the weakness of the people, the text emphasizes the power of Yahweh as redeemer. In the brief section vs. 19–20 Yahweh even moves to position the symbols of divine power between Israel and its pursuers, that is, the angel of God and the pillar of cloud (which also seems to be a pillar of fire, in that it "lit up the night"; cf. v. 24). They serve as a buffer so that the Egyptians are unable to apprehend the Israelites. Then the consummate example of Yahweh's strength is described as the waters of the sea, in response to Moses' outstretched hand, roll back in order to permit the Israelites safe passage. Even the drowning of the army of

Pharaoh is understood by the text to be an example of Yahweh's might, in that "Yahweh tossed the Egyptians into the sea" (v. 27; cf. 14:18).

That which Israel could not do for itself was accomplished by Yahweh, not because Israel deserved to be saved or contributed to its own redemption, but simply because Yahweh, a God of justice and mercy, chose to deliver the people from their oppression. As the authors of the book of Deuteronomy were later to reflect, it was not because Israel was in any manner superior to other peoples that it was saved.

> It was because Yahweh loved you and kept the oath that he swore to your ancestors, that Yahweh has brought you out with a mighty hand, and redeemed you from the house of slavery, from the hand of Pharaoh. (Deut. 7:8)

Another important element in this text is the role extended to Moses. Clearly what happens is the work of Yahweh, yet Yahweh does not work in splendid isolation or, like Zeus throwing thunderbolts, from afar. Yahweh works through the special agent who has been designated to act on Yahweh's behalf. Thus "Moses stretched out his hand over the sea" (v. 21), and the east wind opened a channel of safety. And again "Moses stretched out his hand over the sea" (v. 27), and the waters returned. The result was that "the people . . . believed in Yahweh and in his servant Moses" (v. 31).

And so our text is an important statement about the nature of God's activity in human life in general, and, in particular, it is a statement about the manner in which Moses' ability to lead the people is confirmed in their own minds. The crossing of the sea is as much a right of passage for Moses as it is for the people, for, although grumbling and discontent from the Israelite masses would trouble Moses in the days ahead, there can now be no doubt (at least in the mind of the reader of this text) that Yahweh's promise to be with Moses, made at the burning bush (Ex. 3:12), has been actualized.

Psalm 114

The present depends on what is remembered. Without a pertinent, available memory, the present becomes a chance for distorted perception and careless conduct. Psalm 114 is an act of powerful remembering that leads to present-tense confidence and ends in an awed warning.

In four short phrases, Israel recites its whole memory of life with God, from the slavery of Egypt to the well-being of the Promised Land (vs. 1–2). The first two lines are a dependent temporal clause: "When Israel went out from Egypt . . ." (v. 1). Memory begins for Israel in the exodus, in God's rescue of the slaves from the empire. The preface is lean; it need not be explicated. Israel knows full well that life has begun in a liberating miracle.

God brought Israel to a new home where the slaves had never been, to Judah and to Israel (v. 2). In that new place of well-being, Israel could speak its own language, the language of convenantal fidelity. All the years of suffering, risk, and jeopardy are bracketed by these two lines, beginning in slavery and ending in well-being. The memory invites Israel to be astonished and grateful.

The memory evokes a taunting, gloating, mocking lyric (vs. 3–6). The voice of this psalm is the voice of those long oppressed, now delivered and established, permitted a wondrous moment of exultant well-being. Israel cannot refrain from making fun of those who were so arrogant and abusive, but who could not even for a moment withstand the powerful intrusion of Yahweh. These lines express pent-up hostility; for a long time Israel was subordinated and had had to swallow its rage and resentment. Now Israel can at last say what it has long felt.

Verses 3 and 4 are imaginative descriptions of the past, seen through the trusting, liberated eyes of faith. The four characters are named and addressed: sea, Jordan, mountains, and hills. They are all cowardly failures who thought they could do what they wanted, but were deeply frightened when the Lord of liberation appeared on the scene. The psalm mocks all the powers of oppressive stability, in order that Yahweh should be praised as the One who has overcome and transformed reality.

The description turns to taunt (vs. 5–6). In four questions, the speaker makes fun of the same four characters, the sea, Jordan, mountains, and hills. The RSV phrase, "What ails you?" might well be rendered, "What's to you?" or we might simply say, with the NRSV, "Why is it . . . ?" The lines reflect the recently emancipated, now daring to walk boldly up to the former guards, the former police, the former intimidators, and daring to mock, make fun, tease, pull beards. The tone is that of newly gained bravado. It is Yahweh who "ails" the sea. It is Yahweh who intimidates the Jordan. It is Yahweh who terrorizes the mountains and hills. It is Yahweh, the Lord of freedom, the power of newness, the source of justice. It is Yahweh! It is Yahweh, and these bold witnesses accept life from and with Yahweh. They are free now to mock oppressors the way Easter

Christians mock death (cf. 1 Cor. 15:55–56). There is no more fear or intimidation for these people, because Yahweh has acted.

The psalm ends in an awed warning (vs. 7–8). The "earth"—all natural phenomena, all creation, all rulers and empires, all centers of power and authority—should tremble, quake, and twist in discomfort before "the LORD." The one who comes is *'ādôn;* the Hebrew uses the starkest, strongest word for the sovereign One. None can withstand the "God of Jacob," who has saved the "house of Jacob."

This lyrical psalm is a doxology addressed to the tough, irresistible power of Yahweh. It is praise to God. A by-product of that praise, however, is acknowledgment that the God of power is also the God of justice who will tolerate no practice of oppression. Thus the singers are not theologically indifferent. They are poignant witnesses who have seen that life is inverted from death to life. Such an inversion, an Easter inversion, is indeed cause for singing, free and untroubled, buoyant and unapologetic. Each time the community engages in this taunting celebration, it exercises freedom from the powers of oppression and chaos that weary, deceive, and finally kill. This God is an alternative to the slow, hard death of intimidation.

Romans 14:1–12

Quarrels regarding religious practice plague every Christian generation, perhaps every congregation. In Rom. 14:1–15:13, Paul addresses some specific quarrels and articulates a theological framework for dealing with them. Whether these specific quarrels are characteristic of the church at Rome remains unclear, for Paul does not explicitly say that he knows about such issues being a problem in Rome. The issues themselves could have existed in many early congregations, especially in those that involved both Jews and Gentiles. The quarrels have to do with diet and with special days, although again the specifics are unclear. Some believe that their faith allows them to eat anything, while others (perhaps from concern about contact with food that would be impure according to kosher laws, or eating meat sacrificed to pagan idols) eat only vegetables (14:2). Some observe special days, while others regard all days as the same (14:5).

Despite the remoteness of these specific debates from contemporary Christian practice, many pastors will recognize and identify with the dilemma Paul faces here. How can quarrels be adjudicated without destroying the fabric of the community? What is most striking about Paul's response is that he does not attempt to decide the specific issues of food laws or feast days. He issues no call for an orthopraxis by which believers may be assessed or evaluated. Instead, he makes several important theological observations and trusts that they will lead toward reconciliation. In other words, in this instance the health of the believing community takes precedence over "right" belief or "right" observance.

The central conviction Paul brings to bear in this conflict appears first in vs. 3–4 and again in vs. 6–9: "Who are you to pass judgment on servants of another? It is before their own lord that they stand or fall" (v. 4). Consistent with the argument of the letter as a whole, Paul asserts that Christians belong to God. God created them, and in the Christ-event God has reclaimed them. That relationship takes precedence over all others, without exception. For this reason, the specific religious practices or nonpractices of any individual stem from that person's standing as a servant of God. The one who eats everything without scruple does so to the honor of God; the one who abstains from everything acts likewise. What matters is the integrity of the relationship with God, not the specific religious practices.

In addition to recalling that Christians belong to God rather than, first of all, to one another, Paul urges that people be "fully convinced in their own minds" (v. 5). Further on in this chapter he will articulate the unusual judgment that people who act contrary to their own consciences are condemned (v. 23), underscoring again the importance of conviction. To act contrary to conscience is indeed a dangerous thing. Whatever decision is reached about specific religious practices, the decision needs to have behind it the integrity of genuine reflection rather than the doubt and confusion that grow out of haste or group pressure.

A third aspect of Paul's instruction in this passage is his injunction against judgment: "Why do you pass judgment on your brother or sister?" (v. 10). As is evident already in Rom. 9—11, Paul believes that only God has the right to judge human beings. Christians certainly may not judge one another, for all of them serve the same Lord (v. 4) and must recognize the right of that Lord. Since all human beings are accountable to God, there is no reason for Christians to usurp God's role (vs. 10–12).

To this point, it would appear that Paul is advocating a kind of individualism in this passage. Believers belong to God and are accountable only to God, not to one another. Believers must act out of their individual consciences and convictions. Believers will stand before divine, not human, judgment. A fourth feature of this text places that pluralism firmly within a community context. The entire section of the letter begins with "Welcome those who are weak in faith," and that "welcome" recurs importantly in 15:7. What Paul seeks in this passage is not merely the tolerance of diversity, a grudging acceptance of the inevitability of differences. Instead, he articulates an active welcome for those with conflicting views and practices. If Christ welcomed all people (15:7), then Christians must find a way to welcome one another and to respect the integrity of one another.

We would be quite mistaken to take this passage as an endorsement of any and all behaviors, for Paul elsewhere insists on certain limits. For example, the needs of the larger community dictate what one does in worship (1 Cor. 1). Similarly, sexual practice is not a matter of indifference, but must reflect the fact that human beings belong to God both spiritually and physically. What Paul has in view in Rom. 14—15 is perhaps close to contemporary disputes about forms of baptism or celebration of the Eucharist. What one group regards as permissible another will see as prohibited and another as required. These debates will always characterize the life of the church, as one or another emphasis comes to the foreground, but the debates should not prevent a common understanding of the Lordship of God and the servanthood of believers.

Matthew 18:21–35

The Bible repeatedly tells us that we ought to forgive those who have injured us. We know that. It is ingrained in our minds from the Lord's Prayer and from passages such as the one listed for this Sunday. Congregations are full of people who know they should forgive, who intellectually recognize that there is some positive value in letting go of cherished hurts, but who find it well-nigh impossible to do so. Being cheated on by a spouse or double-crossed by a business partner are experiences that engender shame and rage, that leave the injured party feeling defective, defeated, and never quite good enough. To be told that one *ought* to forgive and let go of the pain simply does not effect a change; in fact, it may aggravate the situation by heaping a load of guilt onto an already enraged and shamed person.

In such a setting, we seek to read and interpret the two pieces of our lesson from Matt. 18. The first piece is a brief exchange between Peter and Jesus about the extent and nature of forgiveness (vs. 21–22). "Seventy-seven times" is Jesus' way of telling Peter that forgiveness is not a commodity to be reckoned on a calculator. Not only is it limitless, but it cannot even be quantified. The language of numbers is inappropriate when one contemplates forgiveness. (This is illustrated in the parable that follows, with the absurdity of the indebtedness of the first servant.)

The second piece of the reading includes the vivid parable of the king who forgives one servant an impossible amount of indebtedness, but that servant is then unable to forgive a fellow servant a reasonable debt. At first blush, the parable evokes considerable consternation. Why does the first servant, having been treated so generously by the king, immediately act so ruthlessly toward his fellow servant? He seems an unrealistically heartless ogre. No one would do that. The king is certainly justified in his harsh retaliation—torture and imprisonment.

But when we sit with the parable awhile and reflect on the difficulty of genuine forgiveness, it takes on a different tone. Does the concluding verse (18:35) mean that if I do not forgive those who injure me, God will withhold forgiveness? Is divine forgiveness conditional on my letting go of grudges and hurts? That seems to be the conclusion here as well as elsewhere in Matthew (6:12, 14–15)—though it is not necessarily so.

Look again at the parable. The most obvious point is that human forgiveness is rooted in divine forgiveness. The king forgives the servant an incalculable amount of indebtedness. Ten thousand talents represents more than the wages of a day laborer for 150,000 years! There is simply no way to measure the extent of God's generosity when it comes to forgiving. "Seventy-seven times" doesn't say it, and neither does "ten thousand talents."

But what happens to the first servant? There is a remarkable gap in the parable. On hearing of his release from the obligation, the servant shows no appropriate response—no rejoicing, no gratitude, no celebrating with wife and children who are spared imprisonment, no reflection about the meaning of freedom. We hear only that on the way out he refuses the pleas of a colleague. The "gap" in the parable has to be taken seriously. The first servant clearly has not "discovered" forgiveness. We already see something of the problem in his initial plea to the king. Though in debt beyond any conceivable capacity to pay, he nevertheless makes his case on a quid pro quo basis. "I will pay you everything" (18:26). He imagines he is dealing with the king on the basis of justice. What he receives but never grasps is the king's mercy.

Forgiveness has to do with something very different from distributive justice. The parable wants us to know that. The first servant still thinks of indebtedness/forgiveness as a power game. He has not come to view himself in a new light as a truly "gifted" person, the recipient of mercy rather than justice. He is not able, therefore, to see himself in the same situation as the second servant, and is not able to show mercy as mercy has been shown. The final verse (18:35) makes it clear that forgiveness is a matter of the "heart," a transformation of the inner disposition of the recipient, something the first servant has not discovered.

How, then, does the passage address seriously injured persons, persons battling with shame and alienation? It portrays in a dramatic story the incredible kindness of God, who surprises people not by dealing with them on the scale of justice, even though they seek it, but by showing mercy. It invites readers to view themselves as forgiven debtors—no more, no less—living with and among fellow debtors. The difference between the debtors is only slight. To be forgiven means to give up the power game of playing innocent versus guilty, and to join a fellowship of forgiven sinners.

PROPER 20

Ordinary Time 25

Sunday between
September 18 and 24 inclusive

Except for the commonality of interest between the Old Testament and Psalm readings, the lections for this day appear to be more horizontally than vertically related. The Epistle reading inaugurates a series of selections from Philippians that lasts four weeks, while the Gospel lection continues the extensive readings from Matthew.

The Old Testament reading from Ex. 16 concerns Israel's primary memory of food given in the wilderness, given where there are no visible sources of life, given in the face of restless protest, given wondrously, inscrutably, saving Israel from both hunger and despair. The passage from Psalms is the fourth citation of Ps. 105 in recent weeks, the present text recalling the marvel of God's grace during the wilderness years and the people's joyful response.

In the lection from Phil. 1 Paul wrestles with the question of God's will with respect to his own leadership. The apostle's imprisonment seems to have cast doubts on his worthiness, at least in the eyes of some. Paul not only explains the meaning of his incarceration, but goes beyond that to explain the meaning of his life: "living is Christ and dying is gain." This reality is valid not only for Paul, but for his readers also.

The Gospel lection from Matt. 20 reminds the reader that in the kingdom of heaven the mercy of God is often surprising, even offensive. Persons are valued not because of their economic productiveness, but because God loves and engages them. That which initially appears to be an outrageous injustice is portrayed as the greatest justice of all—justice motivated by mercy and grace.

Exodus 16:2–15

The story of Yahweh's miraculous feeding of the people in the wilderness is consistent with other narratives of the exodus from

Egypt in that it portrays Israel's God as one who is zealous for the well-being of the people and whose compassion is expressed by continuing intervention in Israel's life. (Compare this text to Num. 11, and note how muted is the interest here in God's anger, a prominent theme in the parallel passage.) This is the same God who promised to be with Moses and the people at the burning bush (Ex. 3), who demonstrated God's awesome care at the Passover (12:1–14) and at the crossing of the sea (14:19–31). Now Yahweh sends manna, Israel's "daily bread," to preserve the people from starvation. Yet the miraculous food is also sent for the purpose of providing a recurring witness to the mercy and presence of Yahweh (16:7).

The narrative is introduced by an account of the grumbling of the people, a recurring theme throughout the accounts of the exodus and wilderness wanderings (14:11–12). "If Yahweh intended to kill us, why not in Egypt where at least our bellies were full?" they complain (16:3). And, as the text makes clear (vs. 7, 8, 9, 11), it is precisely because of the protests of the multitudes that Yahweh acts, as if to demonstrate that their complaints are an example of their foolishness. One is reminded of the remonstrance of the disciples shortly before Jesus' miraculous feeding of the five thousand (Mark 6:35–37). As is the case there, the miraculous food is made to appear, in part at least, as a benevolent rebuke to the shortsightedness of the people.

Apparently there are to be two types of divine food—quails in the evening and manna in the morning (vs. 8, 12–13), but in this passage references to the quails have been given much less prominence than those having to do with the manna (again, cf. Num. 11). Verse 6 appears to suggest that the quails are to be a reminder of Yahweh's intervention in the recent past, while the manna is to bear witness to the present glory of Yahweh. Yet this distinction is only hinted at here and is not developed elsewhere in this text.

The present glory of Yahweh is at the forefront of the text's interest, for there is even a theophany (v. 10), and Moses (together with the people?) hears the words of God giving instructions for the eating of the divine food and drawing attention to the significance of these special meals: "Then you shall know that I am Yahweh your God" (v. 12).

The passage concludes with a description of the arrival of the first foods, quail in the evening and manna the following morning, with, once more, primary interest on the manna (vs. 13–15). The appearance of the divine bread is described, and the puzzled Israelites' question, "What is it?" not only hints at the etymology of the name (*mān hû'*, manna), but extends to Moses the opportunity to provide a theological rationale for this wondrous miracle: "It is the bread that Yahweh has given you to eat" (v. 15).

It is not surprising that many Christian interpreters over the years have related the account of the sending of the manna to the Lord's Supper, for in spite of certain differences, there are many parallels. In both cases, the people are in need of God's grace. In both cases, the beneficiaries of the divine grace do not immediately see the full significance of the food that is before them. In both cases, the food is present as a result of God's intervention in human life. And in both cases, the food is emblematic in that, while it feeds a present hunger, it also fills a deeper need which transcends present appetites. Moses' statement in v.15 is as much at home at the Lord's Table as in the ears of the Israelites in the Wilderness of Sin.

But there is also present in our passage an emphasis on the ability of the miraculous bread to test the faithfulness of the people. Admittedly, part of the expression of this theme lies outside the text as it is defined by the lectionary, but part of it lies within. The bread is to be given daily for six days, but there is to be no miracle on the Sabbath, in order that the people may be tested (v. 4). On the day preceding the Sabbath, the people are to gather twice as much manna as normal, and the next morning—and *only* on the Sabbath morning—the manna will have retained its freshness overnight (vs. 22–24). Later (vs. 16–30), some of the people disobey Yahweh's instructions, only to go hungry! Not even God's miraculous gifts may be taken for granted, but are to be used in the manner and for the purpose for which they are intended.

It is difficult for the reader to understand the callousness and lack of gratitude on the part of these people who have witnessed such powerful expressions of God's mercy, yet prefer grumbling and disobedience to praise. One is reminded once more of the disciples, who often displayed an exasperating inability to understand and be responsive to what Jesus was about (as, for example, in Matt. 16:23). The obtuseness of both Jesus' disciples and Moses' compatriots reminds the reader of this text of how inclusive and patient is the mercy of God.

Psalm 105:1–6, 37–45

The normative account of Israel's past is recited in yet another portion of Ps. 105, as in Propers 12, 14, and 17. In this section of the psalm, there is much less detail, as more events of rescue by God are treated in quick order.

On the summons to doxology in vs. 1–6, see Proper 12.

The body of the recital takes place in three distinct parts, plus one noteworthy "intrusion in the recital."

1. Having skipped over vs. 27–36, our reading treats of the exodus only in vs. 37–38. We are told of only two items about the liberation wrought by Yahweh. First, the Israelites, bond servants as they were and without material resources, did not depart empty-handed. Moses instructed the Israelites that as they departed Egypt they should "ask" the Egyptians for silver and gold. It is likely that the word "ask" is a soft or ironic substitute for "take." These were slaves who had long noticed the economic contrast between establishment affluence and their own deprivation, and they no doubt noticed with resentment. For that reason, when they went they "took," sensing as the disadvantaged frequently do some entitlement to that which has long been denied them. As a consequence, when they arrived in their new place they had some resources. The taking is likely not noble or religiously inspired, but the sort of act any disadvantaged might perform vis-à-vis the "overly endowed."

Second, we are told that Egypt was relieved when Israel finally departed. According to the narrative account of the book of Exodus (12:33), this is in the end correct. What is missing in the terse account of the psalm is that this is a last-minute change of heart on the part of Egypt, brought about by the final plague of the death of the firstborn (v. 36; see vs. 29–30). Up until that desperate moment, mighty Egypt had refused Israel's departure, and accepted it in resignation only when the overriding power of Yahweh had become evident, even to Pharaoh.

2. The second element in this brief recital concerns the wilderness sojourn (vs. 39–41). Two elements of the Pentateuchal account are here accented. First, the cloud and fire are significations of God's guiding *presence* for this people on the dangerous trail of the desert. Second, the two miracles of *sustenance* concerning quail and water bespeak God's powerful, providential care of Israel. The gifts of *presence* and *sustenance* indicate that Yahweh has the capacity to redefine the wilderness into a place of care and support. Israel retells these memories to indicate that by Yahweh's powerful generosity even the wilderness becomes something it was not, namely, a place of viable life.

3. The third element in this retelling concerns arrival in the Land of Promise, the goal of both the exodus (vs. 37–38), and the wilderness sojourn (vs. 39–41). The departure from slavery and the arrival in the land of well-being, the two definitional events in the life of Israel, are a cause for great joy and celebration, because the arrival is

an indication of trust in the God who keeps promises. This long tale of Israel's precarious travel is indeed a move from death to life.

The tradition is candid and unembarrassed that Israel took over the lands that belonged to others, possessing the wealth of other peoples. So long as this tradition is told with theological innocence, the joy for such possession may be unrestrained. We are reminded in this statement, however, that Israel's entry into the land contains an ominous dimension of conflict, violence, and displacement. To treat this treasured memory with "innocence" is not easy, though it may be understood in that way when told of slaves, peasants, and land-hungry seminomads. Here in this psalm, the journey of faith innocently comes to happy fulfillment. God can be trusted! Read in many subsequent contexts, such a move of faith is problematic when it focuses on such abuse of other peoples.

4. Earlier we suggested a noteworthy "intrusion" in this three-event recital. Verse 42 stands out in bold relief as an oddity in the recital. This one verse is not a part of the recital of Mosaic events, as are vs. 37–41, or even of vs. 43–44, which are derivative from Mosaic tradition. This single verse, rather, seeks to go behind Moses and the book of Exodus to the book of Genesis and the promise to Abraham. This verse, introduced by "For," which could be rendered "Because," gives a reason for God to do all these saving miracles. (It has the same function as the parallel statement in Luke 1:48 on the lips of Mary.) The entire saving history, it is asserted, is powered and enacted by God's ancient promise which, circumstance notwithstanding, works its own way in the history of Israel. God is faithful! The promise is trustworthy and overrides all circumstances of bondage, hunger, and death. No wonder Israel sings and rejoices.

Philippians 1:21–30

This is the first of four consecutive Epistle readings taken from Paul's letter to Christians at Philippi, a letter that poignantly reflects on Paul's imprisonment and his intimate relationship with this church. Following the thanksgiving (1:3–11), which expresses Paul's confidence in the partnership of Philippian Christians, he turns to the difficulty posed by his imprisonment. If later generations of Christians see in Paul's imprisonment an indication of his faithfulness, that apparently was not the case with at least some of his contemporaries. Perhaps he encountered the notion that prison meant failure for the church, or that "real apostles" would not find themselves subjected to such humiliation. It is easy to imagine that some

Christians would be shocked at the sight of an imprisoned apostle (see, for example, the attitudes Paul attacks in 2 Cor. 10–13).

Paul's own interpretation of his imprisonment differs dramatically from this negative assessment, as Philippians readily demonstrates. Prison has not hindered, but spread, the gospel, since those around him plainly see that Paul's imprisonment is "for Christ" (Phil. 1:12–13). The fact of Paul's imprisonment has made other Christians bold in their own preaching of the gospel (v. 14). Paul himself will not be shamed by these events, but rather through him the gospel will be exalted (v. 20).

In addition to the need to explain his imprisonment, Paul recognizes that the Philippians have a natural concern about his physical safety. Although Paul seems to anticipate his eventual release (v. 19), he cannot know what the outcome of his imprisonment will be ("whether by life or by death," v. 20). For that reason, he attempts in our passage (vs. 21–30) to show the benefits of either outcome and to encourage the Philippians in what may well be a time of doubt and anxiety.

Paul's stay in prison may lead to his death or it may yield his eventual release. Neither of these outcomes does he regard as failure or loss: "For to me, living is Christ and dying is gain" (v. 21). He could as easily have reversed the two parts of this sentence and written that "living is gain and dying is Christ." Dying, he writes in v. 23, in fact means a departure and the opportunity to "be with Christ." Dying, then, does not signal the end, but rather the culmination of a Christian's hopes in the triumph of Jesus Christ. While death is not to be sought, its arrival is also not to be dreaded. Living in the flesh, on the other hand, also "is Christ." Even the finite life available to flesh nevertheless permits a profound connection with Christ (see, e.g., Gal. 2:20). Continued life in the flesh also means an opportunity for extended labor as an apostle.

Throughout vs. 21–23 Paul juxtaposes the two possibilities that lie before him: to live versus to die, departing to be with Christ versus remaining in the flesh. He even discusses these two possibilities as if the choice is his own, although that probably reflects the need to assure the Philippians that events have not overcome him. With v. 24 the evenhanded consideration of these two options comes to an end: "to remain in the flesh is more necessary for you." Here Paul's vocation comes to the foreground. He has been called as an apostle and labors under a tremendous compulsion to proclaim the gospel in new locales *and* to care for the churches he has already established. He cannot abdicate that commitment in favor of an escape from the world, no matter how attractive that escape might be. The vocation comes first.

As Paul reflects on his own situation and the possibilities that confront him, he also addresses the situation of the Philippians. By expressing confidence about his own future, he exhorts the Philippians to have confidence as well. Moreover, his references to the "progress and joy in faith" (v. 25) of the Philippians functions rhetorically to impress the Philippians with the need to live up to Paul's expectations. Like the parent who praises the good behavior of a child, Paul probably expects that his comments about the Philippians here and elsewhere in the letter will in fact lead to further progress and deeper faith.

The connection between Paul's situation and that of the Philippians becomes explicit in v. 26 with the reference to a future visit of Paul to Philippi, and in v. 27, which marks a transition from consideration of Paul's imprisonment to the situation of the Philippians. Whatever happens to Paul, he wants to be assured that they are secure in their faith. He admonishes them to "live your life in a manner worthy of the gospel of Christ." This brief instruction contains the outlines of Paul's understanding of a Christian ethic. The gospel is freely given to human beings; their appropriate response is to live in accordance with that gospel.

The remainder of the passage announces themes that will carry throughout the letter. The Philippians should be "standing firm in one spirit, striving side by side with one mind for the faith of the gospel." Paul's repetition here of "one spirit" and "one mind" provides a glimpse into his concern for the unity of the church. That unity appropriately reflects the mind of Christ and secures the church against its opponents and the suffering it too may be forced to endure (vs. 28–30). It also would reassure an imprisoned Paul that his own work would survive his death.

Matthew 20:1–16

There is no more cherished word in the Christian's vocabulary than "grace." Simply put, it describes the mercy of God demonstrated in countless ways to undeserving people. It is not surprising that polls show "Amazing Grace" to be by far the most favored hymn of American church members. But just because of its popularity, the notion of grace often loses its cutting edge. It gets acculturated, divorced from the character of a righteous God, resulting in saccharine permissiveness. When that happens, nothing jolts and jars the sentimentality quite like a reading of the parable of the laborers in the vineyard (Matt. 20:1–16). In a vivid and even abrasive story, the radical and offensive nature of grace is depicted, inevitably leaving the reader with the questions, Was the owner really fair? Don't the laborers who worked all day have a legitimate beef?

One word of warning: This is a parable that needs very little explanation or interpretation. Its impact is so forceful, so direct, so engaging that the preacher has to worry about staying out of the way of the parable's confrontation with the congregation. The trick is to let the story have its own way, and then perhaps to help hearers understand their response to the story.

Two dimensions of the context set the parable in proper perspective. First, the audience is primarily the disciples (19:23, 27; 20:17). The passage is a part of their instruction as they make the move from Galilee to Jerusalem (19:1; 20:18). The parable is not in the first instance addressed to the crowds or even to seekers, but to insiders, whose who know, at least in a measure, about divine grace. Second, the story is bracketed by two reversal sayings (19:30; 20:16), sayings that in themselves carry enormous threat for persons who identify themselves as insiders, as the privileged who enjoy a special place with Jesus (see 20:20–28). The parable in effect depicts what it means that the first shall be last and the last first.

As for the parable itself, the radical and offensive character of grace is evident in two sets of relationships. First is the relationship between the owner of the vineyard and the laborers who work all day. The precise telling of the story leaves us with a final scene in which the laborers who work the entire day stand by and watch as the manager pays the other laborers a full day's wages. The first group's anticipation of a bigger wage mounts as they see the generosity shown to the others. When they receive "only" the agreed-upon wages, understandably they grumble against the landowner.

We need to linger a bit over the apparent unfairness of the owner. Imagine what would happen if the world really functioned this way! What if the "equal pay for equal work" principle were not operative? Why, people would sleep late and come to the labor pool only in the late afternoon if they knew they would get paid for the whole day! The owner's action upsets the whole arrangement of societal order, by no means an evil arrangement since it institutionalizes an important principle of justice.

Divine grace, of course, does not rest on the merit system. But because it doesn't, we insiders are prone to grumble. We wonder if grace does not undermine the whole reason for being good, for observing standards, for keeping rules, for living justly. We second-guess a God who breaches the system and equalizes the pay like this. We could support the owner's generosity if the groups of workers that came after noon had merely been delayed, if the truck that brought them to the fields had broken down. But the owner's actions are not the sign of a little generosity to an unfortunate few. They call for a totally different way of viewing God.

But the second set of relationships in the parable gets us even deeper into the offensive character of grace—the relationship between the laborers who work all day and the laborers who come late. The former group express their gripe by saying, "These last worked only one hour, and you have made them equal to us" (20:12). They are envious of the generosity shown the others. Presumably had *they* been the recipients of the owner's gracious method of bookkeeping, they would have been overjoyed. What they cannot take is the beneficence that puts these latecomers on a par with them. The grumblers are not really against grace; they are against grace shown to others and what that implies.

It is an old story. Jonah sat on the brow of the hill outside of Nineveh and pouted when God spared the city. The elder brother thought his father a doting old fool when his father invited him to join the celebrating at the prodigal's return. The Pharisee at prayer thanks God that he is not like the sinful publican. Divine grace is a great equalizer which rips away presumed privilege and puts all recipients on a par. That's hard to stomach when we have burdened ourselves with a merit system and want to see some reward for our labors. That's hard to stomach when we discover those guilty of wrongs we have long opposed (for example, racism, sexism, colonialism, and the like) are brothers and sisters to whom the divine generosity has been shown. Grace no longer seems so sentimental.

PROPER 21

Ordinary Time 26

Sunday between September 25 and October 1 inclusive

The mercy of God, a grace that not even the hardest human heart can frustrate, is a theme that surfaces, in various ways, within the texts for this day. In the Old Testament narrative from Ex. 17, Israel is not sure that God is faithful or reliable. By requesting water and voicing an urgent need, Israel is seen to be testing God, to find out about God's power and inclination. Although water is given and Yahweh is vindicated (that is, passes the test set by Israel), the demand of Israel is judged by the narrative to be disrespectful and inappropriate. God's sovereign intention is not to be questioned!

The lection from Ps. 78 belongs to that genre of hymns within the Old Testament which praise Yahweh, in this instance for Yahweh's grace in liberating the people from Egyptian bondage. In the time of the people's need, Yahweh's mercy sustained and supported them. The ultimate task of the psalm is to teach (v. 1) the people about Yahweh, the bestower of grace and of redeeming love.

The Epistle, the great christological hymn from Phil. 2, sings of God's mercy with an eloquence few biblical texts can match. The passage begins with a statement concerning the need for human kindness and compassion, and then moves to the foundational issue, that work of mercy which motivates human love, namely, the incarnation of God in Jesus Christ. What act of divine mercy could possibly surpass the self-emptying of God, the assumption of servanthood on the part of the Christ? Yet because of this self-giving, God has glorified Christ and has shared with him that same royal majesty of which the psalm passage sings.

The series of readings from Matthew, here 21:23–32, continues with the parable of the two sons, one of whom said he would obey his father but didn't, the other of whom said he would not obey, yet did. The mercy of God, which is extended to those who normally receive no mercy (tax collectors and prostitutes), illustrates not only the inclusive nature of God's grace, but also how different is the kingdom of heaven from the kingdoms of this world.

Exodus 17:1–7

The present text narrates the incident at Massah/Meribah in which Moses struck the rock in order to quench the thirst of the quarrelsome Israelites (compare this text with Num. 20:1–13, which emphasizes the impatience and faithlessness of Moses). In some respects, this passage is a companion piece to Ex. 16:2–15 (Proper 20) where, in response to the grumbling of the people, Yahweh miraculously provides meat and bread to satisfy their hunger. In both texts there is similar thematic movement: the people are in distress, they complain to Moses (interestingly, their distress does not produce repentance—a feature of some biblical texts), and Yahweh responds compassionately to the complaints. In Ex. 16:2–15, the purpose of Yahweh's miracle (in addition to satisfying the needs of the people) is to demonstrate Yahweh's Lordship (16:12). Here, however, there is no such stated purpose, and Yahweh's compassion seems more primitively pragmatic. In fact, if Moses' sentiments reflect those of Yahweh (v. 7), Yahweh provides this miracle grudgingly.

It is difficult for the reader not to entertain some sympathy for the Israelites. The harshness of the Sinai wilderness (note the reference to Mount Horeb in v. 6) is legendary, and even modern travelers through the region have noted a sense of isolation there. If one were not provided with a basic necessity such as water, one's attitude would surely deteriorate with the onslaught of heat and thirst, no matter how intense the euphoria over newly gained freedom. Even liberated slaves cannot live on emotion alone!

But apparently the text condemns the quarrelsomeness of the people precisely because it arises in the aftermath of the miracle of the quail and manna. And the text seems to be asking, Haven't these people witnessed the merciful presence of God in the miracle of the heavenly food? Do they not understand that, having saved and protected them thus far, Yahweh does not intend to let them perish in the wilderness through dehydration? As noted in the comments on Ex. 16:2–15, the dullness of the people reminds the reader of similar instances of obtuseness on the part of Jesus' disciples, who, fresh from some remarkable encounter with the Spirit of God, betray little evidence that they have understood what they have seen or heard or, in some cases, what they themselves have said (see especially

Matt. 16:22–23). Impatience and faithlessness characterize the spirit of the people, an attitude memorialized in the names given to this place, Massah ("Test") and Meribah ("Quarrel").

But if some degree of sympathy with the people is generated in the mind of modern readers of this text, there is much more sympathy with Moses. Poor Moses! Caught between his contentious compatriots and the harshness of the environment, he would also have been tempted to acts of impatience with God, as the Num. 20:1–13 passage, mentioned above, makes clear. Yet in this lection, at least, Moses persists in the role of the mediator, communicating the panic of the people to Yahweh and subsequently enacting Yahweh's instructions as to how to deal with this emergency. How many visionary individuals who undertake leadership roles in the church and in society find themselves incessantly buffeted by the unrealistic demands of those whom they seek to lead, and find themselves trapped between those demands and the realities of a given situation. The portrait of Moses as leader that is found in this and similar texts is a subtle, yet powerful, expression of the difficulties that positions of leadership confer. How much easier, how much less complicated it is to be a follower!

The mention of Moses' staff (v. 5) recalls the incident related in Ex. 7:14–25 in which Moses and Aaron use this object to strike the water of the Nile, transforming Egypt's lifeline into a river of blood. The point is obvious: Yahweh's miraculous power is two-dimensional, in that it can become an instrument either of death or of life. The same Yahweh who can *banish* water from the Nile can *produce* water from a barren rock. Praised be Yahweh! And praised be the relationship between Yahweh and Israel that results in life for the people.

But if this text is describing a present condition (namely, the quarrelsomeness of the people, the discomfort of Moses, and the mercy of Yahweh in sustaining the people), it also points to a future reality. This hint of that which is to come lies in the reference to Horeb (v. 6). Not only are we reminded of the incident of the burning bush (Ex. 3:1), but we are also being prepared for the giving of the Torah at Sinai and the reaffirmation of the covenant which that gift symbolizes. Horeb and Sinai appear to be but two names for the same mountain (Deut. 5:2), and the gushing of the water from the rock, in addition to providing sustenance for the people, also points the reader forward to that other, even greater expression of Yahweh's love for Israel that occurred here. (One need not become excessively entangled in how Israel, already at the mountain, could then travel to the mountain to receive the Torah, Ex. 19:1. We are dealing with more than one literary tradition in this part of the book of Exodus.)

Having fed the people with manna and quail, having quenched their thirst with water from a rock, Yahweh will sustain them in a far more significant manner than with food and drink, and that is with the principles, the ordinances by which they are to live. A narrative of that great act of Yahweh's mercy will provide the Old Testament lection for the next three Sundays (Propers 22, 23, and 24).

Psalm 78:1–4, 12–16

After a rather generic introduction concerning God's miracles as the narrative material of instruction (vs. 1–4), our reading of Psalm 78 focuses on a series of Mosaic miracles (vs. 12–16).

On the introductory verses to this psalm, see Proper 27.

Verse 4 has introduced the subject of Yahweh's "glorious deeds" and "wonders," that is, acts of faithfulness that overwhelm what appeared to be "given" in the circumstance. Now, in vs. 12–16, we take up a specific series of such "wonders" which are normative for Israel's self-identity.

The initial reference in these verses to "marvels" is a use of the same word root as "wonders" in v. 4. First among the wonders cited here is the exodus (vs. 12–13). We are so familiar with the story of the exodus that we often fail to note the remarkable political inversion wrought, according to that account, by the power of God. The event happened in Egypt, a known geographical reference. The term "Egypt" conjures up for Israel a mighty imperial power which treated their ancestors abusively. In the face of mighty Egypt, Israel was indeed small, weak, and insignificant. Yahweh proved to be more than adequate for the crisis, even in the face of Egyptian power. Moreover, Yahweh commanded the very winds and the waters to act as instruments of Israel's rescue (v. 13; cf. Mark 4:41). Pharaoh is certainly a chaotic power who evokes disorder in the earth, but the Creator overrides this force of chaos and puts the powers of creation to positive, saving use. The "wonder" is that Pharaoh's obvious and acknowledged power is overwhelmed and rendered null and void. And when the power of Pharaoh fails, Israel enters a new world of freedom and possibility.

The remainder of our verses concern Israel's experience in the wilderness (vs. 14–16). (On these verses, see Proper 20, concerning Ps. 105.) The wilderness is a place void of resources, where exposure and vulnerability may lead to death. The "marvel" is that this place empty of resources for life is filled with God's resolve to preserve life. God led safely, like a good shepherd (cf. Ps. 23:2–3), in a place endlessly filled with threat, that is, the "valley of the shadow of death" (23:4 RSV). By the signs of cloud and fire, Israel is assured around the clock of Yahweh's mighty, beneficent presence.

More specifically, the wilderness is a place of drought. And in that terrible heat, day after day, Israel is exposed to great danger. So says the teacher to the children: By a stroke against a rock, the arid territory is turned into gushing water (Ex. 17:5–6), and the threat of death is transposed into a long, satisfying drink, which issues in life.

Remember that Ps. 78 is instruction to the children (vs. 1–8). So what is the purpose of telling miracle stories to the children? It is to nurture the children away from excessive realism, which accepts the world's disbelieving verdict about the nature of reality. This fabulous memory asserts that the world, in its most concrete form, is open to healing and transformation by the power of God. The alternative, disbelieving verdict is that the world is a closed system, which remains always the same. Obviously such a view of the world ends in despair. This instruction is to counter despair, and to leave the world as open to hope and possibility as our ancestors have known it to be.

Philippians 2:1–13

The Philippians hymn (Phil. 2:5–11) has already appeared in Year A as the epistolary reading for Palm Sunday. Including as it does the exhortations that precede and follow the hymn, this reading emphasizes the important ethical context in which the hymn occurs. The general movement within the hymn itself is well known. The first half (vs. 6–8) depicts Christ's earthly life as a series of actions in which he gave up his own prerogatives for the sake of obedience ("emptied himself," "taking the form of a slave," "humbled himself," "became obedient to the point of death"). The second half of the hymn (vs. 9–11) depicts God's response ("Therefore") of exalting Jesus, and the resultant universal acknowledgment of Jesus as Lord.

Some questions arise about the precise way in which this hymn is related to the ethical admonitions that appear on either side of it. Is Paul implicitly suggesting that Christians who obey as Christ did will be exalted as Christ has been? That extravagant promise seems unlikely, especially since Paul's experience at Corinth should have taught him that at least some Christians will abuse their own anticipated glorification. Does Paul mean that only Christians who die as Christ did can be regarded as obedient? The answer to that question surely is no, for while Paul recognizes that suffering may come to believers, he does not see it as inherently good.

The introduction to the hymn in v. 5 provides only limited help in understanding the connection between the hymn and the surrounding ethical admonitions, because the Greek of v. 5 is somewhat unclear. If the NRSV translates correctly, then the connection has to do with the "mind," or mind-set, of Christ. Christians are not expected to copy all the actions of Christ, much less to anticipate being "rewarded" as Christ was, but they are able to be shaped by the same way of thinking, the same attitudes. As Christ's way of thinking dictated the obedience that was appropriate for him, so believers will find the obedience that is right for them by sharing in his way of thinking.

Philippians 2:1–4 and 12–13 help to make those attitudes clearer. The chapter opens with a series of appeals to Christian experience ("encouragement in Christ," "any consolation from love," "any sharing in the Spirit," and so forth). The Philippians have experienced some or all of these gifts, which allows Paul to appeal to them as the basis for Christian action. The love, the compassion, the encouragement that they received need also to be displayed in their conduct with one another.

As is usually the case in Paul's letters, the exhortations are to general attitudes rather than to specific behaviors. Here he is concerned with the unity of the community, particularly its unity of thought: "be of the same mind, having the same love, being in full accord and of one mind." The repetitious character of these admonitions underscores the importance Paul attaches to unity within the community. That unity cannot be achieved or maintained if individuals think only of their own interests or care only for their own pride. Unity requires that all share a concern for the common good.

Following the Christ-hymn comes another and different exhortation. Here Paul becomes even more general in his concern, addressing not the specific issue of unity of the community but the larger issue of the way in which Christians approach the living of the faith: "Work out your own salvation with fear and trembling." Even here, however, the salvation Paul addresses is not that of an individual believer, for the "you" in this verse is plural rather than singular. Christians, as those who belong to one another in Jesus Christ, together "work out" their salvation.

Taken out of context, this admonition seems strikingly contradictory to Paul's understanding of justification by grace. Paul does not, of course, mean that Christians bring about their own salvation or that they have the responsibility to earn some part of it. Verse 13 quickly corrects any such misunderstandings, for it is God who is at work in Christians. To "work out" salvation, by contrast, is to take responsibility for understanding what that salvation means in daily life. Particularly in view of the possibility that Paul would not be able to return to Philippi, he urges believers there to make their own judgments about behavior.

Christians work out their salvation with "fear and trembling," acknowledging that they stand accountable before God for their actions. At the same time, they know that God "is at work" within their lives. They thereby trust that God, who has already acted on their behalf and continues to do so, will sustain them and enable them to make judgments that are acceptable and good.

This passage, like others in Paul's letters, makes many Christians uncomfortable. Paul will neither declare that the Christian is free to do whatever she or he likes nor offer a list of rules and regulations to govern behavior and thought. Instead, he insists that Christians may act with confidence, because they have actually been changed by the gospel and because they know that God continues to be at work in their lives.

Matthew 21:23–32

For the next few Sundays, the Gospel lessons from Matthew relate encounters of conflict between Jesus and the Jewish religious authorities—chief priests and elders of the people, Pharisees, Herodians, and Sadducees. The situation of the text obviously reflects historical engagements, both within the ministry of Jesus and within the circumstances of Matthew's community. But our communities and contexts are different, and there are hazards in making the leap from ancient settings to modern ones, especially since these texts in Matthew carry a strong polemic couched in sharp invectives. How do we preach on these passages today?

Two comments about the interpretive move. First, the uniqueness of the ancient contexts prohibits us from generalizing about the Jewish religious authorities. Their picture throughout Matthew's narrative may be something of a caricature, and the modern interpreter must be on guard not to carry over from the passages, directly or subtly, an anti-Jewish sentiment. What was an intramural struggle in the biblical settings would not be so today. Second, the task is to isolate as discretely as possible the *issue* that sets the authorities over against Jesus, often an issue that has immediate relevance to modern audiences. At times there are even pointers within the text itself that tell us that the narrator envisions a wider application.

The brief parable of the two sons follows immediately on the heels of the discussion in the Temple about Jesus' authority (Matt. 21:23–27). The religious leaders are put on the spot when Jesus raises the matter of John's baptism, and employ a face-saving tactic by refusing to answer. In turn, Jesus refuses to answer their initial question about the source of his authority. But there comes from Jesus to the authorities a rhetorical invitation to reflect on the upcoming story to be told ("What do you think?"), a story on which they are to be tested.

A father of two sons directs the first to go and work in the vineyard. He declines, but then changes his mind and goes. The second son is given the same directive, agrees to go, but then doesn't. The authorities are kept in the conversation by Jesus' simple question to them: "Which of the two did the will of his father?" They really have only one option—to say "the first." While their previous face-saving tactic momentarily got them off the hook, there is no possible evasion now.

Before going on to Jesus' conclusion, we can note that the second son's response to the father ("I go, sir [*kyrie*]") may be one of those subtle pointers that suggest a broader application of the parable. The Greek word behind the "sir" is reminiscent of Matt. 7:21, where Jesus says, "Not everyone who says to me 'Lord, Lord [*kyrie, kyrie*],' will enter the kingdom of heaven, but only the one who does the will of my Father in heaven." The second son, who so graciously agrees to work but then fails to fulfill his commitments, recalls all those who declare loyalty and even profess a high Christology, but who exhibit no consistency between words and deeds, between religious activity and obedience. The narrator retells Jesus' parable in such words that those within the Christian community cannot assume that it is directed only to the Jewish authorities and not to them. Doing the will of the Father is as much a Gentile problem as a Jewish one.

The authorities' acknowledgment that the first son is obedient, while the second son isn't, leads to Jesus' pointed application of the story. The tax collectors and prostitutes may not on the surface look much like God's people, especially when compared to the pious religious authorities, but they are identified with the first son, and the religious authorities with the second. The difference lies not in appearances, but in their respective responses to the message of John. The tax collectors and prostitutes believed the message of John, while the religious authorities were resistant.

The prominence of John (cf. 21:25–27) in a narrative written long after his death reminds us that his message lingers on. It is interesting that the text does not exclude the authorities; it does not finally shut the door in their faces. Rather they are invited to rehear John's message and to be open to the reversal it urges. It is the same message Jesus preached; "Repent, for the kingdom of heaven has come near" (Matt. 3:2; 4:17). Through the text, modern-day religious authorities as well as those of Matthew's day are faced with the demand for a similar transformation in the light of God's coming reign, for the same reversal experienced by the first son, who initially rejects his father's directive but changes his mind and obeys.

Proper 22

Ordinary Time 27

Sunday between
October 2 and 8 inclusive

Life before God and life within community may be identified as the related themes in this day's lections. The texts call attention to a reality that is foundational to the biblical proclamation, namely, that finding peace with God and finding peace with one's neighbor are but extensions of the same enterprise—that the former cannot be attained without the latter.

The Old Testament passage from Ex. 20 is so fundamental to the Judeo-Christian-Islamic tradition that it almost beggars comment. It is vital that the Decalogue be considered no litmus test of righteousness or religious purity, but rather a declaration that lies near the heart of the covenant relationship between Yahweh and Israel. Yahweh not only has chosen and redeemed Israel, but has provided the people with an important means by which they may express their acceptance of the divine love. The Torah, or Instruction of God, is that by which the people say "yes" to God's saving initiatives.

Psalm 19 contains one of the most moving meditations on the meaning of Torah in all of the scriptures. Verses 1–6 link the gift of the Torah to other acts of divine creation and furnish important background for the psalm's emphasis on the vitality of the Torah. The balance of the psalm celebrates the strength and beauty of the Torah in poetry of most exquisite formulation, and moves the reader behind the Torah to its Giver, thereby proclaiming the gospel of the well-ordered life.

The reading from Phil. 3 turns to the urgency inaugurated by the Christ-event. Even the accumulated achievements of Paul appear as rubbish in the presence of the reality of the gospel. Paul speaks of himself as leaning into the future ("forgetting what lies behind and straining forward") in response to the manner in which Jesus Christ has invaded his own life.

If Paul urges both himself and, by implication, the Philippians to live in ways that are in accordance with the gospel, the parable of

Matt. 21:33–46 presents a direct and bold affirmation of that same claim. Regardless of the gifts that have been given to God's people, they must live in ways that produce the "fruits of the kingdom." As the wicked tenants could not forever get away with their abuse of the landowner, so those who have been entrusted with God's "property" must not take advantage of that trust.

Exodus 20:1–4, 7–9, 12–20

It does not overstate the case to observe that this passage (along with its parallel, Deut. 5:6–21) is a central pillar in Israel's understanding of its relationship with God and that it is, therefore, one of the most significant contributions of the Old Testament to the church's theology. One may continue by noting that this text also projects a principle that is among the most basic of Western civilization, namely, that there are certain moral postulates that transcend the moment and that may be traced back to the very Creator of the universe. The observation of the American Declaration of Independence that "We hold these truths to be self-evident, that all men are created equal, that they are endowed by their Creator . . ." is one of many instances of the influence of the Decalogue on human life and thought.

In a narrower sense, however, this passage plays a crucial role in the biblical narrative, as it is the consummation of Yahweh's covenant relationship with Israel. On one level, it is an entirely new thing, in that nowhere else in Israel's experience of Yahweh is such dramatic and awesome attention given to the forging of the covenantal union. The description of the theophany in Ex. 19:16–24 leaves no doubt concerning the fundamental urgency of the moment of the giving of the law, and the universal language in which the Commandments are transmitted strengthens the understanding that not only are these instructions from God, but they are intended to shape human life in its every aspect.

On another level, however, it is clear that the giving of the Commandments to Israel is a continuation of that which has gone before. The road to Sinai began at the burning bush (Ex. 3:1–15; Proper 17), where Yahweh summoned Moses to be the instrument of Yahweh's great redemptive activity within Israel's life. And at that time the points of continuity were clearly drawn: "I am the God of your father, the God of Abraham, . . . Isaac, and . . . Jacob" (3:6). Shortly thereafter Moses is directed to declare to the people: "Yahweh, the God of your ancestors, the God of Abraham, . . . Isaac, and . . . Jacob, has sent me to you" (3:15). The covenant that is forged at Sinai is therefore no new departure. It is, rather, the perpetuation and deepening of a relationship that extends back to Abraham. The covenant at Sinai is reaffirmation that Yahweh's activity as redeemer is a continuing affair.

And covenant is indeed the issue here. It cannot be stressed too much that the Torah of God does not descend into human life in splendid isolation from the larger drama. Yahweh's instruction to the people is not the orders of master to slaves, although it is clear that Yahweh and Israel are not equals in the universal scheme of things. The commandments of God are God's gracious gift to the people, by which the people are provided with the means to respond to God's love. They are the instrument placed in Israel's hands by a loving and protective Sovereign, by means of which the people express their acceptance of all Yahweh is and does. Psalm 19, today's psalm, clearly expresses this understanding of the Torah as compassionate and wondrous gift when it identifies the Torah as the greatest of God's acts of creation.

Far too much attention has been given by at least some interpreters of the commandments to the negative language they contain, ignoring the fact that this was a traditional form of legal documentation in the ancient world. In some quarters the result of this bias has been to cast the impression that one attains a posture of faithfulness to God by what one refrains from doing, and, in this mode, individual commandments have been subjected to the most extravagant exegesis. Yet, as Jesus makes quite clear, when the commandments are shorn of their judicial language, they are seen to be ideals of a most positive nature: love God unreservedly, and love your neighbor as you love yourself (Mark 12:29–31 and parallels). And, as original as Jesus' teaching is, the fact that he relies on Old Testament texts (Deut. 6:5; Lev. 19:18) to make his point illustrates that the Torah as positive force was understood in ancient Israel as well.

Paul's discussion of the law (Rom. 7 and elsewhere) highlights the difficulty that even the most faithful persons experience in responding fully to God's loving activity in human life. Idolatry in many forms distracts us from our pure devotion to God, while a concern for self rather than others erodes our social and personal relationships. Only as a man or woman is enabled by the power of God's Spirit may he or she begin to approach the purpose for which the commandments were set forth, that is, to serve as a faithful response to the presence of God's redemptive activity in human life. These gifts of the Spirit (Gal. 5:22–23) permit the man or woman of God to realize an important reality, namely, that even our response to God's loving presence is dependent on and conditioned by God's gracious initiatives in our lives.

This dependence on the Spirit, however, has another dimension. Not only does it illustrate our own weakness and need for God, but it opens the human spirit to more creative avenues of faithfulness and obedience. When one is motivated not by the letter of the law, but by its spirit, possibilities for gracious responses to God's redemptive love are made available that the law, narrowly and literally understood, could never have envisioned. And so Paul can rejoice: "The law of the Spirit of life in Christ Jesus has set you free from the law of sin and of death" (Rom. 8:2).

Psalm 19

Psalm 19 divides into two distinct parts, concerning creation (vs. 1–6) and then the Torah (vs. 7–14).

Creation is a witness to the glory of God (vs. 1–6). Creation is not mute, but speaks powerful, eloquent testimony to the character of God (vs. 1–4b). Notice in these verses that the elements of creation are matched to verbs for speech:

heavens . . . *tell*
firmament . . . *proclaims*
day . . . *pours forth speech*
night . . . *declares*

All of creation is alive to the reality that it is a creature which is derivative of the creator. Creation points beyond itself. Creation in its splendor is glorious—how much more is the Creator glorious.

It is not at all clear what these verses mean, in any precise way. Indeed, if one were not prepared to refer back to the Creator, one might not notice the dimension of witness. But such failure to understand the reference to the Creator is a failure to understand the nature of creation, and reduces the visible world to technical explanations. Those who attend to the intention of testimony, by contrast, discern themselves to be invited to join all the other creatures in praise of the Creator, who is glorious.

But, says v. 3, there is no speech or utterance. The poet knows very well that creation does not talk. Yet the testimony of these wondrous creatures of God is everywhere, open to all, addressed to all who will listen. In these verses there is nothing distinctively Israelite. Even aside from such particularity, those who see creation truly are invited to wonder, awe, and gratitude, and finally even to obedience. The psalm, given its large horizon, is addressed to every human creature and bears witness to the God of all people, as of all other creatures.

The heavens, named in v. 1 as the first witness to God, are now presented as a shelter for the sun. The sun in turn performs as a key witness to the Creator (vs. 4a–6). The poet waxes eloquent about the sun, and does not even refer to the sun specifically as a witness. That is all implied here from vs. 1–4b. But what a witness! The sun rises in the morning with the eagerness of a bridegroom rushing to meet the bride on their wedding day; moreover, the sun does it every day with such eagerness! The sun moves like a strong athlete, who delights in her speed and prowess and cannot wait for the next competitive event. The sun moves all over the earth, and impacts every other creature. About the sun, we are left to improvise from vs. 1–4b. Even the sun refers itself back to the creator of the sun, even more splendid, more eager, stronger, more impacting than the sun. In the context of the hymn, even the sun refers us back to Yahweh, and invites us to wonder and amazement and praise.

The move from awe and wonder to obedience marks the abrupt transition to vs. 7–10. Now we move to particularly Israelite categories, away from the creation categories shared by all human persons and communities. Unlike creation, the Torah commandments are the particular gift of Yahweh to Israel.

The psalmist meditates on the life-giving power of the commandments. The poem contains six parallel statements, using synonymous phrasing. The synonyms are "law [Torah] . . . decrees . . . precepts . . . commandment . . . fear of Yahweh . . . ordinances." The commands are a gift because we do not need to reinvent the wheel, and we do not need to guess about the fundamentals of God's intention for the ordering of creation. That intention has been disclosed to us in the commandments. The commandments are God's way of protecting the human community against dehumanization and barbarism, and the nonhuman creation from excessive exploitation.

The commandments, which arise out of God's own mouth, are truly wondrous. Israel is amazed and grateful for the commands. They are said to be "perfect [i.e., complete] . . . sure [reliable] . . . right [correct] . . . clear . . . pure . . . true . . . and righteous." That is, God got it right. The commandments work. They are adequate. They cover all cases. They will indeed guard, protect, and enhance communal life.

The poet not only celebrates and characterizes the commandments. They are also seen to be active, powerful agents of newness. They have creative force to effect change. The Torah restores one's life, makes one wise, causes one's heart to rejoice, causes eyes to sparkle, lasts endlessly. Obedience to command is a mode of communion with God and a way of being one's true self in the world. The commands not only instruct how to act, but in fact bestow one's genuine identity. Through obedience one gets in touch with one's true self, as that self is willed and destined by God.

This latter affirmation leads to a lyrical claim (v. 10). The commandments, which liberate life from brutality, alienation, anxiety, and guilt, are the richest gift God has given to us. The commands in the end are more treasured than much money, for money cannot give one a true self. The commands are sweeter than honey; in the end honey is ephemeral and the taste vanishes, but obedience gives a taste of sweetness that persists, for all of life is sweetened in the face of anxiety. This advocate of the Torah is not naive, not unaware of ambiguity, not blind to evil. This advocate of a life under command, however, has understood what it means for living to have a settled center outside one's self, to be in trustful communion with the One who rightly orders our life. Such a life is freed from chaos and disorder, and therefore is not wearied about getting through the day.

After this celebration of command, with great moral sensitivity the speaker understands that guilt and sin are subtle (vs. 11–13). The commands themselves are no sure guarantee of an innocent life. The commandments are of course important, but finally, after one's best obedience, one must turn to the Lord of the commandments. Thus the psalm speaks not of complacency but of petition. The prayer offered is a series of imperatives asking God to do for us what we cannot do for ourselves: "Clear . . . Keep back . . . do not let them have dominion." God is not simply a rule giver, but an active agent to guard our life against our own destructive tendencies. It is because of the watchful care of God that one can be innocent and trusting. Thus the commands are only penultimate. They are the threshold over which one steps to the reality of God's profound care. This psalm knows that moral seriousness matters. One must pay attention. The psalm also knows, however, that beyond moral seriousness (vs. 7–10) is trust in God, which counts finally not on obedience but on God's trustworthiness (vs. 11–13).

The psalm ends in a well-known petition of trust and confidence (v. 14). God is the source of well-being, rock and redeemer, point of safe reference and guardian of well-being. It is God who is finally the subject of this psalm, not the Torah. This confident, trusting, innocent petitioner seeks very little. The prayer asks only to have the "words of my mouth" accepted, words of trust and devotion and obedience. It asks to have the meditations of the heart made acceptable, that constant thoughts about command and obedience may be adequate to God (cf. Ps. 1:2). The speaker is under grateful discipline, and so prays with serenity. We are not told how God answered this petition. We share with the psalmist confidence that a life of obedience and a prayer of trust will be honored by God.

The two parts of this psalm on creation and Torah do not belong together in any obvious way. The juxtaposition of the two parts, however, invites us to understand Torah afresh, not simply as rules of conduct, but as the moral shaping of a glorious creation. Creation itself has a moral shape and insistence which cannot be violated and disregarded. But the Torah commands are not primarily prohibitive or negative. Rather, they are life-giving, because they reflect the character of creation, which is designed to "bear fruit." Obedience to Torah, then, is compliance with God's intention for all creation. Adherence to Torah lets us be a life-receiving part of creation.

Philippians 3:4b–14

In the verses that immediately precede this reading, Paul issues a warning against "the dogs," the "evil workers," "those who mutilate the flesh." Scholars debate a number of details about the group Paul has in mind, but it appears that its adherents insist on circumcision for Gentile Christians and boast about their connections with Israel (see Phil. 3:2–4a).

This lection constitutes part of Paul's response to this group. He begins with the claim that he has more reason than they for "confidence in the flesh" (v. 4). Verses 5–6 form a kind of curriculum vitae, beginning with aspects of Paul's life that were decided by virtue of his birth. He was "circumcised on the eighth day, a member of the people of Israel, of the tribe of Benjamin, a Hebrew born of Hebrews" (v. 5). The second half of the list includes matters over which Paul did have a choice: "as to the law, a Pharisee; as to zeal, a persecutor of the church; as to righteousness under the law, blameless" (vs. 5–6). He himself made decisions to pursue and maintain these behaviors.

The picture these phrases create contradicts the general impression many people have, in large part a legacy of Augustine and Luther, that the "pre-Christian" Paul was riddled with guilt over his inability to live as the law demanded. On the contrary, Paul presents himself as an accomplished Jew who had been deeply involved in the best part of his tradition and who defended that tradition zealously. (The reference to persecuting the church does not necessarily contradict this picture, since Paul's persecution may well have been social and economic harassment, which he saw as part of protecting his people.)

The break between v. 6 and v. 7 is dramatic. Without ever even hinting at a vision or a light or a "road to Damascus," Paul marks the change conventionally referred to as his "conversion": "whatever gains I had, these I have come to regard as loss because of Christ." Again contrary to the general impression of Paul, he does not depict his call or conversion as the solution to a problem, the release from some deep moral or psychological or spiritual crisis. Quite the opposite! "Because of Christ," all these accomplishments became for him simply "loss."

Verse 8 restates this assertion more strongly. It was the "surpassing value of knowing Christ Jesus" that led to the radical transformation of Paul's values. He now regards them as "rubbish." At this point the NRSV is somewhat euphemistic in its translation; the more graphic word "dung" is much to be preferred. Even the best that Paul had accomplished he came to regard as nothing more than garbage because of the revelation of Jesus Christ.

What Paul means by "knowing Christ Jesus" becomes more clear in the remainder of the lection. First, it means being "in him" (v. 9), the connection with Christ and all believers that elsewhere Paul terms "the body of Christ." Second, it means leaving aside the righteousness of one's own accomplishments in favor of the righteousness that "comes through faith in Christ" (v. 9). No longer can Paul speak or act or think as if his work is his own alone, or as if his work acquired for him standing before God. The righteousness Paul now seeks is God's own. That righteousness finally ends in the resurrection itself (v. 10).

Despite the significant change Paul has experienced, he is careful to acknowledge that he has not yet arrived at the goal. The goal itself appears to be of two sorts. First, he identifies "the resurrection from the dead" as his goal; that is, he aims at being with Christ following his own death (see 1:23). The second goal is spiritual maturity, but that goal is somewhat obscured by the NRSV. Translated more literally, v. 12 opens with the words, "Not that I have already received this or already been made mature." Paul acknowledges that he has not yet achieved the goal he would set for himself.

He continues to pursue that goal "because Christ Jesus has made me his own." The English translation here needs to be more forceful, as in "because I have been overtaken by Christ Jesus." Paul's understanding is that he was seized or captured by Christ, not that he initiated the relationship, or that he earned it somehow. Because of that seizure, which Paul now understands to have been a gift of grace, he continues to strive toward what lies ahead.

Paul's interpretation of his own conversion is highly suggestive for contemporary reflection on what it means to proclaim the gospel. Unlike many traditional approaches to evangelistic preaching, which offer the gospel as the answer to problems in people's lives, Paul understands the gospel to be just the opposite. It gave him no answers to problems, but instead it disturbed his answers and sent him in search of a new "solution," a new understanding. More precisely, it thrust a new understanding on him, an understanding that required radical reassessment of past, present, and future.

Matthew 21:33–46

For three Sundays the Gospel lessons direct us to consecutive parables in Matthew's narrative that seem pointedly aimed at the Jewish rejection of the Messiah and at the movement of the Christian message to a non-Jewish world. And yet, with all three parables, a careful reading of the text reveals a broader concern and a wider audience than merely the case for a Gentile mission. In last Sunday's passage we discovered that the parable of the two sons (Matt. 21:28–32) was retold in such a way that the fundamental question raised is: Have you heeded John's message of repentance and "change[d] your minds"? In today's reading, Jesus tells "another parable" (21:33), which confronts readers with the need to produce "fruits of the kingdom" (21:43). Likewise, the third parable (22:1–14), with its addendum about the guest at the wedding without proper wedding attire, speaks directly to the non-Jewish community that has come to participate in the festivities.

The first thing to observe about the parable of the wicked tenants is the highly christological cast to the story as it is retold by the narrator of Matthew. The son comes in the line of the prophets who have been stoned and killed (see Matt. 23:37). When the wicked tenants reason that eliminating the son will enable them to inherit the vineyard, they throw him "out of the vineyard" and kill him. The Jewish authorities, who are engaged in dialogue and who inadvertently condemn themselves by their answer (21:40–41), don't initially get the point, but the narrator's citation of Ps. 118:22–23 (in Matt. 21:42) makes it perfectly clear. The rejected stone has become the cornerstone. This is a text the early church used to underscore God's vindication of the prophetic, crucified Jesus in the resurrection (e.g.,

Acts 4:11). Unambiguously the son is Jesus, and the vantage point of the allegorical retelling of the parable is Easter.

Through the citation of the psalm in 21:42, the parable seems to be about the Jewish rejection of the Messiah, cleverly told in such a way that the religious leaders pronounce a verdict on themselves ("put these wretches to a miserable death"). One can imagine the initial readers of Matthew's Gospel, a mixture of Jewish and Gentile Christians in a bit of a squabble with the synagogue down the street, deriving comfort from this word of judgment spoken against their opposition. But then the passage takes a different turn. The vineyard (now the kingdom) is wrenched from the original tenants who have abused their privileged status, and it is given, not to Gentiles per se, but to "a people that produces the fruits of the kingdom" (21:43). There is no reason for Matthew's initial (or modern) readers to gloat over the plight of the original tenants or to take unwarranted pleasure in their own membership in the "right" community. They cannot count on an automatic transfer, as if now they have been guaranteed tenantship. The question is: Are they (we) a people producing "the fruits of the kingdom"?

"Fruit" appears as a frequent and vivid image in Matthew's Gospel. It is prominent in John's message to the Pharisees and Sadducees (3:7, 10) and in Jesus' Sermon on the Mount (7:15–20). True repentance issues in a changed life, in radical obedience to God, in more than talk or right theology—in "good fruit." The whole Gospel, positively and negatively, provides vignettes of what the changed life is like, perhaps summed up in the two commandments to love God and to love neighbor (22:34–39). In the parable, the totality of allegiance demanded by God is hinted at when the owner sends servants "to collect his produce" (RSV "to get his fruit," 21:34), a slight variation from the Markan version ("to collect from them *his share* of the produce of the vineyard," Mark 12:2, emphasis added). For Matthew, God's share is the whole harvest.

The text brings readers face-to-face with the exclusive demands of God, with the challenge of a righteousness that exceeds that of the scribes and the Pharisees (5:20). While the parable does convey the history of God's dealing with the Jewish people, the history is told in such a way that the hearers (and readers) are pushed to examine themselves and not rest easy with a sense of cheap grace. The original hearers perceived this, but unfortunately they felt the only response was violence (21:45–46).

PROPER 23

Ordinary Time 28

Sunday between
October 9 and 15 inclusive

The motif of the golden calf dominates both the Old Testament text and the Psalm lection. The narrative in Ex. 32:1–14 would appear almost comic if it were not so desperately tragic. Hardly have the Israelites received the Commandments from Yahweh on Mount Sinai and entered into the covenant that those commandments were intended to ratify, than they grow impatient. Yet the monumental blindness of the people is not the only concern of the text. Rather, the focus is also placed on Yahweh's intense anger and on Moses' intervention. The result is that Yahweh's mercy prevails, and Moses is revealed as the quintessential mediator that he is.

The text from Ps. 106 recalls the folly of the people in manufacturing the golden calf and amplifies on the significance of the Exodus text. In large measure the sinfulness of the Israelites is laid to their forgetfulness, their lack of memory of the saving deeds of their God. The inability or unwillingness of the people of God to remember is a damning sin, and Israel rightly should be destroyed. But, as in the Exodus text, Moses, the great intercessor, is credited with eliciting from Yahweh that mercy by which the people are saved.

The concluding reading in the series from Philippians (Phil. 4:1–9) draws together a number of themes that run throughout the letter. Perhaps the most important among them is the need for faithfulness to the gospel. As Christ was faithful to death, and Paul has himself endeavored to be faithful to his own calling, he urges the Philippians to "stand firm in the Lord" (4:1). In this way, they may regard both Christ and Paul as examples of Christian behavior.

If Philippians offers a positive example of faithfulness, Matthew's version of the parable of the wedding banquet (Matt. 22:1–14) offers a negative example, in the form of a guest who comes to the wedding without the proper attire. Caught up in their own identification with the outcasts who are finally included in the banquet, Matthew's readers may find themselves confronted with their own complacency and their desire to judge others rather than to reform themselves.

Exodus 32:1–14

The episode of the golden calf shocks and disturbs us, coming as it does so quickly on the heels of Yahweh's giving of the Torah to Moses and to the nation on Mount Sinai. This moment of great importance in the drama of Israel's (and humankind's) salvation by God is followed by a shameful denial by the people of the very love and power that has saved them. Having been compassionately embraced and delivered from their peril, the people restlessly turn away from Yahweh to gods of gold.

The immediate cause of their apostasy is Moses' delay in coming down the mountain. In the sequence of the narrative as we have received it, Moses, sometimes accompanied by Aaron and other leaders of the people (Ex. 24:9), has made a number of trips up the mountain to receive further amplifications of the Torah, laws having to do with a variety of matters, many of them liturgical in nature (Ex. 21—31). Finally, Moses is entrusted with the two tablets of the covenant and, presumably, prepares to return to the people (31:18). But he has delayed too long in the eyes of Israel, and the people cry out for new divine leadership, "gods . . . who shall go before us" (32:1).

The role of Aaron in this affair is difficult to explain. His willingness to desert his brother and to yield to the impulses of the crowd seems incomprehensible, but he offers no recorded protest. Asking for the people's gold, he fashions it into a calf, which the people hail as divine. Why this particular animal should be chosen is unclear, but Aaron's statement in v. 5 implies that the calf was considered a representation of Yahweh (cf. 1 Kings 12:28). Thus the Second Commandment, if not also the First, has been violated in the most flagrant manner (Ex. 20:2–6).

An indignant Yahweh alerts Moses, who is still on the mountain, to what has happened and promises judgment (32:7–10). Although scholars have, with justification, viewed the repetitious nature of vs. 7–8 as evidence of complex redactional activity (notice how v. 8 reproduces v. 4), in its canonical form these repetitions serve to emphasize the heinousness of what Israel has done. Thus we are not completely unprepared for Yahweh's fury: "Get out of my way, Moses, and let me at the people. I shall destroy them, but of you I shall make a great nation." That is at least one possible way of paraphrasing vs. 9–10.

The lection reaches a climax as Moses, who has been rebuffed by the people and, momentarily at least, shunted aside by Yahweh, steps forward to reclaim his role as mediator between Yahweh and the people. The qualifying phrase in v. 11, "whom *you* brought out of the land of Egypt with great power and with a mighty hand" (emphasis added) seems to echo vs. 4 and 8, where salvation is attributed to the calf-god(s). The people may be in doubt as to who has saved them, but Moses is under no illusion, and he is well aware that that divine power which has saved Israel may now destroy it.

In his intercession with Yahweh, Moses makes appeal by means of two arguments. The first goes something like this: "Why give the evil Egyptians the satisfaction of seeing their enemies destroyed by the very God who once saved them? That will only lead them to attribute false and malicious motives to you, Yahweh" (v. 12). The second appeal is to the covenant with the ancestors of Israel (v. 13), although this argument seems to ignore that Yahweh has just announced an intention to fulfill that covenantal promise by initiating a new line of Moses' descendants (v. 10b).

The lection ends with the simple declaration that "Yahweh changed his mind . . ." (v. 14). If the reader is surprised by what may appear to be vacillation on the part of Yahweh, it is well to recall a number of other texts in the Old Testament in which Yahweh restrains judgment on a sinful people because of the intercession of a just mediator (e.g., Gen. 18:22–33; Amos 7:3, 6). The point is not that Yahweh is indecisive, but that Yahweh's justice is tempered with mercy, and that when the two qualities clash the former yields before the latter.

It is important in interpreting this text that the Christian exegete identify with the rebellious people, and not contrast the church's life before God with that of Israel. As observed previously, the portrait in Exodus of the children of Israel anticipates in important respects that of the disciples in the New Testament Gospels. Just as Israel was blind to the initiatives of God and often didn't recognize them even when in closest proximity, so the followers of Jesus often misunderstood and misjudged his teachings and his acts of compassion (see Mark 10:35–45). In both cases, only the patience and mercy of God sustained the relationship, and only the patience and mercy of God permitted the people to move from doubt to faith. Everyone kneels before the golden calf, everyone who has received the saving love of God with less than the full devotion that it demands—and that includes us all.

Not only is this message contained in the text, but we are impressed again with the value of Moses both to Israel and to Yahweh.

To Israel this great man of God served as the channel of divine guidance and strength at a time when the nation so desperately needed both qualities. And to Yahweh, Moses served not only as faithful servant, but as patient voice insisting that justice is not justice unless it is administered in love.

Psalm 106:1–6, 19–23

Israel remembers its past: in this particular account, that past is not a good memory. It is a story of unmitigated distrust and disobedience on the part of Israel. That story should have brought deathly destruction—except for the powerful intervention of Moses.

The hymnic opening of Psalm 106 moves through a series of stylized phrasings of praise and prayer (vs. 1–6). Verse 1 constitutes by itself an independent hymnic expression, which celebrates God's abiding fidelity (cf. Ps. 117; Jer. 33:11). Verse 2 refers to the "deeds of might" (NRSV "mighty doings") which function as the subject of these psalms. These deeds are the substance of Israel's memory and the data from which Yahweh's steadfast love is attested. After these two hymnic affirmations, v. 3 is a very different sort of statement. It echoes wisdom sayings and has a didactic intention. This two-line statement affirms the moral reliability of the world. Those who enact justice and righteousness are the ones who are "happy" (blessed). This verse constitutes a norm for what follows in the psalm, suggesting that disobedient Israel has not done justice and righteousness, and therefore has not enjoyed and will not enjoy "happiness" (well-being).

Whereas vs. 1–3 are quite public and impersonal, these verses are followed in vs. 4–5 by a first-person-singular prayer. The speaker asks God to be attentive to the speaker. But this single speaker immediately turns the petition toward the community and, as is characteristic in Israelite piety, prays as a member of the community, seeking the well-being of "chosen" Israel. That is, the prayer asks God to continue in fidelity and to continue to enact "mighty doings."

All these statements are preliminary, for in v. 6 the prayer comes to its real subject, a confession of sin. The confession is uttered in the context and horizon of God's gracious miracles. The faithfulness and mighty deeds of God are asked in order to override the consequence of Israel's long-standing pattern of sin. This generation of Israelites, perhaps in exile, are the heirs of long generations of disobedience, and are suffering the consequences of a long inheritance of recalcitrance and rebellion. From this point on, the psalm articulates a steady interaction between Israel's sin and Yahweh's graciousness, ending in v. 47 with a petition that God's graciousness will be powerful and constant, for disobedient Israel has no other source of hope.

In our selected verses, the general rebellion of Israel is focused and specified at Mount Sinai (Horeb; vs. 19–23a). The episode of the "calf" in Ex. 32 is regarded in Israel as the paradigmatic act of disobedience. In the complicated history of the "calf" (cf. 1 Kings 12:25–33), three elements made the calf a model of wrongheadedness: (a) the calf is of gold, that is, it is worship of Israel's best "commodity"; (b) the calf was in Israel an emblem of fertility, and therefore fertility religion creeps into Israel's covenantal faith; and (c) both these elements, of commodity and fertility, derive from the larger problem that the calf is self-generated for the sake of Israel's self-sufficiency—the calf is a gesture of self-indulgence, which substitutes worship of self for worship of Yahweh. That is, the calf mediates a religious gesture whereby Israel orders all its life around its own capacities. The "molten image" (cf. Ex. 20:4) is in fact an attempt to harness and capture "holy power" for one's own purposes.

This poem shrewdly articulates the depth of the religious transaction of the calf episode. Israel made an exchange. It was a bad, stupid, costly, unequal exchange. Israel had in its midst God's glory, that is, presence and power for life. Israel gave up that presence for a grass-eating ox, or a calf. Israel was allied with the God of life, and in a moment of self-indulgence it gave away its chance for life to have in its power and possession this alternative religious symbol. (On such an exchange, see Jer. 2:11–13 and Rom. 1:25.)

Our ancestors would not have made the silly exchange if they had remembered; but they forgot (see Ps. 106:7). At Horeb, they forget the exodus. It did not take long to forget. In the very moment when God was making covenant with them, they forgot the deliverance that is the basis of covenant. They forgot the wonders (*pĕlā'ôt*) that created historical possibilities (v. 7). This would explain why they made the silly exchange. They no longer could notice that Yahweh is distinctive, the one who alone can intrude, liberate, and transform. When all of Yahweh's miracles are forgotten, then one god looks as good as any other. The Israelites were no longer able to discriminate among the gods, among the gods who can do nothing (in this case the calf) and the only God, who is known as "Savior." Israel lost its memory, and when memory vanished, the truth of Yahweh's distinctiveness was also forgotten. And when Yahweh's distinctiveness is forgotten, Israel can no longer recall its own peculiar destiny in the world.

The upshot of such an act of rejection would inevitably be destruction: "Therefore" (v. 23a). God will not tolerate such rebellion. Israel's relation with God should have ended in destruction. It did not, however. It did not, because . . .

The sentence in v. 23a breaks abruptly. What we expect to follow next does not appear. The didactic sequence that we anticipate does not occur, because God's own chosen agent, Moses, intervenes (v. 23b). Moses stands in the breach at great risk, and breaks the pattern set in motion by Israel's disobedience. Moses placed his body, his reputation, his very life in the dangerous place between an angry God and a pitiful people. Yahweh would destroy Israel, but could do so only over Moses' dead body (cf. Ex. 32:32). Moses prevented God from doing what God passionately wanted to do and legitimately should have done. Moses is daring intercessor, courageous mediator, and in the end effective rescuer.

Israel recalls the strategic and inimitable role of Moses. Israel also recalls how close to death it came, saved only by the self-risking, self-giving of Moses. Israel's future is sustained by the thin line of Moses' bold resistance to Yahweh. In light of Israel's long story of recalcitrance, the present generation ("we") can be amazed and grateful for the last-minute rescue through the intervention of Moses (cf. v. 8). Israel's life has begun in miracle; it has until now continued as a miracle. In its stubbornness, Israel lives on borrowed time, borrowed from the life of Moses.

Philippians 4:1–9

This lection appears to be a rather loose collection of miscellaneous exhortations, but taken together they repeat many of the important themes of Philippians as a whole. Three admonitions directly relate back to earlier parts of the letter, and three other themes, although implicit earlier in the letter, come to expression here in new ways. First, Paul urges the Philippians to "stand firm in the Lord." These words aptly summarize much of Paul's letter to Christians at Philippi. Writing to them from prison and obviously concerned about their ability to withstand various pressures without his presence, Paul at several points implores the Philippians to steadfastness (1:9–11; 1:27; 2:12; 2:16). Nothing should be allowed to undermine the faith that has nurtured and nourished these people.

One persistent threat to faithfulness is disunity, and so it is not surprising that the second exhortation Paul repeats is for unity. Earlier in the letter he urged that the Philippians be of the same mind (2:1–2) and think of one another's interests (2:3–4). Here that plea for unity becomes quite specific, as Euodia and Syntyche are the objects of concern. No information tells us who these women were, except that they are among those who work on behalf of the gospel. They may well have been leaders in the Philippian congregation, especially since Paul refers to them by name. He can assume that his readers know the women and their circumstances. What is important for Paul to address is their need to reach a common mind.

The third exhortation that repeats earlier material in the letter begins in vs. 8–9 and culminates in the words: "Keep on doing the things that you have learned and received and heard and seen in me." Throughout the letter, both explicitly and implicitly, Paul has offered himself as an example to be imitated. His attitude toward his own imprisonment, his rejection of past values in favor of being overtaken by the gospel of Jesus Christ, his single-minded focus on the citizenship of heaven—all these are aspects of Paul's life that he offers for their instructional value. In the same way, he sees in the story of Jesus Christ an example of obedience that instructs Christians in their own obedience (2:5–11).

Along with these admonitions which clearly recall earlier instructions in the letter there are three themes that, while consistent with the rest of the letter, appear here for the first time. First, 4:6 reads. "Do not worry about anything, but in everything by prayer and supplication with thanksgiving let your requests be made known to God." Paul's earlier refusal to be derailed by his own imprisonment may offer a model of this saying. Later in this same chapter, he reflects on his own experience of learning to cope both with abundance and with need. Contemporary Christians, many of whom make a virtue of worrying about everything, will find this instruction challenging, to say the least! Reminiscent of the language of Matt. 6:25–33, it reflects a profound sense of confidence in God's providence.

A second theme that ties together this reading, reinforcing earlier parts of the letter but becoming explicit here for the first time, is the theme of God's presence and the nearness of the eschaton. "The Lord is near," Paul writes in v. 5. "And the peace of God, which surpasses all understanding, will guard your hearts and your minds in Christ Jesus" (v. 7). The passage closes with a third assurance that "the God of peace will be with you" (v. 9). Unlike most of this reading, these are statements of assurance rather than words of exhortation or admonition. Nevertheless, their connection with the ethic Paul advocates is clear. Steadfastness, unity, reliance on God rather than on anxiety are possible only for those who know that God will indeed be with them.

A third theme in this lection is that of joy. Verse 4 exhorts, "Rejoice in the Lord always; again I will say, Rejoice." Paul has earlier expressed his own joy over the Philippians (1:4) and over the gospel itself (1:18). Here he urges that same joy on the Philippians. This is surely one of the most important—and one of the most neglected—aspects of this letter and of Paul's understanding of the Christian life. Even as his own well-being is threatened, even as he contemplates the possibility of not seeing Christians at Philippi again, he is able to voice joy over them and urge joy on them.

Some contemporary Christians may find this an unexpected element in Paul's letter. Like the proverbial New Englander who fears that "someone, somewhere might be having a good time," some people associate the faith itself with a sobriety that suspects joy of being trivial or of lacking in dignity. Others will welcome Paul's words as a confirmation of the attitude that the church exists in order to make people feel good. Paul would find himself profoundly ill at ease with either group. For him, joy comes as an entirely appropriate response to the good news of God's action in and through Jesus Christ. Joy, then, is a by-product of the gospel, not to be confused with the good news itself.

Matthew 22:1–14

Most preachers, given the option of choosing either Matthew's or Luke's version of the parable of the banquet as the text for a sermon, would unquestionably choose Luke's. The story in Luke (14:15–24) is more straightforward, cleaner, without the violent and complicating features that characterize the allegorical retelling in Matthew. Luke's parable has a powerful quality of engaging the reader with the characters in the plot. The unusual details of Matthew's account, however, result in an unrealistic and unbelievable story.

The meal is a wedding feast hosted by a king. When the servants are sent to tell the invited guests to come, a strange thing occurs: they are made light of, mistreated, and even killed (much as the servants were in the parable of the wicked tenants, Matt. 21:35–36), an odd way to treat servants who have come to perform a positive and helpful function. Understandably, the king reacts with rage, but then the story of the feast itself is interrupted long enough to allow the king time to marshal his troops, destroy the invited guests, and burn their city. The meal is held in abeyance until the violence is over. Then the story is taken up again: the second group of guests are invited off the streets, and the wedding hall is filled.

Apparently Matthew's parable is the result of applying a simpler version of the story of the banquet to the Jewish rejection of the Christian gospel. The servants calling the invited guests are preachers who have been abused and whose message has been rejected by Jewish leaders. The vengeance by the king seems to relate to the havoc wrought on the city of Jerusalem by the Romans in 70 C.E. (perhaps interpreted in the light of Isa. 5:24–25). The guests brought in from the streets are the Gentiles, who end up enjoying the wedding banquet. Just as the parable of the two sons reflects the Jewish rejection of the message of John (Matt. 21:28–32) and the parable of the wicked tenants reflects the Jewish rejection of Jesus, who comes in the line of the prophets (21:33–43), so the parable of the wedding banquet reflects the Jewish rejection of Christian messengers, who bring the invitation to the kingdom.

But just as in the two previous parables, the narrator will not let the audience bask complacently in the judgment pronounced on others. The jolt comes in the added scene—the guest found at the festivities without a wedding garment (22:11–14). Here again there are details in the story hard to fathom. Should a guest invited off the street be expected to have the appropriate clothes? What is implied when the guest is described as "speechless" (22:12)? Is this evidence of guilt, or is he stunned into silence? Isn't "the outer darkness," with its "weeping and gnashing of teeth," a harsh punishment for one who only lacks the proper attire?

In spite of its sharpness, the story works its purpose of challenging the smugness of the audience. The Jewish leaders or people are no longer in view, only the Christian hearers/readers. As in every period of the church's history, Matthew's community is composed of "both good and bad" (22:10). Sometimes the issue is whether the community should rid itself of the bad, pull up the weeds that have grown amid the wheat (13:24–30, 36–43). Here there seems to be no such issue, only the effort to confront the audience with the hapless and disquieting figure of the guest without a wedding garment. Judging others is no business of the audience; rather, they are to tend to themselves, their own preparedness to meet the King, their readiness in the face of judgment.

In this allegorical retelling of Matthew, what does the wedding garment signify? A host of answers have been given, going all the way back to patristic times, but in Matthew's context the wedding garment must symbolize "[doing] the will of my Father in heaven" (7:21), having "a righteousness [that] exceeds that of the scribes and Pharisees" (5:20), producing "the fruits of the kingdom" (21:43). All are expressions to identify the consistency between speech and life, words and deeds, that is appropriate for those who call Jesus "Lord." The garment represents authentic discipleship, and the parable prods the audience to self-criticism lest they find themselves among the bad, who are finally judged.

While the Lukan version of the parable of the banquet seems more to the point and is certainly more popular, Matthew's version presses an ancient issue about the quality of our lives: whether in the ordinary dimensions of our relationships we manifest a genuineness, a trustworthiness. The surprise surrounding the verdict of the king on the man without the wedding garment is reminiscent of the surprise shown by the two groups gathered before the final judgment when they hear words of commendation or judgment (25:37–39, 44). What matters is a life without pretense or guile, that takes seriously the grace given in Jesus Christ.

PROPER 24

Ordinary Time 29

Sunday between
October 16 and 22 inclusive

The Old Testament lesson from Ex. 33 narrates further activity of Moses, the mediator, who is as concerned to represent Israel before Yahweh as he is to interpret Yahweh's ways to the people. Because of their sinfulness the people are worthy of judgment, and on that judgment Yahweh seems intent. But Moses successfully argues that without Yahweh's merciful presence Israel is no nation, and that Yahweh's and Moses' efforts have come to naught.

The Psalm lection (Ps. 99) belongs to that genre of hymns within the Old Testament which praises the kingship of Yahweh. Yet the mention of Yahweh's royal rule brings to mind the human agents of that rule, in this case Moses, Aaron, and Samuel. Each of these leaders facilitated Yahweh's conversation with the people, each facilitated Yahweh's rule over them. And through their faithfulness Yahweh's mercy sustained and supported the people. The ultimate word in the psalm is of Yahweh, the bestower of grace and of forgiving love.

The opening lines from 1 Thess. 1:1–10 raise a question regarding the church's understanding of evangelism. Quite in contrast to some conventional notions that evangelism involves a unilateral act of proclaiming the gospel to a passive recipient, Paul describes a relationship that is anything but one-sided. Paul and his co-workers change because of the Thessalonians. The Thessalonians in turn become a living proclamation of the gospel by virtue of their ready acceptance of it. Particularly those who are working to reinvigorate plans of evangelism need to ponder this text at considerable length.

In the Gospel reading (Matt. 22:15–22) we meet Jesus in an atypical setting. In response to a question designed to catch him and leave him without an acceptable answer, Jesus asks another question, one that is easy to answer but whose implications prove devastating: "Whose head is this, and whose title?" The simple question leads Jesus into a statement that confuses Jesus' "audience" even today. As so often in the Gospels, Jesus' "answers" remain provocative because of the questions they raise.

Exodus 33:12–23

This text, like so many others, cannot be fully appreciated without reference to its larger context. It follows the story of the golden calf, in which Israel broke the covenant that had been graciously forged by Yahweh (Ex. 32; see Proper 23). In one of the many climactic moments in that narrative, Moses shatters the tablets of the covenant which he had brought down the mountain (32:19), as clear a symbol as one could wish of the shattered union between Yahweh and the people. Similarly, the present lection is tied to what follows, namely the restoration of the covenant symbolized in the engraving of new tablets (Ex. 34:1–10). In the present passage, therefore, there is important theological "movement" by which the nation is forgiven and restored, by which the people pass from alienation to restoration. This clarity regarding overall theological themes, however, should not allow the interpreter to overlook significant difficulties within the text of a compositional nature, and attention to one or more of the better critical commentaries would be in order.

Before our lection begins, Yahweh has ordered the people to leave Sinai and to continue their journey to the Land of Promise (33:1–6). They will be protected by an angel and will successfully make their way into "a land flowing with milk and honey." But Yahweh will no longer accompany the people, for the simple reason that their sinfulness would result in their destruction. "You are a stiff-necked people; if for a single moment I should go up among you, I would consume you" (v. 5). That brings us to the drama of our text, vs. 12–23.

Moses, in his now familiar role as mediator, is simply not willing to permit Yahweh to withdraw from the presence of the people. It is not possible to resolve all the problems in this part of the text (vs. 12–17), where the unevenness of the narrative suggests a long and complex literary history. But in essence Moses seems to be saying that, since Yahweh has promised to be the God of Israel and has further assured Moses that he is still regarded benevolently by Yahweh, there is no reason for Yahweh now to abandon the nation. Moses' principal imperative statement, "show me your ways" (v. 13), seems to be something like, "Come clean with me, Yahweh. Explain yourself." For Yahweh responds to Moses' insistence by consenting to go with Israel toward the Land of Promise (v. 14). The meaning of the curious phrase "I will give you rest" is unclear, but is perhaps also a reference to the possession of the land, as in Deut. 3:20.

Yet Moses wishes to nail down the issue once and for all, and so he insists that unless Yahweh is willing to accompany Israel the people should not be sent forward. For only in Yahweh's presence does Israel have any claim to distinctiveness among the nations of the earth (v. 16). Yahweh reiterates that Moses' wishes will be met: "I will do the very thing that you have asked." Gritty Moses has once again persuaded Yahweh to change Yahweh's mind (cf. 32:14).

The second part of the present lection (vs. 18–23) contains fewer problems than the first, again suggesting a very involved history of transmission. In certain respects this passage echoes Ex. 3, in that the focus of attention is on the name of the Deity. The name Yahweh is proclaimed (v. 19) and is connected with God's nature by means of language ("I will be gracious to whom I will be gracious . . ."), which is syntactically akin to the "I AM WHO I AM" of Ex. 3:14.

But more urgent is the parallel between "Show me your ways" of v. 13 and "Show me your glory" of v. 18. Just as the first of these imperative statements by Moses transmits the larger meaning of vs. 12–17, so the second is the key to understanding the significance of vs. 18–23. In other words, having successfully received from Yahweh the promise of a continuing divine presence in the life of the people, Moses now requests of Yahweh personal confirmation that Yahweh is who Yahweh has been presented to be in the past and that he, Moses, is Yahweh's agent. The mysterious ritual that follows, while it contains some familiar elements such as the prohibition against gazing upon Yahweh (Ex. 19:21), frustrates the ability of the interpreter to clarify all details. Nevertheless, now that Yahweh has promised to be with Israel, Yahweh seals that promise by means of a theophany.

Thus several important themes emerge. One is that of Moses the tireless mediator, who not only remains loyal to his people in spite of their disloyalty to him and to Yahweh, but demonstrates tremendous courage in doing so. Another theme is that of Yahweh, the merciful God. Yahweh, with considerable justification, has determined that, while the people will be spared, the covenant cannot be maintained. Yahweh must remain separate from this sinful nation, for their own good. But in response to the work of the mediator, Yahweh has a change of heart. "My presence will go with you, and I will give you rest" (v. 14) expresses a mercy that is reemphasized by the elaboration on the divine name: "I will be gracious to whom I will be gracious, and will show mercy on whom I will show mercy" (v. 19).

Once more, when justice and compassion clash within the heart of Yahweh, compassion prevails.

And so the act of shattering the tablets of the law in consequence of the golden calf is now annulled, and the covenant is renewed, as the new tablets are to attest.

Psalm 99

The Psalm for today combines two very different facets of Israel's faith, the assertion of God's cosmic sovereignty (vs. 1–5, 9) and the celebration of God's concrete fidelity to Israel (vs. 6–8). The connection between cosmic sovereignty and concrete fidelity is voiced in Yahweh's relentless commitment to justice and righteousness (v. 4).

Psalm 99 is a celebration of Yahweh's rule over all the universe (vs. 1–5). The psalm reflects a liturgical moment when Yahweh is praised in a manner that causes the world to tremble in fear, deference, and submissiveness (v. 1). That liturgy and theological affirmation are enacted in the Jerusalem Temple (i.e., "in Zion," v. 2). The Temple liturgy is the arena for Yahweh's sweeping claim of sovereignty.

All peoples, Jews and non-Jews, are brought under this sovereign rule, which changes the shape of the created world. The new shape of the world is given by the will and purpose of the newly enthroned Ruler. Yahweh is a God who "love[s] justice" (v. 4). That is, God intends that the necessary resources of life should be made everywhere available to everyone who has need. God's passion for fairly distributed goods to sustain life is expressed as "justice," "equity," and "righteousness" (v. 4). The last phrase of this portion of the psalm ends with Israel's most sweeping doxological affirmation: "Holy is he!" That is, Yahweh is beyond challenge, beyond resistance, beyond explanation. Yahweh's purpose will indeed be worked out in the earth; none can hinder it.

The psalm makes an abrupt transition to Israel's concrete memory (vs. 6–8). The psalm cites Israel's three great intercessors, Moses and Aaron from the early period, and Samuel from the period just before the monarchy. The three great ones called to God; they cried out in Israel's need. They voiced Israel's desperate need and urgent hope. They are voices of petition in relation to Israel's experience of oppression. Moses and Aaron voiced to Yahweh the abuse of the Egyptian empire. Samuel voiced the heaviness of the Philistine hegemony. In both cases, Israel turned to Yahweh because it had no other adequate help for its time of terrible need. These petitions are the context for the stunning affirmation of the psalm made about Yahweh.

Yahweh answered (v. 6)! Yahweh heard. Yahweh attended. Yahweh was moved to care. Yahweh acted. Yahweh hears and answers because Yahweh has a keen antenna for people who are in situations of desperate need. Such need is the condition most contrasted to the justice Yahweh loves.

Verse 7 is an allusion to the giving of the law (and promise) at Mount Sinai. The Commandments are Yahweh's good and gracious response to oppression and injustice. God's testimonies and statutes assert a massive alternative to injustice against which Israel protests in its need and pain.

After the "cry-answer" affirmation, v. 8 offers a derivative reflection on the character of God. This characterization of God is a counterpart to the statement of v. 4. God is a God who answers, who can be reached and summoned to involvement. God's responding works in two ways. On the one hand, this is a God who forgives (cf. Ex. 34:6). On the other hand, this is a God who requites wrong deeds, who punishes those who perpetrate wrong (cf. Ex. 34:7). The juxtaposition of "forgiving God" and "avenger" means that God intervenes both caringly and toughly to establish and maintain a just order.

The affirmation of God's cosmic sovereignty as justice and God's concrete solidarity as forgiveness evokes doxology in Israel (v. 9). Thus the psalm ends in lyrical celebration, echoing v. 5, which concludes the first part of the psalm. The elevation of Yahweh through praise is to happen in Jerusalem. That dramatic, specific liturgical act, however, affirms an evangelical reality not contained in or limited to Jerusalem. The "holy mountain" is the place where the holiness of Yahweh is known and acknowledged. That awesome holiness overrides and destabilizes every act of injustice. It is God who makes a new covenantal world possible for all peoples. Moses, Aaron, and Samuel evoked in Israel what is everywhere offered by Yahweh to all peoples.

1 Thessalonians 1:1–10

First Thessalonians, probably the earliest of Paul's letters and therefore the earliest written evidence of Christianity, opens with an extended thanksgiving. The thanksgiving begins with 1:2 and continues perhaps as far as 2:16. In the lectionary reading for this week, 1 Thess. 1:1–10, Paul expresses his thanks to God regarding the reception of the gospel among the Thessalonians. What is striking about this passage, however, is that Paul depicts an evangelism that differs from the conventional image of a unilateral action by an evangelist on a receptive yet passive audience. Here evangelism involves the interaction of Paul and his co-workers with the Thessalonians, an interaction that leaves both sides changed, an interaction that results in the Thessalonians themselves becoming evangelists as well.

First, the Christian evangelists make the gospel known among the Thessalonians. Influenced by the public speeches Luke describes in The Acts of the Apostles, most readers will imagine Paul and his colleagues preaching on street corners or at other public places. Paul himself gives few clues as to what forms this early stage of evangelism took; he may have taken advantage of his trade to talk with people in workshops and in small, informal gatherings, rather than in larger, public settings.

Whatever the form of Paul's preaching, he indicates that "our message of the gospel came to you not in word only, but also in power and in the Holy Spirit and with full conviction" (v. 5). Since the gospel itself is more than words, more than intellectual assertions to be affirmed, its reception also must take many forms. The reception of the gospel manifested itself also in the Thessalonians' imitation of Paul and his co-workers: "And you became imitators of us and of the Lord, for in spite of persecution you received the word with joy inspired by the Holy Spirit" (v. 6). The Thessalonians' reception of the gospel extended well beyond intellectual assent. They took the Christian evangelists as their models, specifically as models of joy in the face of persecution.

Even this element in Paul's comments differs from some understandings of evangelism, for Paul clearly has in mind not simply an evangelism of preaching followed by a profession of faith. He understands that an adequate response to the gospel involves action as well as assent. More striking, however, is what Paul says about the way in which the evangelists themselves are influenced by this relationship. Not only did the Thessalonians change, but "you know what kind of persons we proved to be among you for your sake" (v. 5). Paul and his co-workers found themselves to be different because of the relationship that was established. Evangelism involves a mutual exchange, involving both sides. For the sake of the Thessalonians, the evangelists themselves behaved differently. This notion is expanded in the early lines of 1 Thess. 2, where Paul describes himself as a nurse who cares for her own children and as a father with his children. Because of their deep involvement with people at Thessalonica, Paul and his colleagues find themselves vulnerable.

The result of this relationship between Paul and his colleagues and the Thessalonians is not simply the conversion of some people at Thessalonica. The Thessalonians themselves become ministers by virtue of the impact of their conversion on others. Paul writes that "you became an example to all the believers in Macedonia and in Achaia" (1:7), signaling that other Christians find themselves influenced by the lives of the Thessalonians. They have in turn become models of the faith. Both those who are already Christians and those who are not have come to know about the faith by means of the Thessalonians: "in every place your faith in God has become known, so that we have no need to speak about it" (v. 8). Even if we suspect Paul of considerable exaggeration here, the point he makes is nevertheless important. The new Christians at Thessalonica, although they are not formally designated as apostles or preachers, become both by virtue of the impact their conversion has on the lives of other people.

The conversion of these Gentiles to the Christian faith is summed up in vs. 9–10 in very traditional language: "You turned to God from idols, to serve a living and true God, and to wait for his Son from heaven, whom he raised from the dead—Jesus, who rescues us from the wrath that is coming." The first half of this statement draws on a conventional Jewish understanding of what conversion involves. Gentiles turn to the one God from their service of many gods, or better, Gentiles turn to the only real God from their service of false gods. The second half of the statement reflects Christian eschatological expectation, in that those who have joined with the Christian movement live in the knowledge of Jesus Christ's resurrection and in the expectation that he will return as part of God's final triumph over evil. Within the context of 1 Thessalonians, of course, this traditional language will serve a very specific purpose. Gentiles who have turned to the one God must live lives consistent with that understanding and must forgo practices that may have been acceptable in their earlier lives (see 4:1–8). They also live in full confidence that God will accomplish Jesus' return, although the time of that return is not subject to human prediction (4:13–5:11).

Matthew 22:15–22

The passage for the Gospel reading for today has been a favorite one on the basis of which to address issues of church and state. The statement "Render therefore to Caesar the things that are Caesar's, and to God the things that are God's" (RSV) becomes a basis for discussing the extent to which the church is or is not involved with the political process and what responsibilities Christians have to the state. The problem, however, is that the text does not answer very many questions, particularly for those who live in a democratic state. Furthermore, isolated from the rest of the biblical witness about church and state, the passage lays itself open to a variety of interpretations and to sometimes radically different doctrines of church and state. The incident certainly has its place in the broader perspective of both Testaments and as one of several texts to be considered, but alone it hardly provides a basis for a precise definition of Christians' obligations in the political arena.

There is more to the passage than simply Matt. 22:21b, and the other parts are critical to a serious grappling with its meaning. The text begins with the plot of the Pharisees, who try to rig the conversation with Jesus. They send some of their younger protégés, together with a few Herodians, first to flatter Jesus and then to put him on the spot. "Is it lawful to pay taxes to the emperor, or not?" A yes-or-no question like this is bound to get him in trouble, they suppose. If Jesus says yes, then much of the crowd would be disillusioned with him, for there were many voices arguing that paying the Roman poll tax was an act of treason. Even handling the coinage with Caesar's image stamped on it was offensive to some. But if Jesus answers no to the question, then he is guilty of treason, and the Herodians are there in the audience to press their accusations against him.

At one level Jesus' response—asking for a coin, having the questioners tell him whose head is on it, declaring "Give therefore to the emperor the things that are the emperor's, and to God the things that are God's"—is cleverly evasive. He successfully escapes the trap laid for him. He does not answer the query directly, but throws the issue back on the audience, who will have to decide for themselves where to draw the line between the emperor's jurisdiction and God's jurisdiction. Even his questioners (who have already been exposed as "hypocrites") are amazed at his brilliance and go away and leave him alone.

At another level, however, the vignette is much more than an example of Jesus' outwitting the opposition. When Jesus asks for a coin, he also asks, "Whose head [*eikōn,* image] is this, and whose title?" The coin of course bears Caesar's *eikōn,* and belongs to Caesar. Humans, on the other hand, bear the *eikōn* of God. They may pay the infamous poll tax, but they do not belong to the emperor. They themselves belong to God. The declaration of that ultimate belonging has powerful implications.

Another way to put this is to say that the passage does not make

God and Caesar to be equals, nor are they symbolic names for separate realms. If so, one could be led to the notion that the emperor has his realm in which ultimate allegiance can be demanded, and God is relegated to another realm. Quite the opposite is inferred in the text. Humans bear God's image, and wherever they live and operate—whether in the social, economic, political, or religious realm—they belong to God. Their primary loyalties do not switch when they move out of church and into the voting booth.

Read this way, the text does not solve the question of church and state. It does not answer many lingering issues about Christians' obligations to the government—taxation, military conscription, and the like—but it does set allegiances into an ultimate and penultimate order. The text is certainly not iconoclastic regarding governments. It gives space to political arrangements, but at the same time it conditions those arrangements by the reminder that not only we, but all God's children, bear the divine image and therefore belong to God. Furthermore, the text operates subversively in every context in which governments act as if citizens have no higher commitments than to the state. When the divine image is denied and persons are made by political circumstances to be less than human, then the text carries a revolutionary word, a word that has to be spoken to both oppressed and oppressor.

Proper 25

Ordinary Time 30

Sunday between October 23 and 29 inclusive

In the narrative of Moses' death and Joshua's succession in Deut. 34, both the end of Moses' life and the continuation of his influence emerge as dominant motifs. Israel mourns for Moses, but when thirty days have passed the mourning comes to an end and Joshua takes over Moses' role. At the same time that Moses is being replaced, however, his influence continues. It is "because Moses had laid his hands on him" that Joshua has the spirit of wisdom, and the description of Moses in vs. 10–12 reflects his ongoing importance in Israel's life.

Psalm 90 is connected with the Old Testament reading from Deut. 34 by virtue of the fact that it is described in the superscription as "a Prayer of Moses." While there is nothing in the psalm that refers directly to Moses, the tone is suitable to the setting portrayed in Deut. 34. The text speaks in both the indicative and the imperative moods. By means of the first of these, the psalmist reflects on the mortality of all women and men (vs. 1–6). We are "like a dream." In the imperative, however, the writer calls on God to meet our need and to deliver divine assurance, the assurance that results in great joy. "Make us glad. . . ."

In 1 Thess. 2:1–8 Paul continues his recollection of the relationship that existed between himself and the Thessalonians. Not content with proclaiming the gospel in an abstract way, as if it concerned only some philosophical truth about God, Paul and his co-workers acted out their love of neighbor in unconventional ways. They behaved with the Thessalonians the way a nurse would if she were caring for her own children. This "love of neighbor" again becomes possible only because of their prior love of God.

The Gospel reading (Matt. 22:34–46) depicts Jesus once again in a setting of controversy with the religious leaders of the day. Their desire to trick Jesus invariably results in their own humiliation. Here two instances depict their plots and their ineffectiveness. The exchange about the greatest commandment ironically demonstrates that the religious authorities in fact observe none of the commandments because of their inability to understand properly what Jesus calls the "first" and "second" commandments.

Deuteronomy 34:1–12

Mercy and peace are two qualities that may be said to characterize the Deuteronomy narrative of Moses' death. The gentle manner in which God deals with the faithful and diligent servant is paradigmatic of God's mercy not only toward Moses, but toward all Israel. And the serenity with which Moses accepts his own mortality reveals the peace that pervades his heart.

On one level, of course, the text is a statement of judgment. Numbers 20:12, part of the larger narrative of the incident at Meribah, Num. 20:1–13 (cf. Ex. 17:1–7, Proper 21), promises that, because of Moses' lack of trust in God, the leader of Israel would not be permitted entrance into the Land of Promise (see also Deut. 32:48–52). This judgment is echoed in v. 4 of our lection, where Yahweh reminds Moses that "you shall not cross over [into the land]." But the tone of judgment is distant and muted, almost as if the punishment has now been forgotten. Instead, the emphasis is on the natural mortality of the great leader. Moses' tasks are now over (in spite of his enduring physical strength, v. 7), and it is time for new leadership to step forth. To his credit, Moses accepts that which Yahweh has ordained.

Yet before Yahweh allows Moses to pass from the scene, Yahweh treats the old man to a rare delight. Moses ascends Mount Nebo and looks down into the Land of Promise, the goal of so many years' journey. The phrase "Yahweh showed him the whole land" (v. 1) is amplified in some detail, as the sites where various of the tribes are to build their homes are cataloged. If Moses is resentful at not being permitted entrance into the arena that now stretches before him, there is no sign of such emotion in the text. In fact, Moses speaks no word at all (cf. Deut. 32:1–43; 33:2–29), and the experience is consummated as Yahweh points to the fulfillment of the divine promise: "This is the land of which I swore . . ." (v. 4). In spite of all the warnings of judgment, Yahweh's mood is that of mercy, not anger. Moses' attitude suggests acceptance and peace.

The mantle of leadership now falls on Joshua, and the text celebrates that the charismatic endowment that had been bestowed on Moses is now extended to the new leader. Yet even here Moses' influence is vital. Joshua now possesses the "spirit of wisdom, because Moses had laid his hands on him" (v. 9; cf. Num. 27:12–23; Deut 31:1–8). The people follow Joshua, "doing as the LORD had commanded Moses." Moses may be dead, but his example lives on in the hearts of all Israel. The encomium (vs. 10–12) that concludes the text (and the entire Torah) places Moses' ministry in the unique category that it deserves. He was an unparalleled leader "whom the LORD knew face to face" (v. 10).

Such is the poignant climax to the story of the greatest of all the leaders of ancient Israel, a story whose highlights have occupied the lectionary for the last several weeks. During this time we have witnessed a number of ways in which Yahweh has called on Moses to represent Yahweh before Israel, and even before the nation's enemies. We have also seen Moses respond in a variety of emotional moods, from fear and self-doubt (Ex. 3:11, Proper 17) to bravery in the face of great danger (Ex. 14:19–31, Proper 19) and to a gentle reproach of Yahweh (Ex. 32:11–13, Proper 33). But on all occasions, with one exception, Moses has acted with great trust, faithfully carrying out Yahweh's will for his (Moses') life and for that of Israel. Even the one exception, at Meribah, seems to reflect normal human impatience more than it does sinful waywardness. However, in spite of Moses' great accomplishments of the spirit, or perhaps precisely because he is a model figure for all time to come, Moses is forced to pay a dear price. He is refused entrance into the Land of Promise.

Yet, as the Scriptures reveal in a number of places (see Hos. 11:8–9), when God's justice is on a collision course with God's mercy, it is the mercy that prevails. So it is in this text. The veneration with which Moses is viewed almost causes the reader to forget that Moses, like all people, was a sinner. Not only is the judgment referred to in hushed voices, implying Yahweh's great compassion, but the people are awed by the contributions of the one who has now left them. The period of mourning (v. 8) may have fulfilled a ritualistic demand, but the weeping of the people seems genuine.

At the same time, the text is starkly realistic in its recognition that the people must move forward. The notation concerning the end of the period of mourning implies that, when the thirty days had ended, the weeping ceased and the people began to address themselves to the challenges that would confront them under their new leader, Joshua. He may have been ordained by Moses, but he was *not* Moses, and subsequent events would reveal that the demands placed on him would be no less than those placed on Moses, and his responses would be strikingly bold and faithful. There could now be no looking back, no more nostalgia for the "fleshpots" of Egypt (Ex.

16:3, Proper 20). The Promised Land lay before them, and Joshua, as Yahweh's new agent, would lead them into it.

There are enormous lessons of leadership in these verses, lessons for leaders incoming and outgoing, as well as lessons for those who are led. But more to the point, there are timeless lessons about the grace and mercy of God.

Psalm 90:1–6, 13–17

Our verses of today's Psalm reading speak in two different voices, an indicative (vs. 1–6) and an imperative (vs. 13–17).

The indicative voice of this psalm addresses God in a reflective, meditative way, concerning the brevity and fragility of human life (vs. 1–6). The mood of these verses is one of trusting realism, perhaps with some haunting regret at the God-given character of human life, but without sounding any anxiety or protest.

These verses function to establish the profound contrast between God and humankind. At the outset, God is acknowledged to be enduring, abiding, and utterly reliable (vs. 1–2). The initial address to God is "Lord," but it is not the proper name "Yahweh," but rather a generic name for the *sovereign* who must be both obeyed and relied upon. God is "*our* dwelling place" (emphasis added), the only locus that is truly home. This "our" is not the Israelites, but all humankind, who, without God, are left orphaned in the world (cf. John 14:18). This only "true home" (=God) is completely reliable, more enduring than even the mountains, the earth, the world, before time, through time, and beyond time (cf. Jer. 31:35–37; Isa. 54:10).

The speaker of the psalm confesses that this sovereign has uttered a decisive command, "Turn back" (v. 3). Turn back "to dust." Turn back to nonbeing. Turn back to oblivion, to earth, to dust, to ashes. This is an awesome acknowledgment that ponders the God-given reality of death, and understands that the temporary, precarious quality of all human life is willed by God. Those utterly faithful to God willingly accept such reality as right destiny, and live until the end with complete trust and confidence.

The following verses (vs. 4–6) are an exposition of the meaning of God's command to "turn back." God's sense of time is so different from ours that human existence is redefined in God's chronology. Length of time, in fact, matters not at all to the significance or quality of human life. Humankind in God's intended transitoriness is like a dream—one is not sure it had any reality—like grass that has no staying power at all. One must not cling excessively to such life, but must cling to the Lord of life. That Lord of life, unlike us, is Lord of time and Lord of all time beyond time. It is God's reality that is the substance of human hope, for humanity has no lasting hope in the human shape of things.

Nonetheless, the psalm dares to utter an imperative to God, seeking to mobilize God's massive sovereignty in a quite concrete way (vs. 13–17). The psalm speaks a command to God: "Turn!" The command uses the same word as the command uttered by God in v. 3. The petition addressed to God is followed by "How long?" a characteristic complaint of needfulness. The question is not an inquiry about the extent of time for one's life, as we might expect from vs. 3–6. It is, rather, a statement of honest need and passionate yearning, which tries to engage God with the need and the yearning.

The recognition of transitoriness evokes a series of imperatives addressed to God: "Have compassion . . . Satisfy us . . . Make us glad . . . Manifest your work and your power . . . Show your favor (delight) . . . Prosper our work . . . O prosper our work!" The speaker seeks to build a hedge against his own sure nullification and oblivion. The speaker knows, however, that human power cannot generate such protection for the self, and so appeals to God. The speaker asks for compassion and joy, in order to override the haunting sense of grief and loss that is daily present to a reflective, knowing person.

This psalm never challenges the decree of v. 3 or the reality of transitoriness voiced in vs. 3–6. Nonetheless, the speaker dares to ask for some assurance from God, given the reality of that decree from God. The speaker seeks from God the kind of generosity and steadfast love that will endure. There is in the psalm no answer from God concerning these petitions. From the context of Israel's faith, however, we may trust that these askings will not be ignored, but will be granted. Even these gifts from God, however, are given and received only in the context of transitoriness, which is unrelenting. Such gifts from God do not preempt the limitedness of human life, so that the gift most asked for is that the quality of time granted human persons should be marked by companionship and fidelity.

There is a particular wistfulness voiced in the last verse. The human voice yearns to leave a mark in the world that will endure after one is no longer alive. It is, of course, a wistfulness about which many of us know intensely. "The work of our hands" can be any accomplishment valued by the community—an accomplishment in service and caring, an expression of art or intelligence or imagination or fidelity. The psalmist knows that even such enduring markings of significance do not in themselves guarantee any durability, but that only the sanction of God can leave us well remembered. Thus the final petition is a mixture of pathos as well as yearning.

The movement of these two sections of the psalm may focus for us on the two utterances of "turn," one a command of God (v. 3), the other a human petition addressed to God (v. 13). Reflective human life is lived in the tension between these two, the first a voicing of experienced reality, the second a hope that comes from honesty as well as faith. Concerning the first: Life is transitory. Time, like an ever-rolling stream, "soon bears us all away; / We fly forgotten, as a dream/Dies at the opening day." The second is a voicing of hope and yearning that do not readily accept this reality and destiny, but seek to qualify the decree of God in an important and comforting way as an appeal to God. There is no way out of this tension, which is definitional for human life. It is in any case enormously illuminating to see that human persons work both sides of the theological tension as indicative and imperative. Both sides of the tension are marked with profound reality, and both are concerned with the Ruler of all reality, in time and beyond time.

1 Thessalonians 2:1–8

Today's passage from 1 Thessalonians continues Paul's recounting of the ministry he and his co-workers established with and among Christians at Thessalonica. Already Paul has written of the reception the Thessalonians gave to him, and now he turns to the nature of his own work with them. It is important to note that this letter, probably the earliest among the extant Pauline letters, does not begin with Paul's description of himself as an apostle. In fact, Paul uses only the names "Paul, Silvanus, and Timothy." By contrast, his later letters will emphasize his calling as apostle (1 Cor. 1:1; 2 Cor. 1:1; Gal. 1:1; Rom. 1:1), sometimes at considerable length (see the openings of Galatians and Romans). In 1 Thessalonians, where he has not yet taken up this practice, he seems to describe the apostle's work in this passage rather than to identify it succinctly in the letter opening. Perhaps, indeed, Paul is here working out his understanding of what it means to be called "apostles of Christ" (v. 7).

Paul's understanding of apostleship emerges here in three distinct but related characteristics. First, to be an apostle is to have the courage needed to proclaim the gospel: "We had courage in our God to declare to you the gospel of God in spite of great opposition" (v. 2). The fact that Paul refers to opposition and that he prefaces this statement with comments about suffering and mistreatment at Philippi prompts the reader to think of courage as the willingness to act in the face of adversity. But any proclamation of the gospel requires courage, for the gospel inherently and inevitably causes offense to its hearers.

The courage required of apostles comes to them not from their own resources or their own discipline. The apostles have courage "in our God," that is, they receive courage as a gift of the God who empowers and legitimates their task. Alongside this text might be placed the scene in Acts 4 in which the gathered Christian community in Jerusalem prays together for boldness to speak the gospel in the face of threatening officials (Acts 4:23–31). Without such boldness, without courage, the gospel is never proclaimed.

A second characteristic of the apostles is their integrity. Paul describes this integrity in 1 Thess. 2:3–6. The apostles acted without "deceit or impure motives or trickery," without "words of flattery" or with "a pretext for greed," because their task was one of pleasing God rather than human beings. Unlike the unscrupulous salesperson who decides that a sale justifies any strategy or device, the genuine apostle knows that strategies reflect their goals. Strategies that simply attempt to move people, to win their consent or their support, are strategies that ultimately will fail. Because it is God who has authorized the apostles, they cannot select sales techniques that contradict that authorization. It is God who has approved of the apostles and entrusted them with the gospel itself (v. 4).

The third characteristic of the apostle has to do with the character of the relationship between the apostle and the convert. That relationship has already been referred to in 1:2–10 (Proper 24), but it emerges again here in striking imagery about the roles Paul and his co-workers adopted in relationship to the Thessalonians. They treated the Thessalonians as would a nurse who was charged with caring for her own children (v. 7). They exhorted the Thessalonians as a father would, treating each one individually (v. 11). A good case can be made that v. 7 should read "But we were infants among you," rather than "But we were gentle among you" (see the footnote in the NRSV). If that is the case, Paul uses in this brief passage three distinct and even conflicting images to convey the apostolic role. The apostle is as weak and unprotected as an infant; the apostle is as gentle as a mother with her infant; the apostle is as protective as a father.

What ties these three images together is the utter vulnerability they attach to the figure of the apostle. In this interpretation, the apostle is not a powerful and authoritative figure, whose message is conveyed by sheer personal charisma. Rather, the apostle is one who undertakes a profound relationship with others, risking humiliation and painful rejection, so that the truth of the gospel might be made known to others. Small wonder that Paul concludes the passage by recalling that they had determined to share "not only the gospel of God but also our own selves" (v. 8).

Paul says little about the "results" achieved by this apostolic strategy. The indications that come through have nothing to do with numbers of people converted or financial security acquired or influence achieved. He simply asserts that "our coming to you was not in vain" (v. 1). That use of negation for emphasis (technically referred to as litotes) occurs elsewhere in the New Testament (see, for example, Rom. 1:16) and does not reflect a kind of false modesty. It is, however, important to notice that Paul measures the apostolic work by the integrity of response rather than by its size.

Matthew 22:34–46

The two incidents included in the Gospel lesson for this Sunday bring to an end an important section of Matthew's narrative and prepare for the speech of denunciation in chapter 23. Since the triumphal entry into Jerusalem (21:1–11), the story has reported the sharp conflict between Jesus and the religious authorities. More immediately, three parables (21:28–32, 33–46; 22:1–14) and three questions put to Jesus by opposition figures (22:15–22, 23–33, 34–40) bring the conflict to a head, leading to Jesus' initiative in 22:41–46, in which he questions the Pharisees about the Messiah and stymies any further interrogating of him.

The first of the two incidents in today's lesson is carefully linked to the previous questioning by the Sadducees (22:34) and, though asked as a question to test Jesus, raises a fundamental issue for ancient and modern readers: "Which commandment in the law is the greatest?"

Three observations about Jesus' reply are critical.

1. There is an inseparability between the two commandments, to love God with the whole self and to love the neighbor. The second commandment is "like" the first one. It gives it focus and pinpoints the way in which the love of God can find practical expression. The writer of 1 John more specifically than any other New Testament voice spells out the role of the second commandment in relation to the first by his statement: "Those who do not love a brother or sister

whom they have seen, cannot love God whom they have not seen" (1 John 4:20). A failure to honor the second commandment while claiming to observe the first makes one a liar.

Worship, both public and private, becomes the target of prophetic critique when it is divorced from "the weightier matters of the law: justice and mercy and faith" (Matt. 23:23). The close connection between the two commandments keeps the church's liturgy, its confessions of faith, its songs of praise, and its piety genuine.

2. But while the two great commandments are inseparable, neither is dissolved into the other. Discovering the decisive mandate to love one's neighbor as oneself (for example, engaging consistently in acts of service or being intensely involved in struggles for justice) does not mean that the first commandment then is no longer significant. Often atheists or humanists keep the second commandment in a way that far exceeds what most Christians or Jews do.

The first commandment, however, remains the *first* commandment. There is a dimension of loving God that goes beyond or is different from loving one's neighbor. Put another way, God remains the ultimate point of reference for human life. Prayer, public and private worship, the aggressive search for truth about God, and a serious wrestling with issues of faith are essential to the nurture of that ultimate point of reference.

3. For Matthew, Jesus is the one supreme interpreter of the law, and here he declares that the love of God and the love of neighbor are the interpretive keys to understanding "all the law and the prophets" (22:40). Both commands of course come from the law (Deut. 6:4–9; Lev. 19:18). They do not lessen human obligations, but make them more radical and comprehensive. What is owed to God and neighbor is not the carrying out of a specific law, but a total approach to life (so "with all your heart, and with all your soul, and with all your mind"). Love's claim is without restriction.

The second incident in the lesson (22:41–46) raises the christological issue underlying the conflict between Jesus and the opposition. When the Pharisees answer Jesus' question by saying that the Messiah is "the son of David," Jesus confronts them with Ps. 110:1. David, in fact, does not call the Messiah his son, but instead calls him "lord": "The LORD [God] says to my lord [Messiah] . . ."

At one level, it looks as if Jesus has stumped the religious pundits with a riddle they cannot solve, and thus they are speechless in the face of his brilliance. But at another level, they are confronted with the true understanding of Messiahship, and they have nothing to say about it. While the Messiah is the son of David, the career and character of David do not define Messiahship. Readers need not think in terms of expanded national boundaries and a return to the glory days of the Davidic monarchy. Jesus as suffering Lord, whose upcoming days include rejection and death, whose disciples are called to take up the cross and follow him, alone defines Messiahship. He rules not by military prowess, but by love. The ways in which the Messiah is different from David make his reign unique, threatening, and ultimately victorious.

PROPER 26

Ordinary Time 31

Sunday between October 30 and November 5 inclusive

One of the fundamental questions of the Christian experience is how we relate to human authorities in light of God's authority, how we establish and maintain human relationships in light of the relationship God has established with us. There are times when we wish that we had to deal only with God and could avoid the pressure of living in the ambiguous human community, where relationships and decisions are often morally confusing and power struggles are unavoidable. At other times, the idea of God's being in any sense a reference point for a human relationship seems an unnecessary intrusion. What business is this of God?

The texts for this Sunday in no way solve the particular questions we bring. No simplistic answers are offered. The texts do, however, remind us that human decisions, relationships, communities must be rooted in the reality of God, and the texts provide us with interesting models of what such rootage implies.

The thesis, as it were, is expressed by the psalmist:

> O give thanks to the LORD, for he is good;
> for his steadfast love endures forever.

It is exclusively Yahweh's grace and power that render viable the life of the redeemed, both in community and in individuality.

That axiom is illustrated by the story of the crossing of the Jordan in Josh. 3. In important respects, this narrative reviews the more-often-read story of the crossing of the Red Sea, with the same emphasis on the mercy of a sovereign Yahweh. Apart from Yahweh's grace, Israel's life could not be sustained.

The New Testament lessons offer a positive and a negative expression of human relationships that reflect or fail to reflect their rootedness in God. Paul, whose ministry is an expression of the gospel, exhorts the Thessalonians "like a father with his children" (1

Thess. 2:11). He does not deny an authority due him because of his previous relations with his readers. At the same time, he can reverse the image and speak of himself as an orphan when separated from these people (2:17). The possibility of mutuality emerges out of a clear acceptance of the authority of the gospel.

As a contrast, the scribes and Pharisees are singled out in Matt. 23:1–12 for their flaunting of their positions and for engaging in pious activity so as to be praised and courted by others. Their craving of honorific titles illustrates their failure to acknowledge the empowerment of Jesus as teacher and God as Father. The proper recognition of divine authority relativizes all human authorities, our own as well as others'.

Joshua 3:7–17

The story of the entry of the Israelite tribes into the Land of Promise has obvious resonances with the story of the crossing of the Red Sea in Ex. 14:21–31. Differences between the two narratives abound, but they are similar in that in both instances Yahweh works through the divinely chosen leader of the people, Moses and Joshua playing pivotal roles in the unfolding events. Also in both narratives, the waters are miraculously held at bay until the people of God have crossed on dry land, escaping from danger into the safety of the land where God wishes them to be.

In the sequence of Old Testament lections, the present passage forms an appropriate continuation of the story of God's saving deeds in Israel's life, in that the account of Moses' death in Deut. 34 (Proper 25) marks both a close to one epic period in Israel's life and the beginning of another. The promise of Deut. 34:4 now begins to be actualized.

The text begins by making clear that the office to which Joshua has been called is tantamount to that held by Moses (v. 7). In human terms, the problem of succession is always problematic when the earlier leader has been so enormously influential and decisive. To fill the office left vacant by Moses' death would be no small task, even with divine approval. Thus part of the function of the present lection is to assure the reader that Israel will not suffer because of a leadership vacuum: a new Moses has been raised by God (cf. Deut. 31:23).

The ensuing action is designed to authenticate Joshua's leadership as well as that of Yahweh. "By this you shall know that among you is the living God" (v. 10) points to the evidentiary nature of the events. The priests are to walk into the riverbed carrying the Ark of the Covenant, the most sacred object in Israel's inventory and the talisman representing the very presence of Yahweh. Much of the suspense of the narrative lies in whether the waters will acknowledge this divine presence.

(The role of the twelve representatives of the tribes is not immediately clear [v. 12]. They are not to be the bearers of the Ark, since that task can be assumed only by priests. Nor would it seem that they are to form some kind of honor guard, since nonpriestly persons were to keep their distance from the Ark [note v. 4]. Their role becomes evident only in 4:3.)

The text goes out of its way to point to the spring floods as the time of this miraculous crossing. (The "harvest" referred to in v. 15 is not the autumn harvest, which comes at the end of the dry season, but the spring harvest, which occurs at the conclusion of the rains.) Not only would the waters be unusually high at this time of year, but the geographical location—near Jericho—would be significant in this regard, also. All the force of the accumulated waters, some of which had begun to course their way down the slopes of Mount Hermon in the far north, now bear down on the mouth of the Jordan—and on the path that the tribes are to take. The tradition wishes to make it abundantly evident that the people did not enter the Land of Promise because they were able to skip over a trickle, but because Yahweh held back a torrent!

The reference to a "single heap" (vs. 13, 16) is a further sign of the miraculous nature of the crossing. In order that the lives of the people not be placed in peril, the priests who bear the Ark station themselves in the midst of the now dry riverbed, and it is only with the crossing of the last Israelite that the priests climb up to the farther shore—and into the Land of Promise. The Ark is now on the sacred soil of Israel!

The goal of so many years in the wilderness has at last been realized. God, who called Israel out of Egypt so long ago, has kept the divine promises!

Psalm 107:1–7, 33–37

Psalm 107 is a wondrous song of thanksgiving. Distinct from "praise," "thanksgiving" in ancient Israel is characteristically response to a specific, nameable action on God's part. It is this writer's impression that the lectionary verses are inappropriately divided, breaking the psalm in unfortunate ways. For that reason, it has seemed helpful to include vs. 8–9 and 38 in the comment.

The psalm begins with a rather generic summons to thanks (vs. 1–3). Verse 1 is a classic formulation of thanks that is a response to God's "steadfast love." We have encountered this same formulation in Ps. 106:1, and see also Ps. 117. The introduction of God's steadfast love suggests that the specific cases of deliverance that constitute the body of this psalm are expositions from concrete experience about the rescue that is available because God is faithful.

The invitation to thanksgiving in v. 1 is matched in v. 2 by a second invitation. The redeemed, that is, the ones who have concretely benefited from God's steadfast love, are invited to speak, that is, to bear witness and give account of their rescue. God has done two things for those summoned. First, God has "redeemed" from trouble. The term translated "trouble" literally means "a tight, restrictive place." God has broken the abusive confinement. Second, God has "gathered." The verb is often used with reference to "the scattered," those dispersed in exile, so that God's steadfast love is exile-ending and the source of glad homecoming. Thus "redeem" and "gather" might refer paradigmatically in Israel to the exodus from the tight place of slavery, and the homecoming from Babylonian exile. These usages, however, do not refer specifically or singularly to those events, but to many less dramatic, personal and communal experiences of liberation and homecoming that play on the model events. Because Israel is grateful for such acts of God, Israel bears thankful testimony that Yahweh has done this and is the God who characteristically does it. Israel is here summoned to "name its blessing" aloud, as an expression of gratitude and as a witness to others that they also can receive such joyous gifts from this God.

Then follow in the psalm four concrete examples of such "redemption." These include vs. 4–9, which is our text (as extended), plus vs. 10–16, 17–22, and 23–32. Each of these four cases includes four stylized elements of thanksgiving: (a) a statement of trouble which evokes, (b) a cry to Yahweh, (c) a report of Yahweh's powerful intervention, and (d) a response by Israel of thanks to Yahweh. The first case study (vs. 4–9) follows exactly this fourfold pattern of rhetoric.

1. The trouble out of which the thanks arise is wilderness wandering (vs. 4–5). While this reference may be an allusion to the wanderings of Israel under Moses, the characterization is more generic. Much of the territory of ancient Israel is a slightly populated, arid territory which is life-threatening. The experience of travel in that territory may consist of losing one's way and being without food and water, and consequently having one's energy and vitality (= "soul") grow weak. It may be possible to treat the picture metaphorically, as

in the hymn lines "pilgrim through this barren land." First, however, one must linger over the literalness of the picture to sense the poignancy of the threat.

2. Those in such trouble know that they themselves have no resources for the crisis. In the horizon of Israel, this means they must turn to Yahweh, their trusted rescuer (v. 6a). They know to whom they must turn, and they know that they must voice their need and ask for help. Each of these "cases" of rescue depends on initiative from the side of human need. Rescue in this scenario does not begin in God's attentive love, but in Israel's voiced complaint. Yahweh responds, but Yahweh does not make the first move. A thanking people first must become an out-loud, candid, complaining people.

3. Yahweh does indeed hear such a cry, does respond, does act to save (vs. 6b–7). In v. 6 there is no pause, slippage, or uncertainty between "cry" and "deliver." God is immediately responsive. The God who hears and answers acts specifically to bring Israel to an oasis where there is food, water, and new life. Notice that this narrative of trouble and help is somewhat different from the old sojourn narratives of Moses in the books of Exodus and Numbers. The "miracle" here is not bread from heaven or water from rock, but guidance to already existing life-support systems.

4. The completion of this form is Israel's thanks (vs. 8–9), an element that cannot be omitted as the appointed lectionary reading proposes. Thanks consists in a sweeping acknowledgment of God's faithfulness and powerful action given to humankind (v. 8). Then, in v. 9, the saving deed is made quite specific. The rescue matches the trouble. Israel's life begins again, saved and valued by the God who transforms Israel's circumstance.

On the basis of these four examples of need and rescue, vs. 33–38 voice an unrestrained, doxological affirmation of Yahweh's power and beneficence. Yahweh converts rivers into deserts (v. 33), and deserts into waters (v. 35). Yahweh can work inversions in either direction. When Yahweh works a positive inversion, from desert to water, people not only live, they develop working towns (v. 36) and functioning agriculture (v. 37). Verse 38 employs the language of creation (blesses, multiplies, and gives prosperity), which is here measured in cattle. God is powerful, generous, and good, and turns conditions of death into gifts of life. Israel has so much for which to give thanks. Thanks is a glad recognition that the goodness of life is a gift and not an achievement. Such gifts evoke gratitude and not anxiety.

1 Thessalonians 2:9–13

This reading (with vs. 14–20 included in the discussion) continues Paul's recollections, begun in 1 Thess. 1:2, of his earlier stay in Thessalonica. Paul writes, however, not simply to preserve a record of this experience or to reflect on it for himself. His recollections carry within them an exhortation to the Thessalonians to continue in the faith to which they have been called. Much as a teacher or parent uses praise for positive reinforcement, Paul uses memories of his visit with the Thessalonians to introduce issues about which he has some instruction to offer. The eschatological issue that comes to the foreground in chapter 4 already slips into the conversation here in 2:16 and in 2:19 (compare also 1:10). Paul also introduces here the question of the behavior of these former Gentiles (2:12–13), an issue that will come to prominence in 4:1–12. The relationship between Paul and the Thessalonians allows Paul to assert a powerful claim over their behavior. How can they act in ways that contradict the gospel if they are Paul's own "crown of boasting"?

The passage opens with a further remembrance of the apostles' behavior at Thessalonica. The apostles themselves worked "night and day" in order to provide for their own needs and thereby not burden the Thessalonians. Their behavior was "pure, upright, and blameless." Drawing again on the familiar language of 2:1–8, Paul compares the apostles to fathers, who treat each of their children with care, "urging and encouraging you and pleading that you lead a life worthy of God." Despite this appeal to the relationship between the apostles and the Christians at Thessalonica, it is essential that the gospel be understood as God's word rather than a human word (v. 13). What the Thessalonians received was not simply a relationship with Paul and his colleagues, but the gospel of Jesus Christ.

Standing behind the transition from apostle to gospel in v. 13 is the complex relationship between the word that is proclaimed and the agent of that proclamation. As is clear elsewhere in Paul's letters, he understands full well the role of the apostle or preacher. People respond to the integrity of that individual, and the response of believers to the apostles is their sole ground of boasting. The gospel does not find a hearing apart from the human agent who makes it known. Nevertheless, the apostle is simply an agent of the gospel and not the gospel itself. What the apostles proclaim is never their own action but the action of God in Jesus Christ.

What the Thessalonians received is God's word, and that word is now at work not only in and through the apostles, but in and through the Thessalonians themselves (2:13). Paul has already referred to the way in which the Thessalonians have become a form of proclamation (1:2–10). In the present passage he gives as additional evidence the fact that they have become imitators of believers in Judea, in the sense that the Thessalonians have experienced persecution at the hands of their compatriots as have Judean Christians at the hands of the Jews.

Verses 14–16, where Paul comments about Jews "displeas[ing] God" and about the wrath of God, constitute one of the most difficult passages in all of the Pauline corpus. At the outset, the contradiction between this passage and the later passage in Rom. 9—11 is significant. There Paul anticipates the salvation of "all Israel" (Rom. 11:26). Second, the frustration of Paul over the opposition to Christian preaching may give rise to his anger in this particular situation. Third, the final words of v. 16 are quite ambiguous, as the footnotes to the NRSV indicate. This passage should in no way be taken to reflect Paul's considered judgment about the ultimate standing of Jews before God. Instead, it demonstrates his frustration with a particular group over a particular set of behaviors.

With vs. 17–19, Paul turns from his reflection on his initial visit to Thessalonica to his present situation of separation from believers. Again in this passage, as he comments on the separation and his desire to see the Thessalonians once more, he reveals aspects of his understanding of the relationship between them. In v. 17, he writes that "we were made orphans by being separated from you." For those who see Paul operating as a father to his converts, and in an exclusively hierarchical sense, these words will come as a surprise. How can Paul and his colleagues, who are fathers to their Thessalonian children (v. 11), be "orphaned" by their separation? Here again Paul offers a glimpse of the mutuality of this relationship. Not only are he and his colleagues parents to the Thessalonians (as 2:7 and 2:11), but they also somehow are the children of the Thessalonians (see 2:7 and the alternate reading "infants" there). The significance of these converts for the apostles is such that they, the apostles, are indeed bereft when absent from them. Stated positively, Paul and his colleagues depend on the relationship for their own "hope" and "joy" and "crown of boasting" (v. 19).

Matthew 23:1–12

Matthew's narrative sneaks up on you. Over and over again readers assume the text is talking about other people, people in Jesus' day who are an obstacle to the reign of God or whose lives are inconsistent with their words. Then with a word or a phrase readers are jerked out of their remote, uninvolved posture to find their own names being called.

Matthew 23 is like that. It seems like a tirade by Jesus against the scribes and Pharisees for a whole host of failures, and then the narrator turns to speak directly to the readers (23:8). And we discover that the behavior of the scribes and Pharisees is only illustrative, that the real point of the text is not a condemnation of the Jewish religious leaders of Jesus' day or of Matthew's day. Instead, the text is aimed at Christian readers, who can no longer remain in merely an observing position, wondering why Jesus and the religious authorities had such a squabble.

We should have been sensitive to the narrator's tactics from the beginning. While Jesus previously had been debating with Pharisees, Herodians, and Sadducees (22:15–46), the audience subtly changes to the crowds and the disciples (23:1). But the predominantly third-person language lulls us into thinking that the text is still exposing the sins of the Jewish religious leaders, who constitute the hard-core opposition to Jesus. Our strong sense of judgment tends to make us identify with Jesus as he calls a spade a spade and describes the sham and pretense of the leaders. But v. 8 immediately draws the readers into the text, not on the side of Jesus, but on the side of the scribes and Pharisees.

What's the issue? The narrator wants Christian leaders who read the text not to act like the religious leaders of Jesus' day, but to be servants, to be humbly learning from their one instructor, Jesus (23:10–12). At the same time, the narrator intends that the ordinary constituency of the church not fall into the habit of using obsequious titles for leaders (23:9), but instead to "do whatever they teach you and follow it" (23:3).

How do the scribes and Pharisees serve as negative models? Basically, they do not practice what they teach. Their lives give no evidence that they take seriously the very law about which they endlessly debate. Consistency and wholeness are missing. At this point in the narrative, the issue is not the content of their teaching (Jesus has spoken to this throughout the Gospel and will raise it again in this chapter, 23:16–24), but the living out of their teaching.

Several examples are given. First, the scribes and Pharisees multiply the specific demands of the law to such a point that their minute interpretations become a horrendous burden for common people, but the leaders either don't bear those burdens themselves or don't provide help for others to bear them (23:4). The result is an enormous gap between leaders and people, between professionals and ordinary folk.

Second, the religious authorities of Jesus' day make a display of their leadership. They want their deeds to be noticed and their religious status to be recognized. Their badges include enlarged phylacteries (small leather cases worn on the left arm and forehead, containing important Old Testament texts) and extended fringes at the bottom of their robes (tassels worn to signify their bondage to the law; cf. Mark 6:56). They enjoy the attention they receive not only in the synagogue but also in the marketplace and at social functions.

Third, the religious leaders of Jesus' day crave titles: rabbi, father, and instructor. For Christian leaders the pride that cultivates such honorific titles reveals a fundamental failure—the ignoring of Jesus as teacher and instructor and of God as Father. The model of the Christian church is not one in which an authoritarian figure (whether "preacher," "pastor," or "doctor") dispenses truth to fawning followers, but an egalitarian community where all are students of Jesus and children of God. The proper recognition of divine authority relativizes all human authorities.

The concluding two verses of the lesson, employing the familiar pattern of reversal, bring the section to a positive climax. Greatness is manifest in service, and in the economy of God the humble, those who maintained integrity in life and avoid showiness in leadership, will finally be exalted.

Matthew's readers, then, whether leaders or common people, are not allowed by chapter 23 to remain detached critics of the scribes and Pharisees, those so-called bad guys of the first century. Instead, they are confronted with the demand for a righteousness that exceeds the scribes and Pharisees, with a style of leadership and following that acknowledges one divine source of authority. Teachers as well as learners are instructed by Jesus himself, the authentic interpreter of the law, and teachers as well as learners are called to do the will of the heavenly Father.

Proper 27

Ordinary Time 32

Sunday between
November 6 and 12 inclusive

Two of the last three Sundays of the Christian year carry an eschatological focus. Passages from both Old and New Testaments speak of ultimate commitment or of the return of Jesus, or they speak in parables that reflect a protagonist who has been delayed in an anticipated appearance. Living so far from the time of the texts makes it difficult to appreciate the urgency with which the issues arose in various communities and the crises they precipitated.

Eschatology, however, is not to be thought of merely as a speculative venture in which curious religious people gamble on a time when the world will end. In the Bible, eschatology provides the framework for ethics, the context in which believers are called to right conduct. It is the coming advent of God that demands from and warrants for the people of God a distinctive style of life. The texts for this Sunday depict responses appropriate to the end-time.

The text from Josh. 24, while not eschatological in itself, resonates to eschatological themes in its insistence on unswerving loyalty to Yahweh. Israel is given an opportunity at the Shechem assembly to define itself by identifying its God. But, in a manner that resonates to the eschatological hope that helps to shape the church, Israel is shaped by its understanding of the nature of God in whom the people are asked to hope.

Psalm 78, in which the speaker promises to

> . . . open my mouth in a parable;
> I will utter dark sayings from of old

forms a theological bridge in the New Testament lessons. In the parable of the five wise and five foolish maidens (Matt. 25:1–13), Jesus calls for readiness to face the delay of the bridegroom. A lack of preparedness results in a devastating verdict from the bridegroom: "I do not know you."

The text in 1 Thess. 4 comforts anxious believers who are worried about the fate of their deceased parents. Jesus' resurrection is not an isolated event, Paul argues, but the beginning of the resurrection of all people. The prospect of Jesus' return is the basis for hope.

Commitment, preparation, hope, and worship are bold ventures to be risked in anticipation of God's coming reign.

Joshua 24:1–3a, 14–25

The present passage marks an important watershed in the life of Israel-of-old. The tribes have, for all practical purposes, succeeded in their settlement of the Land of Promise—a series of episodes that command the attention of the major part of the book of Joshua. And now that the settlement is complete, the tribes are about to embark on their new life, no longer as nomads, but as permanent residents of the cities and farmlands of Canaan, the primary focus of the book of Judges. Therefore, the Shechem assembly which is described in Josh. 24 is a point of transition from one crucial and formative era into another. At this major junction in their lives, the people are summoned by Joshua to make a fundamental decision concerning their allegiance and concerning their identity.

(It is perhaps worth noting in passing that last week's Old Testament lection from Josh. 3, which records the entry of the tribes into the Land of Promise, forms with Josh. 24 a pair of brackets which frame the events associated with the settlement.)

Joshua 24:1–3a sets the context for Joshua's challenge to the people. Because of its early prominence in the stories of the Israelite confederacy, the town of Shechem, nestled in the trough between the sacred mountains Ebal and Gerizim (note Deut. 27), may be judged to have been an important cultic site for the Canaanites and others who lived in the land before the arrival of the Israelites. Its continuing prominence (note, for example, 1 Kings 12:1–15) extends into the period of the New Testament (John 4:1–30).

Thus it is not sheer happenstance that this site becomes the venue of this important ceremony of covenant renewal. The echoes of Mount Sinai may clearly be heard here. As Moses mediated the presence of God to the people at Sinai, so Joshua does the same at Shechem. That this is not just a popular assembly, but an encounter with Israel's God, is made quite clear by the final words of v. 1.

Joshua begins his address to the people by summarizing their history before God. This entire recital extends from v. 2 through v. 13, but, in order to render the passage into a manageable size, only the first two sentences have been retained in the lection (vs. 2–3a). Comparison may be made with similar historical surveys in Deut. 6:20–25 and 26:4–9 which, like Josh. 24:3–13, may have enjoyed repeated use in the worship of ancient Israel as creedal affirmations. This historical summary plays a significant theological role within the passage, in that it describes Yahweh's role in the covenant with Israel.

"Since Yahweh has done thus and so, Israel is now obligated to respond." Thus we might paraphrase Joshua's reasoning in vs. 14–25.

Verses 14–15 convey Joshua's initial challenge. The mythologies of Mesopotamia and Egypt are held up as negative examples (the "River" of v. 14 is the Euphrates) to the people, on whom Joshua now urges faithfulness to Yahweh. Nor is the divinely chosen successor of Moses content to permit the people to choose their deity by default. "If you won't serve Yahweh, you must declare whom you will serve" is the substance of v. 15a. (In contrast to v. 14, the alternatives to Yahweh here are the mythologies of Mesopotamia and Canaan—"the Amorites.") And then those words which have resounded through time: "As for me and my household, we will serve Yahweh."

This is a defining moment for Israel, in that the people are asked not only to identify their god, but to shape their own self-identity as well.

Verses 16–18 contain the first response of the people, and this unit forms a reprise of vs. 2–15. Once again there is a (much briefer) historical recital, followed by a statement of the people's commitment to Yahweh (v. 18b, which reformulates Joshua's statement at the end of v. 15). "Since Yahweh has done such great things for us, we now wish to respond by means of our commitment."

But Joshua challenges the sincerity of the people in vs. 19–20. Whether Joshua actually believes the people are incapable of living up to the demands of the covenant, or whether he is simply testing them, is not clear. In any event, they understand his words as an accusation concerning their vulnerability. "No, we will serve Yahweh!" (v. 21) is their terse but forceful rejoinder.

After further affirmations (vs. 22–24) Joshua makes clear what has been implicit all along, namely, that this is a moment of covenant renewal for the people: "So Joshua made a covenant with the people that day" (v. 25). Even the references to "the book of the law of God" and to the "large stone" (v. 26—beyond the scope of the lectionary passage) suggest links with Sinai.

And so the result is a renewed understanding of Israel's relation to God. Israel is Yahweh's people, a reality that has been demonstrated by the manner in which Yahweh has been involved in their history. And Yahweh is Israel's God, a commitment now reaffirmed by the people.

Psalm 78:1–7

This psalm is a recital of Israel's normative memory, much like that featured in Ps. 105, which recurs in the lectionary. In Psalm 78, however, the main point is to urge obedience to God's commands, and to warn of the disastrous consequences that follow from disobedience. Thus the sorry history of Israel is recited with a quite pronounced didactic purpose, binding the new generation to the commands of Yahweh as the condition of well-being.

The psalm begins with the speaker taking the role of a teacher, resolving to instruct the community, with particular reference to the younger generation (vs. 1–4). The teacher summons Israel to listen, to be ready to be instructed (v. 1). The teacher promises to speak in "parables" (or proverbs) and in old, well-established utterances ("dark sayings"). That is, the speaker indicates the genres to follow, which are intentionally pedagogical. The term rendered "dark sayings" is unclear in its precise meaning. What is clear is that the instruction is intended to ground members of the community in the ancient conviction that they are part of a coherent, responsible covenantal existence.

The accent is on the younger generation. This speaker knows that explicitly articulated instruction is necessary. Children do not inhale or receive by osmosis the full identity of this community, but depend on the intentional witness of adults. Thus the psalm aims at incorporating the young into the miracles and demands that constitute the identity of this particular community.

The specific substance of this instruction in "sayings" is to testify to the wonders, miracles, and acts of great power that have been performed by Yahweh for Israel. And, of course, those wonders and miracles are preserved and transmitted in the community by narrative. The teacher proposes to "tell the old, old story," so that the telling may evoke a sense of peculiar belonging on the part of the listening, younger generation.

Now the teacher seems to change the subject (vs. 5–7). Where the earlier subject has been miracles, now the subject is testimonies ("decrees") and Torah commands. Today's Old Testament reading of Josh. 24 indicates the way folk ("me and my household") are incorporated into the commands of Yahweh, thus becoming committed to a different, covenantal practice of communal existence. Indeed, Israel is unthinkable without commands, and they must be taught and told.

The purpose of this teaching and telling is "so that":

1. The children should "hope in God." The hope offered in the Bible is not generic confidence or optimism, but is grounded in the specificity of a God who enacts wonders, decrees, and commands. The purpose of instruction is to *combat despair,* which makes the young an easy mark for other hopes that are, in fact, false.

2. The children shall remember the "works of God," that is, be able to tell and trust the grounding, normative stories. These stories are not about Israel's achievements, but about God's overwhelming, inexplicable gifts to Israel. The purpose of instruction is to protect the young and to *combat amnesia,* whereby this defining memory is scuttled, either to embrace a single-dimensioned absolute future, or to opt for a memory that has no saving power and cannot keep its promises.

3. The children should "keep his commandments," that is, live a life of responsible obedience and thereby turn enemies into neighbors and live in joyous, intimate communion with Yahweh. The purpose of such learning of commandments is to *combat autonomy,* whereby the young come to think they are unconnected to anyone and are free to do whatever they please, thereby enacting a life of destructiveness to others and loneliness for self.

This reading of these verses notes a peculiar dialectic between learning *miracle narratives* and *covenantal commands,* or between *story* and *rule.* The reason for this transaction is that Israel regards both story and rule as Torah, and the second derives from the first. Thus Ps. 78 reviews the previous stories, but in each case the narrative ends with a teaching about obedience.

This urgency of instruction is crucial in the life of the contemporary church. Much of the church, both adults and children, is illiterate about the defining tradition that gives the church its life. As a consequence, the church lives much of its life in modes of despair, amnesia, and autonomy. It need not be so. A healthy, faithful alternative, however, requires the careful intentionality evidenced by this teacher on the part of caring adults. Only so will the next generation come to share the definitive passions of this community of faith.

1 Thessalonians 4:13–18

All Paul's letters are pastoral letters, although sometimes the pastoral issues lie far from the surface of the letter itself. Even in Romans, which less clearly addresses a specific pastoral issue than do Paul's other letters, pastoral concerns nevertheless find a place (as in Rom. 14, for example). In 1 Thessalonians, at least one such issue is unmistakable, and that is the concern prompted by the deaths of some within the congregation.The distance of two millennia from Paul's setting makes it difficult for contemporary Christians to appreciate the reaction that must have met the first death of a believer. Paul and the churches founded by him lived with the expectation that Christ's return would occur within the very near future. Since their own future depended on that return, a death within what was probably a small and intimately connected circle would have prompted dismay and grief. If 1 Thess. 4:13–18 reflects the situation at Thessalonica, it appears that Christians there were especially dismayed about the future of those who had died. What would become of them at Christ's Parousia?

Paul's response demonstrates the inherent connection between a theological response and a pastoral one. He addresses both the theological issue that has been raised and the emotional distress of the Thessalonians. The Thessalonians are not to "grieve as others do who have no hope" and they are to "encourage one another." It is equally important, however, that they understand the theological issues raised by their concerns. Indeed, their ability to encourage one another will depend directly on their understanding of the theological issues involved.

Paul introduces the issue with the claim that Christians are not to "grieve as others do who have no hope." Divorced from its context, this claim might be understood as a general guideline for Christian life: Christians should not grieve. And, indeed, Christians do sometimes choke back their own grief with the reminder that a loved one rests safely with God, or they censor the pain of others by using the promise of resurrection almost as a weapon. Paul's words, however, do not forbid grief to Christians. Surely the apostle who longs to be with his converts would understand the simple human longing to be with a loved one once again. His admonition, rather than prohibiting grief in general, distinguishes the grief of a Christian from the grief of those who live without hope.

With the word "hope" Paul reaches to the heart of this issue and to the connection between the theological and the pastoral issues at stake. Unlike other people, the Christian lives in the light of the specific hope stated in v. 14: the fact that God raised Jesus from the dead means that God will also raise those who have died. Jesus' resurrection is not a private miracle, a magic act performed simply in order to secure belief in his unique individual powers. It is, instead, the first stage in God's final triumph over death itself, as 1 Cor. 15 so eloquently puts it.

Paul does not speak here of resurrection as a reward for Christians, or even as the sole meaning of Christian hope. Hope, for the Christian, involves the expectation of resurrection, but, more important, it involves also the expectation of being with Christ Jesus. Christians who remain among the living may expect to be joined with those who have died, but Paul's final words of expectation in v. 17 are "and so we will be with the Lord forever." It is God who *secures* the Christian's hope and also God who *is* that final hope, in the sense that believers anticipate being together with God.

The language that Paul uses in this passage, as is the case with apocalyptic language elsewhere in the Bible, raises concerns for many readers. What does Paul mean when he refers to "the archangel's call" and "the sound of God's trumpet" (v. 16)? Will Christ actually raise believers up into the clouds (v. 17)? Christians remain divided between those who find such imagery so uncomfortable that they want to ignore it altogether and those who wish to use it to predict the exact time and way in which Christ will return. Neither response deals adequately with Paul's words, which (like apocalyptic writings in general) employ images that are larger than life to depict convictions that are also larger than life. To ignore the imagery is to domesticate the convictions by making Christian hope less than it truly is. At the same time, to reify the imagery by reading it literally is also to domesticate the convictions, pretending that they are subject to human verification and testing.

The passage ends by returning to the pastoral dimension of this issue, which Paul introduced in v. 13. Here at the end, however, Paul moves from offering comfort himself (as in v. 13) to admonishing the Thessalonians to comfort others: "Therefore encourage one another with these words." It is not enough for Christians to hear "official" pronouncements about hope from their pastors or teachers. They need to hear and speak those words to one another, enacting once again the mutuality of ministry Paul has already described in chapter 1. Such mutual encouragement carries within itself signs of the ultimate hope of all God's people.

Matthew 25:1–13

The second coming of Jesus is not a very popular topic for preaching in mainline Protestant churches. The somewhat bizarre apocalyptic imagery used in many New Testament texts and the long delay of the Parousia make the issue difficult to handle. Not wanting to seem fanatical about a topic that often has aroused fanaticism, we tend to avoid passages that speak of or allude to the return of Jesus, or we demythologize the images and offer a moral about good behavior. In doing so, however, we miss a critical dimension of New Testament theology and omit the primary event toward which the early Christian hope was aimed.

The Gospel lessons assigned for today and the next two Sundays come from a section of Matthew's narrative that speaks to the delay of the Parousia (24:48; 25:5, 19—admittedly a much shorter delay than we contemplate today) and urges a quality of life to be lived in anticipation. The passages include three of four consecutive parables Matthew records as a part of Jesus' final discourse to the disciples (24:45–51; 25:1–13, 14–30, 31–46).

A careful reading of the parable of the wise and foolish bridesmaids (25:1–13) always raises questions, since the parable contains a number of features that make for an awkward story: the long delay of the bridegroom, his arrival at such a late hour, the notion that shops from which to buy oil would be open at midnight, the willingness of the wise maidens to share their oil with the foolish, and the concluding injunction to "keep awake," when the flaw of the foolish maidens has not been that they slept but that they failed to prepare. Apparently, in the history of the tradition the parable has been allegorized to fit the situation of a community perplexed about the delay of Jesus' return, and the result is a story whose drama is strained.

All the awkward details, however, help to heighten the contrast between the wise and foolish bridesmaids. Five have prepared for the delay of the bridegroom by brining a sufficient supply of oil, while five have not. The latter group want very much to attend the wedding banquet. They are close enough friends of the bride and groom to be attendants. Yet when they return from their search for oil and call out, "Lord, lord, open to us," they are rejected as if they were strangers. "Truly I tell you, I do not know you."

This exchange between the foolish maidens and (apparently) the bridegroom recalls Jesus' words toward the end of the Sermon on the Mount (7:21–23). There, despite the high confession, "Lord,

Lord" and even extensive religious activity, Jesus rejects some with the words "I never knew you."

The obvious connection between the two passages leads to two observations. First, the parable of the wise and foolish bridesmaids is not directed toward outsiders but toward apparent members of the community, those who call Jesus "Lord," those who consider themselves a part of God's family. The foolish are insiders who in the face of the delay of the Parousia ignore the obligation of obedience and whose failure makes them outsiders. Second, the parable's stress on preparedness is given specificity by 7:21. What ultimately matters now and is especially exposed when the bridegroom appears is not the theology of those who wait or their extraordinary accomplishments, but their doing of the Father's will. Watching means seizing the day, loving God and loving neighbors in each moment, not a passive or speculative stance that soon despairs of a delayed return.

In the parable of the two servants that precedes the lection (24:45–51), the wicked servant counts on a prolonged delay and is not ready for the master's return (24:48). In the parable of the wise and foolish bridesmaids, the latter fail to take account of any delay and are ill equipped for the long haul. In both cases, the failure of anticipation prevents a faithful engagement with the present. "When Jesus calls on his disciples to keep watch, he is calling on them to take the reality of God so seriously that they can come to terms with its sudden appearance at any moment within their own lives, precisely because they know that this reality will one day come unboundedly in the kingdom of God" (Eduard Schweizer, *The Good News according to Matthew;* Atlanta: John Knox Press, 1975, p. 468).

Proper 28

Ordinary Time 33

Sunday between
November 13 and 19 inclusive

When people ask about the relevance of so much biblical talk of the return of Jesus, what do we say? If it is not a matter of scanning the skies or reading a divinely determined timetable, what is it? What does it mean to be eschatologically sensitive? The texts for Proper 28, following as they do those of the preceding Sunday, provide at least a few directions to move in reflecting on this critical article of biblical faith.

1. An eschatological awareness means taking God with utter seriousness and wrestling with the implications of God's character. On the one hand, it is clear that God can neither be trifled with nor blatantly ignored (Judg. 4:1–3). On the other hand, the third servant in the parable of the talents illustrates how a misunderstanding of God paralyzes responsiveness and leads to rejection (Matt. 25:24–30). The psalmist gets it right when he contemplates the reality of the established order and declares, "You [O God] are enthroned in the heavens!" (Ps. 123:1).

2. An eschatological awareness undermines a false sense of security. The image of "a thief in the night" (1 Thess. 5:2) disturbs complacency and reminds readers that "destruction will come upon them . . . and there will be no escape" (5:3).

3. An eschatological awareness evokes a daring style of discipleship, marked by the taking of risks and by leaps of faith. The two servants in the parable of the talents assume the responsibility placed in their hands and venture an investment that cannot be guaranteed. They model a faithfulness that takes God seriously.

4. An eschatological awareness clings to God's ultimate intentions—to save and not to destroy. The passage in 1 Thess. 5, despite its disturbing images, calls for hope and encouragement. The words are remarkably reassuring: "God has destined us not for wrath but for obtaining salvation through our Lord Jesus Christ" (5:9).

Judges 4:1–7

The choice of Judg. 4:1–7 as the Old Testament lection for this day is a happy one, for it provides worshipers with an important story of a woman leader of ancient Israel. However, in view of the fact that the text, as specified, is incomplete—at the conclusion of v. 7 one is left "hanging"—the preacher will undoubtedly wish to complement vs. 1–7 with the addition of other verses in order to bring the narrative to some kind of conclusion. The appending of vs. 12–16 would seem to be the most satisfactory solution to the problem.

Verses 1–3 provide an account of the events that have led up to the present crisis, and in doing so they use a formula that is frequently invoked in the book of Judges. The people sin. Yahweh punishes them for their sin by raising up an oppressor. The people cry to Yahweh for mercy. Yahweh's gracious response sets the stage for a divinely chosen deliverer. (Cf. Judg. 3:12–15; 6:1–6, and elsewhere.)

The serious nature of the Israelites' sinfulness is indicated by the enormity of the oppression that King Jabin has inflicted on the tribes. Nine hundred chariots may seem to be an exaggerated number, but as this particular implement of warfare had been introduced into the eastern Mediterranean-Mesopotamian area centuries before the time in which this story is set the number is not totally farfetched. In any event, the image of such vast and tyrannous power is meant to underscore the perilous plight of the Israelites, as is the figure of twenty years (by no means unbelievable!) as the period during which Jabin "had oppressed the Israelites cruelly."

(A good critical commentary on the book of Joshua will point out interesting literary and historical aspects to the study of this text. For one thing, this is one of the few stories of early Israelite-Canaanite warfare situated in the north, in that Hazor is located north of the Sea of Galilee [cf. Josh. 11]. For another, the prose account of this incident, including the chilling narrative of the assassination of Jabin's general, Sisera, by the Israelite woman Jael [Judg. 4:17–22], is paralleled by a poetic version in Judg. 5 which is surely one of the most ancient bits of literature in the entire Hebrew Bible.)

Far to the south of Jabin's center of power, the woman Deborah, who served both as prophetess and as judge (Judg. 4:4), presided over the affairs of the Israelite tribes from her home near Bethel in the central hill country. Like most of the leaders described in the book of Judges, Deborah was probably an individual of primarily local importance, although the suggestion of the text is that Israelites from far and wide came seeking her judgment. For his part, Barak is a son of the tribe of Naphtali, that group most immediately affected by the oppression of Jabin, in that Hazor lay in the territory occupied by the Naphtalites. That Barak responded to Deborah's summons reflects not only the woman's authority as a leader, but also the distress felt by this Naphtalite warrior over the suffering of his people.

The text does not describe the manner in which Yahweh's will is communicated to Deborah, but her words to Barak (v. 6) make it clear that she is acting under divine authority. It is Yahweh's intention that Barak is to lead a combined army of fighters from Naphtali and from nearby Zebulun (no other tribes are mentioned, but note Judg. 5:14–17) against Jabin's army. The prominence of general Sisera in the story (and in 4:17–22!) suggests that he was an individual of uncommon skill. But that skill, and the raw power over which he presided, was no match for the strength of Yahweh. Sisera was completely under the authority of Yahweh, who would bring out the Canaanite general and "his chariots and his troops" to their utter destruction by Barak (v. 7).

(The Wadi Kishon and Mount Tabor [v. 12] are both located near the Jezreel Valley, scene of many battles in antiquity. For example, Mount Gilboa, the site of Saul's mortal encounter with the Philistines [1 Sam. 31:1], is only a few miles south of Mount Tabor.)

When Sisera hears of Barak's movements he counters with his massive army (vs. 12–13), precisely in keeping with Yahweh's promise of v. 7. Deborah's renewed command to Barak (v. 14) again emphasizes the role of Yahweh in what is happening. "Yahweh has given" and "Yahweh is . . . going out before" are two phrases that perfectly summarize the theology of the entire narrative. What is about to transpire is not only an evidence of Yahweh's power over even the mightiest of human armies, but—most important—is also evidence of Yahweh's mercy toward a sinful and suffering Israel.

In vs. 15–16 the encounter is as decisive as Deborah has promised it would be. Barak's force is large (ten thousand warriors, v. 14), but again the emphasis is on the power of Yahweh. It was not Barak's skill as a tactician nor the valor of the soldiers, but Yahweh's might that "threw Sisera and all his chariots and all his army into a panic." Sisera escapes (for the moment), but his army is completely decimated. In keeping with the provisions of the holy war, not one of the enemy was spared!

> The stars fought from heaven,
> from their courses they fought against Sisera.
> (Judg. 5:20)

Admonitions found elsewhere in this volume concerning the danger of projecting the political and social tensions of our own time onto a biblical screen are surely applicable here. To assume that those with whom one has differences are therefore the enemies of God is a tragic misstep of religious faith that has led to incredible suffering and loss in our century, and texts such as Judg. 4 should never be applied in such a manner. But as an ancient tale of the forgiveness and mercy of God it may still play a significant role in the life of the church. Jabin and Sisera stand as symbols of the many oppressive consequences of human sin. Barak's victory is emblematic of God's concern that that oppression not be permitted to stand.

Psalm 123

Today's psalm is a petitionary prayer that begins in doxology (vs. 1–2d), petitions for mercy from Yahweh (vs. 2e–3a), and explores the need for mercy (vs. 3b–4).

The first part of Psalm 123 states the theme of the psalm, *mercy* (v. 2e,f), but precedes the theme announcement by a statement of praise and deference (vs. 1–2d). The psalm begins abruptly with an inversion of normal Hebrew word order. The first word is "To you." The speaker assumes a tone of urgency and need. The eyes (attention, devotion) of the speaker are completely fixed on Yahweh, utterly dependent on Yahweh as the only source of help, not distracted by any other option.

This singular devotion to the Ruler "enthroned in the heavens" is explicated by two parallels. The devotion is as singular as the devotion of a servant to a master, as a maid to a mistress. These "underlings" are characteristically postured in complete obedience. They wait only for the command, gesture, or wish of the dominant person in order to promptly obey. And the same watchfulness for master or mistress is a waiting for an affirmation or a commendation of approval. At the end of v. 2, the speaker returns to his own eyes as in v. 1, except now it is not "my eyes" but "our eyes," as the speaker articulates the faith and need of the entire community of faith.

Finally in v. 2, we reach the point of the foregoing. "My eyes," "our eyes" are fixed only on Yahweh. But to what purpose and for how long? The purpose is to receive mercy from Yahweh. Yahweh is expected to give mercy, and the speaker is confident that God will give it. It turns out that this gaze upon Yahweh is one not only of deferential obedience, as the metaphors accent, but also of expectant hope. The servant expects kindness and consideration from the master, and Israel expects the same from Yahweh. For how long? Until it happens. Until God acts in graciousness. The wait may be long, but Israel will never give up, both because Israel trusts completely, and because Israel has no alternative.

Now the poem turns to a prayer of complaint on the part of the community (vs. 3–4). The shift to community has been signaled by the "our" of v. 2. In these concluding verses, the entire concern of the prayer is communal.

This prayer in rather standard fashion includes a petition (v. 3a) and a reason for the prayer to be answered by Yahweh (vs. 3b–4). The petition voices a double use of "mercy" (*ḥnn*). Between the two uses the name of Yahweh is situated. "Mercy" here refers to a free, undeserved act of enormous kindness. This is what Israel most needs and wants, and counts on receiving from Yahweh.

The reason that the prayer should be answered is that this community is exhausted by the "contempt/scorn/contempt" of its neighbors, "the proud," that is, the ones who are arrogant and condescending. Notice that "the proud" are not identified, nor is the reason for scorn expressed, nor is there answer to the prayer given by Yahweh, any assurance or any enactment of mercy.

The experience of "contempt" must have occurred in a low season of the failure of Israel's buoyant faith. This might suggest, for example, the experience of exile, when the God of Israel has seemed to fail and Israel is taunted by its more successful neighbors (cf. Ps. 137). Nothing, however, is specified and so the experience is generic, permitting us to fill in the details according to our own experience.

We might extrapolate two other dimensions of "contempt." First, the venomous practice of anti-Semitism is often characterized as "the teaching of contempt," that is, the abuse and torment of Jews just because they are Jews. This contempt is evoked by the peculiarity and distinctiveness of Jewishness, which the world has often not tolerated or appreciated. The voice of this psalm, which is exhausted with contempt, surely moves in a jagged line to this contemporary practice. It is no wonder that this Jewish voice is ready to say to God, "Enough!" Second and more broadly, the prayer can be heard as the voice of anyone in the community who is abused and regarded as inadequate, or suffers from a failure of nerve or lack of confidence or effectiveness. The psalm seeks to mobilize Yahweh to be attentive to those whom the world regards as "losers."

The most remarkable claim of this prayer is that *God's mercy* can override the *contempt of the world* (vs. 2–3). Such a prayer of yearning understands God's mercy to be a sense of presence and solidarity with the seeker, and an affirmation of worth. Such a prayer indicates a courageous refusal of the world's verdict, and a capacity to listen for and trust in a verdict that comes from beyond worldly judgments, from the very voice of the Holy One. But then this remarkable community of faith in its long tradition of trust and abrasive speech, and all those dismissed by the harsh world, here trust in a different verdict, as confident of such a verdict from God as they are needful of it.

1 Thessalonians 5:1–11

The previous week's reading, from 1 Thess. 4:13–18, concludes with an admonition that seems to bring to an end Paul's discussion of the anticipated return of Christ. The present reading, however, takes up the topic once again. Paul knows, either from some inquiry on the part of the Thessalonians or from experience elsewhere, that the promise of Christ's Parousia always prompts the question of time. If Christ is to return, when will that be and how can people make sure that they are ready for him?

For most people, the Parousia will be sudden and its consequences unavoidable. It will come "like a thief in the night." Just as a thief enters the houses of those who believe themselves to be secure, so the "day of the Lord" will break in upon those who take for granted that the ways of the world will continue without challenge. When that day does come, it will be inescapable, just as are the pains of a woman in labor. She can find no rest, no escape from her agony.

Paul does not here explicitly say that no one knows when the day of the Lord will be, a theme that is sounded elsewhere in the New Testament (Matt. 24:36–44; Mark 13:32–37; Luke 21:34–36; Acts 1:6–7). Indeed, 1 Thess. 4:13–18 seems to suggest that Christ will return during the lives of at least some among Paul's generation of believers. Nevertheless, the implication of 5:1–3 is that no timetable may be drawn up or predictions offered.

If Christians have no schedule by which to await and prepare for Christ's return, the coming of that day should still not catch them by surprise: "But you, beloved, are not in darkness for that day to surprise you like a thief" (5:4). Christians belong to the light, to the day, and should be constantly prepared for the return of Christ. The metaphors of v. 8, with their martial imagery of a breastplate and a helmet, emphasize the need for constant readiness. In other words, for the Christian the answer to the question "When will the day of the Lord come?" is always "Now!"

The dualism that Paul expresses here exists in a variety of early Jewish and Christian literature, as well as in literature from the larger Greco-Roman environment. Its presence often troubles contemporary readers, who may hear in it echoes of racist or anti-Semitic or other forms of a rhetoric of exclusion, by which one group vilifies another to justify itself. While Paul's language in this passage can be twisted into such a rhetoric, it is important to see that the dualism in this passage serves to admonish the Christian to live a life of watchfulness rather than to vilify the non-Christian. Paul's interest in the passage lies in the way Christians understand and respond to the hope of the return of Christ rather than threatening those outside the Christian circle.

The Christian watchfulness and wakefulness that Paul advocates will sound strangely outmoded for a generation of Christians that lives nearly two thousand years removed from Paul's letter and knows that Christ has not yet returned! But the watchfulness to which Paul urges Christians is not merely a matter of time. It is also a matter of importance. To watch for the Parousia, even two thousand years after its promise, is to confess that God stands both at the beginning and at the end of human life and that humankind remains accountable to God for its behavior.

With vs. 9–11 it becomes clear that the question of time is not, in Paul's judgment, the most important question. What is really at stake in this passage is not so much when Christ might return as what that promise means. Verses 9–11 answer that question: Christ's return means salvation. God's will is to bring about salvation through Jesus Christ (cf. 1:10), and part of that will is that "whether we are awake or asleep we may live with him." As in the previous discussion of the fate of those Christians who have already died (4:16–17), the most important point for Paul is that Christians ultimately will somehow live with Christ. When that life is fully accomplished, how it is to be accomplished, and what it will look like—the answers to these questions lie beyond human understanding. What is important is the confident hope that Christian life culminates in God.

The end of this lection repeats and expands on the exhortation that concludes chapter 4: "Therefore encourage one another and build up each other, as indeed you are doing" (5:11). The "therefore" signals that this exhortation is not an independent refrain, tacked onto the end of Paul's comments but not substantially related to them. Indeed, it is *because* of their confident expectation that the present life in Christ leads to another and unending life in Christ that Christians are able to encourage one another. They also are to "build up each other." More characteristic of 1 Corinthians than any of

Paul's other letters (cf. 1 Cor. 8:1, 10; 10:23; 14:4, 17), "upbuilding" in this context anticipates the exhortations that will follow in 1 Thess. 5:12–22. Upbuilding also involves the general need for Christians to understand themselves as profoundly connected with one another, so that the needs of others within the community are understood to be one's own needs as well.

Matthew 25:14–30

Preaching the parable of the talents in the fall of the year has its hazards. The fall is the time when most congregations face the issue of money and talk about financial pledges to the church for the coming year. Since the parable speaks about responsible stewardship, it is easy to let the two (that is, pledging and stewardship) become intertwined and to let the congregation come away with the implied, if not expressed, notion that making a sacrificial pledge to the church is the essence of stewardship. Such a notion might boost the budget a bit, but unfortunately denigrates stewardship and avoids the hard message of the parable.

In the context in which the parable is found, it clearly presupposes the departure of Jesus and his anticipated return. When would it happen? What would it be like? What does it mean for the church? The narrator discourages speculation and instead provides these parables of Jesus (24:45–51; 25:1–13, 14–30, 31–46), which direct the hearers' attention to the issues at hand, to faithfulness, preparedness, and risk. Waiting and watching for Jesus' return really means being good stewards of all our resources, especially the gospel. Two of the servants in the parable of the talents obviously took that calling seriously.

But what about servant number three? What is his problem?

He is not a dishonest servant who was out to milk his master of whatever he could get. There is no hint of fraud, deceit, or scandal. He had no plans to embezzle the funds or to swindle his master. Neither do we have any indication that he was a philanderer, a prodigal son figure out for a fling (though there is another version of this parable in the apocryphal Gospel of the Nazoreans that depicts the third servant as a wild renegade, rather than as the reluctant servant who hid his money in the ground).

What's so wrong with being cautious? Discretion and deliberateness are virtues, not vices. But with this third servant virtues become vices. Prudence and wariness easily become self-protectiveness and restraint. Inhibition turns to fear, and the servant ends up refusing the risk of trading in the marketplace. By preserving exactly what has been entrusted to him he can at least minimally stay in the good graces of his master—or so he thinks. Though his master has expressed confidence in him, he judges his master to be a harsh man. He deems it better to preserve his own safety and security than to run the risk of losing the money and angering his master.

But love demands risks—marriage, parenting, vulnerability, confrontation, tenderness. For Matthew's intended readers, however, the main risk was not the matter of interpersonal relations, but the risk of the public expression of the gospel, whether they would keep it safely tucked away in a secure context or let it loose in the broader world among the nations. Anticipating Jesus' return meant rejecting the lure of security, with its logic of fear and intimidation, and taking the risk of discipleship, with its dangers and perils.

Look at another feature of the story. The two servants who invested wisely are rewarded for their achievement, and the timid creature who stashed his money away is sharply rebuked, his money confiscated. What do we do with this stress on rewards and punishment? Does this invalidate the image of a gracious, generous God, who accepts people despite their good or bad behavior?

Interestingly, the faithful two didn't get higher salaries or gold watches or plaques to put on their walls. They got two things: First, they got more responsibility. "You have been trustworthy in a few things, I will put you in charge of many things." The reward for taking the risk and managing the investment was the burden of greater risk and the challenge of larger investments. But with the responsibility came a second reward: the joy of the master's presence. "Come on in and share my happiness!" the *Good News Bible* translates it. And the punishment of the third servant? He loses two things: the responsibility of being a steward and the joy of the master's presence.

The parable clarifies the alternatives. To the one choosing security over risk, the Lord remains a hard master, one who seems to reap where he does not sow and gather where he has not planted. Fearfulness breeds more fear. The prospect of joy and the freedom of response are gone. But those who risk discover a Lord ready to share the delight of his presence and participation in his mission. They discover a link with the teller of the story, who knows all about risks and whose love is neither prudent nor calculating.

Christ the King or Reign of Christ

Proper 29
Ordinary Time 34

Sunday between
November 20 and 26 inclusive

The last Sunday of the church year sounds a triumphant, but not triumphalist, note. The universal rule of God, expressed in Christ the Shepherd-King, is a dominant theme in all the texts assigned for the day, giving the occasion for celebration and rejoicing. No power can match the power of the reigning Lord. And yet the Gospel lection, with a sober realism, reminds us that much is yet promised and that Christ's presence is encountered in the world today not with flamboyant demonstrations of power, but amid the needy and the marginalized.

Both texts from the Old Testament dwell on the nurturing, protecting role of the Shepherd-King, whose people we are, "the sheep of his pasture" (Ps. 100:3). Even when in the presence of this ultimate Majesty, the people do not tremble, but "come into his presence with singing" (v. 2). The selection from Ezek. 34 gives the shepherd's guiding and defending role a political twist by condemning the succession of shepherd-kings who have neglected and exploited the flock. Yahweh has to intervene publicly, and will intervene again in the future through a servant-king of the Davidic line (Ezek. 34:23–24).

Both the New Testament passages celebrate the victory of Christ, even echoing sounds from the Old Testament selections—the enthroned Son of man of Matt. 25 separates the flock (as Ezek. 34:16–22), and the risen Christ of Eph. 1 is seated by God "far above all rule and authority and power and dominion" (v. 21). But neither text champions an unbounded flagwaving or religious jingoism.

We live in an interim, for now the Son of Man who suffered and was crucified is manifest among the hungry, the thirsty, the stranger, the naked, the sick, and the imprisoned. But Christ guarantees God's completed reign. There need be no doubt about it. Death will be vanquished, and the suffering Son of Man will rule as judge over all the nations.

Ezekiel 34:11–16, 20–24

As close readers of the book of Ezekiel are aware, the passage at hand is one of several (cf. Ezek. 36:1–15; 37:1–14) that provide messages of hope in complement to Ezekiel's many oracles of doom (note Ezek. 5:1–17; 8:1–11:13, among other texts). Yet the proclamation here is not of unrelieved good news, for the problem of persistent evil must still be dealt with.

The theme of the day of Yahweh is addressed early on in this lection from Ezek. 34. That day was one of "clouds and thick darkness" (v. 12), an occasion for the scattering of the sheep of Israel. But clearly that day is past and the scattered are now to be collected together through the grace of God, the image for God's compassionate concern being the dedicated shepherd. In this first section of the present passage (vs. 11–16) the portrait of the shepherd who seeks the lost sheep of the flock is lifted as the metaphor for Yahweh's redemptive activity. As a good shepherd collects the animals of the flock who are in peril, so Yahweh will bring together the remnants of scattered Israel. The hungry sheep will be fed from the choicest pastures, the thirsty sheep will be led to the mountain watercourses, the purest of all streams. The injured will be healed, the weak will be strengthened.

All of this will be done as the result of the intervention of Yahweh, a personal God who cares for the sheep as Yahweh's own possession. In this section, the immediacy of Yahweh is communicated through the repetition of the first-person pronoun (in Hebrew this is frequently the first-person-singular verb form): "I myself will search for my sheep" (v. 11). "I will seek out my sheep. I will rescue them" (v. 12). "I will bring them out from the peoples" (v. 13). Over and over again the reader is reminded of the personal involvement of Yahweh in the life and fortunes of the nation. Whether or not this imagery is the direct inspiration for Ps. 23, it surely stimulated Jesus' articulation in his own understanding of his role as the good shepherd (Luke 15:3–7; John 10:1–18) who seeks the lost.

The first reaction of the reader to this section is that the prophet is speaking of the restoration to their own land of the Babylonian exiles (among whom Ezekiel lived and worked). This conclusion is gained with good reason, for elsewhere (Ezek. 37:1–14, for example) the prophet speaks as if he has the historical Israel in mind. Yet Ezekiel's concern outreached a narrow nationalism, and so here as elsewhere attention directed at a historical reality becomes a metaphor for the eschaton (cf. Ezek. 40—48 and the description there of the Temple). In other words, the present text is concerned not only with the plight of sixth-century Israel, but with the realities of good and evil in an ultimate sense. Israel's return to the Land of Promise from the Babylonian exile becomes paradigmatic for the redemption of all the people of God. The work of Yahweh, the good shepherd, is not limited in time and space.

The second section (vs. 20–22) is anticipated in v. 16 where, in contrast to the manner in which Yahweh has sustained the weak, Yahweh promises to destroy "the fat and the strong." This promise is rendered more explicit in v. 21, where the text provides a reason for Yahweh's hostility: the fat and strong have been instrumental in the persecution of the weak. Their deprivation has called forth Yahweh's activity as judge (vs. 20, 22) and, in order to save the flock, Yahweh will distinguish "between sheep and sheep." Yahweh's mercy is not lavished without discrimination.

The final section (vs. 23–24), moving beyond descriptions of judgment, identifies the office of the Davidic king as the special instrument in the redemption of the people of God. David, not just as shepherd boy (1 Sam. 16:11), but as reigning shepherd-king, will execute the saving intentions of Yahweh. As Yahweh's representative, the Davidic king will do all those gracious deeds that Yahweh has personally set out to do. Only the activity of "feeding" is mentioned in the text, but the implication is that watering, healing, and strengthening are also intended—in other words, the same gracious deeds of Yahweh specified earlier (vs. 14–16).

If the prophet meant these words as historical promise, he joins others in the prophetic tradition who yearned for the restoration of the Davidic monarchy following the end of the exile (cf. Hag. 2:20–23; Zech. 6:9–14). However that may have been, it is the transcendent, eschatological dimensions of the text that speak to the reader/hearer in our own time. It is the first coming of the Davidic-king-like-no-other, Jesus Christ, soon to be remembered in Advent and Christmas, that is the incarnation of this promise and, in certain respects, the beginning of its fulfillment. And it is the second coming of this same Messiah, also to be commemorated in the weeks ahead, that will constitute the consummation of the promise and of the hope that Christ's people have placed in him.

Psalm 100

This familiar and well-loved hymn is a model example of praise in ancient Israel. The standard form of hymn consists of a *summons* to praise and *reasons* for praise. In this psalm, the pattern of summons and reason is enacted two times.

The first example of summons and reason is in vs. 1–3. The summons to praise consists in three verb phrases—"make a joyful noise," "worship," "come into [God's] presence [=sanctuary]." The speaker invites the community to come to the sanctuary where Yahweh will be rightly worshiped and honored.

The initial work of the psalm, to "make a joyful noise," in fact means to lift a cry of celebration, an acknowledgment of the victory and sovereignty of Yahweh. The "noise" is one of triumph, confidence, and joy. The other two imperatives of summons are matched by an invitation to "gladness" and "singing" which suggests joyous, boisterous, celebrative singing, perhaps in an actual ritual procession of exultation.

While the liturgical markings of this summons are unmistakable, the summons is at the same time political. The liturgical affirmation of Yahweh is a declaration of loyalty to Yahweh which is not to be shared with any other "would-be" sovereign. The "reason" offered, the motivation for such praise, is voiced in v. 3. The reason is normally introduced by the particle "for" (*kî*), which may also be rendered "because." Here the particle is preceded by the verb "know," and is translated "that," but the verb refers not simply to cognitive information but an acknowledgment, as in "confess." What Israel is to confess (which evokes praise) is that Yahweh, Yahweh alone, is the true God and the only God who warrants such an affirmation of loyalty and celebration.

What qualifies Yahweh for such a claim is that Yahweh "created" Israel (in the events of exodus and Sinai), and Israel owes its very existence to the will and passion of Yahweh. In v. 3b, there are two possible readings of a slightly unclear text. One reading (as in NRSV) is that because Yahweh "made us," we are Yahweh's property and possession, and must refer life back to Yahweh, which is done through praise. Thus praise is an acknowledgment of belonging to Yahweh. The other possible reading is that "we did not make ourselves," and therefore have no autonomous existence, and so must cleave to Yahweh who makes life possible. Both readings come to the same affirmation, but by different interpretations of Israel's past and present.

As an exposition of this claim for Yahweh (on either reading), the poet employs the metaphor of sheep-shepherd. In that relationship, the sheep is completely dependent on the shepherd, and the sheep are fully trusting in the shepherd. This is the ground of praise to which Israel is summoned, an awareness of *complete dependence* and an affirmation of *complete trust*. No wonder the praise is marked by triumphant, confident joy and singing!

The same pattern of praise is reiterated in vs. 4–5. The "summons" consists in three imperatives. "Enter," "give thanks," "bless." The first verb is the same as the last verb in v. 2, making clear that this is a liturgical procession. The second verb, "Give thanks," suggests not only an act of gratitude, but also a public acknowledgment of belonging to Yahweh in loyalty, i.e., "confessing Yahweh." The third verb means to assign to Yahweh the capacity of power for well-being. Again the summons asks Israel to give its life in public ways over to Yahweh.

The reason is here introduced by the predictable particle "For." The actual reason here is a stereotypical characterization of Yahweh, rather bland compared to the reason of v. 3. Yahweh is marked by three compelling properties: Yahweh is "good," that is, friendly and capable of giving well-being; and Yahweh practices covenant loyalty and faithfulness. The last two words, *ḥesed, 'ĕmûnāh,* are a classic connectional word pair in Israel, bespeaking God's utter reliability as a dependable covenant keeper.

Two accents in this psalm are noteworthy. First, praise is an act of public affirmation of a definitional loyalty to an agent outside self. Praise is for that reason problematic in a possessive society like ours which champions autonomy and self-possession. Praise is a surrender of autonomy, an affirmation that life is derived from and lives toward an agent who must be obeyed as well as trusted. Thus praise, each time we do it, is an act of identifying ourselves by relation to this other one whom we fully trust and rely on.

Second, the metaphor of shepherd is a powerful and pervasive one in biblical faith. The metaphor affirms that the community (sheep) are vulnerable and dependent. In today's Old Testament reading in Ezek. 34, Yahweh, the good shepherd, does all those attentive, healing, restorative acts we all so need and crave. Israel gives itself over in praise to this Shepherd-Lord, because Israel knows no other who is so concretely helpful to the wounds and dangers of daily life.

Ephesians 1:15–23

See the discussion of this passage under Ascension.

Matthew 25:31–46

The very familiar passage of the separation of the sheep and goats has become a favorite text for sermons calling the congregation to engage in social ministries of compassion to the needy and a popular source for slogans for benevolent institutions. These are not entirely inappropriate uses of the text, for with a powerfully rhetorical flourish it directs the reader's attention to the hungry, the thirsty, the stranger, the naked, the sick, and the prisoner. They become the locus of the Son of Man's presence. And yet the passage offers much more than merely an exhortation to visit the jail occasionally or provide a Christmas basket to the needy. Its demands are more pervasive than that and its promises more binding.

1. It is intriguing to read the passage in its liturgical context, with an eye toward this Sunday's emphasis on Christ the King. Right away, the primary focus moves away from judgment to the Judge, away from what we must do to what the Son of Man has done. The chief protagonist is neither the group on the right hand who are blessed, nor the group on the left hand who are cursed, nor even the neglected, needy people, but the Son of Man, who sits on the throne. He is the Shepherd-King, who separates the sheep from the goats.

The literary context reinforces this christological perspective. Matthew 24 and 25 are chapters that depict the coming end-time. The three preceding parables (24:45–51; 25:1–13, and 14–30) share a moment of climax when the householder, the bridegroom, or the master of the servants after some delay returns to receive a reckoning from those left behind. The passage for this Sunday begins with an already-returned protagonist.

Critical to the interpretation of the passage from the vantage point of the reader is the threefold rendering of the presence of Christ. Most obviously, Christ is anticipated as the exalted Son of Man, who comes in glory with his angelic train and who, sitting on his throne, renders decisions regarding the gathered nations (24:27, 30, 36–37, 39, 44; 25:31). Titles such as "king" (25:34, 40) and "Lord" (25:37, 44) undergird his prominence as the eschatological Judge. Second, Christ is present in "the least of these," the needy with whom he has identified himself and who become the locus of his presence. Third, Christ is present as the Son of Man, who suffers and is crucified (26:2, 24).

Christ the King, the exalted figure whom the Christian community anticipates and before whom the nations are gathered, is present among the outcast and the lowly. They become his designated representatives, so that in serving them one serves the eschatological Lord. But such an identification is only part of the story. The royal rendering and the rendering as the needy cannot be severed from the memory of the Son of Man, who is handed over to be crucified. The Judge has himself been the victim of human judgment; the universal

King has been mocked as king of the Jews (27:27–31). The one who renders verdicts is no less than the Jesus who "will save his people from their sins" (1:21)—an unprecedented Judge. The all-embracing authority of Christ the King makes sense only in light of this threefold rendering of Christ's presence.

2. The judgments declared by the Son of Man and the categories describing the needy who are served or not served carry immense and even threatening power. As commentators have noted, sickness in the Bible often carries the notion of sin and contagion, and nakedness implies shame and powerlessness. Convicts and strangers are included in the list. Some of the categories, at least, connote marginalization, even the experience of being ostracized. Whether "the least of these" are Christians or not, their circumstances nevertheless put them at the fringe of society. To be deeply involved with such people means to be implicated in their predicament, to be incriminatingly linked to their situation, and no doubt to be guilty by association. The passage then demands something more profound than altruistic endeavors.

"The righteous" (25:37, 46), who are invited to enjoy the kingdom prepared for them, are not intimidated by the aura of exclusion that surrounds the needy. Their sense of surprise when recognized by the Judge may suggest not only a lack of self-consciousness on their part but also an awareness that this is simply the essence of discipleship, this is what it means to be a Christian. After all, the Judge was himself accused of being "a glutton and a drunkard, a friend of tax collectors and sinners" (11:19).

ALL SAINTS

November 1 or the
first Sunday in November

All Saints' Day is a wonderful time in the life of a congregation to attend to dimensions of the faith often neglected or relegated to funeral meditations. For a church that exists in a consumeristic society so present-oriented, so eager to forget the past and so unwilling to face what seems like an uncertain future, the themes of this day are needed. They point us beyond our individualism and parochialism. They remind us of our connectedness to a great company of God's people of every age and generation, in whom we are included as sisters and brothers. The themes of this day have the power to reshape our identity, to teach us who we are and what we are about.

For one thing, there is the theme of a community with a single-minded focus on God. The psalmist gives expression to this sort of preoccupation as one who was deeply at risk but wondrously rescued (Ps. 34:1–10, 22). The glorious scene of the Apocalypse depicts the faithful gathered before the throne worshiping God "day and night within his temple" (Rev. 7:15). Though they are themselves people who have suffered, the saints take delight not in their own accomplishments but in God, to whom salvation belongs (7:10).

Such a community is marked by diversity. Its members are drawn from every nation, people, and language, and yet they speak a common voice. Their chorus is not marred by chaotic dissonance. They sing the same song. The images of food (Ps. 34:8) and family (1 John 3:1–2) bespeak a life shared and a communion experienced.

Finally, the community claims a bonding that transcends death. On the one hand, the future is unknown. Its details are blurred. No description is given of heaven's furniture. The images are expansive and evocative. On the other hand, the future is secured. "What we do know is this: when he is revealed, we will be like him, for we will see him as he is" (1 John 3:2).

Revelation 7:9–17

In the larger context of the book of Revelation, chapter 7 forms an interlude between the opening of the first six (Rev. 6) and the last (8:1–5) of the seven seals. The initial part of the interlude, 7:1–8, describes the sealing of those who have been redeemed out of Israel. The precise nature of this sealing is unclear, but it is apparently intended to convey that the redeemed have been formally confirmed as members of the community of the Lamb, Jesus Christ. (Compare Ezek. 9:4, where those who are faithful to the God of Israel are marked on their foreheads in order that they may be spared from the destruction to come.) The number of these individuals, 144,000, is significant, in that it is a thousandfold expansion of the square of the number of the tribes of Israel.

The second part of the interlude, vs. 9–17, constitutes the present lection and is a description of the confirmation of the Gentile members of the community of the Lamb. Unlike the number of the Israelite redeemed, which is very precise and geometric, the number of Gentiles is so "great . . . that no one could count" (v. 9). The sources of the Israelites are, again, quite specific: the twelve tribes; whereas the Gentiles come "from every nation, from all tribes and peoples and languages." They stand before the throne of God (chap. 4) and before the Lamb that had been slaughtered (5:6, 12), dressed in white clothing, symbolic of their purity, and holding palm branches in their hands. The palm branches, associated in Israelite liturgy with the Festival of Booths (Lev. 23:40), seem in this instance to be emblematic of the victory of the Lamb and, through him, of the redeemed (cf. John 12:13). The hymn of the Gentiles lauds both God and the Lamb (Rev. 7:10), an offering of praise that is affirmed and echoed by the host of angels (vs. 11–12).

Verses 13–14 have been provided in order to avoid any confusion on the part of the reader concerning the identity of the Gentile redeemed. One of the twenty-four elders, whose thrones are near the throne of God (4:4), questions John in the matter, but the author of the Apocalypse turns the query back on its owner: "Sir, you are the one who knows." The elder then answers in such a manner that he not only relates the victory of the redeemed to the sacrifice of the Lamb, but implies that they have arrived at their present state only through great struggle and suffering (v. 14). Many commentators have seen in these words reference to the early martyrs of the church.

The elder then breaks into a hymn (vs. 15–17), which, while it echoes several Old Testament texts, appears to have been written with Isa. 49:10 specifically in mind. Verse 15 describes the reason for the continuing services on the part of the redeemed—that is, they are responding in gratitude to the victory won for them by the Lamb. And as a consequence of this service God will provide them constant care. Hunger, thirst, and heat, symbols of all the pain and suffering that accompany human life, are to be banished from the experience of the redeemed (v. 16). The Lamb will be their shepherd (note the irony), and their thirst and their sorrow will be banished by the water and by the consolation which the Lamb and God will provide.

This joyful, radiant portrayal of the life of the redeemed of God has buoyed the spirits of generations of Christian men and women, especially in times of hardship and suffering, and it contains several remarkable proclamations. The first is that victorious though the redeemed may be, and as important in the eyes of God as their own sufferings may be, their victory has been won not by means of their own efforts, but through Christ's sacrificial death and triumphant resurrection. This affirmation lies at the heart of this text. The redeemed are those who have been faithful to God and to the Lamb, but they enjoy their present happiness not because they have made their robes white in their own blood, but "in the blood of the Lamb" (v. 14). The power of Christ's death and resurrection is hereby affirmed.

A second proclamation of this lection has to do with the astonishing scope of God's redemptive activity. The contrast between the sources from which the redeemed Gentiles come (v. 9) and those of the redeemed Israelites (vs. 5–8) undoubtedly reflects a time when the young church had become predominantly Gentile. But the expansive dimensions of v. 9 also announce the activity of a God who knows no boundaries of race, culture, language, or nationality. All groups will be represented before the throne, their faithfulness and their devotion equally held up for approbation. Such a portrayal should forever banish narrowness and bigotry from the hearts of those who serve the Lamb.

A third proclamation concerns the activity of the redeemed: they are busy for God. NRSV's "they . . . worship him day and night within his temple" (v. 15) is an accurate rendering of the Greek, yet the English "worship" may imply to some minds, at least, a passivity which the Greek *latreuō* is not intended to convey, since in nonbiblical Greek the verb can refer to labor that is performed for wages. And so NEB's "minister to him day and night" is perhaps nearer the mark (compare KJV and "old" RSV). In any event, the life of the redeemed of God is not to be characterized by indolence and ease, but by involvement in the life of the kingdom.

Psalm 34:1–10, 22

This psalm is the voice of a trusting, confident poet. The poet wants to affirm in celebrative utterances the way in which the trustworthy God whom he praises has rehabilitated his life. The speaker also wants to invite others to join the celebration, and instructs them in the reality of a reliable God who calls to obedience.

The introduction to Psalm 34 voices a resolve to bless and praise God, and invites others to join in the praise (vs. 1–3). The poet's personal resolve is to bless God and to praise God with great exuberance (vs. 1–2a). The term NRSV renders as "boast" is the same term as "praise"; thus *hālal* occurs twice. The poet exhibits a deep passion and resolve for a life of unending praise. Thus far we do not know why the speaker has this intention.

In vs. 2b–3, others in the community are invited to join the praise, but in these verses the others are not told why either. The ones peculiarly addressed and summoned are the humble, that is, the powerless and vulnerable with whom the speaker stands in solidarity. This praising, thanking community is invited to magnify and exalt God. These two verbs suggest that the praise of Israel impacts God, making God greater and lifting God up for greater honor, so that God can more fully exercise appropriate sovereignty. The praise of the humble poor thus strengthens the hand of God to act on their behalf.

Only now are we told the basis of the invitation to thank (vs. 4–10). In these verses, the speaker twice tells of the personal experience that motivates the invitation to the others. In v. 4, the standard form of thanksgiving in Israel refers back to a situation of trouble, to which God has decisively responded. The statement of trouble is signaled by the phrase "I sought Yahweh," referring back to an earlier complaint and petition that this same speaker has uttered. Yahweh's resolution of that previous trouble is marked by the verbs "answered . . . delivered." This simple transaction of seek-answer is at the core of Israelite faith, for Yahweh is attentive and transformative. In this transaction, both parties, Israel and Yahweh, do what they most characteristically do.

The second personal witness is in v. 6, and reiterates the same transaction. The speaker is "poor," a word closely linked to "humble" in v. 2. This time the transformative transaction is in the words "cried . . . heard . . . saved." No wonder the speaker is exultant!

Most of this section of the psalm, however, is not personal testimony (as in vs. 4, 6), but is invitation and instruction to others. In these verses the speaker seeks to convince "the humble" that they also may share the benefit of Yahweh, as has the "poor" speaker. Turning to Yahweh in trust will transform their faces from shame to radiance (v. 5). This is an allusion to the familiar phrasing, "The Lord make his face to shine upon you." The change in one's face bespeaks a change in circumstance, so that even the vulnerable poor may expect Yahweh to give them new circumstances and a new chance for a good life.

The poet then uses two images to make the possibility of transformation more palpable. First, God's attending angel may go with them to guard and to rescue them (v. 7). That is, the world is potentially peopled with God's political, military entourage. Note, however, that the accompanying protection is not to the "humble," but to the God-fearers, or those who obey God. So now the speaker has fully voiced the tight theological calculus of trusting innocence. Obedience assures God's decisive presence. The vulnerable poor may or may not be God-fearers but they must become so in order to receive what the speaker has received from Yahweh.

The second metaphor is that God is the giver of sustaining food, even to those who have no power to secure food for themselves (vs. 8–10). God's blessing is quite concrete and material. Such an offer of food, which is here a metaphor for well-being (as in our slang term "bread," meaning wherewithal), is assured to those who rely on Yahweh (v. 8). This assertion is explored further by a contrast between the well-fed God-fearers who have no power to get their own food, and young lions, ravenous, powerful, energetic creatures who go hungry if left to their own resources (cf. Ps. 104:21–22). These verses use the term *ḥsr* two times. The word is well known in Ps. 23:1: "I shall not *want*" (emphasis added), that is, "I shall not *lack* anything." Thus those who "fear" (trust and obey) Yahweh will lack nothing. Those who are given everything by God are contrasted with those most "eager eaters," young male lions. But the lions will lack, even when Yahweh's faithful fearers have plenty.

Verse 22 offers a climactic statement which reiterates the claims of the psalm. Yahweh's world is well and reliably ordered. Yahweh redeems, values, protects, frees, cares for those who trust and serve. Yahweh never acts against those who are faithful, that is, the saints. Thus the reading is singularly appropriate on the day in which the honored, faithful, God-fearing dead are remembered. They are the ones who "lacked no good thing."

This is, of course, an innocent statement. Its horizon is well before the troubles that often come to a faithful life left in misery. One eventually may be more suspicious about such a quid pro quo confidence in God. But for now, as a baseline for trust and obedience, faith must begin at this innocent place, fully confident of God's attentiveness and generosity. Such a claim is reassuring. But it is also a challenge to those who find their own competence more impressive and more reliable than childlike trust. This psalm undermines an excessive confidence in self, as well as excessive despair about circumstance. This psalmist stands in the long line of those who have trusted and obeyed, and receive everything needed from God.

1 John 3:1–3

Despite its affirmation by many Christians each Sunday in the Apostles' Creed, the communion of saints remains something of a mystery. Contemporary Christians, especially those in North America, reflect the larger culture's preoccupation with the present and its utter disregard for either past or future. In that cultural context, the assertion that Christians are connected with believers both past and future appears to be nonsense. What is it that the "saints" of various historical periods and societies have in common? While the lection from 1 John does not directly address that question, it does comment on the "children of God" in ways that are suggestive for understanding the communion of saints.

First, the writer asserts that the children of God are characterized by the love given them by God (3:1). Indeed, that is why they are called children of God. The theme of love, both God's love and the love of God's children for one another, of course plays an important role throughout this letter. Over and over, the letter asserts the necessary relationship between God's love of believers and their love of one another. Clearly, however, the starting point in the relationship is God's love, which constitutes the community. The thread that binds all believers together, then, whether past or present, known or unknown, is the love God has displayed to them. That love in turn demands a loving response, both to God and to the "saints" of all ages. It also can become a powerful source of support and encouragement, for solidarity arises not simply from contemporary fellow Christians, but from all those who precede and those who will follow.

This first point feels familiar and comfortable. Whether Christians of this or any other generation actually love one another, talk of loving and being loved strikes a warm and welcome chord. The second point will be far less welcome: "The reason the world does not know us is that it did not know him." Within this particular passage, this reference to the world seems abrupt. The writer has been discussing love, and no transition has marked the move from that topic to this one. Within the letter as a whole, however, the two are closely related, since the writer uses both motifs to enhance the community—one that connects believers to one another and the other that sets them apart from the world.

This saying, that the world does not know the church or God, will cause many Christians to suspect the writer of 1 John of sectarianism. Here the church becomes a world unto itself, set apart and hostile to the "real" world. Within the history of the church, Christian groups have enacted such barriers, setting themselves apart from a world perceived to be evil and hostile. The text, however, reflects not simply a sectarian view of the church-world relationship, but a profound truth about the gospel: in every time and place those who adopt the values and perceptions of "the world" are not able to recognize God or God's children. Humanity remains alienated from God by its own blindness, and is therefore prevented from seeing God or God's people for what they are. What believers in every time and place share, then, is that they become the objects of the world's perennial hostility to the gospel.

In vs. 2–3, the writer turns to the future of God's children. Although believers are already God's children, made so by God's love, the future promises to bring them yet another transformation. That transformation is both known and unknown: "What we will be has not yet been revealed. What we do know is this: when he is revealed, we will be like him, for we will see him as he is" (v. 2). Already Christians live within God's love, shaped and changed by it ("All who have this hope in him purify themselves," v. 3). Their hope for the future is even greater, however, in that they will be made like God ("we will be like him"), although they do not yet know what that transformation will mean.

In terms of understanding the concept of the communion of saints, this discussion of the future means simply that Christians in all times and places have a common future. They share the conviction that death is not the end of their life with one another or with God. Somehow, in ways not at all understood or even glimpsed in the present, they belong to one another even beyond death.

The epistolary readings for the last several weeks have all addressed the issue of the future and its place in Christian faith. Although the readings have come from different points in Paul's life and now from the Johannine tradition, they assert in common the conviction that the future is both known and unknown. The exact details of the life that lies beyond death remain unknown, but each text expresses an utter conviction that God will be shown to be powerful even over death itself. Whatever the future may hold, Christians know that their connection with God and God's Christ endures. That fundamental conviction provides the larger framework for the communion of saints, in that it is God's power and love that hold together believers of God in the past, present, and future.

Matthew 5:1–12

The Beatitudes have been previously commented on in connection with their listing as the Gospel lesson for the Fourth Sunday After Epiphany. What was said there about a beatitude's being a statement of eschatological blessing is particularly appropriate for a consideration of the passage on All Saints' Day.

In a sense, the Beatitudes of Matt. 5:1–12 can be read in two ways. First, the stress can fall on the recipients of the blessings. To whom will the kingdom of heaven belong? Who will inherit the earth? Who will ultimately see God? The answers provided by the text come as surprises. Who would have thought of the poor in spirit, or the meek, or the pure in heart? These rather unlikely candidates become the beneficiaries of God's special attention.

On All Saints' Day, however, we might consider a second way to read the Beatitudes—in terms of the blessings promised. What can the poor in spirit hope for? What do the meek receive? What happens to the pure in heart? Again, in terms of human standards of recompense, the answers are surprises. Moreover, the answers are colossal promises, backed by the commitment of Jesus. They are promises that not only are oriented to an existence beyond death, but also have profound impact on the living of life now.

Take the last two beatitudes. Those who are falsely maligned and who suffer various sorts of opposition and persecution in this life for the sake of the gospel are not only promised a great reward in the afterlife; the kingdom of heaven belongs to them. The history of the church is replete with dramatic examples of those victimized and even killed in the cause of righteousness. "The blood of the martyrs is the seed of the church." The promise holds, however, for those not so dramatically persecuted, those experiencing opposition in less intense forms, those singled out for slander. Rejection, painful resistance, or even death is not the end of the story. Heaven becomes a place of recompense, a place where the long line of persecuted prophets, faithful disciples, and ordinary Christians who have experienced the on-again, off-again pressures of a hostile society are rewarded. On All Saints' Day the church celebrates the promise that

God has not forgotten the poor in spirit, the meek, the merciful, the pure in heart, the peacemakers—and certainly not the persecuted.

But the last beatitude has a strange twist for those who are still alive. They are not invited to expect instant recompense, but rather to be comforted by the eschatological perspective, to take heart in the face of opposition, to trust joyfully the divine promise made about the future ("Rejoice and be glad"). Put another way, the celebration of God's vindication of the saints who have suffered carries with it an encouragement for those who still daily struggle against the forces of oppression in the marketplace, in the home, in the courts, in the government. There may be penultimate battles that are apparently lost, even wounds to be borne, but the final outcome is never in doubt.

There is an additional beatitude in the list that warrants special consideration on All Saints' Day. "Blessed are those who mourn, for they will be comforted" (5:4). When our thoughts move from the host of disciples in the past who have faithfully served the cause of justice in great ways or small to particular departed saints we have known, then the mood of celebration is often tinged with grief. Familiar faces begin to appear—parents, spouses, sons, daughters, grandchildren—cherished individuals whose separation from us means deep pain and remorse. We can celebrate with our heads, but our hearts remain heavy.

The verb "mourn" in the text is an inclusive word, embracing a spectrum of experiences. In context, it most naturally pictures the plight of those who are heartsick because things are not right in the world, because injustice and suffering are still rampant. But it also includes the situation of those who grieve because of loss. Death is a part of what is wrong in the world, "the last enemy," Paul called it (1 Cor. 15:26). Thus the beatitude offers a blessing to those who face the communion of saints with mixed feelings, with grief as well as celebration. They too are not forgotten. Jesus promises comfort.

Index of Lectionary Readings

Old Testament

Genesis

1:1–2:4a 337–340
2:15–17, 3:1–7 183–185
6:9–22; 7:24; 8:14–19 347–348
12:1–4a 193–194
12:1–9 356–357
18:1–15 (21:1–7) 364–366
21:8–21 372–373
22:1–14 522–524
24:34–38, 42–49, 58–67 389–390
25:19–34 398–399
28:10–19a 407–409
29:15–28 417–419
32:22–31 426–428
37:1–4, 12–28 435–436
45:1–15 444–445

Exodus

1:8–2:10 453–455
3:1–15 462–463
12:1–14 471–473
12:1–4 (5–10), 11–14 238–239
14:19–31 478–480
16:2–15 487–489
17:1–7 201–202, 497–499
20:1–4, 7–9, 12–20 506–508
24:12–18 165–166
32:1–14 516–518
33:12–23 526–528

Leviticus

19:1–2, 9–18 147–148

Deuteronomy

30:15–20 138–139
34:1–12 535–537

Joshua

3:7–17 545–546
24:1–3a, 14–25 554–556

Judges

4:1–7 563–565

1 Samuel

16:1–13 210–211

Psalms

2 167–168
8 340–341
13 383–384
15 120–122
16 267–269
17:1–7, 15 428–430
19 508–511
22 248–250
23 211–213, 284–286
27:1, 4–9 112–113
29 93–95
31:1–5, 15–16 294–295
32 185–187
33:1–12 358–360
34:1–10, 22 581–583
40:1–11 102–104
45:10–17 390–392
46 348–350
47 312–313
51:1–17 176–178
66:8–20 303–305
68:1–10, 32–35 321–323
72:1–7, 10–14 84–86
72:1–7, 18–19 12–14
78:1–4, 12–16 499–500
78:1–7 556–557
80:1–7, 17–19 30–32
86:1–10, 16–17 373–375
90:1–6, 13–17 537–539
95 202–204
96 39–41
97 49–50
98 57–59
99 528–529
100 573–575
104:24–34, 35b 331–332
105:1–6, 16–22, 45b 437–438
105:1–6, 23–26, 45c 464–465

Psalms (cont.)
105:1–6, 37–45 489–491
105:1–11, 45b 419–420
106:1–6, 19–23 518–520
107:1–7, 33–37 546–548
112:1–9 (10) 129–132
114 480–482
116:1–2, 12–19 239–241, 366
116:1–4, 12–19 276–278
118:1–2, 14–24 258–259
118:1–2, 19–29 230–233
119:1–8 139–141
119:33–40 149–151
119:105–112 399–401
121 194–196
122 3–5
123 565–567
124 455–456
130 221–223
131 158–159
133 445–447
139:1–12, 23–24 409–411
146:5–10 21–24
147:12–20 75–77
148 67–69
149 473–474

Isaiah
2:1–5 2–3
7:10–16 28–30
9:1–4 110–112
9:2–7 38–39
11:1–10 11–12
35:1–10 20–21
42:1–9 92–93
49:1–7 101–102
49:8–16a 156–158
50:4–9a 229–230
52:7–10 56–57
58:3–9a (9b–12) 128–129
52:13–53:12 247–248
60:1–6 82–84
62:6–12 47–49
63:7–9 65–66

Jeremiah
31:7–14 73–75

Ezekiel
34:11–16, 20–24 572–573
37:1–14 219–221

Joel
2:1–2, 12–17 174–175

Micah
6:1–8 119–120

New Testament

Matthew
1:18–25 34–36
2:1–12 88–90
2:13–23 71–72
3:1–12 16–18
3:13–17 97–99
4:1–11 189–191
4:12–23 115–117
5:1–12 124–126, 585–586
5:13–20 134–136
5:21–37 143–145
5:38–48 153–154
6:1–6, 16–21 180–181
6:24–34 161–163
7:21–29 352–354
9:9–13, 18–26 362–363
9:35–10:8 (9–23) 368–370
10:24–39 377–379
11:2–11 25–27
11:16–19, 25–30 394–396
13:1–9, 18–23 403–405
13:24–30, 36–43 413–415
13:31–33, 44–52 423–424
14:13–21 432–433
14:22–33 440–442
15:(10–20) 21–28 449–451
16:13–20 458–460
16:21–28 467–469
17:1–9 170–172
18:15–20 476–477
18:21–35 484–486
20:1–16 493–495
21:1–11 235–236
21:23–32 502–504
21:33–46 513–514
22:1–14 381–382
22:15–22 531–533
22:34–46 541–543
23:1–12 550–552
24:36–44 7–9
25:1–13 560–561
25:14–30 569–570
25:31–46 575–577
28:16–20 343–345

Luke
2:(1–7) 8–20 52–54
2:1–14 (15–20) 43–45
24:13–35 280–281
24:44–53 315–317

John
1:1–14 61–63
1:(1–9) 10–18 79–81
1:29–42 106–108
3:1–17 198–199
4:5–42 206–208
7:37–39 334–336
9:1–41 215–217
10:1–10 288–290
11:1–45 225–227

13:1–17,
31b–35 244–245
14:1–14 297–299
14:15–21 307–308
17:1–11 325–327
18:1–19:42 253–254
20:1–18 261–263
20:19–31 271–272

Acts
1:1–11 310–312
1:6–14 319–321
2:1–21 329–330
2:14a, 22–32 265–267
2:14a,
36–41 274–276
2:42–47 283–284
7:55–60 292–293
10:34–43 95–97,
256–258
17:22–31 301–303

Romans
1:1–7 32–34
1:16–17,
3:22b–28
(29–31) 351–352
4:1–15,
13–17 196–198
4:13–25 360–362
5:1–8 366–368
5:1–11 204–206
5:12–19 187–189
6:1b–11 375–376
6:12–23 384–386
7:15–25a 392–394
8:1–11 401–403
8:6–11 223–225
8:12–25 411–413
8:26–39 420–422
9:1–5 430–432
10:5–15 438–440
11:1–2a,
29–32 447–449
12:1–8 456–458
12:9–21 465–467
13:8–14 474–476
13:11–14 5–6
14:1–12 482–484
15:4–13 15–16

1 Corinthians
1:1–9 104–106
1:10–18 114–115
1:18–31 123–124
2:1–12
(13–16) 132–134
3:1–9 141–143
3:10–11,
16–23 151–153
4:1–5 160–161
11:23–26 242–243
12:3b–13 332–334

2 Corinthians
5:20b–6:10 178–179
13:11–13 342–343

Ephesians
1:3–14 77–79
1:15–23 313–315, 575
3:1–12 86–88
5:8–14 213–215

Philippians
1:21–30 491–493
2:1–13 500–502
2:5–11 233–235
3:4b–14 511–513
4:1–9 520–522

Colossians
3:1–4 259–261

1 Thessalonians
1:1–10 529–531
2:1–8 539–541
2:9–13 549–550
4:13–18 558–559
5:1–11 567–569

Titus
2:11–14 41–43
3:4–7 51–52

Hebrews
1:1–4 (5–12) 59–61
2:10–18 69–70
4:14–16;
5:7–9 251–252

James
5:7–10 24–25

1 Peter
1:3–9 269–271
1:17–23 278–280
2:2–10 295–297
2:19–25 286–288
3:13–22 305–307
4:12–14,
5:6–11 323–325

2 Peter
1:16–21 169–170

1 John
3:1–3 583–585

Revelation
7:9–17 579–580